Years of Turmoil

Edited by
RICHARD WILKINSON

CONTRIBUTING AUTHORS
ANGELA ANDERSON, NIGEL HEARD,
EDWARD TOWNE

Hodder & Stoughton

A MEMBER OF THE HODDER HEADLINE GROUP

∽ ACKNOWLEDGEMENTS ∽

The authors are grateful to Peter Burton and Harland Walshaw for the photographs of the buildings and of the portrait of George Morley, and to Steve Connolly and Elinor Denman of Hodder & Stoughton for their encouragement and expertise.

The front cover shows the execution of Charles I by an unknown artist reproduced courtesy of the Scottish National Portrait Gallery/Private Collection.

The Publishers would like to thank the following for permission to reproduce material in this book:
Addison Wesley Longman, for a diagram from *Charles I* by Angela Anderson (1998) used on page 14; B.T. Batsford Ltd, for an extract from *Battles of the English Civil War* by Austin Woolrych (1961) used on page 114; Blackwell Publishers Ltd, for extracts from *They Saw It Happen, 1485–1688* (1957) pages 213–4 used on page 209, and from *Women, Work and Sexual Politics in Eighteenth-Century England* by B. Hill (1989) pages 259–60 used on page 327; Cambridge University Press, for extracts from *Charles I* by C.W. Daniels and J. Morrill (1994) page 58 used on page 62, and page 112 used on page 60; Edward Arnold/Hodder Headline plc for an extract from *Authority and Conflict* by Derek Hirst (1987), pages 61–62 used on page 342; Folger Shakespeare Library for an extract from *Three British Revolutions* by C. Carlton in J.G.A. Pocock (ed) (1981) pages 185–6 used on page 61; *History Today*, for an extract from 'The Revolution of 1688 and the flight of James II' by A.A. Mitchell (July, 1865) used on page 219; Hutchinson for the extract from *English Society* by K. Wrighton (1982) page 93 used on page 326; Macgibbon and Key for an extract from *The Pen and the Sword* by Michael Foot (1957) page 152 used on page 259; Macmillan Press Ltd for an extract from *The Origins of the English Civil War* by Conrad Russell (1973) used on page 130; Open University Press Ltd for extracts from *Seventeenth-Century England* by Ann Hughes (1980), Vol 1, pages 56–57 used on page 346, and pages 57–58 used on page 347; Oxford University Press for extracts from *Charles II* by Ronald Hutton (1991) used on page 365, from *Clarendon: Selections* by G. Huehns (ed), (1978) pages 6–7 used on page 61, from 'The Baptists – fount of all heresy' by J.F. McGregor in *Radical Religion in the English Revolution* by J.F. McGregor and B. Reay (eds), (1986) pages 23–26 used on page 361; Penguin Books for an extract from *A Monarch Transformed* by Mark Kishlansky (1996) used on page 165; Routledge & Kegan Paul for an extract from *Women in Stuart England and America* by R. Thompson (1974) pages 74–75 used on page 327; UCL Press for extracts from *Crime and Punishment in England* by J. Briggs et al. (1996) pages 36–38 used on page 339; Weidenfeld & Nicolson for an extract from *The Civil Wars of England* by John Kenyon (1996) used on page 114; A.P. Watt for an extract from *Prides's Purge* by David Underdown (1971) page 260 used on page 365.

The Publishers would like to thank the following for permission to reproduce the following copyright illustrations in this book:
Althorp page 111; Bridgeman Art Library, London/New York/Private Collection pages 126, 141; British Library pages 106, 362, National Portrait Gallery, London pages 18, 51, 62*l*, 69, 77, 109, 118, 145, 159, 172, 176, 178, 180, 199, 223 *l* and *r*, 250, 253, 257, 385, 386, 390, 399, 430; National Trust Photographic Library/Roy Fox page 103; Peter Burton and Harland Walshaw pages 128, 273, 288, 368, 397, 452; The Fotomas Index (UK) page 325; The Royal Collection © 1998 Her Majesty the Queen pages 62*r*, 125; Trustees of the British Museum page 84.

(*r* right; *l* left)

Orders: please contact Bookpoint Ltd, 39 Milton Park, Abingdon, Oxon OX14 4TD, UK. Telephone: (44) 01235 400414; Fax: (44) 01235 400454. Lines are open from 9.00–6.00, Monday to Saturday, with a 24-hour message answering service. Email address: orders@bookpoint.co.uk

British Library Cataloguing in Publication Data
A catalogue record for this title is available from the British Library

ISBN 0 340 69727 X

First published 1999
Impression number   10 9 8 7 6 5 4 3 2 1
Year   2002 2001 2000 1999
Copyright © 1999 Richard Wilkinson, Angela Anderson, Nigel Heard, Edward Towne

Typeset by Wearset, Boldon, Tyne and Wear.
Printed in Great Britain for Hodder & Stoughton Educational, a division of Hodder Headline Plc, 338 Euston Road, London NW1 3BH by Scotprint Ltd, Musselburgh, Scotland.

Contents

～ LIST OF TABLES ～

∽ LIST OF MAPS ∽

∽ LIST OF DIAGRAMS ∽

∽ LIST OF ILLUSTRATIONS ∽

⌒ LIST OF PROFILES ⌒

Preface: How to use this book

1 ⌒ A NEW TEXTBOOK

Years of Turmoil has been written to answer a need. The authors have done their best to write the kind of book that examination candidates at the senior secondary stage will find useful and have tried to produce a narrative that is sufficiently substantial without being overburdened with detail. An analytical approach has been adopted, which is nevertheless intended to be reasonably accessible. Readers are introduced to the disputes currently raging between historians and which feature in examinations. Finally, guidance is offered on the skills essential to those embarking on an advanced historical examination course.

With regard to the book's subject matter, a glance at the table of contents will reveal that Chapters 2 to 7 offer a chronological account of the years between 1603 and 1714. Rightly or wrongly, most examination syllabuses remain rooted to traditional constitutional history. We have therefore made it our first priority to do justice to these political developments so that examinees will not be let down. We have aimed at a strong, coherent, stimulating narrative which offers sufficient detail and analysis of the usual constitutional topics.

However, this title also seeks to do justice to the economic, intellectual and social aspects of the story (Chapters 8 to 10), and a particular feature which we consider important is that the book is a history of Britain, not just England. As it happens, recent studies of the causes, course and consequences of the central episode in the seventeenth century, that is to say the civil wars, have emphasised this British dimension. All of us are aware of this in our writing, and Chapter 11 is specifically concerned with developments in Ireland, Scotland and Wales, and with the emergence of a British united kingdom.

The book is generously illustrated. We have incorporated into the text a considerable amount of documentary evidence, which helps to explain how contemporaries thought and reacted. Where appropriate, the narrative is clarified by maps, summaries, tables, diagrams and graphs. There are several reproductions of portraits of people who played a significant part in the history to be studied and photographs of buildings illuminate the environment of such events as the execution of Charles I.

Particular features of the book are the highlighting in the margin of the issues and questions which are being addressed and the cross-references to other parts of the book, for we are anxious to combat a blinkered approach. We feel that it is a pity to study just the constitutional chapters. Understanding of any aspect of the story is heightened and enriched by a wide awareness of the whole canvas of developments. What kind of society produced the Levellers? What did Pym and Charles I look like? What was Laud's perception of Christianity? The answers to these questions really are crucial to an understanding of the political conflict which occurred – and vice versa. Therefore, readers of Chapters 1 to 7 will constantly be referred to other chapters. A student who shows awareness of social and cultural aspects will impress a good examiner and candidates looking for appropriate topics for individual studies will find plenty of suggestions in Chapters 8 to 10.

We are well aware that the seventeenth century is a difficult period to understand. For one thing the English language has changed over the past three or four centuries, and so the margin frequently contains definitions and explanations of unfamiliar words and technical terms. Such words are collated in an alphabetical glossary on page 458. Another frequent cause of confusion is the involved and baffling unfolding of events. Chronological summaries, or timelines, therefore will be found in the text and on pages 453–5. Controversies between historians are summarised where this is appropriate. At the end of each chapter there is a bibliography where suitable books are frankly described.

2 ⤳ THE ACQUISITION OF SKILLS

A *Mastering the material*

A history examination is a test of knowledge as well as perception. Examiners' criticisms of weak essays often include the comment, 'unsubstantiated assertion'. In other words, the candidate is incapable of justifying argument with supportive evidence. It is no use saying that 'Charles I was an inept ruler' unless you can quote facts to prove it. A good textbook therefore is an aid to the comprehension of relevant material and its commitment to memory. We therefore give advice on note-making, which is an essential skill. At this stage it is enough to stress the importance of adopting a methodical approach to note-making, and of taking trouble over neatness and handwriting. One advantage which accrues from making efficient notes is that it demands concentration on the material as you read it. It is no use trying to make a note on material which has not been understood. Having made a note, it is a good idea to see if it makes sense. If it does not make sense now, it certainly will not in several months' time when final revision occurs.

How does one commit facts to memory? There is no substitute for learning by heart a few necessary dates and names. For instance, the dates of the Stuart monarchs are a useful framework on which to base one's knowledge of the period and are *an absolute minimum of what you should know!* Or again, not to know that the battle of Naseby was in 1645, following Marston Moor in 1644, will inevitably lead to muddle and confusion in the student's mind. To facilitate the memorising of essential

1603	James I
1625	Charles I
1649	The Interregnum
1660	Charles II
1685	James II
1688	William and Mary
1702–14	Anne

TABLE 1
The Stuart Dynasty

facts, we include several chronological summaries which are there to be consulted, or even learnt by heart. Such 'rote-learning', as it is sometimes dismissively called, is time well spent, even if it seems a chore.

A more pleasant way of mastering detail is to argue and debate thought-provoking issues. Knowledge is picked up on the way, without trying. Both in the margins and at the end of chapters we include key issues and questions which can be explored profitably, either in group discussion, or on paper, or by the individual's thought and research.

B *Essay-writing skills*

Some examination papers contain 'structured' essay questions, that is to say questions which are broken down into sub-sections. The essential priority is to answer the questions asked in a businesslike, informed way. We include a structured essay question and give advice on how such questions can be answered efficiently.

For many candidates, however, the uninterrupted 45-minute essay is likely to remain a feature of their examinations. To plan and write such an essay, ultimately in exam conditions, is a skill which has to be acquired if a high grade is to be achieved. It is not easy and does not usually come naturally. We therefore offer a considerable amount of advice and several practice exercises in essay-writing. The crucial point is that almost invariably *analysis* is required, and *not* narrative. This truth is illustrated by the three types of essays which examiners are likely to set.

(i) The first is the 'Explanation' question, where, for instance, you are asked to 'account for' an event such as the outbreak of the Civil War or 'examine' the consequences of the Revolution of 1688–9. 'Account for' is *not* the same thing as 'write an account of', nor is 'examine' the same as 'describe'. The first requires analysis, the second requires narrative. Clearly the relevant causes or results have to be put forward. But to achieve a high mark, you must do more than that. You have to demonstrate your ability to *understand* cause and effect, and therefore to analyse and evaluate their importance so that you can come to an overall judgement.

See pages 79–80.

(ii) 'Yes/no' questions confront you with a proposition with which you are asked to agree or disagree. Sometimes you are presented with a quotation, which you are then asked to 'discuss'. An obvious point here is that 'discuss' does not mean 'digress'. You must stick to the quotation and show that you understand its point, for this will enable you to do justice to the author's argument, though you do not necessarily have to agree with the quotation. After weighing up the pros and cons, you must come to a conclusion – 'yes', 'no', or just possibly 'there is truth on both sides'. But you must answer the question, and leave the examiner in no doubt as to your answer. Again, analysis is essential.

See pages 162–3.

(iii) 'Significance' or 'importance' questions demand an evaluation of the significance of an event, a person or a movement. Clearly you must

See pages 333–4.

know your facts in order to answer the question. But it is a question. Once again, a narrative description of the person or movement is not the answer and will get you a grade D at best. The high grade goes to the candidate who argues analytically just how important the person or event actually was. Comparison with other factors is often necessary. Quite possibly the answer may turn out to be 'not very'.

Clearly, some essays fall into none of these categories, but the majority do. We have used examples of all three in the exercises which we have introduced – and the type of essay is specified in the table of contents (see pages iii–vi). These exercises are introduced by a general note on essay-writing at the end of Chapter 1 (see pages 7–9). Basically, there is nothing mysterious or impossible about writing analytical history essays. The priority is to answer the question, intelligently, perceptively and effectively. Easier said than done? Yes, indeed – especially for students initially embarking on the writing of analytical essays, who may be disheartened by first attempts. This is why we have devoted considerable space to essay-writing skills.

C *Source-analysis skills*

Most examination papers now include at least one document question where candidates have to understand and evaluate primary sources. Even where there is no document question a candidate will acquire credit through displaying familiarity with original sources. After all, this has always been and always will be the only conclusive way to settle a historical controversy, i.e. what do sources say? We have therefore included several document questions which might well appear in examination papers, and also document exercises which simply test the historian's basic skills. For instance, on pages 113–15 you are asked to estimate the numbers killed in the sack of Bolton on 28 May 1644. Amazingly, reputable historians such as John Kenyon accept parliamentary claims that the Royalists butchered 1,600 people. But the only solid evidence suggests that 79 were killed. Where does the truth lie?

Most document questions follow a consistent pattern. There are four or five sources, mostly primary but sometimes including a present-day historian's comment. Then follow structured questions requiring comprehension of the sources and realistic evaluation. The last question often asks you to combine the sources with your own knowledge to answer a general question about the topic to which the sources relate. We have included several such questions and detailed guidance is provided on how to answer them.

One or two general pieces of advice can usefully be offered here. First, spend at least 10 minutes reading the sources carefully. Often the sources set are *meant to be obscure*, otherwise there would be no point in requiring candidates to work out their meanings. This is especially the case with regard to seventeenth-century documents where inevitably the language is liable to be unfamiliar. In order to understand a document therefore, you have to work at it, and this will take time.

Secondly, take careful note of the allocation of marks. Clearly it is bad tactics to spend too long on a question which carries only two or three marks and not leave yourself time for questions for which 11 or 12 marks are awarded. Thirdly, be ready for certain 'buzz-words' such as 'reliable' and 'useful to the historian'. We will give you precise guidance when specific examples materialise. Suffice it to say now that these words will occur and they need methodical treatment. Fourthly, you will probably be asked to compare documents. The trick here is to start with the document with which you are asked to compare other documents, working out first what this document signifies. Do not worry, this will become clear when you tackle a specific example.

Introduction 1

1 ⌐ THE DECISIVE CENTURY IN BRITISH HISTORY?

According to the historian Mark Kishlansky, 'the seventeenth century was decisive for everything'. It was certainly decisive for Charles I, who was put on trial by his own subjects and, on a cold January morning in 1649, publicly executed. This event, which shook the civilised world, symbolises the decisiveness of the *political* developments discussed in this book. But we shall not be concerned only with politics. British society was transformed as well. By 1714, the landed aristocracy shared power with a more broadly-based, monied elite while the gulf between rich and poor widened. Queen Anne founded Royal Ascot, while her subjects played cricket and golf. Rich people drank coffee and tea instead of beer. Much was achieved in religion, philosophy and the arts. Meanwhile an economic revolution occurred. In 1603, the British Isles were off-shore islands of little interest or significance to Europe. Even the cloth trade, which had flourished in the Middle Ages, had declined. By 1714, Britain had become a great naval and military power and London was now the mercantile centre of the world. In Kishlansky's words, 'it is astonishing to reflect on the achievements of Britain's seventeenth century'.

> See Chapter 8 for a discussion of the economy.

Are such claims over the top? Sceptics might ask whether the Stuart age was *that* special while enthusiasts for, say, Tudor history could put up an equally impressive case. More to the point, did contemporaries see their century as decisive? They certainly believed that their world was 'turned upside down', that their times were 'years of shaking', or indeed years of turmoil. Consider the merchant John Okey's tomb in Bolton churchyard:

> In his time there were many great changes, and terrible alterations. 18 years civil war in England, besides many dreadful sea-fights, the crown or command of England changed 8 times, episcopacy [bishops] laid aside 14 years, London burnt by papists, and more stately built again, Germany wasted 300 miles, 200,000 protestants murdered by papists in Ireland, this town thrice stormed, he went through many troubles and divers [several] conditions.

The 'many troubles and divers conditions' through which Okey passed form the subject-matter of this book. Clearly his friends thought them so traumatic that his survival was worth recording. As a mature adult Okey lived through the revolutionary decades from 1640 to 1660.

When he died in 1681, Britain again faced the threat of civil war – years of turmoil indeed.

Arguably they were years of progress. Even Charles I's tragic death had positive results, for the British had shown that a king who was not up to the job could and should be removed. For the same reason note the successful revolt against the pathetic James II in 1688 and the appointment of his successor on Parliament's terms. In no other era has such significant political progress been made. By rising against their King in defence of Parliament, the British resisted the European trend towards absolute monarchy. The subsequent American and French revolutionaries were substantially in Britain's debt. Add the advances made in the economy, literature and the arts, and we can claim a decisive century in *world* history.

See pages 124–30 for the significance of Charles I's death.

2 ∾ THE ISSUES AT STAKE

The issues at stake discussed in this book fall into two categories: those which mattered to contemporaries and those which matter to us. Contemporaries might not agree with us on what the key issues were during their turbulent century and might not even have been aware of their existence. The story goes that a peasant, told to vacate Marston Moor so that King and Parliament could fight a battle, exclaimed, 'Has them two fallen out then?'

So our first concern will be to establish empathy with seventeenth-century people so as to understand their priorities. For instance, the crucial issue for most of them was the next pay packet, or indeed the next meal. For this reason rich and poor alike resented taxation, especially when it was exacted by an incompetent and corrupt government whose policies were widely criticised. Similarly, the army was unpopular during the 1640s and 1650s primarily because it was expensive, which explains the longing for peace during those turbulent decades. Apart from necessitating the existence of the army, war disrupted trade, the fields lay untilled, people starved. Everyone wanted the wars to end so that peace and prosperity could return.

See pages 67–8 for examples of unpopular taxation.

While we can easily empathise with concern for the necessities of life, it is harder to understand the seventeenth century preoccupation with religion. For most of us this is an unfamiliar landscape. There is a story of an air hostess instructing her passengers to fasten their seat-belts on the descent to Belfast since 'we are now entering the seventeenth century'. Northern Ireland's problems today can help us understand religious tensions in Stuart Britain. Bigoted Protestants such as Oliver Cromwell spouted the Old Testament, demanding the punishment of God's enemies. Most thinking people in Stuart Britain were stridently Protestant, to our way of thinking paranoid about the alleged dangers of Roman Catholics extending their control of Ireland to the rest of Britain. Only gradually and reluctantly was toleration granted.

What else? Did *any* seventeenth-century people care about the political and constitutional issues at stake which have interested historians?

Clearly some did. People in the past were not stupid. But constitutional issues were inextricably tied up with concerns of the day. Take the question of the control of the sword. Was Charles I to be trusted with the command of an army to suppress the Irish revolt when it seemed only too likely that he would join the rebels? Why should ship money be paid to build ships which escorted Spanish gold to be conveyed across England for the benefit of troops suppressing Protestants in Germany? In other words, what mattered was the difference that the disputed constitutional issues made when put into practice.

See pages 90–1 for the Irish revolt and pages 72–4 for ship money.

This book will explore the conflicts and controversies of the age of turmoil from the viewpoints of both contemporaries and of ourselves. Political developments will be placed in the context of social, economic and cultural achievements. We shall be especially concerned with the British dimension. Perhaps the most important issue at stake was the emergence of a so-called United Kingdom, with those attendant strengths and weaknesses which were to have such profound consequences for future generations.

3 ⁓ BRITAIN IN 1603

When James VI of Scotland became James I of England, what did his joint inheritance amount to? The new King was dazzled by England's apparent wealth – a far cry, so it seemed to him, from the austerity of backward, primitive Scotland. But appearances were deceptive. He was similarly misled by the welcome he received from his new subjects, failing to understand their short-term relief at the peaceful accession of a ruler who was clearly sane, male, Protestant and 'with the usual number of arms and legs and no tail' (J.P. Kenyon). James was soon to discover that ruling his two kingdoms was no picnic and that there were limits to the wealth at his disposal.

See Chapter 8 for economic background.

Perhaps the salient point to grasp about James's inheritance is that its various parts had very little in common. England, Scotland, Ireland and Wales had their own traditions, cultures, dialects, religions and economies. There was certainly little love lost between them. There were very few ties of loyalty, emotion or mutual self-interest which James could tap in his laudable attempts to unify his lands.

Even England – the largest and richest component of the British Isles – presented its ruler with severe problems. For Elizabeth the 'Great' bequeathed a difficult situation to her successor. Indeed, recent scholars have revised the adulation of Good Queen Bess by seventeenth-century Protestants and pro-Tudor historians. For instance, J.A. Sharpe argues that Elizabeth's only achievements were the Church of England and the Poor Law. This seems harsh given Elizabeth's success in guiding Protestant England through the shoals of a hostile, largely Catholic Europe, maintaining royal authority at home and forging an emotional link between crown and nation. Nevertheless, the 1590s were an unhappy decade, distinguished by bad harvests, a long and unsuccessful war against Spain, a bankrupt treasury, a grumpy House of Commons and increasing resentment against the authority of bishops. A few months before her death the weary monarch had to fend off a full-scale revolt by her favourite, the Earl of Essex, which recalled the bad old days of bastard-feudalism. The only beneficiary from this distressing episode was Essex's rival, the greedy, ambitious, unpopular Robert Cecil.

While the experienced, much-respected Queen had had her problems, what chance had James VI and I? The English struck foreigners as being virtually ungovernable. According to the Venetian ambassador, in recent times 'three Princes of the Blood, four Dukes, forty Earls and three thousand other persons have died by violent death'. Certainly the English were notoriously quick to draw their swords or resort to fisticuffs. Their manners were barbaric. They were proverbially gluttonous and drunken, urinating in public and allowing their women far too much freedom. They were unpredictable and untrustworthy. Visitors to England experienced the widespread hatred of foreigners both among the upper classes and the populace – 'most hostile to foreigners', 'naturally the enemies of all aliens'. That the Protestant English should hate the Roman Catholic French and Spanish was only too predictable. To the amazement and indignation of James I they disliked the Scots even more; according to a tactless MP, Scotsmen were 'proud, beggarly, quarrelsome, they have not suffered three of their kings to die in their beds these last two hundred years'.

Actually, one must be precise when talking about 'the English': 80 per cent of the population were poor, illiterate and from our point of view largely anonymous. Labouring on the land or forming the impoverished workforce of the towns, these unfortunate peasants and labourers were politically powerless, having no voting rights or meaningful representation in Parliament. Only occasionally and in exceptional circumstances did the 'mobile' flex their muscles. Superimposed on them were prosperous landowning yeomen in the countryside, merchants and master-craftsmen in the town, members of the 'learned professions' (the clergy, the medical profession, the law) and the nobility and gentry. Some yeomen and merchants voted in parliamentary elections, the franchise being extraordinarily messy and inconsistent, and they played their parts in town and village politics. Together with the nobility and gentry they formed what historians call 'the political community'. This is a useful term, signifying the minority of educated, informed, wealthy and well-connected men who actually wielded political power. Women, it should be added, were side-lined in a totally sexist way. The most important English men were the nobility and gentry who served as Members of Parliament and as Justices of the Peace, who attended the two ancient universities and the Inns of Court and who occupied all the best livings in the Church of England – in short, the people who mattered socially, economically and politically.

It was this elite – often bigoted, arrogant and unreasonable – whom the English monarch had to humour and manage if success was to be achieved, since the Crown was dependent on the political community for the implementing of policy. A king could not *force* his subjects to obey him: he had neither a standing army nor a professional civil

> **KEY ISSUE**
>
> *How many English people were politically significant?*

service, still less a police force. It was necessary therefore to cajole the political community by flattery, bribery and patronage. For instance, the raising of money was impossible without the good will of the gentry and merchants who paid part of the taxes and administered the amateur and clumsy system of taxation. In theory the monarch was supposed to fund government out of revenue from Crown lands and ancient and cumbersome dues. In an age of steep inflation this was always difficult and in wartime impossible. In such circumstances the ruler had to go cap-in-hand to Parliament.

Still, as the Tudors had proved, the job itself was not impossible. There was an inbuilt feeling of loyalty towards the sovereign. The country was reasonably prosperous, thanks to an agricultural system which functioned well enough unless the weather turned foul, and a thriving if primitive domestic industry. England was a confessional state – that is to say, everyone belonged to the state-church. This was the Church of England, dominated by bishops who were Crown appointments and preached that kings were appointed by God and should be unquestioningly obeyed. The English were taught to be deferential to their social superiors and, in the words of the Book of Common Prayer, 'to do their duty in the state to which it had pleased God to call them'. The greatest dread of the political community was 'overturning', the chaos and disruption which opposition to the Crown would inevitably cause. It was a king-worshipping age therefore, profoundly traditionalist and conservative.

> See pages 337–41 for the confessional state.

Scotland was different. A brilliant past contrasted with a grim present and future. The sixteenth century had been a golden age for the Scottish nation. According to the historian Jenny Wormald, Scotland had been 'intensely outward-looking, self-consciously aware, indeed proud, of her receptiveness and contribution to the political, economic, religious, and intellectual life of Europe'. With four universities (Glasgow, St Andrews, Aberdeen and the recently founded Edinburgh) and cultural ties with Catholic France and Protestant Geneva, Scotland was in some respects more civilised and progressive, more *European,* than contemporary England.

There were, however, reactionary elements which threatened to dominate the future – a social system based on kinship and lordship, the oppressive rule of the Scottish Presbyterian Church (otherwise known as the Kirk), the rivalry between the cosmopolitan, English-speaking, Protestant Lowlands and the remote, Gaelic, Catholic Highlands. Though twice the size of Scotland, England was a more homogeneous country. In the Highlands the great chieftains – Campbells, Macdonalds, Huntleys – exercised a quasi-regal sway. In the Lowlands the lairds survived with difficulty, farming their unproductive estates. Unlike England, where upwardly mobile gentry frequently infiltrated the nobility, the gulf between magnates and lairds was insurmountable, just as the peasantry could do little more than survive. There was no equivalent to the prosperous yeoman south of the border.

Furthermore, the departure of the King was a disaster for Scotland.

While James VI of Scotland enthused about becoming James I of England, Scotland lost its royal Court with all its opportunities for advancement, patronage and, in James's case, whole-hearted participation in the nation's intellectual and cultural life. Intellectually and economically Scotland now tagged along in England's wake, instead of maintaining its own contacts with Europe. James VI and I never forgot Scotland or lost a sneaking regard for it. His rule by correspondence from Westminster was surprisingly effective, given that only once did he return to the land of his birth. But things could never be the same again. The problems encountered by James's ignorant and inept son in his relations with Scotland indicated the widening gulf caused by James's trek south in 1603. In the meantime, the intellectual and cultural influence of the Crown was increasingly replaced by the repressive dead hand of the Kirk. Scotland was on the high road to **theocracy.**

theocracy a state in which the chief political power is exercised by clergy.

Ireland was different again from the other parts of this distinctly disunited kingdom. For centuries the English had exploited and bullied the Irish. The bulk of the population was Roman Catholic, suppressed, ignorant and without hope of economic salvation. They were dominated by their priests who were equally poor, dependent on the charity of starving peasants who had to pay tithe to support the Protestant Anglican Church in Ireland to which hardly anyone belonged. An ancient Catholic nobility co-existed uneasily with English newcomers, some of them Protestant, some recent converts to Catholicism. In the north, Protestant immigrants monopolised the best land. Most of these had come from Scotland as few English people could be tempted to move to such a depressed country. The whole wretched island was in theory governed by the King of England's Lord Deputy, operating from Dublin and controlling the few square miles to the west of the capital known as the Pale. The rest of Ireland was neither governed, cultivated nor civilised – in short, 'beyond the Pale'.

Wales was fully integrated into the English political network. This process dated back to Edward I's reign (1272–1307). But the Welsh were still content to be uninvolved in English affairs, retaining their own language and culture. The Welsh economy was backward and the Welsh Church was impoverished. The English patronised and insulted the Welsh, dismissing them for their alleged dishonesty and inability to speak the truth. Even Shakespeare failed to rise above this prejudice. The Welsh retaliated by turning their backs on their repulsively condescending neighbours.

To sum up, 'Great Britain', as James I called his lands, consisted of an uneasy and unco-ordinated ragbag. The new King boasted about his 'empire' and a cheeky MP suggested that he should call himself 'emperor'. The rulers of the European powers, however, France, Spain and the Habsburg Empire, had understandable contempt for the unpleasant and eccentric British peoples and their ludicrous ruler. Certainly, James I had no idea how to unite his unimpressive and violently disparate possessions. Yet there were possibilities. The sea surrounding the British Isles protected them against the invasions which plagued France and Germany, and provided alternative means of communication to the largely unnavigable rivers and atrocious roads. England, and to a lesser extent Scotland, Ireland and Wales, possessed great natural resources. With its population of 190,000, London was the largest city in Europe – a fact which reflected its economic potential as a centre of international trade and finance. A minority of English men (as opposed to women) had been well-educated in the excellent grammar schools which had been founded at the Reformation. English literature blossomed in a way which the Continent could not match: Shakespeare's plays, Donne's verse and the matchless prose of the Authorised Version of the Bible. For all their faults the leaders of society possessed sturdy independence. They were capable not only of defending their own privileges, but also of showing awareness of the nation's interests. Time would show what sort of a fist the British would make of future challenges.

4 ⌁ BIBLIOGRAPHY

While it is hoped that students will find this book a satisfactory general history of seventeenth-century Britain, there are several works which cover a similar canvas. *A Monarchy Transformed* by Mark Kishlansky (Penguin, 1996) is up to date and studiously objective. *The Stuart Age* by Barry Coward (Longman, 1994) is a substantial and stimulating work, worth consulting, though in general rather demanding and beyond most sixth-formers. *Stuart England, 1603–1714* also by Barry Coward (Longman, 1997) is more appropriate for A level students – brief, attractively laid-out, with some advice on technique – but it too is demanding, being analytical rather than narrative. *The Century of Revolution* by Christopher Hill (Nelson, 1961) is wonderfully provocative and exciting. Written from the Marxist stand-point, it still reads well and is full of thought-provoking ideas. *The Stuarts* by J.P. Kenyon (Batsford, 1970) is an entertaining description of the rulers' strengths and weaknesses. See also *A History of the Modern British Isles 1603–1707* by David Smith (Blackwell, 1998) which is a stimulating, though demanding, volume.

5 ⌁ A GENERAL NOTE ON ESSAY WRITING

1. An essay should consist of:

(a) *Introduction*   Show that you understand the point of the question, in other words why it is a good question. Clarify any possible sources of confusion, definitions, terms of reference etc. which the examiner may deliberately have incorporated in the question to test your awareness. Indicate how you intend to approach the question, but do not reveal your answer at this stage. If possible, begin with a short sentence – try not to put the reader off straightaway with an involved, long and complicated mouthful.

(b) *Development*   This is where you deploy your factual material in order to answer the question. But your approach must be analytical, not narrative. You must develop an argument. To do this you must use paragraphs methodically. Each paragraph should begin with a key sentence which refers back to the question and establishes the point which you intend to make in the rest of the paragraph. Stick to your key sentence's terms of reference, i.e. do not wander off the point. Your line of argument can be clarified by rational use of connectors at the beginning of paragraphs – 'furthermore', 'again', 'indeed' for the continuation of an approach and 'however', 'on the other hand', 'nevertheless' for a change of approach.

Here are examples of key sentences from an essay, 'Do you agree that Charles II showed more ability than the other Stuart monarchs?' 'There is no doubt that Charles showed ability on several occasions.' 'Furthermore, other members of the Stuart dynasty had very little ability.' 'On the other hand, Charles made several serious mistakes which suggest that his ability was limited.' 'Again, if William III is considered to be a Stuart, his ability certainly rivals Charles II's.' Note the use of connectors and note the emphasis on the most important word in the question – 'ability'.

(c) *Conclusion*   Sum up your argument, arriving at your answer to the question. Try not to repeat yourself; if possible, introduce one or two new details or ideas – though not so startling as to disrupt or contradict your argument. It is essential to leave your reader in no doubt as to your answer to the question. In other words, answer explicitly, not implicitly. Ideally, you should end forcefully, with what the Americans call 'a good punch-line'.

2. In general:

(a)   Think before you write, for at least five minutes. Some people find writing rough notes helpful, but this is not necessary and can simply waste time. Underline the most important word(s) in the question, in order to concentrate your thought. This word should feature in your key sentences throughout your essay.

(b)   Only quote the names of historians if you are explicitly debating their arguments – e.g. Christopher Hill's explanation of the Civil War. But do not forget that the examiner is interested in *your* ideas, not Hill's. Reeling off historians' names to create an impression of industry and erudition is counter-productive and ludicrous ('Trevor-Roper says—and I agree with him . . .'). Alas, it is amazing how many examination candidates do this.

(c)   Try to make your essay different, and personal. This is refreshing from an examiner's point of view. Bring in anecdotes and colourful detail derived from your reading and discussions. Do not be afraid to express your own ideas, provided that you can back them up with relevant evidence.

(d)   Presentation matters. Aim at an examiner-friendly script. If at all possible, do not incorporate messages, arrows, 'turn to page 14 for last para' and additions in the margin in illegible, minute scrawl. Remember that the examiner is probably tired and cross, and is only human. Do not turn the examiner against you unnecessarily.

(e)   Sheer length is not a virtue, but you cannot expect to prove a case without backing it up with substantial, supporting evidence. Given average-sized hand-writing, a top-grade answer is seldom less than three sides of A4.

2

The Reign of James I 1603–25

INTRODUCTION

Any historical study beginning with the accession of James VI of Scotland as James I of England in 1603 runs the risk of being distorted by the momentous events that followed – the civil wars of 1637–51, the execution of Charles I in 1649 and the Revolution of 1688–9. The danger is that the events of James's reign will be seen only as a prelude to a crisis which contemporaries neither desired nor expected; and that their importance will be assessed only in terms of how far they caused, or contributed to, its emergence and eventual outcome. Any historical account is necessarily selective; events have to be included on the basis of their importance at the time or in later developments, and an account dominated by a crisis which developed in later years may well overstress the roots of that crisis when compared with other issues.

At the same time, however, the focus of this chapter is political and religious, and the emergence of a political and religious crisis shortly after James died can hardly be ignored in assessing his achievements or lack of them. Historians writing in the past have made judgements in these terms; for the Whig historians, James was a king who alienated his people and handed on an impossible task to his son. It is therefore necessary to maintain a balance between issues that were important to contemporaries and those that interest historians, and to make judgements about the actions and decisions of those involved in the light of both their long-term significance and the situations operating at the time. Indeed, a genuine understanding of how and why future developments occurred can only be drawn from an understanding of how and why contemporaries acted as they did in the light of what they knew and believed. In an attempt to meet these requirements, this chapter will address four key questions:

See page 93 for the Whig interpretation.

1   What did James inherit? Was he heir to a healthy, well-governed kingdom, or to one faced by serious problems? What was required of him as king, and how far was he capable of meeting these requirements?
2   How did he handle it? What did James and his advisers see as important issues, and what steps did they take to deal with them?
3   How far was he successful? What did James's government achieve, why did it not achieve more? What part was played in this process by individuals, and what by circumstances outside their control?
4   What was his legacy? What did he pass on to his successors? How should his reign and his achievements be assessed in terms of seventeenth-century political and religious developments?

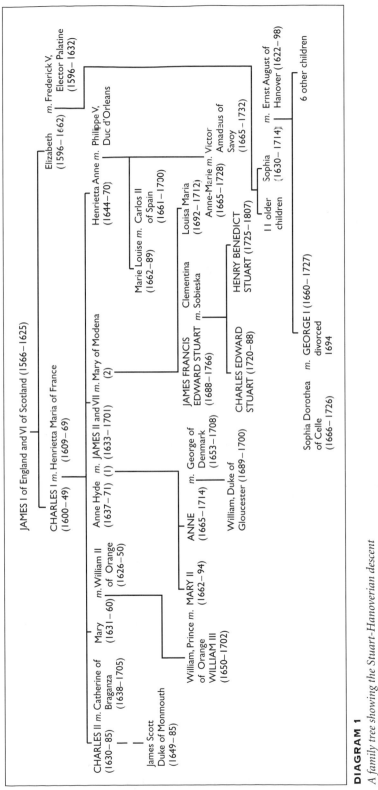

DIAGRAM 1

A family tree showing the Stuart–Hanoverian descent

These questions define the four sections of the chapter. Section 1 considers the state of the kingdom that James inherited in 1603 and assesses his skills and character. Section 2 looks at the early years of his reign, in which attempts were made to introduce necessary reforms. Section 3 examines the deterioration of government in later years, while the concluding fourth section draws together the implications of the preceding analysis, and offers an assessment of the impact of James as a monarch.

1 ✎ THE NEW KING AND HIS INHERITANCE

On 24 March 1603, Queen Elizabeth died, naming James as her successor, and he immediately began his journey south to take up his inheritance. The speed with which he moved reflected the extent to which he had been prepared for this moment by his English contacts, especially Robert Cecil, Elizabeth's Secretary of State, and the wealth, power and status which he saw in his new kingdom. In comparison with Scotland, England was rich, with fertile land, substantial natural resources, an established overseas trade and an effective system of communication by river and sea. While he certainly overestimated England's wealth, there was no doubt that it was the largest and most prosperous of the British kingdoms.

Moreover, its rulers had already claimed control of Wales (incorporated into the English State by Henry VIII) and of Ireland. There, English control had been largely limited to the Pale, around Dublin, but successive rebellions and the planting of English settlers in Elizabeth's reign had enabled it to be gradually extended. In 1594, the anti-Protestant Ulster Confederacy led by Hugh O'Neill, Earl of Tyrone, broke into open defiance and sought Spanish help – but the rebellion was crushed in a brutal campaign by Lord Mountjoy and O'Neill finally surrendered six days after Elizabeth's death. The new King was truly master of three kingdoms, although perhaps exaggerating his status in awarding himself the title 'Emperor of Great Britain'.

> **KEY ISSUE**
>
> *The kingdom of England included Wales and Ireland.*

A *The King's Government*

Source A provides a contemporary view of government, in which a king ruled as well as reigned. He was head of the Church as well as of the State, appointing bishops to administer it as with any other government department, although they were not open to dismissal in the same way. The Church was an essential pillar of royal power, providing a means of communication through pronouncements from the pulpit, an administrative channel through parish officials, and a massive propaganda machine through its teaching of obedience and deference as illustrated in source B.

A From *De Republica Anglorum* by Sir Thomas Smith (1583).

The king distributes his authority and power in the fashion of five things: in the making of laws and ordinances; in the making of battle and peace with foreign nations; in providing of money for the maintenance of himself and defence against his enemies; in choosing and election of the chief officers and magistrates; and fifthly, in the administration of justice. The first and third are done by the prince [king] in parliament. The second and fourth by the prince [king] himself. The fifth is by the great assize [law courts].

Q

What is the significance of the statement that laws and taxes were made by the 'king in parliament'?

B From an Elizabethan homily. These were set prayers that were often read out during Church services and were taught to children.

Almighty God hath created and appointed all things in heaven, earth and waters in a most excellent and perfect order ... Every degree of people in their vocation, calling and office hath appointed to them their duty and order: some are in high degree, some in low, some kings and princes, some inferiors and subjects, priests and laymen, masters and servants, fathers and children, husbands and wives, rich and poor: and everyone hath need of other: so in all things is to be lauded [praised] the goodly order of God.

Q

How would this homily help government to keep order?

The centre of political power lay in the Royal Court, a combination of the monarch's private household, personal friends and government offices – access to the king was the source of both office and influence. For those with political ambitions or strong religious views, the way to achieve their aims was by gaining the king's favour, and putting their friends and allies in office. This led to the existence of political **factions**, which developed from relationships among courtiers and shaped the structure of politics at Court.

The monarch governed with the help of the Privy Council, appointed at his wish and discretion, although the main officers of state – the secretaries, lord treasurer, chancellors, keepers of the privy seal and others – were normally members by virtue of their offices. In addition, the monarch could, and frequently did, take advice from others outside the Council. Originally a council of advisers, by 1603 the Privy Council had acquired important administrative and judicial functions – members effectively headed government departments, acted as judges and supervised local government. They also staffed **prerogative** courts and councils, which had been developed to allow direct application of the monarch's personal authority.

The oldest of these was the Court of Chancery, used to decide cases that fell outside the scope of ordinary law. Councils for the North (based at York) and the Welsh Marches had been established to exercise control in the Tudor borderlands, alongside the Court of Star Chamber which consisted of privy councillors sitting in Whitehall and acting as

factions groups of supporters who gathered around an influential leader because they agreed with his views, owed him some personal loyalty, or believed that he could provide access to jobs and positions.

prerogative describes the personal powers of the monarch, not dependent upon law or Parliament. The prerogative courts were run by the King's Councillors, acting as personal deputies and exercising his personal power in his name.

judges in the king's name. After the Reformation of the 1530s, a Court of High Commission had been added to deal with Church matters. These courts were noted for their speed and detachment from local pressures, and carried out useful administrative and judicial tasks in the monarch's interest. The older law courts – the Court of the King's Bench and the Court of Common Pleas – dealt with criminal and civil cases under the common law, which was a mixture of custom, precedent, royal grants such as Magna Carta, and statute law made in Parliament. The judges, appointed by the monarch, held Assizes in each county.

It is clear from this description that the machinery of central government was extremely limited, and relied a great deal on the co-operation of the nobility and gentry in local government. The backbone of local government were the Justices of the Peace (JPs), who met in petty and quarter sessions to deal with both criminal and administrative matters. They were selected and supervised by the Privy Council. Although the position of JP was unpaid, and increasingly demanding as their functions grew in number, it conferred considerable status in the local community and was therefore widely sought. Duties included dealing with minor crime, the licensing of ale-houses, repair of roads and bridges and, by 1603, supervision of the system of Poor Laws that had been introduced to deal with the problems of unemployment and vagrancy. They supervised, and sometimes appointed, a range of local officials – constables, bailiffs and overseers of the poor, drawn from the 'middling sort' of yeomen, craftsmen and farmers – who put the law into effect at village and parish level. In the 1590s, the needs of war had added another tier of local

SOURCE C (DIAGRAM 2)
The structure of government and the social hierarchy in seventeenth-century England

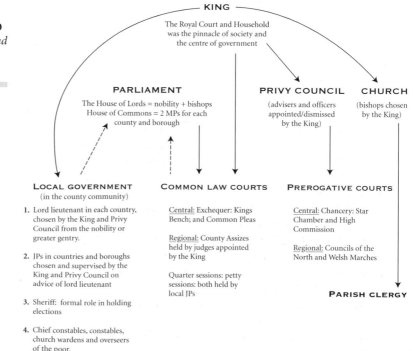

KING

The Royal Court and Household was the pinnacle of society and the centre of government

PARLIAMENT
The House of Lords = nobility + bishops
House of Commons = 2 MPs for each county and borough

PRIVY COUNCIL
(advisers and officers appointed/dismissed by the King)

CHURCH
(bishops chosen by the King)

LOCAL GOVERNMENT
(in the county community)

1. Lord lieutenant in each country, chosen by the King and Privy Council from the nobility or greater gentry.

2. JPs in countries and boroughs chosen and supervised by the King and Privy Council on advice of lord lieutenant

3. Sheriff: formal role in holding elections

4. Chief constables, constables, church wardens and overseers of the poor.

COMMON LAW COURTS

Central: Exchequer: Kings Bench; and Common Pleas

Regional: County Assizes held by judges appointed by the King

Quarter sessions: petty sessions: both held by local JPs

PREROGATIVE COURTS

Central: Chancery: Star Chamber and High Commission

Regional: Councils of the North and Welsh Marches

PARISH CLERGY

government in the office of Lord Lieutenant, responsible for the militia in each county, with the help of a number of deputies.

This system, summarised in source C, reveals a number of important characteristics of English government. In the first place, it relied upon unpaid amateurs at local level. Secondly, it involved a social hierarchy as well as a hierarchy of power. Society and government came together in the concept of a ruling class, based on the ownership of land and 'gentle' birth. Within this governing class there were different levels encompassing gentry and titled nobility, based on their political functions as well as wealth and titles. It was broadly assumed that the monarch should be served and advised directly by those closest to him, the titled nobility, while those below them administered the country at local and regional levels. In practice, it was never that simple – kings had always recruited their servants and advisers from the most talented, regardless of their social position, and men of quite lowly origins had risen through professional 'escalators' such as the Church and the legal professions. Nevertheless, the assumptions of the social hierarchy were recognised in the tendency to reward these ministers with the grant of titles, offering them the necessary status as well as land and wealth, often to the irritation of the older nobility who saw their position both usurped and undermined.

In the localities these hierarchies formed what has been described as the 'county community', meaning the gentry and their associates who governed in a particular region. The county was the basic unit of local government, and the emergence of county Lieutenants and Deputy-Lieutenants in the 1590s had helped to strengthen the sense of county identity. The Lord Lieutenant was usually drawn from the leading families, often titled, and the deputies from those just below them in status. They were often consulted by the Privy Council on the choice of JPs, and met with those chosen at the quarter sessions and county Assizes. Held in the county town, these were important social as well as judicial occasions.

The later sixteenth century had also seen the growth of close co-operation between county and borough authorities. Towns which held a royal charter had their own local government, usually in the form of a mayor and aldermen, although larger towns such as London and York also had a wider group of elected councillors. Often wealthy merchants, these men acted as JPs within the borough, and usually had considerable influence on the choice of MPs – each borough elected two, the same number as the counties. As the importance of Parliament increased, so the competition for seats enabled the boroughs to enlist the gentry to serve alongside members of the corporation. Their mutual interests, the tendency for wealthy merchants to purchase landed estates and for younger sons of gentry to engage in trade, strengthened local links and contributed to a sense of identity.

The strength of county identity varied. In counties like Kent there is evidence of a strong and distinctly 'county' identity – much less so in Warwickshire. In large counties such as Yorkshire and Lincolnshire, loyalties tended to be to smaller regions and sub-divisions. Whatever

KEY ISSUE

The importance of the ruling class as a partner in government.

KEY ISSUE

The gentry and the merchants were often linked in a 'county community'.

patronage the use of
wealth and/or power by
a patron to help,
support or encourage
an individual, with an
expectation of loyalty
and gratitude in return.
In political terms, it was
a way of ensuring
support; it was used by
kings to exercise control
over their subjects, and
by political leaders to
establish factions in a
period before political
parties existed.

their precise form, however, these communities provided the basis of
government in the country and their distinctive identity and loyalties
had to be recognised and accommodated. The machinery was oiled by a
system of **patronage** emanating from the king himself.

As the pinnacle of the social hierarchy and the source of office and
power, a king rewarded his friends and their friends with positions,
pensions and titles. The nobility therefore sought places at Court to
gain access to the monarch, and the lower levels of the gentry sought
the good influences of the nobility. In turn, the leading families cultivated the loyalty of gentry in their localities to increase their standing
with the king and to enhance their power in the political factions competing for the king's favour. A county with more than one such family
was often the scene of bitter rivalries which influenced reactions to
national politics at the local level.

The result was a series of overlapping groups and relationships
binding the localities to the centre. The local communities relied on
patronage from the centre; the Privy Council approved JPs, their
leading families cultivated contacts at Court, the ambitious sought positions and influence through such contacts. The crucial point is that the
existence of strong local communities made government a partnership
in which the authority of the king and the rights of the governing class
were mutually dependent. For the partnership to work, it had to be
managed with a measure of mutual respect. The governing class in the
localities had no doubt of their dependence on the king, not least to
protect them from the masses below and to ensure their own authority.
A king's legal and military powers, his wealth, status and rights made
open defiance both difficult and dangerous, but the limits of central
government machinery left plenty of scope for reluctant enforcement,
passive resistance and plain inertia. The partnership was one-sided, but
it was real, and a successful monarch needed the support of the governing class in its local functions and when it met as the 'political
community' in Parliament.

B *The function of parliaments*

KEY ISSUE

*Parliament was a point
of contact between the
king and the ruling
class.*

The 'political community' is the term often used to describe the governing class in the counties and boroughs, with the addition of those
outside it who could vote. It is difficult to assess numbers of voters, since
the borough franchise varied widely, but Derek Hirst has suggested that
the effects of growing wealth and inflation might have extended the electorate to include about one-third of adult males. If this is accurate, then
it can be argued that seventeenth-century parliaments were probably
fairly representative of public opinion, given the personal nature of
family and employment networks. When parliaments met, their functions were strictly limited. In no sense did they share the responsibilities
of government. They were called by the king, as and when he wished,
and sat for as long as he wished. Their purpose was to enable him
to understand his subjects, to turn certain decisions into statute law –

the highest and most secure form of law – and to grant extra revenue in the form of taxation when the needs of government justified it. They were not designed as a forum for politicians or opposition to the monarch.

MPs were not professional politicians, but representatives of a local community, sent to London to ensure that its needs and interests were protected. They were often local gentry or lawyers, sometimes office-holders, and frequently associated with a member of the House of Lords through loyalty or interest. The Lords was in many ways the superior House, and its members included politicians in the modern sense, i.e. men for whom politics was a normal and regular sphere of activity, by virtue of birth, wealth and positions at Court. It also included 26 bishops, owing their position entirely to the monarch. Parliaments had been created to strengthen the king's power by increasing his legal and financial options, and even in periods of apparent conflict this role continued. Nevertheless, in 1603 a combination of circumstances had made parliaments, and the House of Commons in particular, more politically significant.

Many of these circumstances can be traced back to the Henrician Reformation of the 1530s, in which Henry VIII seized control of the Church and its assets. This had been carried out through parliamentary legislation to ensure that the changes were legally enforceable. Not only had this process encouraged the development of parliamentary procedures and experience, it had also allowed Parliament to legislate concerning religion, the succession to the throne and the monarch's powers. Above all, it ensured that future changes would also have to be made through Parliament, significantly increasing its importance. The Reformation also brought Protestant ideas to England, with religious, social and political consequences. Protestant ideas emphasised the importance of bible-reading, and therefore literacy (see Chapter 9, pages 352–6). Combined with the increasing reliance on educated laymen to fill government posts once held by priests, this resulted in a larger, more powerful, more confident and articulate gentry class. The seizure of monastic lands by Henry strengthened Crown finances in the short term, but the need to ensure support and the costs of Henry's wars ensured that much of it was sold or given to the gentry and nobility, greatly increasing their wealth and creating a market in land which encouraged social mobility.

After the Reformation, religious quarrels divided British society. The issue became important in defining political factions among the nobility, and the existence of Parliament encouraged such factions to play out their rivalries in that arena as well as, more traditionally, at Court. The Catholic counter-Reformation and the influence of Catholic Spain created intense religious fears, and Queen Elizabeth's refusal to eradicate all traces of **popery** from the new Church of England led some MPs to try and bring in reform through Parliament. The Queen forbade such discussions, raising issues concerning the right of MPs to free speech. Extreme Protestants, or 'Puritans', who wanted to purify the Church were silenced, but not satisfied.

KEY ISSUE

Parliament's powers were limited.

KEY ISSUE

Parliament's role had been enhanced by the Henrician Reformation.

popery used to describe Catholic practices, such as richly decorated churches, elaborate ceremonies, praying to saints and the Virgin Mary, and the beliefs that lay behind them. Generally used as a term of abuse, a hostile reference to anything associated with Catholicism.

KEY ISSUE

Financial problems necessitated more frequent Parliaments.

This might well have mattered less if the monarchy had not also faced financial problems, which ensured that frequent Parliaments would be called. To some extent these were the result of a rising population and inflation across Europe, but they were made worse by the frequency and expense of warfare. Elizabeth attempted to control expenditure by avoiding war, but Spanish interference eventually made this impossible. Nevertheless, the political pressures made her reluctant to increase taxation, or update assessments in line with inflation. Instead, she sold Crown lands, underpaid her officials and resorted to financial expedients such as the sale of monopoly rights – passing on to James an outdated fiscal system, a debt of £100,000 and a good deal of parliamentary irritation on the subject of finance.

C *The character of the King*

PICTURE 1
James VI of Scotland, James I of England by Mytens – a portrait of senility

JAMES VI OF SCOTLAND, JAMES I OF ENGLAND 1566–1625

The new King was, in many ways, well-equipped to deal with these problems. The son of Mary, Queen of Scots and Lord Darnley, he was effectively orphaned as a baby and had been King of Scotland since his mother was deposed in 1567. The Scots were no easy nation to rule, since a succession of minority reigns had accustomed the nobility to a great deal of power and independence, and a Protestant Reformation carried out in spite of a Catholic monarch had created a Church that was rigidly Presbyterian and fiercely independent of state control. Nevertheless, James had shown considerable skill in balancing different factions to ensure that he could maintain control without alienating any completely.

His prospects in England were more complex. Physically unattractive, he avoided the dazzling ceremonial in which Elizabeth had wrapped the monarchy, and both contemporaries and historians have suggested that he lacked the dignity required by a monarch. Whig historians like Trevelyan condemned the gluttony and immorality of his Court, and lamented 'the change from a wise Queen to a foolish King', while others referred to his 'mumbling speech and dirty ways...', his blatantly homosexual attachments and his alcoholic excesses'. His portraits, however, suggest a sharp intelligence. They conflict with the descriptions given by hostile commentators like Sir Anthony Weldon who described him as fat, cowardly, forever fiddling with his codpiece, and with a tendency to dribble food because his tongue was too large for his mouth. The difficulty of making judgements regarding his appearance and personality arises from the lack of reliable evidence. Portrait painters found it wise to flatter kings, while Weldon's attitude can be judged from his comment that 'to be bound in marriage to a Scot would be like being chained to carcass and thrown into a stinking ditch'. His view of James was not improved by the fact that, upon hearing of his comments, the King dismissed him from Court. It may therefore be suggested that his descriptions of the new King were not entirely fair.

For the most part, James's characteristics had both good and bad effects on his ability to govern England well. A rigid Presbyterian upbringing had encouraged his scholarly interests, and before becoming King of England he had already published learned works on *The Trew Law of Free Monarchies* and *Basilikon Doron*, which was a manual on kingship. He was known for his desire to bring peace to Europe, an advantage to an England struggling with a long and crippling war with Spain. On the other hand, his high-flown claims of a Divine Right of Kings, who were God's representatives on earth, did not endear him to a political community in England that was much attached to the common law and rights of Parliament. James himself seems to have found relief from his upbringing in personal extravagance, a love of hunting and a tendency to surround himself with handsome male companions which may, or may not, have involved active homosexuality. While his open affection for his young favourites, and a tendency to lavish gifts on them, was offensive to his English subjects (especially if the favourites were Scots), his generosity was in some ways a pleasant contrast to the refusal of Elizabeth to reward adequately those who served her. It was an indication of James's shrewdness in practice that, despite a level of extravagance and self-indulgence in his handling of money, he also made sure that rewards of both wealth and power were spread across all the main factions in both of his kingdoms.

It would appear, therefore, that both the new King and his inheritance were a mixture of good and bad features. England was a potentially well-governed kingdom, with particular problems relating to the limited power of central government, divisions within the Church, and the state of public finances. James was a shrewd politician and an experienced Protestant king, able to handle situations with tact and diplomacy, but with a liking for grandiose schemes and a serious tendency towards self-indulgence. The impact of his reign would perhaps depend on which side of his character came to predominate.

KEY ISSUE

The importance of the King's character in a personal monarchy.

2 ⌐ THE EARLY YEARS AND THE HOPES FOR REFORM

When James arrived in England he was greeted with relief as a Protestant successor, and with hope that problems which had emerged in the old Queen's years of decline could be addressed. His closest ally was Robert Cecil, who had done much to prepare his way. Cecil had served Elizabeth through the 1590s and was skilled in the factional intrigues of the Court. In 1604 he was able to use Catholic plots to discredit his main rival, Sir Walter Raleigh, and confirm his dominant influence in the Privy Council. He recognised the need for reform in the administration and in royal finances. James himself had ambitions to bring about constitutional reform by uniting his new kingdoms, and showed his readiness to work with the political community by summoning Parliament to meet in 1604. In the meantime, he found himself addressed by those desiring changes in the Church – the Catholics who sought relief from persecuting laws and the Puritan reformers who hoped to see the Church in England become more like the one that James knew in Scotland.

A *Church, Crown and People*

THE CHURCH OF ENGLAND AND ITS PROBLEMS

The Church of England, as constituted in 1603, had been established by Elizabeth in 1558–9. Faced with a bitterly divided nation, she had sought to create a flexible institution, capable of embracing a wide range of views. While its doctrine (laid down in **Thirty-Nine Articles** of faith) was clearly Protestant, she had retained many traditional symbols and services because they were familiar, popular and to her own taste. She also ensured that the Church was administered by bishops whom she appointed and controlled. The result was a compromise which was acceptable to the majority, but which left dissatisfied minorities such as Catholics loyal to Rome and Protestant reformers who believed that the Church should be purified further. Their attempts to achieve this were frustrated by the Queen and her bishops, but Puritan ideas remained a significant force within the Church. In 1603, they hoped that a king who had been brought up in the thoroughly Puritan Church of Scotland would have more sympathy with their aims. They therefore presented him with a petition – the Millenary Petition, supposedly signed by a thousand ministers – listing the changes that they hoped he would make. In response, James agreed to attend a conference at Hampton Court in 1604 to debate the issues.

Some historians have suggested that this was a misjudgement in that, by agreeing to a debate, he gave some recognition to Puritanism as a force within the Church. The argument should not, however, be pushed too far. Puritan ideas were already a force which had survived the hostility of Queen Elizabeth, and James had little to lose by hearing their arguments. There were genuine issues to be discussed, not least the

Thirty-Nine Articles
these were published in the Book of Common Prayer and laid down the beliefs and rules of the Church.

KEY ISSUE

Anglicanism – a 'middle way'.

See pages 340–1 for the Church's poverty.

poverty of the Church and the misuse of its buildings and churchyards. Of 9,244 parishes, only 3,804 had a resident, university-trained minister. The Reformation had involved a vast transfer of Church property into the hands of laymen, and in many parishes the tithes, a tax of 10 per cent on all incomes, which was supposed to be paid for the minister's support, had been **'impropriated'** by laymen who chose the minister and paid a salary of some kind. Some parishes were far too large for one minister to serve, and the poverty of others led to the practice of pluralism – holding more than one living. Churches were used for business meetings, sports and games and in one place for storing coal. Churchmen with such widely differing views as the Puritan John Preston and the High Anglican, William Laud (at this time a newly-ordained chaplain), agreed on the need to address the condition of churches. Their proposed remedies, however, were totally opposed, reflecting the deep and serious divisions within the Church over its organisation and forms of worship.

> **impropriation** the taking over of the right to choose a minister for a particular parish and to collect the tithes.

PURITANISM AND REFORM

The nature of religious divisions and of Puritan ideas has been the subject of much historical debate, in which recent research has challenged the established idea of 'Puritanism' as a coherent movement. It is clear that 'Puritans' did not differ in any defined way from other English Protestants in 1603, when the Calvinist theology of predestination – that a minority of souls had been selected by God to be saved as a free gift of grace – was shared by the vast majority. This theology would be challenged by the Dutch thinker, Jacob Arminius, and by a minority of Anglicans who shared his views, but it would also come under fire from 'Puritan' separatists like John Smyth, the founder of the English Baptists. There is similar difficulty in defining Puritans on the basis of Church organisation. While many English Puritans had a preference for the form of organisation used by Calvin in Geneva, and adopted as Presbyterianism in Scotland, there were others who found the office of bishops quite acceptable. Much of the Puritan dislike of bishops in 1603 was the result of Elizabeth's use of them to silence demands for further reform.

> **KEY ISSUE**
>
> *The problem of defining Puritanism.*

See pages 359–63 for Puritanism in action.

This does not mean that Puritan ideas and influence were not real and significant, but it does suggest that they should be seen as strong Protestants, defined by a range of characteristics, rather than as a distinct or coherent movement. In many ways, they are most clearly recognisable in relation to the other religious extreme, the Catholics. For Puritans, the Church of Rome was not an alternative form of Christianity, but an evil anti-Christian force, and the Pope was Antichrist (the Devil) himself. Early Protestants had protested against the corruption and mistaken doctrines of the Church. This corruption for Puritans had been the Devil at work, destroying the purity of the early Church in order to hinder the work of God and lead souls to hell. It was therefore crucial to remove all traces of popery (Catholicism) from the reformed churches, in order to prevent that corruption from creeping back.

To modern ears these beliefs appear extreme and illogical, but there

> **KEY ISSUE**
>
> *The strength of anti-Catholic fears.*

are strong parallels with the anti-Communist fears that gripped western Europe and America in the years after the Second World War, when communist and socialist beliefs were not viewed as a political alternative, but as an alien ideology, secretly supported by a network of spies, the agents of a threatening foreign power. The world was dominated by an eternal struggle between good and evil, in which only permanent vigilance could protect the good. Knowledge of the good was contained in the Bible, the word of God, and it was in the Bible that the correct forms of organisation and worship, as well as doctrine were to be found. The main function of the Church, therefore, was to preach and teach knowledge of the Bible so that individuals could know and understand God, and its key figures were the preaching ministers who fulfilled this role.

What this meant in practice was that Puritans wanted a Church in which educated ministers were free to preach and pray without being distracted by set forms and ceremonies. They wanted the wealth that had been taken from the Church at the Reformation to be used to provide a capable minister in each parish. He should preach at least once in each week, possibly twice, and should be encouraged to hold extra meetings for reading and discussing the meaning of the Bible. All superstitious signs and symbols, such as using the sign of the cross in baptism, should be abolished, and churches should be simple, whitewashed buildings without statues and stained glass which distracted people from listening to the word of God. Ministers should not be forced to wear special robes. Some wished to see a Presbyterian form of organisation, in which ministers were assisted by parish Elders to discipline and control the behaviour of their parishioners, and meetings of ministers and their representatives made the decisions about the rules of the Church. If there were to be bishops, they should be for advice and guidance, and should not have the power to enforce their decisions.

For the most part, these ideas were well within the mainstream of Protestant thinking. Elizabeth's objections to them were political rather than religious, based on the desire to accommodate traditionalists as well as reformers, and upon the threat that such ministerial independence would pose to royal control. She had little interest in the private beliefs of her subjects. She believed that the key function of the Church was to teach obedience to authority, and she had no intention of surrendering control of such a major influence over their attitudes and beliefs. Catholics therefore were fined for **recusancy**, but not for private worship unless there was some suggestion of contacts abroad, which could lead to treason.

Similarly, Puritans were able to preach and work within the Church, but were disciplined for breaches of its rules and denied the opportunity to change them. However, by 1603, some ministers, notably Richard Hooker, had begun to challenge Puritan claims and argue that, far from being a weak compromise, the Church of England represented the true faith of the early Church, inheriting its best traditions without the corruptions brought in by Rome. Those who held such Anglican

---

KEY ISSUE

Puritan demands for an educated Church, cleansed of popish characteristics.

---

recusancy the term means a refusal to attend church on Sundays, which had been made compulsory by law in the reign of Elizabeth. Recusants were fined, providing a useful income for government, or rather, for the courtiers who were granted collection rights.

views believed that, not only was further reform unnecessary, it would damage true faith. Therefore, by 1604, when the Hampton Court Conference met, there was resistance to Puritan demands for reform on both political and religious grounds.

THE HAMPTON COURT CONFERENCE AND ITS AFTERMATH

In 1604, James responded to the Millenary Petition by calling a conference of Church leaders at Hampton Court. Despite his desire to be a peacemaker, he reacted angrily to Puritan demands for reform, which he claimed would have ended 'the dependency of the Church upon the Crown'. It was this perception that lay behind his famous declaration that 'No Bishop' would end in 'no King' and his threat to 'harry them out of the land' if Puritan ministers would not conform. The only positive result of the conference was the authorisation of a new translation of the Bible, which finally appeared in 1611. True to his threat, James approved strict new canons (church rules) in 1604, and appointed the authoritarian Richard Bancroft as Archbishop of Canterbury when Whitgift died in the same year. A number of ministers were deprived of their livings immediately, and others followed. Bancroft also attempted to address the problems of poverty and **pluralism,** putting forward an ambitious scheme in 1610 to raise Church revenues and reclaim impropriated tithes to improve the quality and provision of ministers. The scheme was dropped because of opposition from the propertied classes, in Parliament, the very people who held most of the 4,000 impropriated livings which would be reclaimed.

For some Puritans, James's hostile reaction and the disappointing of their hopes led to a parting of the ways, and they moved into separatism as opposed to reforming the Church from within. Among these were John Smyth and John Robinson, two Cambridge-educated ministers who were deprived of their livings and founded a separatist congregation in Lincolnshire, near Gainsborough. After discovery and persecution, the group left England in 1608 to live in the more tolerant atmosphere of Holland. There they went separate ways, Smyth going on to establish the Baptist movement, while Robinson and his adherents eventually sailed in the *Mayflower* to America and established the first colony in New England, at Massachusetts Bay. This would later provide a refuge for many Puritan emigrants, driven out by the harsher persecutions of Laud in the 1630s.

Having blocked changes in the Church, however, James had no wish to provoke the Puritans unnecessarily. He shared their Calvinist theology, and sympathetic to many of their concerns. His experience of the Presbyterian Church in Scotland made him determined to assert his political control, but he was aware of the importance of an educated, preaching ministry. In the Church, as in many other aspects of government, James sought to bring English and Scottish practice closer together by encouraging the best features of each system. He therefore restored bishops in Scotland, although with more limited powers than their English counterparts. They were initially ordained in England, to establish a link with the wider Christian tradition.

See page 343 for James I's compromises.

pluralism the practice of holding more than one living in order to increase income. It led to the neglect of some parishes and the use of an inadequate and poorly paid deputy.

KEY ISSUE

James I's sensible moderation.

Feoffees a group of Puritans – four lawyers, four merchants and four ministers – who sought to buy up impropriated tithes and use them to provide a preaching ministry in each parish.

KEY ISSUE

Treatment of Catholics.

Arminian was a label attached to the High Church faction who wanted to restore many traditional ceremonies and decorations. It came from a Dutch theologian, Jacob Arminius, who challenged Calvin's views.

In England James approved schemes to improve the quality of the ministry, and when these were blocked by political interests, allowed private endowments, like those later set up by the **Feoffees.** In eight years they raised over £6,000, and by 1633, when Laud brought their work to an end, had at least 18 ministers installed in neglected parishes. At the same time, wealthy individuals, often of Puritan inclination, endowed special sermons or 'lectures', often in towns and boroughs on market days and weekdays, to supplement the work of local churches. The result was that James's reign saw a measure of peace in the Church, based on an informal compromise. When Bancroft died in 1611, James appointed the distinctly Calvinist George Abbot as the Archbishop of Canterbury. Under Abbot's leadership a measure of flexibility was used in applying the rules of the Church, and as long as ministers accepted the authority of the bishops, demonstrated their obedience by occasional use of the correct services and symbols, and did not engage in political campaigns for further change, they were often allowed a measure of choice in how they conducted their ministries. In 1618, Abbot was able to persuade James to withdraw the Book of Sports, which offended Puritans by encouraging games and pastimes to be played on Sundays, but in 1621 his authority was diminished after he accidentally shot a gamekeeper, and he was unable to exercise any restraining influence over Charles I.

A similar attitude was adopted towards Roman Catholics. In 1603, James had tried to soften the recusancy laws, to vociferous protests from both Puritans and the courtiers who benefited from the fines. The Gunpowder Plot of 1605 caused a flurry of anti-Catholic activity, but thereafter enforcement of the recusancy laws was patchy and variable. Government exploited the plot for political purposes, including a grant of money from Parliament, but Cecil was well aware that the majority of English Catholics were both loyal and peaceable. Wealthy families suffered financially from fines and a certain level of harassment – often because of the need to exploit all sources of revenue rather than for religious purposes – but as long as Catholics worshipped privately and discreetly, they were left in peace for long periods. Only when political pressures or events focused attention on the threat of international Catholicism did the anti-Catholic paranoia, which was always present in English thinking, rise to the surface to threaten English Catholics in practice.

In religious matters, therefore, it can be said that James balanced a determination to exercise political control with a measure of tact and diplomacy. In Scotland he proceeded cautiously with reform, and in 1621 attempted to introduce a set form of service, not unlike the Book of Common Prayer. Faced with widespread opposition, he abandoned the scheme with good grace. In England he was careful to promote and encourage leading figures from all parties in the Church, as bishops, deans and royal chaplains. The result was that all varieties of Protestant thought developed within the Church. A small **Arminian** group argued for greater ceremonial and beautification of the churches, a much larger number developed an affection for the existing Anglican practice. A significant Puritan minority, seeing themselves as the 'godly', sought to defend Protestantism and spread their message of devotion to God and the Bible through preaching, bible meetings and classes, and a 'reformation of manners'. Denied the right to change the Church as they had wished, they were nevertheless able to spread their ideas and win hearts and minds to their cause. In that sense, James failed to solve the problem of religious division in England and of conflicting views within the Church. What he did achieve, however, was a situation in which these parties were able to co-exist, to work for the benefit of souls, and to maintain political loyalty to the King and the State in which they lived.

B *Politics and the constitution*

A UNITED KINGDOM?

The issue of most immediate concern to the King himself was that of constitutional reform, to recognise and accommodate the new links between the British kingdoms. His inheritance meant that James ruled three separate kingdoms – England and Wales, Ireland, and Scotland – each with its own parliament, Church and legal system. Not surprisingly, James wanted to create greater uniformity, and saw his accession as an opportunity to bring improvement to all three. Ireland, with its Catholic majority and Gaelic culture, was bound to prove problematical, but James saw no reason why progress could not be made quickly in uniting England and Scotland. There were three possibilities. The favoured option among some Englishmen was for an 'incorporative' union, similar to the sixteenth-century union with Wales, by which Scotland would be reorganised into counties along English lines, send MPs to Westminster and adopt English common law. An alternative, more acceptable to the Scots, was for a federal union, in which the two kingdoms would remain separate entities with their own constitutional identities. The third option, preferred by James, was for a 'perfect' union, in which both countries would adopt a common, reformed system of law and government, based on the best features of both. As in the Church, James saw the situation as an opportunity for improvement, and it was in this spirit that he sought to present the idea to his first Parliament in 1604.

Unfortunately, the session began badly when government lawyers tried to reverse the results of the election in Buckinghamshire, where the 'Court' candidate, Sir John Fortescue, had been defeated because of local quarrels. The attempt was ham-fisted, rather than sinister, but irritated a House of Commons, which had learned to guard its privileges under Elizabeth; the House declared that only MPs had the right to judge the validity of elections. In turn, James seems to have over-reacted, reminding them that parliamentary privileges had been granted by monarchs. By implication, this suggested that what had been granted could be taken away. The incident was smoothed over, since neither side wished to create an open breach, but it helped to sour the

> ### KEY ISSUE
>
> *James failed to establish union between England and Scotland.*

atmosphere. James was further irritated by complaints from some provincial MPs that the peace with Spain, now nearing completion, would only benefit the London merchants who increasingly monopolised the cloth trade. They greeted his plans for British union in the same vein. Genuine concerns about the safety of common law rights were overlaid with anti-Scottish prejudice – complaints were aired about greedy Scots who would flood into England, as well as those who had already accompanied the King south. As a new monarch, James had distributed posts and pensions with considerable generosity; those who complained tended to ignore his equal generosity to English supporters and focus solely on what had been given to the Scots.

In 1604, these tensions created no more than an exchange of words. A Commons' *Apology*, which was in fact a defence of their rights to free debate, was never presented to the King because he defused the situation by proroguing (suspending) the sitting. However, when Parliament reassembled in 1606, he found that little had changed. The aftermath of the Gunpowder Plot and a burst of Protestant unity led the Commons to vote for taxes to help settle royal debts, but on the issue of union, they were immovable. Sir Edwin Sandys suggested that the 'perfect' union could be achieved by abolishing Scottish law and replacing it with the law of England, but even this was unacceptable to some MPs who saw the Scots as penniless adventurers. 'If one man owns two pastures', declared one MP, 'with one hedge to divide them; the one pasture bare, the other fertile and good; a wise owner will not pull down the hedge, but make gates to let them in and out, otherwise the cattle will rush in and not want to return'. Clearly, he saw the 'cattle' in question dressed in kilts and bonnets. By 1607, therefore, it was clear that James's cherished scheme of reform was not going to succeed, and he had the sense to withdraw. In 1608, he persuaded the judges to declare common citizenship for those born after 1603, and in 1607–9 he imposed a campaign of pacification on the border counties, notorious for the lawlessness created by clans of armed robbers on both sides of the border. Apart from such piecemeal changes, however, he abandoned his efforts.

THE PROBLEM OF FINANCE

Constitutional reform had quickly proved unattainable, and the relationship of King and Parliament had clearly been damaged by the process, but James's realism had prevented an open breach. However, a far more contentious problem was building up because of the growing inadequacy of Crown finances. To some extent this was the fault of the King, who never managed to exercise the financial discipline that was required. To a greater extent, however, the problem arose from fundamental weaknesses in the methods of financing government, and expectations of the King as the source of power and patronage.

The origins of the problem lay in the wars of Henry VIII and the inflationary pressures caused by a rising population. This situation had worsened during Elizabeth's reign, with the expense of war against Spain. Elizabeth had tried to limit expenditure, but had failed to address the underlying issues. For political reasons she had neither administered Crown estates commercially, nor updated the tax structure in line with inflation. Tax assessments, including customs' duties, were based on out-dated prices, and the Crown continued to grant lands on fixed rents for long leases. In 1587, for example, Elizabeth leased land in Bermondsey at £68 per annum, which was found to be worth £1,071 per annum when the lease ended in 1636. Tax rates were even more out-dated, but religious and political pressures meant that Elizabeth feared offending supporters, and instead adopted short-term solutions such as the sale of Crown lands or the granting of monopoly patents or income from judicial fines.

The difficulties that James inherited were not insoluble. There was a small surplus on current expenditure, which peace with Spain reinforced. An existing debt of about £100,000 could be covered by parliamentary grants. The core of the problem lay in two factors – the first was the continuing expectation that kings should fund normal government out of their own incomes, increasingly difficult in an age of inflation, and the second was James's extravagant approach to the distribution of patronage. While this was not unreasonable for a new king, anxious to ensure future support as well as reward past services, James's generosity was excessive in both its extent and longevity. Robert Cecil and Thomas Sackville, both of whom had played a significant part in ensuring his peaceful accession, became Earls of Salisbury and Dorset respectively. To maintain political balance, James also elevated Lord Henry Howard to the Earldom of Northampton. Both honours and wealth were granted to his Scottish favourites and the 906 new knights created in the first four months of his reign. These honours were often accompanied by pensions and grants of income. In 1611, James gave away £90,688, with £67,498 of it going to 11 Scotsmen.

While this expenditure does not explain the financial problem entirely, it was distinctly unhelpful and politically unwise at a time when Parliament was being asked to grant extra taxation not normally expected in peacetime. It was particularly unhelpful when Salisbury was attempting to persuade Parliament of the need for structural reform. He addressed the financial problems from two angles. For the long term, he sought to persuade Parliament to make a regular contribution to royal finances through a Great Contract, by which the King would give up certain traditional payments in return for a regular grant of parliamentary taxation. In the short term, he sought to address immediate problems by a more rigorous exploitation of the customs duties, known as **tonnage and poundage**, which were granted to each monarch at the start of their reign. In the event, the two strategies proved contradictory, and contributed to his eventual failure.

The issue of taxation was a delicate one, which could only be dealt with in co-operation with Parliament. Salisbury's aim was to persuade the Commons to grant a regular income to the monarch, to be paid for by parliamentary taxation – an unheard of and fundamental change. He hoped to obtain agreement by offering to abandon some of

KEY ISSUE

The need for financial reform.

tonnage and poundage traditional duties on wine and wool, the right to levy them being usually granted to a king or queen for life by the first Parliament of his or her reign.

wardship was a king's traditional right (and duty) to take responsibility for any females or minors inheriting land held by military tenure. The practice allowed the estates to be exploited for a king's benefit, as well as allowing him to arrange marriages and extract inheritance fines when the heir came of age.

purveyance gave a king the special right to purchase food and supplies for the Royal Court at fixed low prices. It was based on the feudal idea that the monarch had a right to be supplied by those who owed him loyalty.

impositions were new, extra duties levied on imports – so-called because they were not approved by Parliament.

the Crown's traditional rights, such as the payment of **wardship** and **purveyance**.

At one time, when monarchs regularly travelled around the kingdom, purveyance had affected most areas, but with the Court increasingly stationary in and around London, the problem, and benefit from its abolition, affected a relatively small number of counties and constituencies. Similarly, wardship had an uneven impact, since it only came into operation if the head of a family died early, and affected families with great estates more than most. By offering to exchange these rights for parliamentary payments, Salisbury was seeking to put royal finances on a more predictable and rational basis. The financial benefits would not, however, be evenly spread, and success would therefore require a measure of goodwill from Parliament.

Unfortunately, other events combined to reduce such goodwill. Salisbury's hopes of introducing the scheme in the parliamentary sessions of 1604 and 1606–7 were frustrated by the King's schemes for an Anglo-Scottish union, and received further setbacks from parliamentary complaints about the King's extravagance. His exploitation of customs duties was also resented. In 1606, Parliament had granted some subsidies to settle the King's debts. James promptly gave away £44,000 of it to three Scottish friends. Instead, Dorset (the Lord Treasurer) had to sell off land, reducing future income still further. Unable to control the King's expenditure, Salisbury was forced to expand revenue, and the customs were the obvious source. A decision by the judges in Bate's case of 1606, arising from problems in the Levant Company, had clarified the King's control of the rate and number of duties and allowed him to add to, or increase existing levies. In 1608, therefore, Salisbury issued a new Book of Rates, imposing new and increased duties. Financially, it was a rewarding move, bringing in £70,000 per annum by 1610. Politically, and in the longer term, it was a serious error.

When Parliament reassembled in 1610, there were vociferous complaints about the new **impositions** and fears expressed that, if the King became financially independent, the future of Parliament might be bleak. This was hardly the best atmosphere in which to propose the Great Contract that Salisbury envisaged. In return for a parliamentary income of £200,000 a year, the King would abandon his rights to wardship and purveyance, and the use of informers in raising judicial fines. James also hinted that he would add no more new impositions. Members were instructed to consult their constituents during the summer recess, and negotiations would be resumed when Parliament reassembled in November.

By that time, both sides had begun to have serious doubts. The Commons had been shocked by the amount requested, and reaction in the country confirmed these reservations. Many of the gentry were largely unaffected by wardship and purveyance, but more seriously, they feared James's intentions if he were freed from the need to call Parliaments. In the words of the lawyer, James Whitelocke: 'Considering the greatest use they make of assembling Parliaments, which is the supply of money', there seemed little reason to believe that parliaments would survive under a financially independent monarch. James had also begun to have doubts. There was no provision to pay off existing debts, and there were significant disadvantages to a fixed income in a time of inflation. Perhaps more importantly, he was well aware of the political control that he gained over the nobility by the existence of wardship. Moderate inheritance fines, careful management of estates and beneficial marriages for the King's friends, or the opposite for those who had offended him, were powerful weapons in maintaining support.

The result was that both sides began to draw back, and the Contract came to nothing. Its failure, however, destroyed the power of Salisbury, who forfeited James's trust. Although he held on to his offices until his death in 1612, power began to drift towards other factions, in particular the Howard faction headed by Henry Howard, Earl of Northampton, and his nephew, Thomas, Earl of Suffolk. In opposition to their Catholic links and tendencies, an alternative faction gathered around the Earl of Pembroke, Chief Justice Sir Edward Coke, the Lord Chancellor, Ellesmere, and the Calvinist Archbishop of Canterbury, George Abbot. James himself seemed happy to allow these rivalries, confident that by balancing his favours he could manipulate both factions. Instead, his laziness and reluctance to commit himself to any strategy encouraged the government to drift, lacking clear purpose and direction, and slipping deeper into debt, factional rivalry and corruption.

THE FAILURE OF REFORM

It is clear, therefore, that by 1610 the opportunity to reform the system of government had slipped away. The causes of failure do not lie with any single individual, but in a series of errors and misunderstandings: the narrow and short-sighted outlook of many MPs; the greed and faction of lords and courtiers; the contradictory strategies adopted by Salisbury; and the self-indulgence displayed by James himself. Nevertheless, there is also evidence of a more deep-seated problem between King and Parliament, in the suspicions shown by MPs of some desire on the King's part to destroy, or at least weaken, Parliament as an institution.

> **KEY ISSUE**
>
> *The abandonment of financial reform.*

> **Q** *What were the MPs' fears which prompted the* Apology?

D From the Commons' *Apology* of 1604.

All experience shows that the prerogatives of princes may easily, and do daily, grow [but] the privileges of the subject are for the most part, at an everlasting stand. They may be by good providence and care preserved, but once being lost are not recovered but with much disquiet. If good kings were immortal as well as kingdoms, to strive so for privilege were but vanity perhaps, and folly; but seeing the same God who ... hath given us a wise King ... doth also sometimes permit hypocrites and tyrants..., from hence hath the desire of rights, liberties and privileges ... had its just original ...

This was revealed as early as 1604 in the Apology of the House of Commons. Source D, on the previous page, which is an extract from it, shows the fears that arose from the issue of who controlled the choice of MPs when elections were doubtful or disputed.

The Commons therefore saw themselves as under pressure, forced to defend their rights; the existence of parliaments was one of the few guarantees of the rule of law and the liberties of the subject. This mentality was clearly defensive, rather than an attack upon royal power or a wish to increase the importance of Parliament at the King's expense, but it was also significant and potentially damaging.

The reasons for such suspicions probably lay outside James's control, in the events of Elizabeth's reign and in developments in Europe, but there is no doubt that James made them worse. It was not that he acted in a despotic way – indeed he had shown considerable respect for Parliament since his accession – but that his theoretical claims and declarations gave the impression that he might. In 1598 he had published *The Trew Law of Free Monarchies*, in which he laid claim to a high-sounding **Divine Right of Kings.** While Tudor monarchs such as Henry VIII could be tyrannical in practice, and while Elizabeth was always willing to assert her prerogative rights, the Tudor monarchy had established the concept of government by king-in-parliament.

> **Divine Right of Kings** was the belief that kings represented God on earth and were chosen by him. To resist the king was to defy God.

As source A shows, a king governed but conducted certain functions of government in Parliament – specifically the making of law and the raising of taxes. English monarchy was therefore 'mixed' rather than absolute, and the function of the king's laws, made in Parliament, was to define law and protect the subject as well as asserting royal authority. What James's theories stressed, and what MPs feared he might seek to put into practice, was the absolute authority of monarchy as the representative of God on earth and the source of all law. In theory, James's claims placed him above the law – as illustrated in sources E and F.

> **E** From *The True Law of Free Monarchies* (1598).
>
> . . . the king is overlord of the whole land so he is master over every person that inhabiteth the same, having power over the life and death of every one of them. For although a just prince will not take the life of any of his subjects without a clear law, yet the same laws whereby he taketh them are made by himself or his predecessors, and so the power flows always from himself . . .

James is clearly writing in theoretical terms, and, regarding himself as a just prince, made no claim to a right to ignore the law, but the argument left subjects no protection other than a king's sense of justice. Similarly, in a speech made to Parliament in 1610, while declaring his intention of obeying the law, he made it clear that this was a matter of conscience and choice rather than enforceable limits on his power.

F From a speech to Parliament in 1610.

The state of monarchy is the supremest thing on earth; for kings are not only God's lieutenants upon earth, and sit upon God's throne, but even by God himself they are called gods . . . In the first original of kings, whereof some had their beginning by conquest and some by election of the people, their wills at that time served for law. Yet how soon kingdoms began to be settled in civility and policy, then did kings set down their minds by laws, which are properly made by the king only . . . So, as every just king is bound to observe that paction [pact] made to his people by his laws . . . A king governing in a settled kingdom leaves to be a king and degenerates into a tyrant, as soon as he leaves off to rule according to his laws . . . As for my part, I thank God I have ever given good proof that I never had intention to the contrary . . . I will not be content that my power be disputed upon, but I shall ever be willing to make reason appear of all my doings, and rule my actions according to my laws.

Q *Do sources E and F suggest that James I was reasonable, or that he aimed at unreasonable, unlimited monarchy?*

From James's point of view, this was a conciliatory speech, making clear his good intentions. It did not occur to him that some of his subjects might find the prince's conscience and goodwill a small protection for their liberty and property. Nothing in James's actions suggests any intention to dispense with Parliament, despite the irritation that he undoubtedly felt about some of the members' more obstructive attitudes. His manner and words however do explain the defensive attitudes adopted by MPs, which contributed to the failure of necessary reforms.

In the short term, the damage done to relationships between the King and Parliament was limited. Throughout the remainder of his reign, James continued to exercise a measure of tact and avoided any serious breakdown in relationships within the governing class. Nevertheless, the best opportunities for necessary reforms had passed him by, and the long-term consequences for monarchy and government were serious as will become apparent in the next chapter.

> **KEY ISSUE**
>
> *How far had the relationship between James and Parliaments been damaged by 1610?*

3 ↝ DRIFT AND DETERIORATION

A *The years of drift*

The years that followed the failure of the Great Contract and the decline of Salisbury's power can be described as a period in which government drifted, lacking clear leadership or a sense of direction. James did not allow any single figure to dominate government as Salisbury had done, instead dividing it among different factions. Unfortunately, he was also too indolent himself to provide the leadership that was necessary to make such a system function well. The situation was made worse by the death of his eldest son, and heir, the charismatic Prince Henry in 1612.

> **KEY ISSUE**
>
> *James was too lazy to control factions and give government a clear direction.*

His brother Charles was at this time too young and too lacking in confidence to play a significant role in influencing political decisions. Without a strong lead, factions and individuals competed for power, and decisions could be influenced as much by internal rivalries as by the needs of government.

THE ROLE OF FACTION

Rivalries might involve differences of policy, but were often linked to competition for office and the wealth that could come from it. An example of this can be seen in the rivalry between the Chief Justice, Sir Edward Coke, and his fellow-lawyer, the Attorney-General, Sir Francis Bacon. In 1616, Coke was dismissed from office for refusing to interfere, on the King's behalf, in a lawsuit against the Bishop of Lichfield and Coventry. Bacon sided with the King and gained promotion in royal service. In 1618 he became the Lord Chancellor. Coke, having regained favour by forcing his daughter to marry the brother of the Duke of Buckingham (James's personal favourite), went on to lead the parliamentary attack on corruption in 1621; he was able to divert complaints about Buckingham, to protect the Duke and to engineer the dismissal of Bacon on charges of bribery. Personal and political rivalries, interacting with the system of patronage, therefore created an aura, and sometimes the reality, of greed and corruption.

See page 387 for Coke's attitude to his daughter's marriage.

KEY ISSUE

Personal rivalries and lack of leadership create tensions and a sense of corruption in government.

The immediate problem facing the government after 1610 was the perennial one of money. The failure of the Great Contract meant that other methods had to be found to deal with the King's debts, and further impositions on customs would create huge political problems. The result was that the government lurched from one strategy or project to another. In 1611, a new title of baronet was created, specifically to be sold to raise funds. At first this was successful, with new and minor gentry flocking to pay the asking price of £1,095, and by 1614 it had raised £90,000. Thereafter, however, it was vastly oversold, and by 1622 the price had fallen to £220. As a contemporary commentator sourly remarked, 'Gentlemen be made good cheap in England'. The sale of more prestigious titles created great offence among the older nobility.

Even more irritating to the population as a whole was the practice of selling monopoly patents for the production or importing of certain goods. By this method, groups of merchants were given exclusive trading rights in return for payment to the King and bribes to the courtiers who arranged it. While some monopolies might be necessary to protect new industries or high-risk trading ventures, the lack of competition usually led to higher prices (to recover the cost of the patent) and often to a decline in quality. Elizabeth's use of monopolies gave rise to a crisis in the Parliament of 1601, but by 1610 James's financial problems and the need to reward those who served him had led to their renewed use. By 1614 there was growing anger in the country at the extravagance, corruption and self-indulgence of the King and his Court.

THE ADDLED PARLIAMENT

In 1614, the Pembroke faction persuaded James to call Parliament, in the hope that the more anti-Spanish foreign policy that they favoured could be used to obtain a grant of supplies. They had already had some success in creating a more 'Protestant' image, in the marriage of the King's daughter, Elizabeth, to the German protestant prince, the Elector Palatine. Preparations for the election were muddled, with little co-ordinated support for Court candidates, but when the Commons assembled they were greeted by rumours that Court members were 'undertaking' to manage the House and ensure that it complied with royal wishes. The fears generated in earlier clashes with James, and an isolated case of intimidation of electors in Hampshire, were enough to give credibility to these rumours. They may well have been generated by the Howard faction, in order to destroy their rivals' policy, but they were effective because government was ill-prepared for managing the session, and because they were believed. The result was uproar in Commons' debates, with renewed complaints about the tyranny of impositions, which destroyed any possibility of grants of taxation. The opposition of the Lords prevented any open parliamentary protest, but James had little choice but to dissolve Parliament. He did not call another for seven years.

In the short term, the beneficiaries of this 'Addled Parliament' were the Howards, whose influence over the King was increased by their links with his personal favourite, Robert Carr, Earl of Somerset. Although James's affection for him was undoubtedly homosexual in tendency, if not in physical reality, Somerset was in love with Frances Howard, wife of the Earl of Essex. In 1613, her relatives manipulated a hasty divorce, based on claims that Essex was impotent, enabling her to marry Somerset and secure their access to the King. By 1614, with the failure of the Parliament, Somerset dominated the Court and King, and Thomas Howard, Earl of Suffolk, was Lord Treasurer. Not daring to impose new customs duties, they attempted to raise money for the growing royal deficit by selling titles and monopolies, including the ill-advised Cokayne Project, reorganising the cloth trade. By depriving the Merchant Adventurers of their monopoly of unfinished cloth sales to Europe, and developing the cloth-finishing process in England, it was hoped to provide jobs and profit for the merchants as well as money for the King, but the project was badly prepared and underfunded, resulting only in a disastrous slump in sales of cloth. Although hastily abandoned, it damaged the trade and reduced revenue from customs – by late 1616, when the Merchant Adventurers were re-established, cloth exports were one-third down on 1614 levels. By 1618, they were back up to the level of 1603, but the outbreak of war in Europe prevented full recovery.

THE FAILURE OF THE HOWARDS

The failure of the Howards to solve the King's financial problems weakened their position at a dangerous time. By 1616, with the deficit on current expenditure running at £160,000 a year, there were growing

> **KEY ISSUE**
>
> *The dominance of the inefficient and corrupt Howards.*

> See page 297 for the Cokayne Project and page 297 for economic background.

complaints about the corruption and licence of the Court. The system of patronage encouraged a level of corruption, since courtiers and office-holders expected to recoup their costs from the offices that they received, often through bribes. Even a relatively dedicated minister such as Salisbury amassed a personal fortune from his work. In the early years of James's reign, the King's generosity helped to reduce the need for such profits, but as his finances worsened and his gifts became less frequent, his courtiers were, in Derek Hirst's words, 'forced back on to self-help'. Such was Thomas Howard's self-help that he was able to finance a huge palace for himself at Audley End, described by James as 'too big for a king, but big enough for a Lord Treasurer'. It was not surprising that Howard was eventually accused of corruption and tried for embezzlement in the Star Chamber in 1618.

Financial scandals were not the end of the matter, however. There were equally vociferous complaints about the gluttony, drunkenness and sexual licence of the Court. To some extent, James himself was responsible. His appearance of drunken behaviour and a tendency to dribble his food were actually the result of an illness, porphyria, which attacked the nervous system, but his indolence and preference for hunting in the company of young men over attending to matters of state were hard to excuse. His openly homosexual gestures and demonstrations of affection to his favourites were offensive in an age when homosexual acts were a felony, punishable by death. Moreover, James set the tone for others. Matters came to head over the Essex divorce and marriage of the Somersets, when it was revealed in 1615 that Somerset's secretary, Sir Thomas Overbury, had been poisoned in order to smooth the path towards the marriage. In 1616, the matter was brought to trial, and although James commuted the death sentence to one of imprisonment, both the Earl and Countess of Somerset were imprisoned briefly in the Tower of London and never returned to Court.

The Overbury scandal brought the influence of the Howard faction to an end and created the opportunity for renewed attempts at reform, but it is clear that the middle years of James's reign were significantly damaging to government, to the country and to the King himself. It was no coincidence that the glorification of 'Good Queen Bess' and the mythology of Elizabethan England in popular culture began to take shape in these years. In 1610, the government had missed an opportunity for reform; in the years that followed, it had drifted into mismanagement, a growing financial problem and a reputation for extravagance and corruption.

Perhaps more significantly, the leader of the reformist faction that had now emerged was himself a product of court intrigues and of James's liking for handsome young men. George Villiers had been introduced to James in 1613 by the Pembroke faction in an attempt to counteract the influence of Somerset and the Howards. In 1614 he became a Gentleman of the Bedchamber, and by 1616 he had taken Somerset's place. In 1617, he became Earl of Buckingham. Handsome, affable and charming, his power was entirely the result of his personal relationship with the King and his ability to control access to royal

KEY ISSUE

Sleaze at the Court of James I.

See page 388 for the Essex divorce.

patronage. Whether such a man would be able to bring about genuine reform remained to be seen.

B *The Buckingham years, 1618–25*

FINANCIAL REFORM

In 1618, the prospects for reform and an improvement in the quality of government seemed bright. Although the royal debt had reached £726,000, and the current deficit was running at £137,029 a year, Buckingham's purge of the Howard faction had brought in able new ministers, especially Lionel Cranfield, who became Master of the Wards. With Buckingham's power behind him, Cranfield was able to establish a series of interlocking commissions to examine household and government accounts, and reduce wardrobe and household expenses by almost 50 per cent. Contracts for the armed forces were re-negotiated, and waste and corruption greatly reduced. In 1618, James had borrowed money from the London merchants to finance his trip to Scotland, and defaulted on payments, taking his debt to £900,000. Even he was embarrassed by this, and at last made efforts to limit his generosity. In 1621, complaints in Parliament led to the **impeachment** of two monopolists, Mitchell and Mompesson, and of the Lord Chancellor, Sir Francis Bacon, for accepting bribes. This revived a medieval method of bringing powerful criminals to account, in which the House of Commons acted as prosecutors in a trial held before the House of Lords. The use of this device signalled growing irritation among MPs, but it also showed the willingness of some at Court to see the worst abuses of patronage controlled. Cranfield, now the Earl of Middlesex, became Lord Treasurer. By 1624, when he was finally brought down by a quarrel with Buckingham, he had managed to create a small surplus of income over expenditure, although the King's debts had not yet been tackled.

Much of this progress, however, was an illusion. While Cranfield's watchful eye could find out corruption and reduce costs, the system of government depended on patronage and payments from office. Cranfield himself took profits from the Court of Wards, and when he challenged Buckingham in 1624 (significantly by bringing his own, pretty nephew to Court, to catch the King's eye) it was not difficult to find evidence of bribery to enable Parliament to impeach him. The continuing need for MPs to adopt strategies of this kind had much to do with Buckingham himself. By 1620 he was in total control of patronage (though not of policy) and exploited the resources of government to maintain his power. He also had a large and needy family, whose financial security was based on his control of offices and pensions. It is probably unfair to suggest that Buckingham's drive against corruption in 1618 was entirely a ploy to destroy the Howards, but it is clear that his enthusiasm for financial discipline did not extend to himself and his friends. The sacrifice of Bacon in 1621 was partly to deflect criticism from himself. As long as those who held power at Court were products of the patronage system, and as long as factions among the courtiers

> **KEY ISSUE**
>
> *Buckingham supported Cranfield's reforms – as long as it suited him.*

> **impeachment** was a medieval procedure in which the Commons acted as prosecutors in a trial judged by the Lords.

> **KEY ISSUE**
>
> *Genuine reform demanded a completely new system.*

and nobility were able to influence and manipulate the actions of Parliament, a genuine overhaul of the system was impossible, and improved financial discipline was as much as could be hoped for.

In addition, there were significant developments in Europe which might well require expenditure of a different kind – on war. Since the reformation of the 1530s Europe had been divided by religious wars, both within and between existing states, and by dynastic struggles between France and the Habsburg rulers of Spain and the Holy Roman Empire. In 1618, the Czechs of Bohemia rebelled against their king, the Emperor Ferdinand Habsburg, and invited the Elector Palatine, James's son-in-law, to take his place. Against James's advice, the Elector accepted the throne and was defeated by the Habsburgs at the Battle of the White Mountain in November 1620.

Still worse, the Emperor chose to regard the Elector's behaviour as rebellion against his imperial overlord, and used his victorious forces to drive the **Elector** and his English wife out of their original lands, the Rhineland Palatinate. This was an attack on his inherited rights, and a threat to all the princes of the German Empire. The campaign divided Germany, and marked the beginning of the religious and dynastic struggle known as the Thirty Years War. From 1618–48 the Protestant princes of northern Germany fought (with the help of Sweden and France) against the Catholics of the south led by the Habsburgs. Like most civil wars, it was a war littered with atrocities, and it changed the political atmosphere in both Europe and England.

FOREIGN POLICY, WAR AND RELIGION, 1618–22

Since his accession in 1603, James had seen himself as a potential peace-maker for the troubled Continent, and his peace with Spain in 1604 had been motivated by diplomacy as well as finance. As ruler of the largest Protestant power in Europe, he sought to cultivate friendship with that most Catholic of powers, in order to act as a link between the religious factions. Having married his daughter to a Protestant, he sought a Spanish princess as a wife for his eldest son, Charles, to cement an Anglo-Spanish alliance that could, he hoped, bring peace to Europe. However the Spanish viewed his aspirations, they caused little difficulty until 1618. The outbreak of war transformed the situation in Europe, and in England. Many Protestants saw it as the opening of a Catholic offensive, an international crusade by the Pope (Antichrist) and his supporters to destroy the true Protestant religion. For some, it was the beginning of the final struggle between good and evil which, according to the Bible, would prepare the way for the kingdom of God on earth.

At the extreme these were the views of a minority, but there were many who went some way with their ideas. While most English Catholics were loyal, fear of Catholicism was deeply ingrained in England. Memories of persecution under Mary Tudor were fuelled by the Protestant mythology presented in John Foxe's *Acts and Monuments*, more widely known as the Book of Martyrs, which was published in 1563. A copy was placed in each parish church along with the Bible, and became popular reading. The Catholic counter-

KEY ISSUE

The influence of events in Europe.

Elector one of seven German princes who had the right to elect the Holy Roman Emperor. Germany consisted of 329 separate states.

KEY ISSUE

Religious rivalries renewed in Thirty Years War

Reformation, the activities of the Jesuit society and of priests trained in continental seminaries, of Catholic plots against Elizabeth supported by Rome and Spain, and finally of attempted invasion by the Spanish armada in 1588, created in England a widespread belief that Rome was the centre of an international conspiracy that threatened English liberty and independence as well as her religion. In that context, it was unthinkable that England, the largest of the Protestant states, should not play a part in defending the cause of true religion.

By 1620, therefore, James was under considerable pressure to act in defence of his son-in-law. He had no intention of intervening militarily – nor could he afford to do so – but he saw the possibilities of using English opinion as a diplomatic weapon in his campaign for an alliance with Spain and a Spanish marriage for his son. Accordingly, in 1621 he summoned Parliament to meet, and requested supplies to prepare for war. Aware of the dangers of inflaming an already volatile fear of Catholicism, he stressed the need to prepare for war to secure peace, and redoubled his diplomatic efforts. At first it appeared that his strategy might be successful. His request for taxes was heard by a nation facing a currency crisis and slipping into economic depression and MPs were reluctant to face constituents with excessive tax demands. Nevertheless, they voted two subsidies, and then turned their attention to waste, extravagance and corruption at Court.

This was not directed at the King – in fact, many of the attacks were orchestrated by members of the Lords and Court factions anxious to weaken rivals, especially the Duke of Buckingham. Though forced to sacrifice Bacon, the Duke survived, and the session ended quietly. In November 1621, when members reassembled, they were directed once again to consider the need for war finance, and in December they petitioned the King to enter the war against the Habsburgs. However, several MPs raised the issue of what kind of war should be fought. The relief of James's daughter and the re-conquest of the Palatinate would require a land war and the equipping of an army. Many members were aware of the expense involved, and were equally aware that Spanish strength came from its possessions in South America and the flow of gold and silver from its colonies. To them, it made more sense to consider a naval war, with its echoes of Elizabethan glory and possible financial windfalls from Spanish treasure, and they said so in a Commons' debate.

From James's point of view, this overstepped the bounds of parliamentary privilege, and strayed into the formulation of policy, which was the prerogative of the King. Angrily, he reminded members of the limits of their privilege of free speech, and that it came by the will of the sovereign. Provoked in their turn, the Commons set out a protestation, asserting that the rights of Parliament and the liberties of the subject 'are the ancient and undoubted birthright and inheritance of the subjects of England' – which James tore out of the Commons Journal. In essence, the quarrel was the same as that of 1604, turning on the issue of whether Parliament's privileges existed by right or by gift of the monarch.

KEY ISSUE

How could James realistically plan to influence the Thirty Years War?

See pages 296–7 for currency crisis and economic depression.

KEY ISSUE

Deteriorating relations between the King and Parliament.

In this case, however, the claimed right was that of freedom to debate royal policy, arising from concerns over foreign relations and religion. Whatever the rights of free speech, there was no doubt that these areas of policy came within the King's recognised prerogatives, and the Commons were encroaching on royal powers. James had every right to object, although whether his reaction was politically wise is more debatable. To have allowed the debate would have set a dangerous precedent, but once the issue moved on to involve parliamentary privileges, there was little chance of agreement. It was clear to James that there would be no grant of taxes, and there had been some attacks on both his policy and his favourite. Accordingly, he dissolved the Parliament and continued his diplomatic pursuit of Spanish friendship and a marriage for his son.

The legacy of the Parliament of 1621 was complex. While his foreign policy had made little progress, the King had defended his prerogative with some success. Nevertheless, there were some worrying signs and precedents. The Commons had been able to bring some government office-holders to account, using the mechanism of impeachment, by which ministers were accused by the Commons and tried by the Lords. These proceedings had arisen from rivalries among government factions, but there was no guarantee that the Court or the Lords would always be able to orchestrate their use. The quarrel over privilege and prerogative had sharpened existing fears. Above all, the airing of concerns about foreign policy had alerted Protestant opinion to the Catholic threat and raised concerns about the King's attitude towards Spain. Members had expressed concern about a Catholic marriage, and the concessions that would be required by Spain. As the Petition of December 1621 put it, 'If the papists once attain a connivance, they will press for a toleration; from thence to an equality; from an equality to a superiority; from a superiority to an extirpation of all contrary religions'. The Parliament of 1621 had not precipitated a crisis, but the monarch might well find that it had increased the capacity of later assemblies to do so.

THE SPANISH MARRIAGE AND WAR, 1622–5

Within a year, however, a crisis of a different kind had been created by the behaviour of Buckingham and Prince Charles. Frustrated by the delays in the marriage settlement, the two decided upon a romantic gesture. In February 1623, they left London in disguise with only a single servant, and set off for Spain to pursue the match in person. It is difficult to explain their behaviour, but the Prince was young and Buckingham reckless. It is also possible that the Duke had an eye on his future position. The Prince had always disliked his father's favourite, and with James growing visibly older, Buckingham may well have seen an opportunity to establish a friendship with his heir. In that sense the escapade worked, although in every other aspect it was a humiliating failure. The Spanish kept the two young men kicking their heels in Madrid while proceeding no further with the proposed marriage. The English ambassador, the Earl of Bristol, was infuriated by the whole

KEY ISSUE

James I's inability to control his heir and his favourite.

incident, especially as he found Buckingham attempting to shift the blame to him. James's international diplomacy was reduced to a desperate concern to get his son home safely. By 1624 the two had returned, but the Spanish match and alliance were dead.

Nevertheless, there were significant repercussions. Angry at their humiliation (and apparently oblivious of the extent to which it was self-inflicted), Charles and Buckingham were determined on war with Spain. By now the two had forged a friendship which would have a major influence on politics in this reign and the next. They were encouraged by the anti-Spanish mood of the country, never difficult to generate in Protestant England. For the moment they were treated as heroes, and saw no difficulty in raising the necessary funds from Parliament, which was summoned in February 1624. Although James warned that a country suffering from plague and depression might be reluctant to finance war, Charles and Buckingham were confident. They had the support of the 'Puritan' faction, including Pembroke, Southampton and Warwick in the Lords, and seem to have been in touch with leaders in the Commons such as Sir Robert Phelips and Sir Edward Coke. Although they failed in an attempt to blame Bristol for the Spanish fiasco, they were able to destroy Cranfield who opposed their war strategy on financial grounds. In addition, they secured support in the Commons by pressurising James into accepting a law against the granting of monopolies in trade. Faced with this coalition, and in deteriorating health, James could do little to restrain his heir and his favourite; his reservations were set aside, and by the end of 1624, England was at war with Spain and its Catholic allies.

However, this apparent unity disguised serious problems. The failure to impeach Bristol revealed the dislike among the older nobility for Buckingham's power, and suggested that the alliance with the Puritan Lords might be temporary. In support of the war with Spain, Buckingham was negotiating an alternative marriage for Charles with Henrietta Maria, sister of the king of France. That this was also a Catholic marriage, and that the settlement terms included her right to worship freely, was conveniently overlooked. Most seriously, there were fundamental differences between Parliament and the Court as to the nature of the war that was being undertaken. James had tried to clarify the issue by asking Parliament for six subsidies and twelve-fifteenths in taxation, as well as money to repay his debts. This would have financed the intended land war for the Palatinate as well as naval action against Spain. When Parliament refused to vote on such huge amounts, Charles and Buckingham accepted a greatly reduced grant, and promised a naval war only. It was a promise that they no intention of keeping. By the spring of 1625 James was dead and Charles was King. While James may be criticised for attempting a foreign policy which was too grandiose and in some ways unrealistic, it has to be said that the difficulties facing Charles in 1625 were largely of his own making.

KEY ISSUE

Charles and Buckingham's exploitation of parliamentary fears.

4 ⌒ CONCLUSION: THE REIGN OF JAMES I

KEY ISSUE

The legacy of James I to his successors.

It is perhaps fitting that James's reign ended as it began, with England at war with Spain. The key question in assessing James is how much or how little had changed in the 22 years of his reign. He had inherited a country which faced religious, financial and administrative problems, and he passed on to his son a country in a similar condition. This does not mean that James had achieved nothing – indeed some historians would argue that it was an achievement to have avoided a serious crisis. Some improvements in administration and finance had taken place – Cranfield's reforms had some effect and the income from customs duties was growing. In the important area of religion, James had achieved a great deal. While asserting and reinforcing the monarch's control of the Church through bishops and the Book of Common Prayer, he had also created sufficient flexibility for individual conscience, and especially the powerful Puritan tendency, to function harmoniously within it. It could be said that the practical compromises that he established offered a foundation for genuine peace in a key area of national life.

In other areas, however, James's legacy was more problematic. His extravagance and financial irresponsibility created serious problems and weakened the position of the Crown both in, and outside, Parliament. The financial weakness of the monarchy, starkly revealed by the foreign policy demands of the 1620s, cannot be laid entirely at his door – the underlying problems of inflation, the spiralling costs of warfare and the errors of other monarchs all played their part. Nevertheless, James had undermined reforming ministers and had wasted opportunities. His personal life – the indulgence, financial corruption and sexual licence of the Court – had weakened the monarch's prestige at a time when education, growing literacy and a 'reformation of manners' among the upper classes and 'middling sort' were creating new expectations. In 1618 he had issued a Book of Sports, encouraging the population to occupy its Sundays in traditional sports and games. The intention was to occupy the minds of the populace, but it offended many who felt that the Bible and the state of their souls would be a more productive and dignified object of attention.

Perhaps most serious of all, James seems to have created an impression among those who sat in Parliament that their liberties and property were in danger, as well as their souls. In fact, his actions were exemplary – he had sought throughout his reign to work with Parliament, and respected its rights and privileges. Nothing that James did suggests that he had anything but respect for the rule of law, and he often showed considerable patience with the narrow preoccupations of many MPs. The failure of financial reform, and even more of the Anglo-Scottish union reveals the limited abilities and aspirations of England's governing class as well as her monarchs. The problem lay in his words and declarations, his theoretical arguments, rather than his deeds. In an age when the power of monarchy and central authority was growing at the expense of local privilege in many parts of Europe, and when traditional institutions which protected local rights were being significantly weakened, James's claims to divine right and status encouraged fears which were quite unnecessary, and enhanced the defensive mentality which was the chief enemy of reform.

On balance, therefore, it could be said that James was not a bad king, but that he could have been a better one. He had intelligence, vision and tact, but he was also lazy and self-indulgent. He did little to damage his kingdom, but did not greatly improve it either. The verdict of Whig historians that he handed his son an impossible task in 1625, and that England was already 'on the high road to civil war' is not supported by events, but James must bear some responsibility for the later crisis. In the words of the historian Christopher Haigh, his 'self-selected task in life had been to become King of England, and that had been achieved . . . He had tried and failed to achieve political Union, and he had tried, with more success, to reduce religious tensions. He liked to strut as an international statesman and a European scholar, but neither role was for him a full time occupation. There seemed little more for even a conscientious king to do – and James was not very conscientious.' A similar point is made by Derek Hirst, who emphasises James's Scottish experience. In Scotland, James claimed to have learned 'kingcraft', by which he meant the ability to manage men and factions. As Hirst points out, however, 'he failed to appreciate not just the need but the opportunities for reform in England, where kings possessed far more authority than did their Scottish counterparts'. What both historians emphasise is that the reign of James was not a disaster, but a missed opportunity.

5 ⌒ BIBLIOGRAPHY

The most extensive recent study of James is *James I and VI* by Roger Lockyer, in the Profiles in Power series (Longman, 1998), a thoughtful and balanced reappraisal. General text books by Roger Lockyer and Barry Coward contain relevant chapters, while it is still worth looking at older text books such as *Century of Revolution* by Christopher Hill (Sphere Books, 1969). The interpretation has been challenged, but the book deals with aspects of the period which are sometimes ignored, and contains a wealth of useful detail. Among the most accessible of more recent accounts are those provided in *The Early Stuarts, 1603–40* by Katherine Brice in the Access to History series (Hodder and Stoughton, 1994) and the more extensive account in *Authority and Conflict: England 1603–58* by Derek Hirst (Edward Arnold, 1986). There is a useful collection of essays entitled *The Reign of James VI and I* edited by A.G.R. Smith (Macmillan, 1973). Finally, *Stuart England, 1603–1714* by Barry Coward (Longman, 1997) includes useful analysis of particular issues, including a source-based analysis of the character and personality of James.

6 ❧ STUDY GUIDE

1. The first stage in studying any historical period is to establish a clear framework of knowledge of what happened. This involves collecting essential information in a form which highlights key points, and which makes it easy to retrieve the information at a later stage. One of the best ways of doing this is by writing linear notes as you read each chapter. While this can be a slow process, particularly at first, it is one that repays the effort throughout the period of study.

Linear notes should consist of essential information set out under headings and sub-headings which are drawn from the subject matter itself. The first stage of this process has been carried out in the chapter above, by dividing it into numbered sections with sub-sections denoted by A, B etc. Within each of these sections you should try to record information using numbered key points, with sub-points that provide detail or examples about the key point. For example:

(a) *Making clear notes*
(i) Use spatial layout – setting sub-points under the key point to show the relationship between them.
(ii) Use abbreviations – include established ones and others of your own.
(iii) Stick to main points – but include good quotes, precise figures and examples, and extra ideas of your own. They will all help to build up your knowledge and understanding of the subject.

(b) *Using the notes*
(i) To make notes in this way, you will have to think about what you are reading. This helps you to concentrate, to select what you need and to spot anything that you do not understand.
(ii) Writing out the key points in this way helps you to remember them. You will be learning as you go.
(iii) Clear spacing and the use of headings/sub-headings makes it easy to break the material into sections for revision.

If you think that you have got the idea, you should now try making notes on the reign of James I. Work through one section at a time. Use the headings provided and the arrangement of paragraphs to enable you to pick out the main points and include some details from each paragraph as sub-points to support and illustrate them. You will find it slow at first, but you will get quicker with experience.

2. Making notes will enable you to collect information, but in order to use it, you need to define issues and formulate key questions. One issue that Chapter 1 has addressed is whether James can be seen as a successful king, and by implication, how far he was responsible for the problems faced by the monarchy in the seventeenth century. This involves examining the actions of James, but it also requires you to look at other factors which caused problems, and to compare their importance to that of James – you cannot make a judgement about James in isolation.

The first step, therefore, is to identify the factors involved. A *factor* is a number of actions, events and beliefs that are linked to a common theme. Identifying factors enables you to organise the actions, events and beliefs around the theme in order to explain their importance – it allows you to answer questions rather than tell a story. If you take a question such as 'Why did the various attempts to reform the system of government in the reign of James I fail?' you can start by identifying reasons for the failure. If you then look through your notes to find examples, you will be linking the examples together around a common factor. For example, consider the four attempts at reform listed below.

(i) James's plans for Anglo-Scottish union, 1603–7.
(ii) Bancroft's schemes to improve the condition of the Church, 1604–11.
(iii) Salisbury's Great Contract, 1610.
(iv) Cranfield's financial reorganisation, 1618–24.

Read through your notes and make a list of all the reasons that you can find to explain why each of these schemes failed. Highlight any reason that appears more than once. Now give each reason a short title and write a brief explanation of what it involved, all the occasions when it occurred and how it helped to cause failure. When you have done that, you will have identified and explained the *factors* that caused reform to fail. For example, you could produce a list of reasons for failure on each of the occasions, such as:

(i) anti-Scottish feeling among MPs, concern to protect the common law, James's lack of tact over parliamentary privileges;
(ii) cost, concern to protect the rights and influence of existing patrons;
(iii) cost, resentment over impositions, dislike of James's financial extravagance, court factions, concern to protect Parliament's powers;
(iv) James's financial extravagance, court factions, the influence of Buckingham.

You will see that some of these reasons appear on more than one occasion and some problems are common to different attempts at reform. You can therefore compile a list of factors to cover the whole reign, such as:

Parliamentary attitudes – narrow mindedness and suspicion of change, concern over legal rights, fear of high taxes, parliamentary rights.
The influence of courtiers – factions and rivalries, greed, the system of patronage, Buckingham.
The actions of James I – lack of tact, laziness and self-indulgence, extravagance.

If you now write a brief explanation of each factor, including examples from different occasions and explaining how each one helped to cause the failure of reform, you will have analysed the issue and established a framework for answering a number of different questions about it. You will be able to show how the different factors worked together, and to make judgements about the part played by James himself. You will also be able to adapt the material to answer a number of different essay questions in a planned and organised way.

3. Another way of analysing particular issues is to consider them in more detail by looking at primary sources. This involves developing certain skills of interpretation and using the evidence to draw conclusions. The main skills needed are:

Analysis – breaking down the source into main points to pick out the information in it;

Inference – looking beyond what is said to consider what is implied;

Cross-reference – matching information with other knowledge to bring out more possibilities and/or evaluate its reliability. You can cross-reference to other sources, or to your own knowledge of the period;

Synthesis – putting together the information and ideas that you have developed;

Application – using the evidence that you have interpreted to make judgements, test ideas and develop new ones.

For example, the effectiveness of James as a king could be considered by analysing the nature of his relationship with Parliament and whether he caused that relationship to deteriorate. Chapter 1 contains a number of sources which address this issue; use the questions below to analyse, interpret and evaluate the evidence that they provide, in order to assess how effectively James worked with his parliaments.

Q

(a) Read sources A and B on page 13.

  (i) What, according to source A, were the functions of a king? (1 mark)

  (ii) From whom did the king derive his authority? (1 mark)

  (iii) Do the sources suggest that there were any limits to this authority? (3 marks)

(b) Look at source C on page 14. How far does this agree with the evidence provided in sources A and B? (2 marks)

(c) How far do these sources suggest that James was justified in

  (i) his 'impositions' on trade? (2 marks)

  (ii) his reaction to the Commons' debates and protestation of 1621? (3 marks)

(d) How far was his behaviour politically wise? (3 marks)

(e) Read sources D, E and F on pages 29–30.

  (i) What reasons are given for the Commons' concern with their privileges in source D? (2 marks)

  (ii) What claims does James make to absolute power in sources E and F? (3 marks)

  (iii) Source E had been published in 1598. Does this mean that James had created the fears expressed in source D? (3 marks)

  (iv) What limits does James place on kings in exercising their power? (2 marks)

  (v) Do any of his claims conflict with the descriptions of government given in sources A and B? (5 marks)

  (vi) How far do sources E and F explain the attitude shown by MPs in source D? (5 marks)

(f) Using the evidence provided by these sources and your knowledge of the reign of James I, explain how far the tensions between the King and Parliament were created by the attitudes and actions of James himself. (15 marks)

3

The Reign of
Charles I 1625–40

INTRODUCTION

In 1625, when Charles I succeeded his father as King, he was apparently welcomed by a Parliament and political community who supported his policy of war with Spain. Fifteen years later, in 1640, he faced a crisis in which his authority as King had effectively collapsed. Unable to contain a rebellion in Scotland, he was forced to call Parliament in England and to agree to restraints on his power in order to settle his debts and restore his ability to govern. In spite of these concessions, he was regarded with such suspicion by a significant section of the political community that a permanent settlement proved impossible, and by 1642 England had slipped into civil war.

The reasons for this spectacular change of circumstances and attitudes are complex, but must obviously include the personality and actions of Charles himself. Historians have generally agreed that, 'as a King, Charles was not a success' (Conrad Russell). Nevertheless, there are wide differences of view about what other factors influenced developments, and precisely what part the personality of Charles played in the process. The previous chapter challenged the claim that James I had been a disastrous king, who passed on an impossible task to his son, but did not deny the existence of serious problems which James had failed to solve. It can therefore be said that, in 1625, there were difficulties and tensions within the political and social structure of the British kingdoms, and that these combined with the personality and actions of Charles to create a crisis by 1640.

The reign of Charles to 1640 falls into two phases. From 1625 to 1629 Charles tried to pursue his objectives in partnership with Parliament, and failed. After a series of quarrels and confrontations, the relationship broke down in 1629, when the House of Commons ignored the King's orders to prorogue [end the session] and passed Three Resolutions which criticised his religious and financial policies. A furious King dissolved Parliament and declared his intention not to call another until his subjects should understand him better. From 1629 to 1640, therefore, he tried to pursue his objectives without the help of Parliament, and appeared to be succeeding, until he took the decision to extend his religious reforms from England to Scotland in 1637. This sparked a major rebellion in Scotland, and Charles discovered that he lacked the financial and political means to deal with it. He was therefore forced to face an English Parliament united in its determination to redress pent-up grievances, and to withhold necessary support from the King until he did so. What needs to be considered is how this crisis occurred, at what point it became unavoidable, and how far Charles, as an individual, was responsible for it.

1 ⌐ THE PARLIAMENTARY CRISIS, 1625–9

When Charles ascended the throne in March 1625, he appeared to be in control of the situation. In 1624 he and Buckingham had initiated an apparently popular war against Spain, overriding the reservations of his ageing father. MPs had supported the war to the extent of voting three subsidies to fund it. Despite this apparent co-operation, however, his relationship with Parliament was less harmonious than it appeared.

TABLE 2
Key events, 1625–9

June–August 1625	First Parliament
September 1625	The disastrous Cadiz expedition
February–May 1626	Second Parliament
October 1627	The disastrous La Rochelle expedition
November 1627	The Five Knights case
March 1628 to March 1629	The Third Parliament
June 1628	The Petition of Right
August 1628	The assassination of Buckingham
March 1629	The Three Resolutions

A *War, finance and religion in the Buckingham years*

For a start there were fundamental differences over foreign policy. Many MPs viewed the Spanish war as a religious crusade, part of the greater struggle between the forces of good and evil, and saw the best hope of victory in a sea-based campaign. This would also have the advantage of being affordable. They recalled the successes of the Elizabethan privateers in seizing bullion from the Spanish treasure fleets, and they hoped that such a war could pay for itself. Charles and Buckingham, however, were determined to seek revenge for their humiliation over the Spanish marriage, and saw the war as a matter of honour. In addition, Charles was determined to help his sister and restore her husband to his lands in the Palatinate, which required intervention in Germany. In the winter of 1624–5 he therefore equipped both a naval expedition to Cadiz and a land army, vastly overspending in order to do so. Both were expensive failures.

MPs were persuaded to vote a further two subsidies in June 1625, but refused to grant Charles the traditional lifetime right to levy tonnage and poundage (customs duties). Initially this was delayed

> **KEY ISSUE**
>
> *Initial misunderstandings and disagreements between Charles and Parliament.*

because the Commons wanted to review the whole issue of duties and impositions which had caused tensions with King James. This was not necessarily directed at Charles, but it is likely that resentment of the waste of Parliamentary subsidies and the inefficient conduct of the war influenced the decision. Predictably, Charles was infuriated by what he saw as a gross insult.

There were also misgivings in the Commons over the King's marriage and his religious views. To replace the failed Spanish match, Buckingham had negotiated a marriage between Charles and Henrietta Maria, sister of the King of France. While this had diplomatic logic, since France and Spain were dynastic rivals, it ignored the fact that she was a Catholic and that the marriage contract gave her the right to practise her religion at the English Court. Worse still, Buckingham had agreed to help the King of France suppress a Protestant rebellion at La Rochelle, raising suspicion that foreign policy was being conducted without regard to Protestant interests. There were even fears that the King harboured Catholic sympathies. These fears were reinforced by his encouragement of Arminian ideas within the Church of England, which are summarised in the table on the next page.

Arminius argued that God's grace and the gift of salvation for the soul was open to all, not merely to a select band of predetermined 'saints'. For many Protestants, this doctrine was dangerously close to the Catholic belief that salvation could be earned with the guidance of the Church, and these fears were increased in England when Arminian ideas were taken up and developed by a small group of English ministers led by Lancelot Andrewes and William Laud. Their interpretation of the argument restored the central role of the Church in finding salvation, rather than the faith of individuals, and emphasised the common origins of Catholic and Anglican churches as well as a traditional authority passed down from Christ himself.

The problem with the ideas put forward by English Arminians was twofold. In themselves, they reinforced the role of authority within the Church, enhancing the power of bishops and giving their edicts the force of an authority derived from Christ himself. They blocked the path of further reform, for which many Puritans still hoped, and increased the status of the clergy at the expense of the laity, including the gentry and property-owning supporters who enjoyed influence in their local parishes. More threateningly, they allowed Catholic links to be increased, and Catholic influence to operate within the Church. Catholicism was regarded by English Protestants to be an insidious corruption that had destroyed the purity of the early Church.

The issue was brought to a head in Parliament through the case of Richard Montague. His tracts challenged the idea of a single Protestant identity, which linked the Church of England with Protestant churches across Europe, and emphasised, instead, its links with Rome. He argued that the Anglican tradition represented the true inheritance of Christianity, retaining its medieval traditions, which were shared with Rome, and rejecting only the unnecessary ceremonial and superstitions that had become attached to the pre-Reformation Church. In 1624 there were

---

KEY ISSUE

The implications of the Arminian offensive.

TABLE 3

The religious divide – Arminian and Puritan

	Puritan view	Anglican	Arminian view	Catholic
Faith and Salvation	Salvation gained as a gift from God to those who were predestined to be saved. Evidence of predestination was the willingness to accept discipline and seek a godly life.	Salvation by faith alone.	The gift of salvation was open to all who would seek it through a true Church. God offers salvation to all – mankind is free to accept or reject it.	Salvation for all but only through the Catholic faith.
Role of the Church and priesthood	To guide and educate according to the rules laid down in the Bible. The chief function of the Minister is to preach God's Word, and to allow souls to find their way to him. Ministers also apply discipline to support the Saints and control the sinners.	The Church has authority to guide people to salvation.	The Church guides through a priesthood which has special powers and status. Their authority is symbolised by robes and ceremonies. There is a place for preaching, but teaching through set prayers and rituals is as important.	The Catholic Church and its rituals provide the path to God. Taking part offers salvation.
Ritual and preaching	Preaching and private prayer, Bible study and reading are the key to salvation. Sacraments like communion are symbolic only. Ritual distracts the ignorant from true religion and creates superstition and idolatry.	There is a place for some ritual to symbolise aspects of faith – for example Holy Communion.	Ritual creates reverence and brings the ignorant to God. If it is beautiful in itself, it is a form of worship. Ritual is essential to promote order and decency.	Ritual is part of salvation – we are saved by our actions and works, such as taking part in a ritual.
Role and power of Bishops	Bishops have no special power. The parish minister is the true leader of the congregation, and the best organisation would be with committees of ministers, advised by Bishops, if desired.	Bishops have authority to rule the Church and represent the King.	Bishops have a special place and authority, passed down from Christ himself through St Peter and the medieval Church. They receive power to enforce rules from the King.	Bishops have special authority from Christ passed through the Pope.
Attitude to Catholics	Catholicism is evil; the devil seeking to corrupt true faith. The Pope is the Anti-Christ, the devil himself.	Catholics threaten true faith; but many of their errors are not a threat to salvation.	Catholicism represents the early Church, misled by error. It is a sister Church, like those set up by Calvin and Luther, and should be treated as such. There need be no Protestant identity which shuts out Catholics.	The True Church.
Obedience to authority	Obedience should be given to those in authority unless they threaten God's cause and true religion.	Obedience should be given to higher authority except on a few matters vital to salvation.	Obedience to authority in Church and State should be total. If, on rare occasions, conscience makes it necessary to disobey, the subject should surrender to authority and accept punishment.	The authority of the Pope is from God – he is therefore infallible and obedience essential.

complaints raised against him in Parliament and James blocked his promotion in the Church. In 1625, however, he published a tract dedicated to the new King, who promptly appointed him as royal Chaplain. Charles could not have signalled more clearly where his religious loyalties lay, and he followed it up with further promotions for Arminian leaders, including Laud, who became Bishop of London in 1628.

Charles's association with the Arminians raised fears that were both religious and political. Their ideas appealed to his own sense of order and authority, and their emphasis on ritual and ceremonial accorded with his perceptions of the dignified beauty that enhanced majesty in both Church and State. He had been greatly impressed by the Spanish Court when he visited Spain in 1623, and he tried to emulate it in his own Court at Whitehall and Windsor. Equally important, the Arminian insistence on the divine authority of Bishops enhanced his own view of the Divine Right of the King who appointed and controlled them. Aware that they had his support, Arminian writers invoked the King's power to impose their views in the Church, and repaid him by arguing for similar authority in the State. Thus, for many MPs and their associates, the new King and his friends posed a threat to religion by allowing what they regarded as Catholic corruption to creep back into the Church, and a threat to law and liberty by attributing to the monarchy an overweening divine authority.

See pages 343–6 for Charles's Church policies.

B *Tensions, conflicts and the development of the crisis*

By July 1625, Parliament's view of Charles had changed considerably. 'You cannot believe the alteration in the opinion of the world touching his Majesty', wrote the Earl of Kellie. Complaints in the Commons about Montague were compounded by the high-handedness of Buckingham. The Duke's power had increased with the death of James, who had never allowed him to dictate policy. Charles lacked both confidence and experience, and quite naturally relied on his older friend and favourite for advice, while Buckingham was eager to demonstrate his skills as a statesman. Unfortunately, these were limited.

A brief summary of Buckingham's career tends to do him some injustice. In many ways charming and affable, he was neither a complete fool nor a villain. His control of patronage and the resentment of the more established nobility at his meteoric rise encouraged factional rivalry, and some of his critics were motivated by envy. His relationship with James seems to have had a basis of genuine affection, and as a favourite, he was less vicious than some of his predecessors. The real problems seem to have arisen from his relationship with Charles, whom he was able to dominate in a different way to James. It is also probably true that his character deteriorated as his power grew. His most serious weaknesses were shown up when he took control of policy, especially foreign affairs. Firstly, his policies lacked consistency because he had no clear vision of what he wanted to achieve other than fame and glory.

GEORGE VILLIERS, DUKE OF BUCKINGHAM 1592–1628

George Villiers was the son of a moderately prosperous Leicestershire gentleman, who caught the eye of James I because of his good looks and charm. He was rapidly promoted to the post of Gentleman of the Bedchamber in 1615, and his close friendship with the King has led to much speculation as to whether the relationship was actively homosexual. The tone of letters from James to his 'Steenie', his pet name for Buckingham, suggests that this may have been the case, but it is impossible to be certain. What is clear, however, is that Buckingham was promoted for his personal charm rather than his abilities as a statesman. Given control of patronage by the infatuated James, Buckingham supported Cranfield's reforms and exercised a measure of discipline over James's personal finances, which at least improved on the corruptions of the Howards. Unfortunately, as his power grew, so did his arrogance, and by 1620 he had used his influence to place his own supporters in key positions and to advance his own family. Financial restraints never extended to Buckingham himself, and he demanded complete loyalty from those whom he advanced. When Cranfield tried to act independently, Buckingham destroyed him. Nevertheless, while James lived, the problem was contained.

Buckingham's dominance of the Court and of patronage created resentment among the nobility and office-holders whom he replaced, but his personality had further, more damaging effects. In 1623 Buckingham revealed how rash and foolish he could be, by encouraging Charles to embark on his Spanish adventure. To accompany the heir to the throne on a dangerous journey without protection or assurance of success was grossly neglectful of his duty to the King, and seriously undermined James's diplomatic strategy. Faced with the effects of his action, Buckingham tried to shift the blame onto the Earl of Bristol, who was ambassador to Spain at the time. The whole affair revealed the extent of Buckingham's greed and stupidity, summed up in James's own comment, 'By God, Steenie, you are a fool'.

The Spanish adventure was, in some ways, a turning point for Buckingham, in that it allowed him to establish an elder statesman's influence over Charles. James's physical deterioration and death removed the remaining restraints of common sense, and Buckingham was able to use his influence over the new King to indulge his fantasies of glory. Having embarked on a war against Spain to avenge Spanish insults, it was not illogical to seek an alliance with France, and Buckingham succeeded in negotiating a marriage for Charles with the French princess, Henrietta Maria, in 1625. In the process, however, he quarrelled with Cardinal Richelieu, the French king's chief minister, and attempted to seduce his queen. More seriously, the marriage settlement committed England to help crush the

PICTURE 2
This portrait (by an unknown artist) conveys Buckingham's good looks, charm and shallowness

See pages 34–7 for Buckingham's rise to power.

KEY ISSUE

Charles I flexed his muscles in defence of Buckingham.

KEY ISSUE

The damage caused by Buckingham.

independence of French Protestants. The end result of Buckingham's diplomacy was war with both France and Spain, with England having to fight two major powers at the same time. As Lord High Admiral, he also took charge of the conduct of these wars, which he carried out with gross inefficiency. Two disastrous naval expeditions, to Cadiz and to La Rochelle, provided ample grounds for impeachment, from which he was saved only by Charles's determined protection. By 1628, Buckingham had become a liability to his country and the King; he was described by parliamentary leaders in that year as 'the cause of all our miseries' and 'the grievance of grievances'. When he was finally assassinated in August 1628 by John Felton, an ex-officer whose pay was in arrears, the nation celebrated.

Based on convenience, they varied and fluctuated with changing situations. Secondly, they were negligently carried out. Little attention was paid to planning, or to any realistic assessment of likely success. Restrained by James, he was a political irritation; given his head by Charles, he was a total liability.

By 1625 this was becoming apparent in both foreign and domestic affairs. Opposition to 'the favourite' was growing, especially within the House of Lords. As social and political leaders, the Lords acquired and influenced client MPs, who were able to raise issues in the Commons. Buckingham had shown his own ability to exploit this system in the Parliaments of 1621 and 1624. Now, however, he was faced by a powerful combination of personal enemies and angry MPs, infuriated by the expensive failures of the previous winter and determined to have some account of how their subsidies had been spent before granting any more. It was clear that, without some concessions, the government would gain little from this Parliament.

In anger and frustration the King dissolved Parliament. Two months later, in October 1625, the attack on Cadiz ended in humiliating failure, depriving Charles of the hoped-for plunder of the Spanish bullion fleet. With his debts increasing, Charles had no choice but to call a new Parliament in February 1626. To protect Buckingham, he used Court influence to prevent the election of his critics, notably Sir Edward Coke and Sir Thomas Wentworth, whose dislike of Buckingham's inefficiency was well known. Their influence was simply replaced by that of Sir John Eliot, a volatile Cornishman with strong Puritan views, who planned to impeach Buckingham on charges of high treason. Within the House of Lords, the favourite was threatened by a temporary alliance of Puritan sympathisers such as Lord Wharton, Lord Saye and Sele, the Bishop of Lincoln, and the Earl of Bristol, whom Buckingham had sought to make the scapegoat for the fiasco of the Spanish marriage.

Seeing the danger to his friend, Charles warned the Commons that 'Parliaments are altogether in my power for their calling, sitting and dissolution'. In May he ordered the imprisonment of Eliot and Sir Dudley Digges on the charge that their attacks on Buckingham were insulting to the Crown, but the House of Commons refused to conduct further business until they were released. By now Charles had taken the offensive, and, when the House of Commons replied to his request for further subsidies (and tonnage and poundage for life) by demanding the dismissal of Buckingham, he simply dissolved Parliament on 15 June. He then followed up the dissolution with a proclamation insisting on total conformity to his interpretation of the rules governing the Church, and a demand for a forced loan to replace his lost subsidies.

This was collected in 1627, producing well over £230,000 by the autumn, and those who refused were conscripted into the armed forces or imprisoned. Further savings were made by billeting soldiers on the civilian population without payment. In November 1627, five of the knights who had been imprisoned by Charles for refusing the forced loan challenged his right to detain them without trial. The judges supported the King, although they declared that this should not be entered as a precedent for future judgements. In effect, they were declaring that his actions were justified by national needs on this occasion, but they were refusing to pre-empt future decisions.

Meanwhile, the clergy reinforced the King's demands for obedience. Charles had promoted Arminians to key posts in the Church, with Laud becoming Bishop of Bath and Wells in 1626, and Bishop of London in 1628. In 1627 Richard Sibthorpe published a tract entitled *Apostolic Obedience* in which he argued that subjects were bound by God to obey even an unjust king. It appeared that the King was able to impose his will despite resistance, but there were signs of mounting opposition to his actions, and growing difficulties at home and abroad.

In foreign policy, Buckingham lurched from one disaster to another. His arrogance, blundering diplomacy and an attempt to seduce the French Queen led, in 1627, to war with Louis XIII, England's most natural ally against Spain. In the pursuit of this he attempted to relieve the Protestant Huguenots at La Rochelle in September 1627, creating yet another humiliating failure. Meanwhile Charles tried to influence the war in Germany by subsidising a Danish army, which cost £12,000 a month and produced no measurable results. Such expenses ran way beyond the scope of forced loans, and faced with the threat of defeat, Charles agreed to summon a new Parliament in March 1628.

It was clear that there would be complaints about the events of 1627, but there is a good deal of evidence to suggest that, even now, negotiation and co-operation could have resolved the problems. The King still needed money, and he was aware of what he could gain from Parliament. The political community had felt the effects of the King's anger, and MPs who sought to influence him had been reminded of the dangers of provocation. The return of Coke and Wentworth to the Commons reduced the influence of the more volatile Eliot, and it was they who masterminded Parliament's strategy. The complaints against Buckingham were set aside, and Wentworth persuaded the House to vote five subsidies to finance the war. At the same time, however, Coke

> **KEY ISSUE**
>
> *Opposition created by a forced loan.*

> **KEY ISSUE**
>
> *Financial problems forced Charles to call another Parliament.*

the Petition of Right
Devised by Coke and
Eliot in June 1628, it
advocated no
imprisonment without
cause shown, no forced
loans, no martial law
and no billeting.

and Eliot drew up a **Petition of Right** which reversed the judgement in
the Five Knights' Case and asked the King to declare that, in future,
there would be no more forced loans, no imprisonments without trial,
no billeting of soldiers or use of martial law against civilians. When he
had accepted the Petition, and not before, the subsidy bill would
proceed to the House of lords. It was clear to Charles that this was the
price that he must pay for his money. The King's dignity was protected
by a pretence that the judges had misinterpreted the law and that he was
simply being asked to clarify it. With the situation in Germany growing
worse and further losses at La Rochelle he had little option but to agree.
In June 1628 the King gave his assent to the Petition of Right, thereby
giving it the force of law, and the subsidy bill resumed its progress to
the Lords.

The Petition of Right was clearly a defeat for Charles, and showed
what could be achieved by a united Parliament in dealing with a king
who needed money. Nevertheless, its significance needs to be carefully
analysed. Was it, as Whig historians argued, part of a Parliamentary
struggle against a tyrant king, or as Charles himself later claimed, a plot
by a malicious opposition to disrupt the legitimate exercise of his
power? If it was neither, why did it occur, and did it necessarily herald a
crisis between King and Parliament?

C   Source investigation: The forced loan and the Petition of Right

A From the Royal Proclamation issued on 7 October 1626.

With the advice of our Privy Council, We have resolved, for the
necessary defence of our Honour, our religion and kingdoms, to
require the aid of our loving subjects in that way of loan, [there being]
no other possible and present course to be taken, nor this to be
avoided, if we as a King shall maintain the cause and party of religion,
preserve our own honour, defend our people, secure our kingdoms
and support our allies, all of which we are tied to do by that bond of
sovereignty, which under God we bear over you. Nevertheless, we
are resolved that this course, which at this time is thus inforced on us
by that necessity, to which no ordinary course can give the Law, shall
not in any wise be made a precedent for after times.

B From *Apostolic Obedience* by Richard Sibthorpe (1627).

Subjects are bound to obedience by the double obligation of Justice
and of Necessity; except they will suffer as rebels or ill-doers. If
princes command any thing which subjects may not perform because
it is against the laws of (1) God or of (2) Nature, or (3) impossible,
yet subjects are bound to undergo their punishment without either
resistance or railing or reviling, and so to yield a passive obedience
where they cannot exhibit an active one . . .

c From an untitled work by Thomas Scott (1627).

Subjects may disobey and refuse an unworthy king's command and request if it be more than of duty we owe unto him. Yea, gracious subjects ought of duty in their places to discountenance and dishearten graceless tyrants that will not [punish] Agag but in his defence fall out with Parliament and with loans and impositions and exalted services continue to deny right and liberty and to oppress and exhaust the people.

D Reporting the reaction of the High Constables in Bedfordshire to the Forced Loan (1627).

... they made some question whether this course now holden were not against law, and they conceived it was not grounded upon good precedent and they feared future danger by such a precedent. They much insisted that the parliamentary way of raising money was most equal and most indifferent ... [and] so did produce good effects, making good law, redress of grievances if anything were amiss, pardons etc. And they did declare that the general opinion was that in a parliamentary way every man would be willing to contribute to his ability.

E From a letter sent by the King to the loan commissioners for Gloucestershire (1627).

Whereas we did require the aid of our good and loving subjects of that county by lending unto us such competent sums of money as might enable us to provide for our own and their safeties and for defence of the true religion and our kingdoms and dominions ... We understand that divers of them have obstinately refused to assist us. thereby discovering their disaffection to their prince and county. We think fit that such as neglect us and themselves shall serve in person for the defence of our kingdoms ... [and] authorise you forthwith to press or cause to be pressed one hundred and fifty of these persons to serve on foot in our wars.

F From the Petition of Right (1628).

By the authority of Parliament holden in the five and twentieth year of the reign of King Edward the Third, it is declared and enacted, that from henceforth no person shall be compelled to make any loans to the King against his will, because such loans were against reason and the franchise of the land. Yet your people have been required to lend certain sums of money unto your Majesty, and upon their refusal to do so have been imprisoned, confined and sundry other ways molested. And where also by the statute called 'The Great Charter of the Liberties of England' it is declared and enacted, that no freeman may be taken or imprisoned or [deprived] of his freeholds or liberties or in any manner destroyed but by the lawful judgement of his peers, or by the law of the land, nevertheless divers [several] of your subjects have of late been imprisoned without any cause showed but that they were detained by your Majesty's special command.

Q

1. *On what basis did Charles justify the forced loan in source A? (2 marks)*
2. *How did the circumstances in which he dissolved the Parliament of 1626 undermine his claims? (3 marks)*
3. *What reasons did Sibthorpe give in source B for subjects to obey the King? (2 marks)*
4. *Considering sources A and B together, explain why many MPs and their constituents would be worried by such arguments. (3 marks)*
5. *'Agag' was a character in the Bible whose life was mistakenly spared by King Saul of Israel. Who do you think Scott was referring to in this reference? (2 marks)*
6. *What reasons does Scott give for resisting the forced loan? (2 marks)*
7. *What reasons are given in source D for preferring parliamentary taxation? (3 marks)*
8. *Sources B, C and D are all contemporary reactions to the forced loan. Use your knowledge of the period to explain (a) why they are so different, and (b) which would be most widely shared. (5 marks)*
9. *How far do the sources prove that the forced loan was unpopular? (5 marks)*
10. *According to sources E and F, how did Charles deal with resistance? (3 marks)*
11. *Why did he believe that his actions were justified? (2 marks)*
12. *How did the Petition of Right argue that he was not? (3 marks)*
13. *Using the evidence provided in these sources in the context of the period, explain how far this conflict between Charles and Parliament was (a) serious, and (b) avoidable. (15 marks)*

KEY ISSUE

The failure of reconciliation.

The success of the Petition of Right and the granting of subsidies to the King provided an opportunity for reconciliation. However, when the House of Commons began to prepare a bill to approve the King's levying of tonnage and poundage, Charles denied that such authorisation was necessary. This raised the old issue of impositions and some merchants refused to pay duties. More seriously, religion and the Church were becoming a major issue. In June 1628, Eliot produced a remonstrance against the growth of Arminianism, and the King responded by proroguing Parliament. In November he reissued the

Thirty-Nine Articles, which laid down the doctrine of the Church, defined according to his views, and forbade any other interpretation. The preaching of Calvinist ideas was forbidden, and indeed preaching itself, so central to the Protestant belief in education and bible study, was to be laid aside in favour of set prayers and sacramental services. The steady progress of Arminian ideas could not be ignored by MPs who held Calvinist convictions, or who feared that it would open the way to Catholic influence.

In August 1628, the Duke of Buckingham, whose presence had created such conflict between the King and Parliament, was assassinated. While the King wept in lonely isolation, the citizens of London lit bonfires in celebration. His removal provided another opportunity for greater co-operation, and Charles did appoint one of Buckingham's leading critics, Sir Thomas Wentworth, as a Privy Councillor and President of the Council of the North. Nevertheless, a deeper reconciliation between the King and critical MPs was made impossible by Charles's resentment at their obvious pleasure in Buckingham's death, and by their continuing fears over the direction of the King's religious policies. The most ominous feature of the growing tensions that existed between 1625 and 1629 was that the separate issues of religion, finance and the relative rights of the King and Parliament were becoming entangled in such a way that progress in one area was undermined by continuing difficulties in the others.

When Parliament re-assembled in January 1629, there were problems almost from the start. The King was offended by the lack of regret for Buckingham, the issue of customs duties was raised immediately, and in February a Commons committee produced a deeply critical report on changes in the Church. In March, Charles summoned the House of Commons to the Lords, presumably intending to announce a further prorogation. Fearing that they would be dissolved before airing their grievances fully, some members held the Speaker in his chair to prevent the House rising while they passed the Three Resolutions – one against Arminianism in the Church and two against the levying and payment of tunnage and poundage without parliamentary consent. The same day, a furious king dissolved Parliament and declared that another would not be summoned until 'our people shall see more clearly into our intentions and actions' and have 'a better understanding of us and themselves'.

> **KEY ISSUE**
>
> *The Three Resolutions epitomised Parliament's hostility.*

D *The causes of the crisis*

The events of 1629 demonstrate the extent of the breakdown in the relationship between the King and Parliament in the years after Charles's accession. What is less clear-cut is where the responsibility lay for the problems that had emerged. Charles himself was very clear about the causes. In March 1629, he issued a declaration in which he sought 'howsoever princes are not bound to give account of their actions but to God alone' to explain his dissolution of Parliament and his intention to delay the calling of another. In it he claimed that:

> **KEY ISSUE**
>
> *Charles's explanation of the crisis.*

> The House hath of late years endeavoured to extend their privileges, by setting up general committees for religion, for courts of justice, for trade and the like; ... so as, where in former times the Knights and Burgesses were wont to communicate to the House such business as they brought from the countries; now there are so many chairs erected, to make inquiry upon all sorts of men, where complaints of all sorts are entertained, to the unsufferable disturbance and scandal of justice and government ... In these innovations ... their drift was to break, by this means, through all respects and ligaments of government, and to erect a universal over-swaying power to themselves, which belongs only to us, and not to them ...

Charles clearly believed that he was facing a deliberate and coherently planned attempt to extend the powers of Parliament and to curtail his own, with Parliament's control of taxes being used as the chief weapon. While challenging this view, some modern historians have claimed that Parliament was irresponsible, refusing to recognise the genuine needs of government or to supply the King adequately.

A closer examination of the behaviour of MPs does not support either view fully. Certainly government finances were inadequate, but on several occasions the House of Commons had shown itself willing to grant the money that the King required, and had in fact done so. In a period of economic depression and disrupted trade, they did offer sizeable subsidies to support a Protestant war. Their criticisms had been directed mainly at the way in which that money was used under the leadership of the Duke of Buckingham, and what they required was some account of its use before more was granted.

This was not a coherent attack on royal powers. At no point had they sought to take control of policy or shift executive power to Parliament. They did not attempt to control the King's choice of advisers, but they did believe that where ministers acted in a way which was dangerous to the State or to religion, there was a need to call them to account. A degree of responsibility for the situation therefore lies with Buckingham. His arrogance and his inefficiency caused disaster abroad and provoked opposition at home. As frustration mounted, this developed into a desire to impeach Buckingham for his errors, but it was the King who made this an issue of prerogative rights.

It was Charles's stubborn determination to defend his favourite that caused the conflicts over subsidies and the forced loan, and raised a real threat to the sanctity of the law. While there were political and constitutional implications in a parliament seeking to call the King's chosen advisers to account, a more tactful monarch could have found ways around this. Instead, Charles had chosen to assert his will by acts of dubious legality over the forced loan. Only a great deal of royal pressure had persuaded the judges to legally justify his imprisonment of refusers, and Charles had then attempted to have the judgement entered as a precedent for the future. Whether he was fully aware of the implications of his actions is uncertain, but he was, in practice, establishing a basis

---

KEY ISSUE

The case for Parliament.

KEY ISSUE

The role of the King.

for tyranny. It was inevitable that a parliament would oppose such actions, and since the forced loan could not solve his financial problems, it was inevitable that he would have to face one. Whether or not Charles sought to establish absolute monarchy as his critics feared, his actions were, at the very least, politically inept.

To make matters worse, he had initiated changes in the Church which frightened and offended many of his subjects. Where James had been flexible and promoted ministers of all shades of opinion, Charles favoured a minority group at the expense of all others. He associated himself completely with a particular party when political needs required him to stand above such disputes. More dangerously, that party was associated in many minds with the Catholic faith, which had been seen for at least a generation as threat to religion, liberty and to the nation itself. Whether or not the fear of an international Catholic conspiracy was justified, it was real, and a sensible king would have recognised it. Instead, Charles favoured neo-Catholics in the Church and allowed his Catholic wife and her confessors to worship openly and gather converts at Court.

In this context, the behaviour of MPs can be more realistically seen as defensive, rather than as an attack on the King and his rights. Seventeenth-century parliaments did not really allow for an organised opposition party. Sessions of parliament were short, and most MPs were amateurs, called occasionally to represent the opinions of their friends and neighbours. A more organised opposition faction could develop in the Lords, and there clearly was a Puritan faction there, centred around Lord Wharton, Lord Saye and Sele and Lord Robert Spencer. These men had clients in the Commons, such as the MP John Pym, who was lawyer to the Puritan Earl of Bedford, but it is difficult to see that they constituted an organised party. The leading figure in the Commons, Sir Edward Coke, had followed a long career of royal service, and was a client of Buckingham. It was Buckingham who controlled the operation of patronage, an area in which he was extremely efficient. The most acceptable explanation for the opposition that Charles faced in these years is not a political plot, but the fact that he offended the deeply held convictions of a significant part of the political community about religion, Parliament and the rule of law.

This does not mean that Charles alone was responsible for the situation. The situation in Europe created a real need for England to take a more active role than James had allowed, and the English monarchy certainly lacked the means to act as many of the political community wished. Charles did have real problems in financing a viable foreign policy. Moreover, some of those who most insistently demanded action, such as the MP Sir John Eliot, also behaved irresponsibly when the King sought to act. Eliot's Puritan convictions and firebrand oratory did much to encourage fears and suspicions among MPs, to provoke the King, and to bring the political conflicts in Parliament to a head. Nevertheless, his ability to influence more cautious and moderate members owed more to the behaviour and attitudes of a King who gave substance to their religious and political fears.

E *The personality of the King*

In the light of these arguments, the personality and attitudes of Charles I become vitally important in explaining the emergence of a crisis and the drift to civil war. If MPs were not actively seeking to change the balance of the constitution, and problems with the system of government were not impossible to handle, then the King's handling of them must be considered to have played a major part. If the argument that Charles, as an individual, was significant, then it must be shown that his personality, and/or beliefs, led him to act in a way which affected the situation and which was different from other kings at the time. If he simply acted as would any seventeenth-century monarch, then it must be argued that the crisis arose from inherent problems in the system of government, and was probably inevitable given the combination of religious, financial and constitutional difficulties that existed. The source exercise that follows is intended to analyse this issue in greater depth. The sources focus on the personality and beliefs of Charles and the questions should enable his part in the crisis to be considered. In order to draw effective conclusions, it is important to interpret them in the context of the events and problems described in the previous pages.

See pages 129–30 for a discussion of Charles I's role in history.

F *Source investigation: The personality and actions of Charles I*

A The Judgement of Chief Baron Fleming in Bate's Case (1606).

The king's power is double, ordinary and absolute ... That of the ordinary is for the profit of particular subjects, for the execution of civil justice, and this is exercised by equity and justice in ordinary courts, and is known as common law, and these laws cannot be changed without parliament. The absolute power of the king is ... that which is applied to the general benefit of the people, and this power is most properly named policy and government. This absolute power varies according to the wisdom of the king for the common good; and these being general ... all things done within these rules are lawful.

B From a letter by Charles I, 29 January 1649.

The next main hinge on which your prosperity will depend and move, is that of civil justice, wherein the settled laws of these kingdoms, to which you are rightly heir, are the most excellent rules you can govern by ... Nor would I have you entertain any aversion or dislike of Parliaments, which, in their right constitution with freedom and honour, will never hinder or diminish your greatness, but will rather be an interchanging of love, loyalty and confidence, between a prince and his people.

c From *Clarendon: Selections* by G. Huehns (ed). Oxford 1978.

... he will be found not only a prince of admirable virtue and piety, but of great parts of knowledge, wisdom and judgement; and that the most signal parts of his misfortunes proceeded chiefly from the modesty of his nature, which kept him from trusting himself enough, and made him believe that others discerned better, who were much inferior to him in those faculties; and so to depart often from his own reason, to follow the opinions of more unskilful men, whose affections he believed to be unquestionable to his service ...

D From *Three British Revolutions* by C. Carlton, in J.G.A. Pocock (ed) (1981).

[Carlton is considering the effects of the fact that Charles was the second son of James I, that he was small and shy with a distinct stammer, and that he was overshadowed by his elder brother, Prince Henry, until Henry's death in 1612.]

In psychological terms Charles's early years had produced an overde-veloped superego that bottled up his inner tensions. Charles tried to protect himself by seeking affection, currying favour, becoming with-drawn, displaying deference rare in an heir, and above all by submit-ting. Thus when he became king he expected similar behaviour, demanded a similar sacrifice, and insisted upon as great and painful a loyalty as he had been forced to yield. An authoritarian personality, Charles was incapable of conceding at a time when compromises were desperately demanded from the English monarchy. He was full of outward self-certainty (manifest in such doctrines as divine right) that only intense inner doubt can engender ...

E From *The Works of William Laud* (William Laud lived from 1573 to 1645).

The inward worship of the heart is the great service of God... but the external worship of God in his Church is the great witness to the world, that our heart stands right in that service ... Now, no external action in the world can be uniform without some ceremonies; and these in religion, the ancienter they be the better, so [as long as] they may fit the time and place ... and scarce anything hath hurt religion more in these broken times than an opinion in too many men, that because Rome had thrust some unnecessary and many superstitious ceremonies upon the Church, therefore the Reformation must have none at all; not considering therewhile, that ceremonies are the hedge that fence the substance of religion from all the indignities which pro-faneness and sacrilege too commonly put upon it.

F From *The Making of Britain: The Age of Expansion* by L.M. Smith (ed).

In many respects Charles I, more than any of his predecessors, was England's supreme Renaissance prince: his personal style (and within weeks, that ordered for his Court) was majestic, sophisticated and cultivated. The paintings of van Dyck, vividly portraying a king calm and confident ruling unquestioned a country harmonious and peaceful, encapsulate both the man and his vision of monarchy.

PICTURES 3 AND 4

A portrait of Charles I by Mytens (left) and a portrait of Charles I by van Dyck (right)

See page 125 for the for the portrait of Charles I at his trial.

Q

1. *What powers did the King exercise according to source A? Does this explain any of Charles's actions between 1625 and 1629? (3 marks)*

2. *What attitude does Charles take towards parliaments in source B? What is the significance of his phrase 'in their right constitution'? (3 marks)*

3. *Do sources A and B suggest that Charles's political beliefs were in any way unusual? (4 marks)*

4. *How does Clarendon describe Charles in source C? (3 marks)*

5. *Given that Clarendon was one of Charles's main advisers in the 1640s, do you think that his description would be accurate and reliable? (2 marks)*

6. *How does Carlton describe Charles in source D? (3 marks)*

7. *Using sources C and D together, explain (a) how his personality is* *reflected in his actions between 1625 and 1629, and (b) how his personality would influence his interpretation of the powers described in sources A and B. (10 marks)*

8. *Look at source G. How successful were the Court painters in projecting the image of a dignified and self-confident king? (2 marks)*

9. *Using sources F and G together, explain what image of himself Charles wanted to project. (3 marks)*

10. *How does Laud justify the use of new ceremonies in the Church in source E? (3 marks)*

11. *Use sources F and G to explain why these arguments might appeal to Charles. (4 marks)*

12. *Using the information provided by these sources in the light of your own knowledge, explain how and why Charles's personality and beliefs might lead him into the kind of political errors that he made between 1625 and 1629. (10 marks)*

2 ⌁ THE PERSONAL RULE OF CHARLES I, 1629–40

Historians have tended to regard the Dissolution of 1629 as a watershed in the reign of Charles, marking the first stage in an open conflict between King and Parliament. For Whig historians of the nineteenth and early twentieth centuries, it was the beginning of the Eleven Year Tyranny, a conscious attempt to establish absolute monarchy along the lines of the French and Spanish examples. More recently, this interpretation has been challenged, and historians like Kevin Sharpe and J.P. Kenyon have suggested that Charles reacted logically to the short-sighted antics of an irresponsible Parliament. Since he could not rely on the help of MPs in carrying out his duty to govern, he sought to find ways of doing so without them and tried to reform an antiquated system of government and administration.

If this is the case, then why did he fail? And, why did his attempt to govern apparently create so much opposition? Historians like Kenyon have argued that, in fact, opposition was limited and muted until after the Scottish Rebellion of 1638, and that many of Charles's reforms were widely accepted outside a religiously motivated minority. Others, such as Conrad Russell and John Morrill, have agreed that Charles came close to success in balancing the budget and silencing opposition until he stretched his resources too far in dealing with the Scots. Their conflicting interpretations give rise to two key issues. Firstly, what were Charles's intentions in dissolving Parliament? Was he attempting to change, or merely to reform the British monarchy, and did he seek to abolish or make irrelevant the institution of parliament? Secondly, how did contemporaries react to his plans? The extent and nature of the opposition that he created can offer insight into his aims, as well as suggesting reasons for his eventual failure.

> ## KEY ISSUE
>
> *Charles's aims and chances of political success in 1629.*

A *Reactions to dissolution, 1629–31*

In 1629, there seems to have been relatively little hostile reaction to the dissolution of Parliament. Nine MPs who were directly involved in passing the Three Resolutions were arrested, but five were quickly released. Eliot, Denzil Holles and Benjamin Valentine were held in various prisons to avoid writs of *habeas corpus* (which would have secured their release) and finally brought to trial in 1630, after which they were imprisoned in the Tower of London. There is no doubt that their open defiance of the King's instructions to Parliament had taken opposition too far, and few would have challenged their punishment at the time. Holles and Valentine were later released after apologising to the King. Only Eliot refused to do so, and he was held in prison until his death from fever two years later. Like the King himself, he was sufficiently obstinate to provide his cause with a martyr.

More importantly, neither the King nor public opinion portrayed these events as a permanent end to Parliaments. The proclamation issued by Charles in 1629 declared that he would summon no more Parliaments until his people were able to understand his purposes. This suggests that, in the long term, he expected his reforms to be understood and accepted, and to produce more co-operative assemblies. It may well be that Charles had no plans to destroy Parliaments but had simply reacted to the overt challenge implied in the Three Resolutions. Having asserted his authority, he now intended to demonstrate the benefits of good government and to establish his vision of peace and order. It was entirely in keeping with Charles's character to give little consideration as to how far his subjects shared that vision.

B *The Personal Rule, 1631–7*

KEY ISSUE

How efficient was Charles I's personal rule?

The nature of his vision can be seen in the government that took shape during the personal rule, because it was very much Charles's own. The centre of his government was the Privy Council, whose function was to advise the King and to ensure that his instructions were carried out. Its supervisory powers were exercised through the choice of Lords Lieutenant and Justices of the Peace, and more directly through the Councils of the North and Welsh Marches, and the prerogative courts of Chancery and Star Chamber. Members included the heads of major government departments such as the treasury and exchequer; they were therefore responsible to the King for both central and local administration. It also included the leading Bishops who carried responsibility for the Church. Through attention to its meetings and supervision of its activities, the King could, and did, exercise direct control of government throughout the kingdom.

The hallmark of the years of personal rule was the active presence of the King in all these functions. Charles attended meetings of the Privy Council, ensured that his purposes were understood, and checked that they were put into effect. In contrast with the laziness of James, which allowed ministers a relatively free hand, Charles was a dutiful governor who paid careful attention to detail. After the death of Buckingham he never again developed a close personal relationship with any minister or favourite – a situation which both caused and reflected his happy marriage. His chief advisers in these years, Laud and Sir Thomas Wentworth, later Earl of Strafford, were kept at arm's length in personal terms, and his Queen, Henrietta Maria, became his closest companion. Unfortunately, her knowledge of England was limited and her political understanding still less. Although her influence was never as overwhelming as that of Buckingham, in political terms it was potentially damaging. Nevertheless, it is clear that the government of England in the 1630s was very much the personal rule of Charles I, and reflected his aims, his strategy and his personal views in a very direct way.

Two aspects of government, the nature of the Royal Court and the administration of local government, are particularly revealing of Charles's intentions. The Court was the seat of government, containing both the King's private household and the major government departments. It was always a reflection of the monarch's personality. The changes introduced by Charles were described approvingly by Lucy Hutchinson, who would be a staunch supporter of parliament during the Civil War.

> See page 91 for the disastrous influence of Henrietta Maria.

COURT AND KING – THE IMAGE OF MONARCHY

Memoirs of Colonel Hutchinson by Lucy Hutchinson, written between 1664 and 1667:

> **KEY ISSUE**
>
> *The style of Charles I's Court.*

The face of the court was much changed in the change of the King, for King Charles was temperate, chaste and serious; so that the fools and bawds, mimics and catamites [boys kept for homosexual practices], of the former court, grew out of fashion; and the nobility and courtiers, who did not quite abandon their debaucheries, yet so reverenced the King as to retire into corners to practise them. Men of learning and ingenuity in all the arts were in esteem and receiving encouragement from the King, who was a most excellent judge and a great lover of paintings, carvings, [en]gravings and many other ingenuities, less offensive than the bawdry and profane abusive wit which was the only exercise of the other court.

Lucy Hutchinson, *Memoirs of Colonel Hutchinson*, Everyman edition 1928, p.67, printed in C W Daniels and J Morrill "Charles I" CUP 1988 p.17

This dignified and artistic atmosphere was deliberately developed by Charles as the setting for his image of monarchy. Having been greatly impressed by what he saw of the Spanish Court in 1623, he sought to emulate it. Courtiers were given detailed instructions on how to act in a variety of situations, and on their standards of morality. Duelling and sexual infidelity were both discouraged. The King's private apartments were kept private, and access to the monarch was restricted. Court ceremonial and entertainments were designed to uphold the concept of hierarchy and order, with close attention paid to rank and birth to uphold the status of the nobility and of the King. Major ceremonies such as those relating to the Order of the Garter were re-designed by Charles himself to ensure appropriate dignity, and moved away from London to Windsor. Unfortunately this robbed them of their value as a public spectacle.

Hence the Court that Charles had created had a relatively limited impact. Successful monarchs like Henry VIII and Elizabeth had used public magnificence to impress their subjects. Charles was a perceptive and enthusiastic patron of art, commissioning paintings by such major artistic figures as van Dyck and Rubens, but very few of his subjects were able to see or appreciate the beauty and symbolism of their works. His virtues as a man, and as a husband and father, were not necessarily those required of a king.

Similarly mixed results were produced by the King's careful attention to administration. On one level, there were significant improvements. Greater consistency in the administration of justice was achieved through detailed instructions to judges and JPs, and the Prerogative Courts were able to offer quick, and often impartial, decisions. With the advantage of being detached from local interests, they were less likely to be unfairly influenced, and in the President of the Council for the North, Sir Thomas Wentworth, Charles had an able and effective administrator. Similar virtues were apparent in Laud's government of the Church, where rules were enforced, visitations carried out regularly and effectively, and order maintained. The Court of High Commission and the Church courts did their best to encourage better standards of behaviour, dealing with cases of drunken or lewd behaviour among the laity as well as upholding the standards of the ministry. Laud was an energetic and determined administrator, and as Bishop of London from 1628 to 1633, he was able to exercise considerable influence. This power was further increased in 1633, when he became Archbishop of Canterbury. Nevertheless, both he and Wentworth depended on the King for their power, and the policy of 'Thorough' that was associated with them was very much the policy of Charles himself.

The clearest example of this approach can be seen in the 314 Books of Orders that were issued to JPs from January 1631. These contained detailed instructions on a range of legal and administrative matters, covering the collection and distribution of the Poor Rate, treatment and punishment of beggars, control of markets, storage and use of grain, movement of goods and upkeep of roads and bridges. The 1620s had seen a depression in trade and a series of bad harvests, leading to significant unrest in a number of localities. The Books of Orders sought to help the poor and improve provision of support in order to ensure control. To some extent, they were successful. According to the historian L.M. Hill 'The poor were better treated and better cared for than ever before. Grain stocks were better administered and waste was curtailed. The quality of local government was markedly improved and little doubt lingered as to the Council's ability to cause the King's writ to run into local parts with considerable authority . . .'

Unfortunately, this success was achieved at the cost of enormous effort on the part of the Privy Council and some resentment at local

KEY ISSUE

The limitations of Charles's political vision.

KEY ISSUE

'Through' (the policy of central supervision) in action.

level. Many JPs regarded local government as their own, and disliked constant interference from the centre. More importantly, they were unpaid and, therefore, to some extent independent of central pressure. The status of JP was prized for its local influence, and the Council was able to exercise some control by threatening to remove recalcitrant Justices from the list, but there were limits to their power. While open defiance was rare, there was considerable scope for obstruction and inertia. In the setting of wage and price levels, for example, government instructions had to be interpreted and applied by magistrates who were themselves local producers and employers. Similarly, government supervision relied on the energies and priorities of the Privy Councillors, and there was a limit to the time that they could devote to this task. Laud's fussy attention to detail was essential in ensuring that checks were carried out, but this also restricted the range of issues that could be resolved. It is significant that the Books of Orders were most effectively enforced from 1631 to 1635, after which the Council was forced to turn its attention to the collection of ship money and away from other areas of administration.

> **KEY ISSUE**
>
> *The limits of central control.*

These problems highlight one of the main weaknesses of the Personal Rule – its reliance on particular individuals and their energies. While Charles's personal supervision and intervention, and the efficiency of Wentworth and Laud, could provide new energy and enthusiasm, they did little to improve the system in the long term. For the most part they sought to make existing arrangements work better, rather than to review or remake them. While this was a significant limitation on their effectiveness, it is also a possible indication of what Charles was seeking to achieve. The key to absolute monarchy in France and Spain was their possession of a paid bureaucracy, dependent on and completely loyal to the King. Had Charles intended to create such a regime in England, he might well be expected to follow their example. Even with improved finances, however, he took no steps in this direction. If he planned to create an absolute monarchy in England, he went about it very inefficiently, and the evidence of his administration suggests that Charles was more guilty of political naivety than of tyranny.

> **KEY ISSUE**
>
> *Weaknesses of the Personal Rule.*

A similar picture emerges in financial matters, where Charles also sought to reform and improve his situation. The difficulties that he had inherited from his father in 1625 had been compounded by his own errors thereafter. Although Parliament had, on several occasions, voted quite generous subsidies, the costs of war between 1625 and 1629 had swallowed up this, and more. After dissolving Parliament in 1629, Charles had made peace with France and Spain, both of which had more pressing concerns in Europe. Thereafter he set out to attain the financial stability required for effective government. Expenditure was checked and curtailed and every opportunity was taken to exploit existing sources of revenue. Helped by an increase in income from customs duties, brought about by increasing trade, Lord Treasurer Weston was able to balance the budget for current expenditure by 1635, and, by 1637, the King's income had reached one million pounds a year.

The table on page 68 sets out the methods used to achieve this. For the most part, as with administration, they consisted of more effective exploitation of existing rights, with little that was new. The approach has been described by Derek Hirst as 'financial antiquarianism', with new revenue created by researching and reviving old rights. Even the famous 'Ship Tax' was not entirely new, as it was an extension of the King's traditional right to call on coastal towns to provide ships for naval defence. In finance as in administration, Charles established restraint, efficiency and improvement rather than the foundations of absolutism.

FINANCE DURING THE PERSONAL RULE 1629–38

TABLE 4
Finance during the Personal Rule

1630 King established a *Commission for Defective Titles*. This examined the leases by which crown tenants held land and raised rents unless the tenant could prove their right to a fixed rate. Further revenue was raised by fines levied from those who had enclosed waste, common or forest land without payment to the King

1630 Commission for knighthoods set up – by feudal law, all men with land worth £40 per year were entitled to a knighthood on payment of a fine to the King. The commission investigated and fined all those who had failed to take up the option (raising £165,000 between 1630 and 1635)

1634 Judicial commission established to investigate and fine those who had infringed the boundaries of royal forests

Feudal rights

1635 Commission for Defective Titles extended and renewed

Trade and customs

1629–40 'Illegal' collection of Tonnage and Poundage continued
Sale of monopolies renewed through a loophole in the 1624 Act

1634 Ship money levied from coastal towns
1635 Ship money levied and extended to all countries – demand for £199,000
1636 Levy repeated as in 1635 – John Hampden refused to pay
1637 Levy repealed – Judges voted against Hampden by 5 to 3
1638 Levy repeated, but amount reduced to £70,000

Ship Money

The King's traditional right to ask coastal towns to provide ships for naval defence had been adapted to a money payment, this was called **ship money**. (The Government decided on the amount required, and JPs had the responsibility to levy it.)

Ship money different to most taxes because it was not set as a proportion of an individual's goods or income. An area was simply told by the government to raise a certain sum. It was therefore flexible.

THE GROWTH OF OPPOSITION 1633–8

If this is the case, and Charles was not attempting to establish absolute monarchy in England, it becomes necessary to ask why his plans eventually created sufficient opposition to precipitate a crisis in 1640. At the most obvious level, it is likely that irritation would increase as it became obvious that Charles did not intend to call a Parliament for the foreseeable future. The historian, John Morrill, has suggested that this may only have been one option in 1629–30, while 'hardened into a resolve only by about 1632'. It would be logical, therefore, to expect opposition to emerge and increase from that time. Nevertheless, long intermissions between Parliaments were by no means unusual, and that alone would be unlikely to create the depth of discontent that emerged by 1640, unless the absence of Parliament was clearly related to other threats to liberty. Such threats seem to have emerged by 1637, arising from the two key areas of change in the Church, and the collection of ship money. While Charles probably did not intend to create absolute monarchy, his actions and decisions in these areas seem to have created fears of that kind. While his real weakness may have been political naivety and lack of awareness, the steps that he took may well have appeared to others to be moving in the direction of tyranny.

PICTURE 5
A portrait of William Laud by an unknown artist after van Dyck. An officious, humourless man, Laud was the best-hated royal servant in Britain

Religion and the Church

Despite the suspicions that he aroused, Charles was not a Catholic. He was genuinely devoted to the Church of England in which he had grown up, and he desired to improve its position in society and its financial health. Ironically, this was an aim that he shared with his most vociferous critics, who wanted to see puritan reforms. The Reformation had transferred a great deal of wealth from the Church to the laity, and many parishes were badly served by inadequate ministers. Like Bancroft in 1610, and the puritan Feoffees thereafter, Charles and Laud wanted to reform and improve the condition of the Church. What differed was the vision of reform that they had in mind.

This vision can be summed up in Laud's famous phrase – 'the beauty of holiness'. For Charles and Laud, ceremonial and ritual in the Church could only add to worship, creating an atmosphere of reverence and using beauty to celebrate faith. Laud argued that rituals and ceremonies were the outward expression of inner faith, upholding decency and order. Tradition was to be respected, and where possible, traditional forms should be maintained. Many of these were derived from the Catholic Church in the days before the Reformation. While he agreed the Catholic rituals included some unnecessary and dangerous superstitions, his argument was that these alone should be removed, leaving the traditional core intact. 'Protestants' he declared, 'did not protest against the Church, but against the unnecessary superstitions that had been attached to it.' When these were stripped away, the ideal form of worship was achieved.

In addition, Laud and Charles wanted to emphasise the role of the Church as the centre of the community. While this was partly a political strategy, strengthening the government's ability to control its subjects, it also came from a genuine concept of communal identity. In contrast to the fiercely individual faith of the Puritan 'godly', with each saint seeking to follow his or her own path to salvation by inner faith in God, the Arminians saw worship as a communal activity which was expressed more effectively in familiar rituals and congregational activities such as singing and chanting of prayers. While the reforms introduced by Laud were intended to restrict debate and ensure harmony in the Church, he saw this as upholding decency and order rather than threatening the right of individual souls to discover God and 'the Truth'.

In 1633 he issued new instructions to the Bishops which were to be enforced by regular visitations to the parish clergy. Preaching was to be limited to Sundays, and the afternoon sermon was to be replaced by catechising (the teaching and testing of learned doctrine by reciting of set prayers and creeds). Clergy were to wear robes and use key signs and symbols such as the cross in baptism, or kneeling at the sight of the alter. Weekday lectures, often used by puritan clergy to enable them to preach without having to carry out offensive services, were banned. A legal challenge was launched in the courts to prevent the Feoffees from buying up and providing ministers for impropriated parishes, and when the judges voted in the King's favour, the parishes that they had already purchased were taken over by the King. Perhaps the most offensive of all to English Protestants was the removal of communion tables from the centre of churches and placing them at the east end of the central nave, the traditional position of the Catholic High Altar. They were to be decorated, railed off from the laity, and approached only by the clergy.

> **KEY ISSUE**
>
> *The aims of Charles and Laud.*

> **KEY ISSUE**
>
> *Laud's reform of the Church.*

Whatever Laud's intentions, these changes were deeply offensive to many English Protestants. Firstly, they contained echoes of Catholic tradition and appeared to be moving the Church in that direction. Secondly, they were obvious and unavoidable. Whereas the doctrinal disputes of the 1620s had engaged ministers and theologians, these changes to the parish church affected large numbers of ordinary lay men and women. This was compounded by the very efficiency with which Laud ran the Church – not only were the new rules brought in, they were enforced. By 1637, there were deep and widespread fears that Catholicism was being re-introduced as the spiritual counterpart to absolute monarchy.

These fears reflected a deep-seated anti-Catholicism, which lay at the heart of English Protestant society. Against the background of the Thirty Years War, Englishmen, who had grown up with stories of the Marian burnings and Spanish plots against Elizabeth, saw Catholicism as the centre of an international conspiracy to undermine true religion. As far as English Protestants were concerned, the Pope was the Anti-Christ, the devil's servant, and his supporters sought to infiltrate the true Church in order to destroy it. While many suspected that Charles and Laud were secret Catholics, others feared that, even if they were not, they were allowing Catholicism to creep into the Church of England and so doing the devil's work. While Puritan ministers were being driven out and increasing numbers took refuge in New England, Catholicism was becoming fashionable at Court. The Queen exercised her right to worship in the Catholic way, and a growing number of courtiers attended her services. Nothing indicates Charles's lack of political awareness more clearly than his decision in 1637 to welcome an ambassador from the Pope, George Con, as a permanent resident at Court and allow him to become a personal friend.

While Laud has carried much of the blame for Charles's religious policies, they were in fact very much the King's own. Laud's instructions regarding the placing of altars were intended to be a recommendation – it was Charles who made it compulsory. While Laud attempted to restrict the Queen's influence, Charles appointed Catholics like Treasurer Weston to the Privy Council. Laud opposed the arrival of George Con, and advised the King to proceed more slowly with changes in the Church – Charles responded in 1637 by deciding to impose a version of the Anglican Prayer Book on the Presbyterian Church of Scotland.

If Laud has been harshly judged in terms of his attitude to the Church, his other activities and his interference in secular (non-religious) affairs was a significant cause of discontent. From 1633, when Wentworth was appointed Lord Deputy of Ireland, he became the dominant figure on the Privy Council. Not only did he interfere in many areas of administration – he was the moving spirit behind the issue of the Books of Orders – he also sought to place his supporters in key positions. In 1632 his protégé, Francis Windebanke was made Secretary of State, and in 1634 he secured the dismissal of the Puritan Chief Justice, Sir Robert Heath. In 1635, when his main rival, Lord Treasurer Weston died, he was replaced by the Bishop of London, William Juxon.

KEY ISSUE

Fear of Catholicism.

KEY ISSUE

The role of Laud.

KEY ISSUE

The Bishops and anti-clericalism.

This clerical influence was deeply resented by the ruling class, for a number of reasons. As Lord Brooke explained, the landed nobility had some independent power and income, whereas the Bishops were entirely dependent on the King for their appointments and for the future of their families. Hence, they could not be expected to act in any interest but the King's. In addition, they were occupying posts and positions that the nobility and gentry had come to regard as their own. Before the Reformation, the Catholic Church had supplied many of the King's advisers and administrators, but the advent of Protestant influence had produced an educated laity to replace them. The return to clerical advisers threatened the power of the lay nobility, and seemed yet another sign of Catholic influence. Such resentments were increased by the attitude of the Laudian clergy. They claimed to receive their spiritual power through the Church from Christ himself and this raised the status and the pretensions of the clergy. There were numerous complaints of the arrogance and high-handedness of many of the Laudian Bishops. Clarendon described the resentment created by the Court of High Commission, which summoned 'persons of honour and great quality, of the court and of the country' to answer charges of immorality and misbehaviour and 'prosecuted [them] to their shame and punishment ... which they called an insolent triumph upon their degree and quality, and levelling them with the common people ... which was never forgotten ... and which likewise made the jurisdiction and rigour of the Star Chamber more felt and murmured against.' In 1637 three puritan pamphleteers were summoned before the Star Chamber and charged with sedition (stirring up unrest) for their written attacks on Laud and the Queen. Dr John Bastwick was a well-known physician, and his companions, Thomas Burton and William Prynne were a preacher and lawyer respectively. All were members of the gentry class. They were condemned to be placed in the pillory and to have their ears cropped. In addition, Prynne, who had been in trouble before was branded on the cheeks. The sentence was carried out before a shocked crowd, horrified to see such mutilations applied to the gentry.

KEY ISSUE

Religion and discontent.

The widespread resentment created by Laud's influence and actions therefore helped to create opposition to the Personal Rule itself. While anger at the changes in the Church might have been limited to a Puritan minority, the fear of Catholicism and the pretensions of the Laudian clergy had a much wider impact. By 1637 there are signs of mounting discontent and a growing desire for Parliament to be called, since there was no other legal means of expressing grievances. What caused even more concern, however, was that by 1637 Charles appeared to have achieved a method of raising money which could make him permanently independent of parliament and might ensure that the Personal Rule could last as long as he wished. Whether he intended this or not, the introduction of ship money, and the judges' decision in 1637 that he had a right to raise such taxes, appeared to lay the foundation of the absolute monarchy that some feared.

The nature of ship money and the opposition that it created has been the subject of considerable debate among historians. In the words of J.P. Kenyon, 'We are assured by Whig historians ... that this aroused the most furious opposition in the provinces, and this 'fact' is generally accepted'. It is essential to the Whig interpretation of this period that Charles wanted to establish absolute monarchy, that he intended to dispense with Parliament, that the opposition recognised this fact and that the country as a whole resisted it. In this argument, ship money is crucial. If Charles had succeeded in establishing it as an annual tax, and was able to apply it to uses other than naval defence, he could certainly have become independent of parliamentary taxes in all except the most desperate emergencies. It is therefore necessary for Whig historians to show that this was his intention, and that the political community recognised and prevented this by refusing to pay. According to Kenyon, 'there is scarcely any hard evidence for this, and what there is, is associated with predictable individuals like the Earl of Warwick and Lord Saye and Sele [the leaders of the puritan faction]'. The money was used to equip a fleet to put down privateers in the English Channel, and most people were quite willing to pay until after the beginning of the Scottish crisis in 1637. In 1635, the government received all but £5,000 of the £199,000 demanded, in 1636 all but £7,000 and in 1637, all but £18,000. Only in 1638, when the assessment had been reduced to £70,000 by the government, was there a serious shortfall. This may well have been, as John Morrill has argued, a result of an over-stretched administration struggling to cope with collecting ship money and preparation for the Scottish wars.

It would appear, therefore, that the Whig argument is fatally undermined, or at least shown to be significantly overstated. With regard to Charles's intentions, this may well be the case. There is no doubt that ship money was initially applied to building up the navy, and its extension to the inland areas was not unreasonable. As with other aspects of Charles's financial policies, it can be seen as a natural and logical desire to maximise the Crown's resources. With regard to the extent of opposition, however, the revisionists' case is less convincing. As early as 1610, the political community in parliament had shown a clear appreciation of the importance of its control of finance in protecting the rights, and indeed the existence, of parliament. It would be surprising if they did not now appreciate the significance of the new tax. Perhaps even more important, the extent of opposition must be assessed in the light of the difficulties and dangers posed by resistance.

In the first place, there was unlikely to be real resistance until it became apparent in 1636 that the tax would be regularly levied. In that year a test case was set up through John Hampden's refusal to pay. It is unlikely that Hampden was acting alone – his known associates included Pym and the Earl of Bedford, as well as Lord Saye and Sele. Hampden was brought to trial in 1637, and the famous split decision of the judges in favour of the King, by seven to five, was not published until 1638. Many who were considering resistance would probably wait for this decision before taking any risky action. Resistance was certainly dangerous. A King who had imprisoned men for refusing to pay a

KEY ISSUE

Hampden's resistance.

forced loan would be unlikely to tolerate those who resisted an apparently legal tax. By 1638, resistance was clearly quite widespread. It has been suggested that this was because the Privy Council were pre-occupied with the Scottish Rebellion, and they were unable to supervise the collection of the tax with the same efficiency as before.

An alternative explanation is suggested, however, by evidence taken from Clarendon's memoirs and other contemporary records. According to Clarendon, there was little resistance to the tax until after the judges' decision against Hampden. The argument of the majority who found for the King was that he had the right to levy such taxes for the good of the country. In the words of Clarendon this was 'a spring and magazine that should have no bottom'. The ship money verdict gave the King the right to demand a sum of money, fixed by himself, and force the JPs to collect it as best they could. For many gentlemen who had previously been willing to pay out of good will to the King, this established a legal duty which had no limit. As such, it was not only an infringement of Parliament's right to consent to taxation, but also an attack on their basic property rights.

This is supported by documents which relate the reaction of the gentry in Kent to the news of the verdict. These documents can be found in C.W. Daniels and John Morrill's study of Charles I (see the 'Bibliography' on page 79). While it is clear that the Kentish gentry accepted the need to pay for naval defence, it is equally clear that they disliked this method of raising it. It was felt that Parliamentary taxes which related payments to income were fairer than the imposition of a lump sum on each county, and it was also believed that control of the amount and timing of taxes should rest with Parliament. There is little doubt that ship money was unpopular and that it did cause considerable resentment. In the words of Clarendon 'the damage and mischief cannot be expressed, that the Crown and State sustained by the deserved reproach and infamy that attended the judges, by being made use of in this, and like acts of power'. Their role was to uphold law, and by interpreting it to enable the King to act as he chose, Clarendon argued, the law was brought into disrepute. Such an opinion, expressed by a royalist and servant of the King, does suggest that ship money was a significant cause of resentment among the political community. Little could be done, however, to express resentment openly unless a Parliament should be called.

C The Scottish rebellion and the end of the personal rule, 1637–40

By 1637, the monarchy was solvent in terms of income and expenditure, although little had been done to reduce debts. More importantly, a period of prolonged peace had benefited trade, so that revenue from customs duties had risen by more than 50 per cent, promising a possible route to long-term financial security. The situation was still finely balanced, and there is no doubt of the discontent felt by some, but

July 1637	Riots in St Giles's Cathedral, Edinburgh greeted Charles I's prayer book	**TABLE 5** *Key events, 1637–40*
February 1638	The Scottish Covenant	
June 1639	The First Bishops' War ended with the Peace of Berwick	
April 1640	The Short Parliament	
June–October1640	The Second Bishops' War	
June 1640	The battle of Newburn – 'Never did so many run before so few'	
October 1640	The treaty of Ripon	
November 1640	The Long Parliament met	

opposition was muted, with little opportunity for open expression. There was clearly some resentment of ship money, of the failure to call Parliament and of the changes in the Church, but little hope of reversing them and the leaders of the Puritan faction were considering emigration as their only way out. Charles appeared to be in control.

It was at this point that Charles made his greatest error, in deciding to extend his reforms from England into his other kingdoms. In Ireland he had already withdrawn the Graces, which had given Irish Catholics a measure of religious freedom, and Strafford's iron grip as governor appeared to preclude any difficulties. In Scotland the independence and strength of the Presbyterian 'Kirk' created difficulties for the monarchy, as well as an encouragement to English Puritans, and King James had already taken some steps towards greater uniformity. Unlike his Scottish father, Charles had little understanding of Scottish politics or culture, and made this worse by seeking advice from a small group of Scots living in London rather than the Scottish Privy Council in Edinburgh. James had attempted to create stronger links between the English and Scottish churches, persuading the Scots to restore the office of Bishop, albeit with much less authority than their English counterparts. In 1621 he had suggested a set liturgy, similar to the English Prayer Book, but had accepted that the fierce opposition it aroused made the scheme impossible. Charles was not only less Scottish than his father, but considerably less tactful.

In 1637, he ordered that a new prayer book, based on the one used in England, should be formally adopted and read in Edinburgh churches. The order was imposed by proclamation and without reference to either the Scottish Parliament or the Assembly of the Kirk. When the book was read in St Giles's Cathedral in Edinburgh, a woman named Jenny Geddes was so incensed that she threw her stool at the Bishop who was reading it. The service erupted into a riot, which rapidly sparked off riots elsewhere among a people who were infuriated by both the book and the manner in which it was imposed. The Scottish Council withdrew the book but Charles insisted that his orders be carried out. This seems to have united the Scottish clergy and nobility in anger at such arbitrary English domination. Early in 1638 they met to draw up a **covenant** (agreement) to defend the Kirk. Charles was outraged by their defiance especially as the Covenanters claimed to be acting in God's name, and the stage was set for confrontation.

> **KEY ISSUE**
>
> *Charles takes the offensive in Scotland.*

> **covenant** an Old Testament term for a solemn agreement, now used by Scots to commit themselves to determined resistance to unpopular innovations.

The confrontation had to be military. Charles regarded the Covenanters as rebels, and had no hesitation in using military force to put down such a rebellion. The Covenanters saw the Kirk as the embodiment of both their religion and culture, and regarded the King as unwittingly serving the cause of the Anti-Christ by restoring devilish ceremonies in the Church. They would fight to defend their religion and felt justified in resisting their sovereign in the name of God. As a result they were united in their determination to resist, while the English were not.

Many of the nobility had no wish to fight, and the JPs were half-hearted in their preparations, perhaps alienated from the King or pre-occupied with the need to collect ship money. The militia was locally based, and men were reluctant to move from their home areas. When they did, the number who became involved in attacking Church ornaments or joining local rioters in pulling down enclosures demonstrates their lack of enthusiasm for the cause for which they were asked to fight. Even Charles realised that he did not have the strength to win, and signed the Treaty of Berwick in 1639. This allowed the Scots to decide on their own religious settlement, and they immediately exercised their freedom by abolishing both the Scottish Prayer Book and the Scottish Bishops.

If Charles had ever intended to respect the Treaty, this action ensured that he would not do so. His political isolation is clear. The London merchants refused to lend him money to raise a new army, and some of the English nobility among the puritan faction, such as Lord Saye and Sele and his son Nathaniel Fiennes, were already in contact with the Scots to encourage them to intervene in England. Charles, however, was unaware of the depth of resentment that he faced, and determined to reassert his authority. To do so, he recalled Sir Thomas Wentworth, now Lord Strafford, from Ireland.

It is difficult to assess how much Strafford could have been expected to know of the situation, but he certainly appears to have misjudged it. He advised Charles to call a Parliament, hoping that traditional anti-Scottish feeling would enable him to rally support. The number of petitions sent to Westminster to greet the MPs who assembled in April 1640 suggests that it was already too late. If not, Charles's handling of the situation ensured that the possibility rapidly disappeared. Without offering any concession, or even perhaps realising that it was needed, he demanded money to defend the kingdom from a crisis that he had created. The result was a chaotic session in which the 'opposition' began to assume shape and structure. The key figures in the Lords were the Duke of Bedford, Lord Saye and Sele and Lord Montague, later Earl of Manchester. In the Commons the dominant figure was John Pym, Bedford's legal adviser. Nathaniel Fiennes was already in touch with the Scottish army and awareness of these contacts may have encouraged Charles to dissolve parliament so quickly as to earn it the name of the Short Parliament; had he had proof, it is likely that Fiennes would have faced a treason charge.

KEY ISSUE

The effect of the Stuart Parliament.

THOMAS WENTWORTH, EARL OF STRAFFORD 1593–1641

Wentworth came from a Yorkshire gentry background. In a contemporary's words, 'a northern lad who has become baron of I know not where', Wentworth changed sides after Buckingham's assassination. President of the Council of the North (1628–32) and Lord Deputy in Ireland (1632–40), Wentworth was not popular at Court and was employed on the frontiers. His especial *bête noir* was the Queen, whom his ally and friend Laud nicknamed 'Lady Mora' ('mora' is Latin for 'delay'). Laud and Wentworth on the other hand believed that they personified 'Thorough'. Wentworth made Ireland profitable and orderly while he built up a small but efficient royal army there. He was detested by the Anglo-Irish nobility whose corruption and inefficiency he pursued with merciless single-mindedness. From Dublin he advised Charles I to have Hampden, a gentleman, whipped for opposing ship money. He was summoned home in April 1640 to tackle the Scottish crisis – too late.

PICTURE 6
A portrait of Thomas Wentworth, Earl of Strafford, by van Dyck. Van Dyck effectively portrays Strafford's ruthlessness and arrogance

Despite the failure of the Parliament, Charles was determined to restore his authority. His lack of political awareness is revealed by his willingness to borrow from Catholics and use Catholic officers, while the rank and file busied themselves in burning altar rails and other catholic symbols. Not surprisingly, the under-equipped and unenthusiastic English army proved unable to match the Scots, who had by now entered England. After a brief battle at Newburn on Tyne it disintegrated, leaving the Scots in control of Newcastle and able to force their terms on the King once more in October 1640, in the Treaty of Ripon. Their conditions – a further truce, payment by Charles of their expenses at £850 a day and the postponement of further negotiations until a parliament met – were designed to give that parliament the advantage. In fact, Charles had already accepted the need to call a new Parliament, and had concluded that some concessions would be needed to gain support. He had little idea of how great these would be, or that the Parliament itself would outlive him.

Q

Does the description of Wentworth suggest that he was a suitable character to handle this crisis?

3 ↬ CHARLES I AND THE CAUSES OF CRISIS

By 1640, Charles's power had collapsed in a crisis covering three kingdoms. The Scots had successfully challenged his right to reform their Church, and the Irish would mount a similar campaign once Strafford's hand was removed. In England, the Parliament which met in November was united in its determination to reverse at least some of the measures that the King had introduced since 1629, and to ensure that in future he

KEY ISSUE

Charles was not trying to establish absolutism. He was inept rather than tyrannical.

KEY ISSUE

Reasons for Charles I's failure.

would have to meet with Parliament at regular intervals. Whatever Charles had sought to create in his decade as ruler, he had failed.

It seems clear, however, that he had not sought to establish an absolute monarchy on the continental model. An examination of his personal government reveals a consistent effort to introduce order, hierarchy and uniformity in both Church and State, and across all three kingdoms, but there is little evidence that Charles expected serious resistance to his plans. A conscious desire to destroy Parliament, the rule of law and the rights of the political community could not have been undertaken in such a naive fashion. Charles's willingness to retreat into a strictly ordered Court, his failure to monitor the effect of his reforms, and his refusal to make meaningful concessions in the emergency of 1637–40, all suggest that he had little idea of the groundswell of opposition that he had created within the political community. The most likely explanation for this, apart from his undoubted lack of political awareness, is that he did not expect opposition because he had no intentions which might justify it. An examination of his actions in the decade of personal rule suggests far more strongly that he intended to do precisely as he had promised in 1629 – to press ahead with reforming the British monarchies according to his vision of order and harmony, and to call Parliament again when he had succeeded and when his subjects 'should better understand' the benefits of what he had done.

If this is the case, then why did he fail? If his objectives were neither tyrannical nor unreasonable, why were they not accepted and supported by the majority of his subjects? While it is difficult to assess the exact extent of opposition, his failure to rally support in the face of Scottish invasion is clear evidence that he did not have the willing support of the English political community. A number of factors contributed to this, but the evidence described above and the nature of the grievances for which Parliament sought redress in 1640–1 suggest that resentments focused on two key areas – the failure to call Parliament while collecting new and unparliamentary taxation, and the attempt to reform the Church to a degree which was opposed by most of the nation. This does not imply that a majority of the English were 'Puritan' in belief, although an active minority certainly were, but that the majority disliked the pretensions of the Laudian clergy, and more importantly, feared the revival of popery which could result from them. These fears were enhanced by contemporary developments in Europe. The Thirty Years War appeared to represent a Catholic crusade to reclaim control in Europe, and in the 1630s it appeared that there was every chance of it succeeding. The Treaty of Prague, signed in 1635, has been called 'the high water mark of the counter-Reformation', marking the height of Catholic recovery before the intervention of France against Spanish and Habsburg influence brought much needed help to the Protestants. Stories of Catholic atrocities revived the anti-Catholic hysteria which was never far from the surface of English life. In these circumstances, an authoritarian king who entertained Catholics at Court and sought to shift the Church in a Catholic direction was bound to rouse opposition to some degree.

Nevertheless, opposition itself does not guarantee failure, and for several years Charles had been able to press ahead despite resistance, because resistance had no legal means of expression. What allowed the opposition in England to be expressed and organised was the rebellion in Scotland and the King's inability to control it with his existing resources. Charles was forced to recall Parliament in 1640 by his need for money; but that need for money was created by his own misjudgement in pressing ahead with reform in Scotland. Ultimately, therefore, the crisis of 1640 was provoked by the character and the political inadequacy of Charles I. Although his political beliefs were not those of a tyrant, his authoritarian personality, his inability to understand the views of others and his political naivety, led him to behave as if they were. In the 1620s, this led to a breakdown of his relationship with Parliament and to his attempt to establish reforms without it. In that attempt, that same personality led him to pursue his vision too rigidly, too fast and too far. To that extent, his failure, and the crisis that it provoked, were almost inevitable, because the personality of Charles made them so.

4 ⌐ BIBLIOGRAPHY

Most of the books recommended at the end of Chapter 1 are also useful for further study of the reign of Charles I. In addition, you could look at *The Causes of the Civil War* by Ann Hughes (Macmillan, 1991) and *Charles I* by A. Anderson (Longman, 1997). The work of Kevin Sharpe is interesting and informative, but his major title, *The Personal Rule of Charles I* (Yale, 1992), is 950 pages long. An easier way to absorb the work of major historians is through collections of essays, which allow reading to be undertaken in smaller chunks. There are useful collections of essays edited by Conrad Russell and John Morrill; titles vary, but anything written by these historians which is of a length that you can cope with will be helpful. *Origins of the Civil Wars* by Conrad Russell (Macmillan, 1973; latest reprint, 1991) contains essays by a variety of authors and covers a wide range of issues. There is also an excellent collection of documents with a commentary provided by C.W. Daniels and J. Morrill under the title of *Charles I* (CUP, 1988), from which many of the sources used in this chapter were taken. Another way to make wider reading accessible is to look for biographies, such as *Buckingham* by Roger Lockyer (Longman, 1981) and the interesting psychological study entitled *Charles I: the Personal Monarch* by Charles Carlton (Routledge and Kegan Paul, 1983).

5 ⌐ STUDY GUIDE

As with Chapter 2, the first task is to make linear notes to organise and record the most important points of information contained in this chapter. Having consolidated your knowledge and understanding of the period by this means, you should then consider how to apply it to the key function of writing essays. The causes of the 1640 crisis often form the subject matter of examination questions, both as a topic in itself and as a major part of essays about the causes of the Civil War. The following exercise is intended to enable you to address this issue in such a way as to allow you to practise planning and writing an essay, and to prepare material which would allow you to deal with a range of essay questions in the future.

1. If we begin with a straightforward question, such as, 'Why was there a crisis between the King and Parliament in England in 1640?', the first task is to answer it. The best way to plan an essay of this kind is to identify causal factors, as in the study guide for Chapter 2, but a good starting point for this is to simply try to answer the question as it is asked. As we often find that the last material that we read is most immediately memorable, a starting point for many students would be: Because Charles was forced to call Parliament and they would not give him money unless he redressed their grievances. Already, we have introduced three factors, Charles, money and grievances. We have also raised some new questions, perhaps phrased as: Why did Charles need money? and Why did MPs have grievances? In turn, this introduces the factor of the Scottish rebellion, which triggered off the crisis in England, and the factor of Charles's failure to call Parliament since 1629 and his religious and political reforms. By this method, it is possible to trace the process by which the relationship deteriorated, and the factors that caused the process back through the reign of Charles I. We could end up with a list of causal factors such as: the financial problems of the Crown; the rights of King and Parliament; religious divisions and fear of popery; the need to rule three kingdoms; and the personality and attitudes of Charles I. By explaining each of these factors, and considering how they worked together, you can plan an essay to answer the question.

2. At this point, however, you will find that it is necessary to go back beyond the reign of Charles. Explaining financial problems, religious divisions, the existence of three kingdoms and tensions between the King and Parliament will require you to go back into the reign of James and even earlier. They are what we call long-term factors, which usually play a conditional role in creating conditions which allowed the crisis to occur. If your essay is not to become impossibly long, you will have to be selective about how much detail you include, and it is here that considering the part played by different factors, and how important each one was, helps you to make sensible decisions. Consider the question: Were these conditional factors (combined together) so strong and important that some kind of crisis was almost bound to develop? If your answer is 'yes', then you will need to explain these factors and how they built up before 1625 in some detail. If, however, you believe that they could have been dealt with fairly easily, and perhaps separately, then you will need to explain them briefly as problems that Charles inherited, and place

more emphasis on explaining how and why Charles let them build up into a crisis which he triggered by provoking the Scottish rebellion. The Scottish rebellion involved all the conditional factors – religion, three kingdoms, money and tensions between the King and Parliament – which is why it brought the crisis to a head.

3. To plan this essay, you therefore need to prepare outlines, in note form, for each of the main factors – religion, finance, multiple kingdoms, King and Parliament, and Charles I. You would also find it useful to construct two flow charts, or spider diagrams, to illustrate how these factors worked together. The first should show how the conditional factors combined and reinforced each other up to 1625, the second should show how they interacted with the personality of Charles I thereafter.

4. You can then use these outlines to construct an essay plan. Start by roughing out your conclusion as an overall answer to the question, then arrange your factors to support and explain it. Finally, plan an introduction to set the essay up. This should define or analyse the question, lay out the issues, and possibly provide some background. Then you can actually write the essay by reversing the order of your planning.

5. By organising your material in this way, you will find that you can also use it to plan and write other essays. Any question on the causes of crisis will require you to use all the factors that you have defined – the way in which you use them depends on the question. Consider the examples below, and work out how you could use the five factors listed in point 3 to plan an answer to the question that is asked.

   (a) The main cause of the crisis of 1640 was the personality of Charles I. How far do you agree?
   (b) How far were religion and the problems of the Church responsible for the crisis that led to civil war?
   (c) Was the crisis of 1640 inevitable?

4

Civil War and Regicide 1640–9

INTRODUCTION

The years to be studied in this chapter were arguably the most momentous in British history. First, when Parliament met, the King's opponents tried to exploit his temporary weakness by imposing on him radical reforms in the government of the Church and State. This campaign was only partially successful. What was achieved however was enough to generate intense disagreement among the political community and its representatives at Westminster. Tension escalated during the summer of 1642 so that eventually England lurched into armed conflict. As a result, between 1642 and 1646 Britain was devastated by sporadic but damaging war. But despite immense bloodshed and victory by Charles I's opponents, no settlement emerged. Between 1646 and 1649, Britain was a land of hope and chaos. Radical movements emerged, terrifying conservative defenders of the establishment. A second civil war arose out of the mistrust between the intransigent Charles and his equally determined opponents. Charles's second defeat brought him to public trial and execution – a totally unprecedented event. What a decade! It was all happening.

For contemporaries, these events were exciting, traumatic and baffling. Blood and tears flowed abundantly, and so did adrenalin and ink. It is essential to be aware of the tragedy of the drama, of the emotional commitment of those involved and of their bewilderment at the complexity of events. If contemporaries were confused, what hope have history students three and a half centuries later? This chapter is offered in the belief that finding a way through the morass may be taxing, but not impossible.

Long Parliament so-called because it met in November 1640 and did not dissolve itself until March 1660. It defeated Charles I, abolished monarchy, the Lords and bishops, established a republic, subjected Ireland and Scotland to England and allowed the restoration of monarchy in 1660.

1 ⌐ THE LONG PARLIAMENT, 1640–2

The previous chapter explained how the personal rule of Charles I ended in deadlock. The combination of the King's ambition and incompetence caused the collapse of royal government in Scotland, a tax-payers' strike in England and defeat in the two Bishops' Wars. But the King could claim that he had done nothing illegal, that his critics had no *right* to impose themselves or their ideas on him and that once he had overcome local difficulties such as the Scottish occupation of Northumberland, Durham and Yorkshire, normality would return –

that is to say, royal government unimpeded by Parliament. The King's critics were aware of these facts. How could they convert Charles's temporary embarrassment into a permanent settlement which would make impossible a repetition of the 'personal rule' and of Charles's objectionable personal policies? The conservatism and legalism of the age meant that radical innovations might offend even the King's most virulent critics. Nothing was inevitable as the MPs rode back to Westminster for the second time that year.

In particular, historians are convinced that civil war was neither necessary, nor expected, nor desired. We have come a long way from 'the high road to war', which Whig historians used to believe could be traced back to James I's reign. The fashionable explanation nowadays is that in the summer of 1642 England's politicians stumbled and bumbled into an armed confrontation, caused by miscalculation and misunderstanding.

Just conceivably this **revisionism** has gone too far. While it is important not to read history backwards and identify 'inevitable' developments which were nothing of the sort, people in the past were not stupid. Intelligent politicians could see that there were issues at stake which could lead to confrontation. There was a sense not only of expectancy but also of foreboding among the MPs who assembled at Westminster. For instance, Sir Henry Slingsby records in his diary his high hopes for the coming session:

> The 2nd of November I took my journey to London to be at the Parliament and came thither two days after it had begun. Great expectance there is of a happy Parliament where the subject may have total redress of all his grievances; and here they apply them to question all delinquents, all projectors and monoplizers, such as levied ship money, and such judges as gave it law.

But Slingsby's optimism contrasted with John Hampden's pessimism. Philip Warwick asked him to identify a scruffy back-bencher who was pleading for the release of the political and religious **radical,** John Lilburne:

> I came into the House well clad (we courtiers valued ourselves much on our good clothes) and perceived a gentleman speaking (whom I knew not) very ordinarily appareled. I remember a speck or two of blood upon his little band, which was not much larger than his collar. His hat was without a hat band. His stature was of a good size, his sword stuck close to his side; his countenance swollen and reddish; his voice sharp and untunable, and his eloquence full of fervour. 'Pray, Mr Hampden, who is that sloven?', I asked. 'That sloven? That sloven whom you see before you hath no ornament in his speech. But that sloven, I say, if we should ever come to a breach with the king (which God forbid) in such a case, I say, that sloven will be the greatest man in England'.

KEY ISSUE

The likelihood of war as the eventual outcome of disagreement between the King and Parliament.

revisionism the tendency of modern historians to revise drastically the assumptions and arguments of their predecessors.

What hopes did Slingsby entertain with reference to the coming Parliament?

radical someone who adopts a new approach to problems, being prepared to uproot previous assumptions.

Why did Hampden predict that Cromwell would be 'the greatest man in England'?

Now 'that sloven' was Cromwell. It is a good story, some may think too good a story. Incidentally, Warwick was unaware that he was criticising Hampden's cousin. But there is nothing inherently improbable in the well-informed Hampden being aware of the likelihood of confrontation. Charles had already shown his colours by arresting his critics in 1629 and waging war on his own Scottish subjects in 1639 and 1640. However inept, a man who appealed to force was unlikely to compromise. With Charles I around, confrontation was always on the cards.

For a war to occur, however, there had to be two organised sides. These did not exist in November 1640. Not only was Charles isolated, but his opponents could count on the consistent loyalty of only a minority of MPs. Of all the anachronistic misunderstandings about the Long Parliament, the greatest is that it contained an organised opposition, similar to nineteenth- and twentieth-century parties, led by a party leader called John Pym. In truth, the majority of MPs were uncommitted country gentlemen. They were not necessarily ignorant or ill-educated, most having attended Oxford or Cambridge universities, or the Inns of Court in London. Nor were they inexperienced. Virtually all were involved in local government in their respective counties. They had views on the political, religious, social and economic issues of the day. But their obligations were to their constituents, who, as Derek Hirst has demonstrated, were not to be sneezed at, constituting between 25 per cent and 40 per cent of the male population. If back-benchers had been asked to name their allegiance, they would have specified God, the King, the law of the land and their 'country', by which they would have meant their own locality. They might well have belonged to one of the informal groups owing loyalty to great noblemen or landowners who exercised patronage over their clients. But they would have rejected any suggestion that they were led by Pym, whose domination of the early sessions of the Long Parliament was exceptional.

KEY ISSUE

The attitude of MPs in 1640.

PICTURE 7
An engraving of John Pym by Glover. This portrait contrasts with those of Fairfax, Goring and Cromwell. It shows him as a civilian in restrained, sober clothes and carefully clipped beard and moustache. The expression is shrewd, calculating and cautious.

JOHN PYM 1584–1643

John Pym was from the West Country, educated at Pembroke College, Oxford and at the Middle Temple in London. A widower, he was devoted to his two sons – who played no part in public affairs. Pym was a lawyer and an accountant. His attempts to set up as a country gentleman failed. He had no sympathy for the pursuits of typical back-benchers: hunting, hawking and suchlike. His interests were his Puritan faith and his dislike of everything Charles I stood for. He sat as MP first for Calne (Wiltshire) and then for Tavistock (Devon). In the early parliaments of Charles I he opposed the King's religious policies. As secretary of the Providence Island Company, he encountered the aristocratic clique opposed to Charles I's policies during the personal rule. These men became his patrons: the Earls of Warwick, Essex and Bedford; Lords Saye, Mandeville and Brooke; John Hampden; and Oliver St

John. Pym was a persuasive speaker, had a flair for publicity and was a clever tactician. He was hand in glove with the Scots in 1639–40

Indeed, during the Short Parliament, Pym emerged as the leader of his former patrons who are described by Conrad Russell as 'Pym's Junto'. He established a remarkable domination of the House of Commons. When the Long Parliament met, it was Pym who masterminded the attack on the royal prerogative and managed the trial of Strafford. Pym negotiated the unwritten alliance between Charles's opponents in Parliament and the radical leaders of the London mob. He orchestrated Parliament's propaganda war against the King until the actual Civil War began. Not even then was Pym replaced as leader. Though he never donned armour, he continued to dominate the opposition to the Crown, keeping the various Parliamentary factions together and devising methods of raising money, such as the excise. His crowning achievement was the Solemn League and Covenant with the Scots (September 1643). His death from cancer of the bowel in December 1643 was a disaster from which Parliament never recovered. Pym was irreplaceable as the man who ruled from the centre. Had he lived, Cromwell would never have become Protector.

What was the secret of 'King Pym's' success? His portrait is revealing, showing us his 'sly, burgher's face' (Hill). What intelligent, calculating eyes! Pym had the gift, valuable in a politician, of timing. He was a fine manager of men, always seeming to follow the wishes of others while in fact leading them. Did he have principles? There is no need to question his Puritanism. Otherwise, he was a moderate, certainly no revolutionary or republican. He believed that compromise could eventually be forced on Charles I as a result of Parliamentary victory on the battle-field. If he could have 'fixed' Charles I, he really would have proved his genius. In the meantime, every option had to be explored, including negotiations with the King. He had Henry Marten committed to the Tower for making subversive remarks about the King – *during the Civil War!* When Pym insisted that for his part he 'neither directly nor indirectly ever had a thought tending to the least disobedience or disloyalty to his Majesty', he was probably sincere.

Q

What can you learn from the portrait of John Pym?

A *Consensus*

The challenge facing Pym in November 1640 was to maintain the consensus which temporarily united the House of Commons. Only then could he force the King to make the necessary concessions. There was agreement among the vast majority of MPs on what had to be done in a negative sense. The King's capacity to rule in an arbitrary way, ignoring the wishes and interests of his subjects, must be curtailed. The Church of England must be saved from the alleged Romanising tendencies of

KEY ISSUE

Pym's struggle to maintain the unity of the House of Commons.

Archbishop Laud. Those who had advised the King to adopt these undesirable policies must be punished. But this programme was not as straightforward as it sounded. Charles was not likely to abandon his principles or his ministers without a fight. While Charles's opponents might well agree in their disapproval of what he stood for – or rather, what they *thought* he stood for – there would be less agreement on how to replace the King's personal rule. This was especially the case with regard to religion.

Typically, Pym straightaway concentrated on what *everyone* approved – the hounding of the King's unpopular ministers. For a cautious traditionalist like Pym it made sense to attack the King's ministers, for traditionally there was no such thing as a bad king, only bad ministers who misled the king. So Laud was impeached and packed off to the Tower. The judges who had found for the King against Hampden were also impeached. Lord-Keeper Finch and Secretary Windebank wisely fled to the Continent. But the greatest quarry, to be pursued with relentless determination, was 'Black Tom Tyrant', whose impeachment was moved by Pym on 11 November. Why did Pym and his colleagues hate Strafford with such intensity? Perhaps they could not forgive him for abandoning the Parliamentary cause in 1628, for he was for ever regarded as 'the lost archangel', the good man gone wrong. Perhaps they blamed him for Charles's appeals to force – the establishment of 'Thorough' in Ireland, the Scottish wars and the alleged intention of using troops in England. Perhaps Strafford's head was demanded by Pym's Scottish friends, for the trial had a truly British dimension. Pym had good reason to fear Strafford, for his own life was at risk. Charles I, who was not a forgiving man, looked to Strafford to put a violent strategy into practice. So the only safe solution was to get in first and kill the King's great minister. As the Earl of Essex remarked, 'stone dead hath no fellow' (a dead man can do no further damage).

'I am tomorrow to London with more danger beset, I believe, than ever a man went out of Yorkshire'. Strafford's apprehension was to be fully justified. Yet his King had promised him that no harm would come to his person or his estate. At first, Charles's support was not needed, for Strafford proved well able to look after himself. It was not simply that, when he was surrounded by rioting London youths, one look from Black Tom 'was enough to affright the apprentices', but that the impeachment, though masterminded by Pym, went wrong. In truth, the charges were absurd, and at one stage Strafford and the King, who was watching from the gallery, burst out laughing. It was hard to prove Charles's most faithful servant guilty of treason. The prosecution's key evidence was Strafford's note to the King filched from Secretary Vane's desk by his son, which stated, 'You have an army here with which to subdue this kingdom'. The note was ambiguous and to any fair-minded person more likely to refer to rebellious Scotland than to peaceful England. Yet the prosecution's case was that Strafford wanted to use Irish troops against England. As for the other charges, Strafford, though wracked with illness and anxiety, demolished his enemies. The crowd in the public seats, fortified with bread, cheese, onions and beer, and

Q *Why did Strafford express fear when he journeyed to London in autumn 1640?*

KEY ISSUE

Pym's assault on Strafford.

relieving themselves where they sat, were moved to admiration for the accused. It looked as though Strafford would get off.

But Strafford must die! Pym now resorted to a bill of **attainder.** That Pym had to ressurect this medieval device was a tribute to Strafford's skill and an admission of the prosecution's weakness. If the attainder had failed, Pym's credibility would have disappeared, and he would have faced a vengeful adversary. He now played two trump cards. First, he released details of the so-called Army Plot, a crazy scheme whereby officers would march on London, release Strafford and arrest the King's enemies. George Goring, the commandant of the Portsmouth garrison, had, for reasons best known to himself, betrayed the plot to Bedford who passed the details to Pym. Pym held on to them for a month – indicating how seriously he took the plot – and then divulged them to a shocked Commons. Hysteria resulted. Strafford was clearly guilty! Secondly, Pym asked his allies in the City, notably the radical alderman Isaac Pennington, to let loose demonstrations against Parliament and the royal family. If Strafford was spared, the King and Queen would pay for it! For days, baying hooligans raged around Westminster. Against this background the bill of attainder passed the Commons by 204 to 59. It is significant that so many dared to vote against the attainder, and that so few out of a total of 507 voted at all. The Lords, who were especially targeted by Pennington's 'rent-a-mob', passed the bill, relying on Charles's promise to reject it. But Charles signed, blubbering through his tears, 'My lord of Strafford's condition is happier than mine'.

On 12 May 1641 Strafford was executed on Tower Hill before a crowd of 100,000. From his prison window Laud watched his friend pass by and gave him a final, silent blessing. When Laud first heard of Charles's act of betrayal, he wrote in his diary that the King 'knew not how to be or be made great'. Does this explain why Charles signed? Was it defeatism or fear for his wife's safety? Or lack of sympathy for a man he had never warmed to? Whatever the truth, Charles never forgave himself. Shortly before his own death nearly eight years later, he said, 'An unjust sentence that I suffered to take effect is now punished by an unjust sentence on me'.

Charles's betrayal of his chief minister was by no means his only concession. The King had already accepted the Triennial Act, which stated that Parliament had to meet once every three years whether he summoned it or not, yielding what he rightly called 'one of the fairest flowers in my garland'. On the same day that he abandoned Strafford, Charles signed a bill which stated that the present Parliament could only be dissolved with its own consent. In June, the Tonnage and Poundage Act and in August, Acts making ship money, knighthood and forest fines illegal, demolished the financial expedients of the personal rule. In July, the prerogative courts – Star Chamber, High Commission, and the Councils of Wales and the North – were axed, while the Privy Council lost its powers over law suits. All these measures the King accepted. It was extraordinary. What was going on?

First, the constitutional implications must not be exaggerated. These measures did not amount to **parliamentary sovereignty.** They were

attainder an Act of Parliament which stated that an accused person was guilty of treason. No charge had to be proved. It simply had to receive the assent of the Commons, the Lords and the Crown.

KEY ISSUE

Why did Charles I agree to Pym's demands?

See page 191 for Shaftesbury's use of London hooligans.

parliamentary sovereignty Parliament's right to control the government's legislation and policies. Ministers are responsible to Parliament.

KEY ISSUE

The constitutional significance of the acts of the Long Parliament, 1640–1.

purely negative, making a repetition of the personal rule impossible. Even the Triennial Act, though it had a great future, was an *ad hoc* measure to reassure financiers who had loaned money to pay the Scots. The crucial control of policy and ministers was still an unsettled issue. Secondly, humiliating and damaging though these concessions undoubtedly were, Charles could always withdraw them should his circumstances improve, for he had conceded them under duress. Thirdly, Pym's game plan must be understood; he cannot have been under any illusion as to the durability of Parliament's achievements. The real questions were, 'How can we pin the King down?' and 'Where do we go from here?'

Pym contemplated a package. The money to pay off the Scots would be found in return for which the King would appoint his leading critics to posts of responsibility. In fact, the money was eventually found through loans from the City and subsidies were unwillingly granted so that the northern counties could be evacuated by the Scots before the end of August. The King did make some 'bridge appoinments', as historians call them. St John became Solicitor General, Saye was made Master of the Court of Wards and Warwick became Lord Admiral. Pym, on the other hand, was *not* made chancellor of the exchequer as Bedford – whose brainchild these bridge appoinments were – had recommended. Given the distrust between Charles and Pym, the scheme would never have worked. Bedford died in May 1641.

In truth, Pym had immense problems. By releasing the Army Plot he had raised the public temperature. Fear was everywhere – fear of papists, fear of foreigners, fear of religious and political extremists, fear of the mob. When two fat MPs stood up to hear an inaudible speech and the plank supporting them snapped like a pistol shot, somebody screamed 'gunpowder!' and the House of Commons stampeded. It was a hot summer, plague raged in the city and MPs longed for home. Several drifted away before Parliament was prorogued. Even more worrying for Pym was the recovery of the King's fortunes. Until May Charles had done everything wrong, making concessions which he should either have made much earlier in order to rally support or which he should not have made at all, alternating between truculence, as recommended by his wife, or abject surrender. Now he had recruited a new adviser and his stock rose.

See page 176 for profile and portrait of Hyde.

KEY ISSUE

The King's recovery, summer 1641.

Edward Hyde personified reason and compromise. He had disliked the personal rule and had supported Pym's reforms. But now he became worried by the dangers of religious extremism, he was distressed by the injustice of Strafford's fate and he thought that Pym had clipped the prerogative enough. So he changed sides, becoming the Stuart dynasty's most effective servant. He urged Charles to ignore the extremists at Court and bid for the support of men of moderation and reason. Charles, being Charles, never wholly accepted this advice, often simultaneously listening both to Hyde and his wife – who not surprisingly loathed each other. In the summer of 1641, however, by following Hyde's advice, Charles attracted supporters. He received deputations and conferred honours. Sometimes he got confused, on one occasion bestowing an unwanted knighthood on a kneeling petitioner. But it was the right idea. Even the political concessions which had been wrung from him made him look reasonable and won him support.

It was an indication of Charles's recovery that when he announced his intention of going to Scotland to negotiate directly with his subjects there, Pym and his colleagues were dismayed. What if he returned with an army at his back? They begged him not to go. Charles replied sardonically that he was pleased to be in such demand in both his kingdoms, but rejected their request and departed for Scotland on 10 August. All Pym could do was dispatch John Hampden to keep an eye on Charles's clumsy attempts to create a party which culminated in a mysterious plot to kidnap the King's enemies, known as 'the Incident'. Meanwhile, gloomily presiding over the remnants of his 'party' at a deserted Westminster, King Pym had to accept that the consensus in his kingdom was disintegrating. Worse was to come.

B *Bifurcation*

As it happened, Charles did not return with an army, though when he travelled south back to London in late November, he was welcomed all the way. He was no longer isolated. For by this time two issues had surfaced which totally demolished Pym's consensus against the King. The first was religion. The second was the Irish revolt.

In December 1640, 1,500 Londoners had presented a petition carrying 15,000 signatures demanding the abolition of bishops, 'root and branch'. Recognising how divisive this proposal would be, Pym referred the **Root and Branch** petition to a committee. However, the issue could not be so easily swept under the carpet, so strongly did MPs feel. It is a measure of Laud's folly that his Arminian campaign not only provoked a theological backlash but led to massive condemnation of the very institution of bishops. Strictly speaking this was illogical, for there had always been bishops Puritan in outlook and Calvinist in theology. But a substantial element both inside and outside Parliament concluded that the bishops' track-record was so abysmal that total abolition was the only answer. The fact that the most impeccably Protestant churches, such as the Genevan and the Scottish, did without bishops was a further inducement, especially bearing in mind the importance of keeping in with Parliament's Scottish allies. Indeed, the necessity of paying the Scots made the abolition of bishops, deans and chapters ('dens of loittering lubbers' as one extremist described them) a most attractive proposition, given the money which could then be garnered. It would resemble the dissolution of the monasteries. In Nathaniel Fiennes's words, 'To speak plain English, these bishops, deans and chapters do little good themselves by preaching and otherwise, and if they were felled, a great deal of good timber might be cut out of them for the use of the church and kingdom at this time'. The axe would indeed be wielded – but not yet.

> **Root and Branch**
> pressure for the total abolition of bishops expressed by the 'Root and Branch' petition presented to Parliament in December 1640.

See pages 345–8 for hatred of bishops.

KEY ISSUE

*The case for the
retention of bishops.*

For a number of reasons the debates in the Commons on Root and Branch, which took place in May and June 1641, revealed some support for the retention of bishops. All agreed that Laud's excesses in worship and ritual should go. The trouble was that it was difficult to call a halt. The line between do-it-yourself reform and vandalism had already become blurred, and the removal of 'popish' altar rails led to smashing of stained glass, splashing paint on 'superstitious pictures', defacing monuments, demolishing organs and playing football with prayer books. The restoration of the altar, now rechristened 'the table', was an invitation to extremists. Thomas Cheshire, preaching at St Paul's Cross, deplored the influence of Puritan rabble-rousers who encouraged contempt for the priesthood. 'There goes a Jesuit, a Baal's priest, an abbey lubber, one of Canterbury's whelps', had become common talk. The permissive climate was abused by cobblers, weavers, feltmongers, tailors and butchers who felt free to preach. Cheshire had found a woman encouraging her child to urinate on the communion table at St Sepulchre's. Against this background, bishops were seen as guarantors of social and religious stability. There was no enthusiasm for replacing geographically remote bishops with local ministers. A petition from Cheshire county argued, 'The aim of the reformers is to pull down 26 bishops and set up 9,234 potential popes'.

Pym's problems were compounded by a fierce row with the Lords. Attempts by the radicals in the Commons to abolish the bishops' voting powers and membership of the Lords were rejected by the Upper House. Pym's policy of maintaining unity between the two Houses was now in tatters. When Charles at last signalled his abandonment of Laudism by promoting moderates to vacant seats – Williams (an old enemy of Laud) to York, Hall to Norwich and Ussher to Carlisle – the best that Pym could salvage was a general order forbidding crucifixes, candles, images and bowing to the name of Jesus. Indeed, the crux of the problem was how to replace bishops if they were abolished. The Root and Brancher, Oliver Cromwell, summed it up, 'I can tell you, sirs, what we would not have, but I cannot what we would'.

KEY ISSUE

*The importance of the
Irish revolt.*

Consensus was irretrievably wrecked by news of a revolt by the Ulster Catholics which reached Westminster on 1 November 1641. The desperate, much-persecuted Irish seized the chance to exploit English weakness. Charles had rejected Strafford's advice to appoint the capable Marquis of Ormond as Lord Deputy. Instead he appointed two joint Deputies, Borlase and Parsons, weak ultra-Protestants who were neither respected nor liked by the Catholics. Decades of exploitation and cruelty were now avenged in a few days. If a fraction of the atrocity stories were true – which they probably were – there was ammunition enough for the outrage expressed at Westminster. In fact, tales of pregnant women's wombs ripped open, Protestant bishops found naked in ditches, babies impaled on pikes and people driven into cottages and burnt alive, improved with the telling. Rumour alleged that 200,000 Protestants were massacred – far more than the total population of Ulster. But even Clarendon estimated 40,000 dead, reduced by the historian S.R. Gardiner to 4,000 – which was bad enough. Not only was anti-Catholic prejudice fuelled. The revolt had to be suppressed. For this an army was needed. Who was to command the army? This was a question which not even Pym could fudge. The armed forces had always been part of the prerogative. But could Charles I, who was widely suspected of being in league with the Catholic Irish, be trusted with the control of an army, commanded by one of his favourite firebrands? Pym's suggestion that funds should only be advanced if the King employed counsellors approved by Parliament, and Haselrig's demand that any army that was raised should be led by a Parliament-approved commander, outraged conservatives such as Hyde.

Pym responded on 22 November with the **Grand Remonstrance.** This was a clever document. First came a statement of the King's mistakes since his accession and a list of Parliament's reforms. Few MPs disagreed so far. References to religion were ambiguous. 'We confess our intention is to reduce within bounds the exorbitant power which the prelates have assumed unto themselves', while the nation's religious practices were to be referred 'to a synod of the most grave, pious, learned and judicious divines'. Again, most MPs agreed. But the sting came between these platitudes: 'The king's ministers were to be such as the Parliament may have cause to confide in'. Hyde, Falkland and Culpepper attacked the Remonstrance for raking up past grievances and trespassing on the King's prerogative. Even more contentious was the proposal to publish the Remonstrance. As Dering put it, 'When I first heard of a Remonstrance, I presently imagined that like faithful councillors we should hold up a glass to His Majesty. I did not dream that we should remonstrate downwards, tell stories to the people, and talk of the King as of a third person'. The debate raged by candlelight. It was noisy, bad-tempered and physical. Members drew their swords and grappled with each other. The vote was taken at 1 a.m.: 159 in favour, 148 against. It was a victory of a sort for Pym. Cromwell muttered that if the Remonstrance had been lost, he would have emigrated forthwith. Yet this marked the final defeat of Pym's attempts to lead a united Commons. The two sides which fought the Civil War can be traced back to that November night.

If Pym's hopes were in ruins, Charles now came to his rescue – or rather Henrietta Maria. She was the founder of the club of disastrous foreign queens who destroyed their husbands (Marie Antoinette and the Tsarina Alexandra were later members). It was to be expected that the King should reject the Grand Remonstrance out of hand. But, on 23 December, he alienated moderate opinion by appointing as Lieutenant of the Tower the Queen's favourite desperado, Sir Thomas Lunsford who was believed to breakfast off new-born babies. Worse was to follow. On 4 January 1642, Charles marched into the House of Commons accompanied by 400 troops to arrest five MPs – whom together with Lord Mandeville he accused of high treason. The secret of Charles's foray was badly kept, for its originator, the Queen, was as indiscreet as she was foolish. The five members – Pym, Hampden,

Grand Remonstrance
Pym's summary of the King's misdeeds which justified radical change.

KEY ISSUE

The importance of the Grand Remonstrance.

KEY ISSUE

The attempted arrest of the five members.

Holles, Haselrig and Strode – left the Commons by the back door as the King entered by the front. The trap was perfectly baited. 'I see my birds are flown', exclaimed the King while Speaker Lenthall refused to co-operate, claiming that he was the House's servant. What difference would it have made if Charles had got his men? It is impossible to say. What is certain is that when he left the House to indignant cries of 'privilege!', he had not only put himself in the wrong but had made himself ridiculous. The moderate support accumulated by Hyde had been dissipated. Charles gathered up his family and fled to Hampton Court – where no beds were made up. He was only to return to the capital for his trial and death.

Was war now inevitable? Certainly compromise between people who so deeply distrusted each other would have been difficult. In March, the Lords and the Commons claimed control of the trained bands by issuing the **Militia Ordinance.** The King countered with **Commissions of Array**, calling on his supporters to raise troops. In June, Parliament published the Nineteen Propositions, a beefed-up version of the Grand Remonstrance, demanding Parliamentary control of the government, the armed forces, foreign policy and religion. This was a claim to sovereignty. Charles's shrewd reply was composed by Lord Falkland: 'These being passed, we may be waited upon bare-headed, we may have our hand kissed, the style of majesty continued to us, but as to the real power, we should remain but the outside, but the picture, but the sign of a king . . . the common people would destroy all rights and properties, all distinctions of families and merits'.

During the summer both sides prepared for war. The national mood was apprehensive. The leaders of society in many counties desperately tried to prevent war, while here and there hotheads appealed to arms. Lord Strange attacked Manchester, but was frustrated by the local Puritans. Charles demanded entry into Hull – invaluable since its arsenal was full of arms intended for the Scottish wars and Henrietta Maria had already gone overseas with the crown jewels, which she intended to exchange for troops. But Sir John Hotham refused to admit the King, and Parliament would not co-operate in prosecuting Sir John for treason. The colleges of Cambridge University sent their plate off to the King, but it was hijacked on the Great North Road by Cromwell. War was formally declared on 22 August 1642 by Charles I when he raised his standard at Nottingham. It read, 'Give Caesar his due'. It was blown down during the night.

Militia Ordinance an ordinance not a law, because it never received the royal assent. It appointed lords lieutenant to control the militia, responsible to Parliament, not the King.

Commissions of Array issued by Charles I to his supporters who were commanded to raise troops. Their early sixteenth-century origin was stressed by the fact that they were written in Latin.

Q

Was Falkland's reply to the Nineteen Propositions fair comment?

2 ⌒ THE CAUSES OF THE FIRST CIVIL WAR

The causes of the Civil War have been hotly debated – and rightly so, for it was an extraordinary phenomenon. As we have seen, most contemporaries neither expected war, nor desired it. They were totally bewildered by the outcome of events. For example, horror and perplexity as to what had occurred were expressed by the Parliamentary general Sir William Waller in a letter to his friend Sir Ralph Hopton – who happened to be the general on the other side: 'That great God who is the searcher of my heart knows with what a sad sense I go on upon this service and with what a perfect hatred I detest this war without an enemy'. So why did Waller and Hopton – and thousands like them – fight each other? They *were* enemies, however much they deplored it. What had gone wrong?

Propagandists on both sides were obsessed with conspiracy, attributing to their enemies deeply laid schemes of villainy. Both sides described their opponents as 'delinquents', i.e. war criminals. Edward Hyde, Earl of Clarendon in his *The History of the Great Rebellion* (1702) produced the classic statement of the Royalist case. The war had been deliberately planned by ambitious power-addicts such as Pym who had conned the gullible into following them, despite the overall excellence of royal government. 'The people were sick of well-being'. Parliamentarian apologists on the other hand depicted a conspiracy to establish an absolutist state dedicated to the overthrow of Protestantism in the British Isles. A weak, foolish, henpecked King was manipulated by sinister forces surrounding his foreign, Catholic wife. Irresponsible swordsmen plotted with scheming Jesuits to overthrow religion and liberty.

History is 'an unending dialogue between the present and the past' (E.H. Carr). For this reason, in the aftermath of the Civil War and the Restoration, historians were Royalist in sympathy. But the emergence of parliamentary liberalism in nineteenth- and twentieth-century Britain produced far more sympathy for Parliament than for the Crown. The result was **the Whig interpretation.** Historians such as Macaulay, Gardiner, Trevelyan and Ogg, depicted the Civil War as necessary and beneficial. Stuart absolutism *had* to be defeated to make way for the emergence of Parliament and religious toleration. The Stuart kings and their ministers were consistently denigrated, while Parliamentary leaders – Pym, Hampden, Cromwell – were canonised. This bias is especially apparent in Whig accounts of 1688–9. Whereas James II was cruel and tyrannical, William III was 'the Deliverer', the noblemen who invited him over from Holland were 'the Immortal Seven' and it was a 'Glorious Revolution'. A feature of the Whig interpretation was its middle-class, elitist lack of sympathy, not only for the Stuarts but also for the poor, the illiterate and the unrepresented. So Whig historians gave little emphasis to radical movements such as the Levellers. G.M. Trevelyan, for example (M stands for Macaulay), whose book entitled *England under the Stuarts* (Methuen, 1904) was 'written with gusto' (J.H. Plumb), dismisses the Levellers in a few paragraphs and relegates the Diggers to a patronising footnote. So the Whig explanation of the Civil War plays down social and economic issues, concentrating purely on the political and religious confrontation

KEY ISSUE

Rival conspiracy theories.

the Whig interpretation historians argued that Parliament's victory in the civil wars was desirable because it led to the replacement of royal absolutism by parliamentary sovereignty.

See pages 223–30 for the revolution of 1688–9.

Marxist Karl Marx argued that the means of production should be owned by the workers who should replace the upper classes by violent revolution if necessary.

between Charles I and his opponents which, due to Charles's obstinacy, could only be resolved by war.

This interpretation was challenged by the **Marxists.** While historians such as R.H. Tawney, Christopher Hill and Laurence Stone can be called Marxist in only a general sense, they agree in giving far more importance to social and economic causes. Tawney argued that Protestantism encouraged individual landowners, merchants and manufacturers to maximise their profits through thrift and hard work, believing that God made his favourites successful. This success gave the rising landowners and merchants self-confidence and the determination not to be pushed around by a reactionary court and aristocracy. Therefore the 'rise of the gentry' explains the Civil War. Hill developed this argument by showing how frustrated the forward-looking gentry and merchants were by outdated taxes, restrictive monopolies and generally unsympathetic government attitudes to the protection of British trade. Not surprisingly the economically advanced parts of England fought for Parliament. Hill stressed the beneficial effects of the Parliamentary victory on British overseas expansion and the establishment of the Republic. Hill and Stone have argued that typical Parliamentarians were rising gentry and merchants, representing the bourgeois revolution of Marxist ideology which preceded the proletarian revolution. This was the *English* revolution, comparable with the first stages of the French and Russian revolutions, which in due course led to the triumph of the proletariat.

For Marxist historians the Parliamentary leaders were greedy capitalists, to be admired for their efficiency compared to the feudal dinosaurs in the Royalist ranks, but nevertheless selfish and hypocritical. They caused the wars through their pursuit of what they understood as liberty. But Hill argued in his *Century of Revolution* (Nelson, 1961) that for Pym and Hampden 'liberty' in fact meant 'privilege'. He quotes the contemporary judgement of the Restoration: 'the gentry brought back the king not out of love for him but out of love for themselves'. The 'free parliament' promised by Charles II meant 'a parliament of the free', i.e. the propertied. In Marxist eyes the heroes who really campaigned for liberty were the radicals, especially the Levellers. Hill followed H.N. Brailsford in writing sympathetically about them, and about the Independent sects which flourished as a result of the lifting of censorship. These were the real believers in freedom, who understood the meaning of democracy. 'Which side would you have been on at Marston Moor?', demanded a prominent liberal. 'Which side would you have been on at Burford?', was the Marxist reply.

Like the Whig interpretation, the Marxist interpretation has been acrimoniously criticised. For example, H.R. Trevor-Roper gleefully produced plenty of *prosperous* gentry who fought for Charles I and plenty of de*clining* gentry who fought for Parliament, preferring to see the Civil War as a conflict between an all-

See page 123 for what happened at Burford.

pervasive court and excluded outsiders. Hill has revised and refined his arguments, though by no means abandoning his fundamental contention that a feudal hierarchy was defeated and replaced by a more bourgeois meritocracy, with incalculable social and economic effects for the future. However fallible their overall interpretion has proved to be, Marxists have performed a service by demolishing the monopoly previously exercised by political and religious interpretations.

Influenced by the Marxists, historians now scrutinise the behaviour of ordinary people and of local communities. The interaction of central government and local interests has been explored by historians such as Alan Everitt (Kent), Ann Hughes (Warwickshire), J.T. Cliffe (Yorkshire) and John Morrill (Cheshire). David Underdown has investigated West Country loyalties, showing how much more radical the isolated pastoral upland communities were than the more traditional arable centres. The former played individualistic games such as stoolball (the ancestor of cricket), while the latter played football. Co-operation in sport marched with deference to social superiors. The sturdy individualists joined the ranks of Parliament. Historians now realise how close links were between Westminster and local communities. While politicians and people were naturally preoccupied with local affairs, there was widespread awareness of national and international disputes. MPs kept their own constituents in touch with Westminster so that the Commons performed an educative role, becoming a seminar for the nation.

'Revisionist' historians, such as Anthony Fletcher, while rejecting the sweeping, dogmatic explanations of Royalists, Whigs and Marxists, adopt a 'functionalist' approach, stressing the day-to-day interaction of personalities, coincidences, miscalculations and misunderstandings. They reject the long-term causes beloved by Whigs and Marxists in favour of the short-term causes originating in the crises which suddenly sprang up between 1639 and 1642. In this context, Conrad Russell argues that the Civil War must be seen as a *British* event. He believes that historians have attached too much importance to English developments. The Stuart kings ruled three kingdoms, all of them with their own problems and priorities. Charles I's inadequate response to the challenge of ruling all his subjects caused crises in Scotland and Ireland which brought his government crashing down and affected the course and outcome of the wars. Charles's successors likewise grappled with problems posed by the British dimension – with uneven results. The Restoration, like the Civil War, was triggered by events in Scotland.

Where does all this get us? One conclusion is that you can usually find evidence to support *or demolish* any theory if you look hard enough. While any historical interpretation must be based on facts, only too often the facts are either inconclusive, or point in different directions. For example, two historians, D. Brunton and D.H. Pennington, analysed the members of the Long Parliament. Perhaps salient characteristics would emerge (religion, professions, family

KEY ISSUE

Revisionist explanations.

KEY ISSUE

The British dimension.

ties, geography etc.) which would justify an explanation of why they fought for or against the King. The causes of the Civil War would then be revealed. After much time and effort the following conclusion emerged: members who fought for Parliament were on average ten years older than those who fought for the King. There was virtually no other identifiable difference. So what?

KEY ISSUE
Similarities and contrasts.

A salient point, perhaps not sufficiently stressed, is that the similarities between the two sides are much more striking than the contrasts, at least when the war began. Here the Marxist analysis is especially vulnerable. The Civil War was not a class war. It was the result of a split between members of the governing classes. In 1647, a Leveller petition to the Commons put this point succinctly: 'The ground of the late war between the king and you was a contention whether he or you should exercise the supreme power over us'. Certainly the two sides looked like each other. This was especially the case before the first recognisable uniform was issued – to the New Model Army in 1645. On 28 May 1644 the commander of the Bolton garrison, Colonel Rigby, with admirable presence of mind, joined the Royalists as they stormed into his town. A few weeks later, Sir Thomas Fairfax was able to ride straight throught the Royalist army at Marston Moor without anyone being able to tell that he was an enemy. There certainly were differences in social and economic background between the two sides, but almost all generalisations have to be qualified, making it hard to construct sweeping theories.

Really there are two questions to be answered. First, why did disagreements between monarch and Parliament which had been resolved or fudged by previous generations through discussion, prove insoluble – or unfudgeable – in 1642? In other words, to quote Winston Churchill, why did 'jaw-jaw' become 'war-war'? Secondly, why did individuals fight for one side or the other?

With hindsight, the answer to the first question lies in the irreconcilable conflict between two rival concepts of government – monarchical and representative. In other words, the Whigs were right: the basic issue was sovereignty. This issue was implied in the Grand Remonstrance, and stated explicitly in the Nineteen Propositions and in Charles's reply. Contemporaries, however, would not have accepted such clear-cut alternatives. Both Royalists and Parliamentarians believed in the basic principle of government by king-in-parliament under the rule of law. This was the best way to guarantee the welfare of Church and State. But how was this to be achieved? Compromise was difficult in the summer of 1642 because the supporters of the King and Parliament disagreed about the implementation of policy. How was government by king-in-parliament to be carried out in practice? Furthermore, pride and distrust explain why neither side would back down. Charles was blowed if he was going to surrender his God-given prerogative to the

KEY ISSUE
Why was compromise impossible?

likes of Pym, who for his part had deep distrust for the policies and priorities of a Romish, absolutist court. Pym and his colleagues feared for their own safety and distrusted Charles's word.

Both sides stumbled into war as a last resort, which they hoped and believed would not be necessary. Throughout the spring and early summer of 1642, the King and Parliament manoeuvred for position. But Charles could not believe that gentlemen would break their oath of allegiance, which explains his indignant incomprehension when Sir John Hotham denied him entry into Hull, his own royal property. Pym, on the other hand, did not think that Charles could raise a side. In the spring of 1641 this was a reasonable assessment, and very possibly true after Charles's disastrous blunder in trying to arrest the five members. But thanks to the good sense of Hyde and Falkland, the tide of loyalty, conservatism and apprehension concerning where Pym would stop flowed Charles's way so that he was able to recruit support. War was now on.

Secondly, why did men – and women – fight? There would have been no war if the population had stayed at home. No doubt there were five and a half million different answers. Men enlisted for drink or to evade the law, as they have always done. Many had to conform to the orders of their local superiors. The influence of the Earl of Derby in Lancashire or of the Earl of Warwick in Essex are examples of the pressures which obliged stay-at-homes to get involved. Marxists are right to stress social and economic pressures such as the impatience of merchants with government restrictions. Many responded to emotional and idealistic considerations. Loyalty to the Crown brought Sir Edmond Verney to his death as the King's standard-bearer at Edgehill. Many Royalists felt a deep affection for the Anglican Church which was clearly under threat from Parliamentary extremists. Those young Royalist MPs whom Brunton and Pennington identified may even have felt drawn to Laud's 'beauty of holiness' in which they had been brought up. On the Parliamentary side, religion was similarly influential. The conviction that they were fighting God's battle counteracted the guilt of rebels in a monarch-worshipping age. Both Royalists and Parliamentarians, both leaders and led, were convinced that theirs was a crusade against wickedness in high places. It takes a lot for decent and civilised men to abandon their homes and set off to kill their fellow human beings. But this is what happened. Why it happened, is so often anybody's guess.

There was an *emotional* difference between the two sides, the one committed to loyalism and the Anglican Church, the other to Parliament and Protestant hatred of Rome. The emotions of the two sides – and their prejudices against each other – gave rise to the abusive terms Cavalier (irresponsible swordsman) and Roundhead (close-cropped Purian killjoy). These were caricatures, brilliantly parodied in *1066 and All That* by W.C. Sellar and R.J. Yeatman (Methuen, 1930): 'The Cavaliers were wrong but romantic, the Roundheads were right but repulsive'. Parodies only approximate to the truth. Cromwell wore his hair long, Hyde was a killjoy and so on. But contemporaries were aware of these emotional contrasts. Preaching before the King at Oxford in 1643,

> ## KEY ISSUE
> *Why did people fight?*

Edward Chillingworth anticipated *1066 and All That*: 'All the scribes and pharisees are on one side, all the publicans and sinners on the other'.

Emotion and reason combined to motivate both sides. Royalists were convinced that Pym's irresponsible attempts to 'overturn' (the seventeenth-century term for revolution) the constitution and demolish such social landmarks as the bishops would lead to rule by the mob. 'Tradesman and illiterate people of the lowest rank' were preaching. Soon they would be replacing their superiors in Parliament and local government. No bishops, no gentry. Men of property and rank must rally round the Crown to stop this dangerous nonsense. Combined with this apprehensive conservatism was hatred of the Scots who were self-evidently in league with Pym. Parliamentarians believed profoundly that Charles I operated malevolently, not only in a British but in a European dimension. In the great struggle for the survival of Protestant Christianity, England's king was *on the wrong side.* Whether Charles was duped by sinister advisers or whether he realised what he was doing was a secondary issue. Events in Scotland and Ireland demonstrated what would happen if Parliament did not establish its right to control events. To restore traditional, English, Protestant values was worth fighting and dying for. Failure to intervene would be cowardly and immoral, and would have devastating results. While both sides claimed to fight for the Protestant religion, did *any* Roman Catholics fight for Parliament? One suspects not.

See page 345 for the attractions of Anglicanism.

3 ∽ DOCUMENTARY EXERCISE ON THE OUTBREAK OF THE FIRST CIVIL WAR

Study sources A, B and C and attempt the questions that follow. In so doing, you must demonstrate your awareness of the problems that propaganda poses for the historian.

A The Militia Ordinance, 5 March 1642.

Whereas there hath been of late a most dangerous and desperate design upon the House of Commons, which we have just cause to believe to be an effect of the bloody counsels of papists and other ill-affected persons who have already raised a rebellion in the kingdom of Ireland, and, by reason of many discoveries, we cannot but fear they will proceed not only to stir up the like rebellon and insurrections in this kingdom of England, but also back them with forces from abroad. For the safety, therefore, of His Majesty's person, the Parliament, and kingdom, in this time of imminent danger, it is ordained by the Lords and Commons now in Parliament assembled, that Henry, Earl of Holland shall be Lieutenant of the County of Berkshire . . .

B The King's letter sent with the Commission of Array to Leicester-shire, 12 June 1642.

Whereas a small number of both Houses have attempted by way of Ordinance to put in execution the militia of the kingdom, we there-fore, considering that by the laws of the realm it belongeth to us to order and govern the militia of the kingdom, have prohibited all manner of persons whatsoever upon their allegiance to muster ... and considering that in ancient time the militia of the kingdom was ever disposed of by the commissioner of array, and that by a statute upon record in the Tower, made in the fifth year of Henry the fourth, we have thought fit to refer it to that ancient legal way of disposing the power of the militia by commissions of array for defense of us, our kingdom and our country; authorising you to find arms for other men in a reasonable and moderate proportion ...

C From *The History of the Great Rebellion* by Edward Hyde, Earl of Clarendon (1702).

The parliamentary party attempted underhand to persuade the people that the marquis [of Hertford] was come down to put a commission of array into execution, by which commission a great part of the estate of every farmer or substantial yeoman should be taken from them; and so, taking advantage of the commission's being in Latin, translated it into what English they pleased. Although the gentlemen of ancient families and estates in that county [Wiltshire] were for the most part well affected to the king, yet there were also people of an inferior degree who, by good husbandry, clothing and other means had gotten very great fortunes. From the beginning, these people were fast friends to Parliament, and many of them were now entrusted by them as deputy-lieutenants in their new ordinance of the militia.

Q

1. *Explain the differences between the 'Militia Ordinance' (source A) and the 'Commissions of Array' in the context of 1642 (source B). (3 marks)*
2. *Contrast the explanations of the need for mobilising troops in sources A and B. (4 marks)*
3. *How does Clarendon (source C) explain the responses of Wiltshire people to sources A and B? (4 marks)*
4. *How reliable are the three sources as evidence on the reasons for people joining the two sides during the summer of 1642? (4 marks)*
5. *Using these sources and any other information known to you, explain Parliament's success in raising military forces to fight the King. (10 marks)*

4 ⌐ THE FIRST CIVIL WAR

TABLE 6
The civil wars

1642	October	Battle of Edgehill (Charles I v Essex – drawn)
	November	Battle of Turnham Green (Rupert v Essex – drawn)
1643	June	Battle of Adwalton Moor (Newcastle v Fairfaxes – Royalist victory)
	July	Battle of Roundway Down (Hopton v Waller – Royalist victory)
		Capture of Bristol by Prince Rupert
	August	Failure to take Gloucester, Plymouth and Hull prevents Royalist advance on London
	September	First Battle of Newbury (Charles I v Essex – Parliamentary victory)
		Solemn League and Covenant ratified
1644	May	Rupert's campaign in Lancashire – sack of Bolton
	July	Battle of Marston Moor (Rupert v Leven, Fairfax, Manchester – Parliamentary victory)
	August	Essex trapped by Charles I at Lostwithiel
	September	Battle of Tippermuir (Montrose v Covenanters – Royalist victory)
	October	Second Battle of Newbury (Charles I v Manchester – drawn)
	December	The Self-Denying Ordinance
1645	January	Creation of the New Model Army
	June	Battle of Naseby (Charles I v Fairfax – Parliamentary victory)
	July	Battle of Langport (Fairfax v Goring – Parliamentary victory)
	September	Rupert surrendered Bristol to Fairfax
		Battle of Philiphaugh (Montrose defeated)
1646	April	Charles I surrendered to the Scots at Newark
	June	Surrender of Oxford
1648	April	Royalist risings in Kent, Essex, Cornwall, Yorkshire and south Wales
	July	Scottish invasion linked up with Royalists
	August	Battle of Preston (Hamilton v Cromwell – Parliamentary victory)
1649	August–December	Cromwell's campaign in Ireland
1650	September	Battle of Dunbar (Cromwell v Leslie – Parliamentary victory)
1651	September	Battle of Worcester (Cromwell v Charles II – Parliamentary victory)

Table 6 conveys the general shape of the war. On the whole the Royalists had the upper hand until the winter of 1643–4, though they proved incapable of maximising their relative success. The balance was overturned by the Scottish intervention, which led directly to Parliament's victory in the greatest battle of the war at Marston Moor. Even then, however, total victory proved elusive. The decisive event proved to be the creation of the New Model Army during the winter of 1644–5.

MAP 1
Britain during the Civil Wars

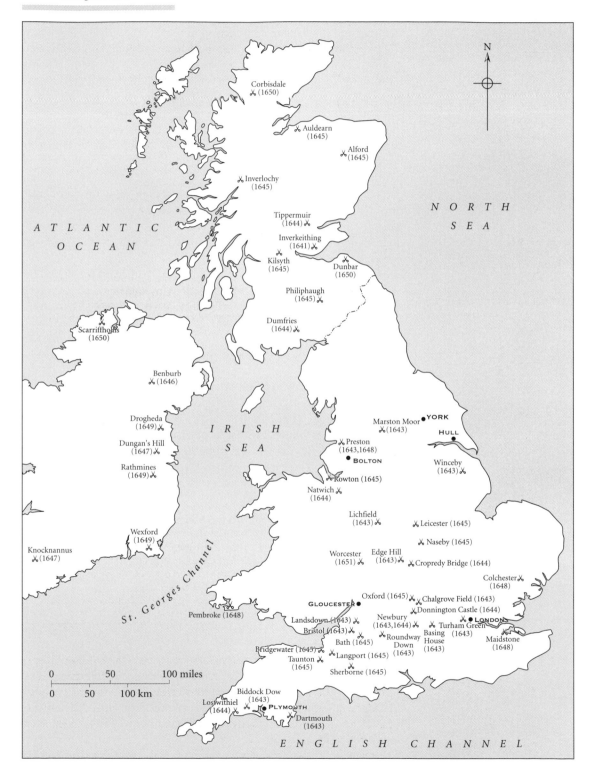

N

Corbisdale
(1650)

Auldearn
(1645)

Alford
(1645)

Inverlochy
(1645)

NORTH
SEA

Tippermuir
(1644)

ATLANTIC
OCEAN

Inverkeithing
(1641)

Kilsyth
(1645)

Dunbar
(1650)

Philiphaugh
(1645)

Dumfries
(1644)

Scarriffholls
(1650)

Benburb
(1646)

Drogheda
(1649)

IRISH
SEA

Marston Moor
(1643)

●YORK

HULL

Dungan's Hill
(1647)

Preston
(1643,1648)

Rathmines
(1649)

●BOLTON

Winceby
(1643)

Rowton (1645)

Natwich
(1644)

Lichfield
(1643)

Leicester (1645)

Knocknannus
(1647)

Naseby (1645)

Wexford
(1649)

Worcester
(1651)

Edge Hill
(1643)

Cropredy Bridge (1644)

Colchester
(1648)

Oxford (1645)

Chalgrove Field (1643)

St. Georges Channel

GLOUCESTER ●

Donnington Castle (1644)

Pembroke (1648)

Landsdown (1643)

Newbury
(1643,1644)

Turham Green
(1643)

LONDON

Bristol (1643)

Bath (1645)

Basing
House
(1643)

Maidstone
(1648)

Bridgewater (1645)

Roundway
Down
(1643)

Taunton
(1645)

Langport (1645)

Sherborne (1645)

0   50   100 miles

0   50   100 km

Biddock Dow
(1643)

Lostwithiel
(1644)

●PLYMOUTH

Dartmouth
(1643)

ENGLISH   CHANNEL

KEY ISSUE

The problem of equipping troops.

Thirty Years War
fought in Germany
(1618–48) between the
Catholic imperialists
and the Protestant
princes, proverbial for
its devastation and

Victories at Naseby and Langport led to the King's surrender to the Scots and the fall of Oxford. Militarily the war was over.

The war was initially a conflict between incompetent leadership and training, and inadequate administration. Both of the rival armies were equipped with obsolete weapons and ammunition, and both were urgently in need of experienced officers who could train recruits. Historians such as John Kenyon have researched the amazing success of both sides in clothing and equipping their armies. Until 1645 neither side had a recognisable uniform; but troops had to be protected against the weather, and against bullet, sword and lance. It was a major preoccupation of the military administrators to find boots, essential for marching troops. Cromwell's army, for example, called in at Northampton on its way north in 1648 to pick up several thousand pairs of boots. Campaigns were won and lost depending on the acquisition of horses and fodder. Seventeenth-century people seem to have been unsentimental about horses. While we know the name of Rupert's dog, we do not know the name of a single horse in the war. Cromwell, however, was knowledgeable about horses – one of his qualities as a cavalry general. Both sides banged away at each other with artillery, but with uneven results. Guns which could be moved were not powerful enough, guns which were powerful were hard to move. There were, however, some famously successful guns such as 'Sweet Lips', called after a Hull prostitute, which demolished Scarborough Castle in 1645. The guns Cromwell took to Scotland in 1650 were called 'the Twelve Apostles'.

Charles was seen at his best after he had raised his standard at Nottingham. He toured Cheshire and Shropshire, recruiting men, equipment and money. The Catholic Marquis of Worcester led the way with £300,000. Others followed with gifts of jewels, arms, retainers and above all themselves. At Shrewsbury more recruits streamed in from the Welsh Marches. The King welcomed his nephews Rupert and Maurice from Germany, spirited young men with experience of the **Thirty Years War**. Rupert soon displayed ability as a strategist and cavalryman. Another high-profile recruit was George Goring, the heir to the Earl of Norwich. Goring had charm and intelligence. When sober, he was a good general. Unfortunately, he was usually drunk and his failure to stop his men plundering and beating up civilians was to damage the King's cause. Clarendon believed that Goring 'wanted nothing but industry (for he had wit and courage, and understanding, and ambition, uncontrolled by any fear of God or man) to have been as eminent and successful in the highest attempt in wickedness of any man in the age he lived in, or before'.

With the Royalists there was no doubt who in theory should be in charge. Could the King, however, control his generals in practice, to say nothing of politicians such as Digby and Hyde and his own wife Henrietta Maria who fancied herself as 'she-generalissima'? If so, Charles had a good chance of making the most of his temporarily promising assets and finishing the war quickly.

Parliament's best chance of winning was to prolong the war. For

PICTURE 8
A portrait of Lord George Goring, (right), and Mountjoy Blount, Earl of Newport (left), both prominent Royalist commanders, by van Dyck. Van Dyck has captured the essence of Goring: drunken, pitiless and irresponsible. But there is intelligence and flair as well. No doubt Goring had leadership potential, even though his 'crew' had the lowest of reputations

Q

Does van Dyck's portrait support the low opinion that Clarendon advances about Goring?

KEY ISSUE

Parliament's advantages.

only then would their several solid advantages be exploited. First there was the possession of London, the administrative and economic as well as the political centre of the country. The capital's trained bands, organised and led by the veteran Philip Skippon, were the best in the country, though more suited for defence than attack. The navy had declared for Parliament, therefore cutting off the King from Continental assistance being organised by his wife and making possible the supply from the sea of Parliamentary strongholds such as Hull, Plymouth and Gloucester. On the whole, the wealthier parts of the country, such as the home counties, had declared for Parliament – the result of the King's ill-advised departure for the north in March 1642.

For most of the war Parliament's military leadership was uninspired. This problem was epitomised by the commander-in-chief, the Earl of Essex. Socially, Essex was an asset. It was reassuring for gentlemen contemplating high treason to be led by such an impeccably respectable aristocrat. John Adamson has argued that the Civil War can be seen as a baronial revolt and that its leader, the Earl of Essex, aspired to be a medieval Lord-Protector. His entries into London at the end of the campaigning seasons of 1642 and 1643 resembled Charles I's return to his capital in 1641. Since the portly, pipe-smoking Essex was an affable and popular figure, men were glad to 'live and die with the Earl of Essex'. Unfortunately Essex was indecisive and strategically inept. He was to display a genius for allowing the enemy to get between him and his base. His lack of determination and elan was symbolised by his habit of carrying his coffin and winding-sheet around with him on campaign. In the long run he was to prove a liability.

The first major battle of the Civil War was fought at Edgehill in October 1642. It was in many ways typical of future encounters. First, for several days before the battle the two armies marched parallel before discovering each other's existence, for there were no means of telecommunication, still less aerial reconnaissance. Secondly, the artillery bom-

KEY ISSUE

Edgehill – a typical Civil War battle.

bardments of both sides were largely ineffectual. Thirdly, Rupert's cavalrymen swept all before them, only to disappear in pursuit of plunder when they should have been exploiting their success on the battlefield. They proved unstoppable in more senses than one. Meanwhile a confused infantry mêlée occurred with no decisive result, though the Royalists remained in possession of the field while the Parliamentarians withdrew to Warwick, leaving open the road to London. Fourthly and most importantly, it was a horrible battle, with high casualties on both sides; the dying left out in the open on a cold October night and the wounded incompetently nursed. The full horror came as a shock. 'Lord, I shall be very busy this day. If I forget Thee, do not Thou forget me', prayed the Royalist Sir Jacob Astley. God had clearly forgotten his Englishmen to allow such a tragedy.

Perhaps horror and disgust undermined Charles's capacity for action. To march on London forthwith as Rupert recommended was to be his best chance of winning the war. But Charles dithered. He moved to Oxford, which became the Royalists' headquarters. Then he advanced so slowly up the Thames valley that even Essex was able to overtake him. Rupert was unleashed against Brentford, which he stormed and plundered. 'The sack of Brentford' was a gift to Parliamentarian propagandists who compared it to the sack of Magdeburg, the worst atrocity of the Thirty Years War. When the Royalists got to the suburbs of London at Turnham Green, they found a force twice their size in the way. Essex's men were reinforced by the city's trained bands, ready to die for their homes. After an eyeball confrontation, Rupert withdrew virtually without firing a shot. The chance had gone. To be fair, negotiations for peace had been in progress for several days. Rupert was not to know that these would prove abortive.

Historians have depicted the 1643 campaign as a three-pronged Royalist attack on London. But this flattering picture owes something to hindsight. There certainly were three areas in which the Royalists achieved success. In the north, the Earl of Newcastle dominated Yorkshire, defeating the Fairfaxes at Adwalton Moor, but an advance into Lincolnshire was checked in a skirmish at Gainsborough where Colonel Cromwell's cavalry fought stoutly. This force was part of the army raised by the counties of Hertfordshire, Cambridgeshire, Norfolk, Suffolk and Essex, called the Eastern Association. In the midlands, Rupert sacked Birmingham and Lichfield, and won a skirmish at Chalgrove in which John Hampden was mortally wounded. The most impressive Royalist progress was made by Hopton in the West Country. At the head of 8,000 men he advanced on Bath. The Parliamentarians, under Waller, however, had the better of a drawn battle at Lansdowne outside Bath in which Hopton was wounded and temporarily blinded when his ammunition blew up. The Royalists limped into Devizes, which seemed a death-trap for them, hopelessly outnumbered, their general on a stretcher and Waller complacently overlooking them from Roundway Hill. But Hopton sent horsemen across the downs to Oxford. Maurice and Wilmot responded immediately. Achieving surprise they bundled the Parliamentarian army off Roundway while

KEY ISSUE

When were the Royalists nearest to victory?

Hopton's infantry attacked from Devizes. The battle of Roundway Down led to the capture of Bristol by Prince Rupert. But victory was not followed up. Royalists were reluctant to advance further while Plymouth, Gloucester and Hull remained defiant. The year ended in stalemate.

Pym held the Parliamentarian war effort together. He reconciled the disagreements between the peace party (Denzil Holles), which argued for negotiation with the King and the war party (Vane, Marten, Hazelrig), which pressed for all-out defeat of the Royalists. Pym headed a centre party which included Hampden and Essex. This party was handicapped by Essex's lack of military success and by Hampden's death in battle. Pym's leadership was essential to Essex's survival and to the maintenance of Parliamentary unity. Pym also raised money through monthly **assessments**, which far exceeded those raised by Charles I, by confiscating Royalist estates and by an **excise** tax. To an increasing extent the King's money problems exceeded Parliament's. Much of the credit goes to Pym for persuading counties to co-operate with each other in the Eastern, Northern and Midland Associations. The overall war effort was controlled by a Committee of Safety. Now Pym was to achieve one last service before he died. During the hot summer months he negotiated with the Scottish commissioners for a military alliance. The Scots demanded money – £30,000 a month – and religious conformity with the Presbyterian Church of Scotland. Pym gave them the money, but haggled over religion. He knew how unpopular a Presbyterian settlement would be. In the end he managed to persuade the Scots to accept a typically clever evasion. The English Church was to be reformed by the Westminster Assembly of Divines 'as may be agreeable to God's Holy Word'. By bringing in the unpopular Scots, Pym took risks. He widened the conflict and raised the stakes. But the military balance unquestionably shifted Parliament's way.

The immediate result of Pym's dying master-stroke was another Scottish invasion. The city of Newcastle was besieged. The Earl of Newcastle shut himself up in York and screamed for help, while the Yorkshire Parliamentarians re-emerged and joined the Scots. The army of the Eastern Association moved on York for the kill. Charles responded by dispatching Rupert into Wales on a recruiting drive. As a result of the **Cessation** Irishmen joined Rupert's army, which was swollen to 12,000. He conducted a whirlwind campaign in Lancashire, bypassing Manchester through Trafford Park, brutally storming Bolton, taking breakfast off a terrified mayor of Preston, capturing Liverpool and relieving the Countess of Derby at Lathom House. This young man in a hurry, crossed the Pennines through the Clitheroe gap, drew the Parliamentary army away from York by taking Knaresborough and by a brilliant feint to the north through Boroughbridge marched into York unopposed. This was the peak of Rupert's career. He had done his job. He had redressed the balance in the north and relieved York. His enemies scuttled for cover, the Scots retreating to Tadcaster and the Eastern Association hastily heading for their unprotected homeland.

KEY ISSUE

Pym's contribution to Parliamentary victory.

assessments a land and property tax modelled on ship money. It hit the gentry whereas in the past the burden had fallen on merchants and smaller property owners.

excise the equivalent of the modern purchase tax, levied on such commodities as beer, meat, salt, starch, soap and paper. It affected everyone, especially the poor, and was very unpopular.

Cessation a truce permitting Irish volunteers to fight for the King in return for temporary toleration of Catholicism. This truce damaged Charles's reputation, apparently confirming his links with the Irish and sympathy for Catholicism.

PICTURE 9
The Bloody Prince and his poodle, Boy. Birmingham and Daventry were sacked by Prince Rupert. His satanic reputation is conveyed in this Parliamentary cartoon

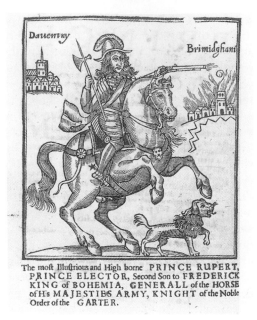

The most Illustrious and High borne PRINCE RUPERT, PRINCE ELECTOR, Second Son to FREDERICK KING of BOHEMIA, GENERALL of the HORSE of His MAJESTIES ARMY, KNIGHT of the Noble Order of the GARTER.

Tendentious knowingly misrepresenting the truth in a plausible way.

Tendentious pamphlets depicted Prince Rupert as a Satanic sadist, rejoicing in the destruction of cities and massacring women and children. His dog, Boy, often featured, since Boy was a famous animal. Royalists admired his ability to bark excitedly at the word 'Charles' and urinate when 'Pym' was mentioned. But for Parliamentarians Boy displayed more sinister accomplishments. Not only was his hide impervious to sword and bullet, but he caught musket balls in his teeth, spoke Hebrew and offered unspecified sexual favours.

RUPERT OF THE RHINE 1619–82

Rupert was the son of the Elector Frederick and James I's daughter Elizabeth. He fought for the Protestant cause in the Thirty Years War, learning his trade as a cavalry leader, deriving his code of conduct from the mercenary armies of war-torn Germany and experiencing imprisonment for three years. After he and his brother Maurice had rallied to their uncle's cause in 1642, he soon established a reputation for strategic ability and leadership in battle. Rupert introduced the cavalry charge as practised by Gustavus Adolfus of Sweden, first at Edgehill and subsequently at Chalgrove, Marston Moor and Naseby. He captured Bristol in 1643 and surrendered it two years later, to Charles I's disgust.

Rupert built up a terrific reputation: 'his very name is half a conquest'. Charismatic, generous and impetuous, he was hero-worshipped by his men, respected rather than liked by his colleagues and loathed by aristocrats such as Digby and Newcastle for whom he could not conceal contempt. At court his nickname was 'the German'. Until Marston Moor, Rupert was dreaded by his opponents. His speed and ruthlessness were proverbial. He was believed to be in league with the Devil. Rupert and his dog, Boy, allegedly galloped round the countryside at superhuman speed. Sulphur could be smelt after he had passed. Rupert's record for humanity was mixed. His savage treatment of Brentford and Birmingham earned him a rebuke from Charles I. When he stormed Bristol on the other hand, Rupert belaboured his own men with the flat of his sword for maltreating civilians. But there was also the sack of Bolton.

After leaving England following a quarrel with his uncle in 1645, Rupert achieved distinction as a sailor, or to be more accurate, as a pirate. He evaded capture by the Parliamentarian navy. At the Restoration he returned to England and became a member of the Royal Society. He never married, though he had a mistress who bore him a daughter, Ruperta.

Having relieved York and checkmated his enemies, Rupert threw his advantage away. Despite being outnumbered he 'offered the enemy a field', as a contemporary put it. Marston Moor was the result. Why did Rupert fight? His defenders say that Charles had told him to do so. But Rupert had no regard for his uncle's judgement. The answer is that he was on a high. He was unstoppable. He would win. Indeed he could have won. When he led his forces out to Long Marston (six miles outside York) only the Scottish rearguard and a few Yorkshiremen faced him, while horsemen galloped off to Tadcaster to tell Manchester and Leven to come back. But Rupert waited for the dilatory Newcastle, whom he had offended. By the time the sun set, about 18,000 Royalists faced 28,000 Parliamentarians. Rupert reckoned it was too late to fight and stood his men down, while Newcastle withdrew to his caravan to light a pipe. In a violent thunderstorm the Parliamentarians suddenly attacked. The battle lasted two hours followed by a nightmare pursuit under a full moon. This was the one occasion when Cromwell and Rupert faced each other. Rupert's cavalry broke and ran. Despite a neck-wound, Cromwell kept his triumphant troops under strict rein until Sir Thomas Fairfax located him and directed him against the Royalist centre. Newcastle's whitecoats fought on to the last. About 2,000 Parliamentarians and 4,000 Royalists were slain. The next day a Royalist captain surveying the carnage remarked, 'Unhappy King Charles!' At one stage all three victorious commanders, Lords Manchester, Fairfax and Leven, ran away while their deputies won the battle. After the battle, Newcastle rode to Scarborough and took a ship to the Continent 'to avoid the laughter of the court'. Rupert, whose dog, Boy, was a casualty, rallied the remnants of his men. With the generosity of one fine soldier for another, he christened Cromwell 'Old Ironsides'.

Among the Parliamentarians slain was the eldest son of Colonel

What does Cromwell's letter to Valentine Walton reveal about the writer's values and opinions?

Valentine Walton, Cromwell's brother-in-law. Cromwell broke the news to his father, who was not present at the battle:

> Truly England and the Church of God hath had a great favour from the Lord. We never charged but we routed the enemy. The left wing, which I commanded, being our own horse, save a few Scots in our rear, beat all the Prince's horse. God made them as stubble to our swords ... Sir, God hath taken away your eldest son by a cannonshot. It broke his leg. We were necessitated to have it cut off, whereof he died. This is your precious child full of glory, to know sin nor sorrow more. He was a gallant young man, exceedingly gracious. God give you his comfort.

Such letters are not easy to write, and we do not know how Walton reacted to it. It his highly Cromwellian in its emotional grief, though some might suggest that his sympathy could have been put less abruptly. The typical pride in his own men's accomplishment, however, could not be better put. Typical also was the wholly inaccurate and unjust belittlement of the Scots and the claim that Parliament's victory was all God's doing, 'God made them as stubble to our swords. . .'.

Actually, Marston Moor made surprisingly little difference. Certainly the north of England was lost. But in Scotland the Marquis of Montrose achieved a series of dazzling victories over Parliament's allies, Argyll and his Covenanters. Further south Charles I pursued Essex down into Cornwall. At Lostwithiel the cavalry broke through the Royalist lines. But the commander-in-chief had to escape in a boat leaving his infantry to surrender and prompting the witticism that if they had been prepared to live and die with the Earl of Essex, he was not prepared to live and die with them. This fiasco was followed by the Second Battle of Newbury in which the Royalists escaped due to poor co-ordination between Essex, Manchester and Cromwell. The politicians at Westminster expressed their frustration by yanking Laud out of the Tower and condemning him to death by attainder. Alone and helpless the old man defended himself surprisingly well, infuriating his judges by insisting that both he and his King were totally Protestant. He behaved bravely on the scaffold, remarking that 'it was an uncomfortable place to preach in'.

Meanwhile, Essex's disgrace brought to a head a row which had been smouldering in Parliamentary ranks ever since Pym died. It was summed up in a heated exchange between the Earl of Manchester and his second in command, Oliver Cromwell. Manchester agreed with Essex and other moderates that the war should be ended by compromise and deplored the pursuit of outright victory: 'If we beat the king ninety and nine times, he is king still. But if he beat us but once, we shall all be hanged and our posterities undone'. Cromwell who believed in as decisive a victory as possible replied, 'If that be so, why did we take up arms in the first place? This is against fighting ever hereafter'. There was more to the row than this, however. Cromwell horrified his superi-

KEY ISSUE

The results of Marston Moor.

KEY ISSUE

Disagreements in the ranks of Parliament.

PICTURE 10
*Walker's portrait shows
Cromwell at the height of his
military career – self-confident,
forceful and effective*

ors by recruiting and promoting on merit as opposed to rank. And he
had somewhat eccentric ideas about 'merit'. After Edgehill, Cromwell
had told Hampden that Parliament would never win with their present
riff-raff: 'old decayed serving-men and tapsters'. It was essential to
recruit 'men of spirit, that are likely to go on as far as gentlemen will
go', or as Cromwell was to say on another occasion, men with 'the root
of the matter in them ... who know what they fight for and love what
they know'. In practice this meant religious enthusiasts, irrespective of
their social origin. Cromwell trained such men to follow him against
the odds. Marston Moor vindicated his methods of recruitment, training and leadership. When Cromwell wrote to the Speaker describing
Marston Moor, reference to the creditable role of his own precious,
godly soldiers was censored.

But Cromwell was not alone. The war party, now led by the influential northern magnate, the Earl of Northumberland, supported him
in pursuit of victory. They were sympathetic to his methods of promotion and leadership, several of them being political or religious radicals.
They agreed with Cromwell that the old gang – Manchester, Essex,

Self-Denying Ordinance passed by the Commons in December 1644. Members of both Houses had to resign their commands so that they could be replaced by new appoinments.

New Model Army created by Parliamentary ordinance in January 1645. The armies of Manchester, Essex and Waller were merged to produce an army of 22,000 men – 14,400 infantry, 6,600 cavalry and 1,000 dragoons (mounted infantry).

KEY ISSUE

How effective was the New Model Army?

leaguer bitches the women who accompanied armies. Leaguer is a seventeenth century term for the camp of an army on campaign.

Waller – had to be removed. Their master-ploy was the **Self-Denying Ordinance** by which members of both Houses had to resign their commissions. The Lords resented this insult and never passed the ordinance in its original form. The ordinance not only threatened the high command but also the rights of aristocrats to control their local levies. Nevertheless, peers and commoners eventually bowed to moral pressure and resigned. Hand in hand with the ordinance went the creation of the **New Model Army.** This was to be a 'go-anywhere, go-anytime' army, unlike the stay-at-home armies of the Associations. Its creation was overtly anti-Scottish, designed to remove Parliament's dependence on its unpopular ally. The New Model Army was to be properly equipped and paid. Its commander-in-chief was the impressive, non-political, enigmatic Yorkshireman, Sir Thomas Fairfax, to whom no-one could take exception. Philip Skippon, another non-political professional, commanded the infantry. Who should command the cavalry? 'A.N. Other' was pencilled in. Yet everybody knew that only Cromwell deserved the job. But he was excluded by the ordinance and was anathema to the conservatives. In fact, he was indispensable and continued to serve on a temporary basis throughout the spring of 1645 until his position was made permanent on the eve of Naseby.

In its early days the New Model Army was not the force it subsequently became. Its cavalry mostly came from the Eastern Association and knew its job. The infantry, however, was unreliable, recruited from various armies, both Parliamentary and Royalist. When Charles I rejected Rupert's advice and challenged the New Model Army at Naseby in June 1645, nobody could be confident about the result. If Charles had waited for Goring to arrive with reinforcements, he could have won. As it was, just before the battle began, a great cheer from the Parliamentary camp announced that it was they who had been reinforced: 'Old Ironsides has come among us!' This time Cromwell and Rupert were on opposite wings, with predictable results. Both swept the opposition before them. Rupert lost control as he had done at Edgehill. Cromwell wheeled his cavalry and returned to cut down the Royalist infantry. After the rout the New Model infantry plundered the Royalist baggage and butchered the **'leaguer bitches'.** In the King's baggage was found his correspondence with Catholic Irish chieftains, which Parliamentary propagandists were glad to publish. *The King's Cabinet Opened* confirmed the allegations of Charles's critics.

After Naseby the Royalists had little hope of victory, though Manchester's adage held good: Charles was King still. But Goring was defeated at Langport, thereby losing the south-west. Basing House, the stronghold of the Catholic Marquis of Winchester, was ruthlessly sacked by the New Model Army. The defenders were slaughtered, including several priests, and women were stripped naked. Rupert surrendered Bristol to save pointless slaughter, was publicly admonished by his uncle and left for the Continent in disgust. In Scotland, Montrose was at last beaten at Philiphaugh. In 1646, Oxford surrendered. As a final act of defiance Charles gave himself up, not to Parliament, but to the Scottish army at Newark. The First Civil War was over.

PICTURE 11
A portrait of Sir Thomas Fairfax attributed to Edward Bower c.1646. Fairfax was called 'Black Tom' by his troops. This Yorkshire nobleman had respect for culture and tradition. We owe to him the survival of York Minster's stained glass and the preservation of the Bodleian Library in Oxford. Walker's portrait conveys some of the high moral quality which contemporaries respected, as well as something of the steel which made him an outstanding commander-in-chief.

Q

What does this portrait reveal about Fairfax? He must have been a remarkable man to have obtained – and retained – the command of the New Model Army in his early thirties. He was widely respected.

It had been a traumatic experience. Whig historians argued that because it was a war of principle, the Civil War was fought humanely. No-one believes this nowadays. Apart from anything else, 'a humane war' is a contradiction in terms. The number of deaths shows that the British civil wars were no exception. The statistics for the total period are represented in Table 7.

These figures should be treated with caution and are at best 'something like the truth'. Certainly infantrymen suffered more than cavalrymen, four legs being better than two when it was prudent to run away.

TABLE 7

Deaths due to the British civil wars, 1642–51

	Total pre-war population	Dead	Percentage loss
England and Wales	5,000,000	190,000	3.7
Scotland	1,000,000	60,000	6
Ireland	1,500,000	618,000	41
Total	7,500,000	868,000	11.6

quarter not to be confused with 'free quarter', which meant uninhibited plundering of civilians, 'quarter' alone meant 'mercy'.

The horrendous experience of Ireland, out of all proportion to the rest of the British Isles, will be explored in the following chapter. The overall point is valid. The proportion of British men killed equalled the proportion killed in the First World War. Add the unknown total of people wounded in body and mind, and we have a major disaster. As it happened, nature conspired with man to increase the suffering. The weather during the 1640s was wet and harvests were abysmal. Plague and venereal disease accompanied the troops. Rocketing taxation, sometimes violently extracted by troops, the quartering of unruly soldiers on reluctant civilians in return for paper promises of payment at a later date (euphemistically called 'free quarter'), and the theft of movable property by soldiers living off the land, compounded the misery.

As for alleged atrocities, on the whole there seems little evidence of rape. Civilians were not normally butchered when a town fell – except in Ireland. The accepted rules were usually observed – that if a town was summoned *twice*, **quarter** was refused to soldiers, but in no circumstances was it acceptable to kill civilians. But even in England atrocities occurred. When due allowance is made for propaganda, the Royalist storms of Bolton and Leicester and the Parliamentarian slaughter of the leaguer bitches after Naseby and the capture of Basing House were bad businesses. Clearly some soldiers thoroughly enjoyed the wars, as they have always done, for the worst reasons.

One reaction of those who definitely did *not* enjoy the war was to try to stop it. We have noted the abortive peace manoeuvres and attempts to keep the war out of specific localities. Towards the end of the war ordinary people banded together for self-protection and become known as the Clubmen. This movement initially flourished in Shropshire and then in south Wales, Somerset, Wiltshire and Dorset. The Clubmen were driven to action by the ill-disciplined conduct of both sides. If anything they were Royalist in sympathy to start with. However, because it was paid relatively promptly and disciplined, the New Model Army on the whole behaved itself better than the Royalists. Furthermore, Parliament made more determined attempts to recruit local support. Gradually, therefore, Clubmen favoured Parliament. Fairfax negotiated courteously with the Dorset Clubmen, though Cromwell had to mount a brief though bloody attack on them in order to stop them obstructing supplies.

When localities refused to support the King, they had to be coerced. Sir Henry Bard ordered the countrymen of south Worcestershire to bring taxation for six months to Worcester within a week, otherwise 'you are to expect an unsanctified body of horse among you from which if you hide yourselves (as I believe each of you has his hole) they shall fire your houses without mercy, hang up your bodies wherever they can find them and scare your ghosts into your drabbling garrison'. 'Goring's crew' had an especially bad reputation. But his policy of unlicenced frightfulness was self-defeating. 'In the last analysis it was the local community, not Parliament, which defeated Charles I, not from hatred of his cause but from hatred of the war itself' (Ronald Hutton). Parliament also coerced localities, but their troops were slightly less unpopular and looked more likely to win.

See page 395 for 'Goring's crew'.

Why did Parliament win? Ultimately, widespread disgust with the war, impatience with half-measures and determination to finish the business caused the creation of the New Model Army which was, with due respect to Hutton, the single greatest reason for Parliament's victory. Superior resources, the Scottish intervention, control of the sea and Charles I's inadequacy as a supreme commander all played their part. But the stalemate was broken by the New Model Army's competent leadership, discipline and equipment. It even had an artillery train which lumbered round the country blowing up town walls and medieval castles. Professionalism triumphed over amateurism. Whether this professional military triumph would lead to political success was another matter. The Royalist commander in the west, Sir Jacob Astley, sitting on a drum at Stowe-in-the-Wold, perceptively addressed his captors, 'You have done your work and may now go and play – unless you will fall out among yourselves'.

KEY ISSUE

Reasons for Parliamentary victory.

5 ⌐ DOCUMENTARY EXERCISE ON THE SACK OF BOLTON: WAS IT A WAR CRIME?

On 28 May 1644 Prince Rupert stormed and sacked the Lancashire cotton town of Bolton, known as the 'Geneva of the North' for its Puritan sympathies. According to Parliamentary sources a disgraceful massacre was perpetrated, with over 1,600 slain. In September 1651, the Earl of Derby, Rupert's second in command, was tried as a war criminal because of his involvement in the sack and executed in Bolton market-place ('a town of his own' – Clarendon), Rupert himself being 'unavailable'. The questions for the historian are: precisely what happened, how many were killed, were the accepted rules of war broken, and if so, why?

Study sources A to F and attempt the questions that follow.

A From *History of the Great Rebellion* by Clarendon.

The rebels in Lancashire were reduced by the Prince, much blood having been shed in taking places by assault which were too obstinately defended.

B From *Memoirs of the House of Stanley* (1644).

His Highness, being greatly irritated and ruffled by this repulse, but especially with the barbarous cruelty of the enemy who murdered his soldiers taken in the first assault, gave orders that the Town should be carried forthwith, and no quarter was to be given to men in arms.

C *An exact relation of the bloody and barbarous massacre at Bolton in the Moors by Prince Rupert, penned by an eye-witness miraculously preserved, 22 August 1644.*

And now there was nothing heard but 'Kill dead! Kill dead!' in the Town killing all before them. Some they slashed as they were calling for quarter, others when they had been given quarter. Will Bolton was fetched out of his chamber with scorn, saying that they had found a praying saint, and fetched him to kill him before his wife's face who being great with child and ready to be delivered fell on him to have saved him but they pulled her off without compassion, and bade him to call on his God to save him while they cut him in pieces. James Syddall was heard to give a groan and presently one discharged his pistol at his heart ... Katherine Saddon, an aged woman of 72 years old, run with a sword to the very heart. Of their and our side it is conceived that there were slain about 1,500 folk.

D St Peter's Parish Church, Bolton.

St Peter's Parish Church register names 79 people buried on 29 May 1644 after the town had been stormed by the Royalists. These names include Will Bolton, James Syddall and Katherine Saddon.

E From *Battles of the English Civil War* by Austin Woolrych (1961).

Bolton's turn came three days later, and the manner of its taking brought a whiff of the German wars in which Rupert had been nurtured. Only 700 of its defenders were granted quarter, after 1600 had been slain, and the town was given over to sack.

F *The Civil Wars of England* by John Kenyon (1996).

Rupert pressed on to Bolton, where the defenders were suicidal enough to hang a royalist prisoner before his eyes; he stormed the town and this time put it to the sack in true continental fashion, with the loss of 1600 civilian lives.

> **Q**
> 1. *Discuss the reliability of the six sources. (5 marks)*
> 2. *How many people were killed during the sack? (5 marks)*
> 3. *What is the significance of the explanations given in the Royalist accounts? (6 marks)*
> 4. *Refer to the biography of Rupert and his portrait (pages 106–7). What do you make of his role in the massacre? (4 marks)*
> 5. *From your examination of the documents and from other information known to you, how do you explain the sack of Bolton? (5 marks)*

In assessing the seriousness of the massacre, the numbers killed are clearly important. It is amazing that several modern historians such as Woolrych and Kenyon accept the claims of Parliamentary propaganda. The only solid evidence is the parish register. But whose names would the vicar or his clerk have entered? Obviously he would enter people whose names he knew, i.e. civilians who were killed. Of course 79 is a high figure – but it is way short of 1,600! Hundreds of unknown soldiers from both sides were presumably buried, so a total of several hundred from both sides, soldiers and civilians, is possible. But one should always be sceptical about biased statistics. It is significant that Royalists admit that something unusually unpleasant occurred. Can the excuse that the garrison openly murdered Royalist prisoners be believed? Kenyon admits that this was amazingly foolhardy conduct – if it ever happened. Is it not more likely to be a Royalist invention? If atrocities were committed by the attackers, and Royalist admissions are significant, why was this so? Was it the fault of Rupert the German, with his low standards of conduct and impatience to be on his way? What role did religion play in provoking the Royalists? The First Civil War may not have been 'a war of religion', but Bolton may have been an exception. Were rules of war broken? Did Derby deserve to die?

6 ↩ PARLIAMENT, THE ARMY AND THE KING: THE SEARCH FOR A SETTLEMENT

The war had apparently settled nothing. Despite widespread war-weariness and longing for the return of normality, peace remained elusive during the period between the King's surrender and his execution (April 1646 to January 1649). Indeed, war broke out again in 1648. What went wrong?

Five consistent factors need to be appreciated if a way is to be found through these complex events. First, Charles remained a key figure, stubborn and duplicitous, unaware that his ability to deceive others was exceeded by his ability to deceive himself. Secondly, Parliament was theoretically in charge since the King was its prisoner, but MPs were divided among themselves, bewildered as to how to achieve a settlement

KEY ISSUE

Five crucial factors: Charles I, Parliament, the Scots, the Irish and the Army.

TABLE 8

Key events, July 1646 to April 1649

1646	**July**	Propositions of Newcastle offered to Charles
1647	**February**	Scots handed Charles I over to Parliament and left England
	April	Army petitions and the election of agitators
	June	Seizure of Charles I by Cornet Joyce at Holdenby House
	August	Heads of the Proposals presented to Charles I
		The Army entered London and ejected leading Presbyterian MPs
	October	The debates in Putney church between the grandees and the agitators
	November	Charles I escaped to the Isle of Wight
		Leveller mutiny at Ware suppressed by Cromwell
	December	Charles I signed the Engagement with the Scots
1648	**April**	The godly prayer meeting at Windsor
		Royalist risings in Kent, Essex, Cornwall, Yorkshire and south Wales
	July	Scottish invasion links up with northern Royalists
	August	Battle of Preston – Cromwell v Hamilton – Parliamentary victory
	September	Fairfax captured Colchester
		Parliamentary commissioners renewed negotiations with Charles I
	December	Pride's purge
1649	**January**	Trial and execution of Charles I
		Abolition of monarchy and the House of Lords – England now a republic
	April	Leveller risings suppressed at Burford

given the King's refusal to settle. Thirdly, the Scots could not be ignored, even though they departed home after handing Charles over to Parliament. Their leaders had intervened in 1643, intending to impose their own Presbyterian system of church–government on England. Now they watched resentfully as the English failed to comply. They were a brooding presence, not to be ignored. Fourthly, the Irish revolt continued, while hardline Catholics headed by the papal nuncio quarrelled with men prepared to compromise with Protestants in order to resist the inevitable English counter-attack. Indeed, Parliament never forgot the urgent necessity of suppressing the Irish revolt and re-establishing English control, though MPs disagreed as to the best method of achieving this objective. Finally, the New Model Army remained unbeaten, unpaid and now unemployed. As events unfolded, it emerged as the ultimate dominating factor.

The attempts at a settlement are summarised in the table on page 117. First, the Scots pressed Charles to sign the Covenant but Charles refused. So the Scots supported the Propositions of Newcastle, submitted by Parliament in July 1646. These were tough terms. Charles prevaricated, the Scots lost patience and in January went home, exchanging the King for £400,000. Charles's comment, 'I am ashamed to be sold for so much more than my Redeemer', illustrates his determination to be a martyr if he could not have his way. Now imprisoned at Holdenby House, he complacently watched his enemies fall out. Parliament

Nineteen Propositions, June 1642. Parliament to control the militia, the King's choice of ministers, the education and marriages of his children, the reform of the Church and the conduct of foreign policy. A general pardon for Lord Kimbolton, the five members and everyone else involved on Parliament's side.

Propositions of Newcastle, July 1646. Triennial parliaments. Parliament to control the militia for 20 years and permanently to nominate the senior ministers of state. Bishops abolished in favour of a Presbyterian Church settlement for three years. Fifty-eight Royalists excluded from a general pardon.

The Heads of the Proposals, August 1647. Biennial parliaments to sit for at least 120 days, constituencies to correspond with the distribution of population, Parliament to control the choice of ministers and the militia for ten years. Bishops and the Book of Common Prayer not to be imposed by law or abolished, an act of oblivion for all involved in the war, seven Royalists excepted. New laws to be negotiated with regard to papists. Parliament to remedy grievances such as the excise and the legal system.

The Engagement, December 1647. The constitution of 1642 to be restored, Presbyterianism to be imposed for a trial period of three years and the Independent sects to be abolished. (This was the only settlement offered to Charles I which he actually signed.)

TABLE 9
The settlements offered to Charles I

KEY ISSUE

Attempts to settle with Charles I.

See page 158 for Ireton's idealism.

modified the Newcastle Propositions, but by this time the Army had made up its mind not to accept a Presbyterian Church settlement. Cornet Joyce removed the King from Holdenby House. When Charles asked to see his warrant, Joyce indicated the soldiers at his back. Charles smiled grimly and said it was the best-written warrant he had ever seen. Negotiating from strength, the Army now presented to the King the Heads of the Proposals, the most generous terms Charles was to receive: Parliament to control the Army for ten years, a tolerant Church settlement which included bishops and only seven Royalists excluded from pardon. These terms were drawn up by Henry Ireton, Cromwell's cool-headed son-in-law. In rejecting the Heads of the Proposals, Charles said to Ireton, 'You cannot do without me, you will fall to ruin if I do not sustain you'. Ireton was unimpressed. In fact the two men instantly disliked each other. Ireton rumbled Charles's dishonesty. Charles resented Ireton's lack of deference. Even so, Charles was a fool to reject the Army's terms.

Something very strange was happening to the Army. Historians disagree about the extent to which the New Model Army was politically and religiously radical. Until recently contemporary descriptions of soldiers preaching, of godly prayer meetings, of lower-class men promoted on merit have been taken at face value. Leveller influence and republicanism have been seen as the political results of this social and religious radicalism. The Army's idealism – or ideology – allegedly explains its military effectiveness. Mark Kishlansky, however, has questioned all this, arguing that contemporary conservatives such as the Presbyterian Richard Baxter overreacted and that the soldiers were more interested in their pay and conditions than in building a new Jerusalem. Sheer professionalism explains the New Model Army's victorious track

PICTURE 12

A portrait of Henry Ireton by Walker. This portrait of Cromwell's son-in-law, a Nottinghamshire landowner, represents the drama and the tragedy of the Civil War. Walker depicts him in armour – a professional soldier despite himself. Ireton never displayed an impressive military talent, but he had a lucid mind. He was also a man of high principles. Walker shows a formidable, humourless Puritan who was involved in politics to do what was right

Q

What can be learnt from Walker's portrait? Ireton is depicted as a soldier rather than as a politician or political theorist. His face is intelligent, a little complacent and humourless.

KEY ISSUE

The radicalisation of the Army.

See pages 359–64 for an intellectual background to the radicalisation of the Army.

record. But perhaps Kishlansky is too sceptical. While the exciting and unprecedented achievements of the Levellers and their left wing associates may have over-impressed sympathetic historians, there is surely no mistaking the unusual characteristics of the New Model Army. In fact its growing radicalism made it unique in history.

The extraordinary events which the soldiers had both witnessed and caused must have profoundly affected their impressionable young hearts and minds. To see their social betters robbed and humiliated when a castle was taken, to defeat in battle the leaders of the nobility and gentry, to spearhead a successful rebellion against the King – these were heady days. Towards the end of the fighting a 'wanted' notice appeared in one of the New Model Army's journals 'for a man called Charles, recognizeable by a stammer and an inability to speak the truth'. There is a real possibility that when Cornet Joyce removed the King from Holdenby this was the spontaneous initiative of the radical rank and file. Cromwell protested to the King that he had had no foreknowledge of Joyce's coup. Charles's reply 'String him up, and I'll believe you' might seem a reasonable reaction, but possibly Cromwell was speaking the truth. The soldiers guarding Charles I nicknamed him 'Stroker' – a flippant and disrespectful reference to the King's alleged power to 'touch' for the 'king's evil' (i.e. scrofula). When drunken Royalist officers tipped a chamber pot out of a window, soldiers of the New Model Army rushed into the room and demanded an apology – with drawn swords. A sword had always been the symbol of aristocratic superiority over the lower classes. Now no longer.

Now the Army flexed its muscles. It was disturbed by Parliament's deafness to its points of view. Initially it had simply been a question of money. The Presbyterians in Parliament should have paid off the soldiers promptly, and £200,000 would have satisfied the New Model Army. But it was not easy. Taxes were high enough already, given the impoverished state of the counry. So the Army was fobbed off. In the meantime, Parliament pursued repressive policies against the Independent sects, popular in the Army. The soldiers' hero, Lilburne, was prosecuted for defying the censorship laws by his old colleague, the de-eared Bastwick. In February 1647, Parliament voted to disband the New Model Army without pay and without indemnity for alleged war crimes such as requisitioning horses for military use. A minority of the Army was invited to volunteer for service in Ireland under officers who had to take the Covenant. 'Fairfax, Cromwell – and we all go!', was the indignant response. When the soldiers petitioned against these terms, Holles had them declared 'enemies of the state and disturbers of the public peace'. The cavalry, the most educated and articulate members of the New Model Army, responded to this arrogant and stupid provocation by electing 'agitators', that is to say, representatives who would act for them. In June 1647, the agitators, who, like all shop-stewards were to the left of their constituents, persuaded the Council of the Army to issue the '*Declaration of the Army*', a demand for toleration and the dissolution of the Long Parliament, to be followed by frequent elections. It was drafted by Ireton.

In the autumn of 1647 matters came to a head. After the Presbyterians in Parliament, supported by the London apprentices, had tried to call the Army to order, independent MPs sympathetic to the Army left Westminster, the Army moved on London and its enemies in the Commons ran away. So did the King. From his new refuge at Carisbrooke on the Isle of Wight, Charles negotiated yet another settlement, the Engagement. This was a deal with the Scots. Or rather it was with some of the Scots, for the more realistic appreciated that Charles's promises to accept a Presbyterian Church for three years were worthless. They also damaged his admirers' campaign to depict him as an Anglican martyr.The more gullible Scots, led by the Marquis of Hamilton, agreed to invade England on the King's behalf. This was to coincide with nationwide Royalist risings before the Second Civil War, which flared up in April 1648.

This war was a bitter affair, with widespread Royalist protests against

> ## KEY ISSUE
> *The Army lost patience with Parliament.*

Parliament and the New Model Army, notably in Kent and south Wales, but in general all over England. Recent research has stressed the spontaneous, desperate nature of this 'revolt of the provinces'. What a marvellous opportunity Charles I had to negotiate a settlement if only he had been less obstinate and less dishonest! Even with another Scottish intervention, however, this Royalist nationwide campaign never had a chance against the New Model Army, which not only fought with frightening efficiency but with ever-increasing bitterness and brutality.

Convinced that unnecessary blood was now being shed, the Army treated Royalists mercilessly. Bloody-mindedness on both sides surfaced during the siege of Colchester. The Royalists fired dum-dum musket balls – their surfaces deliberately doctored to inflict horrible wounds. Fairfax methodically wrecked the town's water supply and refused permission to women and children to leave the besieged town. When a group of women tried to get out, Fairfax's men stripped them and drove them back. Two Royalist leaders were summarily shot by Fairfax after Colchester surrendered. A rising in south Wales was quickly suppressed by Cromwell. The Royalists' accidental killing of a left-wing officer, Colonel Thomas Rainsborough, at the siege of Pontefract, prompted savage counter-measures. Prisoners of war were auctioned as slaves for the Plantations. When 21,000 Scots, incompetently led by Hamilton, invaded down the west coast, Cromwell, despite being outnumbered, caught them vulnerably strung out along the main road through Preston and butchered the survivors at Warrington – a victory for professionalism. Cromwell's instinctive feel for a situation combined with Lambert's natural élan.

Sheer naked force, latent for so long, now erupted on the political scene. Though the Presbyterians in Parliament tried to reopen negotiations with the King (the Treaty of Newport), the New Model Army had had enough. In December 1648, Colonel Pride ejected 186 MPs, while another 86 voluntarily withdrew. As promised weeks earlier in a godly prayer meeting at Windsor, it was now time to achieve a final settlement with 'that man of blood', as demanded by political and religious radicals. The die was cast.

See page 145 for Lambert's role at Preston.

KEY ISSUE

The Army took control of London.

A *Presbyterians and Independents*

These terms have been widely used by contemporaries and historians, and are frequently causes of confusion. The chief reason is that while the two terms were religious in their origin, they came to be applicable to many who were not necessarily Presbyterian or Independent in religion. Initially, Presbyterians were people who believed that a disciplined State Church organised on Presbyterian lines similar to that in Scotland was desirable. The chief features were local churches dominated by Elders (from the Greek *presbus*), both clerical and lay, and a nationally elected assembly to co-ordinate the Church. In practice, this system made possible harsh censorship of other beliefs. Independents stood for local self-governing congregations. If there was a national structure, it was loose and permissive. There was far greater opportunity for members to think for themselves. Many Independents were Baptists or Congregationalists. Others were less easily defined.

In the chaotic conditions of the 1640s, many politicians veered towards the two religious attitudes, but the correlation was only approximate. On the whole, political Presbyterians stood for a conservative settlement with the King by which the aristocracy would retain power. The New Model Army was to be put in its place. The Presbyterians had some sympathy with the Scots. Typical political Presbyterians were Manchester and Holles. Political Independents were sympathetic to the Army, disliked the Scots, were socially less aristocratic and less sympathetic towards the King. However, Independents were not necessarily radicals. Indeed, left-wing rank and file Independents in the Army were soon referring to 'gentlemen-independents' or 'grandees' (e.g. Fairfax, Cromwell and Ireton).

7 ⌐ THE LEVELLERS

The term 'leveller' was derived from the anti-enclosure protesters who demolished fences enclosing common land. The implication was that the political and religious radicals who emerged in the 1640s were social levellers, trying to abolish private property and class distinctions. Though the term was originally abusive and in any case not particularly accurate, it stuck and was soon accepted with pride. The term should be used cautiously in that the Leveller movement was amorphous, comprising several different groups and opinions, and was never organised along the lines of a modern political party.

The Levellers emerged in the chaotic conditions of the 1640s. Their original inspiration was biblical, for the Bible is a subversive book if you think about it. Texts such as 'blessed are the poor' prompted the conclusion that 'Jesus Christ is the Head Leveller'. This religious background is explored in Chapter 9. The assaults on the social and political establishment arising from the Civil War and the collapse of censorship were the ideal conditions for the emergence of radicalism. But these spontaneous stirrings of relatively low-born and impoverished subversives would have been of minimal political significance had it not been for two factors. First, the Levellers flourished in London, near the centre of power. Secondly, and even more alarming for conservatives, the Levellers established a foothold in the New Model Army.

While historians disagree on the extent of religious radicalism in the New Model Army, certainly the relatively literate cavalry was both religiously and politically aware. Initially, the high command was prepared to adopt Leveller proposals. Cromwell and Ireton agreed with the Levellers in desiring toleration and opposing the Presbyterians. Furthermore, the Levellers shrewdly threw their weight behind Fairfax's campaign to have the soldiers properly paid. Ireton, Cromwell and Lambert included Leveller sentiments in their *Representation of the Army,* published in June 1647, which argued for religious toleration and the right to petition Parliament. It contained the ringing phrase 'we are not a mere mercenary army'.

Disagreement, however, arose between the high command or the 'grandees' and the rank and file. The agitators felt that they had not been consulted over the Heads of the Proposals and suspected Cromwell and Ireton of selling out to Charles I. The Levellers produced their own constitution, the Agreement of the People, which was significantly more radical: no monarchy or Lords, one House democratically elected, equality before the law, complete toleration and no impressment into the armed forces. John Wildman appointed himself spokesman for the Army in his *The Case of the Army Truly Stated*, in which he questioned the grandees' commitment to the freedom of the people. Cromwell was most anxious to maintain the Army's unity and was by now seriously worried by Leveller influence. A meeting of the Army Council was therefore summoned to Putney church in late October 1647, where disagreements were to be thrashed out. Whether the meeting could be called a success, is open to question. Both sides failed to convert the other, while Cromwell's attempts to fudge disagreements in godly rhetoric fooled no-one. The meeting, however, was memorable for the classic statements of the conservative and radical positions, expressed by the lucid Ireton and the emotional Rainsborough:

> *Rainsborough:* For really I think that the poorest he that is in England hath a life to live as the greatest he; and therefore truly, sir, I think it's clear, that every man that is to live under a government ought first by his own consent to put himself under that government.
>
> *Ireton:* I think that no person hath a right or interest or share in the disposing of the affairs of the kingdom, that hath not a permanent fixed interest in this kingdom. As for the rest we should not refuse to give them air and place and ground and the freedom of the highways and other things to live amongst us.
>
> *Rainsborough:* Sir, I see that it is impossible to have liberty but all property must be taken away. If you say it, it must be so. But I would fain know what the soldier hath fought for all this while. He hath fought to enslave himself, to give power to men of riches.
>
> *Ireton:* I will tell you what the soldier hath fought for. The danger that we stood in was that one man's will must be law.

Q *How did Ireton counter Rainsborough's arguments that government should be based on the consent of all, including 'the poorest he'?*

There was no possibility for compromise. When Charles's escape from Hampton Court on 11 November brought debates to an end, the Levellers demanded a general rendezvous. The grandees defused the situation by dividing the Army into three, directing the different regiments to separate assembly areas. At Corkbush Field near Ware in Hertfordshire cavalry troopers refused to remove copies of the *Agreement* from their hatbands. Cromwell, with brutal courage, rode into their ranks and personally confiscated the offending pamphlets. Three ringleaders were arrested and condemned to death. One had to be shot by the other two. They diced for their lives. Richard Arnold lost. The

Second Civil War caused ranks to close. When officers and agitators met in a godly huddle at Windsor in April 1648, they sank their differences by resolving 'that it was our duty, if ever the Lord brought us back again in peace, to call Charles Stuart, that man of blood, to an account for the blood he had shed and mischief he had done to his utmost against the Lord's cause and people in these poor nations'. When indeed peace of a sort was restored, Ireton's *Remonstance of the Army* showed Leveller influence in its demand that the King should be brought to account. After Fairfax had failed once more to negotiate with Charles, the Council of Officers accepted the Remonstrance. There was some Leveller input into the trial of the 'man of blood', but England's new masters stood no nonsense from the Levellers. In the spring of 1649, Leveller mutinies were ruthlessly suppressed. Robert Lockyer was executed in April, and Cromwell and Fairfax chased mutineers from Salisbury to Burford where the ringleaders were shot against the church door. The two victorious generals celebrated their victory by receiving doctorates from a grateful Oxford University.

It is as easy to belittle the Levellers as to exaggerate their importance and modernity. They never advocated adult male, still less female, suffrage. For all Rainsborough's disagreement with Ireton, they advocated the vote only for men of independent means, not for servants or paupers. The true democrats were the Diggers, the radical offshoot from the Leveller movement. There is magnificent outrage in the Diggers' pamphlet entitled *More Light Shining in Buckinghamshire*: 'Mark this, you great curmudgeons, you hang a man for stealing for his wants, when you yourselves have stolen from your fellow-brethren all their land, creatures etc. So first go hang yourselves for your great thefts and then afterwards you can hang your poor brethren for petty theft.' Actually, many Levellers showed acquisitive instincts. For instance, Rainsborough tried to hold onto his commission in the Army when he was appointed vice-admiral of the Fleet. He would not be 'the poorest he'! While the Levellers showed compassion for debtors and for urban poor, they missed an important opportunity in not campaigning for the land-rights of peasants. At best, they were agitators in the modern sense and brilliant propagandists whose journal, *The Moderate* (what a title!), had a wide circulation. They were capable of organising impressive demonstrations, for example the 20,000 at Robert Lockyer's funeral.

With all their limitations, the Levellers should be seen as remarkable products of the 'world turned upside down'. They were unique in Europe. They gave the upper classes the fright of their lives. Anyone who cares for democracy and freedom must still be moved by the Leveller Richard Rumbold's assertion that 'there was no man born marked of God above another, for none comes into the world with a saddle on his back neither any booted and spurred to ride him'. Historians who belittle the Levellers are guilty of 'wonder-blindness'. One should never lose the capacity to be impressed by the surprising, the shocking, the funny, the appalling. In the background of seventeenth-century Europe the Levellers were *different* – as Cromwell certainly appreciated.

See pages 365–7 for repression of radicals.

8 ∽ THE TRIAL AND EXECUTION OF CHARLES I

The King's defeat in the Second Civil War in no way discouraged the conservative Presbyterian majority in the House of Commons from further negotiations with the King. Indeed, the flood of petitions from the political community in favour of a negotiated settlement suggested that the Presbyterians truly represented majority opinion. The war's outcome did not alter Charles's belief that he could continue to play his enemies off against each other, making promises left, right and centre which he had no intention of keeping. The result was the so-called Treaty of Newport, though its terms were never finalised, for the Army intervened, making clear its refusal to tolerate further dealings with the 'man of blood' on a 'here we go again' basis. This emphatic intervention by the Army was the final result of its politicisation since the end of the First Civil War. The combination of Leveller radicalism and religious conviction that God's declared will had to be implemented, drove the Army's leaders to legalised murder of the King.

Only decisive action by the Army's leaders made this possible. MPs were divided over the next steps to be taken, and a majority were definitely opposed to the trial. David Underdown has identified five distinct groups: 45 were so enthusiastic for an agreement with the King that they were imprisoned by the Army, 186 were 'purged' by Colonel Pride, 86 deliberately absented themselves from the proceedings, 83 accepted the King's death in retrospect and a mere 71 actively supported the trial and execution. Given this breakdown it is clear that the initiatives of the grandees were essential for the trial to proceed. Of none was this more true than of Cromwell. But as was so often the case at great crises in his life, Cromwell dithered while he sought the Lord's will. He deliberately busied himself up in Yorkshire with the siege of Pontefract while Ireton and Pride got on with things in London. When he returned to London, Cromwell made a last, desperate attempt to negotiate with the King. Having failed where so many others had failed, Cromwell made up his mind. When the pernickety lawyer Algernon Sidney objected on two grounds, 'this court cannot legally try the king, this court cannot legally try anybody', Cromwell thumped the table and shouted, 'I tell you, we will cut off his head with the crown upon it'.

The trial was a farce, a botched affair. It was difficult to persuade enough men of stature to attend to give the court credibility. For instance, the President was John Bradshaw, an obscure Cheshire solicitor. Though his hat was lined with steel, Bradshaw cut a poor figure in court, fussy and indecisive. The King climbed the steps from the river while his enemies still argued about the indictment. Henry Marten came to the rescue: 'In the name of the Commons in Parliament assembled and all the good people of England'. As Charles took his seat, he looked round in bewilderment, for he recognised hardly any of his judges. Royalist propaganda exaggerated when it talked of 'a court of brewers and draymen'. Charles's judges were minor gentry – and reli-

KEY ISSUE

What to do with the King?

KEY ISSUE

The trial was a public relations disaster.

A portrait of Charles I at his trial by Bower. This is a wonderful portrait, commemorating Charles I's finest hour. Calm, dignified and self-possessed, he has a penetrating glance. There is a real touch of arrogance too, of totally unyielding inflexibility. Did the artist admire Charles I or not?

gious radicals. What cannot be disputed is that of the 135 judges nominated in the ordinance to try the King, only 87 consented to serve. The absentees included the republicans Vane and Sidney, and Commander-in-Chief Fairfax whose wife interrupted the trial by shouting, 'Oliver Cromwell is a traitor!' Only 59 signed the death warrant. In fact, the warrant is a revealing document. It is covered with crossings-out and corrections. Some of those who signed later claimed that Cromwell forced them. During the disorderly signing, Cromwell and Henry Marten flicked ink at each other.

What also cannot be disputed – and Royalist propaganda naturally exploited this – was that Charles behaved impressively. Here the managers of the trial miscalculated, believing that the King could be relied on to make a mess of his own defence. Not so. Charles was confident, decisive and intelligent. He even conquered his stammer. He consistently fastened on the absurdity of the court trying him, the King, for treason. He could have prolonged proceedings indefinitely by pleading 'not guilty'. But because he was interested in victory rather than stalemate – even though victory would cost him his life – he refused to

PICTURE 14
Charles I's Death Warrant. The cleaned up version.

KEY ISSUE

Charles, saint and martyr?

plead, for to do so would have admitted the court's legality. There were moments of high pathos such as when he dropped his cane – and no-one rushed forward to pick it up. There was drama too when Bradshaw told the clerk to do his duty. 'Duty?', shouted the King.

After the inevitable sentence had been pronounced, Charles died bravely on a scaffold erected outside Inigo Jones's banqueting hall, reminiscent of happier times. The King wore two vests against the January frost so that he would not shiver – and be misunderstood. For unlike his father, Charles was not a physical coward. He was not afraid now, convinced that what he was doing was right. He refused to make the usual gesture of forgiveness towards his executioner, for no-one could forgive the murderer of the Lord's anointed. Bishop Juxon was allowed to pray with him on the scaffold. Charles made a brief speech, which only those close to him could hear as cavalry kept the crowd at a distance. The last words Charles heard in this life were ironic. As the executioner adjusted the King's hair so that he could make a clean cut, Charles thought that the blow would follow immediately, and told the executioner to wait for his signal. 'I will, an'it please Your Majesty', was the executioner's reply. A moment later the King gave a sign. The axe flashed. The crowd groaned. A woman fainted. The Man of Blood became Charles the Martyr.

While law and pity were on Charles's side, his speech on the scaffold justified his enemies' actions:

> For the people truly I desire their liberty and freedom as much as anybody whatsoever; but I must tell you, their liberty and freedom consists in having government, those laws by which their lives and their goods may be most their own. It is not their having a share in government; that is nothing appertaining to them. A subject and a sovereign are clear different things.

With such a man compromise was impossible.

While 30 January 1649 was a profound tragedy for Charles and for his loving family, and a very sad day for the House of Stuart, in a real sense it was a great day for representative government and for political freedom. First, there was something grand about the way that the King was tried and executed in public. As Harrison the regicide said at his own trial 11 years later, 'it was not a thing done in a corner'. Secondly, despite the dubious claims of Charles's judges to represent the English people, they were more representative than Charles I. By these representatives of the nation the principle was established that no-one is indispensable, not even the monarch. Charles I was clearly not up to the job. Like the rest of us when we are unfortunate enough for this to be clearly the case, he had to go.

Because of his devotion to high principle, or obstinate stupidity, Charles refused to compromise and to accept that because of his inadequacy he had to be replaced. His death, tragic and illegal, was the inevitable consequence. One could almost argue that it was his own choice. What else could his enemies have done with him? As a prisoner he had proved his capacity for trouble-making. As an exile he would simply recruit another army and invade. He had to die. There is a story that Charles's corpse was visited on the night of 30 January by a hooded figure – Cromwell. 'Cruel necessity!', exclaimed the figure. The source for the story is suspect and Cromwell would more likely have invoked the will of God. But there is an element of truth in the suggestion that the King's death was 'cruel necessity'.

KEY ISSUE

Was the trial and execution of Charles I 'cruel necessity'?

See the contemporary picture of Charles's execution on the front cover.

PICTURE 15

The banqueting hall, Whitehall – an illustration of Inigo Jones's architectural genius and the scene of Charles I's death

9 ⌐ BIBLIOGRAPHY

The Civil Wars 1640–9 by Angela Anderson (Hodder and Stoughton, Access to History series, 1995) is an invaluable guide and inspiration for this difficult decade. See also *The English Civil War* by Martyn Bennett (Addison Wesley Longman, 1995). Students interested in warfare will find endless material on the battles and campaigns of the civil wars. *The King's War* by C.V. Wedgwood (Collins, 1958) is well written and detailed. A more up-to-date treatment is provided by *Going to the Wars* by Charles Carlton (BCA, 1992), *The Royalist War Effort* by Ronald Hutton (Longman, 1982) and *The Civil Wars of England* by John Kenyon (Weidenfeld and Nicolson, 1988). There are some enjoyable biographies of Cromwell, recommended at the end of Chapter 5 (page 162). See also *Freeborn John*, a biography of Lilburne by Pauline Gregg (Dent, 1986). *Debate on the Civil War Revisited* by R.C. Richardson (Routledge, 1991) is a lucid summary of the historians' arguments about the causes and nature of the civil wars.

10 ~ DISCUSSION POINTS AND ESSAY QUESTIONS

1. Does Charles I's career illustrate the importance of the role of the individual?
This is a fascinating issue, well worth discussing orally, perhaps in a seminar, though it is unlikely to occur as such in an exam. The following parargraphs provide some relevant factors and ideas.

Was Charles I the master or the prisoner of events? Was he the victim of impersonal forces which he could no more resist than Canute could turn back the tide? Or has his own influence on events been underestimated? The answer no doubt is: both.

Certainly there were impersonal forces at work that affected all seventeenth-century rulers. Perhaps the most important was the inflation that had raged since about 1550. This rise in prices made tax yields pay for less, government more expensive and war in particular cost more. Charles had to grapple with the problem of ruling three kingdoms. It was no coincidence that the so-called English Civil Wars were in fact imposed on England by rebellions first in Scotland and then in Ireland. Also, Charles could not help the fact that Europe was convulsed by a cataclysmic struggle which threatened the survival of Protestantism – the Thirty Years War. This background of religious conflict made it hard for Charles's subjects to assess his religious and foreign policies in a cool and rational way. Charles's job was very difficult.

On the other hand, Charles I had a lot going for him. He operated in a conservative, king-worshipping age. He was the fountain of patronage. He had considerable sources of wealth. He could select his own ministers and policies. His opponents and critics could not easily organise opposition – unless he summoned Parliament, which he did not have to do. Charles's success in building up a strong position during the first eight years of his 'personal rule' shows that he was not the prisoner of circumstances.

Indeed, the role of the individual is perfectly illustrated by the career of Charles I. Take the collapse of the personal rule. The conclusion of Chapter 3 proves that this occurred because of Charles's unnecessary and quixotic decision to take on the religious prejudices of his Scottish subjects. By this foolish policy he dissipated the strength which he had laboriously built up. Similarly, by his attempted arrest of the five members he threw away the support of the moderates whom he had attracted following Hyde's advice. Charles's ineffectual record as a war leader and his devious manoeuvres between 1646 and 1649, brought him to the scaffold. Given the resurgence of royalism in 1647 and 1648, and the anxiety of everybody – even Cromwell – for a settlement involving Charles, his rejection of anything that did not include full restoration of his power was tragic. His dignity at his trial and death saved the monarchy. He was more use to his cause as a dead martyr than a living leader. His personal input was considerable.

In the early modern period even an unsuccessful king *had* to be important. The structure of politics and society thrust him into the limelight. His actions influenced millions for good or ill. One can argue that it was a stupid system, but it was there. In particular, it gave even a politically ungifted king the opportunity for imposing his *style*. Here Charles was extremely successful. He created a cultured, dignified court. He was a devoted husband and parent, in contrast with his father and sons. His devout Anglicanism, better understood in retrospect than at the time, was very much his own peculiar form of Christian commitment. This was all part of his style, his special contribution to his age, which he influenced profoundly. Charles I may have been a tragic figure in many ways. He cannot be considered a successful ruler. But as John Kenyon remarked, Charles 'looked well behind bars'. He was a very successful martyr.

2. Was Charles I's trial and execution a case of 'cruel necessity'?
3. How do you account for the defeat of the Royalists, 1642–8?
4. Were the Levellers democratic?
5. How do you explain the political influence of the New Model Army?
6. How humane was the conduct of the First Civil War?
7. Read the following extract from *The Origins of the English Civil War* by Conrad Russell (1973), and answer the questions that follow: 'The English Civil War was not an isolated event. Charles ruled over three kingdoms, and within three years he faced armed resistance in all three of them, Scotland in 1639, Ireland in 1641 and England in 1642.'

(a) How important were events in Scotland and Ireland in causing the rift between Charles I and his opponents? (10 marks)
(b) Why did armed resistance in England not occur until 1642? (10 marks)
(c) What impact did Ireland have on the outcome of the First Civil War? (5 marks)

While structured questions are broken down into separate parts (such as in question 7), there is always a unifying theme which a good candidate remembers when writing the answers. Here it is the interrelation between England, Ireland and Scotland during the Civil War. Clearly the failure of Charles's attempt to impose a new prayer book on the Scots and the outbreak of revolt in Ireland caused the unresolvable rift in the summer of 1642 (question (a)). It is essential to keep these developments in mind when answering (b). Similarly, a strong candidate will stress such factors as Charles's recruitment of Irish troops and the Cessation in answering (c), while at the same time doing justice to other factors. Note the distribution of marks.

5

The Search for a New Constitution 1649–60

INTRODUCTION

'*Exit tyrannus, regum ultimus*' ('Out goes the tyrant, the last of the kings'). These triumphalist words were engraved on the pedestal of a statue of Charles I, which was removed after his execution. Yet the King's unceremonious exit shattered its perpetrators almost as much as the rest of Britain. As we have seen, although there were a few Republicans among the King's enemies, there was no deep-laid plot to abolish monarchy. In fact, various members of the Stuart house were considered as replacements for Charles I. Yet no-one appropriate was available. So the miscellaneous politicians, lawyers and soldiers responsible for the King's death settled for a republic. Several republican MPs, such as Algernon Sidney and Edmund Ludlow, who had opposed the King's trial, now supported and strengthened the new regime.

See page 124 for Sidney's argument with Cromwell.

This chapter explores the experiments between 1649 and 1660, which aimed at political stability. Sections will be devoted to the Commonwealth, or to give it its less flattering name, the Rump (1649–53), Barebones Parliament (April–December 1653) and the Protectorate of Oliver Cromwell (1653–8). The chapter ends with the failure to preserve the Republic after Cromwell's death, leading to the Restoration of the Monarchy.

Although these constitutional experiments were ultimately abortive, the Interregnum (the period between kings, 1649–60) was not the 'sterile aberration' which some historians have indentified. This chapter also includes the advances made in the context of economic, social, cultural and intellectual spheres. Since some of these achievemments are dealt with in separate chapters, they will merely be alluded to here. The Interregnum was also a fruitful time in the contexts of imperial and foreign policy – topics which will be covered here in greater detail. Perhaps of most significance for the future was the welding together of England, Scotland and Ireland. All in all this was an exciting period, especially in the realm of ideas. This intellectual liveliness merits a separate section, as does the extraordinary man who dominated this decade, even from the tomb. For Cromwell's death led to the Republic's collapse – though this was not inevitable.

See pages 307–9 for economic initiatives.

1 ⌐ THE COMMONWEALTH OR THE RUMP PARLIAMENT, 1649–53

Commonwealth this word had a long history, dating back to Tudor times. It suggested an idealistic concept of the State, which allegedly existed for the benefit of all. This flattering name chosen by the new government contrasted with the term applied to it then and since – the Rump.

KEY ISSUE

Problems facing the Republic.

The Republic was initially known as the **Commonwealth.** Its supreme authority was Parliament, or more exactly the House of Commons, for the House of Lords was abolished along with the monarchy in March 1649. Government was implemented by the Council of State, responsible to Parliament. Since so many of the originally elected MPs had departed for one reason or another (some were Royalists, some were killed in the wars, some had retired into private life and some had been imprisoned or purged), both contemporaries and historians have called the survivors the Rump, the unseemly backside of the Long Parliament. Actually, recent research has shown that there was a steady stream of purged MPs back to Westminster. The presence of such conservatives in Parliament and the Council of State explains the caution of the Rump's policies and achievements with which this first section is concerned.

It was a bleak world into which the infant English Republic was born. It was 'English' rather than 'British', for Ireland was still in revolt and Scotland welcomed Charles II. He was recognised in Europe as well, for the trial and execution of Charles I were universally condemned. The Republic was outlawed by the monarchies of the civilised world, and was soon at war with its only fellow republic, Holland. The Republic's ambassador to Spain, Anthony Ascham, was assassinated while Isaac Dorislaus, a Dutchman who had helped to prosecute Charles I and who represented the English Republic at the Hague, was also murdered by Royalist hitmen whom the Dutch government declined to pursue. There was an open season as well for the destruction of English shipping. Exiled Royalists planned and plotted with their sympathisers at home, while organisations such as the Sealed Knot caused headaches for republican regimes.

The execution of the King doomed the Republic to irreversible unpopularity at home. Charles I's reflections from prison, *Eikon Basilike,* ghosted by John Gauden, proved a best-seller. Thirty-five editions appeared within a year. The government countered by reintroducing censorship. This illiberal move was defended by the apostle of freedom of expression, John Milton: 'More just it is that a less number compel a greater to retain their liberty, than that a greater number compel the less to be their fellow slaves'. In other words, the English were to be *forced* to be free, and there was no doubt from where the force came. Like all the republican regimes, the Rump depended on the New Model Army. As long as this was so, no free election would return a sympathetic parliament. No way round this dilemma was ever discovered. The killing of the King and the reliance on the hated Army necessitated repression. Not that anyone could repress John Lilburne. The last chapter discussed how the Leveller influence in the Army was destroyed, but Lilburne still operated as a loose cannon. In February 1649, he published *England's New Chains Discovered.* Its title was self-explanatory. Lilburne was arrested and brought before the Council of State. Waiting to be interrogated, he overheard Cromwell smash his fist on the table and shout, 'You have no way with these men – either you must break them, or they will break you'. Lilburne was imprisoned in the Tower and then exiled. But he remained irrepressible. The Commonwealth had not heard the last of him.

Cromwell was more successful in repressing the Catholic Irish. He brought to this task his uncomplicated racism: 'I had rather be overrun with a Cavalierish interest, than a Scotch interest: I had rather be overrun with a Scotch interest, than an Irish interest; and I think of all this is the most dangerous – all the world knows their barbarism'. Much of the preliminary spade-work had already been done by the Irish themselves, who totally failed to co-operate with each other, and by the competent Colonel Michael Jones who defeated the army of the Catholic Confederacy at Rathmines in August 1649. When Cromwell landed a few days later with 10,000 well-paid, well-equipped troops complete with artillery, there was no field army capable of facing him. But there was still a long hard slog if the rebels' strongholds were to be reduced. Cromwell thought he could solve the problem. He showed his hand at strongly-fortified Drogheda, which he stormed on 10 September. Cromwell's letter to Speaker Lenthall explains what happened:

See profile of Milton on page 364.

See page 362 for a profile of Lilburne

KEY ISSUE

The suppression of the Irish revolt.

> Upon Tuesday the 10th instant about five o'clock in the evening we began the storm; and after some hot dispute we entered, about seven or eight hundred men; the enemy disputing it very stiffly with us. Divers [several] of the Enemy retreated into the Mill-Mount: a place very strong and difficult of access. The Governor, Sir Arthur Ashton, and divers considerable officers being there, our men getting up to them, were ordered by me to put them all to the sword. And indeed, being in the heat of the action, I forbade them to spare any that were in arms; and I think that night they put to the sword about 2000 men. Whereupon I ordered the steeple of St Peter's Church to be fired, when one of them was heard to say in the midst of the flames: 'God damn me, God confound me; I burn, I burn'. When they submitted, their officers were knocked on the head; and every tenth man of the soldiers killed; and the rest shipped for the Barbados. I am persuaded that this is a righteous judgement of God upon these barbarous wretches, who have imbrued their hands in so much innocent blood; and that it will tend to prevent the effusion of blood for the future. Which are the satisfactory grounds to such actions, which otherwise cannot but work remorse and regret. And now give me leave to say how it comes to pass that this work is wrought. It was set upon some of our hearts, that a great thing should be done, not by power or might, but by the Spirit of God. And is it not so, clearly?

Q

How did Cromwell explain his soldiers' success at Drogheda?

This letter will be discussed in the section devoted to Cromwell (see page 143) for the light that it sheds on his personality and values.

134 *YEARS OF TURMOIL*

KEY ISSUE

The effects of the Cromwellian conquest of Ireland.

See pages 418–19 for Ireland under Cromwell.

KEY ISSUE

The Rump's conquest of Scotland.

Covenanters Scottish Presbyterians who swore allegiance to the Covenant to resist popish innovations and introduce Presbyterianism into England. Their leader was the Marquis of Argyll.

Suffice here to point out that the Commonwealth's soldiers regarded themselves as fulfilling a God-given mission to suppress once and for all the revolt launched by 'these barbarous wretches'. Cromwell took Wexford a few weeks later in even more appalling circumstances. While the slaughter of Drogheda's defenders could be justified by the currently accepted rules of warfare, there was no excuse for the massacre of Wexford's civilians, including several Catholic priests.

Whether these methods of barbarism actually worked as Cromwell intended and predicted is doubtful. He had in fact ensured that Irish resistance would never die. When he returned home in March 1650 to conquer Scotland, he left his son-in-law, Henry Ireton, much to do. The completion of the conquest killed Ireton. His last words, 'I will have blood', were prophetic of the repercussions of Cromwell's intervention in Irish affairs. The Commonwealth drove Catholic landowners westwards into the wastes of Connaught, confiscating their lands so that they could be awarded to English speculators who had lent money to Parliament since 1642. This policy was extended by Fleetwood and Henry Cromwell during the Protectorate. Landowners who refused to co-operate were deported *en masse* to Barbados. In fact, many turned to terrorism, earning the nickname 'Tories', meaning robbers who operated from the bogs and marshes.

Persecution of Irish Catholicism was combined with economic exploitation to plunge Ireland into a man-made dark age – not the Republic's finest achievement. Furthermore, while as a purely military undertaking Cromwell's campaign in Ireland was remarkably successful and sophisticated, combining sea-power and psychological warfare with well-planned military blitzkrieg, it was unquestionably the greatest blot on his reputation. His contribution to Irish history was uniquely deplorable. While Cromwell has to be acquitted of deliberate genocide, and there certainly had been a Catholic revolt in which Protestants were murdered, he overreacted by spearheading an unnecessary and vicious assault on Irish religion and culture. As Cromwell wittily put it, Dublin was to be a purely English city in which there were to be 'no Macs or Os'. Comparison with the Nazi 'settlement' of Eastern Europe is irresistible.

The Scots, on the other hand, were another matter. Until recently they had been Parliament's allies. They were indisputably Protestant. However, in 1650 they argued that the recent public murder of their King had dissolved their only link with England. They therefore welcomed Charles II. It was inconvenient that the **Covenanters** had just executed the leading Scottish Royalists, Hamilton and Montrose. But this apparently worried neither Charles II, who cheerfully took the Covenant, nor the leading Covenanter, the Marquis of Argyll, who personally crowned Charles at Edinburgh. This happy event was followed by a day of fasting for the House of Stuart's sins. Indeed, the 'Ayatullas of the Kirk' (John Kenyon) insisted on the amiable royal lecher expressing public remorse for his father's crimes and his mother's idolatry. Still, Charles was now an anointed king. He and his new-found subjects prepared an expedition to enforce the Covenant on England. But that was enough to bring Cromwell crashing down on them. He got his blow in first.

Fairfax having turned the job down, Cromwell was appointed by the Rump as commander-in-chief, assisted by Monck, Fleetwood and Lambert. They were a formidable team. Despite being drenched by appalling weather, decimated by sickness, outmanoeuvred and out-numbered, on 3 September 1650 Cromwell won the most impressive victory of his career at Dunbar. He spotted that his opposite number, David Leslie, had complacently extended his line. His right wing was therefore dangerously exposed and could be crushed before the rest intervened. Cromwell decided on a dawn attack. An eyewitness described him shepherding his cavalry over the swollen Bronx Burn, 'riding on a little nag, the blood running unheeded down his chin'. It was a tense moment indeed before a watery sun rose, 'and I heard Nol say, "Let God arise and let his enemies be scattered!" ' Most of the Scots were asleep, and 11,000 of them ran before 3,000 English – until a halt was called for the singing of Psalm 117. Cromwell now avoided the vin-dictiveness that he had shown to the conquered Irish. In fact, he was Christian charity personified. He begged Covenanters and the Kirk to accept God's verdict: 'I beseech you in the bowels of Christ, consider that ye may be mistaken'.

But some of the Scots were not even convinced after further victories had clearly indicated the Almighty's preferences. In the following summer, when Cromwell deliberately left the west coast route open, Charles led his followers south into England, hoping for a general upris-ing. The response was disappointing. English people, however much they disliked the Republic, had no wish for a third civil war. Charles and his dispirited army were trapped at Worcester and destroyed – 'the crowning mercy' as Cromwell predictably named his last victory, which occurred on 3 September 1651, exactly a year after Dunbar. Charles, 'a tall black man, about two yards high', in the words of the numerous 'wanted' notices circulated by the government, had several dramatic escapes, hiding in the recesses of country houses and oak trees until he finally reached the Continent. Apart from the absence of a whisky bottle, his abandonment of his followers and his lucky escapes antici-pated Bonnie Prince Charlie's adventures a century later. Cromwell confidently dismissed Charles II from his future calculations: 'All he needs is a leg of mutton and a whore, for he is so damnably debauched that he would undo us all'.

These impressive military achievements, followed by naval victories over the Dutch, did not make life easy for the Rump. Garrisons in Ireland and Scotland, plus the construction and maintenance of 70 battleships, had to be financed. The monthly assessment rocketed to £90,000 while the hated excise remained in place. Furthermore, soldiers and politicians got on best when actually fighting the common foe. After victory had been won, the soldiers had time to look critically at the politicians' achievements – if that was the right word – since the members of the Rump showed their conservatism by their extreme caution towards reform. Very little seemed to be happening. All that

> **KEY ISSUE**
>
> *The Rump's achievements.*

they could show, for example with regard to legal reform, was the establishment of a commission under Matthew Hales and an act replacing the absurd, incomprehensible mixture of Latin and Norman French with English – a thoroughly sane measure which made the law more accessible to ordinary folk. In all other respects, however, the law remained cumbersome, expensive and the exclusive gravy-train for lawyers which it has always been. There was nothing done to relieve debtors or improve the conditions of prisons. As for legislation to improve the common lot, there were stringent laws against 'the detestable sin of prophane swearing and cursing', aimed at religious radicals such as Muggletonians and Ranters, laws enforcing sabbath-day observance and laws imposing the death penalty for adultery, fornication and incest. Four women were hanged – proof of the prevailing double standard. Acts for the Propagation of the Gospel imposed well-paid clergy on the impoverished Welsh and Irish.

The rich and privileged on the other hand had little fault to find with the Rump. All moves to abolish **tithes** were resisted, tithes being considered as property since for the most part they no longer maintained clergy but had been bought up by the rich as a safe investment. As discussed previously, left-wing sects such as the Levellers and Diggers were hammered. In August 1650, a Council of Trade was established, signifying a more sympathetic attitude towards mercantile interests. Its most notable achievement was the Navigation Act of October 1651, which decreed that trade with England and her colonies should be carried in English ships or ships from the country of origin. This act drove out Dutch middlemen from England's trade to West Africa and the New World, to the immense benefit of English merchants. Above all, the Rump kept order, defeating enemies abroad and at home. Men of status and property became satisfied republicans.

The rich and privileged, however, did not have the final say; that belonged to the New Model Army, its pushy career-officers and its weird commander-in-chief. By spring 1653 the question of what was to happen next had emerged. The wealthy oligarchs of the Rump's leadership were in no hurry to face this question. Why should they, given their monopoly of honours and perks? But there was no justification for their perpetual tenure of power. Even the Rump admitted this by debating 'a Bill for a new representative', involving elections in November. It used to be thought that their determination to ensure their own control over these elections persuaded Cromwell to intervene. Alternatively, genuinely free elections were proposed, which would inevitably produce a Royalist result. As the Rump's scheme never re-emerged from Cromwell's pocket, we cannot be sure. Perhaps he shared the soldiers' disillusionment with the lack of reforms. Something certainly ignited that strange man's touch-paper, driving him to action, 'the contemplation of the issue whereof made his hair stand on end'. But he acted just the same. The result was the most outrageous scene in Parliament's history.

On that unforgettable day of 20 April Cromwell listened to the debate, glaring at the MPs from under his hat. After a few moments he

tithes a tax to support clergy, consisting of a tenth of the payer's income. The tax was universally resented, especially by people who did not belong to the State Church.

KEY ISSUE

Reasons for dissatisfaction with the Rump.

had had enough: 'This is the time I must do it!', he whispered to Major-General Harrison, and strode onto the floor of the House. 'Drunkards! Whoremasters!', he shouted, 'You are no Parliament, I say you are no Parliament, I will put an end to your sittings.' Murmurs of protest rose to an indignant crescendo. 'Fetch them in', Cromwell ordered Harrison, and troops flooded the House, ejecting the Speaker and hustling outside the protesting members. 'This is not honest', exclaimed Sir Henry Vane, 'this is against morality and common honesty!' 'Sir Henry Vane, Sir Henry Vane. The Lord deliver me from Sir Henry Vane!', Cromwell sonorously replied. In the middle of this mayhem a flunkey appeared carrying the mace, the symbol of the House's authority. 'Hey, what shall we do with this bauble?', shouted the great iconoclast. 'Take it away!' Did Cromwell savour the comparison with the scene 24 years earlier when the Speaker had been held down in his chair by Holles and Eliot? Probably not. Irony was never his strong suit. Next day a notice was pinned to the locked doors of Parliament: 'This house to let, now unfurnished'.

Cromwell subsequently claimed that 'not a dog barked' when he expelled the Rump. Historians have been too ready to accept a similarly dismissive approach to the Rump's achievements and apparently deserved demise. The leading luminaries were, so we are told, selfish, uninspired second-raters who had no ideals and no self-belief. The republicanism of the Rump was 'a mere improvisation, triumphant by default, unconvinced and largely unprofessed' (Blair Worden). The revisionist, Sean Kelsey, has questioned this portrayal, arguing that the Rumpers believed in their mission to fight for England's true interests, taking themselves seriously and projecting the regime with flair and self-confidence. Cromwell, on the other hand, acted cynically and unjustifiably, bidding for the support of his more ruthless and ambitious military colleagues who perceived that their own power was threatened by the civilians. What Cromwell did was undemocratic and irresponsible: 20 April 1653 was a tragic day for English liberty. Cromwell, whose statue undeservedly stands outside Parliament, destroyed English representative government as surely as General von Schleicher destroyed the Weimar Republic in 1932. Cromwell, however, was his own Hitler. His subsequent military dictatorship and his failure to achieve consent – about which he emitted self-pitying bleats – were inevitable. This failure is usually attributed to the execution of the King. But the expulsion of the Rump did even more harm to the prospects of a constitutional settlement.

> See page 167 for Vane's fate.

> **Q**
> *Why did Cromwell expel the Rump?*

2 ⤳ THE BAREBONES PARLIAMENT, 1653

When Cromwell had told the Rump a few weeks earlier that there was no more fitting moment for a dissolution, the irrepressible Harry Marten had replied that there was no more fitting moment to replace Cromwell, the Lord General. But in truth, the Lord General was irreplaceable. He alone now stood between the country and anarchy. As so

millenarianist one who believed that the world was about to end and the 1,000-year reign of Christ and his saints begin. This belief often went with fifth monarchist interpretations.

fifth monarchy people believed that the four monarchies of ancient civilisation – Babylon, Assyria, Greece and Rome – were now to be replaced by the fifth monarchy, which was prophesied in the books of Daniel and Revelation. This would be the kingdom of Christ on earth.

KEY ISSUE

Barebones – reality and myth.

---

often in his career, however, this impulsive man had acted first and thought afterwards. What was to be done now? Influenced by Harrison and his dottier military colleagues, Cromwell had apparently become a convinced **millenarianist.** He believed that the **fifth monarchy** was about to be established. The reign of King Jesus was at hand. This explains Cromwell's action in forming an interim committee of four generals, which asked the Independent Churches throughout the country to nominate members. The Council of Officers then added several of their own candidates and whittled the total down to 140. A remarkable feature was that six members sat for Scotland, five for Ireland and five for Wales – hardly a generous allocation but at least the beginning of a British assembly.

'Truly you are called by God to rule with him and for him', the excited Lord General told the assembled Saints. 'I confess I never looked to see such a day as this. Jesus Christ is owned today by your call. You are at the edge of the promises and prophesies. Truly something is at the door.' Cromwell's millenarianist enthusiasm was shared by many, though by no means all, of the nominated members. They promptly declared themselves a true Parliament and addressed the problems of reforming the country.

There are several myths about the Nominated Parliament. Its other names perpetuate the Royalist slurs on its composition: the 'Parliament of Saints', in other words religious nutcases; and the 'Barebones Parliament', a snobbish allusion to a prominent member, Praise-God Barbon, a London leather-seller. In fact, 60, almost half, had sat in previous Parliaments, while the majority were lesser gentry. Another myth is that the Nominated Parliament pursued absurd, doctrinaire goals. Actually, most of its policies were sensible The Dutch war was vigorously continued. The union of England and Scotland was explored. Humane measures were introduced for the relief of debtors and the care of lunatics. The abolition of tithes was discussed with compensation for the present owners and for the payment of clergy. Steps were taken to abolish the dilatory and expensive Court of Chancery. Machinery was created for the registration of marriages, births and deaths. Civil marriages could now be solemnised by Justices of the Peace. Nothing too zany there.

Unfortunately, the Barebones Parliament came up against the same problems that every Parliament of the Interregnum encountered: how to satisfy radical demands for reform without alienating conservatives. Perhaps too much was expected by way of a new Jerusalem – encouraged no doubt by the Lord General's initial millenarianism. Soon, saints were complaining that sinners exercised too much influence over government policy. When John Lilburne returned from exile and was promptly re-arrested, hundreds attended his trial and applauded his attempts to prolong proceedings by denying his own identity, claiming he could not read the indictment and demanding adjournments for calls of nature ('Officer, help me to a chamber-pot'). Lilburne's acquittal, which was cheered uproariously, discredited the government with both radicals and conservatives. On the other hand, men of property were horrified by the suggestions to abolish tithes and reform law. Where would it end? Even Cromwell was alarmed. He complained that he was now troubled more by the fool than by the knave. He may have been aware of the plot to terminate the reign of King Jesus, which was masterminded by the practical Yorkshireman, John Lambert.

On 12 December 1653, the moderate members met by prior arrangement while the extremists were holding a prayer meeting. They voted their own abdication, collected the mace and handed it over to the Lord General. This time the government's assassins were ready with an alternative constitution. Within three days, Major-General Lambert presented the Instrument of Government to the Lord General, which he promptly accepted, ending the most extraordinary political experiment in seventeenth-century Europe. With due respect to the revisionists, this combination of the divine right of the godly with the principle of representative government was *not* run-of-the-mill. It was quite remarkable. It was a determined attempt to put into effect the religious and political radicalism of the time.

KEY ISSUE

The fall of the Barebones Parliament.

3 ⌒ RELIGIOUS AND POLITICAL RADICALISM

Chapter 9 explores in depth the relationship between religious and political radicalism. In the context of this chapter, it is worth exploring how people living in the 1640s and 1650s had the *nerve* to declare war on their king, abolish bishops, execute the Lord's anointed and experiment with the government of Church and State. Belief in an imminent day of the Lord, when the present governing classes would be swept aside in favour of the saints, was a morale-booster. So was the Calvinist conviction, based on St Paul's Epistle to the Romans, that the only distinction which mattered was that between God's elect and the damned, especially if God indicated where his favours lay by bestowing victory. The sturdy individualism of the Puritans was to be seen in the ranks of Cromwell's troopers and in the Leveller movement. Such men (and women) were no longer prepared to accept authority without question.

'Think for yourself', was part of the Puritan philosophy, which achieved its apogee in the 1650s. 'If I should worship the sun, or the moon, or the stars, or that pewter pot upon the table, what is that to you?', demanded a soldier in the New Model Army. Religious radicalism had always been politically dangerous. Charles I maintained that Puritan lecturers were liable 'to stir up and continue the rebellion raised against me'. For conservatives, a disciplinarian State Church was far preferable to toleration. Thomas Edwards argued that the prevalent religious heresies, if left unchecked, would lead inexorably to the belief that 'by natural birth all men are equally and alike born to like property, liberty and freedom'.

Between 1640 and 1655 censorship collapsed, making possible the publication of thousands of pamphlets, newsletters, cartoons and broadsheets. George Thomason, a London bookseller, collected 18,000 items, which are now in the British Library. They are a wonderful monument to the liveliness of the English mind and to the exhilarating opportunities available for self-expression during those heady years. Christopher Hill argues that the best illustration of the new approach to truth, 'look at the evidence, work it out for yourself', can be found in the realm of scientific research. But in general, everything was thrown into the intellectual melting-pot – religion, politics, science and education. It was even suggested that schools and universities should stop majoring on Latin and Greek, and do something useful such as mathematics and science. The Leveller movement might have been smashed by Cromwell's troops, but their propagandists continued to publish subversive tracts. Levellers even asked what right Englishmen had 'to deprive a people of the land which God and nature had given them and impose laws without their consent'. They meant the Irish.

In the lively, permissive atmosphere of the 1650s, the establishment was not only challenged by the eccentrics of the left. There was a lively market for Royalist provocation as well. Jibes against Parliamentarian reliance on Scotsmen, Welshmen and, worst of all, women abounded: ' "And thus it shall go", says Alice, "Nay, and thus it shall go", says Amy, "Nay, thus it shall go", says Taffy, "I trow", "Nay, thus it shall go", says Jamie.'

An example of Royalist radicalism was *The Man in the Moon*, edited between April 1649 and June 1650 by John Crouch. This scurrilous, down-market broadsheet catered for the low-brow right, the 70 per cent of London's artisans who could read a little (in other words, a seventeenth-century version of the *Sun*). The moon proverbially created lunacy, which explains the title. Serious criticism of the Republic's assaults on propriety and justice marched with attacks on prominent figures. Favourite characters were 'Nose' or 'Nose Almighty' (Cromwell) and 'Tom Ladle' or 'the Cuckold General' (Fairfax, who was allegedly hen-pecked). Selling at only a penny, readable and outrageous, its survival for over a year, despite the Rump's attempts to suppress all the various subversive Royalist tracts, proves its popularity. *The Man in the Moon* compares well with the *Mazarinades* circulating in contemporary Paris – bitter and negative, with obscene attacks on the chief minister, Cardinal Mazarin. Paris produced nothing like the intellectual liveliness of the British Republic.

4 ∽ OLIVER CROMWELL: SOLDIER AND STATESMAN, 1599–1658

Compare the portrait on the next page with that by Walker on page 109. Clearly this is a portrait of an older man. His face has filled out and the famous warts are prominent. What else is there in the face? Humour? Emotion? Sensitivity? Despite Cromwell's aversion to flattery, to what extent has Cooper been too kind to him? Is this portrait what one would expect, knowing the man?

PICTURE 16

A portrait of Oliver Cromwell by Cooper. Samuel Cooper's remarkable miniature shows Oliver Cromwell in later life. It inspired Lely's portrait which prompted Cromwell's desire to be painted 'warts and all'

No-one better personified the paradox of the 'Puritan Revolution' than Oliver Cromwell. A radical in both religion and politics, he made the republican regime respectable by smashing the Levellers and torpedoing the Parliament of the Saints. Indeed, the contradictions of his career baffled his contemporaries, who concluded that he was a power-hungry hypocrite: 'You shall scarce speak to Cromwell, but he will lay his hand on his breast, elevate his eyes and call God to record, he will weap, howl and repent, even while he doth smite you under the fifth rib.' The Leveller, Richard Overton, has been echoed by Cromwell's critics ever since. Here is the Puritan at his worst: sanctimonious, dishonest and pitiless.

But Cromwell was not as straightforward as that. To dismiss him as a Uriah Heep in armour will not do. He was a complex man. He must be

Q *Was Cromwell a hypocrite?*

1625–40	Failed Huntingdonshire farmer and businessman MP for Huntingdon and Cambridge
1640–2	Radical opponent of Charles I in the Long Parliament
1642–5	Colonel in the army of the Eastern Association
1645–9	Second-in-command of the New Model Army
1650–8	Lord General, Commander-in-Chief
1653–8	Protector

TABLE 10

Date chart of the key events in Oliver Cromwell's career

the best known, most often quoted, but least understood figure in British history. While he exhibited some characteristics of the typical Puritan – and there is no need to doubt his religious commitment – he was not really a typical anything. He was an eccentric.

He certainly did not look or behave like a Puritan. With his scruffy clothes, red face and long hair, he resembled the conservative back-woodsman that in some respects he remained all his life. Furthermore, no greater mistake could be made than to visualise him as a killjoy. Cromwell enjoyed company, music, a glass of wine and a pipe. He got on well with women, though Royalist allegations of impropriety with Mrs Lambert were libellous. He had a vivacious personality and a forth-right sense of humour, which sometimes descended to a friendly fight, such as when he threw cushions at his generals, and to the earthy, such as when he told a lawyer that he had no time for 'Magna Farta'. He could be kind and charming, especially when he wanted to recruit someone he valued. Lucy Hutchinson, who disliked him, describes how Cromwell tried to win over her formidable husband: 'He went to the end of the gallery with the Colonel, and there embracing him said to him: "Well, Colonel, satisfied or dissatisfied, you shall be one of us, for we can no longer exempt a person so able and faithful from the public service, and you shall be satisfied in all honest things".'

Cromwell's vibrant personality clearly helps to explain his success both as a soldier and as a statesman. He was liked and respected even by people with whom he quarrelled or disagreed. It was much to his credit that he was able to hold together his generals, men of character and independence, some of them quite difficult and touchy on occasions. George Monck spoke for them all when he remarked that, 'Richard Cromwell forsook himself, for I would have sustained him out of the regard which I had for his father.'

How good a soldier was Cromwell? Military historians are reluctant to put him in the top flight, arguing that he never faced a formidable continental foe. David Chandler rates him below Marlborough and Wellington. From our point of view Cromwell was better than Essex and Manchester, and much better than Rupert and Goring. He was a natural cavalryman, with an eye for country and horseflesh. He was a superb trainer of men – witness his firm control over the charge at Marston Moor or his ability to move cavalry at night across the swollen river at Dunbar. His Irish campaign was a model of methodical plan-ning and effective leadership. Part of Cromwell's success was due to his enjoyment of war. He preferred the informal bonhomie of the camp to the back-biting of Westminster and revelled in victory: 'I profess they run!', he yelped at Dunbar. A quality which he shared with Julius Caesar was that he took up soldiering very late. He was 43 when the Civil War began. If for no other reason, this makes his military career remarkable.

Cromwell on the other hand was not a natural politician. The best that can be said for him is that he learnt from experience. The naive backbencher of 1640 and the puzzled, ineffectual debater at Putney became the unchallenged head of state who was ultimately offered the crown. But he failed to solve the problems which he tackled, to some

KEY ISSUE

Cromwell as soldier and statesman.

See page 155 for Richard Cromwell's fate.

extent because they were insoluble but also because he made mistakes. He mishandled his Parliaments and misunderstood public opinion. His objectives were unrealistic because he stood almost alone in considering them desirable. But he could claim achievements nevertheless.

What are we to make of Cromwell's claim, echoed by so many politicians, that he was only involved in politics for the public interest? This claim he invariably expressed in religious terms: he was God's servant, entrusted with the welfare of God's people. Cromwell never entirely lost his sympathy for the oppressed and the poor. His advice to MPs after Dunbar rings true:

> Own your authority and improve it to curb the proud and the insolent, such as would disturb the tranquillity of England; relieve the oppressed, hear the groans of poor prisoners in England; be pleased to reform the abuses of all professions; and if there be anyone that makes many poor to make a few rich, that suits not a Commonwealth.

Cromwell consistently stood for two principles: a return to political stability based on the consent of the governed and the establishment of religious toleration for peaceable Protestants. As we shall see, his tragedy was that these two objectives conflicted, since the vast majority of the political community were incapable of Cromwell's vision and generosity. It is surely impossible not to sympathise with him as he pleaded over and over again for toleration: 'Notions will hurt none but them who have them', 'Your pretended fear lest error may creep in is like the man who would keep all wine out of the country lest some would become drunk', 'It is a fine thing to have fought the oppression of the bishops only to impose a worse tyranny ourselves'.

What about Drogheda and Wexford? Some of Cromwell's biographers such as Antonia Fraser and Maurice Ashley are too kind, claiming that he got 'carried away', or that like President Truman and the atomic bomb, the prime aim was to save life. This is to defend the indefensible. Cromwell was not the only seventeenth-century Englishman who persecuted the Catholic Irish, and arguably his greatest crime in his Irish campaign was to be so effective. But his prejudice was grotesque. That terrible letter to the Speaker about Drogheda says it all: the barbarous wretches had got what was coming to them, with God's approval. What was the point of the man in the steeple who shouted 'I burn'? I am afraid that Cromwell thought it funny.

Cromwell's Christianity did not extend to loving the enemy if he happened to be Irish. Indeed, it is fair comment that the Old Testament rather than the New inspired Cromwell. His imagery was often taken from the Old Testament. When he rejected the crown, he explained that he would be like Moses leading the Israelites back into Egypt. Or it would be tantamount to rebuilding Jericho. He resisted the temptation to enrich himself – 'the sin of Achan'. In his crusade to reform morality, he referred admiringly to Phineas who harpooned two fornicating

Q Was Cromwelll a genuine idealist?

See pages 133–4 for the military context of Drogheda.

iconoclasm literally the defacing of 'icons', i.e. statues, stained glass and organs. In general terms it means the destruction of previously respected institutions and assumptions.

Israelites. There is not much here about love and forgiveness, though in practice Cromwell was a generous and merciful man, which he demonstrated by supporting John Lilburne's widow after the death of her impossible husband. But she was not Irish!

Perhaps Cromwell's most remarkable quality was his **iconoclasm.** He consistently displayed a willingness to smash the relics of the establishment: 'Take away that bauble!'; 'I say you are no parliament!', 'We will cut off his head with the crown upon it!' At times this destructiveness was prejudiced and boorish, such as when he interrupted the Reverend Henry Hitch saying Evensong in Ely Cathedral: 'Leave off your fooling and come down, Sir!' But there is a splendid dismissiveness of snobbish convention in his readiness 'to shoot the king just like any other enemy soldier' and in his preference for men 'with the root of the matter in them' rather than the pampered sprigs of the aristocracy. In his willingness to dispense with formality and precedent he showed his true originality. What a character!

5 ⌐ THE PROTECTORATE, 1653–8

December 1653 was a watershed in more ways than one. Cromwell himself was bitterly disappointed and disillusioned by the failure of the Barebones Parliament. Clearly, the reign of King Jesus, which he had welcomed so effusively, was not at the door. Both saints and sinners would continue to demand his attention. This was the moment too when the revolution, if there was such a thing, turned right. These developments were personified by the replacement of Harrison by Lambert as the man to whom Cromwell listened. Practical common sense replaced visionary idealism.

KEY ISSUE

The Instrument of Government – a realistic compromise?

Certainly the Instrument of Government was realistic. It was modelled on the Heads of the Proposals and anticipated the Great Reform Bill of 1832. Cromwell's title, Lord Protector, had a reassuringly conservative ring, with its echoes of Tudor times. While he headed the government and continued to command the New Model Army, he shared power with the Council of State, whose members held office for life. Parliament, consisting of one House only, met at least once every three years. Triennial elections returned members from 460 seats, of which two-thirds represented the counties, as opposed to the former one-third. Although borough representation was curtailed, seats were found for the first time for growing conurbations such as Leeds, Halifax and Manchester. Thirty seats each went to Ireland and Scotland, the members to be nominated by the Protector in Council. Elsewhere, the vote went to men owning property worth £200. The New Model Army was to be reduced to 30,000, adequate taxation being provided through assessment and excise. There was to be a decentralised State Church, with toleration for all Christians except Anglicans, Catholics and those who threatened public order. In other words, the aim was to create a tolerant, orderly state, a well-paid and well-disciplined army and a

MAJOR-GENERAL JOHN LAMBERT 1619–84

Born of minor gentry stock in the Yorkshire Dales, Lambert was educated at Kirkby Malham Grammar School and Trinity College, Cambridge. With no military training he rapidly achieved senior rank, virtually winning the Battle of Preston for Cromwell at the age of 29. He was a popular leader, showing concern for his soldiers' welfare. He played a prominent part in the politics of the Interregnum and was lucky to escape a death sentence at his trial in 1662. He spent the last 24 years of his life in captivity. Lambert and his pretty wife shocked the more po-faced members of the Republican establishment by their ostentatious and wealthy lifestyle in their house in Wimbledon. 'Able and impressionable, daring and outspoken, Lambert the tulip-fancier was incongruous in a society which set an excessive premium on piety or the reputation for it' (David Ogg). Walker's portrait depicts a realist. Can one read into it Lambert's cynicism? Is this a picture of a dandy on the make or of the statesman-like architect of the Instrument of Government?

PICTURE 17
Major-General John Lambert by an unknown artist after Walker, 1655

See page 120 for the Battle of Preston.

properted electorate. The MPs representing Scotland and Ireland were reliable placemen who would do as they were told by the government.

Since Parliament was not to meet until 3 September, Cromwell's lucky day, the Protector in Council had to fill a power vacuum until then. These eight months were arguably the most constructive period of the Interregnum. Eighty-four ordinances were issued achieving numerous reforms. Chancery was restored with reduced fees. Traitors were no longer to be disembowelled. Bear-baiting and cock-fighting were abolished. Roads and postal services were improved. Triers and ejectors were appointed to dismiss scandalous ministers and schoolmasters. 'Scandalous' was defined as frequenting ale-houses, playing with dice or cards, misusing the Lord's Day, associating with loose women – and using the Book of Common Prayer. Tithes were to be paid only to worthy ministers. Laws were passed against drunkenness and blasphemy.

When the first Parliament of the Protectorate eventually met, however, sweetness and light evaporated. The members refused to recognise the Instrument of Government as it had never received parliamentary approval, and they refused to implement the Protector's 84 ordinances. When Cromwell required them to swear loyalty to the Protector in Council, 90 refused and had to be purged. The rest objected to the size of the New Model Army and demanded persecution of the Independent sects. Cromwell offered to renegotiate the Instrument if four essential priorities were accepted by the MPs: government by a

KEY ISSUE

The refusal of the first Protectorate Parliament to co-operate.

single person and Parliament, Parliaments not to be perpetual, control of the New Model Army to be shared by the Protector and Parliament, and liberty of conscience. The MPs refused to accept these priorities. So Cromwell, in disgust, dissolved his first Parliament. It had been a fiasco.

The dissolution of Parliament triggered Republican and Royalist protests, the most threatening of which was Penruddock's rising in Wiltshire. Two significant points need to be grasped. First, these protests failed pathetically. Penruddock could only muster 400 followers who paraded through the streets of Salisbury before they were scattered by Lambert's troopers. Penruddock and a handful of his lieutenants were executed. Cromwell's efficient and well-informed head of security, John Thurloe, ensured that further Royalist attempts were snuffed out before they happened. Secondly, Cromwell and his Council overreacted to the threats posed by these symptoms of defiance, the reason for the Major-Generals.

It is not difficult to see why the experiment of the Major-Generals was exceedingly unpopular. First, their soldiers – 500 picked cavalrymen per district – had to be paid for by an additional tax, a 10 per cent levy on Royalists who had incomes over £100 per annum. Secondly, the interference of Cromwell's snoopers in people's private lives in the pursuit of godly reform was understandably resented. This was especially the case because there was no consistency between Major-Generals. Therefore, the energetic Charles Worsley closed over a hundred ale-houses in the Blackburn district, whereas the feeble and diffident William Gough closed none at all. Thirdly, the Major-Generals were outsiders (apart from Philip Skippon) and relatively low-born, compared with the aristocratic county officials whom they attempted to supersede. Fourthly, and most importantly, they were there, on the spot, with soldiers at their backs. Previous initiatives by bossy governments had been rendered bearable by the distance from London. But the Major-Generals were not distant at all. Defy them, and you would find them coming down on you like a ton of bricks, at once, with soldiers at their backs. This was intolerable.

The Major-Generals did not improve their popularity ratings by attempting to influence the elections for a second Parliament in September 1656. This had been necessitated by the gap between the government's income (£2,250,000) and military, naval and civil expenditure (£2,611,532). The Major-Generals actually advised Cromwell to call Parliament on the grounds that they could ensure the return of compliant members, but they failed. When Parliament met, 100 Republicans had to be excluded. Relations between the Protector and Parliament deteriorated further over the case of the Quaker, James Nayler, who rode into Bristol on a white donkey, apparently impersonating Christ's entry into Jerusalem. Parliament reflected the unanimous horror at this blasphemy by demanding the death penalty for Nayler. Cromwell held no particular brief for Nayler, but he felt that Parliament had exceeded its authority, and, as a merciful man, thought that the death penalty was too harsh. He was not very much happier with the barbaric punishments which Parliament reluctantly settled for as a

KEY ISSUE

The failure to achieve consent.

second best: Nayler was whipped, his tongue bored through with a hot iron and he was imprisoned for life. 'Reflect', the Protector urged the bigoted MPs, 'that the case of James Nayler might be your own'. It was good advice.

When Parliament rejected John Desborough's bill to renew the decimation tax which financed the Major-Generals, Cromwell let this ill-starred experiment lapse. In doing so he had a hidden agenda. He was bidding for the support of a group which Austin Woolrych has called the 'new Cromwellians', mostly civilians of moderate opinions who proposed a revised constitution. This was offered to him by Parliament – a great attraction in Cromwell's eyes. ('That which you get by force, I look upon as nothing.') He was not deterred by the obvious intention of the conservatives to limit his power, rather than increase it. The new constitution was the work of prominent lawyers such as Bulstrode Whitelocke and William Lenthall. It was supported by influential civilians such as the Irish magnate Lord Broghill and by some, though by no means all, of the senior army officers, such as George Monck. It was presented to Cromwell in March 1657.

The new constitution was called the Humble Petition and Advice. This offer to Cromwell marked a further move to the right. It was an attempt to return to the good old days when the monarch's powers were checked by the rights of Privy Council and both Houses of Parliament. The Privy Council and a second House were restored. Cromwell was invited to become king.

Cromwell agonised for more than a month as to what he should do. In the end, he accepted most of the Humble Petition but rejected the crown. Why did he turn down this immensely flattering offer, which held the supreme attraction of a final return to normality? Perhaps because it *was* so flattering, for as a modest man Cromwell was aware of the sin of pride. 'King Oliver'! Not bad for a failed Huntingdonshire businessman! But God had already expressed his dissatisfaction with Cromwell by causing the failure of the Western design. What would be the Almighty's reaction if Cromwell were now to fly in the face of Providence and accept the crown? Perhaps Cromwell was also deterred because the majority of his senior officers were against the idea, though Cromwell had outfaced them on previous occasions. Perhaps he flinched at a step which would appear to corroborate his enemies' charges of hypocrisy and ambition. Perhaps he believed that the constitutional innovations which he accepted gave him all he needed. He was even invited to nominate his successor, and could have used his prerogative powers in order to spare James Nayler. In the event Cromwell's decision disappointed his new-found civilian allies, while his dithering alarmed his radical friends in the New Model Army. In fact, he had to dismiss John Lambert from the Council for refusing to take an oath to the new constitution.

If Cromwell had hoped that his acceptance of the new constitution would improve relations with Parliament, he was disappointed. Because the Instrument of Government had now been replaced, the 90 MPs purged in September 1654 returned. They had lost nothing of their

See page 367 for Nayler's stance.

KEY ISSUE

Cromwell rejected the crown.

See page 153 for the Western design.

KEY ISSUE

Cromwell's failure to get on with Parliament.

militant republicanism. Led by Haselrig and Vane, they attacked the Humble Petition and Advice because the Protector had too much power and demanded the recall of the Rump which had been illegally expelled in April 1653. Cromwell could do nothing with them. Even though the £1,300,000 granted by the Humble Petition fell short of actual expenditure by £500,000, Cromwell decided to dissolve Parliament. His son-in-law, General Fleetwood, wept with frightened apprehension. 'Go to! You are a milksop', retorted the old man. 'Let God judge between you and me', he shouted at the departing MPs.

Cromwell was in fact depressed by his failure to get on with his Parliaments. 'I am as much for consent as any man', he lamented, 'but where shall we find that consent?' Historians have been much intrigued by this question. Hugh Trevor-Roper argued that, as an inveterate backbencher, Cromwell failed as a parliamentary manager. He could not change his spots. There is clearly something in this – more in fact than Trevor Roper's critics allow. Cromwell actually prided himself on not intervening in parliamentary debates, disingenuously assuring the Parliament of 1656 that he had no idea what they had been debating. In truth, Cromwell was not a good parliamentary tactician. He was vulnerable to the charge of political naivity and incompetence in failing to present a government programme for his Parliaments to discuss. It was inept of him to promote his ablest parliamentary debaters to the Upper House in January 1658. His speeches to Parliament – long-winded, hectoring and patently economical with the truth – are reminiscent of James I on a bad day.

Nevertheless, Trevor-Roper identifies a secondary as opposed to the primary cause of the trouble. No amount of brilliant political footwork could have concealed the fundamental problem. Cromwell, as head of state, and his Parliaments had different, indeed flatly contradictory, goals. He was not prepared to relinquish control of the New Model Army and still less to agree to its disbandment, whereas the majority of MPs wanted the Army to be reduced and its political influence abolished. And the reason why Cromwell needed the Army was because it guaranteed the toleration of the sects, which remained Cromwell's supreme aim. On this he refused to compromise.

If Cromwell's record as Protector might seem uneven, there were considerable achievements. Cromwell himself would have welcomed the argument of the Whig historian, Sir Charles Firth, that the establishment of English Nonconformity was his ultimate triumph. This was also especially the case in Wales. Cromwell practised toleration by admitting Jews and by winking at Catholic and Anglican worship. He also enjoyed friendship with the prominent Quaker, George Fox. Attempts to reform the morals of the nation were unpopular and ineffectual, but not always to be despised as killjoy snooping. More kindly treatment of lunatics, prisoners and animals for instance has much to commend it, nor can one quarrel with the attempted foundation of Durham University. The next section will detail Cromwell's undoubted achievements in foreign policy. The forging of the union between England, Scotland and Ireland was the basis for future developments

See pages 366–7 for Quakers.

such as the Act of Union (1707). Above all, Cromwell did the job. He filled the bill so far as the political community was concerned. He kept order. He ensured that the republican regime became acceptable at home, while England was respected abroad as never before in its history.

Peter Gaunt has demonstrated how impressive was Cromwell's *style*. While the 'sloven' of November 1640 had come a long way, Cromwell was not a natural showman, still less was his wife – cruelly satirised by Royalist pamphleteers as 'Queen Joan'. The undignified could become the ludicrous if good taste and restraint were abandoned. Cromwell in fact seems to have got it right. He was never ostentatious, and his own lifestyle remained modest. But when he became Protector he signed his letters 'Oliver P', he was addressed as 'Your Highness' and was treated with deference by his colleagues. A sword of state was borne before him in June 1657 and he carried a golden sceptre. He created over 30 knights, a dozen baronets and a couple of hereditary peers. There is no evidence that even hostile contemporaries found all this unconvincing or inappropriate. His demeanour was perceived to match his achievements and his personal qualities.

Was he a military dictator? He tried not to be. He consulted Parliament. His Council ran the country, so far as detailed business was concerned, since for about half the time Cromwell did not even attend Council meetings, whether due to other business or ill-health. There was no doubt, however, that Cromwell took the important decisions, for instance over foreign policy. He did not even consult his Council over his dissolutions of Parliament. Sometimes the mask slipped even more dramatically. In November 1654, the London merchant George Cony refused to pay customs on silk. Both he and his lawyers were sent to the Tower, while Chief Justice Rolle resigned rather than try the case. When Cromwell was told that nine out of ten people in the country were against him, he retorted, 'What if I should disarm the nine and put a sword in the tenth man's hand? Would not that do the business?' He knocked down Parliaments in a way no Stuart ever attempted. Levellers and Royalists were suppressed. His power rested on the New Model Army. He was a military dictator.

Cromwell, however, tried to use his power responsibly. He was relatively uncorrupted. While he had his blind spots, he remained a basically decent man. His greatest claim to be respected is his battle for the right of Protestant Christians to make their own choices without being persecuted by other Christians. 'Religion was not the thing first contested for, but God brought it to that in the end', he remarked: meaning that the civil wars ultimately were fought to defend religious toleration. 'To be a seeker is the next best sect after a finder, and such a one shall every faithful, humble seeker be in the end', was his philosophy, and he fought for the seeker's right to seek and to find.

Cromwell's health failed in the summer of 1658. He was depressed by the death from cancer of his favourite daughter, Elizabeth. He was laid low by malaria. He died during a storm on 3 September – his lucky day. Antonia Fraser plausibly suggests that Cromwell fought to prolong his failing life until that memorable date. Nothing illustrates Cromwell's

> **KEY ISSUE**
>
> *Cromwell, the military dictator.*

stature better than the collapse of the Republic after his death, to which we shall shortly turn. But there was nothing inevitable about that collapse. Who can say what would have happened if Cromwell had lived for another ten years, or if he had nominated his formidable, pushy, younger son Henry instead of his eldest, the easygoing, ineffectual Richard? But history is not concerned with might-have-beens.

Summary of the constitutions of the Interregnum

1 The Commonwealth (the Rump), 1649–53
England was a Republic, governed by a Council of State whose 41 members had been nominated by the New Model Army and were responsible to the House of Commons. There were 34 MPs on the Council. The monarchy, the Lords and the bishops had been abolished. The MPs were originally members of the Long Parliament, elected in 1640. Ireland and Scotland, both of which were rebellious in 1649, had no representation.

2 Barebones Parliament, 1653 (otherwise known as the Nominated Assembly or the Parliament of Saints)
The Army asked the Independent Churches to submit the names of members of what was originally intended to be a constituent assembly which would propose a constitution. The Army selected 140 members, who immediately declared themselves to be a Parliament. Ireland returned five members and Scotland six members – the first occasion that these areas had been represented at Westminster.

3 The Instrument of Government, 1653–7
A single chamber Parliament composed of 400 MPs from England and Wales, plus 30 each from Ireland and Scotland. Executive power held by a lord protector and a council of state. Parliament to meet at least once every three years for at least three months. Votes to men with property of at least £200 in value. Constituencies redefined to reflect distribution of population.

4 The Humble Petition and Advice, 1657–9
The offer of the crown was rejected by Cromwell, who remained Lord Protector and now could nominate his successor. The Privy Council was restored, also a second chamber of 40 members who were appointed for life by the Protector in Council. The second chamber could veto the proposals of the Lower House. Otherwise the provisions of the Instrument of Government stood.

6 ⇝ THE FOREIGN POLICY OF THE COMMONWEALTH AND THE PROTECTORATE

England cut a sorry figure at home and abroad during the first half of the seventeenth century. The ineffectual foreign policies of James I and

1651	October	The Navigation Act
1652	May	Anglo-Dutch war began
1653	July	Battle of the Texel
		Admiral Tromp killed
1654	April	Treaty of Westminster concluded the Anglo-Dutch war
1655	April–May	Failure of the Western design
		Capture of Jamaica
	October	Trade treaty with France
		War declared on Spain by Europe
1656	July	Commercial treaty with Sweden
1657	September	Stayner destroyed Spanish treasure fleet
1657	May	Blake captured Spanish treasure fleet at Santa Cruz
1658	June	Battle of the Dunes
		English occupation of Dunkirk

TABLE 11
Summary of key events, 1651–8

Charles I provoked contempt. This contempt was not wholly deserved since both kings appreciated that the Thirty Years War (1618–38), which their critics thought England could influence, was a contest between heavyweights. Since England would be outclassed, non-intervention was the correct policy. Nevertheless, it was galling for patriotic, Protestant Englishmen to have to watch helplessly the apparent destruction of European Protestantism, just as it was equally galling when in 1623 the Protestant Dutch massacred English merchants at Amboyna in the Spice Islands without any restitution.

As for Ireland and Scotland, they were simply potential jumping off places for England's continental enemies, if they could be bothered. There was the possibility during the Civil War that Charles I's European relations would support him. Indeed, Henrietta Maria persuaded her brother, Louis XIII, to consider intervention on Charles I's behalf in 1640. But nothing came of it, since Louis's Chief Minister, Cardinal Richelieu, knew a loser when he saw one. During the First Civil War, Parliament's control of the navy made it difficult for the Royalists to introduce foreign recruits, and during the Second, when part of the navy went over to the King, France was devastated by the Fronde revolt and the rest of Europe was exhausted by the Thirty Years War.

The execution of Charles I, however, and the creation of the Republic, provoked a universally hostile reaction in continental Europe. Charles II appealed to his fellow monarchs to help him recover the throne for the House of Stuart. The Republic reacted by bringing Ireland and Scotland under its direct control. Charles never managed to exploit Irish discontent, while his campaign in Scotland ended disastrously at Worcester in September 1651. The failure of these and subsequent Royalist invasions and insurrections was by no means inevitable, and resulted in part from the harrying of the Royalists by the Republic's foreign policy. Similarly, Prince Rupert's flair as a piratical admiral could have paid off had it not been for the Rump's far-sighted and intelligent construction of 40 battleships and Admiral Blake's effective leadership. Rupert was blockaded at Lisbon and his fleet dispersed.

The leaders of the Rump looked to Holland for support. The murder of their envoy, Dorylaus, was to some extent cancelled by the death of William II in November 1650 and the consequent eclipse of the pro-Stuart Orange party. Holland was Protestant. Politicians sympathetic to mercantile interests, such as St John and Strickland, feared and admired Dutch efficiency. A determined attempt was made to forge a union with Holland based on mutual economic interests leading to a Protestant crusade against Spain: but it all went wrong. Part of the problem was the Navigation Act of October 1651, which decreed that goods brought into England, Ireland or the New World colonies should be carried by English ships or ships from the country that had produced them, and that fish could only be sold in England if it had been caught by Englishmen. This Act was clearly anti-Dutch. It has been hailed as an epoch-making innovation, anticipating the future colonial system run on mercantilist lines. In sober fact it was an *ad hoc* measure to protect British naval and trading interests. Furthermore, it could not be enforced, due to the infuriating Dutch ability to do anything better that the English did: and the Dutch had far more ships.

See pages 304–7 for the results of the Navigation Act.

Attempts by the English navy to search Dutch ships and to force them to dip their flags to the Republic provoked war (May 1652 to April 1654). Despite initial victories by the Dutch Admiral Van Tromp, the English did well. Van Tromp was killed at the battle of the Texel (July 1653), Admiral Blake proved a commander of genius, and Dutch trade was devastated by the blockade of their coast. In the spring of 1654 the newly appointed Protector Cromwell and the anti-Orange Dutch burghers saw sense and agreed the Treaty of Westminster. 'You have appealed to the judgement of Heaven: the Lord has declared against you', thundered the Protector at the chastened Dutch delegates. Nevertheless, Cromwell's critics maintained that the Treaty was a sell-out. It was true that he had never liked this war against fellow Protestants and that he was already seeking to build up an anti-Spanish coalition, but it was a pity that the Dutch made no economic concessions, for example over fishing disputes. The Dutch did agree to abide by the rest of the Navigation Act, to honour the English flag, to pay compensation for Amboyna and not to harbour the Stuarts – not entirely worthless concessions.

See page 151 for Amboyna.

Whatever the terms of the treaty, contemporaries were sufficiently impressed by English victory to court the Protector. England now negotiated favourable trade agreements with Portugal, Denmark and Sweden. This was to the credit of England's ambassador, Bulstrode Whitelocke, who had established an affectionate, almost sexual relationship with the eccentric Queen Christina before she abdicated in favour of the formidable Charles X. He too, however, was glad to negotiate with England at the expense of the Dutch, whose shipping in the Baltic was now replaced by the English. The Protector was courted as well by the rival Catholic super-powers. According to an English observer, a scurrilous pamphlet published in Paris showed Cromwell sitting on his commode 'at his business with the King of Spain on the one side and the King of France on the other, offering him paper to wipe his breech'.

Cromwell chose France. Mazarin was ready to respond positively, though he had been worried about Leveller John Sexby's visit to Bordeaux in 1651 where the *ormee* revolt defied the government in Paris. A trade agreement was signed with France in October 1655, and in addition Mazarin promised to expel Royalists while Cromwell refused asylum to ex-Frondeurs. Cromwell now implemented his cherished project of a crusade against Spain.

There is some doubt as to Cromwell's direct influence over foreign policy. The documents suggest that often the whole Council was involved in decision-making. On one occasion, however, a Swedish delegation complained of delays lasting a fortnight while the Protector was too busy to see them before they were eventually fobbed off with a meeting with the Latin Secretary, 'a blind man, a Mr Milton'. But the decision to mount an expedition against Spain was certainly Cromwell's, indeed it was his pet project. There was a heated disagreement in Council when Lambert expressed totally justifiable doubts about the project's viability.

The 'Western design' was, untypically for Cromwell's projects, ineptly planned. Perhaps the explanation lies in his absurd, bigoted instructions to the expedition's leaders: 'The Lord himself hath a controversy with your enemies, even with that Romish Babylon'. But the Romish Babylon proved fully capable of repelling the badly equipped, badly led collection of jail-birds whom the Protector dispatched. The idea was to capture Hispaniola. But if the expedition was supposed to bring back the days of Drake and Hawkins, Buckingham was a better precedent. The troops ran away, caught dysentery and died like flies. The two commanders quarrelled. Admiral Penn had ability, as he was to prove on later occasions. But General Venables already had a poor track record, having been ambushed twice in the same place near Westhoughton in Lancashire during the First Civil War. He now contrived to be ambushed twice in the same place in Hispaniola. This must be a record. The remnants of the expedition abandoned Hispaniola and staggered on to the largely unoccupied island of Jamaica. Its value was not immediately apparent and it served as a poor consolation prize. Cromwell was devastated, and turned to domestic reform of manners. The nation's sins must be cleaned up, for England had clearly alienated the Almighty: 'The Lord hath mightily humbled us'.

The alliance with France, however, yielded better results. Cromwell interceded effectively on behalf of the Protestant Vaudois, whom France's ally, the King of Savoy, had been persecuting. In return for the promise of Dunkirk and Mardyke, he committed 6,000 well-equipped redcoats to fight under Turenne's leadership in Flanders. The combined Anglo-French army defeated the Spaniards in the Battle of the Dunes (June 1658). Dunkirk surrendered to Louis XIV, who immediately handed it over to the English. It was a bizarre situation. Catholic France led by Charles II's cousin and a Roman cardinal was grateful for the assistance of Protestant Republican England to whom it surrendered an invaluable channel port. Unbelievable!

In the meantime, the navy showed England's flag all over the world,

> **KEY ISSUE**
>
> *Failure in the Caribbean.*

> See pages 299–302 for the economic aspect.

blockading enemy ports, suppressing piracy and supporting English trade. English shipping teamed in the Baltic and in the Mediterranean, which was freed from the curse of piracy when Blake captured Tunis. English merchants frequented Russia, the New World, China and the East Indies, under the protection of the Republic's warships. Sea power guaranteed the failure of the Spaniards to recapture Jamaica in 1657. It enabled the government at home to re-establish control over trans-oceanic colonies. American independence could well have occurred a century earlier had it not been for the Republic's navy. Naval stores now came from America, 'to free us [sic] from dependence on Dutch-carried Baltic supplies', as Christopher Hill puts it with un-Marxist patriotism.

Are Marxist historians such as Hill right to echo the naive and arrogant enthusiam of Whig historians? Logically, Hill admires the entre-preneurial success of England's mercantile republic in establishing the first British Empire – a crucial stage in the triumph of the bourgeoisie. Recently, however, revisionist historians such as Derek Hirst and Ronald Hutton have stressed the flaws in the foreign policy of the Rump and the Protectorate. For one thing it did not pay its way. Although in September 1656 Captain Richard Stayner destroyed Spanish ships containing £700,000, £200,000, of which was brought from Portsmouth to London in 38 wagons, and Blake captured an even larger fleet in May 1657, the cost of building battleships was ruinous and the various overseas expeditions beggared the Treasury. Cromwell made Sweden too powerful in the Baltic from Britain's point of view, and he helped to set up Louis XIV's domination of Europe. The Western design was an abysmal fiasco. If Cromwell hoped to lead a Protestant crusade against Spain, he failed. Clarendon's oft-quoted compliment to Cromwell – that his greatness at home was but a shadow of the glory he had abroad – and the various nostalgic references made by latter-day patriots, reflected disillusionment with Charles II's foreign policy rather than an accurate appraisal of Cromwell's. Clarendon in particular may have been influenced by the fact that his own disgrace was foreign-policy led.

An assessment of the foreign policy of the Interregnum to a great extent depends on what kind of a patriot you are. If you like to see Britain 'great' and respected by other powers, you have to be impressed by the acquisition of Jamaica, St Helena, Pulo Run, Surinam, Dunkirk, Nova Scotia and New Brunswick. You will enthuse about the establish-ment of British sea-power, and naval and military victories over the Dutch and the Spanish. Whereas England had been humiliated with impunity by European powers during the reigns of the first Stuarts, now it was respected and its alliance was widely sought. Whereas in 1633 England had an ambassador at Constantinople and nowhere else, in the 1650s English diplomacy operated on a world scale. The sheer scope of Cromwell's vision is breathtaking. Hill has a good case when he argues that during the Interregnum, London became the centre of world trade, that the foundations were laid for the eighteenth- and nineteenth-century British empires based on British industry and agriculture, and

KEY ISSUE

The case for and against the foreign policy of the Interregnum.

The collapse of the Republic, 1658–60

that British sea-power enabled British entrepreneurs to exploit colonial trade to the benefit of themselves and the mother country.

If you regard all this as foolish or deplorable, as in neither Britain's nor anyone else's true interests, you will not be impressed by the foreign policies of the Commonwealth and the Protectorate. One particular point should be stressed. The greatest source of British profit in the eighteenth century was the slave trade, which was already thriving in the seventeenth century. Cromwell's acquisition of Jamaica soon became the central supply depot of the New World's slave plantations, both in the islands and on the American continent. London and Bristol thrived on this trade. 'Every brick is cemented by the blood of a slave', was said about Liverpool. This is a dreadful story. Did *any* seventeenth century writer or thinker – apart from Aphra Behn – protest?

> **KEY ISSUE**
>
> *British involvement in the slave trade.*

> See pages 301–2 for the slave trade.

7 ⌐ THE COLLAPSE OF THE REPUBLIC, 1658–60

'Oliver Cromwell ruled England from his urn', remarked a contemporary. It was indeed the case that Richard Cromwell succeeded without protest, the New Model Army expressed its loyalty, European rulers acknowledged the new Protector and indeed the French court went into mourning. But 'Tumble-down Dick' or 'Queen Dick' had inherited few of his father's qualities. Amiable and well-meaning, he simply did not have the personal clout to dominate the scheming Army officers who quickly exploited his good nature, and despite some civilian support, he did not have the skill to tackle the truly horrendous problems which faced the new regime.

> **KEY ISSUE**
>
> *The failure of Richard Cromwell.*

The country seethed with rivalries and conflicts: the Army versus civilians, Republicans versus conservatives, Presbyterians versus sectaries. A trade recession added to a series of bad harvests to drive up prices and create a food shortage. The Army clamoured for its pay, £900,000 in arrears in January 1659, while the Protectorate's debt amounted to a staggering £2.5 million. Clearly, the recall of Parliament was unavoidable. But no help came from that quarter. Sir Arthur Haselrig crowned a dazzling career of obstruction by torpedoing every attempt at a settlement until he was finally silenced by the return of Charles II. Haselrig's Republicans insisted on the Council of Officers sitting only with Parliament's approval and handing over the local militia to Parliament. The Council of Officers held a prayer meeting, an ominous sign, and ordered the Protector to dissolve Parliament and recall the Rump. Richard complied, and when the Rump restored the Commonwealth in May 1659, Richard abdicated. His final comment does him credit: 'I will not have a drop of blood shed for my greatness which is a burden to me.'

There now followed a year of anarchy, which can only be understood if the sequence of events is grasped and if four overriding factors are borne in mind. First was the dread of violence and 'overturning'. Episodes such as 'the great fear' of autumn 1659 illustrate this factor, as

TABLE 12
Summary of key events, 1658–60

1	September 1658 to May 1659	The Protectorate of Richard Cromwell
	January–April 1659	The Third Protectorate Parliament
2	May 1659 to February 1660	The restored Commonwealth
	May–October	The Rump recalled
	May	Abdication of Richard Cromwell
	August	Booth's rising in Cheshire suppressed by Lambert
	October	Lambert dissolved the Rump and established a Committee of Safety
	December 1659 to February 1660	The Rump recalled – again
	January–February	Monck's march on London
3	February–March	The Long Parliament restored – and dissolved itself
4	April–May	The Convention Parliament
	April	Publication of the Declaration of Breda
	May	The return of Charles II

does the obsession with the Quakers who had not yet acquired their pacifist, idealistic reputation. Secondly, there was a widespread desire for a return to normality and an end to sword government. Thirdly, there was hardly any overt royalism. Fourthly, the New Model Army was still the key to the situation: it could still dictate events – as long as it remained united.

The Rump proved totally incapable of rising to the occasion. Its appoinment of General Charles Fleetwood as commander-in-chief was a mistake. The 'milksop' commanded little respect from his fellow officers, 'his tendency to weep in public being considered unbecoming in a cavalry officer' (David Ogg). Radicals and conservatives were equally disillusioned, and a national panic ensued. Royalists attempted to exploit a seemingly promising situation. Sir George Booth led a rising in Cheshire that looked threatening until it was smashed by General Lambert. The New Model Army still had its teeth. Lambert, who was now understandably on a high, lent his authority to an Army petition demanding that the Rump's authority be controlled by a second House. Sir Arthur Haselrig responded by proposing that Lambert and his petitioners should be dismissed and jailed. But it was not to be. In October, Lambert occupied London and dissolved the Rump.

There now occurred an event of incalculable importance. The commander-in-chief in Scotland, George Monck, protested at the high-handed actions of his military colleagues in London. So the New Model Army was no longer united! In vain, Lambert and his paladins set up a Committee of Safety containing a few cardboard cut-out civilians to conceal military dictatorship. The officers could shrug off the petitions that flooded in from all over the country demanding a 'free Parliament' and an end to military rule, but they could not shrug off George Monck. When they sent Lambert north to negotiate, his troops melted away. The Army Council realised that the game was up, disbanded the Committee of Safety and recalled the Rump, yet again.

Meanwhile, Monck had decided to clear up the mess in London. On New Year's day he crossed the Tweed at Coldstream (hence the Coldstream Guards). As Monck marched south, he was inundated with petitions to 'restore Parliament'. At Marston Moor he met Fairfax who emerged from retirement to support a conservative settlement, whatever that might entail. Monck kept his cards close to his chest, continued south and entered London to a cautious welcome. Inspired by Haselrig, the Rump attempted to purge the Army's high command and officiously told Monck to control the volatile capital. Monck, however, was standing no nonsense from Haselrig and recalled all the surviving members who had been excluded since Pride's purge. Old campaigners such as the de-eared Prynne re-emerged. In fact, Prynne – the rhinoceros in blinkers – for once charged in the right direction by proposing that the militia should be entrusted to known Royalists. The Long Parliament now had the necessary virility to implement the Act of 1641 and dissolve itself.

Writs were issued for a new Parliament, which met in April. This was the Convention Parliament, so-called because it had not been summoned by royal writ. There was still no commitment to a restoration of the monarchy. There was a considerable Presbyterian element among the MPs and while one of the sermons was preached by the Royalist Dr Gauden, the other came from Richard Baxter, ex-New Model Army. Monck, however, seems to have made his mind up that the King's return was the only practical way to restore stability. He was in touch with Charles II who was still in exile at the Dutch town of Breda. Monck advised Charles to issue a statement of his intentions. Edward Hyde responded by drafting for Charles's signature the Declaration of Breda, which Monck duly put before the two Houses of Parliament.

The Declaration of Breda was a clever document. On Hyde's advice Charles promised a general pardon and religious toleration. He referred the contentious issues of the Army's pay arrears and the question of land ownership to Parliament. The land issue in particular was bound to cause anguish. Would Royalists who had sold all to support their king or who had been victimised by Parliament get their estates back? What would happen if property had changed hands several times? Difficult! Charles passed the problem over to Parliament, therefore neatly side-stepping the inevitable blame.

Having accepted the Declaration, on 8 May Parliament declared England to be no longer a republic, government again residing in King, Lords and Commons. On 14 May parliamentary delegates invited Charles II to return to reign. On 26 May Charles landed at Dover, greeted Monck as 'Father' and made him a duke. He received a Bible from the Mayor, which he declared to be the most precious thing in his life. On 29 May, his thirtieth birthday, Charles entered London to universal acclaim. The streets were full of flowers, the balconies crowded with women and the fountains ran with wine.

Whose fault was it that the Republic had fallen? This question no doubt exercised the minds of those to whom the Restoration brought grief and disaster since Charles II was unable to keep the promises of pardon set out in the Declaration of Breda. Not only was it a matter of personal tragedy for regicides and pseudo-regicides such as Vane, but the sects were persecuted, the navy was humiliated by the Dutch, and sleaze returned to Whitehall. The Republic was dead and buried. What had gone wrong? It is not necessary to be a republican to see the importance of this question.

The most obvious explanation is political. The search for a constitution ended in failure. Arguably it could never have succeeded from the moment that the King's head was severed. Because this legalised murder was committed by a tiny clique, its perpetrators could never face a free electorate. As long as they relied on the Army, consent was out of the question. There was no way to square this circle. Even so, historians should beware of inevitability. Time might have healed if Cromwell had lived or if his heirs had remained united. But they quarrelled once the unifying presence of Oliver P had gone. This was the crucial flaw in the Republic's armour. Politicians and soldiers had respected Cromwell however much they might have disagreed with him and with each other. Now they quarrelled. Furthermore, the generals fell out among themselves – the ambitious Lambert versus the tearful Fleetwood versus the inscrutable Monck – and, as a contemporary remarked, 'the soldiers say that they will form a ring in which their officers can fight'. For in the last months of its life the New Model Army was no longer a band of brothers. Officers exploited their men by buying up the debentures (or IOUs) with which they had been paid – and then cashing them in at a profit. This explains why Lambert's troops would not follow him, whereas Monck paid his men in full.

How important was the appeal of monarchy? What about Charles II's raptuous reception? On their way north in 1650, when Cromwell and Lambert were applauded, Lambert remarked to Cromwell how gratifying it was to be so popular. 'These very persons would shout as much if you and I were going to be hanged', replied the great realist. This would have been fair comment on the euphoria of 1660. Undoubtedly there was widespread disillusion with the expense of military rule and impatience with Cromwell's campaign to improve morals. It was believed that the King – uniquely qualified as he was to restore phallic maypoles – would banish both swordsmen and snoopers. Still, the failure of Royalist revolts was undeniable up to and including Booth's fiasco in August 1659.

By the same token, however, Puritan idealism had much diminished. In 1650, Ireton refused a parliamentary gift of £2,000 a year because others were more deserving of the State's generosity – 'And truly, I think he was in earnest!' (Ludlow). Contemporaries noted with amusement how concerned 'saintly' officers such as Major-General Berry, Colonel Barkstead and Colonel Pride had become about their salaries and plush residences. By 1658 'The Good Old Cause' had few defenders. Few now shared the enthusiasm of the regicide Major-General Harrison who was heckled on his way to the scaffold – 'Where is your Good Old Cause now?' 'Here', he replied, clapping his hand to his heart, 'and I will seal it with my blood.' But Harrison's generation who had tasted the exhilaration of Marston Moor and Preston were long gone or had joined the establishment, like Monck and Holles. So the Good Old Cause was abandoned or sold by politicians such as Haselrig, Vane and Prynne, and generals like Fleetwood and Lambert who should have known better. 'Saints' such as Richard Baxter were deluded by Charles II's promise of toleration. All in all it was as though the defenders of the revolution gave up without a fight, displaying far less political sense than Charles and his advisers, and a sad lack of backbone. Milton was right to dread 'the perpetual bowings and cringings of an abject people' should monarchy be restored. The 'Saints' *should not* have been so feeble!

On the other hand, the well-born and the well-heeled knew exactly what they were doing. They had worked out where their best interests lay. They realised how much they had to gain from the restoration of the monarchy. For back with the King would come lords, bishops and squires. The Restoration marked the triumph of the gentry who, as a contemporary observed, 'restored the king not out of love for him but out of love for themselves'. When they extracted a 'free Parliament', they knew that that meant 'a Parliament of the free', and freedom meant privilege. This is the chief reason for the fall of the Republic.

GEORGE MONCK, 1608–70

Monck came from an aristocratic Devonshire background. In his youth he accidentally killed a man and ran away to become a soldier of fortune in the Thirty Years War. He returned to the King's army in Ireland, fought for Charles I in the English Civil War and was captured and imprisoned in 1644, after which, like many in such a predicament, he changed sides. Parliament sent him back to Ireland where he distinguished himself, and then to Scotland. After two successful years as a sailor in the Dutch war, he returned to military service in Scotland. He played a crucial role in restoring Charles II, for which he was made Duke of Albemarle and Lord Lieutenant of Ireland. In 1665, he shared command of the fleet with Prince Rupert.

Monck is an elusive character. He was proverbially taciturn, and did not believe in giving himself away. His portraits show a coarse though humourous face and a portly frame, which suggests much good living. He was fond of saying that as a soldier he believed in obedience. His skill lay in spotting whom it was prudent to obey. But he was no cynical turn-coat. Cromwell respected him. He had the nation's welfare at heart when he intervened in early 1660, however well he came out of it himself. With his distinguished service in all three kingdoms he effectively represents the *British* dimension in the events of 1640–60.

PICTURE 18
A portrait of George Monck by Lely

Monck's wife was the victim of unkind gossip because she was plebeian. Aubrey's account of the background to the marriage throws light on Monck's low-key personality. (Aubrey was a contemporary of Monck.)

In 1644 he was prisoner in the Tower, where his seamstress, Nan Clarges (a blacksmith's daughter) was kind to him; in a double capacity. It must be remembered that he was then in want, and she assisted him. Here she was got with child. She was not at all handsome or cleanly. Her mother was one of the five women barbers. Her brother Thomas Clarges came on shipboard to G.M. and told him his sister was brought to bed. 'Of what?' said he. 'Of a son'. 'Why then,' said he, 'she is my wife.' He had only this child.

HISTORIANS' DEBATE

See pages 372–3 for intellectual and religious aspect of the English Revolution.

The 'English Revolution'

When late seventeenth-century people referred to 'the Revolution', they meant the political coup of 1688. But then 'revolution' for them meant the opposite to its modern usage; for them it meant a return to the previous state of affairs. Nowadays revolution means 'a radical alteration of the status quo'. If that definition is accepted, clearly the period between 1640 and 1660 is a promising candidate. But contemporaries used expressions such as 'the years of shaking', while Clarendon referred to 'The Rebellion'.

The modern understanding of the word 'revolution' dates back to the French Revolution of 1789–99. Since then historians have applied it to the period 1640–60 in British history. S.R. Gardiner thought that there was a Puritan Revolution, identifying Puritanism as the driving force behind the radicals. G.M. Trevelyan produced the classic Whig interpretation, claiming that because of their idealism the leaders of the English Revolution were nobler than the French revolutionaries. Christopher Hill sees the Revolution in Marxist terms, but he argues for the widest application of 'revolution'. His *The Century of Revolution, 1603–1714* is appropriately named. In his Introduction he writes: 'The transformation that took place in the seventeenth century is then far more than merely a constitutional or political revolution, or a revolution in economics, religion, or taste. It embraces the whole of life. Two conceptions of civilisation were in conflict. One took French absolutism for its model, the other the Dutch Republic'.

Historians disagree on when the 'English Revolution' occurred. Mark Kishlansky argues that the execution of the King on 30 January 1649 inaugurated the Revolution – 'The English Revolution was born of the axe'. Trevelyan too emphasises this watershed, calling the constitutional experiments of the Interregnum 'the Revolutionary governments'. Martyn Bennett (*The English Civil War*, Addison Wesley Longman, 1995) identifies three revolutions: 1639–41 in

Scotland, 1640–1 in England; and 1648–9. David Underdown *(A Free-born People*, OUP, 1995) goes for 1642–9 and claims that it was a revolution that failed: 'Any explanation of why a revolution (under some definition of the term) occurred between 1642 and 1649 gives us little help when we go on to ask why that revolution failed and there was a Restoration in 1660'. John Adamson believes that there was a revolution all right, but it only lasted for a few weeks (December 1648 to March 1649).

Revisionist historians, however, deny that a revolution occurred at all. Conrad Russell questions both the revolutionary nature of events between 1640 and 1660 and of the intentions of the chief participants. He stresses the role of coincidence and confusion in the developments which led to civil war. A recent collection of his essays is significantly entitled *Unrevolutionary England*. J.C.D. Clarke is unimpressed by the political achievements of both the mid-century 'Revolution' and the 'Glorious Revolution' of 1688–9. He is impressed by the power of the Crown in the eighteenth century, arguing that the real English Revolution did not happen until 1832. 'The rebellion of the 1640s delayed the rise of the English monarchy, but failed to stop it', he maintains. While he allows that changes occurred in the seventeenth century, he disagrees with historians such as Hill and Kishlansky who believe that it was special. Why should the seventeenth century be more 'important' in British history than the sixteenth or the eighteenth? And if there was indeed some significant change, Clark reckons that, 'at local level, too, it was not the Civil War but the 'Exclusion Crisis' and the 'Glorious Revolution' which fundamentally altered the issues and the alignments'.

The student has a wide choice. 'A century of Revolution' perhaps goes too far. The conservative rather than the revolutionary nature of Puritanism is now stressed. Many, however, will agree with Barry Coward that 'it is surely semantic quibbling to deny the unique revolutionary nature of the abolition of episcopacy, monarchy, and the House of Lords, the involvement in politics of masses of people from outside the normal political sphere, and the ventilation of radical ideas of universal importance in the late 1640s'. It seems perverse to deny that the dramatic and traumatic events of the period 1640–60 constituted a revolution, though it was a revolution that began to be reversed from 1649 onwards. Was it a revolution that failed? This is a hard question. The Restoration settlement, detailed in the next chapter, certainly restored a persecuting Anglican Church, a monarchy with considerable executive power and a squirearchy that dominated the localities – hardly the aims of the English revolutionaries. But in other respects – the economy, the sciences, philosophy and political thought – the advances made during the English Revolution proved permanent. The Church, Crown and gentry were not unscathed – how could they be? What had happened could not be erased from people's minds as if they had never happened. So perhaps *something* had been achieved!

8 ∽ BIBLIOGRAPHY

The Interregnum 1649–60 by Michael Lynch (Hodder and Stoughton, Access to History series, 1994) is absolutely first-rate: clear, readable and up-to-date. *The British Republic 1649–60* by Ronald Hutton (Macmillan, 1990) is a lively treatment, emphasising the British dimension. *Inventing a Republic* by Sean Kelsey (Manchester University Press, 1997) explains how seriously the Rumpers took themselves. *The Century of Revolution, 1603–1714* by Christopher Hill (Nelson, 1961) provides a marvellously stimulating and provocative analysis of the Interregnum. There are several interesting biographies of Cromwell: *Oliver Cromwell* by Pauline Gregg (Dent, 1988); *Oliver Cromwell* by Barry Coward (Longman, 1991); *God's Englishman: Oliver Cromwell and the English Revolution* by Christopher Hill (Weidenfeld and Nicholson, 1970); and *Our Chief of Men* by Antonia Fraser (Collins, 1978). *The Stuart Constitution* by J.P. Kenyon (Cambridge University Press, 1966) is a useful collection of documents, with helpful commentary.

9 ∽ DISCUSSION POINTS AND ESSAY QUESTIONS

A *This section consists of questions that might be used for discussion (or written answers) as a way of expanding on the chapter and testing understanding of it.*

1. How do you explain the failure of the Rump to command loyalty and respect?
2. Was the Interregnum a 'sterile aberration'?
3. How close was the relationship between religious and political radicalism?
4. 'A brave bad man.' Do you agree with Clarendon's description of Cromwell?
5. 'Where shall we find that consent?' Why was Cromwell unable to do so?
6. How successful was the foreign policy of the governments of the Interregnum?
7. Why did the Republic collapse after Cromwell's death?

B *This section suggests two ways in which you might compare the Interregnum with other seventeenth-century regimes*

1. Is it fair to contrast the alleged contempt in which England was held under the first two Stuarts by foreign governments with Britain's high reputation during the Interregnum?
2. Compare the religious and intellectual freedom achieved by the governments of the Interregnum with the intolerance of governments before and after.

C *Writing discussion essays.*

On pages xi–xii you were introduced to different types of essays. In this section, we will examine discussion or 'yes/no' questions. In these you will very often be presented with a statement in quotation marks, followed by the words 'Discuss', 'Comment', or 'Do you agree?' Sometimes the wording and format are different, but this question type can logically be answered by the words 'yes' or 'no'. 'Yes' or 'No' questions are often asked.

Consider the following question:

'No human being who ever lived could have made a permanent settlement out of the situation left by King and Parliament in 1648' (G.M. Trevelyan). Do you agree?

INTRODUCTION

This is a clear 'yes' or 'no' question. But it is not completely straightforward. You cannot simply say 'Yes, I agree', and pass on to the next question. If it was that straightforward, the examiners would not ask you to consider Trevelyan's proposition. In the introduction it is essential to show the examiner that you understand why this is a good question. While there is no perfect introduction, a sensible approach would be to explain the point of Trevelyan's remark. What else could be done with the King except kill him? Having killed him, none of his enemies, not even Cromwell, could achieve a permanent settlement. In other words, the failure of the Republic and the restoration of monarchy were inevitable. You would impress the examiner if you could remember that Trevelyan was a Whig historian and therefore likely to favour Cromwell. The failure to achieve a stable regime in the 1650s was especially Cromwell's failure. Is it really true that he was attempting the impossible? Is Trevelyan too kind to Cromwell? Was Cromwell's failure really his own fault?

DEVELOPMENT

Use paragraphs to marshal your arguments in favour of the quotation and against. Your key sentences should indicate the line that you intend to take in the paragraph, and should refer back to the question. Possible key sentences might be: 'The case for killing the King amounted to "cruel necessity" '; 'The majority opinion among the political community that the execution of Charles I was wrong meant that no government could rule by consent'; 'Indeed, the never-ceasing attempts by Cromwell to achieve a permanent settlement suggest that he was attempting the impossible'; 'Furthermore, the association of monarchy with stability meant that only the Restoration could ultimately achieve political permanency' (note the use of appropriate connectors). Then argue against the quotation: 'On the other hand, nothing in history is inevitable, for Trevelyan is indulging in "might have beens" '; 'As a matter of fact, Cromwell can be shown to have made identifiable mistakes, such as the expulsion of the Rump to say nothing of the execution of the King, which doomed his attempts to achieve consent'; 'Indeed, Cromwell's most admirable beliefs wrecked the possibility of consent, namely his passion for religious toleration – which virtually no-one else shared'.

CONCLUSION

This is the kind of essay where you can argue either way – and achieve an A grade. There really is a good case for and against Trevelyan. The essential thing is to come down on one side or the other – 'yes' or 'no'. Leave the examiner in no doubt. It is good tactics to introduce new ideas into your conclusion so that it is not too repetitive, but the ideas must not be too disruptive of your arguments. For instance, you might throw in the thought that Trevelyan is not necessarily correct to imply that the execution of the King was inescapable.

Even so, given that it happened, was there a chance of stability? What if Cromwell had remained loyal to the Republic? What if he had accepted the crown? Arguably the situation when he died would have been unaltered. 'Queen Dick' would not have been any more capable of swinging it as 'Richard IV' as he was as 'Richard P'. On the other hand, the House of Cromwell might have been just as successful as many other usurping Houses in European history. We shall never know.

10 ∽ DOCUMENTARY EXERCISE ON OLIVER CROMWELL'S REJECTION OF THE CROWN

Study sources A to F and attempt the questions that follow.

A Cromwell to Bulstrode Whitelock, April 1650.

What if a man should take upon himself to be king?

B Cromwell to the first Protectorate Parliament, September 1654.

There are some things that are fundamental and some that are not. Government by a single person is a fundamental. As for who the person should be, even if I seem to plead for myself, I do not.

C Anthony Morgan, MP, to Henry Cromwell in Ireland, February 1657.

Sir Christopher Packe offered this paper to the House [offering Cromwell the crown]. Many opposed him, but upon the question whether it should be read or not the House divided: 144 were for it, 54 against it. General Lambert is violently against it. All the lawyers are keenly for it. The Irish all for it except three. All the Yorkshire-men are against it except Charles Howard.

D Cromwell's speech to the Commons Committee, April 1657.

You do necessitate my answer to be categorical, and you leave me without liberty of choice save as to all. I must needs say, that which may be fit for you to offer, may not be fit for me to undertake. I have not been able to find it my duty to God and you to undertake this charge ... I tell you that there are such men in this nation that are godly. I cannot think that God would bless me in the undertaking of anything that would justly and with cause grieve them. I would not seek to set up that which providence hath destroyed and laid in the dust, and I would not build Jericho again.

E From *History of the Great Rebellion* by Clarendon (1669).

There is no question that the man was in great agony, and in his own mind heartily desired to be king, thinking it the only way to be safe. The answer from some principal noblemen was that if he would make himself king they should easily know what they had to do, but they knew nothing of the submission and obedience which they were to pay to a Protector.

F From *A Monarchy Transformed* by Mark Kishlansky (1996).

At first, Cromwell hesitated. Though he had no desire to be king in name, he knew that he would be king in fact. He had apparently set his mind to agreeing when a number of senior army officers informed him that they would not serve a monarch. In the end he chose loyalty to his comrades-in-arms. He averted a crisis by persuading Parliament to decouple the crown from the constitutional reforms.

Q

1. *Using sources C, D, E and F, explain who you think was in favour of offering Cromwell the crown and who was against. (5 marks)*
2. *How do you explain the disagreement between sources E and F as to whether Cromwell himself wanted the crown? (4 marks)*
3. *From your study of sources A, B and D, what would you say was Cromwell's attitude to taking the crown? (9 marks)*
4. *Compare the usefulness to the historian of these six sources in understanding this episode. (7 marks)*

This is a typical document question in that success can, to a great extent, be achieved by reading the documents carefully. If you are allowed, say, 45 minutes, spend ten minutes reading the documents in order to understand them fully. For instance, source D is crucial to answering question 3. But Cromwell's tortured, involved oratorical style is not easy to understand. You must wrestle with it. Clearly you have to take into account the background of the authors of these sources in assessing their reliability and usefulness to the historian. Can you trust Cromwell? Many would answer 'no'.

6

The Restoration of the Monarchy 1660–88

INTRODUCTION

Exit Respublica, never to return? Certainly not for a long time, if ever. The pass was surrendered, the 'Good Old Cause' sold down the river; for the King was restored on outrageously generous terms. While the reforms of the Long Parliament up to and including those of the summer of 1641 remained on the statute book, all the innovations thereafter were scrapped. It was as though civil war, regicide and the Republic had never been. Or was it? This chapter explores the way that king and political community exploited the strangely ambiguous political settlement that was cobbled together in 1660–1. However favourable the conditions on which Charles II returned, it is never possible to turn the clock back. As Charles himself remarked, he was determined not to travel again – just as he perceptively remarked to his ungifted sibling, James, Duke of York, 'Brother, I fear you will travel'. In the same way, politicians and the political community were ineradicably affected, scarred or inspired by 'the years of shaking'. The legacy of those years will now be explored.

1 ⌐ THE RESTORATION SETTLEMENT

A *The King's Return*

Charles's skilfully drawn up Declaration of Breda of 4 April 1660 truly had something for everyone: an undertaking to meet the New Model Army's arrears of pay, an indemnity for all, bar a few irreconcilable regicides to be identified by Parliament, a religious settlement that pledged 'liberty to tender consciences' and a just settlement of the land issue. The Convention Parliament, approximately half of whose members were Royalists, assembled on 25 April and accepted the Declaration on 1 May. The contentious matters addressed by Charles at Breda would be referred to Parliament, as would the questions that had not been mentioned at Breda, such as the issue of Charles's powers as king. When Charles was formally proclaimed in London and invited to return, the ambitious rushed to seek places and favours. The only obstacle to Charles's immediate return was contrary winds in the North Sea.

When the King landed at Dover on 26 May from the *Naseby*, which had hastily and appropriately been renamed the *Royal Charles*, he began a triumphal progress towards London. During his brief sojourn at Canterbury, the Book of Common Prayer was used for the first time since 1645, and his arrival in the capital was greeted by scenes of frenzied rejoicing. The diarist John Evelyn was moved to write, 'I stood in the Strand, and beheld it, and blessed God'. As the King contemplated his fervent welcome, he no doubt reflected on the expectations which his return had aroused, and on the immediate problems that he had to tackle: his constitutional powers, the religious issue (including a possible accommodation between Anglicans and Presbyterians), the land question, the armed forces – especially the New Model Army – and an amnesty for former opponents. For the moment, Charles vowed not to go on his travels again, and remarked that it was his fault that he had been away for so long.

KEY ISSUE

What immediate problems faced Charles II?

B *The Restoration Settlement and the Convention Parliament*

This last task was dealt with first by the Convention Parliament, since without an indemnity, treason charges were still possible, and the New Model Army could not be disbanded without a pardon. The Declaration of Breda had promised a general pardon, with Parliament to decide on exclusions, but many Royalists – well represented in the Convention – wanted revenge against regicides and others.

Charles assented to the eventual bill (for 'Pardon, Indemnity and Oblivion') on 29 August 1660. Apart from 30 exclusions, it extended a general indemnity for all offences committed since 1637, but it could not prevent excesses of vengeance being carried out against those who were already dead. The bodies of Cromwell, Ireton, Bradshaw, Blake and others were exhumed, mutilated and displayed. Cromwell's head was in fact exposed for 25 years outside Westminster Hall, before finding its way to the chapel wall at Sidney Sussex College, Cambridge. Despite this, the Act does seem to have been a genuine and successful attempt to bind up the nation's wounds after the Interregnum, for only a third of the exempted candidates eventually suffered the death penalty, and no cult of martyrdom seemed to emerge around them. The case of the unrepentant Republican, Sir Henry Vane, hounded to his execution by Charles himself, was exceptional. Otherwise, a relatively lenient and sensitive settlement of this issue reconciled many former Republicans to Charles II.

See page 380 for the Act of Indemnity in operation.

See page 137 for Vane's opposition to Cromwell in April 1653.

Next for consideration came the question of a land settlement. This was to be a more complicated matter, as there were three broad kinds of land changes during the Interregnum, amounting to the greatest shift in land ownership since Henry VIII's dissolution of the monasteries in the 1530s. The first category was the diocesan lands sold off, often to former leaseholders, following the abolition of bishops, deans and

KEY ISSUE

The question of former royal or Church land had to be faced.

chapters in 1646. The second embraced lands confiscated from Royalists and Roman Catholics and subsequently leased or sold, although many former owners had managed to recover their lands by 1660. The third category was Crown estates sold off after the abolition of the monarchy, and often bought by members of the New Model Army.

The land issue presented Charles and Parliament with a dilemma. Former landholders had high expectations of recovering their property, while the King was anxious not to upset powerful groups which had done well out of the past 18 years: soldiers, Presbyterian politicians, city merchants, businessmen and tenants. The total rental value of the disputed lands exceeded £6 million a year, and when Parliament failed to agree on the matter, Charles set up a Commission of Sales in October 1660 to fix terms of compensation for existing owners of ex-Church land, although some ecclesiastical owners had also begun to recover possession and to grant new leases. However, Royalists and Catholics often found redress more difficult, being compelled to rely on the courts. Yet if they could show that their lands had been confiscated rather than surrendered voluntarily, they enjoyed greater success. This impression is confirmed by Joan Thirsk's research, which concluded that 70 per cent of land taken in the south-east was restored: 45 out of 179 properties pre-1660 and 81 afterwards.

It seems reasonable to conclude that most Royalist families with lands at risk in the 1640s and 1650s retrieved most of their lands in the 1660s – if they had not already done so before through intermediaries, or by mortgaging at the favourable rate of 6 per cent set in 1651. A few disillusioned Royalists nonetheless lost heavily, particularly those lesser gentry whose loyalty to the monarchy led to them suffering fines, high taxes, billeting of troops, plunder and rent arrears from their tenants. While Charles II was personally generous to some hard-pressed Cavaliers, the disenchantment of a few may have contributed to a weakening of loyalty to the King and the Court later in the reign.

KEY ISSUE

Did the land settlement satisfy anybody?

The third immediate problem was that of the New Model Army, which, together with the navy, amounted to 40,000 men. Many political and religious radicals remained in uniform, and they were costly to maintain, yet Charles had promised at Breda to settle arrears of pay and to re-engage. At Charles's and Monck's urging, the troops were paid off by monthly instalments, and garrisons were reduced to 1637 levels. Gradually the New Model Army's personnel were reabsorbed into civilian life, but the vexed question remained of how to replace it in a persisting atmosphere of insecurity.

The Convention's achievements in religion were less impressive, mainly because of the intractable problems left by 20 years of religious upheaval. The familiar institutions stemming from the Elizabethan Church Settlement of 1559 had collapsed – episcopacy, convocation, the Court of High Commission, had all disappeared during the Interregnum, and in their place had arisen a Presbyterian form of ecclesiastical organisation and a welter of radical sects – Independents, Baptists, Quakers and others – to challenge the idea of a national and inclusive Church. The Declaration of Breda had expressed the pious hope that religious differences could be overcome and that liberty of conscience could be established, but there seemed to be little agreement about the nature and organisation of a State Church, or about what should happen to those who chose to remain outside it. In other words, how far could a new structure be comprehensive and indulgent? The Convention's one contribution to religious settlement was to reinstate Anglican ministers dispossessed and ejected during the 1640s and 1650s, provided that they compensated those whom they supplanted. Roughly 700 out of 9,000 parishes suffered some disruption as a result. Parliament adjourned in September 1660, having agreed to call a conference of learned divines at Worcester House, the London home of Edward Hyde, Earl of Clarendon and Charles's Lord Chancellor, to settle the outstanding issues.

The Conference published its declaration on 25 October 1660, recommending a single Protestant Church to guard against 'popery', with diocesan and suffragan bishops and rural deans, co-existing with synods and presbyters; this had the effect of 'reducing' episcopacy and mingling the traditional Anglican ecclesiastical organisation with Presbyterian arrangements. Indeed, a number of bishoprics were offered to leading Presbyterians, although most of Charles's early episcopal appointments were staunchly Anglican. On the other hand, revisions of the Book of Common Prayer were referred to a synod, containing equal numbers of Anglicans and Presbyterians, to meet in the spring of 1661. The difficult question of what to do about sectaries, or for that matter Roman Catholics, was deferred to the next Parliament. With a rudimentary militia in place and a grant of the excise to the King, Charles dissolved the Convention on 29 December 1660. He hoped that a new Parliament, elected at his command, would be seen as more obviously legal, and would be predominantly Royalist. The Convention nevertheless had important achievements to its credit: it had settled an indemnity, it had disbanded the Cromwellian soldiery and it had established a land settlement; however, it had not arrived at a final religious settlement, and the King's prerogative powers still remained unclear.

> **KEY ISSUE**
>
> *How far was the 1660 settlement a success?*

C *The Restoration Settlement and the Cavalier Parliament*

The Convention failed to solve the problem of Charles's penury by coming up with an absurdly low estimate of the King's fiscal needs. After a generation of argument and royal attempts at fiscal reform, the Stuarts' major weakness remained: it was more than ever impossible for a monarch to live 'of his own'. In fact, Charles had held elections in early 1661: both to affirm the coronation and to make himself financially secure, and in May 1661 a Parliament gathered that was almost too Royalist for the King's liking. When Charles asked for supply he was granted a benevolence, but his real need was to increase regular taxation. Yet the Commons' prolonged inquiries into the excise came to nothing. Finally, in November 1661, they authorised a new tax, the Hearth Tax, expected to yield £250,000 a year and assessed on the

> **KEY ISSUE**
>
> *Charles II's main need was for regular taxation income.*

KEY ISSUE

Why were royal finances still weak?

number of hearths in a household. Sadly, the new tax's yield was disappointing: in the fiscal year of 1662–3 it brought in only £87,700 just a third of the expected take, and indeed it only once raised more than £200,000 before 1678. For all its ingeniousness it was unpopular and hard to collect; while the number of hearths gave a rough indication of wealth, the gentry tended to assess each other and evaded the full rate. Royal finances remained in a parlous state, partly because of the financial ignorance of most Members of Parliament and partly because many MPs relished their financial hold over the monarch.

The most difficult problem faced by the Cavalier Parliament was, however, that of security. Persistent rumours of plots and the reality of Venner's rising in Yorkshire in January 1661 revived fears of sedition and religious extremism. However, standing armies were still unpopular – many MPs remembered all too well the activities of licentious troops during the Interregnum. The Militia Act of July 1662 placed all local militias under royal control, and gave Charles enough money to maintain his personal bodyguard for a further three years.

When the Cavalier Parliament came to debate religion, it was clear that the more tolerant mood of 1660 had changed to a more obviously Anglican one. Elected against the background of Venner's Rising, Parliament now contained far fewer Presbyterians. It proceeded to require MPs to take communion according to the Anglican rite, and ordered the public hangman to burn the Solemn League and Covenant. It went on to repeal almost all the ecclesiastical legislation of the 1640s, therefore restoring the Church courts and the bishops' position in the House of Lords – only High Commission remained abolished. In April 1661, Charles called a synod of divines to meet at the Savoy, the Bishop of Lincoln's lodgings, in order to discuss the format of the Book of Common Prayer. Here the Presbyterians were divided and an Anglican prelate who knew what he wanted, Gilbert Sheldon, forced through a Prayer Book that made few concessions to Presbyterianism. Sheldon was Bishop of London while Juxon was Archbishop of Canterbury from 1660 to 1663. He became **Primate** on Juxon's death and re-established episcopal government in the Church of England.

Parliament now moved on to pass the first of a series of Acts, misleadingly known as the Clarendon Code after the Earl of Clarendon. Not only was the Lord Chancellor not responsible for most of this legislation, he moreover opposed a good deal of it, including the first such measure, the Corporation Act of 1661. This Act required all those holding municipal office to take the oaths of allegiance and supremacy, to abjure the Solemn League and Covenant and to receive Anglican Holy Communion during the year. The second measure was the Act of Uniformity of May 1662. This draconian piece of legislation required all ministers of religion to be ordained by bishops, and to declare their conformity to the new Prayer Book and the 39 Articles by Saint Bartholomews' Day, i.e. 24 August 1662. For good measure, they were also to renounce the Solemn League and Covenant. At least 1,800 clergy failed to conform and were deprived of their livings, including almost 1,000 on the qualifying day itself, when in the 'Great Ejection' nearly

Primate the Archbishop of Canterbury.

KEY ISSUE

A persecuting Church of England.

one-third of London clergy resigned. Charles havered as long as he could (at one point claiming indisposition through gout), before he reluctantly signed the bill on 19 May 1662.

Charles had opposed the Act of Uniformity because he hoped that tolerance of Presbyterians might lead to tolerance of Catholics. Many members of his family were Catholics, and he was about to marry Catherine of Braganza, herself a Catholic. However, while it is tempting to label Charles as a Catholic himself, his precise religious views are not clear – at least in the early part of his reign. On 26 December 1662 Charles issued a Declaration of Indulgence, stating that he wished to assert the right to dispense individuals from the Act's provisions in the spirit of his remarks on tolerance in the Declaration of Breda. Indulgence could be justified as encouraging the unity of the established Church, but on the other hand the King was on dangerous ground in apparently creating a precedent that he could dispense with a law. In fact, Charles quietly withdrew the Declaration under pressure from Sheldon, but he was to use this device twice in the future.

Parliament now passed further measures against Dissenters, who were believed to be conspiring against the regime. The Quaker Act of 1662 picked on the dissenting group that was regarded as the most dangerous: they refused to subscribe to oaths, to doff their caps or to refrain from preaching equality, and they resorted to direct action to disrupt acts of worship. The Act forbade more than five Quakers to meet together, and laid down fines, imprisonment and even transportation to punish defaulters. The Conventicle Act of 1664 forbade anyone over 16 to attend a religious meeting of more than five people without the use of the Anglican prayer book and the Liturgy, while the Five Mile Act drove dissenting ministers away from their centres of urban support – especially London.

In trying to assess the religious settlement, it must be asked to what extent it restored the pre-Interregnum *status quo*. There was now once again an episcopal State Church, hostile to religious dissidence and enjoying the restoration of lands, revenues and Church courts. Moreover, in the country, lay, i.e. gentry, domination over the Church was revived and even advowsons (gentry appointments to clerical jobs) and impropriated tithes (payments made by parishioners originally to the Church) were renewed. The appeal of Anglicanism was clear: it offered order, discipline and an attachment to the Church's traditional doctrine – in short, it gave an ideology to that group in Parliament that were to become known as Tories.

Yet the established Church of the 1660s was not the Laudian Church of the 1630s with its strong Arminian influence. At least a third of the bishops sympathised with a moderate Presbyterianism, and in 1669 nine of them backed a Comprehension Bill in the Lords. In other words, something evidently survived from the 1640s and 1650s, and the effectiveness of persecution in support of the Clarendon Code was variable to say the least. Many Justices of the Peace must have followed Lord Wharton of Woburn near High Wycombe in failing to see Dissenters as a threat, and indeed Bishop Compton's census showed the

See pages 365–70 for ecclesiastic background to the persecution of Dissenters.

KEY ISSUE

Religious differences survived from the 1640s and 1650s.

KEY ISSUE

What was the appeal of Anglicanism in the 1660s?

presence of 110,000 Dissenters (i.e. five per cent of the population), concentrated more in the south and east than in the north and west, and found them both in large towns and industrial centres as well as in remote villages and upland areas. At times repression of dissent intensified, for example during the second Dutch war from 1664–6, when many converted prudently to Anglicanism before returning to their former allegiance. Finally, the bickering of the early 1660s showed that the King was in favour of toleration and comprehension – both of Dissenters and of Roman Catholics, and his Declaration of Indulgence indicated that he was prepared to insert a spanner into the religious works. The events of the last few years of the reign were to show that anti-popery, which had done much to cause and to shape the upheavals of the 1640s and the 1650s, remained a potent force.

2 ∽ CHARLES II: PERSONALITY AND PRIORITIES

PICTURE 19

Charles II in his coronation robes, by John Michael Wright. Sinister, cynical and ruthless, he took his job seriously and was determined to defend the reputation of his throne

CHARLES II 1630–85

Charles was born in 1630 and created Prince of Wales in 1639. He fled abroad after the First Civil War in 1649. He assumed the title of King of England on his father's execution in January 1649 and was proclaimed King of Scotland the following month. In Scotland, he signed the Covenant and was crowned at Scone in 1650. Defeated at Worcester he again went abroad, setting up a Cavalier court in exile. After the death of Oliver Cromwell and the intervention of General Monck, he issued the Declaration of Breda promising a moderate restoration. He returned in May 1660 to a rapturous reception, and agreed the terms of his restoration with the Convention Parliament. Now aged 30, Charles was a mature, tough and shrewd survivor – with attractive qualities: he was witty and convivial, a patron of science and learning, accommodating and resilient. His Court soon showed that the era of Puritanism was over, and the King's sexual athleticism was not universally unpopular. While he had no children with his long-suffering wife, Catherine of Braganza, he acknowledged no less than 17 bastards - four of them by Barbara Villiers (Countess of Castlemaine) alone. He claimed that he rarely had more than one mistress at any one time, and he maintained that he 'could not believe God would damn a man for taking a little pleasure by the way'.

However, Charles was also a cynic, and the only Stuart monarch to lack a long-term vision of what he wanted. His immediate aim seemed to be to survive, and he failed to support his ministers when they encountered difficulties: Charles allowed the young 'bloods' at the Court to oppose Clarendon publicly, thus undermining Clarendon's authority in the period leading up to his fall in 1667. Danby (in the 1670s) and Rochester (in the 1680s) suffered similar problems – under Charles II a beleaguered minister was on his own. The King was unlikely to fight many issues of principle out to a finish.

He gave, moreover, the impression of laziness, and this lack of concentration and application led him to miss chances. He made little effort to understand financial affairs, as profligate spending at Court kept him poor. He failed to develop effective public-speaking skills, or the ability to deal with Parliament. Yet too much could be made of this point, for two other Stuarts, his father Charles I and his younger brother James II, failed at least partly because of their determination to intervene frequently.

Finally, in his approach to religion Charles showed a strong mystical streak. He made clear his own personal attachment to the semi-divine powers of kingship by ardently resuming the practice of 'touching for the king's evil', i.e. touching the victims of the skin complaint scrofula, or allowing them to touch him. No king touched so much. He was also, as we know, strongly drawn to Roman Catholicism. Catholics had been, after all, conspicuously loyal to his father, and many of the son's favourite courtiers were of

See pages 171 and 211 for Charles's marriage to Catherine of Braganza.

See pages 389–92 for profiles about Charles II's mistresses.

the Roman faith. He also was attracted by the Catholic doctrine of grace, and may have been a 'Church papist', in other words one who was a private Catholic, but who conformed on Sundays. However, his secret allegiance to Rome may not in itself explain the Secret Treaty of Dover in 1670, for it is quite likely that this was signed to indulge his favourite sister Henrietta, married to the Duke of Orleans.

Finally, three quotations may approach the essence of his character. The best known of all his *bons mots* remains his deathbed remark about his mistress, Nell Gwyn: 'let not poor Nelly starve'. Macaulay recorded his apology: 'he had been, he said, an unconscionable time dying, but he hoped they would excuse it', and Halifax, (the **'Trimmer'**), paid a generous tribute to his political skills: 'As a sword is soonest broken upon a feather bed than upon a table, so his pliantness broke the power of a present mischief much better than a more immediate resistance'.

Trimmer someone who 'trims' or adapts to the prevailing wind, i.e. changes sides as expediency dictates.

The Restoration Settlements still left considerable prerogative powers in the King's hands: he could appoint and dismiss ministers, maintain the security of the State, devise and direct foreign policy, enjoy an inalienable life revenue and, above all, call, prorogue (i.e. suspend) and dissolve Parliament. It seems reasonable, therefore, to look at the man who effectively took over the reins of executive power in May 1660.

KEY ISSUE

Factions prevailed at Charles II's Court.

Cynicism seems to have been one of Charles's principal traits, for his exile had given him a low estimation of human nature. He could not believe that anyone could serve him out of affection or loyalty, and he enjoyed playing one minister off against another – a habit made easier by the labyrinthine layout of Whitehall Palace. The ensuing factionalism and instability soon became a characteristic of Restoration politics, and ministers rapidly learned that the Court was a jungle and office precarious. Clarendon, who fell from office in 1667, is the best example of a minister who found out the hard way that the King could not be relied upon to protect him from his enemies. It is hardly surprising, therefore, that ministers became less concerned with long-term strategy, and more interested in short-term expedients.

The historian Geoffrey Holmes may well be right in saying, 'William apart, Charles II was beyond argument the cleverest of the Stuarts', but this is not saying much when one looks at the competition. He showed little interest in the minutiae of theological disputation, and was prone to sleep through sermons: a predilection noted by Dr Robert South who, when preaching to King and Court, remarked to Lauderdale, 'My Lord, I am sorry to interrupt your repose, but I must beg that you will not snore quite so loud, lest you should awaken His Majesty'. It is true that he converted to Catholicism on his deathbed, but during his reign he outwardly respected Anglican forms. While he disliked Presbyterianism from his Scottish experiences in 1650–1, he was naturally tolerant and from time to time even looked to the Presbyterians for support in his inclination to tolerate Catholics.

KEY ISSUE

What were Charles II's own religious views?

In foreign policy Charles tended to prefer the French to the Dutch: a preference encouraged through affection for his mother, a French princess, and for his sister, Henrietta Anne, who had married Philippe, Duke of Orleans and Louis XIV's brother. Moreover he admired French manners, culture and language, while disliking the Dutch for their commercial success, their treatment of his sister Mary and for their humiliation of England in the Medway disaster. He may also have felt patrician disdain for a bourgeois republic, and, as a monarch without an effective army of his own, he valued more an ally with an army like France, than the Dutch who had little military power until 1672. Nevertheless, a pro-French inclination was likely to arouse fears in England of absolute rule and rampant Catholicism – fears which Charles was slow to appreciate. These anxieties were enhanced by Charles's marriage to the Infanta Catherine of Portugal, daughter of John IV. The marriage settlement brought a dowry of £360,000 and possession of both Tangier and Bombay, but it also brought England into closer alliance with France.

Charles was above all an idle king, only really applying himself consistently to government during the Exclusion Crisis between 1678 and 1681, when his family's legal rights of succession were under attack. In the wider context of the Stuart dynasty as a whole, sloth may not be such a negative factor: the two Stuarts who lost their thrones, Charles I and James II, were highly active innovatory monarchs, while the more relaxed James I and Charles II kept theirs. Charles's tastes for the regal pleasures of Newmarket, the arms of his mistresses and the brothels of Covent Garden make him seem more human. Charles's aggressive sexuality and the promiscuity that prevailed at Court did outrage contemporary morality, and may well have damaged the Crown's prestige. However, the charge of absolutism which has sometimes been levelled at Charles II is another matter entirely. Yet it is difficult to press this charge too far in his case. One has only to look at the policies of Louis XIV in France to see that his English cousin had a long way to go before he could reasonably be described as 'absolute'.

3 ⌐ THE MINISTRY OF CLARENDON, 1660–7

The Chancellor's enemies never lacked for issues to raise against him. In 1660 the King's brother, James, Duke of York, secretly married Clarendon's daughter, Anne, a move that seemed likely to perpetuate Clarendon's predominance. His enemies at Court relished his embarrassment, but Charles's suggestion that he might legitimise the Duke of Monmouth, one of his several illegitimate children, seemed to put paid to the spectre of a Hyde dynasty. Yet his detractors seized on every failure to attack him.

Clarendon, the architect of the Portuguese marriage, was blamed for the expense of keeping up Tangier, part of Catherine of Braganza's dowry, at a time when the King was committed to heavy expenditure elsewhere. He lost further favour with Charles when he advocated the

See page 88 for Clarendon's role in 1641.

sale of Dunkirk to the French to recoup losses, and his unpopularity was compounded by his criticism of the Court and its lifestyle. He failed to attend Court dinners and entertainments, underestimating the importance of card games as opportunities for informal policy contacts. Therefore his opponents increasingly had the ear of the King: Buckingham, whose savage and ill-judged impeachment attempt of 1663 was to backfire, and Bennet, Berkeley, Fitzharding, Coventry and Downing. Meanwhile, fresh fears were aroused by the consequences of his daughter's marriage to the heir, as the threat of a Monmouth succession waned. By May 1665 Clarendon was thinking of retiring, and resumed work on his *History of the Great Rebellion.* He feared increasingly that there would be a Dutch war for which he would be blamed, rightly as it turned out, and Charles began to blame him for problems with the ostensibly loyal Cavalier Parliament. The high-principled Clarendon was loath to intervene in elections to secure the return of Royalist candidates, nor would he consider bribes or other inducements. Charles even accused him of having encouraged the elopement of his mistress, Frances Stuart.

PICTURE 20

This portrait of Edward Hyde, Earl of Clarendon, by an unknown artist after Hanneman, illustrates Clarendon's humourless devotion to duty and to high principle

EDWARD HYDE, EARL OF CLARENDON 1609–74

Edward Hyde first came to prominence as a member of the Long Parliament when he criticised Ship Money and the Star Chamber. He supported the impeachment of Strafford, but, as a moderate Parliamentarian, opposed proposals to abolish bishops. In 1642, Hyde opted to join Charles at York and became the King's chief negotiator. In exile he was Charles II's chief minister, helping to draw up the Declaration of Breda, and from the Restoration until 1667, he was the King's head of government, a position reinforced when his daughter married James, Duke of York. His name is given to the so-called Clarendon Code – a series of laws to curb the activities of religious Dissenters – but it is doubtful whether he supported this draconian legislation. In foreign affairs he negotiated the sale back to France of Dunkirk in 1662, and spoke out against the Dutch war, although his reputation suffered when the English cause failed to prosper. He was dismissed by Charles in 1667 and impeached by the House of Commons for alleged corruption and authoritarian government. He fled to France and remained in exile until his death. During his last years he wrote an account of the English Civil War entitled *History of the Great Rebellion* from a conservative standpoint, and an autobiography. He was the first, but by no means the last, victim of Charles II's tendency to use his prerogative right to dismiss cabinet ministers when his own personal policy came under attack.

Clarendon in fact urged caution when the second Dutch war loomed, but his enemies clamoured for military action, inspired partly by the prospect of huge profits. A new Parliament sought scapegoats as the war dragged on, and the Great Fire followed hard on the heels of the plague, and ravaged much of the capital. When the Dutch fleet sailed up the River Medway in June 1667, and towed away the *Royal Charles,* Clarendon inevitably shared the opprobrium.

The attacks on the chief minister reached a pitch of intensity in the late summer of 1667, when the familiar group of conspirators put the knife into their victim. Bennet, ennobled as the Earl of Arlington in 1665, Buckingham, Coventry and Lady Castlemaine, yet another of Charles's mistresses, had the measure of Clarendon, supported only by York. Clarendon's old ally, Lord Treasurer Southampton, had recently died. On 30 August 1667 Charles dismissed Clarendon as chancellor after he had refused to resign. His minister's disdain had long irked the King, and he felt that he was becoming an increasing liability – especially as he had failed to control the Commons. Moreover, in foreign policy Clarendon had failed to deliver a French alliance, or a successful conclusion to the Dutch war – the Peace of Breda seemed an insubstantial end to such a bruising conflict. The nagging of Castlemaine and that of the other 'little people' at Court dragged up other issues from the past: the Stuart elopement and the prospect of Anne Hyde becoming queen.

Parliament debated the impeachment of Clarendon on charges of treason, and mindful perhaps of the fate that had befallen Strafford in 1641, Clarendon fled to continue his historical writing in the south of France. An era seemed to have come to an end, and Charles's reign passed definitively out of its Restoration phase. Future ministers were not slow to learn the lesson that they could not depend on the King to protect them from Parliament's wrath. They were now more likely to form alliances with Parliament than to carry out royal policy, and above all, to put their own interests first. Superficially Clarendon's fall appeared to free the King from a major obstacle, but in the long run royal power was weakened.

4 ⌁ THE CABAL, 1667–73

No one chief minister emerged after Clarendon's fall; rather, Charles entrusted ministerial responsibility to the Cabal, an acronym for the names of the five members, who in no sense represented a faction. Indeed, they rarely agreed and frequently vied with each other, being mainly concerned to advance themselves and their supporters. Sir Thomas Clifford had a background in diplomacy, and shared the King's anti-Dutch prejudices and his conversion to Catholicism. He was a successful manager of the House of Commons and worked stolidly on the Treasury Commission from 1667, until he was rewarded with the post of Lord Treasurer in 1672. Sir Henry Bennet, Lord Arlington, was preoccupied with foreign policy, and advocated a French alliance from 1668. He had a reputation for caution and pragmatism, but he too

See page 430 for profile of Lauderdale.

embraced Catholicism on his deathbed. Buckingham, the son of Charles I's favourite, was an unpredictable and unreliable figure, who often fell out with the King. He tried to curry favour by supporting indulgence for Dissenters, and strongly backed the French alliance. Anthony Ashley Cooper, soon to be raised to the peerage as the Earl of Shaftesbury, was appointed Lord Chancellor. He supported the Dutch war and Charles's second Declaration of Indulgence in 1672. Finally, John Maitland, created first Earl and then Duke of Lauderdale, was pre-occupied with Scottish affairs, to the extent of proposing an abortive Anglo-Scottish union.

Two members of the Cabal, Arlington and Clifford, signed the Secret Treaty of Dover with France in 1670, and the other members were made aware of its terms. The treaty envisaged another Dutch war, and this duly broke out in March 1672, by which time the government had secured a generous grant of supply from Parliament, and had repudiated its debts in the 'Stop of the Exchequer' of January 1672, which further eroded royal credit. Everything hinged on the war: if it was successful Charles could dispense prizes and redeem his debts; if, on the other hand, it failed, then debts would rise and Charles could expect trouble from Parliament.

PICTURE 21

A portrait of Henry Bennet, Earl of Arlington by an unknown artist after Lely. Arlington was a member of the Cabal, 1667–73. The scar on his nose was the result of a wound during the Civil War. Courtiers used to amuse Charles II by imitating Arlington behind his back. They would strut around with black patches on their noses

Just before the outbreak of war Charles issued a further Declaration of Indulgence on 15 March 1672, the preamble of which asserted that 12 years of persecution had failed to bring religious peace. All penal laws were to be suspended, and both Nonconformists and Catholics were free to meet – the former in premises specially licensed by the King, the latter in private houses. No attempt was made to secure parliamentary agreement to the Declaration; indeed Parliament was not even in session at the time, and it was clearly based on an exaggerated impression of the numbers of both categories. Most opponents of the measure assumed that it was to benefit Roman Catholics, and many presumed that it was probably issued in accordance with some secret clause of an agreement with Louis XIV. Furthermore, Charles seemed to be displaying alarming absolutist tendencies by appearing to dispense with the law. When the war went badly, Parliament would have to be recalled, and Charles was likely to have a rough ride.

Parliament reassembled on 4 February 1673 and witnessed the greatest policy reversal of the reign so far, when on 8 March Charles, apparently bowing to Protestant pressure, revoked the Declaration of Indulgence. Parliament in return granted a supply of £70,000 per month and proceeded to pass a Test Act, which vividly demonstrated the strength of anti-Catholic feelings. The Act required all civil and military office-holders to take the Oaths of Allegiance and Supremacy, and to affirm a declaration against various tenets of Roman Catholicism, including **transubstantiation**. In addition, they were to take Holy Communion publicly according to the Anglican rite at least once a year. Suspicions that Catholics had infiltrated into senior positions, including military commands, were confirmed when neither York nor Clifford took Anglican Communion that Easter, and both resigned their offices in June.

Indeed, the overt Catholicism of James, Duke of York, was to be the main political issue for the next 15 years. James's first wife, Ann Hyde, herself a Catholic convert, had died in March 1671, and while the two daughters of this marriage, Mary and Anne, were being brought up as Protestants, James remarried, by proxy and with French mediation, the 15-year-old Mary Beatrice of Modena, yet another papist and a client of France. Indeed, for many Protestants Mary of Modena was the most bigoted Roman Catholic in Europe, and allegedly the Pope's daughter. Moreover, if James were to have sons by his new marriage, they would take precedence over the daughters of the first marriage. The spectre of a Catholic king loomed, and indeed of a whole Roman dynasty; the more so as Charles still had no legitimate children, although he admitted to 17 illegitimate ones. Shaftesbury led renewed suggestions in the Privy Council that Charles should divorce Catherine of Braganza, and that the Duke of York should be excluded from the throne.

When Parliament met on 27 October 1673, the Commons considered a request for supply from the King, but they refused it on the grounds that it would further a Catholic war to the benefit of France, and would provide Charles with a pretext to raise an army, which he was unlikely to disband. Charles therefore would have the essential

KEY ISSUE

Charles tried to achieve religious freedom for all non-Anglicans.

KEY ISSUE

The first Test Act thwarted Charles's toleration plans.

transubstantiation is the belief that the bread and wine when consecrated at Mass become the body and blood of Christ.

instrument for absolutism. But after nine days Charles did prorogue the session on 4 November 1673 after an acrimonious meeting. On 9 November 1673 Shaftesbury was dismissed by Charles as Lord Chancellor, and then expelled from the Privy Council and from the Lord Lieutenancy of Dorset for supporting the Test Act and opposing York's marriage. With Clifford dead and Lauderdale still north of the border, little was left of the Cabal. Its fate was finally sealed by the recall of Parliament in January 1674. Although Charles promised that there was no secret treaty with France, and even offered Parliament scrutiny of future treaties, Buckingham came under heavy attack in the Commons, until Charles dismissed him too from Court and Council, and as Master of the Horse. Charles announced the terms of the Treaty of Westminster to the House of Commons on 2 February 1674, and prorogued Parliament again on 24 February. Charles's 'Grand Design' was dead.

KEY ISSUE

The Cabal dissolved following Shaftesbury's dismissal.

PICTURE 22

A portrait of Anthony Ashley Cooper, Earl of Shaftesbury by an unknown artist after Greenhill. This portrait depicts a clever politician who changed sides during the Civil War and worked for both Cromwell and Charles II

ANTHONY ASHLEY COOPER, EARL OF SHAFTESBURY, 1621–83

Born Anthony Ashley Cooper, he changed sides during the Civil War to the Parliamentary cause in 1644. He fell out with Cromwell, and was a member of the delegation to the Hague that discussed terms for a restoration with Charles II. Advancement came quickly: in 1661 when he was made Chancellor of the Exchequer and created Lord Ashley. He was a member of the Cabal ministry and was made Earl of Shaftesbury and Lord Chancellor in 1672. When the Cabal fell in 1673 he joined the opposition. During the Exclusion Crisis he schemed with Monmouth, at one point even making a spectacular personal appeal to Charles to legitimise his bastard son on the steps of Christ Church Hall in Oxford. He attacked Catholics during the Popish Plot hysteria, and tried his best to get York impeached as a popish recusant. Courted by Charles II, he resisted the King's wiles, and was the main figure behind efforts to pass an Exclusion Bill. When Charles II emerged triumphant in 1681, he was accused of treason, but fled abroad into exile.

Charles II's nickname for Shaftesbury was 'Little Sincerity'. How well does his portrait match his nickname?

By 1674 Parliament had won two important victories: peace with the Dutch through the Treaty of Westminster, and the abandonment of the Declaration of Indulgence. Charles could console himself with the theoretical recognition by the Dutch of English control over the North Sea, but he had to pay a high price for this 'success'. Death and disgrace had ravaged his group of advisers, a process completed with the demotion of Arlington from Secretary of State to Lord Chamberlain. He had incurred further debts to exacerbate his financial problems, and he had lost the trust even of his ally, Louis XIV. However, to balance this impression, it could be argued that the failure of Charles's first and only major policy initiative ultimately made him a wiser and more experienced monarch. Moreover, the Cabal looks less like an instrument of absolutism and more like a disparate, but fundamentally cautious group of ministers with no coherent or aggressive policy to increase royal power. It is also clear that Charles's own policy relied very much on Parliament; he could not dispense with it even if he wanted to. Yet this is not to deny that a good many MPs believed that Charles was trying to emulate his father's policy of ruling without Parliament, such as in the 'Eleven Years Tyranny' from 1629 to 1640.

A further revisionist argument has been to state that there was a 'financial revolution' during the period of the Cabal. There does indeed seem to have been a better exploitation of customs duties and reform of the treasury, since revenue from sugar and tobacco customs certainly increased. It may also be the case that tax-farmers did well, but Charles abolished them in 1671 and replaced them with paid commissioners. Indeed, the whole treasury was put into commission after the death of Lord Treasurer Southampton in 1667, when bureaucrats such as George Downing worked there. Further points to note are the application of the 'Rule of Specific Sanction' to ensure that all revenue was controlled by the treasury in the interests of better accuracy and scrutiny, and Charles's ability to borrow more easily at lower interest rates. Regarding the latter point, Charles's debts remained very large, and there was still, at least in the short term, a decided reluctance to lend to him. In this light the term 'financial revolution' looks like an overstatement: the King's settled financial policy was still to call Parliament, and whatever changes were implemented needed more time to take effect than the short span of the Cabal period.

5 ⌐ THE MINISTRY OF DANBY, 1673–8

From 1673 to 1678 government was officially in the hands of Clifford's successor at the Treasury, Sir Thomas Osborne, known after 1674 as the Earl of Danby.

Danby had disapproved of most of the Cabal's policies: the Treaty of Dover, the French alliance, the Stop of the Exchequer and indulgence of Roman Catholics and Dissenters. While the historian Mark Kishlansky rightly describes Danby as a man whose 'principles were untainted by idealism', he nonetheless offered an alternative agenda: to reconstruct a parliamentary majority for the Crown through a policy of Anglican supremacy, to keep this majority loyal with an anti-French foreign policy and to solve Charles's financial problems for good, by making him solvent and less dependent on parliamentary subsidy. This last policy would require a reign of austerity to challenge the King's extravagance – or an increase in revenue.

The fundamental weakness, however, in Danby's approach was that he lacked the wholehearted support of the King at every turn, to the extent that Charles often seemed to be following an alternative policy to that of his chief minister, especially in diplomacy. Charles retained the whip hand in dealing with Parliament, for he could prorogue it at will and did not hesitate to do so. Indeed, there were no fewer than four parliamentary sessions between April 1675 and July 1678. Charles also

KEY ISSUE

The ministry of Danby followed the Cabal.

KEY ISSUE

Danby's strengths and weaknesses.

THOMAS OSBORNE, EARL OF DANBY
1631–1712

Thomas Osborne came from a Yorkshire gentry family, and was elected MP for York in 1665. From then on he enjoyed a steady climb to power: Treasurer of the Navy in 1668, a member of the Privy Council in 1673 and Lord High Treasurer in the same year. At the same time he was advanced through the peerage, becoming Lord Osborne in 1673 and Earl of Danby in 1674. From 1673 to 1679 he was Charles II's chief minister after the collapse of the Cabal – a careerists's dream. Cynically he saw the House of Commons, in Maurice Ashley's words, 'as a body to be corrupted or tricked', the precursor perhaps of Walpole or Newcastle in the next century. He favoured strong measures against Catholics and Dissenters and peace with the Dutch, negotiating the Treaty of Westminster which ended the third Dutch war in 1674. Hostile to Louis XIV, he brokered the marriage of Princess Mary to William of Orange in 1677, but he had to acquiesce in Charles's persistent friendship with France in return for subsidies. His role in these talks became known during the Exclusion Crisis, and Charles sacrificed him: he was impeached in 1678 and languished in prison until 1684.

He opposed James II's Catholicism and style of government, and signed the invitation to William of Orange in 1688. He persuaded York to declare for William and backed the Lords' offer of the crown to William and Mary. His reward was further promotion: Marquis of Carmarthen, President of the Council, Lord Lieutenant of the three Ridings of Yorkshire and Duke of Leeds in 1694. From 1690 to 1694 he ran the government, but he was impeached for bribery in 1695 and resigned all his offices in 1699.

continued his flirtations with France, scorning Danby's efforts to appease parliamentary opinion by seeking a Dutch alliance. The minister's sole success with his pro-Dutch policy was to persuade Charles to allow his 15-year-old niece Mary to marry William of Orange.

As if this was not enough, Danby also found himself thwarted in financial policy by Charles's continuing prodigality, when Danby needed a good two years of rigorous retrenchment to put his policy into effect. At the same time, Danby failed to secure the rapport with Parliament which he had promised the King, when in 1675 there was an attempt to impeach him for treason and attacks on Lauderdale and Lord Keeper Finch as well. The parliamentary opposition stepped up their offensive in other ways: by trying to pass a **Habeas Corpus** bill in 1674, by challenging the succession rights of any prince who made an unacceptable Catholic marriage, by opposing a standing army and by denying Charles's right to conduct foreign policy – a clear threat to the royal prerogative. Above all the opposition demanded the dissolution of what they called the 'Pensioner Parliament' and a fresh general election.

Habeas Corpus a law allowing a person to be released from prison if no cause is shown.

Shaftesbury added his voice to those calling for the end of the Cavalier Parliament, first elected in 1661 and rapidly becoming, in his words, a 'standing Parliament'.

What were Danby's aims? What obstacles stood in his way? Danby could make little headway against a devious monarch and a fractious Parliament, as changes in the climate and structure of politics occurred. In the autumn of 1678 his career seemed threatened with ruin by the 'discovery' of the so-called Popish Plot.

6 ⌐ THE EXCLUSION CRISIS, 1678–81: THE EMERGENCE OF PARTIES

A *Anti-Catholic feeling*

In order fully to understand the hysterical reaction to the Popish Plot in 1678, it is important to grasp the reasons for anti-Catholic paranoia, which had been a powerful factor in English life for well over a century.

Many English Protestants believed that their country was an elect nation – in other words, chosen by God at a time of militant Catholic resurgence to keep the flame of religious reform burning brightly. Having survived Mary Tudor's short-lived experiment in counter-reformation, Protestants could recall their heroism and the evil of their confessional opponents by reading works such as John Foxe's *Acts and Monuments*, popularly known as *Foxe's Book of Martyrs*. First published in 1563, this rapidly became a best-seller, describing in graphic terms the bloody persecution of Protestants under Mary, and as the sixteenth century wore on, there was no shortage of fresh examples of Catholic villainy. In France the Massacre of St Bartholomew in 1572 reinforced the perception of Catholicism as a cruel and bloody religion, as did the series of plots against the great Protestant queen herself, Elizabeth I.

March 1661 to January 1679	The Cavalier Parliament
March–May 1679	First Exclusion Parliament
	Exclusion passed by the Commons
October 1680 to January 1681	Second Exclusion Parliament
	Exclusion defeated in the Lords
March 1681	Third Exclusion Parliament meets at Oxford
	Exclusion passed by Commons and Lords

KEY ISSUE

Anti-Catholic feeling was a strong issue in seventeenth-century England.

TABLE 13
Key events, 1661–81

See page 24 for the Gunpowder Plot.

KEY ISSUE

The rationale of anti-Catholicism.

The seventeenth century produced more examples to fuel anti-Catholic demonology, the first being the Gunpowder Plot of 1605, an attempt to liquidate *en masse* all the members of both Houses of Parliament and to kill the King. Charles I's opponents alleged that his policies were Catholic-inspired – he had after all married a French Catholic princess, Henrietta Maria, and Archbishop Laud's religious reforms seemed to have more than a hint of popery about them. The full horror of rampant Catholicism reared its head in the 1641 Irish Rebellion, when tales of massacres of Protestant settlers lost nothing in the telling.

KEY ISSUE

*Charles's political
enemies also accused
him of absolutism.*

By the second half of the seventeenth century Catholicism had also become firmly linked to the political doctrine of absolutism, most clearly shown in the reign of Louis XIV of France from 1661 to 1715. France had a beleaguered Protestant minority (the Huguenots), who were increasingly persecuted despite the 1598 Edict of Nantes, which was intended to protect their rights. Louis expelled them from France at the height of anti-Catholic feeling in England in 1685. As we have seen, many people suspected that Charles II, also married to a Catholic, had reached some sort of diplomatic accommodation with Louis, involving the destruction of the Protestant Dutch and an eventual re-Catholicisation of England itself. Indeed it was widely believed that Charles was already beginning to emulate his cousin by embarking on absolutist and tyrannical policies, such as the Declaration of Indulgence. The revelation that the autocratically-minded James, Duke of York, had 'come out' as a Catholic in 1673, when he had failed to attend Anglican Holy Communion and had resigned his post of Lord Admiral in conformity with the 1673 Test Act, did not come as a great surprise. As Charles had no legitimate children, and the Queen showed no sign of producing any, the succession would inevitably pass to the Catholic James, who had recently remarried, this time an Italian Catholic closely linked with France.

Was there objectively, however, a genuine Catholic threat? The answer appears to be in the negative. Bishop Compton's census of 1676 suggested that there were in fact very few Catholics in England, and John Bossy estimates their number as around one per cent of the population in 1680. Older Catholic families lost ground through deaths or conversions, and there were few priests: perhaps 230 secular clergy and 255 regular clergy. Moreover there had been no Catholic bishop in England since 1655 and papal interest had dwindled too. Existing legal sanctions also played their part in subduing Catholics, who had to attend Anglican services on pain of fines, and who could face treason charges if they tried to convert anyone, or to shelter a recusant priest.

While Protestants might have accepted at least some of the above points, they liked to draw a distinction between recusancy and popery. Recusants – Catholics living quietly in the countryside, and often enjoying good relations with their Protestant neighbours – were not seen as the real target. The real fear was of an international phenomenon, involving hidden or secret Catholics, mainly in London. In other words, they argued that the precise numbers of papists were immaterial, as the real threat came from a few highly placed Catholics in the capital. These included Queen Catherine with, it was said, no less than 14 priests in her household, the Duke of York and his new wife, the leading royal mistress Louise, Duchess of Portsmouth, wealthy Catholic peers hearing mass in their private chapels and London recusants flocking to foreign ambassadors' chapels. Why, asked many Protestants, were the recusancy laws not being applied with rigour, either in the countryside, where local JPs often seemed to err on the side of leniency, or in London, where the laws seemed to be flouted in a manner offensive to many Protestants?

Many of these anti-Catholic arguments were outlined in Andrew Marvell's book, *Account of the Growth of Papacy and Arbitrary Government*, which appeared in the autumn of 1677 at a particularly testing time. Parliament was not in session, rumours of plots involving foreign agents proliferated, and Charles seemed reluctant to pay off his army of more than 20,000 men – all these could be seen as signs that the charges against the King were justified. Marvell's book rehearsed the familiar theological arguments used against Rome: Catholic disdain for the Bible, the very bedrock of the Reformation, their idolatrous respect for images of Christ and the saints, the apparent divinity and worship of the Virgin Mary, the power of the priest in the confessional, the 'obscenity' of the doctrine of transubstantiation in the Mass and Catholic arrogance in insisting on Rome as the one true Church. Feelings were therefore already running high when Titus Oates made his allegations of a 'Popish Plot' in September 1678.

KEY ISSUE
Why there was so much anti-Catholic feeling in seventeenth-century England.

B *Titus Oates and the Popish Plot*

The previous section showed the historical reasons for anti-Catholic feeling in England, stemming from the Reformation in the previous century. Yet religious hysteria was not a constant feature of English life throughout the whole Early Modern period; it was a phenomenon that waxed and waned. The year 1678 produced a mixture of events and circumstances, which led to a crisis that gripped the country for the next three years, paralysed the government, unleashed a witch-hunt, and caused many apparently rational people to believe that accusation was as good as proof, and that the whole apparatus of law and trial by jury could be dispensed with. The man responsible for letting the genie out of the bottle was Titus Oates.

Titus Oates had had, to say the least, a chequered career. He had been expelled from school and from two Cambridge colleges before ordination into the Anglican Church. He was dismissed from two livings, one in England and one in Tangier, for drunkenness and sodomy, when he decided to try his luck in the Roman Catholic Church, where he fared no better. Enrolled as a Jesuit novice, he was expelled from both the English College in Vallodolid, Spain and the Jesuit College at St Omer in Flanders. With this seedy background behind him, he embarked on his final career, as a professional plot-detector and liar, with a partner, Israel Tonge, who was a beneficed clergyman, a former Fellow of University College, Oxford, a Doctor of Divinity of that university, a successful schoolmaster and the translator of Catholic tracts, as well as a historian of the Society of Jesus. He was also a fanatical anti-papist, and like Oates, a homosexual. In the summer of 1678 the two men concocted a bogus conspiracy for want of a genuine one.

On 6 September 1678 the two swore 43 articles before a Justice of the Peace, Sir Edmund Berry Godfrey, alleging a plot to assassinate Charles II, and to extirpate English Protestantism with an invasion from France, as well as simultaneous Catholic risings in England and Ireland. Every-

KEY ISSUE
Anti-Catholic hysteria, fanned by Titus Oates.

one seemed to be involved in the plot: Jesuits, Benedictines and Dominicans, the Catholic peer Lord Arundell of Wardour and, of course, James, Duke of York and Louis XIV. Oates and Tonge enjoyed two important advantages when it came to making allegations: they were prepared to tell brazen lies, and they had almost total recall under questioning. Danby, who was both anti-French and anti-Catholic, was impressed by the evidence for a plot, and he was asked by the King, who remained more sceptical, to investigate.

Emboldened by his success, Oates now came up with a further 38 articles, making 81 altogether, and laid them before the Privy Council on 28 September 1678. Here Oates enjoyed the first of two strokes of luck, when he suggested that the former secretary to the Duke and Duchess of York, a Catholic convert called Edward Coleman, might have in his possession certain papers implicating him in the plot. The ensuing search of Coleman's premises did indeed reveal correspondence with Pere La Chaise, Louis XIV's confessor, the Papal Nuncio in Brussels and Cardinal Howard. The letters uncovered apparently treasonable designs, for Coleman made no bones about his hopes to reverse the Reformation, to reconvert England from 'heresy and schism', and to overthrow English parliamentary government with French help.

The second piece of good fortune was the discovery of the corpse of Sir Edmund Berry Godfrey, the very same magistrate who had taken down a sworn statement of Oates' and Tonge's allegations 11 days before. The murder of Godfrey seemed to be further proof of the papists' violence and malice: clearly he had been killed and his body dumped at Primrose Hill because he knew too much. In this fevered atmosphere trials of suspects began, and the recusancy laws began to be enforced with renewed vigour, with 1,200 prosecutions in London alone in 1679. At the same time the Cavalier Parliament reconvened for its sixteenth and final session.

The parliamentary session began on 21 October 1678 with MPs convinced that there must indeed be a plot. On 2 November, Shaftesbury demanded York's exclusion from the Privy Council, but Parliament fought shy of bringing in an exclusion bill to debar York from the throne. On 15 November, Oates appeared before the House of Commons and accused Catherine of Braganza of plotting to kill her husband – the day before an important anniversary in the Protestant calendar, the accession of Queen Elizabeth I. Parliament went on to impeach five leading Roman Catholic peers, including Lord Arundell of Wardour, alleged by Tonge to be the intended first minister in a Catholic regime, Lord Bellasis, said to be the captain general of Rome's army of invasion and Lords Powis, Petre and Stafford. Finally, the House passed the Second Test Act on 21 November 1678.

The Second Test Act was an attempt to extend the provisions of the 1673 Act, following rumours about possible Roman Catholics in the Commons. No MP could sit in the Commons or Lords without taking the Oaths of Supremacy and Allegiance, affirming a declaration repudiating transubstantiation, and condemning certain 'superstitious and idolatrous' Roman practices. Any member refusing the Test was presumed to be a popish recusant, subject to legal penalties and debarred from the Court. The Duke of York, however, a peer and a devout Roman Catholic, was exempted by a proviso clause, 'provided always that nothing in the Act contained shall extend to His Royal Highness the Duke of York'. The clause squeaked through the Commons by the bare margin of 158 votes to 156.

Meanwhile, the proceedings against the accused rumbled on. On 27 November, Coleman's trial for high treason began, followed by his execution and that of three others on 3 December, while a grateful Commons awarded Oates a pension for life of £1,200 per year. Then two further events occurred, which hastened the dissolution of Parliament. First, Ralph Montagu, former ambassador to France and with a grudge against Danby for the loss of his job, revealed to the Commons letters implicating Danby in negotiations earlier that year for a French subsidy of £450,000. Immediately the House initiated proceedings for Danby's impeachment, and Charles prorogued Parliament on 30 December, fearful of further revelations of his secret treaties with France and an embarrassing enquiry into his foreign policy over the past ten years. The prorogation and the ensuing dissolution of the 'Pensioner Parliament' on 30 January 1679 was also hastened by Shaftesbury's extension of his attack on James, Duke of York. Shaftesbury, a senior member of the Privy Council, led bids in November 1678 to exclude James from Charles's counsels and from the Lords. As he quoted the precedent of Henry VIII's alteration of the succession by Act of Parliament, a campaign to exclude York from the throne itself seemed only a matter of time.

C *The First Exclusion Parliament, March–May 1679*

Charles's decision to call a general election in the spring of 1679 was a highly risky option, for it was bound to take place in the heady atmosphere whipped up by the Popish Plot, the ensuing further revelations and trials, and the fevered debates of the final session of the Cavalier Parliament. The eventual election results of February 1679 showed that the King could count on the support of roughly 137 MPs, with about 218 making up the country opposition and a potentially dangerous and subversive force, while around 167 MPs seemed undecided. It was highly likely that the opposition, or Whigs as they now began to be called, would attempt to pass an Exclusion bill, and plunge the Crown into the worst crisis since Charles I's refusal to accept the Militia Ordinance in 1642 as an affront to his prerogative. Charles would need all his stamina and diplomatic skill to survive the storms of the next two years.

Before examining the deliberations of the three Exclusion Parliaments, it is necessary to look at the two distinct political groups that emerged from the elections of early 1679. While it is true that half of the MPs who gathered at Westminster in March 1679 were newcomers, many of whom saw their role as essentially to represent the interests of

KEY ISSUE

Parliament began to discuss 'exclusion', that James, Duke of York, should be excluded from the throne.

Whigs were originally Scottish outlaws.

KEY ISSUE

How did Whigs and Tories differ?

Tories were originally Irish bandits.

their own constituents, and that a large group of MPs remained unde-cided throughout the crisis, two distinct groups did emerge in 1679, who were to dictate political argument for the foreseeable future.

Whigs argued passionately for the exclusion of the Duke of York from the throne, on the grounds that James's Catholic faith would inex-orably lead him to impose popery and absolutism by force. For them the spectre of the Irish Revolt of 1641 was at the forefront of their minds: quite simply 1641 could come again. They pointed to examples elsewhere, such as Louis XIV's France, where a combination of militant counter-Reformation Catholicism and political absolutism had led to the very scenario that they dreaded in England. Parliament, they main-tained, had the right to dictate the succession, and indeed had a duty to do so, given recent revelations. The Whigs were therefore arguing a conservative ideology against the claims of an innovative monarchy, which in their view was aping the actions of the King's father on the eve of the Civil War.

Tories, on the other hand, maintained that it was unjust to condemn James untried, and that, in reality, the Whigs had another agenda – namely to unleash another civil war and to overthrow both Church and monarchy. In their view the Whigs were not really interested in 'Popery' at all, but were merely using the furore over the Popish Plot as a pretext to push for a revolutionary agenda. Tories buttressed this view by a resort to Divine Right theory – they held that the existing order was divinely ordained, and that resistance to authority was therefore resis-tance to the law of God. They drew upon a tradition of obedience that went back to Tudor times and beyond, and some went even further, arguing that subjects were obliged, like the early Christians, to suffer patiently what a Roman Catholic king might do to them. James might never become king, they suggested, and even if he did, he might not turn out to be as bad as all that. Moreover, he had, as yet, no legitimate heir.

As MPs assembled for the new session, Charles ordered a reluctant James to leave the country, while he faced an undoubtedly Exclusionist House of Commons. James therefore began three years of intermittent exile in the Low Countries, watching from a distance the attempts to deny him the throne. The parliamentary session began inevitably with the prosecution of Danby. Charles avoided the danger of a trial and the exposure of his complicity in talks with France, by dismissing his minis-ter on 25 March 1679. He followed this up with a royal pardon, and the award of a huge pension and a marquisate. The Commons were furious and proceeded to impeach Danby, who for the next five years lan-guished in the Tower, in the company of the five disgraced Catholic lords.

Charles now set up a new Privy Council in an attempt to deflate charges of arbitrary government, and to wean away members of the opposition from their attachment to Exclusion. His new Council was slimmed down, 30 members instead of 46, with a varied membership including Halifax, Sunderland, Laurence Hyde, Sidney Godolphin, Mulgrave and even Shaftesbury himself, a remarkable attempt to turn a

KEY ISSUE

The reasons why Danby was dismissed.

poacher into a gamekeeper. While Lord Chancellor Shaftesbury remained a devotee of Exclusion, the King's refashioning of the Council did divide and weaken the opposition, cutting them off from their grass roots support, and distracting their efforts towards an institution that enjoyed little real power.

Inevitably the parliamentary onslaught on the Duke of York continued: on 27 April 1679 the Commons resolved that his Catholicism had caused the Popish Plot, and hard on the heels of this resolution came the First Exclusion Bill itself. This was in effect a Third Test Act for the office of king; to disinherit one named individual (the Duke of York) and to replace him in the succession by his daughter Mary. James, it was claimed, had incited a papist conspiracy, his succession would destroy Protestantism in England and his rule was bound to be absolute. The bill included the death penalty for York, if he asserted his succession or entered the realm. It received its second reading on 21 May 1679, passing by 207 votes to 128, a majority of 79, with a substantial number of MPs choosing not to vote. Charles killed the bill by resorting to his power of prorogation on 26 May 1679, followed by dissolution on 10 July 1679. This was the first example, but by no means the last, of Charles making judicious use of these prerogative powers to defeat Exclusion. Faced with this tactic, the Exclusionists had an insuperable problem: any bill had to pass the Commons, and the Lords, with its Royalist majority including many of the Anglican bishops, and it then had to receive royal assent – by no means a foregone conclusion in the seventeenth century. In any case, Charles could short-circuit the whole process by prorogation, as soon as the bill had been debated in the Commons, and at a time of peace, low military expenditure and with customs revenue at a healthy level, Charles could afford to thumb his nose at the Commons. Moreover, Charles had a further card up his sleeve: limitations. He could agree to limit the powers of a popish successor, for example over the Church, the judiciary and the armed forces, to offer a credible alternative to outright Exclusion. If Charles seemed to be offering a compromise, the irreconcilable Exclusionists might be seen to be the unreasonable ones.

> ## KEY ISSUE
>
> *Charles II could always prorogue Parliament and he did so several times during the Exclusion Crisis.*

D   *The Second Exclusion Parliament, October 1680 to January 1681*

Fresh elections held in August and September 1679 produced an even more overwhelmingly Exclusionist Parliament than the last one: while the government could rely perhaps on up to 220 MPs, the opposition could muster around 310 with hardly any undecided members. At this dangerous point the King fell ill, James returned and the Exclusionists began an intensive and sophisticated propaganda campaign to urge the King to summon Parliament, using pamphlets, newspapers, petitions (one of which was 100 yards long), cartoons, sermons (some written by Oates), ballads, playing cards and suchlike. Two hundred pamphlets were issued in the 1679–81 period with titles such as: 'the Character of a

Popish Successor' and 'a Just and Modest Vindication of the proceedings of the Last two Parliaments'. The petitioners ran no less than 30 political clubs, the best known being the 'Green Ribbon Club', but there were limits as to what they could do if the King refused to let Parliament meet – in fact he prorogued it no less than eight times. His finances were sound, unlike in 1641, and he was at peace: in Ireland, on the Scottish border and abroad too. He also initiated a series of prosecutions for seditious libel, and denied that he had secretly married Monmouth's mother. In this way some Whig journalists were silenced, in spite of the lapse of the Licensing Act.

At the same time Tory and Whig propaganda competed, as the 'Abhorrers' also issued their own material, denouncing the petitions as unconstitutional and challenging Shaftesbury's claim to represent the nation. The problem of James, Duke of York was solved by packing him off to Scotland where he was well received, and could embark on what the historian Michael Mullett calls 'the beginning of a long, slow climb back to acceptance that would culminate in his triumphant accession in 1685'. Monmouth, Charles's illegitimate son and the likely beneficiary of a successful exclusion policy, was dismissed from his military command and sent to Holland, from where he returned in the summer of 1680, before being sent by Shaftesbury on a tour of the West Country.

Charles dismissed Shaftesbury as Lord President of the Council in October 1679, and four other Whigs resigned from the Council in January 1680, but Shaftesbury was still determined to achieve Exclusion. With Parliament prorogued, he tried to have James presented by a Westminster grand jury for trial as a recusant, but this ruse was foiled by Lord Chief Justice Scroggs. He also tried to have the Duchess of Portsmouth tried as a prostitute, but the charge was thrown out. Finally, the King called Parliament on 21 October 1680 and the Second Exclusion Parliament began.

Charles called Parliament partly because his financial position had suddenly become more difficult, in part owing to the expense of defending Tangier. Indeed, the Exclusionists offered him supply and the right to name his successor in return for Exclusion: Charles refused and a new Exclusion Bill passed its three readings in the Commons by mid-November 1680. Shaftesbury was confident that the King would now give way: after all this was the same monarch who had abandoned Clarendon, Arlington and Louis XIV, and who had given way on so many other issues: the Declaration of Indulgence, the two Test Acts and Mary's marriage to William of Orange. He had, however, reckoned without the Upper House, for on 15 November the Lords defeated the Second Exclusion Bill at the first reading, partly through the block vote of the Anglican bishops. Charles II himself was present in the Lords throughout the ten-hour-long debate, and silently made his views plain via a series of nods, winks, smiles, grimaces and scowls. He also received powerful backing from Halifax, the advocate of limitations who argued that exclusion of James would establish a bad precedent for all inherited titles to property (such as those enjoyed by their lordships). He also played on fears of civil war, pointing out that James might resort to armed rebellion to assert his rights if the bill passed. This latest reverse for the cause of Exclusion seemed to show that only systematic obstruction and intense coercive pressure might succeed.

In this frame of mind the Commons began the impeachment of Viscount Stafford, who had been named by Oates at the time of the Popish Plot, and who had spent two years in the Tower with the other four peers. Stafford was impeached, convicted and executed on a majority vote of 50 to 30 in the Lords. On Hyde's advice Charles prorogued Parliament on 10 January 1681 and dissolved it eight days later. A new Parliament would be called at Oxford in March 1681.

E *The Third Exclusion Parliament, March 1681*

The elections of February 1681 produced a House of Commons that little differed in temper from its predecessor: the Whigs lost a handful of seats but still held 309, while the Tories' gains only brought them up to 193. Charles decided to use military measures to try to browbeat the Commons, by deploying cavalry along the main road to Oxford, as well as more troops in Oxford and London. The choice of Oxford was not coincidental either: the Whigs would be separated from their London mob, for example, Shaftesbury's 'brisk boys' and anti-Catholic thugs from the East End. Moreover, the Whigs' absence in Oxford would prevent them from convening an alternative Parliament in the City – as had happened in 1642. Oxford also had a powerful symbolic value, for it had after all been the base for the Royalists during the Civil War, and its rich associations with Charles I boosted the martyr cult that was important in Tory image-making.

See page 87 for Pym's use of the London mob.

The King opened the proceedings in Wren's Sheldonian Theatre by making two conciliatory points: first he promised to look at any expedient, short of outright Exclusion, that would safeguard both religion and monarchy. He made clear that he was prepared to consider the so-called 'Orange Option', whereby William and Mary would act as Regents under a form of limitations, gambling that the Whigs were likely to spurn his offer. Secondly, Charles asserted his own distaste for arbitrary government. Charles's ploy worked: Whig intransigence and extremism in the face of the King's apparently reasonable suggestions were seen as the main danger, and the mooted disinheritance of the Duke of York seemed to threaten all titles to property. Charles held his trump card of prorogation, while the majority of Whigs rejected any alternative to Exclusion, and proceeded to launch an impeachment of Fitzharris, a government agent caught while trying to plant treasonable papers on leading Whigs. Fitzharris chose to co-operate with his accusers and began to incriminate James's associates. Whigs began to believe that Charles would not contemplate dissolution for fear of being seen to suppress vital evidence.

KEY ISSUE

Why did Charles hold the Third Exclusion Parliament in Oxford?

The discussion of a new Exclusion Bill started on 26 March with its first reading. Littlejohn spelt out Charles's specific limitation proposals, that is the 'Orange Option' to secure government in Protestant hands under a nominal Catholic monarch, who could be permanently exiled while keeping the title of king. The session held on 28 March 1681 was in the hall of Christ Church, the college which had been his father's headquarters during the Civil War. Charles II had smuggled into the building the robes, crown and other trappings of monarchy necessary for the dismissal of Parliament, and he suddenly appeared in full regal fig to announce yet another prorogation. These turned out to be the last words that Charles ever uttered to Parliament, as he held no more during his lifetime.

Shaftesbury had hoped that sheer fiscal need would force the King to yield, but the royal finances were now on the mend, thanks to the work of Laurence Hyde, Earl of Rochester and First Commissioner of the Treasury, who had insisted on cuts in government spending and had dissuaded the King from spending the surplus that began to accrue. In addition, customs and excise collection had become more efficient, peace ensured a cheaper foreign policy and trade with France was now booming. Finally, unbeknown to the Whigs in Parliament, Charles had signed another agreement with Louis XIV, who agreed to provide a subsidy of 2 million livres in the first year, to be followed by 1.5 million livres annually thereafter. With the promise of £300,000 from France over the next four years, Charles could afford to do without Parliament.

F *Conclusion to the Exclusion Crisis*

The 1681 dissolution shattered Shaftesbury's belief that the King could be forced to accept Exclusion; although Charles pledged a further Parliament in his April Declaration of 1681, he called no more Parliaments during the four years that remained of the reign. Unless Shaftesbury used force or the threat of force, Exclusion looked like an increasingly lost cause. Indeed, civil war was never likely at any stage of the crisis, and there was very little violence at all between 1678 and 1681. Perhaps memories of the 1640s dampened enthusiasm for rebellion, and Charles held most of the military cards as well: an adequate army, a militia with reliable officers and, above all, money.

Most historians agree that the outcome of the Exclusion Crisis was a triumph for Charles II: J.R. Jones writes, 'not only did Charles emerge from the Exclusion Crisis as incontestably the strongest Seventeenth Century monarch, but he did so as a constitutional ruler'. There is also considerable consensus about the reasons for the result of the crisis. It is clear first of all that the Whigs, for all their impressive parliamentary strength, were weakened by divisions. One or two like Halifax ('the Trimmer') were weaned away from Whiggery by Charles's blandishments, but, as we have seen, not all the Whigs appointed to the Council were prepared to back the King on the main issue. The fundamental division arose over who should rule in the event of James's exclusion: some favoured Princess Mary, the Duke of York's elder daughter by his marriage to Anne Hyde, who was a Protestant and married to William of Orange, another Protestant, and indeed her claim was asserted in the Second Exclusion Bill. Another possibility was William of Orange.

KEY ISSUE

There was no agreement among exclusionists about who should succeed if James did not.

himself, able and of international stature and with a blood claim of his own as the son of Charles II's younger sister Mary and William II of Orange. William was, however, wary of committing himself, since he distrusted Shaftesbury and compared the Whigs to his own Dutch republican opponents. Shaftesbury himself pressed the claims of the Duke of Monmouth, Charles's bastard son by his mistress Lucy Walter. Monmouth's charisma appealed to more reckless Whigs like Harbord, Ralph Montagu and Colchester, but Charles refused to legitimise him and he remained the darling of only a minority of parliamentary Whigs. It is true that the Third Exclusion Bill omitted any reference to Mary's claim, thus appearing to leave the way open for Monmouth, but Charles adamantly denied that he had married Lucy Walter, and in any event showed his disdain for his son by dismissing him.

A major weakness of the Whigs was their failure to control Parliament as a whole. While they could dominate the Commons, they never controlled the Lords, where the bench of bishops led by Archbishop Sancroft represented a powerful Tory lobby. Charles would probably have had to sign a bill passed by both Houses, but he preferred to use his prerogative powers of prorogation and dissolution, a tactic that the Whigs were powerless to resist. They could stir up strong feelings – anti-papalism, anticlericalism, hostility to the court and to France – but they found it hard to maintain their campaign during prorogations.

At the same time Tory propaganda was stepped up too, and the Tories had their own intellectuals such as Filmer, whose 'Patriarcha' of 1680 stressed the importance of hereditary descent from God to Adam and beyond. The Whigs were portrayed as civil warriors proposing essentially an elective monarchy, and with the increasing backing of the Anglican Church and the country gentry for the Tories, the Whig claim to represent the nation exclusively looked more and more tarnished. Charles himself could also make a direct appeal to the nation over the heads of the Whig majority in Parliament, as he did in his opening speech to the Oxford Parliament and in his April Declaration.

The final question to be addressed is the extent of Charles's own responsibility for the outcome. Here again most historians stress Charles's skill and judgement in defusing by far the most serious threat to the monarchy during the reign. 'Throughout the crisis', writes Jones, 'his judgement was almost faultless.' It is not hard to find examples of restraint and cunning on the King's part: the admission of opponents to the Privy Council, the exile of James, Danby's dismissal and his refusal to interfere with the trials stemming from the Popish Plot. While he was building up his strength in the country, he tricked Shaftesbury into thinking that there was hope of Exclusion, and he resisted the temptation extended by Shaftesbury, Sunderland and the Duchess of Portsmouth to grant Exclusion in exchange for a vague promise to reduce Whig pressure on the King. When it was safe to do so, Charles deployed his prerogative powers with a touch of theatricality that emphasised the sanctity of kingship. His regal bearing at the Oxford Parliament in 1681 is the most prominent example.

> **KEY ISSUE**
>
> *The weakness of the Whigs.*

> **KEY ISSUE**
>
> *The contribution of Charles II.*

Ronald Hutton presents a contrary view. He believes that the government was never in a critical position and that the monarchy was always fundamentally strong. He sees the 1681 dissolution as a failure for Charles, the clear sign that the King could not work with Parliament. If Charles had wanted to fight a foreign war he would have been able to do so, Hutton maintains, unless he ate humble pie by recalling Parliament and appealing for subsidies. 'Put like this', he states, 'March 1681 was not a victory for Charles so much as a nadir.' It may be that the monarchy was stronger than it seemed, but that was certainly not Charles's impression at the time, or that of his advisers and opponents. It is not clear whether Charles was interested in embarking on another war in 1681, but, as we have seen, he felt able to dissolve Parliament at Oxford because his immediate financial needs were met.

7 ⌐ ROYALIST REACTION, 1681–5

Historians have had some difficulty in arriving at an acceptable description of the last four years of Charles II's rule. For the Whigs it was the 'Second Stuart Absolutism', the first being Charles I's period of rule without Parliament from 1629 to 1640 – the so-called 'Eleven Years Tyranny'. It is true that Charles II reneged on his promise to call a further Parliament after his dissolution of the Oxford Parliament in March 1681, and that Charles's action was a breach of the Triennial Act, which required that Parliament be summoned every three years. Moreover, this was also the classic period of European Absolutism, principally in Brandenburg-Prussia under the Great Elector from 1640 to 1688, and in France under Louis XIV from 1661 to 1715. Charles, however, lacked many of the advantages enjoyed by his continental counterparts: he had no standing army, no police force and no proper bureaucracy – Louis' *intendants* bore no resemblance to English JPs. Besides, Charles's whole manner was far more relaxed and, while his potential powers were very extensive, he was aware that the need to call Parliament in order to raise really substantial sums of money was always a powerful obstacle in his way.

The term 'Tory Reaction' has also been suggested. Certainly, as we shall see, Tories increasingly controlled local government, but Charles's commitment to them was not open-ended. This period may be better seen as a recovery of the advantageous situation that Charles had inherited in 1660 – a 'Second Restoration' perhaps in Michael Mullett's words. Charles began by trying to undermine the independence of the judiciary, and increasingly it became possible to secure capital convictions for sedition. Indeed, one of the early victims of the new crackdown was the wretched Oates, fined the enormous sum of £100,000 for slandering the Duke of York, and whipped into the bargain. Shaftesbury himself was arrested in 1681 on a charge of treason, and when a Whig sheriffs' grand jury refused to indict him, he fled to Holland where he died in 1683. The government enjoyed powerful support in its proceedings against its political enemies from the poet Dryden, who lampooned

See pages 63–77 for Charles I's 'personal rule'.

KEY ISSUE

Why did Charles hold no further parliaments after 1681?

the Whigs Monmouth and Shaftesbury in his brilliant satire, *Absalom and Achitophel,* which first appeared on the anniversary of Elizabeth I's accession in 1681 (also coincidentally the eve of Shaftesbury's trial).

Dryden was a poet who attracted an audience from the elite; the mass propaganda market needed a coarser, more robust form of Tory propaganda, and this was provided by Roger L'Estrange in the *Observator,* which first appeared in April 1681. L'Estrange's cartoon 'the Committee' (otherwise known as 'Popery in Masquerade') was an attempt to link the Whigs with Protestant Nonconformity and 1640s type Puritan zealotry, by arguing that Dissenters could advance the cause of popery. The cartoon depicted Nonconformists plotting the downfall of monarchy, property, order and even sexual morals as the Pope urged them on. Similar sentiments were expressed in sermons, plays, ballads, poems and playing cards; all very reminiscent of the Whig 'Petitioners', who campaigned during the Exclusion Crisis.

There is evidence of a popular response to this campaign, in the form of addresses to the King in his support from major landowners and more humble folk such as craftsmen and apprentices from many towns and cities, including Norwich, Lichfield, Yarmouth and London itself. This was sometimes linked to xenophobia in reaction to Flemish and Huguenot immigration, in a climate of fierce competition for employment opportunities and Whig backing for dissenting minorities. Dissenters, on the other hand, paid a high price for their Whiggery, as the Corporation and Five Mile Acts were more stringently enforced, Quakers in particular being imprisoned in large numbers – especially after the Rye House Plot of 1683 when 1,800 were held. They faced powerful legal obstacles in court, often lacking counsel, briefing papers or even knowledge of the charges. Indeed, anyone failing to take Anglican Holy Communion at least once a year could be debarred from pleading at law or from exercising the vote, and even in some cases, being denied poor relief. Roman Catholics, by contrast, were treated fairly mildly as recusancy convictions declined; in Middlesex for example 70 per cent of convictions for non-attendance at church had involved Roman Catholics; by 1681 this figure had declined to six per cent.

The period was marked by a series of local power struggles as the government strove to regain control of local administrations. Charles was especially determined to re-establish his hold over London, which had become the headquarters of Shaftesbury and the Exclusionists, where the ultra-Whig Green Ribbon Club had met in the King's Head tavern in Chancery Lane. While Charles depended on London financiers for loans, he was anxious to oust the Whig sheriffs who had empanelled the Whig jury, which included a brother of Sir Edmund Berry Godfrey and had acquitted Shaftesbury. The Tories won the sheriff elections in 1682, and Shaftesbury fled to Holland to protect himself from Charles's wrath. After Attorney-General Sir Robert Sawyer's trumped-up charges against the London Corporation in the following year, which led to Charles issuing a *quo warranto* writ against them, the Lord Chief Justice ruled that London could be taken into

KEY ISSUE

The charter campaign.

Charles's hands in this way. *Quo warranto* writs called for the surrender and legal scrutiny of a charter of rights, and were used by the governments of both Charles II and James II against borough charters of incorporation. In this case Charles refrained from granting a new charter to the capital, but he did appoint a new mayor and aldermen, while several livery companies were heavily fined and had new charters imposed upon them, whereby the Crown could veto the election of executive officers.

In 1682–3 14 new charters were issued with a further 76 in 1685, allowing the King to nominate officials, to veto elections and in some cases to restrict the franchise. Norwich and Bristol were among these: both had been seething hotbeds of Whig dissent. The King could now, in theory, dissolve Parliament, but this may well not have been his aim as he did not intend to call fresh elections; he may simply have preferred to be in greater control of the localities. Local Tories were often behind the impetus for change, for example local landowners such as the Earl of Bath, who surrendered 21 charters in Devon and Cornwall, used the new policy to increase their own powers.

KEY ISSUE

Monmouth remained the real problem.

James, Duke of York's return to England from Scotland in 1682 triggered a fresh series of Whig protests, but James received a rapturous welcome in Great Yarmouth where he landed and in Norwich and Newmarket. He was lionised in London too, where he was the guest of honour at a dinner of the Honourable Artillery Company. But Monmouth was the real problem.

James, Duke of Monmouth, was one of the Whigs' few assets. He had been excluded from Court in December 1681, but he remained enduringly popular, sometimes even dubbed 'the People's Prince'. Now he seemed to be openly bidding for the throne, and in September 1682 he embarked on a tour of the Midlands and the north-west. He was snubbed in Lichfield and mobbed in Chester, the latter long being a centre of Whiggery and Dissent. On 20 September 1682 Monmouth was arrested and a Commission of 'Oyer and Terminer' was sent to Chester under the formidable Sir George Jeffreys, followed by the inevitable *quo warranto* action against Chester's charter.

KEY ISSUE

The Rye House Plot of 1683 was the last scare for Charles II.

Monmouth's arrest and the lack of a parliamentary platform drove some Whigs to desperate measures. The Rye House Plot, hatched in the spring of 1683, came to light in June. The plotters intended to kill Charles II and the Duke of York as they passed the Rye House on the main road from Newmarket to London, but the scheme failed when the two brothers left Newmarket early after a fire at their lodgings in the town. Tory propaganda talked of another Gunpowder Plot and urged strong measures against the conspirators and against Monmouth, whom the plotters intended to place on the throne. The government's revenge was savage, and executions followed, among them those of Algernon Sidney, son of the Earl of Leicester and a known Republican militant, and Lord William Russell, heir to the earldom of Bedford and the man who had carried the Exclusion Bill from the Commons to the Lords. Both were members of the Council of Six founded to further Whig aims after the 1681 dissolution, but direct evidence of their involvement in the Rye House Plot was slight. Guilt by association was sufficient, however, to convict in the fearful atmosphere of 1683. The plot completed the destruction of the Whigs and Monmouth fled to Holland, and the Duke of York returned to favour, being appointed to the Cabinet Council and to the Privy Council, and restored to his old Admiralty command with the support of most Tories including Rochester, Sunderland and Portsmouth.

The Rye House Plot was the last scare to ruffle the calm of Charles's final years. With the Whigs broken, booming trade, and the legal system and much of municipal government in friendly hands, Charles could enjoy the few months of life left to him. Danby and the Catholic peers were released, and in July 1683 came the announcement of the marriage of James's younger daughter, Anne, to Prince George of Denmark. The succession after the death of James, Duke of York, seemed to be assured to Protestant hands.

Charles died on 6 February 1685 from a stroke, which his doctors tried to allay using emetics, enemas, bleeding and blistering in an effort to draw out the evil humours thought to be responsible for his affliction. On his deathbed he asked James to look after two of his surviving mistresses, Nell Gwyn and the Duchess of Portsmouth and his 'poor children', but he refused Anglican Communion. Instead, the Duke of York summoned Father Huddleston, the priest who had helped Charles to escape after the Battle of Worcester in 1651. Asked whether he was now prepared to embrace the Catholic Church, Charles replied, 'with all my heart'. With that Huddleston heard the King's confession and administered the sacrament of extreme unction. This public act of conversion to Rome is sometimes cited as evidence that Charles was always a Catholic; perhaps he was merely taking out a last minute insurance policy.

> **KEY ISSUE**
>
> *Charles II had a deathbed conversion to Roman Catholicism.*

8 ∽ CONCLUSION TO CHARLES II'S REIGN

The task of assessing the success or failure of a ruler is always a difficult one. In the case of the Stuarts it is doubly difficult as the dynasty contains two obvious failures: Charles I who lost his throne and his life, and James II who lasted a mere three years before fleeing into exile. Compared with such blatant failures a lacklustre monarch might appear a heroic success. It might be wiser, therefore, to try to reach an assessment of Charles II by taking account of his problems, and by comparing him with the widest possible variety of contemporary rulers, both English and continental.

First it has to be repeated that Charles II kept his throne – in contrast with his father and brother. Yet he achieved more than this: he fought off a major challenge from 1678 to 1681, and set up a strong regime from 1681 to 1685, leaving the Crown in a more powerful position in 1685 than it had been in 1660. He had not done this by arrogating to himself new powers; rather he had successfully asserted key prerogative

> **KEY ISSUE**
>
> *How absolute was Charles II?*

powers to face down a series of major challenges in Parliament. All this meant that the throne was safe for James and for his daughters, both of whom had married Protestant husbands. Secondly, in religious policy Charles had re-established leadership over the Church of England, which by the end of the reign had become a bulwark against both Catholicism and Dissent. The Anglican Church was the established Church, preaching passive obedience and upholding the unity of Church and State. Thirdly, Charles also left an enviable financial legacy, which would have amazed his father, for by 1685 ordinary income had finally reached the levels projected for 1660. Royal expenditure and royal income were at long last in equilibrium, boosted partly by the trade boom that followed peace with the Dutch. There was also a modest imperial expansion despite the abandonment of Tangier in 1684 on the grounds of expense. Fourthly, local government was now more securely controlled from the centre, a development appreciated by Tories who looked back on Charles's reign as a golden age of Anglicanism and benevolent monarchy. Whigs of course could not be expected to agree, denied the forum of Parliament where they had thrived, and increasingly marginalised in the last years of the reign. They tended to look back on the years of Charles's reign as a baleful example of unrelieved tyranny.

Finally, similar claims could be made for Charles's success in foreign policy. In 1685, England was neither at war nor entangled in a major alliance. Charles might be able to claim no great victories to his credit, but he had sustained no crushing defeats either. He had managed to preserve an army of 10,000, minute by continental standards but substantial in the English context, at a cost of £200,000 per year. Michael Mullett concludes, 'all in all, James II inherited an enviable legacy of royal power from his brother'.

Against this broadly favourable view of Charles II, it has been said that he could have made more of his reign with less idleness and more willpower, and this view is supported by the contemporary diarist John Evelyn whose obituary of Charles read, in part, as follows:

Q

What are Evelyn's arguments about Charles II's strengths and weaknesses?

> A prince of many virtues and many great imperfections, debonair, easy of access, not bloody or cruel, an excellent prince, doubtless had he been less addicted to women ... [in public affairs he had the chance] to have made himself, his people and all Europe happy had not his too easy nature resigned him to be managed by crafty men and some abandoned and profane wretches.

This censorious view was taken up by nineteenth-century Whig historians who criticised Charles's dissolute private life and accused him of despotism. Unfavourable comparisons were made both with his predecessors and with his successors: Elizabeth I, it was said, raised England to a high point of prestige from which the Stuarts dragged it down, while the Hanoverians were praised for restoring the kingdom to a lengthy period of tranquillity. Both assertions now look highly contentious, and modern historians would be less inclined to censure

Charles's private conduct, and more likely to forgive his apparent sloth as they note the meticulous administration of ministers such as Clarendon and Danby. There is no harm in restating the argument that of all the seventeenth-century monarchs the least successful tended to be the active ones, and it may not be going too far to say that at least some of the roots of Britain's political stability in the eighteenth century may lie in Charles II's reign.

KEY ISSUE

What sort of legacy did Charles II leave?

9 ～ JAMES VII OF SCOTLAND, JAMES II OF ENGLAND: PERSONALITIES AND PRIORITIES

JAMES VII OF SCOTLAND, JAMES II OF ENGLAND 1633–1701

James was the second son of Charles I and Henrietta Maria. Created Duke of York at birth, he escaped to Holland in 1648 and remained in exile until the Restoration when he was created Lord Admiral. He commanded the fleet ably against the Dutch in the Second Dutch War. In 1669, he secretly converted to Roman Catholicism, and revealed his new faith publicly in 1673, when the Test Act forced him to resign as Lord Admiral.

The alleged Popish Plot of 1678 brought pressure in Parliament for him to be excluded from the throne on the grounds of his religion, and he spent the period of the Exclusion Crisis from 1678 to 1681 abroad, mostly in the Spanish Netherlands or in Scotland. He returned to England in 1681, recovered his old post of Lord Admiral and was reappointed to the Council. As his elder brother Charles had no legitimate children, James succeeded to the throne in early 1685.

James was extremely obstinate, possibly aggravated by his premature mental decline. For one who had plenty of experience – as a soldier, sailor and administrator – at the centre of affairs in his brother's reign, James displayed an astonishing lack of political sense. His religious policy is surprising as he had few Catholic friends and little contact with the native Catholic community. Foreign diplomats were struck by his haughtiness, James receiving them with his hat on in a special room. At the same time James was almost as much an adulterer as his older brother had been. He was 'lusty and amorous', to use Kenyon's words, and racked by the symptoms of venereal disease contracted in the 1660s. Catherine Sedley and Arabella Churchill (by whom he had a son, the Duke of Berwick) were among the best known of his mistresses.

PICTURE 23
A portrait of James VII of Scotland, James II of England by Kneller. This is very much a court portrait. James is depicted as both an admiral and a monarch

Q

How successful has the painter been in concealing James's obstinate stupidity?

James was a convert to Roman Catholicism, and his first and second wives were also Catholic. Once on the throne he was resolved to secure

KEY ISSUES

James II had converted to Catholicism in 1668 and had 'come out' as a Catholic in 1673.

for Roman Catholics the same political and religious rights as Protestants enjoyed. This would involve freedom of worship and the removal of all civil disabilities affecting Catholics, enshrined particularly in the two Test Acts of 1673 and 1678 and the Corporation Act of 1661. He did not want to establish Catholicism as the country's sole religion or to eradicate Protestantism by force: rather he believed that Catholicism would triumph without State compulsion, and that many Anglicans were really, in their heart of hearts, Catholics. However, many contemporaries were convinced that he intended to go further He did not appreciate the fears of many Anglican clergy that they stood to lose their livelihoods, or of landowners who dreaded losing their land in any attempt to restore monasteries. He saw Nonconformists as the common enemies of both Anglicans and Catholics, and he justified persecution of Dissenters on political grounds; they were, he felt, essentially Republicans. James gave, in short, powerful arguments to his Whig opponents, and indeed to later Whig demonology, that his agenda was nothing less than the total eradication of any form of Protestantism.

James was aware of powerful practical reasons that would prevent him from trying to impose his religious views by force. In any case, only about one per cent of the population was Catholic, and James's army was small with a predominance of Protestants in its ranks. He had, moreover, no Catholic heir after 11 years of marriage: the heir presumptive was his daughter Mary, married to the Calvinist William of Orange, and he fully expected Mary to succeed him. Nevertheless, some Catholics did fear that James might endanger all toleration by acting too hurriedly and alienating the mainly Anglican Tories. When William and Mary took over, they believed, Catholics would suffer if they had tried to gain too much during James's lifetime. Non-Catholics naturally felt that Roman Catholicism was simply erroneous, that Catholics were by their nature restlessly ambitious, and that the Test Acts were a simple necessity. If Catholics were employed and admitted to Parliament, it was felt, they would soon achieve a monopoly of power and use it to extirpate Protestantism.

James's political views were similarly plain: he was quite simply divinely ordained as monarch, free to reject Parliament's advice and he saw no room for sharing power or delegating it. Government was a one-way process, and God's design was bound to succeed. He was not, however, seeking to become an absolute ruler such as Louis XIV, since he did not envisage wanting to overthrow the existing laws and constitution. Indeed, in James's address to the Privy Council on his accession he made it clear that he did not seek arbitrary power, and he was happy to repeat these assurances to Archbishop Sancroft and Bishop Turner of Ely a few days later.

Unfortunately, for all James's good intentions he suffered from basic weaknesses: a lack of intelligence and an inability to weigh up what was and what was not politically feasible. He was therefore open to manipulation by more clever men, and was stubborn when he had made up his mind. We must now look at what James made of what was arguably the strongest position of any monarch since the accession of Henry VIII.

KEY ISSUE

James II's personal limitations.

10 ∽ THE REIGN OF JAMES II, 1685–8

A *The parliamentary elections of 1685*

James made few changes in government personnel: Henry Hyde, second Earl of Clarendon, was his Lord Privy Seal and his brother Laurence, Earl of Rochester served as Lord Treasurer, while Halifax became Lord President of the Council – all were pillars of the Anglican Church. James also preferred two former Exclusionists, Godolphin and Sunderland. The latter, as Private Secretary; was James's closest political adviser, converted to Catholicism, but seemed to have no settled religious convictions. Sunderland was directed to ensure the return of 'good members' to the Parliament elected in spring 1685, but there was little need for management. Only nine Whigs were elected from the 195 members representing boroughs with new charters, and only 79 elections were actually contested. When the House of Commons assembled on 19 May 1685 the Tory Earl of Ailesbury exclaimed, 'such a landed Parliament was never seen', and indeed the loyalty of only about 40 MPs was in any doubt.

The new Parliament hastened to provide James with the money that he requested, making a life grant of the Crown's hereditary revenues and of the customs, which James had in fact been taking illegally since his accession. James therefore enjoyed £1.5 million annually with an extra £400,000 a year for eight years to settle his brother's debts and refurbish the navy. Further grants were immediately forthcoming as the threats of invasion from Argyll and Monmouth loomed: James began his reign as the wealthiest monarch since Henry VIII.

B *Monmouth's rebellion, 1685*

Monmouth was Charles II's natural son by Lucy Walter, whose good looks and jovial nature had enabled him to emerge as a Whig and Protestant icon during the Exclusion Crisis. According to G.M. Trevelyan he was 'a weak, bad and beautiful young man'. Thereafter his travels in the West Country and the north-west kept the flame alive until, in the aftermath of the Rye House Plot, Monmouth fled to Holland, where he joined a motley crew of fellow English exiles: Republican ideologues, dissenting ministers and outlawed peers. Here the preparations for an invasion of England dragged on over six months, as the plotters bought arms and chartered ships in Amsterdam, and tried to co-ordinate their plans with the Earl of Argyll, who intended to launch a simultaneous rising in the West Highlands. Finally, Monmouth set sail with 150 followers and landed at Lyme Regis in Dorset on 11 June 1685, hoping to cash in on dissenting opinion in the West Country.

Monmouth proclaimed his platform: annual Parliaments, no standing army, the repeal of all laws against Dissenters, the restoration of charters, elective sheriffs, free juries and independent judges. He also plucked up the courage to make an outright bid for the throne,

MAP 2
The progression of Monmouth's rebellion

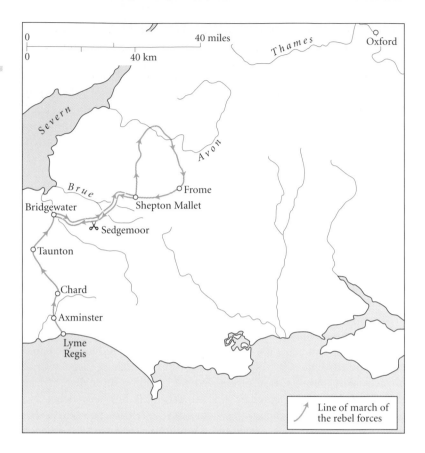

denouncing James II as a usurper and the murderer of Essex and of his brother, the late King, demanding a parliamentary enquiry into his father's death and declaring himself Charles's legitimate son, prepared to submit his title to the throne to a free Parliament. Parliament reacted swiftly to the threat and passed a bill of attainder against Monmouth, so that he could be executed at once as a traitor without further trial. An emergency grant of supply was offered of £400,000 with £5,000 for Monmouth's head, and the Earl of Feversham was sent west to deal with the threat with James's erstwhile page, John Churchill, as his second-in-command.

Monmouth gathered a force of 4,000 on foot and 500 on horseback, including few gentry and few trained men, and moved via Taunton to Bristol, which resisted his rather half-hearted attack. Finally he gambled everything on a night attack against Feversham's army at Sedgemoor on 5 July, where trained royal troops made mincemeat of his volunteers, and the wretched Duke was captured while in disguise and asleep in a ditch. The Act of Attainder was soon invoked, and Monmouth perished at Tower Hill on 15 July 1685. This was the end of what Sir George Clark called 'the last popular rising in the old England'. Lord Chief Justice Jeffreys conducted the mopping-up operation in the aptly named 'Bloody Assize', presiding over trials in Winchester, and then moving to Bristol, Salisbury, Dorchester, Exeter, Taunton and Wells.

He handed down 300 death sentences altogether, of which approximately half were carried out, and sentenced a further 1,000 to transportation to the West Indies. Jeffreys was elevated to Lord Chancellor with a reputation not only for judicial severity, but also for intimidating witnesses, jurors and his colleagues. Most of his victims were humble Nonconformists, freeholders, miners and cloth-workers from small towns such as Axminster and Shepton Mallet, hit by poverty and unemployment. Jeffreys was often inebriated in court, since he drank heavily in order to escape the agony caused by gallstones.

James emerged strengthened from the events of the summer, when Argyll's rebellion had also collapsed. There had been no general rising against him, and he had enjoyed consistent support from the Anglican hierarchy, and even from William of Orange who had offered troops. The repression that followed the rebellion, though harsh, was not unduly so by the standards of the period, and James convinced himself that his success was a sure sign of divine approval, and that God wanted him to advance the Catholic cause. He now began to throw his earlier caution to the winds.

See page 409 for the problem of gallstones.

KEY ISSUE

Why did Monmouth fail?

C *James's campaign against the Test Acts – the Hales case*

Emboldened by the crushing of Monmouth, James met Parliament for a brief and acrimonious session between 9 November and 20 November 1685, when he explained that he wanted to keep approximately 90 Roman Catholic officers in the army in defiance of the provisions of the Test Acts. It is true that Parliament had sanctioned their deployment against Monmouth, but even the Tory loyalist Sir John Reresby blanched at supporting the King, who really seemed to be asking for a standing army of 20,000 men – an unprecedented force. The Commons' reply was to grant £700,000 in return for militia reform, but James prorogued Parliament on 30 November 1685, stung by the protests of Henry Compton, Bishop of London, and the Whig Earls of Devonshire, Nottingham and Bridgewater against the King's demand for freedom to grant any civil or military office to a Roman Catholic. Parliament never met again during the reign.

James now began to try to infiltrate Catholics into important positions: with Sunderland's connivance he began to fashion a new inner cabinet, comprising Sunderland himself, Jeffreys, and Father Edward Petre, James's Jesuit confessor. Halifax was dismissed in October 1685, and four Catholic peers were advanced to the Privy Council, while the King began a policy of 'closeting' – pressurising individual MPs to support repeal of the Test Acts. Catholics began to infiltrate the magistracy; 250 in 1686 alone, and James re-established diplomatic relations with Rome in September 1685 for the first time since 1558. In November, a papal envoy arrived, soon to be advanced to the full status of nuncio, and James pressed on towards further initiatives.

Clarendon, Lord Lieutenant of Ireland, was ordered to dismiss

KEY ISSUE

James's relationship with Parliament deteriorated after the defeat of Monmouth's rebellion.

KEY ISSUE

James II's pro-Catholic campaign.

Protestant officers and to promote Catholics, and James decided to bring a test case to obtain a ruling that he could dispense with the Test Acts. This was the famous case of *Godden v. Hales* of June 1686, when James, having dismissed six out of the twelve judges, asked the High Court to agree that he could dispense Sir Edward Hales, governor of Dover and a staunch Catholic, from the 1673 Act. All but one judge found in favour of the King, and Lord Chief Justice Herbert used the biblical story of Abraham and Isaac to buttress his ruling. Hales was instantly promoted to be Governor of the Tower and Master of the Ordnance; there now seemed to be no legal barrier to stop James from appointing Catholics to any other office. Tyrconnel ('lying Dick Talbot') was appointed as Deputy Lord Lieutenant of Ireland, and he began to purge the officer corps of Protestants, replacing 3,500 with Catholics, fuelling Protestant fears of massacre. James pressed on regardless, appointing the Catholic Strickland to command the Fleet, and promoting three Catholic peers to the treasury commission – Lords Bellasis, Dover and Arundell of Wardour. Rochester and Clarendon clung on grimly, but both lost office at the start of 1687, as James moved ahead with his Catholicisation programme: Catholic schools and friaries, Benedictine houses and more Catholic presses all began to appear, the Inns of Court were urged to admit papists and four Catholic bishops were appointed. Despite James's rather poor relations with Rome (the Pope refused to appoint Petre to the cardinalate), and the fears of many English Catholics that James's policy was jeopardising a good working relationship with English Protestants, and with William and Mary, who stood to succeed on James's death, he now began to put pressure on the Anglican Church.

D *James's campaign against the Anglican Church*

As 1686 wore on the King came to believe that the greatest obstacle to further change was the Anglican Church itself. In February he complained to the hierarchy about anti-Catholic sermons, and, not wishing to exercise the royal supremacy himself, James set up in July a Commission for Ecclesiastical Causes under Jeffreys to silence Anglican critics. This bore a close resemblance to the hated Court of High Commission abolished by the Long Parliament in 1641, and Sancroft, the Archbishop of Canterbury, refused to serve, but the Commission went ahead under Sunderland. James himself issued 'Directions to Preachers', ordering the clergy to confine sermons to doctrines in the catechism and to avoid attacks on Rome, and in May 1686 he suspended Compton, the Bishop of London, for failing to discipline the Reverend John Sharp of St Giles's in the Fields from preaching. When Compton refused to comply, James used the newly founded Commission to bring him to heel. Archbishop Sancroft resigned, but James pressed on, believing that as Catholics were still a minority, it was reasonable to weigh the scales blatantly in their favour. The climax of this policy was the Declaration of Indulgence issued in April 1687, suspending the penal laws against Catholics and Dissenters. James believed that Dissenters were a large and powerful force, and he succumbed to the charm of William Penn, founder of a Quaker colony in North America in 1682, who assured him that Dissenters would become loyal subjects once the persecution against them ceased. Accordingly, 1,000 Quakers were now released from prison.

James now turned his attention to the universities, the main institutions for training clergy. These pre-Reformation foundations should, he thought, benefit Catholics, who should be allowed to matriculate, take degrees and hold college fellowships without having to take the oaths of allegiance and supremacy. During 1685–6 James had some success with a few colleges: a Catholic master was forced on Sidney Sussex College, Cambridge in defiance of its Elizabethan statutes, a Catholic was appointed as Dean of Christ Church, Oxford and a Catholic convert, Obadiah Walker, kept his position as Master of University College. Magdalen College, Oxford, remained, however, James's main target, and when the president died in March 1687, the Fellows were told to elect a Catholic convert, Anthony Farmer, in his place. The Fellows demurred, and chose another candidate on the grounds that their statutes obliged them to elect a former Fellow of Magdalen or of New College, and Farmer was neither of these. James dropped his preferred candidate on the Ecclesiastical Commission's advice, and offered a pluralist Catholic bishop, Samuel Parker, instead, and both James and the Commission went to Oxford to browbeat the Fellows. Eventually, the 25 Fellows of Magdalen College were deprived, and Catholics replaced them, the College becoming in the words of Roger Lockyer, 'to all intents and purposes a seminary for training the future rulers of Catholic England', especially under the Presidency of Bonaventura Giffard, Parker's successor from March 1688.

> **KEY ISSUE**
>
> *Why did James attach such importance to control over the universities?*

James still hoped to obtain a Parliament prepared to repeal the Test Acts, although he maintained that he would not interfere with the established Church or disturb the holders of ex-monastic lands. He still set great store by his relationship with the Dissenters, although the 1676 census had seemed to show that their numbers were quite small, and they were in any event deeply divided – Presbyterians, Independents, Baptists and Quakers. Moreover many Dissenters understandably distrusted James, sensing that his long-term aim was to impose an intolerant Catholicism. Surely, they mused, toleration and Catholicism were incompatible? Halifax played on these doubts in his *Letter to a Dissenter,* published in the summer of 1687, asking whether they wanted 'to be hugged now, only that you may be the better squeezed at another time'.

James, advised by Sunderland and Jeffreys, was determined to fill the next Parliament by altering the county representation. Accordingly most lords lieutenant were replaced, yet by 1688 less than a quarter of JPs and deputy lieutenants were Catholics, and able to give favourable replies to the three questions described by Mark Kishlansky as 'the litmus test for employment in local government'. These were:

1 Would you vote for repeal of the penal laws and tests?

2 Would you support candidates willing to do so?

3 Would you support the King's Declaration of Indulgence by living contentedly with those of all persuasions?

New appointments of JPs took place early in 1688 to supplant those who had replied unsatisfactorily to the three questions, but there was sufficient opposition to James's plan to force him to drop the idea of a Parliament in 1687. In fact, most lords lieutenant refused to put the questions and were sacked.

On 7 May 1688 James issued a second Declaration of Indulgence, repeating the terms of the previous one and envisaging a meeting of Parliament in November that year at the latest. All Anglican bishops were to distribute the Declaration throughout their dioceses, and it was to be read in all churches on two successive Sundays: 20 and 27 May. This move provoked a confrontation with the Anglican hierarchy, and Archbishop Sancroft and six others asked James to withdraw the order. Compliance with its terms was indeed very patchy: in London it was only read in seven churches, and it reached only six dioceses. Under these circumstances Jeffreys, Sunderland and Petre urged the King to ignore the snub to his authority, but James ordered the prosecution of the bishops for publishing a seditious libel, and they were thrown in the Tower. The verdict of the court acquitting the seven bishops came as a bombshell. The four judges and the jury were divided, but they returned a verdict of not guilty. James was humiliated and his opponents rejoiced: in London bonfires were lit, church bells rang and an effigy of the Pope was burned. Even the troops on Hounslow Heath cheered. The trial of the seven bishops is the clearest indication of James's incompetence: to alienate the Church of England and to provoke a rebellion by no less than seven of its prelates, including the primate, took some doing.

A rebellion against James was unlikely however. He could only be effectively challenged by a professional army from abroad, and his son-in-law, William of Orange, remained the heir presumptive as long as James's 15-year-old marriage to Mary of Modena failed to produce a child. On 20 June 1688 the unbelievable happened: Mary of Modena gave birth to a live son.

> **KEY ISSUE**
>
> *James was determined to indulge Catholics fully with a further Declaration of Indulgence.*

> **KEY ISSUE**
>
> *The birth of a son to James's second wife, Mary of Modena transformed the situation overnight.*

See page 410 for the birth of James the Old Pretender.

E *The birth of James's son and William's disembarkation*

The child lived and was named James Francis Edward Stuart. For James's political and religious enemies a period of unbroken Catholic rule seemed to open up, despite Protestant attempts to cast doubt on the authenticity of the birth – the so-called 'warming pan' rumour. At once contact was established between William and the 'Immortal Seven' – Shrewsbury, Devonshire, Danby, Sidney, Russell, Lumley and Bishop Compton who pledged their support to the Prince of Orange if he came

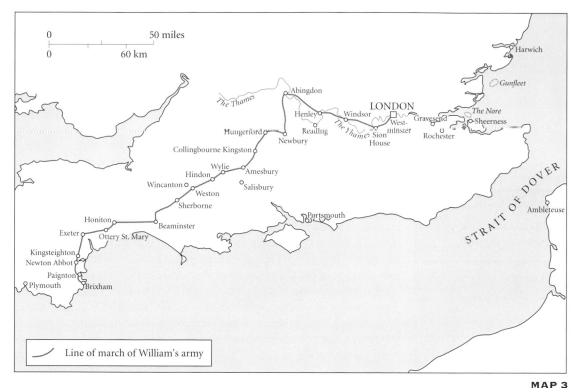

MAP 3

The progression of William of Orange's invasion

over with an army. Contacts continued, but many members of the political community hesitated to become involved, including Halifax, Nottingham, Churchill and Sunderland. To these men contact with William was treason, and there was still hope that James's policies would fail or that the child might die. Ideas of obedience and non-resistance remained strong, and the outbreak of civil war was the worst possible outcome.

Nevertheless, William told one of the seven in the spring of 1688 that he was ready to invade, and sent his envoy Zuylestein to obtain a letter of invitation from leading figures in England. William's reply was the Declaration from the Hague of 20 September 1688, confirming his intention to rescue Englishmen from absolute power and to restore their liberties. There was no mention of seeking the Crown himself; William confined himself to ridding James of his evil counsellors and to securing the election of a free Parliament. William's motives in invading England formed part of his wider diplomacy, for he was sworn to oppose French expansion in Europe, particularly since Louis XIV's encroachments after the Treaty of Nijmegen in 1679, the siege of Vienna by his Turkish allies in 1683 and the Revocation of the Edict of Nantes in 1685, which caused thousands of expelled French Protestants to flee to England and Holland. In 1686, William began to organise the League of Augsburg, and he valued England as a potential ally. He was also concerned to protect his wife Mary's rights to the English throne, which were threatened by the birth of James's son. However, William could not sail for England if Louis still posed a military threat to

KEY ISSUE

William of Orange was now poised to invade England.

Holland, but this danger was removed when Louis launched an attack on the Rhine fortress of Philippsburg in September 1688. Now the States of Holland agreed to William's invasion plan.

James reacted by calling a Parliament to meet in November, and by promising to reverse many of his policies: Compton's suspension was removed, London and other cities had their charters restored, newly appointed lords lieutenant were dismissed, the Fellows of Magdalen returned and the Ecclesiastical Commission was abolished. James even offered to exclude Catholics from the Commons, but he would not remove Catholic officers from the army, or abandon his use of the dispensing power.

KEY ISSUE

What factors delayed William's arrival?

On 29 October 1688 William's fleet set off, but was driven back by storms (the so-called 'Popish Wind'), but he made a fresh start a few days later when the wind had veered round to the East ('the Protestant Wind'). Such a risky enterprise by the cautious Dutchman seems out of character, but James's naval commander, Admiral Dartmouth, could not put out of port, and the navy was never deployed against William, while James's army of more than 20,000 men waited in the south-east for a landing that never occurred. Finally, William landed at Brixham in Devon on 5 November, a day of omen for pious Protestants. He had overcome the considerable practical problems of operating in winter with an uncertain reception in England, and began to move towards Exeter. Immediately, local magnates such as Sir Edward Seymour and the Marquis of Bath openly declared for him, and his forces swelled to more than 14,000 men, of whom a substantial proportion were still foreign mercenaries: Swedes, Brandenburgers, Dutch, Swiss and French Huguenot volunteers.

James nominally disposed of a force of 25,000 men, but he was faced with a dilemma: if he tarried in London he would give time for William to gather support, but if he left the capital, there was no guarantee that he would be able to bring William to battle. Meanwhile William set out towards London via Wincanton, Sherborne, Hungerford and Reading, assembling more support as he went, for example from Lord Delamere in Cheshire, and the Earls of Devonshire and Danby elsewhere. It was still not clear, however, that William and his supporters wished to depose James.

The King decided to leave London on 17 November for Salisbury, which he reached two days later, but he soon lost his nerve and returned to the capital. His morale was hardly improved on the way back when he learned of further defections: Churchill, Grafton, Drumlanrig, Ormonde, Prince George of Denmark (husband to his younger daughter Anne), and even Anne herself. James meanwhile was offered conflicting advice: there were those who urged him to withdraw to France and to return under more favourable circumstances, while others urged him to treat with William, and to take at face value William's affirmation that he had not come to depose the King. James, however, was intransigent, sending his Queen and the young Prince of Wales to France. On 27 November, James met with a group of peers in London to discuss the summoning of Parliament, and he was advised to pardon Orange, and to dismiss all Catholics in his employment. In the meantime James had sent three commissioners to meet William: Halifax, Nottingham and Godolphin, who met him at the Bear Inn at Hungerford. William was unwilling to return to Holland, his task complete; instead he pressed on towards London where he arrived on 18 December, as anti-Catholic riots were breaking out there.

James left London a week earlier intending to go to France. His apparent abandonment of his responsibilities removed the final impediment to a change of monarch. He even bungled the attempt to flee, when he was recognised by some Kentish fishermen on 16 December and returned ignominiously to Whitehall. An eyewitness described James's sufferings when he was captured:

> Some seamen put off in quest of a prize, and about eleven at night they took a Custom-House boat, in which proved to be the king, Sir Edward Hales and Ralph Sheldon. The king was in a particular disguise and so not known that night; but, as if destiny deigned to be severe upon him, the seamen treated him very roughly above the rest. One cried out 't'was Father Petre, they knew it to be so by his lean jaws'. A second called him an old hatchet-faced Jesuit. A third swore it was a cunning old rogue. He was detained at sea all night, and brought up from Owse, where he landed, to Feversham, where he was presently discovered. He seemed cast down at the noise of the rabble, and at last asked me plainly, 'What have I done? What are the errors of my reign?' He was really very melancholy at times and often shed tears. His guards were so severe upon him . . .
>
> From a letter by a gentleman who came to the King when he was taken, printed in Tindall's Continuation of Rapin's *History of England* (1751).

Q *Which of James II's characteristics come across in this account?*

On 22 December James tried again, hurling the Great Seal into the Thames, and at last setting sail for France from the Kent coast for Ambleteuse. On 28 December he was reunited with Mary of Modena and his infant son in St Germain-en-Laye, a few miles to the west of Paris, where a French courtier remarked, 'when you speak to him, you realise why he's here'.

11 ⌐ THE CAUSES OF THE GLORIOUS REVOLUTION

By 1688, if not before, it was quite clear that James II had lost the allegiance and trust of a large section of the political community; in other words his relationship with the upper classes in Church and State had quite simply broken down. James had aroused, in a more acute form, the two fears that had bedevilled the reigns of his father and brother: popery and absolutism. Unlike them, however, James was an admitted and committed Catholic, and showed from an early age a worrying authoritarian streak. After Monmouth's rebellion he seemed to be imposing on England a Roman Catholic despotism similar to that exercised by Louis XIV of France. His reign coincided with the most flagrant example of Louis's persecution of the Huguenots, the French Protestant minority, when in October 1685 Louis revoked the Edict of Nantes of 1598 that enshrined civil and religious rights for Huguenots. Thousands of Huguenots fled abroad, many to Holland and England, where they had lurid tales to tell of the *dragonnades*, vicious military action against Protestants carried out by Louis's soldiery. James's quarrel with the Anglican leadership and his determination to dispense with the Test Acts, and eventually to repeal them, put him on a collision course with the English elite. James was indeed an anointed king, but he tested the Anglican doctrine of non-resistance to tyranny to breaking point.

There is also plenty of evidence of more widespread opposition to James's rule. Many common people joined Monmouth in 1685, when the ruling order backed the King, the replies to James's three questions of 1687 showed significant dissent and, once William had landed in 1688, support for the Prince of Orange surged as soon as it was clear that James was unable, or unwilling, to use his superior military and naval resources to bring the interloper to battle. William's accession was the more acceptable, as he was himself a royal prince married to a Stuart princess, and the couple were both Protestants, committed to ensuring a Protestant succession. Yet when William invaded, it was not ostensibly with the intention of seizing the throne. James II fled abroad, leaving the throne vacant and a major constitutional crisis for William and the establishment to resolve.

KEY ISSUE

Why did James II's departure cause a constitutional crisis?

---

12 ∽ FOREIGN POLICY AND NAVAL STRATEGY, 1660–85

A *The making of foreign policy*

Most monarchs considered the making of foreign policy as their most important function, and while there were many other inputs into English diplomacy, courtiers, ministers, politicians, trading companies and the wider public, Charles II regarded it as his personal policy and the Restoration Settlement established this right as unchallengeable. There were secretaries of state responsible for following overseas developments: the Southern Department concerned itself with France, the Iberian Peninsula and the Ottoman Empire, the Northern Department with the Empire, the United Provinces, Scandinavia and Russia; but Charles was quite capable of conducting his own foreign policy through alternative channels as the Secret Treaty of Dover was to show. Parliament could do little to constrain the King: it met infrequently (for only seven months in total from 1679 to 1689), in brief sessions interspersed with long prorogations, and it usually had little information on which to reach a view. To a large extent Parliament did of course control the royal purse strings, especially in time of war and so an ambitious foreign policy was normally difficult.

The issues that divided nations were varied by the late seventeenth century. Religion was less of a divisive factor than it had been, but it could still form part of the motivation for diplomacy, as Louis XIV's persecution of French Protestants proved. Trading rivalry was an important factor, especially in Anglo-Dutch relations, as was rivalry for the acquisition of territory. Finally, monarchs were often motivated by affronts to their own or their family's honour and prestige, which may well appear trivial to the modern mind, but which offended rulers in this period.

B *The international situation in 1660*

Charles II began his reign with some important advantages, for he owed no obligations to fellow monarchs and he had regained his throne without powerful foreign support. However, England was not a major power, and, as we have seen, an ambitious forward policy was financially impossible. Indeed, Charles sold Dunkirk to France in 1661 and disposed of Tangier in 1684 for reasons of penury. The major issue looming on the European Continent was that of the Spanish Succession, in which England could not expect to play a major part. The huge Spanish Habsburg Empire included much of Italy, the southern Netherlands, other territories on France's eastern frontier, and of course the New World. Philip IV's death in 1665 was followed by the accession of the sickly Carlos II, a syphilitic paralytic, who seemed unlikely to survive for long, and who had no direct heirs. Who then would inherit this bonanza?

Louis XIV's France was well placed to profit from Spain's demise, as it was probably the only European superpower after the treaty of the Pyrenees in 1659. Charles was attracted by friendship with Louis; England could gain from the seemingly inevitable break up of the Spanish Empire, and a Franco-Dutch alliance was to be avoided at all costs. There was also a ready-made conduit for secret negotiations with France in Charles's sister, Henrietta Anne, who had married Louis's brother, Philippe, Duke of Orleans.

Charles was hostile to the United Provinces, which had forced Spain to recognise their independence after 80 or more years of war in 1648 at the Treaty of Münster. This was a commercially ascendant and economically aggressive state, which was likely to clash with English trading interests in the Baltic, West Africa, India, the Far East and North America. They also disposed of a formidable navy, and they were Protestants. Charles would need to tread carefully to avoid upsetting English anti-Catholic sensibilities. Charles found his bride in Portugal, England's oldest and most reliable ally, and Catherine of Braganza brought with her a substantial dowry of £500,000 in cash and possession of Bombay and Tangier. Other states which need to be put into the equation include Sweden, a declining force in the Baltic area under Charles X; Austria under another branch of the Habsburgs and threatened by Hungarians, Poles, Swedes and Turks; and the Ottoman

Empire, itself expanding westwards and even besieging Vienna in 1683. The European diplomatic power game was therefore one which even large states entered at their peril.

C *The second Dutch war, 1665–7*

Anglo-Dutch commercial rivalry was fierce. In short, the Dutch had secured for themselves a lucrative slice of Spanish trade from which English merchants felt excluded. A powerful lobby of London-based companies protested, especially the East India Company and the Royal Africa Company. The burden of their complaint was 'unfair' trading practices, such as bribery to obtain monopolies, and firing on those who would trade with English merchants. There were some particular issues between the two states that remained unresolved. Above all, Pula Run, an East Indian island promised to the English by the Dutch back in 1654, and the outstanding compensation claim dating from 1643 for two English ships seized by the Dutch, the *Bonaventure* and the *Bona Esperanza*, valued at £100,000.

See pages 298–300 for the economic implications of the Dutch Wars.

The Dutch nursed their own grievances: a series of Acts of Parliament seemed directed against them – the 1660 Navigation Act, the Statute of Frauds of 1662 and the Staple Act of the following year. Charles's ambassador at the Hague did not help. Sir George Downing displayed a virulent hatred against the Dutch, and he assured London that they would concede any English demand, fearing a repetition of the first Dutch war and an outbreak of internal unrest. They also, hinted Downing darkly, harboured English regicides sought by the English courts.

As war loomed the Council divided. Clarendon, who was later to be made a scapegoat for the failure of the campaign, opposed war, but he was outnumbered by Bennet, Clifford, York and Charles himself, lured by the prospect of huge profits. The Duke of York was the governor of the Royal Africa Company and he was also Lord Admiral, craving glory and action. Parliament too was caught up in the heady war fever, and voted a supply of £2.5 million over three years at its session of November 1664; on 22 February 1665 Charles formally declared war against the United Provinces. At first things went well; York won the first major naval engagement off Lowestoft on 3 June 1665, when 20 Dutch ships and 5,000 men were lost, the worst Dutch defeat in all three Anglo-Dutch wars, and hailed by Pepys as 'a greater victory never known in the world'. Yet the victory was not followed up, and York could do little to protect vulnerable English shipping in other theatres such as the Mediterranean.

In January 1666, Louis XIV joined the Dutch cause, worried about English naval hegemony, and two further naval engagements ensued: the inconclusive Four Days Battle of June 1666 and a victory over the Dutch at the North Foreland in July. However, the best known event of the whole war could not in any sense be described as an English victory: on 12 June 1667 a Dutch fleet under De Ruyter broke the boom defend-

---

ing the Medway Estuary and the approach to Chatham dockyard, burned several English warships and made off with several others, including the flagship *Royal Charles*, the very vessel in which Charles had crossed the North Sea seven years previously to reclaim his throne. This was as much an administrative and political defeat as a naval one, since at Chatham ships' crews had been paid off, ship-repairing cut back and shore defences neglected, and the search was on for scapegoats – Catholics, Buckingham, Charles himself and Clarendon all came under suspicion. War was the acid test of seventeenth-century government, and Charles's apparently indolent and incompetent administration seemed to have failed it.

On 25 July 1667, England and the Dutch signed the Treaty of Breda, whereby England abandoned its claim to Pula Run and Surinam in exchange for New Amsterdam (later renamed New York), New Jersey and New Delaware. Charles therefore dominated the eastern seaboard of North America, but the treaty hardly addressed the issues which had led to the war's outbreak, and Clarendon's fall followed very shortly.

KEY ISSUE

Why was England hostile to the United Provinces in the 1660s?

D *The secret Treaty of Dover (1670) and the third Dutch war (1672–4)*

The real goal of Charles's personal diplomacy was an alliance with Louis XIV, and secret talks began in 1668 through 'Madame', Charles's sister, Henrietta Anne, who was married to Louis's brother. This was at a time when England was technically allied to Holland and Sweden in the Triple Alliance of January 1668, aimed ostensibly at containing French expansion through a Protestant coalition. The treaty of Aix-la-Chapelle brought Louis's War of Devolution in the Spanish Netherlands to an end, and the Triple Alliance decayed. The terms of the Treaty of Dover were agreed with Madame on 16 May 1670. Charles agreed to send 4,000 troops to help Louis against the Dutch in return for an annual subvention of £225,000 and a promise to give England three strategic areas controlling the Scheldt Estuary – Walcheren, Sluys and Cadzand. The secret clauses were that Charles would rescind the penal laws against the Catholics, and would himself convert to Rome in return for a further £150,000 from France. It is easy to see why Charles might want to wage war against the Dutch, as fierce trading rivalry between England and the United Provinces was still prevalent, and the Medway disgrace could be avenged. An alliance with France would also give England a chance to make huge territorial acquisitions when the Spanish Empire eventually disintegrated. It is, however, less easy to see why Charles agreed to the secret clauses, of which only a small circle consisting of James, Duke of York, Arlington and Lord Arundell of Wardour was aware. There was the ever-present danger that the truth might leak out, and indeed Charles's political opponents often suspected that there was more to the Treaty of Dover than met the eye; there was also scope for Louis to blackmail Charles.

KEY ISSUE

The secret Treaty of Dover has long been a problem for historians. Why was Charles prepared to sign an alliance with France, and to promise the French King that he would convert to Catholicism?

KEY ISSUE

Why did Charles agree to the religious clauses of the secret Treaty of Dover?

The secret religious clauses have puzzled historians. It may be that Charles was genuinely attracted to Catholicism, to which the French general Turenne and the Duke of York had already converted; and it may also be that Charles genuinely appreciated the role of Catholics in enabling him to escape in 1651. It has also been suggested that Charles wanted to please his favourite sister Henrietta Anne ('Minette'), who was mortally ill and married to Louis XIV's brother, Philip, Duke of Orleans. However, the strongest argument seems to be that they improved his bargaining position with Louis, and were the best way to achieve a special relationship with a stronger partner.

Charles declared war on the Dutch on 17 March 1672 following continuing disputes over the Indies and Surinam, and an apparently trivial incident involving the failure of Dutch ships to salute the English flag on Lady Temple's yacht. Parliament agreed a supply of £800,000 and hostilities commenced. The English fleet bungled an attack on the Dutch fleet returning from Smyrna, and had to settle for a draw at Sole Bay off Southwold on 28 May, when two ships were lost and Admiral the Earl of Sandwich drowned. The 1673 naval campaign directed by Prince Rupert fared little better. The French army surged into the Netherlands and quickly overran five provinces, whereupon the States General offered reasonable terms in 1673. Louis rejected the deal and the war dragged on. Under mounting criticism at home Charles cut his losses, and concluded the Treaty of Westminster, ratified on 24 February 1674. The colonial and commercial issues that separated the two powers remained unresolved, while the Dutch conceded the flag issue and offered a modest indemnity.

KEY ISSUE

In reality Charles was conducting two separate foreign policies.

The reality of two foreign policies emerged starkly in Danby's ministry. Danby wanted to strengthen ties with the Dutch, and he engineered the marriage of James, Duke of York's elder daughter Mary to William of Orange; while Charles wished to avoid a breach with France which could lead to the nightmare of a Franco-Dutch rapprochement and the revelation of the Dover treaty. To this end he hoped, ever the optimist, to defuse his subjects' hostility to France.

E *Isolation, 1674–85*

The war went on between France and the Dutch, as the two sides talked terms at Nijmegen from 1674. Charles's policy remained one of avoiding a breach with the French, and also of preventing a formal alliance between Louis and the Dutch, should hostilities cease, and Louis be tempted to publish the terms of the Dover treaty. Relations with France, however, remained warm: Charles received secretly an annual subsidy in 1676 from Louis for three years in the teeth of opposition from Danby, and in the following year, at St Germain-en-Laye, this was reinforced by a commercial agreement. The twin track approach of English foreign policy resumed in 1678, as demands grew in the Commons for a more belligerent stance towards France. In March, England concluded a new defensive treaty with the United Provinces, and in May Charles reached another secret accord with Louis. Parliament, however, was appeased by the signing of the Treaty of Nijmegen, and the marriage between William of Orange and the Duke of York's elder daughter, Mary.

Once Charles had survived the Exclusion Crisis, he was able, as we have seen, to dispense with Parliament after March 1681, since Louis renewed the subsidy of £300,000 per year over four years, on condition that Parliament remained prorogued. Meanwhile, in 1683, James's younger daughter, Anne, married the Lutheran Prince George of Denmark, and England's Protestant succession seemed assured – unless a son was born to James's new wife, Mary Beatrice of Modena.

What then had Charles achieved in foreign policy? There were, as we have seen, strong reasons for hostility against the Dutch, but there were equally strong reasons for being suspicious of Louis's aggrandisement on the Continent. Charles could claim to have done something to check French aggression in 1668 and 1678, but Louis's attack on the Netherlands in 1672 did arouse strong opposition, which intensified when it seemed that his aims were to destroy the United Provinces. In 1681, when he was technically at peace, Louis acquired Strasbourg as part of his 'Reunions' policy and proceeded to make further gains on his eastern frontier without formal declaration of war. Charles was usually able to prevent a Franco-Dutch alliance (this happened briefly only once), but he was dogged by rumours from the early 1670s that he must have concluded some sort of deal with Louis. In 1685, England was neither at war nor in a dangerous alliance, but Englishmen were entitled to wonder whether the policy of alternating sops to Parliament and the commercial lobby through an anti-Dutch policy, at the same time as treating with the unreliable in Louis XIV, was in England's best interests.

> **KEY ISSUE**
>
> *Did England gain anything from Charles II's foreign policy?*

F *James II, 1685–8*

James continued his brother's policy of friendship with France by signing an agreement in 1686 with Louis to settle outstanding colonial claims in North America. However, as James struggled to keep his throne at home, a major European war was looming as a powerful anti-French coalition gathered under William of Orange – the League of Augsburg, set up in 1686 to check Louis's aggressive designs on the Holy Roman Empire. When James sought refuge in France in December 1688 and was supplanted by William, a reversal of the foreign policy of the previous 25 years looked probable. The English throne was attractive to William partly for foreign policy reasons, and Louis could now use the exiled James as a pawn in his own wider diplomatic ambitions.

13 ⌐ BIBLIOGRAPHY

For a succinct general survey of the Stuart period see *A Monarchy Transformed, Britain 1603–1714* by Mark Kishlansky (Penguin, 1996).

The Making of a Great Power, Late Stuart and Early Georgian Britain 1660–1722 by Geoffrey Holmes (Longman, 1993) is a lively, stimulating and highly detailed survey with a most useful compendium of information after the main text. *The Stuart Age, England, 1603–1714* by Barry Coward (Longman, 1994) is highly detailed and comprehensive, while a rather older and more concise textbook is *Country and Court, England 1658–1714* by J.R. Jones (Edward Arnold, 1978). *The Stuarts* by J.P. Kenyon (Batsford, 1958) still reads well. Specifically on Charles II and James II see *The Restoration, 1660–1688* by Paul Seaward (Macmillan, 1991), *Charles II and James II* by Nicholas Fellows (Hodder and Stoughton, 1995) and *James II and English Politics 1678–1688* by Michael Mullett (Routledge, 1994), which includes valuable coverage of the 'Popish Plot' and the Exclusion Crisis. There are two lively and highly detailed biographies of Charles II: *Charles II* by John Miller (Weidenfeld, 1991) and *Charles the Second, King of England, Scotland, and Ireland* by Ronald Hutton (Oxford, 1989), while the best account of James II's reign remains *James II, a Study in Kingship* by John Miller (Wayland, 1978 and Methuen, 1989). The pamphlet entitled *Politics in the Reign of Charles II* by K.H.D. Haley (Blackwell, 1985) is also useful. Finally, John Miller's essay on Britain in *Absolutism in Seventeenth Century Europe* by John Miller (ed) (Macmillan, 1990) addresses the question of how far Charles's or James's reign approached the levels of absolutism achieved in other European states.

14 ᔕ DISCUSSION POINTS AND ESSAY QUESTIONS

A *This section consists of questions that might be used for discussion (or written answers) as a way of expanding on the chapter and testing understanding of it.*

1. How far had Charles II solved his financial problems by 1662?
2. How successful was the Restoration religious settlement in establishing toleration and comprehension?
3. Why did Clarendon fall in 1667?
4. What were the consequences of Clarendon's fall?
5. What attracted Charles II to Louis XIV's France?
6. Did the Cabal follow a consistent policy?
7. Why did the ministry of the Cabal come to an end?
8. Is it possible to distinguish between Whigs and Tories under Charles II?
9. Account for the prevalence of anti-popery in late seventeenth-century England.
10. How far was Roman Catholicism a threat in Charles II's reign?
11. Why did Titus Oates's allegations arouse such concern in 1678?
12. Why was no Exclusion Bill ever passed between 1678 and 1681?
13. Did Charles II emerge stronger or weaker from the Exclusion Crisis?

14. Why did Monmouth's rebellion fail?

15. What evidence is there that James II intended to eradicate Protestantism?

16. Why did William of Orange come to England?

17. Why did James II flee his kingdom?

B *Essay questions.*

1. How successful was the Restoration Settlement in solving England's problems in 1660?

2. How far did the Restoration Settlement represent a return to the past?

3. How important was the succession problem in the reigns of Charles II and James II?

4. How 'absolute' were Charles II and James II?

5. How successful was Charles II in dealing with the Exclusion Crisis?

6. Are there any consistent features of Charles II's foreign policy?

7. Were the Dutch or the French the more serious threat to English interests in this period?

8. Why did Charles II keep the throne and James II lose it?

15 ～ DOCUMENTARY EXERCISE ON ABSOLUTISM

There now follows a number of documentary extracts which all describe in one way or another the theme of 'absolutism', the fashionable political doctrine on the Continent in the seventeenth century and the crime of which Charles II's and James II's enemies accused them. Some are primary sources, i.e. written at the time by contemporaries involved in the issue; others are secondary sources, i.e. written later, for example by historians. There is no reason to suppose that primary sources should necessarily be more reliable than secondary ones; equally, you should not think that just because a document is clearly biased it is useless to a historian. Any document will tell you, at the very least, what the writer believes, or what he or she wants the reader to believe.

Take account of the number of marks allocated for each question; common sense should indicate that the more marks available, the more detail and length is required – particularly supporting detail. First, read the sources carefully and take note of the attribution of each document – in other words, when it was written, who wrote it and for whom.

Questions based on documents are likely to ask you all or some of the following sorts of questions:

1 To explain the meanings of words or phrases within documents.

2 To say what the significance of a source is.

3 To summarise the argument of a given source.

4 To compare and contrast a document with another source or sources, and to draw conclusions.

5 To assess the reliability of documents.

6 To be aware of the uses and limitations of documents: an unreliable source may be useful.

7 To synthesise, in other words to examine the plausibility (or otherwise) of a particular assertion by reference to a particular set of documentary sources.

It will be useful to know that Bossuet was a cleric, who approved of Louis XIV's assertion of absolutism (at least in theory). Bossuet was delighted, for example, when Louis grasped the nettle and expelled the irreconcilable Huguenots in 1685. G.M. Trevelyan was a Whig historian writing at the beginning of the twentieth century, who saw both Charles II and James II as aberrations in the progression of England towards liberal institutions and human rights. Likewise, A.A. Mitchell is hostile to James II's pretensions to be a Divine Right monarch, but he writes more recently. Charles II's declaration of December 1662 is a primary source, but also one that attempts to set out the King's view. Finally in the case of *Godden v. Hales* Lord Chief Justice Herbert is delivering the court's judgement and the reasons for it.

Study sources A to E, and attempt the questions that follow.

A J.B. Bossuet writes about the theory of absolutism in 1670.

Royal authority is sacred ... paternal ... absolute ... subject to reason ... God establishes kings as his ministers and reigns over people through them ... Therefore princes act as ministers of God and as His lieutenants on earth. It is through them that he exercises His empire ... The person of the king is sacred ... God has had them anointed by His prophets with a sacred ointment, as He has had His pontiffs and His altars anointed. But even before being in fact anointed, they are sacred by virtue of their task, as representatives of His divine majesty, delegated by His providence to execute His design ...

Religion and conscience demand that we obey the prince ... Even if kings fail in their duty, their charge and their ministry must be respected. For Scriptures tell us: 'Obey your masters, not only those who are mild and good, but also those who are peevish and unjust'. Thus there is something religious in the respect which one renders the prince. Service to God and respect for kings are one thing ...

The prince need render Account to no one for what he orders ... When the prince has judged, there is no other judgement.

B From *England under the Stuarts* by the Whig historian G.M. Trevelyan.

The secret motive of Charles's actions, unknown to the knavish ministers who thought that because he was their boon companion he was also their fool, unknown in after years to generations of Englishmen who laughed over and loved the memory of their merry monarch, was his design to erect a Second Stuart Despotism, far more terrible in its nature than the First Despotism which his grandfather had inherited and his father lost. The hero of the tennis-court and the ball-room, whom no one in Whitehall respected and no one but his Queen feared; the King of idleness who set on his Councillors to mimic their rivals like schoolboys; the humorist whose thick licentious lips were a fountain of wit, seemingly his only defence against servants who robbed and statesmen who opposed him; the hunter of moths, the friend of little dogs, was plotting an overthrow of our religion, our liberties and even our racial independence, far more revolutionary than the papal vassalage into which old barbarous England had once been sold by its grim King John. Charles II was negotiating treaties with Louis XIV to subvert Protestantism and to establish personal government in Britain by the help of French arms.

C From 'The Revolution of 1688 and the flight of James II' by A.A. Mitchell (*History Today*, July 1965)

His entire political philosophy was out of date, being established on fundamental principles of Divine Right inherited from James I and Charles I, and nourished, during his earlier years, by the first Earl of Clarendon's antique conception of a merely co-operative Parliament. It is characteristic of James's inability to learn from the past that Clarendon's fall, in large part due to Parliament's refusal to remain subservient ... To the day of his own death in 1701, James II remained true to the doctrines of Divine Right: the first article of the 'King's Advice' to his son, the Pretender, reads like a quotation from the works of James I: 'Kings are Accountable to none but to God alone for their Actions'.

D His Majesty's declaration to all his loving subjects, 26 December 1662.

Our principal aim in this declaration is to apply proper antidotes to all those venemous insinuations by which (as we are certainly informed) some of our subjects of inveterate and unalterable ill principles do daily endeavour to poison the affections of our good people by mis-leading their understandings, and that principally by four sorts of most false and malicious scandals ...

The first, by suggesting unto them, that having attained our ends in re-establishing our regal authority, and gaining the power into our own hands by a specious condescension to a general Act of Indemnity, we intend nothing less than the observation of it; but on the contrary by degrees to subject the persons and estates of all such who stand in need of that law to future revenge, and to give them up to the spoil of those who had lost their fortunes in our service.

Secondly, that upon pretence of plots and practices against us, we intend to introduce a military way of government in this kingdom.

Thirdly, that having made use of such solemn promises from Breda, and in several declarations since, of ease and liberty to tender consciences, instead of performing any part of them, we have added straiter fetters than ever, and new rocks of scandal to the scrupulous, by the Act of Uniformity.

Fourthly … that at the same time as we deny a fitting liberty to those of other sects of our subjects, whose consciences will not allow them to conform to the religion established by law, we are highly indulgent to papists, not only exempting them from the penalties of the law, but even to such a degree of countenance and encouragement as may even endanger the Protestant Religion.

E *Godden v. Hales*, King's Bench, 16 June 1686. Godden, Sir Edward Hales's coachman, brought an action against him for holding a colonel's commission without complying with the Test Act. On 29 March Hales was convicted at Rochester assizes, but he pleaded a dispensation and appealed to the Court of King's Bench, where Lord Chief Justice Herbert presided.

We think we may very well declare the opinion of the court to be that the king may dispense in this case; and the judges go upon these grounds:

1. That the kings of England are sovereign princes.
2. That the laws of England are the king's laws.
3. That therefore 'tis an inseparable prerogative in the kings of England to dispense with penal laws in particular cases, and upon particular necessary reasons.
4. That of those reasons and those necessities the king himself is sole judge …
5. That this is not a trust invested in or granted to the king by the people, but the ancient remains of the sovereign power and prerogative of the kings of England, which never yet was taken from them, nor can be. And therefore, such a dispensation appearing upon record to come time enough to save him from the forfeiture, judgement ought to be given for the defendant.

Q

1. *Summarise the argument put forward by Bossuet in souce A. (3 marks)*
2. *Compare sources B and D. Which gives the more reliable account of Charles II's motives? (6 marks)*
3. *How useful to a historian are sources C and E in reaching an appreciation of James II? (6 marks)*
4. *'Charles II and James II set up an absolute state in England'. To what extent do your own knowledge and sources A to E support this conclusion? (15 marks)*

7

Towards Constitutional Monarchy 1689–1714

INTRODUCTION

What a mess! If ever there was danger in reading history backwards, the so-called Glorious Revolution reminds us that *at the time* things were not as cut and dried as they may appear to later generations of historians. For example, the Whig historian Macaulay was quite certain that the 'Glorious Revolution' represented a further seismic advance towards the liberal and constitutional progress that all true Whigs sought. William III and the men of 1688 occupy a place in the liberal Pantheon scarcely less important than the alleged founding fathers of the 'English Revolution' from 1642–1660: Pym, Hampden, and Oliver Cromwell himself. Yet the situation in December 1688 was frought in the extreme. James II had run away, twice, and had eventually made it to the engulfing arms of his magnificent cousin, the Sun King. His rather less magnificent nephew, the hunchbacked asthmatic dwarf, William of Orange, was now in London, seemingly monarch of all he surveyed. Or was he? No-one seemed to know. As the following chapter explains, several alluring options suggested themselves for the solution to the constitutional crisis, into which James II's apparent abandonment of the throne had plunged the nation.

Over the following few years a settlement of sorts was thrashed out, though whether it could rightly be called 'constitutional monarchy' historians heatedly debate. This chapter explores the way in which the masterful little Dutchman exploited his good fortune in order to exact revenge from the French bully who had attacked peaceful Holland in 1672. Unfortunately, the English did not share their new king's outrage. Or rather, the Whigs who favoured war with France did not wish to relinquish the gains of the anti-monarchical Glorious Revolution, while many Tories would not accept the validity of William's claims to the throne. William found himself empathetically closer to the Tories 'because they were the party of monarchy'. But then, as the Earl of Sunderland remarked, 'Your Majesty should reflect that you are not their monarch'.

1 ⌒ THE GLORIOUS REVOLUTION

PICTURE 24
A portrait of William III after Lely. The artist has caught William's austere devotion to duty

PICTURE 25
Mary II by William Wissing, 1685

WILLIAM III (1650–1702) AND MARY II (1662–94)

William's father was William II of Orange, his mother was Charles I's daughter, Mary. He was therefore half-Stuart. His claim to the English throne was enhanced by his marriage in 1677 to Mary Stuart, daughter of James, Duke of York. In the United Provinces his titles were less regal but nonetheless important: he became Captain-General, Admiral-General and Stadholder in Holland by 1672, at the age of 22. He showed early autocratic tendencies, as in his attempt to suppress the liberties of the provinces of Guelderland in 1675. 'Not a man', writes Maurice Ashley, 'who radiated love.' He fought a defensive war against Louis XIV of France in the Dutch war from 1672 to 1678, reinforcing his reputation as a hard man. His relationship with his father-in-law, James II, worsened after he had given refuge in Holland to Huguenots fleeing Louis XIV's persecution, following the Revocation of the Edict of Nantes in 1685.

Asthmatic, a cripple and nursing a tubercular lung, William subordinated everything – wealth, health and happiness – to the greater goal of defeating Louis XIV. For him English politics were anathema; he never trusted either English politicians or generals, but he used them in pursuit of his grand design. William did not live to see the gains of the Treaty of Utrecht (1713); he died shortly after a riding accident in 1702, and the succession passed to his sister-in-law, Anne. William assented to the Act of Settlement of 1701 following the death of Anne's son and heir, the Duke of Gloucester, in 1700. Under this measure, the succession passed to the Electress Sophia of Hanover.

Mary was the elder daughter of James, Duke of York from his first marriage to Anne Hyde. She married her cousin, William of Orange, in 1677, but there were no children from the union. She was brought up as a Protestant on the instructions of her uncle, Charles II, despite the protestations of her Catholic parents. Her early married life was spent in Holland (1677–88); she saw little of her husband and played no part in political affairs. Nevertheless, as a devout Protestant, she supported her husband in his opposition to James II's Declaration of Indulgence in 1687, in his backing of the seven bishops in 1688 and in his acceptance of the invitation to invade Britain.

She rebuffed all her father's attempts to persuade her to convert to Rome, refused to countenance the idea that she should succeed as sole sovereign in 1688, but accepted joint sovereignty and coronation in 1689 – but no executive power. During the period from 1689 to 1694 she exercised control over affairs during William's frequent absences on military campaigns, but her inclination was to leave political affairs in her husband's hands. In short, she did what she was told. Her close friendship with her sister, Anne, was jeopardised by Anne's attachment to the Marlboroughs, and indeed relations between the two sisters were broken off after Marlborough's disgrace and imprisonment in 1692. Two years later Mary died from smallpox.

A *William of Orange*

KEY ISSUE

William's claim to the English throne.

William's hereditary claim to the English throne stemmed from two sources: first via his mother Mary, sister of Charles II and James II, and secondly via his wife, also called Mary, whom he had married in 1677 and who was James II's elder daughter by his first marriage to Anne Hyde. William's status in the United Provinces was rather more confused; the more so since they were a loose federation of seven provinces, each headed by a pensionary, a kind of chief minister chosen from the mercantile oligarchy, and represented in the States General. The Orange family enjoyed quasi-royal status in Holland, one of the states, but William's prestige there derived more from his office of Stadholder or governor in Holland, and his military command as Captain-General, especially during the Dutch war of 1672–8, when Louis XIV invaded the United Provinces.

In 1677, William married Mary. He was also a staunch Protestant, partly because it would improve his chances of succeeding to the English throne, which might enable him to bring England into an anti-French alliance. One of William's principal concerns was to confront the danger of French expansion under Louis XIV. In 1685, on Charles II's death, William's wife, Mary, became heir presumptive to the English throne. In other words, if James II's second wife, Mary of Modena, failed to produce a son, the throne would pass to Mary on James's death. There was every reason to suppose that Mary of Modena would not become pregnant again – she had not had a pregnancy since 1682 and her husband was now 51. William took no part in Monmouth's rebellion of the summer of 1685; he preferred to keep in touch with events in England through contacts such as the Whig Bishop of Salisbury, Gilbert Burnet, and his own diplomats, who included Dijkvelt and Zuylestein. Late in 1687 William's informants told him of Mary of Modena's pregnancy, and in the spring of 1688 William began to prepare contingency plans for an invasion of England.

See pages 201–3 for Monmouth's rising.

The birth of a live male child to James II's wife in June 1688 sent shock waves through both England and Holland, and rumours soon began to circulate that the infant had been smuggled into the Queen's bed in a warming-pan. William now began to step up his links with English opinion, since he was now more worried than ever that there might be a successful rebellion against James from inside his kingdom, while he was unprepared to benefit from it. As we saw in the last chapter, the so-called 'Immortal Seven' had been in touch with William for some time. But one factor held William back – the danger that Louis XIV would invade the United Provinces while William's best troops were abroad. Louis chose fortuitously to attack towards the Holy Roman Empire, when he launched an assault on the fortress of Philippsburg on the Rhine in 1688. Louis's stupidity in shifting the emphasis of his aggression to the East played into William's hands. Louis's forces would move away from the United Provinces in the direction of other members of William's carefully formed League of Augsburg. The English coast was clear for the invasion of England.

KEY ISSUE

William's preparations to invade England.

B *The Protestant wind*

The last successful naval invasion of England had taken place in 1485, and conventional wisdom said that an autumn crossing was hazardous. In fact, William had to return to port after a fierce storm blew up in the North Sea shortly after his embarkation on 20 October. He also faced the threat posed by the Earl of Dartmouth's fleet and James's well-equipped army, and the difficult propaganda task of explaining the reasons for his action to English public opinion. In short, the normally cautious William was running extraordinary risks – if only in military terms, invasion was nothing less than a crazy decision. Accordingly, on 30 September 1688, William issued his declaration to the English people, pledging to 'preserve and maintain the established laws, liberties and customs'. In particular he promised to protect the established reli-

KEY ISSUE

What was William's declared aim in invading?

gion, to ensure judicial independence and to call a 'free and lawful Parliament'. For good measure he added his wish to protect his wife's hereditary rights to the English throne, and cast doubt on the genuineness of the Prince of Wales's birth. He did not mention the need to have English help, or at least English neutrality, in the growing struggle against France.

On 5 November 1688, an important date for all English Protestants, William of Orange landed at Brixham, and by 9 November he had arrived at Exeter. On stepping ashore William is said to have turned to Bishop Burnet, and to have exclaimed, 'Now, Doctor, what do you think of predestination?'. In our less religious age we can speculate on the combination of skill and sheer luck which aided the Dutchman without attributing the 'Protestant wind' and the nosebleeds that demoralised his unhappy father-in-law to 'predestination'. Yet what amazing luck for William that James should crown a career of dazzling incompetence by running away! Truly fortune favoured the brave.

C *The proclamation of William and Mary*

KEY ISSUE

The problem of the succession.

James's flight produced a serious constitutional crisis, and William summoned an advisory assembly in London at Christmas 1688 to discuss the next steps. This group contained peers, men who had sat in the Commons during Charles II's reign (mainly Whigs unsurprisingly), and aldermen and common councilmen from the City. Their advice was to call a Convention Parliament following fresh elections. The members of the Convention assembled in January 1689 with 232 Tories and 319 Whigs, and a Tory majority in the Lords, after a civilised election campaign, during which William agreed to keep his troops away from parliamentary boroughs. The new Parliament's task was to address the tricky constitutional problem, under the disadvantage that it had not been called by a ruling sovereign. Their first responsibility was to decide who should reign.

A small group argued that James II should return as king, but his desertion of his kingdom and his unpopularity, even with many Tories, made this proposal, backed by Sancroft and four of the original seven bishops, a non-starter. Its proponents suggested, as a second choice, a regency under William or Mary, or both. Many peers, including the Bishop of Ely, supported this option to show James that England could be governed without him, and to persuade him to return as a limited monarch. Regency did have the advantage that it avoided a break in the legal succession, but James, who was in any case being supported by Louis XIV, was unlikely to agree to it, and William, Mary and Anne made it clear that they opposed it too. The regency idea was rejected by the Commons, and defeated in the Lords by three votes.

An alternative solution, sponsored by Danby and Sir Edward Seymour, was to offer the throne to Mary, with William acting as regent for her. This would involve no infringement of the laws of succession, and accepted that James had deserted his kingdom and assumed that the Prince of Wales was an impostor. Its weakness was that Mary would not accept the unnatural position of commanding her husband, and William also objected to it since he would lose power on Mary's death, when Anne would succeed to the throne. Indeed, William is said to have expostulated, 'I will not be my wife's gentleman-usher'. The way was now open for a more radical Whig proposal.

William's adviser, Bentinck, suggested that William should rule alone, James being deemed to have abdicated and to have broken his contract with the people. Radical Whigs approved the idea of an elective monarchy and contractual theories, which this proposal seemed to enshrine. They also received powerful support from the political philosopher John Locke, whose 'Two Treatises of Government' was published in 1690. However, there was vociferous Tory opposition, provoked by the fear that William would become the prisoner of the Whig party and by the revolutionary assumption that the throne was vacant. No traditional monarchist would ever accept that the throne was vacant. The search resumed for a compromise solution.

The eventual deal was for William and Mary to rule as joint sovereigns. William had already stated that he would not be a regent or prince consort, and Anne was willing to let William take precedence over her in the succession – provided that Anne and her children came before any children born to William by a putative second marriage. This was not a perfect solution, and John Miller comments, 'The legal basis for such a solution was decidedly shaky, but it did fit the facts while doing as little violence as possible to deeply-held legal and constitutional beliefs and prejudices'. A short period of argument ensued between Lords and Commons when the Upper House insisted on the word 'deserted' rather than 'abdicated' to describe James II's behaviour in December 1688. Eventually, the Lords backed down at a special conference held in early February 1689, and on 13 February 1689 the Crown was formally offered to William and Mary at the Banqueting House in Whitehall. On this occasion William and Mary jointly promised to accept the throne, to rule according to law and to be guided by Parliament.

KEY ISSUE

William and Mary were jointly offered the throne.

D *The Declaration of Rights*

The Declaration of Rights was solemnly read to William and Mary before they formally accepted the Crown in February 1689; in December 1689 it was passed into law. The justificatory preamble to this document placed the blame for misgovernment fairly and squarely on James II, accused of tyranny 'by accumulative misdeeds' in J.R. Jones's phrase. Yet the declaration did preserve a good deal of the traditional royal prerogative: the monarch could still choose his own ministers, make his own policy, influence opinion in Parliament and exercise his own patronage.

However, many of the powers that James II had claimed were now declared unconstitutional. The suspending and dispensing powers used by James II to invalidate statutes were declared illegal, as was the packing of juries and the collection of taxes without parliamentary consent. The monarch was also forbidden to revive a prerogative court such as the Court of Ecclesiastical Commission or to maintain a standing army in peacetime without parliamentary permission. All this seems to entrench parliamentary ancient rights, which were re-established and secured; no new rights were envisaged, and to that extent the document was conservative rather than innovatory.

The bill nevertheless contained one clearly innovative part: it established the succession in a restrictive sense by barring from the throne any Catholic or anyone married to a Catholic. In other words, it extended to the monarchy the principle beneath the Test Acts, and, had it operated earlier, would have disqualified all previous Stuart kings. The Continental maxim '*cuius regio eius religio*' (whereby the hereditary ruler determined the State's religious complexion) seemed now to be reversed in England, since now the sovereign was to practise the same faith as the people rather than the other way round. From this it followed that all James I's descendants in the Orleans line (i.e. the descendants from the marriage of his youngest grandchild, Henrietta Anne, to Philippe, Duke of Orleans, brother of Louis XIV) would be cut out of the succession, as would James II and his son and heirs. After Anne and her heirs and any issue of a subsequent marriage by William of Orange, the throne would pass to the heirs of the union of James I's daughter, Elizabeth ('the Winter Queen'), and Frederick Elector Palatine. In 1689, it looked most likely that this would mean the claim passing to their third child, Sophia, Electress of Hanover, and her son, George, born in 1660.

KEY ISSUE

Did the Declaration of Rights introduce new rights?

Finally, the Declaration included some rather vague statements of intent on outstanding grievances from the previous reign: subjects could petition the King, parliamentary elections should be free – as should the debates and proceedings – and Parliaments should be held 'frequently'. Juries should be duly empanelled, excessive bail and fines should be avoided and no 'cruel and unusual punishments' should be inflicted. However, the final bill did not contain a number of political safeguards that might have satisfied radical Whigs: there was no repeal of the 1661 Militia Act; there was nothing to prevent overlong Parliaments such as the Cavalier Parliament from 1661 to 1678, the sovereign could still use *quo warranto* actions against boroughs to alter charters, there was no prohibition of buying or selling offices; and no independent judiciary.

The Declaration was read to William and Mary before they accepted the throne in February, but the offer of the Crown was not conditional on their accepting it. Naturally, they assented to it later in the year when it passed into law, but it does seem in many respects a conservative and rather disappointing document. This is partly because ambitious Whig politicians knew that William wanted a strong royal prerogative and the Whigs expected to dominate any future government. It is also the case that many MPs were anxious to fill the throne quickly, and to avoid wasting time drafting complicated legislation. The Convention lacked the time and unity of purpose to legislate on more than a few subjects. Nonetheless, the Bill of Rights was the nearest approach yet to a written constitution, and it implied a contract between ruler and ruled. The sovereign had to swear to maintain 'the Protestant reformed religion established by law', and to govern 'according to the statutes in Parliament agreed on and the laws and customs of the same'. There was at least a tacit implication that William and Mary were constitutional monarchs.

E *The Oath of Allegiance and the Toleration Act*

The Oath of Allegiance acknowledging William and Mary as king and queen was designed to maximise support for them, and to accommodate as many people as possible who had scruples of conscience. The phrase 'rightful and lawful' is therefore missing: jurors merely swore to accept them as *de facto* monarchs. A handful of Jacobites and nonjurors refused, including Sancroft, seven other bishops and 400 clergy; the Church therefore suffered a further upheaval such as that experienced in 1660. All office-holders, MPs and clergymen were obliged to take the oath if they wished to retain their posts.

The Toleration Act, which became law on 24 May 1689, was a misnomer. It followed the failure to pass the Comprehension Bill after heavy attack from the Anglican hierarchy. Dissenters were exempted from penalties, provided that they took the Oath of Allegiance and accepted the 1678 Test Act. In other words, they were not obliged to attend Anglican services, but their meeting-houses had to be registered by a bishop or at quarter sessions. By 1709, 3,900 had been licensed, and by 1714 the number of Dissenters was calculated at 400,000; 7.6 per cent of the population. In reality religious pluralism became an established feature of national life, especially after the ending of press censorship in 1695. The Toleration Act in theory did exclude Roman Catholics, Socinians (an extreme sect who doubted the divinity of Christ, and were later known as Unitarians), anti-Trinitarians and Jews, but in practice religious liberty was extended to Catholics too, partly because of William's own efforts. The King was loth to prosecute papists since he had guaranteed their security to his Catholic allies in the League of Augsburg. However, the Test Acts still were in force, and office-holders who would not comply with them could not hold State or municipal office, attend university, join the army, practise medicine or be called to the Bar. Moreover, tithes and Church rates were still expected from everyone. Nevertheless, many Anglicans disliked the Toleration Act, and eagerly awaited Anne's accession, lamenting both 'the Church in danger' and the existence of many towns where the Anglican Church seemed to be permanently weakened.

> **KEY ISSUE**
>
> *Toleration and the Toleration Act.*

> See pages 368–72 for the emergence of toleration

F *The financial settlement*

William sought a permanent financial settlement, but even Tories such as Clarges and Seymour were reluctant to make him independent of Parliament, preferring to keep him dependent on them. In March 1689, the first session of the Convention Parliament agreed to allow William

KEY ISSUE

William was the first English king since the fifteenth century (bar Charles I) not to be offered the customs revenue for life.

to collect existing ordinary revenue for a three-month period provided that the Hearth Tax was given up. Parliament brought up the old 1660 figure of £1.2 million per year as the 'reasonable' figure for the King's needs, but this was an arbitrary figure, and scarcely adequate even in peacetime. William intended to send military assistance to the Irish Protestants, and to have sufficient funds for war against France that was already looming in 1689. The lack of a permanent provision was irksome to say the least. At the second session of the Convention Parliament in October 1689 Parliament offered a £2 million war supply, but in January 1690 William prorogued Parliament, dissolving it a few days later. William exulted in his use of prerogative powers: 'he was not a king', he confided, 'till that was done; without that the title of a king was only a pageant ... the worst of all governments was that of a king without a treasure and without power'. The King was more direct to his confidant Halifax: the Commons, he thought, used him like a dog.

A new Parliament met in March 1690, and granted William the excise for life, but the customs, whose yield was already reduced by the French war, were granted to him for four years only (this was in practice extended to 1699 and beyond). William was therefore the first king since the fifteenth century, apart from Charles I, not to be granted the customs for life. Dislike or distrust played a part in some MPs' minds, but most (Whig or Tory) were determined not to surrender a powerful weapon. Under William the financial needs of war permanently ended the chance of the English monarchy becoming financially independent; William had to return cap in hand to the second session of the 1690–5 Parliament to request supply for an army of 69,000, and a vote of £2.3 million to pay for it. William learned the hard lesson that the Declaration of Rights was one thing, effective control over financial policy while Parliament held the whip hand was another.

2 ⌐ THE DEFENCE OF THE REVOLUTION IN IRELAND

TABLE 14

William III's campaign in Ireland

12 March 1689	James II landed at Kinsale
1 April 1689	James began to blockade Londonderry
28 July 1689	The siege of Londonderry was lifted
30 July 1689	Jacobite army was defeated at Newtown Butler
Winter 1689–90	Schomberg retreated to Lisburn
14 June 1690	William III landed at Belfast Lough
1 July 1690	William III's victory over James II at the Boyne
September 1690	Churchill took Cork and Kinsale
October 1691	Capture and Treaty of Limerick

The Earl of Tyrconnel had been appointed Lord Deputy in Ireland by James II in 1687, and he immediately began a rigorous programme of Catholicisation. By the end of 1688 most judges, sheriffs and army officers were Catholics, and some Protestants began to leave, alarmed at the increasing papist ascendancy. On his accession William III's talks with Tyrconnel failed, although he was prepared to offer religious liberty and

MAP 4
Ireland during the Years of Turmoil

security of property. By the spring of 1689 the Catholics controlled all of Ireland except for Londonderry and Enniskillen.

In February 1689, James II left his exile fastness of St Germain-en-Laye for Ireland, the first English king to set foot there for 300 years. On 12 March he landed at Kinsale in south west Ireland, where he was greeted by the Earl of Tyrconnel. James brought with him an expeditionary force provided by his mentor, Louis XIV, and commanded by the Comte de Lauzun. This frustrated Tyrconnel's tentative negotiations with William III, who was in any case more concerned with developments on the Continent. James moved rapidly to Dublin, and soon controlled all of Ireland except Londonderry and Enniskillen.

KEY ISSUE

James was the first English king to visit Ireland for 300 years.

James began his siege of Londonderry on 1 April 1689, placing a boom across the River Foyle to prevent supplies from getting in. The first relief expedition was turned back, but on 28 July the boom was cut and two ships lifted the blockade, to find the city's 7,000 defenders reduced to 3,000. After 105 days the siege had broken up, and on 30 July the men of Enniskillen crushed a Jacobite army at Newtown Butler and Ulster was saved. James prudently moved to Dublin where he opened the 'Patriot Parliament' in May 1689. They were an overwhelmingly Catholic body, with only six Protestants out of 224 MPs. They soon enacted a series of Catholic measures, including the repeal of the Act of Settlement, restoring many estates confiscated since 1641 to Catholics. Parliament also determined that no English Parliament could legislate for Ireland and that there should be full toleration of all religions. They also passed no less than 2,400 Acts of Attainder to dispossess Protestant landowners. 'This was the Catholics' revenge for the Cromwellian settlement', writes John Miller, 'it ensured that the Protestants in their turn would impose an equally vindictive settlement when they regained power.'

However, James faced formidable practical problems if he was to sustain his position in Ireland, let alone use it successfully as a springboard for an assault on the mainland. He had a confused, uncoordinated military structure with plenty of scope for feuds between French and Irish advisers. His troops were of poor quality, and were ill-disciplined under inexperienced officers. There was a shortage of equipment, uniforms and weapons, and many of his men had to resort to living off the land. The Irish Parliament offered a stingy £20,000 per calendar month, when five times that much was needed; and when James debased the coinage, prices rose. William's much greater wealth as King of England and his personal military skill seemed likely to prevail.

William, however, also faced military problems, and England was arguably in greater danger of defeat in 1690 than at any time up to 1815. For one thing the Glorious Revolution had disorganised the English army. William suspected that many were secret Jacobites, a suspicion reinforced by a series of mutinies, including one at Ipswich in March 1690. Accordingly, many English units were dispatched to Flanders, while William deployed his trusted Dutch regiments in England, and raised fresh forces for Ireland, for example from Denmark. However, military administration remained inefficient and corrupt with inexperienced officers and men, and defective or even non-existent equipment and provisions. Schomberg's arrival at Belfast in August 1689 to swell the Williamite forces failed to rally the King's cause. He showed excessive caution by declining to fight James II near Dundalk, and by retreating to Lisburn for the winter of 1689–90, where 7,000 men from his Dutch, Huguenot and English regiments died of disease or exposure. Idleness and corruption played their part, as did lack of supplies, the autumnal rains, and inadequate food and shelter. Under these circumstances William decided, against Whig advice, to take charge himself, while Mary headed a regency council.

William set sail on 11 June 1690, landing at Carrickfergus on Belfast

KEY ISSUE

What disadvantages did William suffer in Ireland?

Lough three days later. From there he moved south, reaching the River Boyne by 30 June with his impressive force of 36,000 troops, supported by good quality artillery and equipment, and stiffened by more experienced elements from the Continent: Huguenots, Danes, Brandenburgers and Finns. Meanwhile, James II moved up to Dundalk and prepared to defend the south bank of the River Boyne with 25,000 troops. Reaching the River Boyne first, James deployed his troops by a bend in the river at Donore, overlooking Oldbridge, and observed the arrival of William's army of 15,000 men on 30 June. William himself was in fact slightly wounded on that day, leading the Jacobites to believe briefly that he had been killed. Having sent a third of his army upstream – a tactic that drew a large part of James's force in their pursuit – William forded the river and defeated the Jacobites at the Battle of the Boyne on 1 July 1690 for the loss of only 400 men to James's 1,000. Thus ended the largest pitched battle in Ireland's history, and the only serious challenge to William's rule. James fled to Dublin and then to Duncannon from where he sailed back to France. Galloping into Dublin, James shouted, 'The Irish ran away', to which a lady of the Court replied, 'But Your Majesty has run even faster'.

While James had been driven out of Ireland (for good as events turned out), and while there was clearly no chance of him now conquering Ireland, the Irish war went on, since the Jacobite army was far from destroyed, falling back into Connaught on the line of the River Shannon, and repulsing William's attempts to take Limerick and Athlone. After failing to take Limerick with the loss of 2,300 casualties, and the failure of his declaration at Finglas, requiring surrender by 1 August 1690, William left Ireland in September 1690 without total victory. The King's place was taken by John Churchill, who landed in Ireland in September 1690, and rapidly recovered Cork and Kinsale in Munster, isolating the Jacobites west of the Shannon. Five weeks after setting sail, Churchill was back in England. The Dutch general, Ginkel, carried on the campaign the following year, taking Athlone on 30 June 1691 from the French general, Saint Ruth. On 12 July Ginkel won the bloody Battle of Aughrim, when 7,000 Irish were killed, including the heads of many leading Catholic families. Limerick held out until 3 October 1691: the Orange triumph was complete.

The Treaty of Limerick offered free passage back to France for any of the remaining 12,000 French troops, or the opportunity to join William's service. There were civilian articles too, guaranteeing a limited religious toleration and the property of Catholic landowners. However, the Westminster Parliament repudiated the terms of Limerick when it repealed the legislation of the Patriot Parliament, and imposed an Anglican test on all office-holders and MPs. Unsurprisingly the Dublin Parliament of 1692 was dominated by Protestants. Catholic proprietors lost nearly one million acres, about 14 per cent of the land, and new penal laws ignored Limerick's promises of toleration. Papists were to be disarmed, and their bishops and regular clergy banished. Indeed, following the 1704 Act, which forbade Catholics to buy land outright or to pass on estates intact to their heirs, by 1776 only five per cent of Irish land was in Catholic hands, and they (and, for that matter, Presbyterians), were completely excluded from political power. Ireland, writes Barry Coward, 'again was reduced to a colonial subservience, which was reinforced by subsequent enactments of the English Parliament aimed at preventing Irish economic competition with English agriculture and industry'.

The apparently successful outcome of the Irish campaign persuaded English public opinion that it had been necessary – to preserve the Glorious Revolution, to stop the invasion of Scotland and to prevent the return of James II as a French puppet. The Jacobite risings of 1715 in England and Scotland evoked no echo in Ireland, where William III remained (and remains) such a cult figure. It may be, in fact, that 1688 is an even more significant date for Ireland than for other parts of the British Isles, for if James II had held the English throne, the Catholics could well have overrun all Ireland. William, however, tried to restrain the Irish Protestants' lust for revenge as he contemplated what was for him a more important task: the struggle against France. It seems ironic now that such a naturally tolerant man as William should be so closely identified with Protestant bigotry in Ulster.

KEY ISSUE

What was the significance of 1688 for Ireland?

3 ⌐ THE DEFENCE OF THE REVOLUTION IN SCOTLAND

TABLE 15
William III's campaign in Scotland

March 1689	Scottish Convention Parliament proclaims William and Mary
May 1689	The Claim of Right and Articles of Grievances
July 1689	Bonny Dundee's Jacobite victory at Killiekrankie
August 1689	Government victory at Dunkeld
May 1690	Final defeat of the Jacobites
February 1692	Massacre of Glencoe

William and Mary's accession was greeted with unease in Scotland because a Stuart king and his heir had been disinherited, and there were fears of a new interregnum. While a few convinced Protestants did back the new king, many magnates remained confused, and preferred to delay making a definite commitment, and only a handful rallied to James II. In this atmosphere a Scottish Convention Parliament met in Edinburgh in March 1689 to consider its attitude to James's suplanters. Despite a goodly representation of Jacobites and Scottish Patriots, the Convention swung behind the new regime and declared the Crown forfeit, following James's abandonment of his kingdoms. In April they therefore offered the throne of Scotland to William and Mary, who accepted on 11 May. A week later they issued the Claim of Right, absolving the late Duke of Argyll, condemning the quartering of troops on civilians and denouncing bishops in the Scottish Kirk. Hard on its heels followed the Articles of Grievances, which refused to accept the Lords of the Articles, a royally appointed steering committee to control the work of the Scottish Parliament. The Articles went on to assert that no Catholic could be monarch or hold office, the royal prerogative

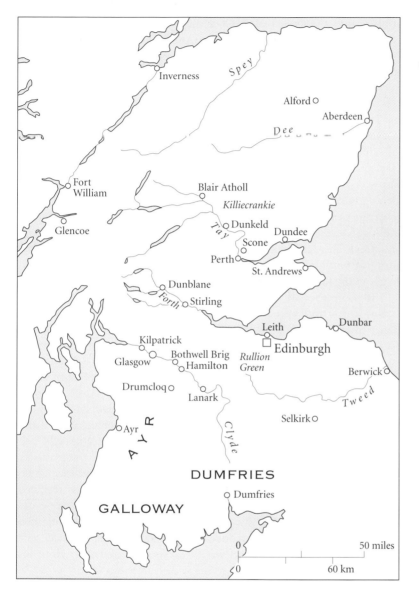

MAP 5
Scotland in the late seventeenth century

could not override the law, Parliament should meet more frequently and its consent was required for supply.

William accepted the Scottish Parliament's assertion of independence and the shift from an episcopalian church (i.e. one with bishops) to a Presbyterian one in June 1690. The General Assembly of the same year deprived several hundred episcopalian ministers in a process known as 'rabbling'. William felt weak in Scotland, unfamiliar with its affairs, and mindful of the danger of Scotland joining the Jacobite rebellion in Ireland. Scottish magnates now began to divide more clearly according to their view of the settlement. The Jacobite faction included many Roman Catholics in the Highlands such as the Macdonalds, and Graham of Claverhouse, Viscount Dundee, alienated by the promotion

> **KEY ISSUE**
>
> *The settlement between William and the Scottish Parliament.*

of his enemy, the Duke of Hamilton, to Commissioner of the Convention. William's supporters included Archibald Campbell, the tenth Duke of Argyll, restored to his forebear's estates, Sir James Montgomerie (described by Michael Lynch as 'an expert in the murky underworld of revolution, plots and double-dealing'), Sir John Dalrymple, appointed the Scottish Secretary of State and forgiven his Jacobite past, and Hamilton himself.

The two sides soon came to blows at the Battle of Killiekrankie on 27 July 1689, when Dundee's Highlanders beat Major General Hugh Mackay of Scourie's government troops in a brief skirmish that killed 30 per cent of Dundee's 2,000 men and 60 per cent of Mackay's 4,000 men. However, 'Bonny' Dundee was himself slain by a stray bullet, and government forces held a fresh Highlander force at Dunkeld in August, and finally defeated the rising at Cromdale near Granton-on-Spey on 1 May 1690. The danger of collaboration between Scottish and Irish Jacobites had passed, but the authorities still faced the question of what to do about the Jacobite clans.

The Campbell Earl of Breadalbane issued orders in mid-August 1691 that all chiefs and vassals had until the end of the year to swear allegiance to William III, and this was reinforced by James II himself from his French exile, who wrote to release his Scottish supporters from his cause. However, one clan did not conform before the deadline: the MacIains of Glencoe. Troops under Captain Robert Campbell of Glenlyon carried out the Massacre of Glencoe on 13 February 1692, when 38 members of the MacIain or MacDonald clan were killed. This was not the worst government atrocity in Scotland in the seventeenth century, but it left a legacy of bitterness – especially as the Campbells had recently received hospitality from their victims. Therefore the massacre was, in Kishlansky's words, 'a brutal violation of one of the basic codes of social conduct in Scotland'. Dalrymple, the Lord Advocate, resigned after the incident, but the 1695 enquiry exonerated almost everyone and William refused to punish those responsible. The Highlands remained ungovernable, and further Jacobite rebellions loomed with Glencoe as a rallying cry. William's attention was, however, diverted away from his intractable problems in Scotland to the wider European war.

> **KEY ISSUE**
>
> *The Massacre of Glencoe.*

4 ⌐ WILLIAM III AND THE ENGLISH MONARCHY

A *William's first ministry*

William lost no time in exercising his prerogative powers to choose ministers. Halifax was an obvious choice for the post of Lord Privy Seal. He had the advantage of having been dismissed by James, and rapidly became a close confidant of the new King, although he had not signed the invitation for William to invade. His lack of a party label also appealed to William, who was at first baffled by English party political labels, and who saw the elevation of men such as Halifax as a chance to balance Whigs and Tories. Perhaps the clinching factor in his appointment was his leadership in the House of Lords during the Convention's deliberations on the settlement, and his opposition to regency. Meanwhile, Danby, now elevated to the marquisate of Carmarthen, became Lord President of the Council. He had signed the invitation to William, and had been the instigator of the plan to marry Mary to William in the first place. He was an undoubted Anglican, had raised his native Yorkshire for William in 1688 and was decidedly anti-French – an inclination especially likely to endear him to the new monarch. William tried to establish a balance between Whigs and Tories in his choice of Secretaries of State, appointing the Tory Earl of Shrewsbury and the Whig Earl of Nottingham, while Lord Delamere (advanced to the earldom of Warrington) became Chancellor of the Exchequer, and Sir John Holt became Lord Chief Justice. In all these appointments William seemed to be falling back on those who had served Charles II; however, none had a powerful grip on English politics and a number of them, including Halifax, Shrewsbury and Godolphin, resigned within the next year. William then had to pluck his ministers amid the shifting rivalries of the inter-party struggle.

See page 181 for a profile of Danby's background.

Finally, William confided in a group of his Dutch cronies, including Zuylestein and Ouwerkerk who had been involved in the original negotiations with English notables that preceded the invasion. However, the best known of this group is William Bentinck, ennobled as Earl of Portland, who quickly became the butt of criticism on account of his foreign origins and his rapidly acquired wealth.

B *William and the political parties*

Whigs and Tories had emerged initially during the fraught period of the Exclusion Crisis from 1678 to 1681, but these party labels should not be confused with modern political parties and their mass organisation, whips and discipline. Party allegiance was but one concern among many that pulled Members of Parliament, who were also very conscious of their constituents, and of the current stance of Crown and Court. William was well aware that his elevation to the throne had been backed by the Whigs, who proclaimed their belief in parliamentary sovereignty and their commitment to a Protestant succession. Moreover, they also favoured religious toleration for Dissenters and the prosecution of war against France, while the principle that had brought them into being (namely that of Exclusion) had been irrelevant for a while. Yet William initially distrusted (and completely misunderstood) the Whigs as intransigent and irresponsible neo-Republicans, and he expected to be able to achieve a closer rapport with the Tories.

The Tories were natural supporters of the monarchy, who had paradoxically acquiesced in James II's removal. Some Tories were beginning to have second thoughts, wondering whether William was not a usurper and an enemy of the Anglican Church.

The Tories themselves were increasingly distrustful of the executive, were beginning to lay less stress on Divine Right, and were not slow to

Junto the word means a
political clique and is
applied to a group of
wealthy and powerful
Whigs in the reigns of
William III and Anne.
They favoured war
against France. Their
leaders were Somers,
Halifax, Orford and
Wharton.

express their opposition to the heavy expense of the French war. At the
same time, after the defection of the old 'country' Whigs, the remnant
of the Whig party reconstituted itself from 1690 as the **Junto** Whigs,
urging the need for a strong executive and strong support for William's
war. The seeds of party rivalry during Anne's reign were therefore sown
during that of her sister and brother-in-law. Barry Coward writes, 'The
character of the political parties which thrived during Queen Anne's
war was moulded by the events which had taken place under the pressure of King William's war.'

Divisive party rivalries persisted, albeit in a different form, and Parliament emerged as a permanent part of the constitution, confronted by
growing political instability, as William's accession created both a revolution in foreign policy (from Francophilia or isolationism to active
intervention against France), and a revolution in public finance to cope
with it. One result of this was more frequent meetings of Parliament.
From 1660 to 1688 there had been a mere five general elections, but
from 1689 to 1715 there were 11, encouraged no doubt by the Triennial
Act of 1694, which was not repealed until 1716 by the Septennial Act.
More frequent elections led to more seats being contested: 60–70 from
1660 to 1689, but over 100 thereafter, and political excitement was
easier to maintain through a constantly changing parliamentary membership. Above all it became harder for the Crown to build up a party of
its own in the House. Political stability was also affected to some extent
by the anomalies of the electoral system, whereby many large towns
such as Manchester, Birmingham, Leeds and Sheffield sent no MPs to
Parliament, while Cornwall had no less than 44 MPs (18 of them representing small villages) and Wiltshire had 32. However, these inconsis-
tencies appeared much more blatant later, but provoked relatively little
criticism in Parliament at the time. There is no doubt, however, that
William and Mary's reign saw the growth of a more sophisticated and
better informed electorate, numbering some 200,000 by 1688; 4.3 per
cent of the population. This was assisted in part by the lapsing of the
1695 Licensing Act, which marked the formal end of Church and State
censorship. Political journalism flourished among a more volatile electorate in what J.H. Plumb has called 'the rage of party', for there was no
shortage of issues: the succession, the individual's right to resist
tyranny, toleration, etc.

Yet the main issue was the role that England should play in European affairs, and especially in the wars against Louis XIV. The division
was between those who wanted to prevent a Bourbon and Roman
Catholic hegemony in Europe, and those (including a number of out
and out xenophobes) who preferred a policy of isolationism. Even
within the pro-war camp a series of further questions provided a flash-
point for debate: how should the war be conducted, and how should it
be ended? Occasionally other issues intervened: Protestant succession,
union with Scotland etc. It became increasingly clear that only when
these issues were resolved would a genuine political stability return. For
the first time perhaps, the English electorate could sway the fortunes of
parties, and even influence the composition of governments; as Geof-

frey Holmes puts it: 'the English electorate emerged in the 1690s and remained for two decades a force genuinely, if crudely, representative of the will of the politically-conscious classes in the country'. One of the issues that exercised the electorate was foreign policy, which is discussed in the next section.

5 ⌐ WILLIAM III'S FOREIGN POLICY

A *The War of the League of Augsburg*

The war that raged in Europe from 1689 to 1697 is called the War of the League of Augsburg, or the War of the English Succession, and sometimes the Nine Years War. Perhaps, however, King William's War is a more apt title, for William made many of the big decisions himself – advised by his Dutch confidants such as Hopp and Bentinck. He negotiated the terms of the Treaty of Ryswick that ended the war, and the two Partition Treaties that arguably ushered in the next conflict: the War of the Spanish Succession. Moreover, the King personally spent no less than six years of the war abroad on campaign.

William's aims in foreign policy were to maintain what he called the 'liberties of Europe', in other words the traditional balance of power to ensure freedom from French domination and dictation. A side effect of the restoration of the balance between Habsburg and Bourbon would, he hoped, be recognition by Louis XIV of his claim to the English throne. William was therefore attempting a fundamental realignment of English foreign policy, away from friendship with France and towards a sustained military commitment to the containment of France. Such a policy would be hard to establish; not least because the English were unused to the long and gruelling (and expensive) military effort that would be involved. Indeed, William was much criticised by contemporaries for apparently subordinating English interests to those of the Dutch. At the same time William had to preserve allied unity in the League of Augsburg – a fragile entity containing the Spanish and Austrian Habsburgs, England, Savoy and several German states. Finally he had to find the huge funds needed for the long haul from representative institutions that found such demands unprecedented.

Louis XIV, on the other hand, enjoyed the paradoxical advantage of having no allies with whom to bicker. His high degree of personal authority in France meant that he could, for example, repudiate the Partition Treaties and accept the will of Charles II of Spain at his own whim, using, in J.R. Jones's words, 'indefeasible legitimacy and divine right'. Moreover, France's population was three times that of England and Scotland combined, and he controlled an army of 250,000 rising to 400,000 with excellent generals of the calibre of Luxembourg, Villars and Berwick, and Vauban, the finest siege engineer in Europe.

For William, differences of interest between England and Holland were likely to surface from time to time, especially at the start of the war when William was concerned to secure English independence and when

1691	Successful French siege of Mons
1692	French capture of Namur. Anglo-Dutch victory at La Hogue Drawn battle of Steenkirk
1693	Drawn battle of Neerwinden
1695	William III recaptured Namur
1697	Peace of Ryswick

TABLE 16
The War of the League of Augsburg or the Nine Years War

KEY ISSUE

What advantages did Louis enjoy between 1689 and 1702?

Dutch help was crucial, particularly in Ireland from 1689–91. At the same time Dutch diplomacy was essential to keep the Habsburgs in the war. William also needed to keep English politicians interested in prosecuting the war. Certainly at first more Whigs than Tories accepted William's argument that war was being waged in the name of mutual security, to protect England and the Protestant religion.

After 1691 the emerging country party favoured a limited English participation in hostilities, suggesting a national contribution of a mere 10,000 men and 30 ships, which was bound to be seen by William as national selfishness and a bad example to other allies. By 1695 William had recruited 68,000 men (including 48,000 British), and opened each session of Parliament with a royal speech reviewing progress in the war (or reverses in the case of the years after 1693). The King's difficulty in raising such huge forces for a long period is summed up by J.R. Jones who writes, 'William had to persuade a comparatively uninformed assembly of country gentlemen to finance a foreign policy of expensive commitments which few of them could understand fully, and to take account of their frequently irrelevant representations'.

William's chief military commitment was the defence of the Spanish Netherlands (roughly the present day Belgium), which was a key strategic area for both England and the United Provinces, and where the bulk of Louis XIV's troops came to be deployed. Louis followed up his destruction of Mannheim and Heidelberg in the Palatinate by using Vauban to besiege Mons successfully in 1691, Namur in 1692, Huy in 1693 and Charleroi in 1694. Pitched battles also went Louis's way: in 1692 he won the battle of Fleurus, but the battle of Steenkirk was inconclusive. The King's difficulties in waging war successfully against the Continent's supreme military power were not unnoticed by England's burgeoning public opinion, increasingly aware of foreign policy issues. The influx of Huguenot refugees from 1685 brought many Englishmen into contact with the consequences of Louis's intolerant religious policy, and a flood of returning Whig exiles in 1688 complemented the improvement in the English diplomatic corps and the extension of press freedom.

Domestic criticism centred on a number of points: the apparent preference for foreign commanders or for those who had been in Dutch service such as Tollemache and Cutts; attacks on the conduct of the war at sea; the failure to deal effectively with French privateers; the allegedly ineffective blockade of France; and the complaints of the mercantile community that the war was having an adverse effect on trade. The issue of commanders came to a head in 1691, when Marlborough demanded the command of English land forces in the next campaign. He complained about the large proportion of foreigners in the English officer corps, and rejected sneers that his rank was still too low to warrant such advancement. It is known that he was in touch with the Jacobite Court at St Germain, and it was indeed the allegation of Jacobite links that justified his dismissal from all his offices in 1692. Anne stood by Marlborough's wife, Sarah, who was her close confidante, and it seems that Mary and Anne never spoke to one another again. Marlborough was to remain in disgrace until 1699, and without a command until 1701.

The 'country' opposition was behind the disparagement of English naval conduct at sea: the fleet had expanded with 160 ships in 1688, and naval tonnage had risen by a further 60 per cent between 1689 and 1697, yet James II, accompanied by a French naval escort, had reached Ireland unmolested in 1689. This Tory-inspired opposition advocated a 'blue water' strategy, whereby England would concentrate on naval deployment and abandon pretensions to be a military power. They approved of the dismissal of the Earl of Torrington who had commanded the 1688 invasion fleet, and had high hopes of Edward Russell, who replaced him and led an Anglo-Dutch fleet to an important victory over the French at La Hogue in May 1692. Nevertheless, the scourge of French privateers remained a serious problem, since Jean Bart and Duguay-Trouin and their ilk preyed upon English shipping from St Malo and Dunkirk with impunity throughout the 1690s and 1700s. At the same time a few Dutch merchants continued to trade covertly with France, as did many Swedes and Danes, jeopardising the blockade and causing the mercantile community to wonder whether the war was indeed such a good idea.

There is little doubt that the war affected the trading community adversely, and most historians agree with J.R. Jones when he writes, 'there is no evidence to support the view that William's war was either encouraged by, or popular with, mercantile interests. Only those directly engaged in credit and financial operations, or in victualling and supplying the army and navy, had any interest in continuing the war'. In fact, in 1693, trade with the Mediterranean was suspended for three years when the Anglo-Dutch Smyrna convoy, poorly escorted by warships, lost 100 out of 400 ships to Admiral Tourville's plundering off Lagos in Portugal. Merchants were dismayed by the ruin of African trading posts, by the pressing of men for the navy – leaving few recruits for the mercantile marine, and the government subsidies for allies and for the army which caused exchange rates to plummet.

By 1694 William was relying on the Junto Whigs to raise sufficient funds to continue the prosecution of the war, and Professor Jones remarks, 'in the ordeal of the last phase of the war the Junto came close to experiencing the almost continuous and intolerable strains, and fearfulness of unpopularity, that William had imposed on himself and his Dutch ministers since 1672'. Meanwhile, William himself continued to arrogate the main decisions to himself: dispositions of troops, preparing campaigns, conducting negotiations (often through Portland) and fixing the levels of subsidies. After the recovery of Namur in 1695, Louis XIV's persuasion to make a separate peace in 1696, William's and Louis's increasing bankruptcy and the stalemate of the 1696–7 Flanders campaign, both sides were ready to enter peace talks.

The deliberations at Ryswick were, as often happened in this period, long drawn out, since the war continued simultaneously with diplomacy. The Holy Roman Emperor in Vienna wanted the war to go on, lured by the prospect of the Spanish inheritance. The French diplomats

KEY ISSUE

The war was opposed in Britain from the start.

at Ryswick delayed, making and then withdrawing proposals, and refusing to compromise on what was for William the central issue: recognition by Louis XIV of him as King of England, and repudiation of support for the exiled James II. French delegates would routinely refuse to address William's delegation as representing a usurper, they worked hard to detach minor allies such as Savoy from the League of Augsburg and they showed a keen awareness of the extent of opposition to the war in England.

War weariness was, however, pretty well universal and was skilfully articulated in England by the Tories and their 'country' Whig allies, who focused attention on high taxes (especially the Land Tax), spiralling food prices and the need for a standing army of no more than 7,000 men, shorn of foreign detachments such as the Dutch 'Blue Guards'. Barry Coward has said the peace party in late seventeenth-century England was 'a popular conservative reaction of pacifism and provincialism: a demand to end England's military involvement in Europe and to return power to the traditional rulers of provincial England'. In September 1697, the peace treaty was finally signed.

France agreed to abandon most of its territorial claims in Germany and the Netherlands, and settled for Strasbourg and a part of Alsace from its gains since 1678. Louis undertook to accept William III as the rightful English king, but was not required to expel James II from France. William seemed to have recovered a real balance of power, with the King of France giving ground, but all the participants knew that Ryswick was only a preliminary to agreement over a more intractable problem – namely the Spanish succession. No-one in 1697 could be sure whether this issue would be resolved by diplomacy or by a war.

DIAGRAM 3

The Spanish succession

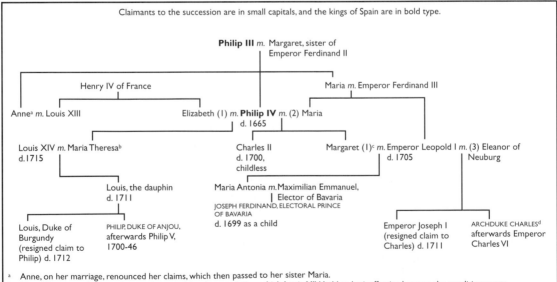

Claimants to the succession are in small capitals, and the kings of Spain are in bold type.

Philip III *m.* Margaret, sister of Emperor Ferdinand II

Henry IV of France

Maria *m.* Emperor Ferdinand III

Anne[a] *m.* Louis XIII

Elizabeth (1) *m.* **Philip IV** *m.* (2) Maria
d. 1665

Louis XIV *m.* Maria Theresa[b]
d.1715

Charles II
d. 1700,
childless

Margaret (1)[c] *m.* Emperor Leopold I *m.* (3) Eleanor of
d. 1705   Neuburg

Louis, the dauphin
d. 1711

Maria Antonia *m.* Maximilian Emmanuel,
Elector of Bavaria
JOSEPH FERDINAND, ELECTORAL PRINCE
OF BAVARIA
d. 1699 as a child

Louis, Duke of
Burgundy
(resigned claim to
Philip) d. 1712

PHILIP, DUKE OF ANJOU,
afterwards Philip V,
1700-46

Emperor Joseph I
(resigned claim to
Charles) d. 1711

ARCHDUKE CHARLES[d]
afterwards Emperor
Charles VI

a   Anne, on her marriage, renounced her claims, which then passed to her sister Maria.
b   Maria Theresa, on her marriage, made a conditional renunciation, which Louis XIV held to be ineffective because the conditions were
     not fulfilled.
c   Margaret was recognised in her father's will as heiress after Charles II and any descendants he might have. The claim of Joseph Ferdinand
     was derived from her.
d   Charles's claim was derived, through his father, from Maria, the daughter of Philip III.

B *The Spanish succession*

The succession to the throne in Spain was the central issue in inter-national relations during the latter part of the seventeenth century. The wretched Carlos II acceded to the throne in 1665, but failed during his 35-year reign to sire an heir. In some ways this was perhaps just as well, as he had a combined physical deformity and mental retardation, the result of centuries of interbreeding among the Spanish Habsburgs. Three alternative claimants emerged: Louis XIV's second grandson Philip, Duke of Anjou; Joseph Ferdinand (the 'Electoral Prince'), child of Maximilian, Elector of Bavaria and Marie Antonia, daughter of Leopold I; and Leopold's younger son by his third marriage to Eleonora of Neuburg, the Archduke Charles.

It was hard to decide who had the best claim, and such speculation was in any event irrelevant as the matter would probably be determined by diplomacy or war. Philip's mother, Maria Theresa of Spain, was Charles II's elder sister, but it was unclear whether she had renounced her rights to the Spanish Crown on her marriage. In any case, Philip's accession would seriously endanger the balance of power laboriously reconstructed at Ryswick, and revive the spectre of a union between France and Spain. Similar fears would be evoked if Charles succeeded: he could come to preside over a revival of Charles V's sixteenth-century Europe-wide empire.

Compromise did, nonetheless, seem possible at the end of the century as Louis and William were both exhausted, and William faced a suspi-cious Parliament, public opinion apparently indifferent to the looming crisis and a standing army of only 7,000 men. Under these circumstances William and Louis signed two Partition Treaties to divide the Spanish Empire on Charles's death in order to preserve a reasonable balance.

The first of these was agreed in 1698, and assigned to Joseph Ferdi-nand the Spanish Netherlands (the key to English and Dutch security), Spain itself and its colonies in the New World, while the Archduke Charles would receive Milan and its hinterland, and Anjou would get Naples, Sicily, the Tuscan ports and Guipuzcoa in northern Spain. Louis showed that he did not want to provoke another war against France by asserting his legal claim to the whole Spanish inheritance, using the argument of the non-payment of Maria Theresa's dowry back in 1661.

Unfortunately, the Electoral Prince died in 1699, and Louis and William thrashed out a Second Partition Treaty in 1700. This time the Archduke Charles would receive Spain and the Spanish Netherlands, with the Spanish lands in Italy going to Philip of Anjou. Leopold, freed from his commitments by the 1699 Treaty of Carlowitz with the Turks, refused to accept either treaty as the terms became known. However, Charles II's death in November 1700 rendered both treaties redundant, when Louis XIV decided to accept the terms of Carlos's will: the whole Spanish Empire was to go to Philip, and, if he refused it, to Archduke Charles. Louis's acceptance of the will ensured war between France and Austria, but such a conflict was likely anyway under either partition

> **KEY ISSUE**
>
> *Attempts at compromise.*

> **KEY ISSUE**
>
> *Why did Louis agree to accept Carlos II's will?*

treaty. Most English politicians welcomed Louis's decision and looked forward to a bruising campaign between Bourbon and Habsburg in Italy; they saw no reason why England need be directly involved.

Louis, however, embarked on the first of a series of provocations when he occupied the eight 'barrier fortresses' located in the Spanish Netherlands, and garrisoned by the Dutch under the terms of the Treaty of Ryswick. The Dutch were thoroughly alarmed by this move, although Louis maintained that the action was taken out of fear that William was about to reconstruct the Grand Alliance and to threaten France. Louis went on to undertake further provocative acts. He seemed to threaten Dutch security further by enrolling Bavaria, Cologne and Liège as allies, and the whole of Europe was concerned when Louis persuaded the Parlement of Paris to ratify Philip of Anjou's claim to the Spanish throne.

However, the Tory-dominated House of Commons feared another war, and hoped that Ryswick had removed the main cause of tension with France. Indeed, the Commons proceeded to impeach four MPs for their alleged part in framing the Partition Treaties, and they welcomed the publication in England of the terms of Carlos II's will. There was also considerable anti-Dutch hostility, stemming from three previous Anglo-Dutch wars, a long history of trading rivalry, William's frequent visits to the United Provinces and his manifest reliance on Dutch advisers. In fact, Coward writes of 'the focus for an outbreak of escalating national xenophobia'.

KEY ISSUE

Why did English public opinion initially support the war?

Over the next few months a gradual realisation permeated English public opinion that Louis's expansionist aims were indeed a threat to English interests, as the French King introduced trading embargoes, overran the towns of the southern Netherlands and made no bones about his desire that Philip of Anjou should inherit both the kingdom of France and the kingdom of Spain in the event of the Dauphin's death. Pro-war opinion was fanned by pamphlets and petitions, for example by the Kentish petition, which accused the Tories of sabotaging an effective foreign policy. Warwickshire and Cheshire submitted similar advice, and in June 1701 Parliament began to vote sums of money for war.

In September 1701 the exiled James II died, and Louis recognised his son as James III of England. This was a flagrant infringement of the spirit of Ryswick. Public opinion was now more obviously opposed to Louis XIV, and William withdrew his ambassador; the French retaliated by introducing harsh duties on English trade, and a further general election produced a more balanced Parliament as between Whigs and Tories. Just before William succumbed to his final illness, brought on by a fall from his horse in the park at Hampton Court, Parliament opened on 31 December 1701, temporarily united in favour of war. William urged a declaration of war on France in the name of European responsibility, to defend the Continent against French aggression and to sustain his 'Grand Alliance' of the previous August. This impressive coalition included Heinsius for the Dutch government, Marlborough (retrieved from disgrace at the King's behest) for the English, and the Austrian Habsburgs, who would not receive the Spanish Crown itself, but who would be compensated with Naples, Sicily, Milan and the southern Netherlands. The United Provinces would be rewarded with a strengthened barrier, French trade with the Spanish Indies would be forbidden and the Crowns of France and Spain would be rigidly separated. On 18 March 1702 William died, and on 4 May 1702 war was declared.

The War of the Spanish Succession began with the Allies in an overall weaker strategic position than the one they had had in 1688–97, since Louis XIV was in effective possession of much of the Spanish Empire, and Philip of Anjou enjoyed the loyalty of all (or nearly all) of its inhabitants. Moreover, Louis occupied the entire southern Netherlands, had obliterated the obstacle of the Dutch barrier and French-occupied Italy, and Louis's allies in Germany separated Leopold, the Habsburg Emperor, from his allies in the west. The result of this emerging conflict was by no means a foregone conclusion.

6 ⤳ THE BANK OF ENGLAND AND THE NATIONAL DEBT

The war of 1689–97 put unprecedented pressures on the English financial system. Over 13 years William succeeded in raising no less than £58 million in taxes, a quite extraordinary achievement compared with James II, formerly the most affluent Stuart, who could only average an income of £2 million per year. The huge costs of the ongoing naval campaign and the Irish expedition alone concentrated parliamentary minds wonderfully, and royal income rapidly doubled after 1688 as taxation receipts averaged a yield of £4 million a year between 1690 and 1699.

This was achieved partly by increasing the excise on salt and alcohol, and partly by extending it to coal, tea, coffee, spices, tobacco, leather, windows, glass, building and even bachelors. At the same time the land tax became a permanent and flexible part of the fiscal scene, fixed at approximately four shillings in the pound, and bringing in about one-third of the money required through local commissioners who seem to have collected it reasonably conscientiously despite the pitfalls of self-assessment. Indeed, it contributed to a total tax yield that was now even higher than under the Long Parliament and Cromwell. Geoffrey Holmes writes of 'the English taxpayer's coming of age', and Barry Coward comments on 'an impressive affirmation by the landed classes of their support for the war'. The English propertied classes committed themselves to the Protestant succession, and in the words of a contemporary: 'Where their treasure was, there were their hearts also'.

A higher revenue from direct taxation was, of course, partly accomplished by an enhanced tax yield. However, it can also be explained by an extension of treasury control over income, and the demise of the subcontracting of customs and excise revenues to private individuals or consortia; in short, by greater centralisation and efficiency. It was also achieved by the emergence of a phenomenon known as the National

Debt, which amounted to no less than £17 million by 1698, and required around 30 per cent of the Crown's annual revenues to service it. This was not the prodigal debt amassed by the earlier Stuarts through personal profligacy; rather it was a truly national debt – a war debt declared by Parliament as 'the debt of the nation'. Moreover, it was underwritten by Parliament, and investors were therefore prepared to lend to the government on a permanent, secure basis – not a temporary and speculative one.

In this way annual Parliaments would be a simple necessity to maintain the monarchy's financial credit, and particular future taxes were tied to pay the interest on what came to be called 'funded debt'. A State lottery and annuities were established to attract creditors, and in 1697 an Act set up a general consolidated (or 'sinking') fund to make good the deficits on the various accounts. This measure institutionalised government creditors, giving them a secure and privileged status, but William and Mary's reign is best known for the setting up of the Bank of England in 1694.

The creation of the Bank of England was far and away the greatest financial innovation of the reign, the brainchild of Charles Montagu, Chancellor of the Exchequer, and fiercely opposed by Tories such as Rochester, Halifax and Nottingham, who described it as 'fit only for republics'. The Tonnage Act of the same year effectively created the Bank, assigning to it the revenue from beer, ale and vinegar to service a particular loan of £1.2 million. Meanwhile, the subscribers to the loan were incorporated as a bank, and allowed to deal in bullion and bills of exchange, as the Bank lent more money to the government to help it to weather the storms of 1695–6. Interest rates fluctuated between 8 and 14 per cent, and Montagu's reminting of the coinage restored confidence in the worn and clipped coins, that had bedevilled the quantity and quality of coinage since 1660. Forgers, the poor trade balance with France, the large exports of the East India Company and substantial subsidies to the Allies were all factors tending to devalue the coinage, but the 1696 reminting helped to establish a sound coinage, developing a successful long-term credit system, and enabling England to emerge from the wars less exhausted than France. As the London money market grew, it prepared the way for London to replace Amsterdam as Europe's financial capital. In the words of Mark Kishlansky: 'all of this shifted the balance of power in London from commerce to finance. In a world at war, the security of funded debt was more prudent than the risk of overseas trade'.

7 ⌐ THE ACT OF SETTLEMENT, 1701

On 28 December 1694 Mary died of smallpox at the age of 32. Her death was naturally a blow to William, whom she had always loyally supported, and for whom she had regularly acted as regent during his frequent absences. She had also been an important symbol of continuity, as the daughter of James II and therefore both a Stuart and

See pages 290–4 for the Bank of England.

KEY ISSUE

London began to supplant Amsterdam as Europe's main financial centre.

English. In the absence of children from the marriage of William and Mary, the Protestant succession would now pass to Sophia of Hanover, daughter of Charles I's sister, Elizabeth, and mother of George, Elector of Hanover, after the death in July 1700 of the Duke of Gloucester, Anne's only surviving son from 17 pregnancies.

Accordingly, Parliament passed the Act of Settlement in 1701 to settle the throne on Sophia after Anne. The full title of the measure was: 'An Act for the further limitation of the Crown and better securing the Rights and Liberties of the Subject'. Sophia's older siblings were debarred on account of their Catholicism, and the Hanoverians were expected to remain Protestants and not to marry Roman Catholics. Yet there were further clauses. Judges were to hold office during their good behaviour (a technical term indicating that judges would continue in office provided that they proved to be efficient – as opposed to simply retaining the King's favour), their salaries were to be paid from the Civil List and they could only be removed by parliamentary vote. All holders of offices of profit under the Crown were debarred from sitting as MPs in the Commons from now on, and all major decisions were in future to be made by the full Privy Council. Also, no future foreign sovereign would be able to engage England in war for the defence of his foreign dominions, and even naturalised persons of foreign birth could not hold office in England or own English land: a measure that would affect Portland, Albemarle, Athlone and Galway. Finally the sovereign had to ask permission to leave Britain, and had to be a communicant member of the Church of England. Barry Coward comments, 'the Act is much more significant as a reflection of majority opinion among MPs and their constituents and their disenchantment with William's war and its effects on their country'.

KEY ISSUE

The Act of Settlement attempted to control the monarch.

8 ⮂ THE ACHIEVEMENTS OF WILLIAM III AND MARY II

Bishop Burnet, a contemporary diarist, wrote of William's foreign policy: 'the depression of France was the governing passion of his whole life', and indeed Louis XIV himself regarded William of Orange as his principal enemy. Under William, England became far more committed to European affairs than ever before, since he used his new kingdom as a pawn in his grand design, greatly expanding the navy and creating a mass army for the first time (numbers of troops rose above 60,000). John Miller commented: 'it was William rather than Marlborough who made the English army formidable; without that army, England could not have become a major European power'.

In Ireland, William's achievement was especially striking, as he completed the process of Protestantisation, and denied the island to Louis XIV as a base from which to strike at the English mainland. Indeed it is ironic that the country in which he was least interested should be the one where his name is most revered. Yet in England the settlement of

1688 remains his enduring achievement, if only as the only way to get rid of James II, and as ushering in important changes in government, politics, economic and social trends, and in intellectual history. Arguably, in fact, William's settlement did more to alter the course of English history than the rather more exaggerated events of 1640–60, since within the wider European environment of absolutism, William helped to engender a relatively liberal political system within a comparatively free society, for all his apparent image as a natural autocrat.

The settlement marked an important advance in political theory, as it made resistance to tyranny an acceptable concept, and paid lip service to the idea of an original contract. The rule of law was established, as Parliament (and not the judges) emerged as the arbiters of politically contentious points. At the same time the King ceased to use the courts for political purposes, and the 1701 Act of Settlement asserted that the King could not dismiss judges at will. William in fact, for all his authoritarian instincts, presided over a demystification of monarchy, as he abandoned 'touching' for the 'king's evil', and over a developing party system in Parliament.

Under William, England enjoyed a significant financial advantage over France, engaging Louis XIV in a struggle for survival, fearful that Louis might attempt to restore James II. Soon the Land Tax was yielding £3 million per year when not that long before Charles II's total income had been no more than £870,000. Moreover, William tapped the wealth of private investors, who were willing to extend long-term loans on security, at a time when few French financiers would contemplate lending money to the Crown, except at very high interest rates. 'The war', comments John Miller, 'then made England a major European power for the first time. The financial apparatus developed to meet the needs of the war was to enable England to intervene regularly in European affairs and to defend and extend its colonial empire.'

Therefore it became easier to make a fortune in the City, as land now seemed more unattractive as an investment. It is true that social status and political power had been associated with land, and that business and professional people had bought country estates, had invented bogus pedigrees and tried to marry their children into the gentry. The reality in late seventeenth-century England was that land was now less attractive as an investment: profits were likely to be low, and land could be heavily and accurately taxed. It is reasonable to date the rise of a 'moneyed interest' from this time, causing perhaps the first cracks to appear in what had been until now a homogeneous ruling class, as impecunious gentlemen were squeezed out of borough seats, perhaps in favour of someone described now as belonging to the 'chattering classes'. Miller concludes: 'land was still the main determinant of social status, but not the sole source of political power'.

While it is arguable that the 1689 Act offered less religious toleration than even Charles I and James II had been prepared to extend, William's refusal to enforce the penal laws, and the abolition of press censorship in 1695 may well have led to the virtual end of religious persecution. This approach was lent powerful intellectual support by the philosopher John Locke, three of whose important works, *Two Treatises of Government*, *A Letter Concerning Toleration* and *An Essay Concerning Human Understanding*, all opposed the notion of original sin, stressing instead that knowledge and values are acquired by experience as well as by a man's senses as interpreted by his intellect. From this it was a short step to assert that man could be taught and led to improve, and opening the way to the possibility of human progress. This was contrary to the traditional Christian view of the world as a vale of tears, to be endured but never improved, since perfection was only attainable in the afterlife. Many in the Church were ready to adapt their idea of God, who could now be seen as the benevolent architect of a rationally ordered and smoothly functioning cosmos. The Church could be expected to promise less hell fire and persecuting zealotry, and more practical morality.

> See pages 370–2 for the emergence of toleration.

The 'Glorious Revolution' in fact encouraged intellectuals such as Locke to take an active part in government. Locke himself toiled at the Board of Trade, Newton was employed as Master of the Mint and the distinguished statistician, Gregory King, was employed at the treasury. Indeed, dabbling in science was encouraged as new problems emerged to be solved, and the Revolution positively seemed to welcome criticism and change.

The most traditional and most simplistic view of the Revolution is that of the nineteenth-century historian, Macaulay, who saw it as having saved England from popish despotism, and making possible the growth of liberty and parliamentary government. According to Macaulay, England avoided a bloody revolution in the nineteenth century by having a bloodless one in the seventeenth century. For him, England was being propelled unerringly towards liberal democracy, and, Macaulay asserted, all the changes that followed the Revolution were both intended and foreseen. It may be that one of William's contemporaries had a more shrewd and modest idea of William's true achievement. Bishop Burnet clearly saw him as hard and single-minded in his determination to defeat Louis XIV, and impatient and unscrupulous in the face of opposition. 'I consider him', he wrote, 'as a person raised up by God to resist the power of France and the progress of tyranny and persecution… After all the abatements that may be allowed for his errors and faults, he ought still to be reckoned among the greatest princes that our history, or indeed any other, can afford.'

> **Q**
> *Do you agree with Burnet's view of William III?*

9 ⌒ ANNE: PERSONALITIES AND PRIORITIES

When Anne was born on 6 February 1665, it seemed unlikely that she would succeed to the throne, since Charles II had only been married for three years and she had an elder sister, Mary, who would probably marry and have children of her own. Her mother was Anne Hyde, Clarendon's daughter, who died in 1671 when she was six and her father, James, Duke of York, then married Mary of Modena. Her step-mother gave birth to a son, James Edward, in June 1688, who would be expected to be next in line to the throne. On the eve of the Glorious Revolution, Anne's chances of being crowned queen still seemed slim. Anne received a Protestant upbringing despite her father's efforts to convert her to Rome. At first she had been tutored by Edward Lake, and from 1675 by Henry Compton, the Bishop of London. Mark Kishlansky asserts, 'by word and deed she was as staunch an Anglican as it was possible to be'.

In 1683, Anne married Prince George, the younger brother of the Danish king and a staunch Lutheran: Anne therefore became the first Queen regnant of England in her own right to combine the throne with a fecund marriage, when she acceded in 1702. Nobody could allege that Anne and George did not try hard to produce an heir to the throne, for Anne experienced no less than 17 pregnancies, but none of the children

PICTURE 26

A portrait of Queen Anne by an unknown artist, after Kneller. The artist sums up Anne's rasion d'être to produce children and her tragedy as the unhealthy mother of a doomed child

See page 408 for Anne's gout.

QUEEN ANNE 1665–1714

Limited intellectually, but conscientious, stubborn and calculating, Anne was a dull, taciturn monarch with a mean and petty streak, declaring for example in her opening speech to Parliament, 'As I know myself to be entirely English...'. She relied very much on advisers and friends, particularly on Sarah Churchill and her husband Sir John, soon to be raised to the peerage as Earl of Marlborough. Indeed, the close relationship with Sarah even developed a private language with quaint soubriquets for the two women and their consorts, 'Mr and Mrs Freeman' and 'Mr and Mrs Morley'. Nurturing her friendship with the Churchills and despising, even hating, a good many prominent politicians, Anne contemplated the issues that lurked ahead: the Whig/Tory party battle, the condition of the Anglican Church and the looming war in Europe over the Spanish Succession, to which England seemed irrevocably committed.

The old view of Anne as an unintelligent puppet needs to be revised. She presided over weekly cabinets, and made personal decisions over crucial events such as the declaration of war in 1702, the union with Scotland in 1707 and the negotiation of the Treaty of Utrecht in 1713. She can lay claim to being the last monarch to attend Commons debates incognito, and indeed the last one to 'touch for the king's evil'. She took seriously her role as Supreme Governor of the Church of England, seeing it as a bulwark against Rome and a guarantee of social peace, and made sensible episcopal appoinments. She also cherished her role as defender of the wider European Protestant cause. She was loyal to favourites (at least until they lost favour), and showed a genuine concern for the happiness and welfare of her subjects. Devoted to her dull-witted husband, she gave birth or suffered miscarriage no less than 17 times. Her greatest pleasure in life was eating.

born survived, and only one lived for more than a few years. Anne became second in line to the throne on the death of her uncle, Charles, in 1685, but the birth of a son to James II's queen in 1688 distanced her. The Glorious Revolution put her back into the succession stakes, especially when it became clear that William and Mary would not have children of their own. The birth of Anne's own son, William, Duke of Gloucester, in 1689 briefly encouraged hopes of a sturdy Protestant Stuart line, but Gloucester's death in 1700 put paid to these hopes, and necessitated the passing of the Act of Settlement, which passed over no less than 52 Roman Catholic aspirants to fix the succession on the Hanoverians. Anne's sister, Mary, died in 1694, followed by her exiled father in 1701. When William died in 1702 Anne ascended the throne at the age of 37, ill and prematurely old, and having to be carried in a sedan chair to her coronation on 23 April 1702 because of gout.

10 ∽ POLITICAL PARTIES AND THE REIGN OF ANNE

A *Whigs and Tories*

Most MPs could be clearly identified as either Whig or Tory in the period from 1702 to 1714. Indeed each side frequented different social milieus: the Whigs to be found at the Kit-Cat Club, the Tories at the Society of Brothers. They even visited different coffee houses: Whigs gathered at the Cocoa Tree in Pall Mall and the St James's Coffee House; Tories made for Ouzindo's Chocolate House in St James's Street or the Smyrna in Pall Mall. A kind of political *apartheid* operated; Halifax, for example, spurned a dinner party invitation when he realised that Harley, the Earl of Oxford, would also grace the occasion in 1713. Moreover, the parties were also polarised in the newspapers that they read: Whigs preferred the *Observator* and the *Post Man*, enlivened by the scribbling of Addison, Steele and Defoe, while Tories turned to the *Post Boy*, *Rehearsal* and the *Examiner*, enlivened by the journalism of Jonathan Swift. By 1712 it is estimated that 67,000 copies of all newspapers were sold each week, read perhaps by as many as 670,000 people, i.e. by three times as many as the number of electors.

County society was also affected by what has been called 'the rage of party'. Party affiliation was an issue for the lieutenancy and the magistracy, especially at the seven periods of election between 1701 and 1715. Landed magnates such as Wharton and Seymour declared their party identity, and even formed caucuses among like-minded notables. All the usual signs of party activity were there: agents, literature and canvassing – even emblems (portraits of Dr Sacheverell for the Tories, and chamber pots for the Whigs).

Of course stereotypes existed for both parties. The typical Tory was a landed Anglican, enjoying a declining rental income and harassed by rising land tax demands. He was critical of expensive foreign wars and could even be a xenophobic English nationalist; a few flirted with Jaco-

> ### KEY ISSUE
>
> *What were the main issues at the start of Anne's reign?*

bitism. The stereotypical Whig represented the moneyed interest: City businessmen and merchants, beneficiaries of the Bank of England, pillars of Protestant dissent and supporters of foreign wars. Yet in reality there were no clear-cut religious or socio-economic divisions between Whigs and Tories. Most MPs of either party were Anglicans, but not all Tories were landowners, and for that matter not all Whigs were businessmen. Indeed, landowning and Anglican Whigs were commonplace, while some Tories were active in finance and trade – in fact several directors of the Bank of England were Tories. Barry Coward says of Tory entrepreneurs, there was 'no significant barrier of social prejudice preventing them from extensive entrepreneurial activities outside their estates'.

KEY ISSUE

Tory and not Whig opinion was more typical in Anne's reign.

However, Whigs and Tories were not two numerically equal groups, even with very few independent and uncommitted MPs. Prevailing opinion, it must be emphasised, was Tory and not Whig – in fact the Whigs hardly ever had a majority in the Commons, as the serious Whig defeat of 1710 showed. Tory ideology had put down deep roots, reinforced perhaps by recollections of wars in the sixteenth and seventeenth centuries, when war represented high taxes and an extension of central government powers. In short, the Tories were in many ways the inheritors of the long 'country' tradition of the seventeenth century.

Some historians have wondered whether the 'rage of party' threatened the country's political structure, but there was no crisis on the scale of that of the 1640s, and indeed the memory of what had happened then seemed to discourage politicians from pressing too far. Geoffrey Holmes has argued that rising living standards also helped to defuse political tensions, and Barry Coward states, 'Whig and Tory political rivalries in the reign of Queen Anne were intense but they did not threaten the established social and political order'. Not everyone in public life was a party politician. Godolphin, Harley and even Marlborough managed to distance themselves from the party battle; yet all three were forced to ally with one party or another – Marlborough and Godolphin with the Whigs from 1705–10, and Harley with the Tories from 1710–14.

B *Occasional Conformity*

Occasional Conformity was the practice whereby Nonconformists (or Dissenters) evaded the Test and Corporation Acts by occasionally (for example, once a year) attending an Anglican service. They therefore qualified for office.

The central political issue of the period from 1702 to 1704 was a religious one. High Churchmen welcomed the accession of the English, Anglican and Stuart Anne, following the foreign and Calvinist William, and they hoped for a High Church revival as High Tories picked up ministerial appointments, and the Queen resumed 'touching for the king's evil', which William had allowed to lapse. Francis Atterbury, later appointed Bishop of Rochester, led the campaign to attack 'Latitudinarian' bishops, i.e. those who wanted the Church of England to be a widely inclusive body, as Archbishop Tillotson urged.

In 1702, the High Churchmen introduced the **Occasional Conformity** Bill into the Commons to prevent Dissenters from being permitted to take Holy Communion in an Anglican Church to evade the penalties of the Test and Corporation Acts, and prior to attending Dissenter services. The Tory cry of 'The Church in Danger' resounded as they complained of the activities of Quakers, Baptists, Presbyterians, Unitarians and Occasional Conformists, but in 1703 the bill was shelved when it passed through the Commons, only to be amended by a margin of a mere two votes. Tories were determined to present the bill again; for them occasional conformity was little less than sacrilege, and the sort of deceitfulness and hypocrisy that they expected from the Whigs. If the bill could only pass, not only would the Church be more secure, but Dissenters would be kept out of local and national office, ushering in an era of Tory predominance in the localities and in Parliament. The Tories' campaign had a powerful spokesman, Dr Henry Sacheverell, Fellow of Magdalen College, Oxford, and in Coward's words, 'the major mouthpiece of the High Church movement'. Sacheverell's first sermon in Oxford in June 1702 showed that the learned doctor intended to start

See pages 370–2 for the religious context of Occasional Conformity.

PICTURE 27

A portrait of Robert Harley, Earl of Oxford, by Kneller

as he meant to go on. Entitled 'The Political Union: A Discourse Showing the Dependence of Government on Religion', it was an emotive and highly-charged appeal aimed at inflaming public opinion.

However, the bill was defeated for the second time in Parliament in December 1703, when the Lords rejected it by 71 votes to 59, and in November 1704 the third bill (the so-called 'tack', when it was attached to the Land Tax Bill in an attempt to force it through) was beaten in the Commons by 251 votes to 134. The question must therefore be asked why, despite popular support in the country, in the House of Commons and from the pulpit, three bills all failed.

The Whigs were consistently opposed to the legislation, for they after all had the most to lose, since their supporters stood to lose both vote and office. The secure Whig majority in the Lords was most useful, and indeed the Upper House voted against the various bills no less than three times. In fact many who were in no way Whigs also opposed the bill: Marlborough and Godolphin felt that it was too controversial for wartime, and Harley managed to suborn Francis Atterbury away from his advocacy of the bill, by offering him the Deanery of Carlisle and other blandishments. The Queen herself was less than keen, no doubt partly because her dissenting husband stood to lose his command in the English armies. Finally, there is no doubt that Daniel Defoe's powerful press campaign played its part. His witty parody of High Church propaganda, *The Shortest Way with Dissenters*, was published in 1703 as a biting attack on the bill, immediately after his release from Newgate Gaol.

There can be little doubt also that the High Church leaders themselves contributed to their own demise, since extreme Tory tactics lost them the support of more moderate Tories and even of the Queen herself. For example, a meeting of 150 Tories at the Fountain Tavern in the Strand decided to 'tack' an occasional conformity clause on to the Land Bill in 1704. In other words this group was saying that it would refuse to grant money for the war unless their Church demands were met. The Tories then divided between 'tackers' and 'sneakers', the latter reviled as apostates by those who backed the bill. Harley, St John and Queen Anne found themselves in the latter camp; devout Anglicans but alienated by the cynical contrivance of the 'tackers' to get the bill through. By 1705 the High Church cause was in disarray, as shown by the Whig gains in the general election of June that year.

C *The Sacheverell Riots*

The irrepressible doctor emerged again in November 1709, when he preached an inflammatory sermon in St Paul's Cathedral against Dissenters, toleration and the whole Revolution Settlement. The sermon, entitled 'In Peril Among False Brethren', was expressed in extreme and provocative language, and at once stirred up popular excitement and involvement. Printed copies sold quickly, 60,000 before the end of 1709. In this heady atmosphere the Whig ministry took the fateful step of impeaching Sacheverell, partly because Godolphin himself was men-

KEY ISSUE

Why did the Occasional Conformity bills fail?

See pages 370–2 for the religious aspect of toleration.

tioned in the sermon, and partly because it was seen as a personal and a political attack against the Glorious Revolution itself. The charge was sedition and subversion, and soon began to turn the accused into a Tory martyr. The trial began on 27 February 1710 in Westminster Hall, which was still bedecked with the standards captured at Blenheim six years before. Such was the crush of spectators that Wren was asked to design extra galleries for onlookers at a cost of £3,000, and a special vantage point for the Queen.

There could be no doubt of the massive popular support enjoyed by Sacheverell. Huge popular demonstrations and a series of riots in London, only outclassed by the Gordon Riots of 1780, enlivened the first few days of February 1710. In an orgy of unprecedented violence, far worse than anything seen in the English Civil War or the Exclusion Crisis, the residences of prominent Whigs and Dissenter meeting-houses were attacked by mobs. Sacheverell had struck a rich vein of paranoia and prejudice, which was xenophobic and opposed to the war, whose targets were Dissenters perceived to have done well out of the war, the 'moneyed interest', and Dutchmen, Jews and foreigners in general. This was no spontaneous combustion, for the targets attacked were selected; nor was it an uprising of the poor and the oppressed, for the 'middling sort' seem to have been well represented.

In this fevered atmosphere, Sacheverell was found guilty by the margin of 69 votes to 52, but his sentence was a lenient one: suspension from preaching for three years, and the original offending sermon to be burnt before the Royal Exchange. Shortly afterwards the accused picked up a lucrative living in Shropshire, and the Tory cause received powerful support from Jonathan Swift's incisive attacks in the Tory press. 'The Sacheverell Case', writes Jones, 'seemed to show that there was nothing that the Whigs would not do in order to extend and defend their near-monopoly of power and office.' The fall of the Whig Junto ministry was not long delayed. The 1710 general election produced the biggest swing of opinion in the reign and returned a Tory Parliament, elected on a pro-Sacheverell and anti-war ticket. With a majority in the Commons of 151, the Tories were in a very strong position.

> **KEY ISSUE**
>
> *What conclusions can be drawn from the support enjoyed by Sacheverell?*

11 ⌢ FOREIGN POLICY: WAR BY LAND AND SEA

The origins of the War of Spanish Succession predated Anne's reign: William of Orange's agreements with Louis XIV in the two Partition Treaties, the death of Carlos II of Spain, Louis XIV's acceptance of Carlos's will, Louis's recognition of James III as the rightful King of England and his annexation of the barrier towns in the Spanish Netherlands all occurred before 1702. Anne therefore inherited a war with a set of clearly defined war aims that was to last until 1713. It aimed to stop French domination of the Mediterranean and American trade, to safeguard the Protestant succession in England (i.e. Anne and the Hanoverians) and to maintain England's interest in keeping a European

1704	**B**lenheim
1706	**R**amillies
1708	**O**udenarde
1709	**M**alplaquet
Key	BROM 4689

TABLE 17
Marlborough's victories

KEY ISSUE

Controversies about the correct strategy.

KEY ISSUE

What were Anne's war aims?

balance of power. She also inherited a distinct party rift in respect of those declared aims.

The Whigs had no doubts about furthering the foreign policy aims outlined above, while Tories had their doubts. Tories such as Rochester favoured a 'blue water' war strategy, whereby England would act as an auxiliary and concentrate on an effort against Spain's and France's colonies and shipping. The Tories argued that in this way France and Spain would be hit at the weakest part of their defences, maritime war was much cheaper, and England had more defined aims in the New World than on the Continent. Rochester's ideas were initially very persuasive to many MPs, who, during the 1702–3 parliamentary session, doubled the sum of money devoted to the navy, but there were those who wondered whether the 'blue water' idea was a sensible one. A solely naval strategy was an expensive option, and the only real way to defeat Louis XIV militarily in Europe was through the 'common cause'. Therefore, securing Spain for the Habsburg claimant Charles III became a major war aim, and the slogan emerged, 'no peace without Spain'.

Marlborough was 52 years old at the onset of hostilities, and married to Sarah Churchill, Anne's principal confidante. He had acquired few claims to fame: he had deserted James II in 1688, reduced Münster in 1690, and falling foul of William III's dislike, had languished in the Tower since 1692. However, the war enabled him to display many fine qualities: he was aggressive and bold, and his 1704 plan to march eastwards along the Danube Valley showed these qualities to the full. Brushing aside Dutch and English scepticism, Marlborough took Bonn, Huy and Limbourg in the spring of 1703, before advancing rapidly towards Vienna through Bavaria, Louis XIV's ally. Accompanied by his allies, Prince Louis of Baden and Prince Eugene of Savoy, Marlborough took Schellenberg near Donauworth on 21 June 1704, before moving on to Blenheim to engage a French army of 60,000 troops under Marshal Tallard on 13 August. Marlborough's stunning victory shattered the myth of French invincibility, for no French army had been decisively beaten since the early seventeenth century, and now all Bavaria lay open to the Allies.

A grateful nation gave its hero the manor of Woodstock in Oxfordshire in 1705, on which he proceeded to build what Kishlansky calls 'the greatest prodigy house of the age', designed by Vanbrugh, Wren's second-in-command at the Board of Works, and Nicholas Hawksmoor. Meanwhile, Marlborough's successes on land were complemented by victories at sea: Sir George Rooke seized the rock of Gibraltar on 23 July 1704, and Sir Cloudesley Shovell successfully escorted Charles III to Spain to assume his kingdom. On 13 August Shovell defeated the French Toulon fleet off Malaga, proving that the navy could defend Britain and keep open vital supply lines.

Further successes followed in 1705, when the Earl of Peterborough, with an English and Dutch fleet and accompanied by Charles III, took Barcelona and triggered off a separatist revolt in Catalonia. In 1706, Marlborough defeated Villeroi at Ramillies in the Netherlands in the

PICTURE 28
A portrait of Thomas, Earl of Wharton by Kneller. 'Honest Tom' represented all that Queen Anne loathed about the Whig Junto. He had played a prominent role in the Revolution of 1688 and was a libertine and an atheist. His violent and corrupt life was illustrated by his 'management' of parliamentary elections and his record as a duellist. He boasted that he had fought 40 duels, had never challenged a man, never refused a challenge and never killed anyone

Q

Has Kneller succeeded in conveying Wharton's cheerful cynicism? The pious Anne had good reason for disliking Wharton, an atheist who had allegedly defecated in a church pulpit.

first massed battle on the plains of the Netherlands since 1692. In June 1706, the Huguenot Earl of Galway left his fastness in Lisbon with an Anglo-Dutch force and seized Madrid, but in the following year Marlborough's half-brother, Berwick, beat the Allies at Alamanza, killing or capturing no less than 5,000 of them. The Whig cry of 'no peace without Spain' seemed to be dangerously over-extending allied resources in Iberia, Italy and north-west Europe.

Developments in the war on the Continent had close links with the party battle at home, and in 1708 the prevailing Whig Junto ministry forced Harley to resign. The Junto blamed Harley for the lack of advancement for Whigs, for a spy scandal in his office and for his failure to defend the war effectively in Parliament. Harley's position became impossible when the Whigs made it clear that they would not serve under him, and when Harley himself realised that the alternative to resignation was impeachment and a probable death sentence. The elections of May 1708 resulted in the largest majority Whig Parliament since 1688, and Anne finally relented on the death of her husband, George, in October, to Whig pressure. In November, a Junto ministry took office, including Somers, Sunderland, Wharton, whom Anne cordially disliked, and St John, raised to the earldom of Orford.

Yet the Junto administration lasted a mere two years since parliamentary support soon eroded, partly in opposition to the Junto's plan to defeat Louis XIV at all costs. Marlborough did beat the French at Oudenarde in July 1708, ending the threat of a French invasion of Holland, but his next victory with Prince Eugene at Malplaquet in September 1709 was a more pyrrhic affair: the allies lost 20,000 men to the French 15,000. What has been called 'the bloodiest battle of the eighteenth century' led to Tory deprecation of Marlborough as the 'butcher' and the spread of anti-war feeling.

The country was now war-weary, and the Whigs seemed unlikely to remain in power, especially as they were accused of profiting personally from the hostilities and for the recent run on the Bank of England. Moreover, Louis XIV now appeared to be prepared to offer realistic concessions, including the withdrawal of French claims in Spain, the Indies, the Low Countries and Italy. He was even ready to recognise the Protestant succession in England and to conclude a barrier treaty with the Dutch. The Tories therefore urged withdrawal, racked by falling rental income stemming from the recent poor harvests and the harsh winter of 1708–9, and stung by the tax rises needed to raise £13 million per year for the war. The Tories also feared a military coup led by Marlborough, the perpetuation of a huge standing army and the Whig scheme to naturalise all foreign Protestants, such as the Dutch and refugees from the Palatinate.

The Sacheverell affair also led to the downfall of the Junto ministry in 1710 and its replacement by Tories such as Dartmouth, Harley, Rochester, Buckingham and St John. Indeed, the general election of that year returned a Tory Parliament in the biggest swing of opinion of the reign. Support for Sacheverell and an immediate peace led to a Tory majority of 151 in the House of Commons.

From their coming to power, the new government began secret talks with France to seek a separate negotiated peace, especially following the evacuation of Madrid in November 1710 and Stanhope's defeat at Brihuega the following month. The death of the Austrian Emperor, Joseph I, in 1711 accelerated the peace process, since Joseph's brother, Charles, evoked the spectre of a union of the two wings of Habsburg territory, Spain and the Empire. The danger of a Habsburg superpower seemed now to be as great as Bourbon hegemony on the Continent, and St John broached in his talks with Louis those issues that mattered to Britain: the *Asiento* (an exclusive contract awarded by the Spanish Crown to supply slaves to Spain's New World colonies), Gibraltar and Port Mahon; Acadia and Newfoundland in Canada; and the privateers' use of the Dunkirk fortifications. Spain would go to Philip V, the Bourbon claimant, the barrier fortresses would be partially restored to reassure Dutch sensitivities and Louis would recognise the Hanoverian succession to the English throne. The Tories therefore believed that their three main aims would be achieved: a division of the Spanish Empire between the rival claimants; a new barrier deal to protect Holland; and concessions to English traders in the New World.

The Whig reaction to the published peace terms was shrill. They were denounced as a sell-out by Tories too (like Nottingham who feared eclipse under a Hanoverian monarch and a Jacobite restoration backed by France and Spain), and by allies such as Prince George of Hanover. However, Jonathan Swift's propaganda in favour of peace was an effective weapon. In November 1711, he published *The Conduct of the Allies*, a savage attack on Marlborough, the Whigs and their Dutch allies for conniving in the prolongation of the war. The Dutch, Austrians and Portuguese, Swift pointed out, had done little to prosecute the struggle.

An example of Swift's satire was a piece for *The Examiner* (see below), in which he defended the government from the accusation of treating Marlborough ungenerously. In two columns he listed 'Roman gratitude' (the modest way Romans treated their generals) and 'British ingratitude' (the way in which Marlborough had been loaded with wealth donated by the State). The amounts are in old-fashioned money.

When the issue came to be discussed in Parliament, the government was outvoted in the Commons by the combined ranks of the Whigs and the 'Whimsicals', Tories who supported the Whigs on this issue. However, Anne was able to overcome the stumbling-block of the permanent Whig majority in the Lords by creating 12 new peers. On 31 December 1711 Marlborough was dismissed after unexplained shortfalls were found in his military accounts, and after Anne's quarrel with his wife Sarah. The Dutch were now forced to the peace table. Few obstacles remained in the way of the signing of a treaty, and Barry Coward encapsulates Whig opinion well when he writes, 'the events of the spring and summer of 1712 showed that a majority in Britain were willing to sweep aside all considerations of national honour and Britain's international obligations in the pursuit of peace'.

Q *How effective and how fair do you think it is, as satirical comment on Marlborough's wealth – and alleged greed? Are Marlborough's gains in fact understated?*

A Bill of Roman Gratitude	£	S	D	A Bill of British Ingratitude	£	S	D
For frankincense	4	10	0	Woodstock	40,000	0	0
A bull for sacrifice	8	0	0	Blenheim	200,000	0	0
An embroidered garment	50	0	0	Post Office grant	100,000	0	0
A crown of laurel	0	0	2	Mildenheim	30,000	0	0
A statue	100	0	0	Pictures, jewels etc.	60,000	0	0
A trophy	80	0	0	Pall Mall grant	10,000	0	0
A thousand copper medals	2	1	8	Employments	100,000	0	0
A triumphal arch	500	0	0		540,000	0	0
A triumphal coach	100	0	0				
Casual charges	150	0	0				
	994	11	10				

TABLE 18
The 'Roman gratitude' and the 'British ingratitude'

12 ⌒ THE PEACE OF UTRECHT

In April 1713, the Treaty of Utrecht was signed by Britain, France and the Dutch. The terms resembled closely those that Harley had discussed two years before: Philip V would inherit the Crown of Spain; some Dutch barrier fortresses would be restored; Louis agreed to recognise the Hanoverian succession (even agreeing that the Jacobite pretender would never return to France); and Britain gained the *Asiento* for 30 years, Gibraltar, Minorca, St Kitts, Acadia (in Nova Scotia) and Hudson's Bay. Utrecht therefore established Britain as the greatest maritime power in the world, preponderant on two Continents and on the oceans. Britain had gained important naval bases in the Mediterranean, which would enable it to achieve a stranglehold over the Levant trade, and to compete successfully with the Portuguese. Britain had also benefited from France's eclipse in the New World, since it now controlled the growing Canadian fisheries and might eventually control all North American trade. Finally, the Dutch were excluded from the South American trade, and the South Sea Company looked forward virtually to printing money, since the slave traded continued as a very profitable enterprise. Moreover, for the first time foreign policy became a major talking point in Britain. J.R. Jones sums up the treaty as follows: 'Britain had now emerged as the new great European power, acting as arbiter in conflicts and problems that had previously stood well outside the range of her interest and power'.

13 ⌒ THE SUCCESSION CRISIS

As the Queen's health deteriorated, the Succession Crisis loomed as an issue. Whigs were unanimous for the provisions of the 1701 Act of Settlement: they looked forward to a Hanoverian succession. Some Tories backed the House of Hanover, notwithstanding its Lutheran associations; others were prepared to consider a Jacobite succession – indeed, George of Hanover's known predilection for the Whigs fuelled Tory fears of a Whig supremacy. A few Tories even talked with James Francis Edward Stuart: Marlborough, Harley and Bolingbroke all discussed matters with James, possibly as an insurance policy in case a Hanoverian succession did not work out. Bolingbroke was in fact spotted at the opera in Paris with James in August 1712. However, many Tory MPs were frankly undecided.

Anne's health declined further, and by December 1713 she was too ill to attend the Utrecht celebrations. At the same time she despised the Hanoverians, and refused to allow the Duke of Cambridge, the Electress Sophia's grandson, to come over to England to attend the House of Lords. Moreover, James Stuart continued to correspond with her, although he refused to abandon Catholicism. In the event the Electress Sophia predeceased Anne on 8 June 1714 – otherwise she would have become queen by the 1701 Act of Succession. Because Anne's only surviving child, William, Duke of Gloucester, had died in 1700, the Act of

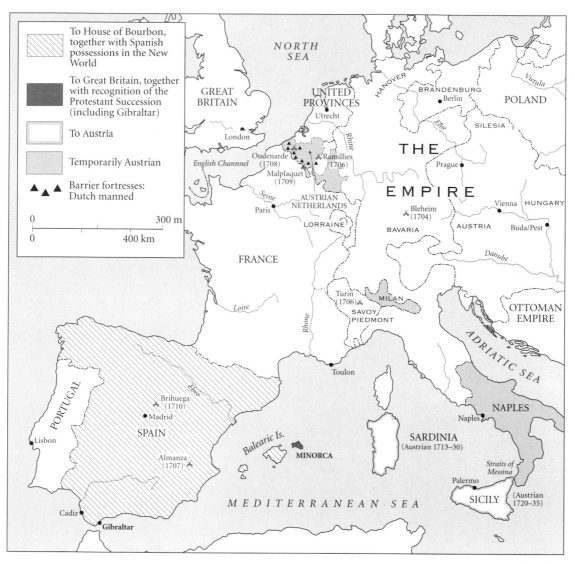

MAP 6
The Spanish succession and the Treaty of Utrecht

Settlement came into operation and Anne at last became reconciled to George's accession. When Anne eventually died on 1 August 1714, George was proclaimed her successor and he immediately announced his disdain for the Tories, who had been responsible for the ending of subsidies to Hanover in 1713. As England awaited the arrival of the new king, the Tories were truly discredited by their bitter divisions, by the small crypto-Jacobite group and by the corruption of leading Tories such as Harley and Bolingbroke. In contrast, the Whigs were united and disciplined, enjoying a wide appeal through their support for the Glorious Revolution and the Protestant succession.

14 ⌐ ANNE'S LEGACY

The main impression of Anne's reign is of constant and successful warfare. Martial success on this scale had been unknown since Henry V in the fifteenth century, and was not to be seen again until the Waterloo campaign of 1815. Louis XIV's grand design was shattered, and contemporaries became used to a standing army of well-trained, largely Protestant troops, whose financing now was accepted as an essential part of the royal budget. The Treaty of Utrecht came to be seen as the signpost to an imperial future unhampered by a union of the Crowns of France and Spain, or by the assertion of French claims in the Low Countries. The acquisition in 1713 of Port Mahon, Gibraltar, Newfoundland and Hudson's Bay led to British naval supremacy in the Mediterranean and to a thriving group of colonies in North America.

New opportunities for economic prosperity were soon seized as the prospect of Britain as the greatest financial and commercial power in the world opened up. In both the economic and strategic contexts, the union of England and Scotland (to be discussed in Chapter 12) was profoundly significant. Patriotism grew, epitomised by John Bull, who from 1712 was identified with a curious mixture of British beef and xenophobia. The essayist Addison lampooned this archetypal English figure in an imaginary conversation:

> ... finding him such a critic upon foreigners, I asked him, if he had ever travelled; he told me he did not know what travelling was good for, but to teach a man to ride the great horse, to jabber French, and to talk against passive obedience: to which he added, that he scarce ever knew a Traveller in his life who had not forsook his principles, and lost his hunting seat.

Q *What is the point of Addison's remarks?*

This mood of national confidence and pride is also shown in the great Augustan country houses of the early eighteenth century (Chatsworth and Castle Howard), and also in the city churches of Hawksmoor and Wren. Alexander Pope's heroic couplets were complemented by a huge growth of political satire by Addison, Steele and others, whereby newspapers and journals thrived: the Tory *Examiner* and *Post Boy*, and the Whig *Observator* and *Post Man*. The *Spectator* initially essayed a neutral course from its foundation in 1711, but soon quarrelled with the *Examiner*. Literary figures were closely involved in party affairs, making this a landmark period in British journalism. The Anglican Church had emerged as a bulwark against both Roman Catholicism and Nonconformity, and indeed, in theory at least, Catholics, Unitarians, Deists and atheists were all proscribed. James II's overt popery and Charles II's secret leanings to Rome seemed a long way in the past.

See page 372 for the religious settlement.

Finally, Anne's reign marked the end of a period of revolution in royal finances. Subsidies, feudal prerogatives and benevolences disap-

peared to make way for regular taxes on land and wealth. The people as a whole were now responsible for maintaining a solvent government. Landowners now paid up the land tax, mindful perhaps of the anarchy into which the kingdom had lapsed during the previous century.

15 ~ BIBLIOGRAPHY

There is a number of useful Stuart textbooks that deal with the period from 1688–1714, such as *Tudor and Stuart Britain, 1471–1714* by Roger Lockyer (Longman, 1964), *Country and Court, England 1658–1714* by J.R. Jones (Arnold, 1978), *The Stuart Age, England 1603–1714* by Barry Coward (Second Edition, Longman, 1994), *The Making of a Great Power, Late Stuart and Early Georgian Britain, 1660–1722* by Geoffrey Holmes (Longman, 1993) and *A Monarchy Transformed, Britain 1603–1714* by Mark Kishlansky (Penguin, 1996).

Among biographies the two relevant volumes published by Weidenfeld and Nicolson in 1972 are *William and Mary* by John Miller and *Queen Anne* by Gila Curtis. *Queen Anne* by Edward Gregg (Routledge, 1980) and *Sarah Duchess of Marlborough* by Frances Harris (Oxford, 1991) can be recommended, while the Glorious Revolution itself is well served by *The Glorious Revolution* by John Miller (Longman, 1983), and *Reluctant Revolutionaries, Englishmen and the Revolution of 1688* by W.A. Speck (Oxford University Press, 1988). The idea of absolutism is covered in *The Myth of Absolutism, Change and Continuity in Early Modern European Monarchy* by Nicholas Henshaw (Longman, 1992) and *Absolutism in Seventeenth Century Europe* edited by John Miller (Macmillan, 1990). Purely political developments are also dealt with by *Politics under the Later Stuarts, Party Conflict in a Divided Society, 1660–1715* by Tim Harris (Longman, 1993) and by *Monarchy and Revolution, the English State in the 1680s* by J.R. Western (Blandford, 1972). A selection of essays entitled *Britain after the Glorious Revolution, 1689–1715* by Geoffrey Holmes (Macmillan, 1969) still contains useful material on a variety of topics, as does an older book entitled *England in the Reigns of James II and William III* by David Ogg (Oxford University Press, 1955). The best selection of relevant documents is *The Eighteenth Century Constitution, 1688–1715* edited by E.N. Williams (Cambridge University Press, 1960).

Finally, *The Growth of Political Stability in England, 1675–1725* by Sir Jack Plumb (Macmillan, 1967; Peregrine, 1969), puts forward a stimulating thesis that England eventually became more stable as a result of the Revolution Settlement of 1688–90, leading to greater political activity and interest in politics, the birth of a Whig oligarchy and the emergence of effective executive power.

16 ⌒ DISCUSSION POINTS AND ESSAY QUESTIONS

A *This section consists of questions that might be used for discussion (or written answers) as a way of expanding on the chapter and testing understanding of it.*

1. What were the intentions of William of Orange when he landed in England in November 1688?
2. Why did the 'political community' eventually prefer the option of a joint monarchy of William and Mary in 1689?
3. Was the Declaration of Rights of 1689 a conservative or a radical document?
4. Does the Toleration Act of 1689 deserve its title?
5. To what extent was the financial settlement of 1690 an obstacle to the exercise of William III's kingship?
6. Account for the success of William III's Irish policy in 1690.
7. To what extent was William III successful in subduing Scottish resistance to his rule up to 1693?
8. Did distinct differences emerge as between Whigs and Tories during the reign of William and Mary?
9. Why did William's war policy arouse criticism during the War of the League of Augsburg, 1689–97?
10. Why did England become involved in the War of the Spanish Succession, 1700–13?
11. Account for the founding of the Bank of England in 1694.
12. Is it possible to distinguish clearly between Whigs and Tories during the reign of Queen Anne?
13. Why did all three attempts to get an 'Occasional Conformity' bill passed fail during Anne's reign?
14. What, if anything, do the Sacheverell Riots tell us about late Stuart England?
15. Why had the War of the Spanish Succession become so unpopular in England by 1710?
16. How significant was the growth of popular opinion during this period?

B *Essay questions.*

1. Why, and in what ways, was there a redefinition of the powers of the Crown in the period 1688–1714?
2. To what extent was there a revolution in all three kingdoms in 1688–90?
3. 'Pragmatism and ambiguity were the hallmarks of the Revolutionary Settlement.' Is this a reasonable assessment of the events of 1688–90?
4. 'Restoration rather than innovation.' Discuss this view of the Glorious Revolution.
5. Which groups profited most from the Glorious Revolution?
6. Discuss the importance of the succession question between 1689 and 1714.

7. To what extent did a genuine two-party system operate in English politics between 1689 and 1714?

8. 'Between 1689 and 1714 the powers of the monarchy were weakened more in theory than in practice.' Discuss this view of the reigns of William and Mary and Queen Anne.

9. Account for British success in warfare from 1689 to 1713.

10. To what extent were religious issues a cause of disagreement during the reign of Queen Anne?

11. How far had political parties developed by 1714?

12. How far were Britain's interests well served by the foreign policy of William and Mary and Queen Anne from 1689 to 1714?

17 ⌁ WRITING ESSAYS ON CONSEQUENCES

Examiners are fond of asking candidates to identify the consequences of an event or of a series of events. Such a question can be a trap for the unwary: a sound answer will require a thorough knowledge of the event itself, and a shrewd assessment of the consequences that followed. One type of essay that might be asked about the reign of William and Mary is something along the lines of: 'Was it the Settlement or what happened afterwards that determined the role of the monarchy?'

It is easy to fall into the trap of assuming that the answer to such a question must be to take one side or another, i.e. that the reign was wholly decided by the terms of the Revolution Settlement, or that subsequent events made the terms of the Settlement entirely relevant. It is most likely, however, that the answer to such a question will in fact be more complicated, i.e. the Settlement had an important bearing on what happened later, but that it did not dictate William's actions as the reign wore on. The essay therefore involves a skilful interweaving of William's expectations of the possibilities open to him from 1689 onwards, and the realities of his circumscribed power resulting from the Revolution Settlement.

The introduction of any essay is absolutely crucial: you have the opportunity to outline the problems and the issues as you see them, and to set 1688–90 in the widest possible British and European context. It would therefore be reasonable to set out William's motives for being anxious to become King of England; especially his ambition to confront Louis XIV of France using the added resources of England. However, William did not accede to the throne in a vacuum. He succeeded to replace James II, who had been unsatisfactory and who had seemed to a majority of the 'political community' to represent a return to the worst aspects of Charles I's government. Therefore a new definition of royal power was inevitable in 1689–90.

Whatever conclusion you reach in this essay, you will need to get to grips with the main provisions of the Revolution Settlement. The Bill of Rights clearly gave William the right to choose his own ministers, but it also severely limited his ability to raise money: no taxes were to be levied without parliamentary consent and no peacetime standing army would therefore be possible without Parliament's permission. The bill also established the succession, and required the new monarchs to swear to maintain the Protestant succession. The Oath of Allegiance was designed to be inclusive rather than exclusive, and the Toleration Act aimed at a broad rather than a narrow Church, but the Financial Settlement ensured that William would have to ask Parliament repeatedly for cash.

After William's campaign in Ireland he was able to embark on the European expedition that was dearest to his heart – the defeat of Louis XIV of France. This war policy was hampered partly by the limitations imposed on monarchical power by the Settlement, but also partly by the provisions of the Triennial Act of 1694, that required fresh elections every three years, and by the parliamentary battle between Whigs and Tories, which was not foreseen in the 1689–90 legislation. Moreover, the electorate was in any event becoming more sophisticated, especially following the lapsing of the Licensing Act in 1695. Political arguments about the merits, or otherwise, of a war policy raged throughout the reign, as William tried to achieve a revolution in foreign policy towards active hostility to France. The Treaty of Ryswick in 1697 should be seen in part as the King's response to the doubts of at least some of his subjects about the wisdom of a forward policy on the Continent. It should also be seen as his preparation for the 'big one': the conflict that had been brewing for a while over the Spanish succession.

William remained determined to secure French recognition of his status as King of England, and to oblige the exiled James II, currently exiled in France, to renounce his claim to the English throne. Indeed for a while his ambitions were supported by public opinion following Louis XIV's incautious occupation of the barrier fortresses. A kind of war hysteria in fact marked the early years of the War of the Spanish Succession. Mary's death in 1694 was eventually followed by the 1701 Act of Settlement, which settled the line of succession on the Electress Sophia of Hanover and her heirs. Neither event was predicted in the Revolution Settlement.

Now we come to the essay's conclusion, which is as vital as the introduction since you have the chance to tie up any loose ends and to summarise your view in the light of the points made in the body of your essay. You are most likely to argue that the Revolution Settlement was a powerful restraint on the monarchy, faced with the demands of almost continuous warfare; but also that William had an agenda of his own that predated his accession, for which he won important backing – at least until war weariness set in. Finally, you should remind the reader that events subsequent to the Settlement also played their part: Louis's provocative military policies in the years from 1688; the death of Mary II; the passing of the Act of Settlement in 1701; and growing opposition to the war from mercantile and financial interests all need to be mentioned. In this way your conclusion should emerge as a balance: both factors mentioned in the title were instrumental in shaping royal policy – and this situation continued into Anne's reign too.

18 ~ DOCUMENTARY EXERCISE ON THE REVOLUTIONARY SETTLEMENT

Study sources A to E and attempt the questions that follow.

A From *History of His Own Time* by Bishop Burnet (1727).

When the debates began to come on, there appeared three different parties upon the matter of settling the nation. The first was for calling back the King, the second for appointing a Prince Regent, and the third for setting the Prince of Orange on the throne. Those who were for restoring the King were at the same time for laying him under such restraints, and treating with him for such security to religion and the laws, as might put them out of danger of an arbitrary and dispensing power for the future . . .

Those who were for . . . [the second] expedient [among whom the Earls of Nottingham and Clarendon were chief in the debate] were of opinion that the King, by his maladministration, having brought himself into an incapacity of holding the exercise of the sovereign power any longer in his own hand, there might another be appointed to exercise thereof . . . Those who were for setting aside King James, and placing another on the throne, were of the opinion that, both from precedents in history and the ancient forms of coronation still in use, there was a mutual contract between the King and the people of England, that as the one promised obedience to their prince, the other engaged to defend his subjects, and govern according to law; and that when he acted contrary thereunto he had forfeited his title to their allegiance and all right to rule over them. Now the King, they said, had broken the laws in many public and avowed instances, had set up an open treaty with France, had shaken the settlement with Ireland, had assumed a dispensing power to invalidate all laws, had set up an Ecclesiastical Commission to oppress the Church, and had finally deserted his people, and fled to a foreign and known enemy to the nation . . .

B From Sir John Reresby's *Memoirs* of 29 and 30 January 1689.

The Lords entered into consideration of the same matter [as the Commons] . . . Some were for recalling the king upon conditions [but those very few]; others for the government to be continued in the King's name, and the Prince to have the executive power of it by the name of regent or protector; others for having the King forfeit the crown and the Prince of Orange elected into it; others for having the said Prince and Princess crowned, as it was in the case of Philip and Mary, and to hold it by descent in the right of his wife, without taking notice of the Prince of Wales, who was to be made incapable to succeed because a papist, being christened in that Church. At last the Lords voted to agree with the Commons in the main as to the vacancy of the crown, only differing in some words . . .

C From *History of His Own Time* by Bishop Burnet.

There was nothing now remaining but to frame an instrument setting forth the chief heads of King James's ill government, and in opposition to these the rights and liberties of the people of England, to be like a Magna Charta between prince and subject, and to instruct posterity in the reasons of this new establishment. And to make all uniform and of a piece, it was thought advisable to adjust the oaths of allegiance etc., to this settlement, and in the beginning of a new government at least to make them as general and comprehensive as might be.

D From the Bill (and earlier, Declaration) of Rights (1689).

Whereas the late King James the Second, by the assistance of divers evil counsellors, judges, and ministers employed by him, did endeavour to subvert and extirpate the protestant religion, and the laws and liberties of this kingdom . . .

And whereas the said late King James the Second having abdicated the government, and the throne being thereby vacant . . .

II. The said lords spiritual and temporal, and commons, assembled at Westminster, do resolve, That William and Mary prince and princess of Orange be, and be declared, King and Queen of England, France and Ireland . . .

E From the Bill of Rights (1689).

The said lords spiritual and temporal, and commons . . . declare:
1. That the pretended power of suspending of laws, or the execution of laws, by regal authority, without consent of parliament, is illegal.
2. That the pretended power of dispensing with laws, or the execution of laws, by regal authority, as it hath been assumed and exercised of late, is illegal . . .
6. That the raising or keeping of a standing army within the kingdom in time of peace, unless it be with consent of parliament, is against law . . .
8. That elections of members of parliaments ought to be free . . .
13. And that . . . parliaments ought to be held frequently.

1. *Summarise the argument in source C. (3 marks)*
2. *Compare sources A and B. Which gives the more reliable account of the options available in 1689, and the support for them? (6 marks)*
3. *How useful to a historian are sources C, D and E? (6 marks)*
4. *'The Revolutionary Settlement of 1689–90 was more conservative than innovatory'. Using your own knowledge and sources A to E, examine this view of the Glorious Revolution. (10 marks)*

The Economy in Transition

8

INTRODUCTION

When James I came to the throne in 1603 the British Isles were still economically backward and militarily weak. In contrast, by 1714 British colonial commerce, protected by a powerful royal navy, had begun to dominate the world. The reason for this dramatic change was the expansion of the English economy. For most of the Stuart period there was a distinct difference between the economies of England and Wales and those in Scotland and Ireland. By 1603 England and Wales had become integrated under the Tudors, and had begun to develop a market economy that was to expand under the Stuarts. In contrast the Scottish and Irish economies remained backward and showed no sign of growth until they were absorbed into the buoyant English economy in the early eighteenth century. For this reason the bulk of this chapter discusses how and why economic growth developed in the English economy. There will be a short section towards the end of the chapter to discuss the contrasting situation in Scotland and Ireland.

See pages 3–7 for Britain in 1603.

1 ⌐ HOW TO STUDY THE STUART ECONOMY

It is quite difficult to pinpoint exactly why there was such a transformation in the Stuart economy. Problems of interpretation are increased because the period falls into two very distinct parts. Until the 1650s the economy remained comparatively depressed before undergoing a period of sustained expansion. This phenomenon has been explained by describing the period between 1500 and 1650 as the 'long sixteenth century'. There has been considerable debate among historians and economists to explain why economic recovery should have started in the 1650s. Some see the 'long sixteenth century' as a period during which the economy was dominated by outdated 'feudal' methods of production. The Parliamentary victory in the Civil War is seen as a 'watershed', or dramatic turning-point, which supplied the dynamic for economic expansion. The case for this view has been advanced convincingly by, among others, C. Hill in *The Century of Revolution* (1961) and L. Stone in *The Causes of the English Revolution 1529–1642* (1972). Another view is that the population level was the major motor driving the economy. A century of rapid demographic growth from the 1540s had driven up demand, and then a period of population stability after

See pages 94–5 for
Marxist interpretations.

demographic relating
to the study of
population.

1650 had allowed economic growth. This is seen as a more evolutionary process, and writers of the Cambridge Group, such as P. Laslett in *The World We Have Lost* (1971), saw little evidence of revolutionary change in Stuart England

Apart from the broad issues of interpretation, it is necessary to identify how and why the economy had expanded by the later seventeenth century. This means that the economy has to be broken down into its various sectors to see if, and how, each one contributed towards economic growth. Agriculture was by far the largest sector and employer in the economy, and by 1700 the farmers were producing food surpluses. However, it can be argued that this was no great achievement because **demographic** growth had ceased and population levels were static. The spectacular growth in overseas trade and financial markets, and the establishment of a colonial empire in the Americas and the Far East, can be seen as the most important economic change. Yet, such growth was largely based on the shipping and exporting of colonial raw materials and Far Eastern luxury goods, which could be said to have done little to improve the domestic economy. Growth of internal trade, boosted by ever-rising demand from the growing towns, particularly London, may well have had a greater economic impact. Although it has been suggested that there was a seventeenth-century industrial revolution, production and employment levels remained low in heavy industries such as coal mining and metal extraction. More significant was the expansion in rural and craft industries, particularly in the Midlands and the north.

There is no consensus among historians as to which of the economic sectors was the most dynamic. This means that the student has to weigh the evidence and the arguments put forward in order to reach a balanced judgement. The economy is governed by both long- and short-term fluctuations and care must be taken to recognise and assess the importance of both these types of influence. It must also be remembered that the economy does not exist in isolation. Economic change can be created by outside forces, such as wars, government intervention, religious attitudes, cultural changes, scientific advances or social developments.

These topics and issues will be discussed more fully in the following sections, and a conclusion will try to draw together the conflicting interpretations.

2 ∾ POPULATION

There are no reliable population statistics for England and Wales until the first census of 1801. All demographic calculations for Stuart England are estimates based on such sources as parish registers of births, marriages and deaths, taxation returns, muster lists of able-bodied men, or local parish and town censuses. The difficulty with all such sources is that they were not originally intended to record the size

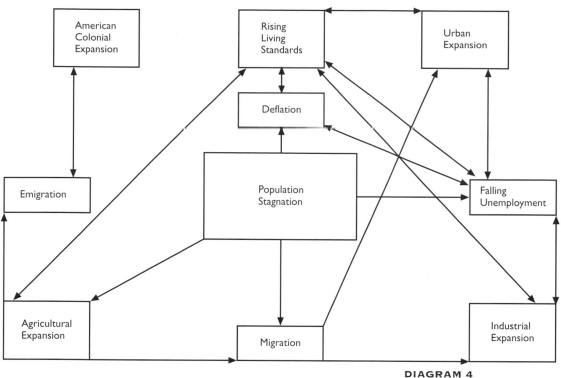

DIAGRAM 4
Late Stuart population stagnation

of the population and were often inaccurate. In any case, in a male dominated society, women and children were often left out of these listings. Another serious problem is that many of these sources have been lost or destroyed so that it is difficult to gain a clear or consistent national picture. Apart from the parish registers, the most helpful demographic source for the seventeenth century is the Hearth Tax which was introduced in the 1660s. This new tax was based on the number of hearths (fireplaces) in a house, and so every household in towns and villages was recorded.

Calculations of population levels before 1801 are now largely based on a process known as family reconstruction, which was begun in the 1960s by the Cambridge Group. Starting from the known demographic structure in 1871, the group used parish registers, supported by other sources, to project the population figures back to 1541. In 1981, E.A. Wrigley and R.S. Schofield published the results in *The Population History of England 1541–1871*. Although based on a small sample, 404 out of 10,000 parishes, falling to only 45 parishes for 1541 after some revision, these estimated population figures are now generally accepted as the most accurate available.

Many economists consider that fluctuations in population levels were the major economic influence on pre-industrial economies. This means that demographic trends are a key starting point for any study of the Stuart economy. Recovery from the late medieval demographic collapse, caused by the Black Death of 1381 and ensuing plague cycles, began in the 1450s when the population was about 1.5 million. By the 1520s the population had increased to some 2.3 million, and then from the 1540s rose rapidly to reach 4.1 million in 1601. Demographic growth continued at about the same rate until the 1650s, rising to 5.28 million by 1656. This marked the end of a long phase of expansion, and by 1684 the population level had fallen back to 4.8 million. From then on population growth was slow, reaching 5.1 million by 1701, and not regaining the 1650 levels until the 1730s. Although these figures are only projected estimates it is interesting that they compare relatively well with contemporary figures. Gregory King, a seventeenth-century economist and statistician, using government records estimated that the population in 1688 was 5,500,520.

In overall terms it is calculated that the population rose by an average of 0.5 per cent a year between 1500 and 1700. This was not a steady increase because there were considerable fluctuations in the rate of growth over the whole period. Expansion in the sixteenth century was much faster at one per cent a year than it was over the next 100 years. The Tudor population increased by some 2.3 million, whereas under the Stuarts it only rose by about 1.1 million. It used to be thought that fluctuations in pre-industrial population levels were largely governed by the food supply. Unrestrained by any form of birth control, population levels rose until they exceeded the available food resources. This caused a check, and population fell until the farmers were able to produce additional food, either by cultivating more land or by improving output. Such situations are called 'malthusian crises', being named after Thomas Malthus, the eighteenth-century economist who proposed the theory. It is very true that there were 'malthusian crises' in medieval England, and that they occurred in continental Europe until well into the eighteenth century. However, it is thought unlikely that there was any such crisis in Tudor England, and certainly not under the Stuarts.

DIAGRAM 5

A graph to show seventeenth-century population trends

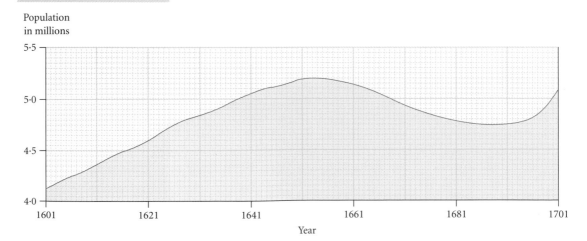

3 ∽ LIVING STANDARDS

It is generally accepted that by the beginning of the eighteenth century the gulf between the rich and the poor was still widening. Local and individual variations make it difficult to do more than reach broad generalisations about changing living standards in Stuart England. Economic changes affected every level of society in different ways. Some sections of society fared better in different parts of the country. Individual fortunes varied in every walk of life; a nobleman might gamble away the family estates, a merchant could be bankrupted because his ship was captured by pirates, or a labourer might be injured and his family fall into destitution. This meant that there was about as much downward as upward movement at all levels of society. The situation was made even more complicated because at all levels of society people could have several different occupations. A landowner might also be a successful lawyer or politician, or he might own extensive plantations in America. Yeoman and husbandmen often ran inns or shops or had interests in cloth-making, brewing and other local industries. Among the lower orders the 'dual economy', whereby both men and women had more than one job, was wide-spread. Cottage industries (see page 313) provided employment for all members of the family in their own home. In addition to seasonal work in agriculture, such as sewing, weeding and harvesting, members of the family might find part-time employment in fishing, mining or the building trades.

PICTURE 29
A nobleman's house, Castle Howard, designed by Vanbrugh

See page 292 for for improvements in communications.

DIAGRAM 6
A graph to show seventeenth-century prices and wages trends

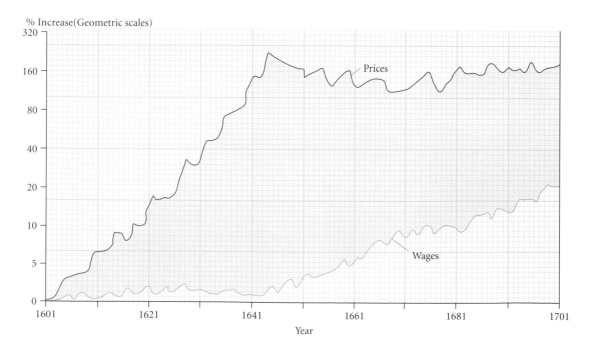

A *Landed elites, yeomen and husbandmen*

For most of the sixteenth century the ownership or possession of land had continued to be the mark of status within society. The nobility and the gentry (baronets, knights, esquires and gentlemen) with their landed estates formed the social elite. Yeomen, farming several hundred acres of land, dominated the middle orders, ranking above tradesmen and even merchants who had no land. Husbandmen, with their small farms of 50 or 60 acres, were the upper tier of the lower orders. Even in the sixteenth century this situation had begun to change as rich lawyers and merchants became more important, but they still had to buy landed estates to confirm their new status. During the seventeenth century living standards were changing, and wealth was becoming as important as land as a status symbol. Improvments in communications, in particular in roads, and the expansion of world trade helped to hasten this process. People from all walks of life were moving around Britain, visiting or settling in towns, emigrating to the Colonies or sailing around the world as merchants or sailors. Travel widened and changed attitudes and began to break down the old rigid hierarchical concepts of society. This helped to promote more social mobility as those people successful in making money were able to rise in society more easily.

See page 289 for improvements in roads.

The nobility, with their wealth and great landed estates, had benefited from the long period of inflation, and continued to prosper in the deflationary conditions after 1650. Until the mid-seventeenth century the nobility had to do very little to ensure a rising standard of living. The steady rise in the price of foodstuffs and an increasing level of rent from their tenantry, had ensured a sustained growth in income. After 1650 stagnating prices and a less buoyant land market meant that the nobility had to invest money to improve their estates, and needed to run them more efficiently by employing estate agents and managers.

The main upshot of this was the amalgamation of many inefficient smallholdings into larger and more productive tenant farms (see pages 277–86). The nobility, or their younger sons, also took full advantage of opportunities to augment their wealth from trade, banking and the colonies. Their ranks were swollen by new creations, such as the Earl of Craven, who having made a fortune in the City, built up a large landed estate in Berkshire. By the eighteenth century the aristocracy were even more firmly established at the top of the social elites. Their increasing wealth allowed them to build sumptuous Palladian mansions on their landscaped estates, and to enjoy a leisured and lavish life style.

The prospects of the gentry with their medium-sized estates were less secure. They too had benefited from the long period of inflation for the same reasons as the nobility. However, the 'rise' of the gentry seems to have ended after 1650. Unlike the nobility most of the gentry did not have the resources to modernise their estates. At the same time many gentry families on both sides had suffered from the Civil War. Some had their estates confiscated or sequestered and never regained them. Others were so impoverished that they were forced to sell up their estates to men such as the Earl of Craven. The greater gentry (baronets and knights), with estates almost as large as those of the nobility, continued to prosper and to enjoy the same lifestyle as their immediate social superiors. Many other gentry families could no longer afford the leisured, lavish lifestyle of the elites, and had to sell their estates and seek their fortunes in the colonies, law, banking and commerce.

The yeomen suffered much the same fate as many of the gentry. They, too, had benefited from the inflationary conditions to 'rise' alongside the gentry. Yeomen, although prosperous, had a more modest and less ostentatious standard of living than the gentry. Apart from their farming activities they frequently owned shops and inns, and engaged in business and industry. Like many of the gentry they could not afford the outlay to improve their small estates and make them competitive in the new economic conditions. As a group yeomen had largely disappeared by the eighteenth century. Some had sold their land to become tenant farmers on the modernised estates of the nobility. Others abandoned their farming interests to concentrate on their other activities and became merged with the ever-expanding 'middling sort'.

Husbandmen, with their smallholdings of under 60 acres, had struggled to be competitive even during the period of inflation. The great landowners were anxious to get rid of uncompetitive smallholdings, and by the end of the century many smaller tenancies had been amalgamated into large commercial farms. Like the yeomen, some of the more prosperous husbandmen became tenant farmers or tradesmen. The majority became cottagers and landless labourers, therefore falling into the ranks of the lower social orders. This development has been described as the 'disappearance of the peasantry' by many Marxist and left-wing historians, who blame the demise of the peasantry on enclosure and greedy landowners. Possibly the husbandman was more the victim of long-term economic change than any concerted policy by the landowners.

B *The pseudo-gentry and the middling sort*

Throughout the seventeenth century the landless middle orders of society were expanding. This was partially due to the large families of the landed elites. As only the eldest son could inherit the estate, younger sons had to find alternative careers in the professions, finance, the administration, industry, commerce, and the army or the navy. The expansion of London and other towns gave people from all ranks of society the chance to find openings and employment. The quickening pace of economic expansion after the 1650s further enhanced the opportunities for investment and employment. At the same time, falling prices gave the middle orders greater spending power and so increased their standard of living. This was a very dynamic section of society undergoing constant changes, which makes it difficult to categorise changes in living standards.

A clear example of the growing middle order prosperity was the emergence of the 'pseudo gentry'. This is a title coined by historians to describe a group that, although they had no land, were regarded by their contemporaries as having the same status as the landed elites. They were drawn mainly from the younger sons of the nobility and gentry who created successful careers for themselves. They had the same education and background as their landed relations and they moved in the same social circles. Their wealth enabled them to build and furnish town houses in the same Palladian style as the country mansions of their relatives. The newly rich, without the same background, who had made their wealth from commerce and finance, were generally scorned by the elites. However, by educating their sons at university and sending them on the 'grand tour', and by marrying their daughters into impoverished noble families, they too were gradually absorbed into the ranks of the elites.

The majority of the 'middling sort' did not have the wealth or ambition to join the elites. On the other hand, they were anxious to use their prosperity to emulate elite lifestyles as far as their means would allow. Their houses and furnishings were modelled on those of their social superiors. They employed increasing numbers of domestic servants, and bought a wide range of the cheaper luxury and consumer goods.

C *The lower social orders*

It is equally difficult to form a clear picture of changes in living standards among the lower social orders. Conditions varied all over the country. Prices and wage levels differed from town to town and from county to county. In the industrialised parishes of the Midlands, although there was little or no poor relief, wages were higher. A cottager with a plot of land and a large family could be quite prosperous. He could keep a cow, a pig and some chickens and grow his own vegetables. He might do some weaving and seasonal work in any of the local industries. His wife and children would help in the garden, take in spinning, and go out to do seasonal work. In contrast, labouring families in the agricultural south had lower wages, less opportunities for seasonal work and were more reliant on poor relief. Apart from the 'impotent poor', newly married couples with very young children and older couples whose children had left home were most likely to suffer poverty.

Historians have conflicting views as to whether lower social order standards of living were rising or falling in Stuart England. The optimistic view is that once the Elizabethan Poor Laws had been established they provided an effective safety net to provide for the very old, the young and the infirm. More efficient farming methods had reduced food prices and greatly lessened the fear of famines and starvation. After the 1650s, wages were rising, and, as the economy expanded, employment was becoming more readily available Indeed, it is suggested that it was the increasing demand from the lower social orders for consumer goods and small luxury items that helped to fuel the economic growth. A more sombre interpretation is that the success of commercial farming was only achieved by driving the smallholders off the land to create larger farms. This created increasing numbers of landless labourers who were becoming increasingly dependent on poor relief. Furthermore, the gulf between the rich and the poor was widening rapidly. A great cultural divide was opening up with the educated elites and middle orders on one side and the illiterate masses on the other.

D *Conclusion*

The continued, if slightly slower, rate of population increase after 1600 meant that the inflation of the sixteenth century lasted until the 1650s. Then, the end of population growth and a slight fall in population levels was followed by a period of demographic stagnation. Whether this was the result of increased mortality, or a drop in fertility caused by later marriage among the lower social orders, is uncertain. The effect of this deflation upon the economy and upon living standards was beneficial. The lessening in basic demand forced both agriculture and industry to reorganise in order to maintain their profit margins. This led to increased output, which lowered prices still further. At the same time, opportunities for emplement increased and levels of unemployment began to fall. Although lower prices had little impact on the already high living standards of the elites, they did benefit those of the middle orders, and possibly to a lesser extent those of the labouring poor.

> **Q** How did changes in population levels influence living standards?

4 ⌁ AGRICULTURE

There is wide agreement that improvements in agriculture were the key to economic growth in Stuart England. One of the main indicators of advances in pre-industrial economies is a change in patterns of employment. Until the seventeenth century the bulk of the population was employed in farming or agriculturally related activities. By 1714, although England was still predominantly rural, an increasing number of people were leaving farming to engage in other forms of employment. The number of people living in towns of all sizes may well have risen to 15 per cent of the population by the end of the century. As towns were reliant on the surrounding countryside for their food supplies, this meant that agricultural output had to increase accordingly. It must also be remembered that, although demographic growth had virtually stopped after the 1660s, the total population of England and Wales had grown by over a million during the seventeenth century.

Such improved agricultural productivity is seen as a major success, which enabled other sectors of the economy to expand. Indeed, by the end of the century, England was exporting grain to the Continent instead of having to import it. Moreover, the extra production was achieved with a smaller workforce, using less land. What is more difficult to decide is how such a transformation, particularly after 1640, was brought about. Some historians, such as E. Kerridge in *The Agricultural Revolution* (1967) saw it as a revolutionary breakthrough, while others, such as J. Thirsk in *Agrarian History of England and Wales* Vol. 4

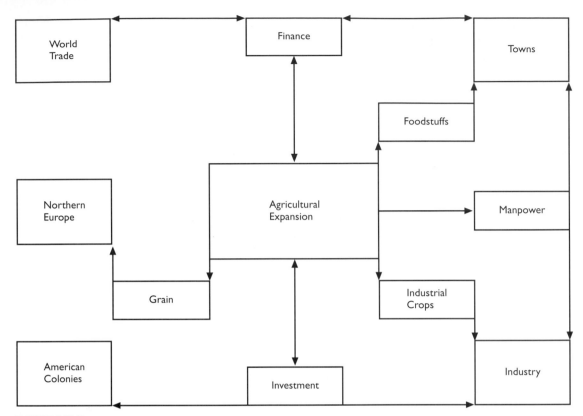

DIAGRAM 7

Late Stuart agricultural expansion

1546–1640 (1967), now prefer to think in terms of slow evolutionary development.

The main problem with the revolutionary approach is to identify how Stuart farming was any different from that in the sixteenth century, when greater production was not achieved. The use of enclosure, new crops and new techniques have all been cited as amounting to an agricultural revolution. But, as they were all in use in the previous century, they cannot really be seen as revolutionary. Similarly, Tudor farmers used commercial methods and specialised in particular crops for market.

For this reason more historians are favouring the idea of evolutionary development, and see changes in the pattern of demand and investment as the reason for increased production. The Tudor economy was too small to encourage any dynamic expansion in agriculture. During the sixteenth century too many people were still growing their own food for there to be any real demand. Towns, although expanding, did not yet offer a sufficiently buoyant market to encourage landowners and farmers to invest in large-scale improvements for higher production. In any case, poor road and river communications made it difficult to move food supplies over more than short distances. While population levels were rising rapidly, landowners, yeomen and husbandmen did not need to invest money in their land in order to make profits. Until the 1560s and the collapse of the Antwerp cloth market (see pages

310–13), it was still more profitable to maintain large sheep runs and to sell wool to the expanding cloth industry, than to grow grain.

During the seventeenth century patterns of demand changed. The rate of urban growth expanded rapidly. London became a metropolitan market, and its food markets attracted supplies from an ever-widening hinterland. Similarly, other developing towns built up market demands in their immediate neighbourhoods. In order to supply the metropolitan and urban markets it was necessary to improve the transport communications by both road and water. Landowners and urban authorities combined to invest in schemes to open up the navigation of rivers, such as the Thames, the Severn and the Ouse, and to start to build canals to link up the river systems. Barges and wherries could then take goods from the growing fleet of coastal vessels to transport along the inland waterways. New toll roads and bridges were built, along which larger carts and waggons, and fast coaches could carry goods and people ever more quickly around the country.

Such developments encouraged landowners and farmers to improve their land, to introduce new techniques and to grow specialist crops. At the same time, industrial expansion made it more profitable to grow non-agricultural crops such as flax, tobacco or oil seed rape. After the 1650s, demographic stagnation meant that it was no longer possible just to rely on population growth to make a profit from agriculture. However, it was expensive to improve and enclose land; some of the gentry and many yeomen and husbandmen could not afford the outlay, and had to sell their now unprofitable land. Only the great landowners, the aristocracy and greater gentry, were wealthy enough to embark on large-scale improvement and modernisation on their estates. They were able also to buy the land of their less fortunate neighbours and amalgamate smallholdings to create large commercial farms. It is this process that is seen as leading to improved agricultural production in the second half of the seventeenth century.

> **KEY ISSUE**
>
> *Was the improvement in agriculture revolutionary or evolutionary?*

A *Enclosure*

Enclosure is a highly controversial and emotive subject. Economic historians consider enclosure to have been very beneficial and central to improvements in Stuart agriculture. Left-wing and Marxist historians regard it as socially divisive, and the means by which greedy landlords drove the peasantry off the land. Enclosures were certainly highly unpopular with the lower orders and central government during the sixteenth century. The Tudors legislated against them throughout the century as they considered that enclosures depopulated the countryside, created unemployment, and provoked riots. However, during the seventeenth century the Stuarts no longer considered them a problem, and by the end of the century the authorities were encouraging a greater use of enclosure. Clearly there is no easy answer to the rights and wrongs of enclosure, and it is necessary to consider the evidence and various arguments carefully before coming to any conclusion.

The enclosure of individual fields with fences and hedges was not a new idea even in the sixteenth century; it had been in use since farming was introduced into Britain some 5,000 years ago. Many parts of the country, especially in the West Country and parts of the north, were already enclosed. It was only in the agricultural Midlands and southern-central England that the medieval open field system was still widely in use. For most of the sixteenth century the usual form of enclosure was the fencing of abandoned land to create sheep runs. This was highly profitable because of the high demand for wool from the rapidly expanding rural cloth industry (see pages 312–13), and sheep pastures required a much smaller workforce than arable farming. At the same time, enclosure was also being used to separate land from the common fields in order to grow more specialised crops. One of the reasons for the lack of agricultural productivity before the seventeenth century was that farmers all grew a mixture of the same type of crops. This was mainly because poor communications meant that supplies could only be transported over short distances to supply local markets, which only required small quantities of mixed foodstuffs. This meant that there was no incentive to specialise and produce large quantities of a particular crop if there was no demand. In any case, in open field regions, the farmers' strips of land were all mixed together in large common fields of several hundred acres, and everyone had to grow the same crop as his neighbour.

As London and other towns began to expand during the sixteenth century, there was an increase in demand from the urban food markets. London began to draw in food supplies not only from the Home Counties, but also from counties bordering the Thames as far west as Oxfordshire because the river provided easy transport to the capital. A similar process was occurring around all the major towns. This provided the incentive to landowners and husbandmen living in the hinterlands of such towns to enclose their land and to specialise in growing the most profitable crops. After the decline of cloth exports by the 1580s there was a further incentive for landowners to turn from sheep raising to grain production in order to meet the needs of the rapidly expanding population.

The question is: why was enclosure and specialised commercial farming not widespread before the seventeenth century? The obvious answer is that it was just not worth the trouble and expense when food prices were rising. In any case, landowners who enclosed land were liable to incur the wrath of the government and risk riots among their tenants. However, the Stuart governments soon began to see enclosure as a means of economic expansion and a source of employment. At the same time, the establishment of the Elizabethan Poor Laws had eased social tensions, and enclosure riots were becoming less of a problem. These changes meant that the pace of enclosure began to increase. Another reason for the slow adoption of new ideas was that most farmers were not really aware of the advantages brought by such improvements. As early as 1523, John Fitzherbert had demonstrated the benefits of enclosure in his *Book of Husbandry,* as had Sir Thomas Smith in *The Commonwealth of England* in 1583. However, before the rapid growth in education and literacy (see pages 352–5) from the late sixteenth century, few of even the elites possessed or could read such books.

The spread of literacy among the male elites and middle orders by the 1660s meant that the great estate owners and estate managers were familiar with these and other books on agricultural improvement. By then the fall in food prices had made it necessary to use land more productively. Estate owners with sufficient wealth embarked on a further extensive programme of enclosure, which resulted in the creation of large commercial farms. Landowners wishing to enclose their estates had to obtain a private Act of Parliament before embarking on the work. This usually was not difficult because most MPs and members of the House of Lords were fellow landowners. By 1700, 71 per cent of agricultural land in England and Wales was enclosed compared with only 47 per cent in 1600. The process of parliamentary enclosure lasted into the nineteenth century, and resulted in the familiar field patterns in the countryside today.

B *Increasing use of new crops and techniques*

The knowledge and use of new ideas introduced under the Tudors spread rapidly during the seventeenth century. Rising levels of literacy meant that even many husbandmen read the increasing number of books written about agricultural improvements. Another sign of a more scientific approach towards farming was that many farmers, such as Henry Best from Yorkshire, kept account books and diaries recording where and when they could obtain the highest prices for their produce. Farmers at all levels were realising that in order to survive they had to be more efficient, and that it was no longer practical to grow the same traditional range of crops. At the same time, there was an increased awareness that to obtain the best returns, crops had to be selected to suit the types of soil available. A growing demand for raw materials from the expanding rural industries was a further incentive for farmers to produce industrial crops. Farmers with enclosed fields were no longer restricted by the customs and regulations governing the crops that could be grown on the communal open fields. This gave farmers a better opportunity to experiment with new crops and methods.

Enclosure was instrumental in facilitating a number of technical advances. Possibly the most important of these was the development of improved crop rotation. In the traditional open field system a three-course rotation was used. One large field was used for cereals, one for peas and other vetches, and the third was left fallow (as pasture). Apart from wasting one-third of the available arable land by using it for grazing, the rotation was not large enough to allow the soil to regain fertility. This meant that it became exhausted and crop yields were low. The new system of convertible husbandry was based on rotating crops

> **KEY ISSUE**
>
> *How was enclosure helping the spread of new crops and techniques?*

and pasture between a number of smaller enclosed fields. Not only could a greater variety of crops be grown, but the new system was four times more productive. Moreover, it maintained a better balance between arable and pastoral farming.

The balance was further improved by the use of floating water meadows, where sluices were used to flood riverside fields every year to cover them in silt to improve their fertility. Artificial grasses, such as clover, lucerne and sainfoin, improved grazing and increased soil fertility. A range of new root crops, such as carrots, potatoes and turnips, was experimented with to extend the crop rotation. Crop rotation was also augmented with a whole range of industrial crops. Saffron and woad were grown for dyeing cloth, hops for the expanding brewing industry, flax for linen manufacturing, oil seed rape for oil, tobacco, and hemp for rope making. Another important advance enabled by enclosure was the selective breeding of livestock, since animals could be separated from the communal herds roaming the common pastures. New breeds of sheep were reared for their wool and meat, while cattle were bred to satisfy the growing demand for both dairy products and meat.

A number of other significant changes were taking place to raise efficiency, variety and productivity. In various parts of the country agricultural pioneers were experimenting to improve their estates. Soil quality was enhanced by adding lime, sand and marl, while in coastal districts seaweed was used as a fertiliser. Seed quality was raised by importing new strains from the Netherlands, and by cross-pollinating older varieties. Such advances, and the invention of the seed drill by Jethro Tull in 1701, greatly improved cereal yields. Harvesting was speeded up through the gradual introduction of the scythe to replace the smaller sickle. There was a steady improvement in the efficiency of farm machinery, such as ploughs, carts and harrows. The more versatile horse was continuing to replace the cumbersome ox for ploughing and other agricultural activities on even the smaller farms. Considerable investment was made in draining the Fenlands around the Wash, the Lincolnshire silt lands and the Somerset Marshes.

Much of this work was carried out by Dutch engineers brought to England because of their expertise in land drainage and building sea defences. They were part of a large influx of political and religious refugees from Holland and the Netherlands. They settled largely in the south-east and East Anglia. Such emigration was encouraged by both Tudor and Stuart governments, who welcomed their expertise because the Netherlands was the most advanced industrial and agricultural region in western Europe. Their arrival encouraged the development of horticulture in the Home Counties to supply the London markets. Orchards of fruit trees and soft fruits, conservatories to raise more exotic tropical fruits, and market gardens producing a wide range of vegetables were established. These met the increasingly sophisticated tastes of affluent London society. Flower cultivation was another Dutch speciality and East Anglia became noted for its bulb fields and nurseries, as well as for the raising of geese and turkeys.

C *Specialisation*

Different types of specialisation steadily increased during the seventeenth century. More understanding of climate and soil conditions led to the greater development of specialist regions. Geologically and climatically the country was basically divided into two main farming regions separated by a line running from Exeter in the south-west to Newcastle in the north-east. To the north and west of this line the terrain is largely hilly and mountainous with thin soils, and the climate is cool with a high rainfall. In contrast, the lowland south-east has deeper soils and is drier and warmer. This difference meant that the south-east was more suited to arable farming, while the north-west was more appropriate for pastoralism. Before the seventeenth century small-scale farming and poor communications had meant that farmers in both zones had to produce all the basic food supplies needed in their immediate neighbourhood.

Improvements in transport by road and river, and the development of regional and national markets allowed farmers to specialise in the produce most suited to their locality. Thereafter, the south-east became predominantly arable, while raising livestock became more characteristic of the highland region. At the same time, there are considerable variations in soil types within both the broad agricultural zones. The limestone Cotswolds and Downs in the south were 'sheep and corn' areas growing mixed crops and grazing sheep. East Anglia, with its light chalk soils, became the major cereal producer. The heavy, damp soils of the Midlands, extending from Yorkshire to Wiltshire, provided excellent 'wood-pasture' for pastoralism, stock rearing and dairy farming. However, the wolds of Yorkshire were more suited to mixed farming and sheep rearing. By the end of the seventeenth century regional specialisation was becoming ever more complicated and governed by the demands of a national market centred on London.

Specialised, commercial production was increasing at all levels, from the small market gardener and the husbandman still farming his traditional 30 acres, to the great estate owner. Wiltshire became a major producer of dairy products, and Somerset and Cheshire were already centres for cheese making. Both these operations suited the husbandman and smallholder because they required only a small capital outlay and brought in a regular cash return. In contrast, the graziers of the Home Counties, fattening the cattle brought along the drove roads from the highland zone, needed capital to buy the stock, and then had to wait to receive a return on their money by selling on to the London meat markets. Oil seed rape grew well in the Fenlands, and by the early eighteenth century the river port of Wisbech in Cambridgeshire had become a major oil centre. Its seven crushing mills annually supplied a thousand tons of oil to the cloth industry.

Hop growing for the rapidly expanding London breweries became a speciality in Kent. Barley became an important crop to supply the brewing, distilling and vinegar industries. Tobacco was another crop that was particularly popular with the smallholders because it could be cultivated with family labour, the initial outlay was small, and returns could be as high as £40 an acre. Other industrial crops needed greater outlay and acreage, but, because they were labour intensive, provided a valuable source of employment. A 50-acre field of woad, for example, gave employment to four women and children at four pence a day for a third of the year. However, although examples of specialisation could be found all over the country, it still depended on the demand from local industry and the urban markets. Many farmers continued to grow the traditional range of crops for sale in the local market towns, and brew their own beer.

D *The large commercial farm*

Possibly the most significant long-term development was the growing dominance of the great estate and the emergence of the large commercial farm after the 1650s. In the deflationary period following the end of a rapid population increase, the greater land owners had the wealth to undertake large-scale improvements to their estates in order to raise production and maximise profits. A normal part of such programmes was the enclosure of common lands, and the buying out of as many freeholders and smallholders as possible. The advantages of this policy are well set out by Edward Lawrence in his book, *The Duty and Office of a Land Steward*, which was in its third edition by 1731:

> A Steward should not forget to make the best enquiry into the disposition of any of the freeholders within or near any of his Lord's manors to sell their lands, that he may use his best endeavours to purchase them at a reasonable price, as maybe for his Lord's advantage and convenience – especially in such manors, where improvements are to be made by inclosing commons and common-field; which (as every one, who is acquainted with the late improvement in agriculture, must know) is not a little advantageous to the nation in general, as well as highly profitable to the undertaker.

As far as possible, smaller, and potentially less profitable, farms were amalgamated to create large farming units of some 600 acres. After being enclosed and modernised, these were then leased out at a commercial rent, often to former yeomen or husbandmen. The terms of the lease usually laid out strict instructions on the maintenance of buildings and hedges, and soil quality. In order to be able to afford the higher rents, tenants had to make sure that their farms were productive and competitive by making further improvements, growing new crops and adopting the latest techniques. As this would enhance the value of the estate, landlords often gave their tenants low interest, long-term loans to help them to carry out the work. Such large modernisation schemes were generally restricted to areas close to large markets to ensure a return on the outlay. Often neighbouring landlords formed partnerships to finance road and river improvements in order to widen the market for their produce. However, even by 1714 such estates were by no means common, and it was not until the nineteenth century that the great estate with its tenant farmers came to dominate British farming.

It is this type of commercialisation that has been condemned by left-wing historians for driving the smallholders off the land and creating rural poverty. Most historians tend to agree with contemporary governmental opinion that such improvements were highly progressive, created employment and added to the wealth of the nation. Edward Lawrence is clearly expressing the governmental line when he goes on to say:

> ... and, whereas the common objections hitherto raised against inclosure are founded on mistakes, as if inclosure contributed either to hurt or ruin the poor; whilst it is plain that (when an inclosure is once resolved on) the poor will be employed for many years, in planting and preserving the hedges, and afterwards will be set to work both in the tillage and pasture, wherein they may get an honest livelihood.

It is clearly difficult to decide the rights and wrongs of this particular issue. Certainly, yeomen and husbandmen were losing their former prominent position as the backbone of the farming community, but they remained active in many areas until well into the nineteenth century. Equally, employment opportunities in both farming and rural industries were beginning to absorb the pool of surplus labour. There are strong resemblances with present day debates on whether bypasses and out-of-town supermarkets create local employment and improve the amenities, or destroy the countryside.

KEY ISSUE

Was the commercialisation of farming promoted more by specialisation or by enclosure?

E *Conclusion*

There is little evidence to support the view that there was any revolutionary breakthrough in seventeenth-century farming. Improved performance came mainly from the steady development of ideas and techniques introduced in the previous century. Progress was achieved by many small advances, not by any sudden major leap forward. The slowdown of population increase after the 1650s had taken the pressure off the agricultural sector, but the need to maintain profit margins accelerated the adoption of new crops and techniques. Demand was fuelled by the continuing growth of London and other towns. Rising living standards, especially among the middle orders, and the expansion of rural industry enabled the sale of an ever-widening range of agricultural products. Distribution was facilitated by an increasingly sophisticated market structure.

However, although specialisation and commercial farming were certainly expanding, they had not changed the face of rural England by 1714. Stuart agricultural developments were part of a long, slow, evolutionary process that is still continuing today. While agricultural improvement had removed the threat of famines and 'malthusian crises', many historians consider that there was a distinct downside to the process. Although enclosure may not have been guilty of sweeping the 'peasant' off the land, some sections of the lower social orders may well have suffered a loss of social and economic status. Certainly, it does seem that on many estates in the agricultural south, lower order living standards were depressed. Landlords, by preventing settlement on their land, maintained a subservient labour force with low wages, which were supplemented by poor law relief. Writers of women's history see commercial farming as detrimental to working women, reinforcing the sexual double standard, and establishing the long tradition of female low pay. Patriarchal Stuart society considered women too unintelligent and weak to be able to cope with new agricultural techniques and the heavier ploughs and scythes. For this reason they were no longer employed in higher paid work such as harvesting, and were only given menial low paid tasks such as weeding, stone clearing and bird scaring.

See pages 326–8 for attitudes to women's employment.

5 ◃ LONDON, URBAN GROWTH, BANKING AND THE NATIONAL MARKET

Many historians consider that the spectacular growth of London during the seventeenth century was the engine that powered Stuart economic expansion. London became the centre of a national market, which by 1714 was growing increasingly sophisticated. The major towns and ports and industrial centres were becoming linked to the capital, and to each other, through an expanding road, river, canal and coastal shipping network. This allowed the increasingly rapid transport and exchange of a growing volume of goods.

The need to supply food to the London markets provided a considerable incentive for such improvements. By the 1680s it required 200,000 quarters of grain a year to provide bread for the capital compared with only 60,000 quarters at the beginning of the century. In turn, the internal market was linked through the ports to the expanding overseas market, which speeded up the shipment of exports and the distribution of imports. The transfer of goods was further enhanced by developments in banking, credit facilities and bills of exchange. This is seen as a benign circle, which, once established, continued to expand almost of its own volition, fostering economic growth. Once again the question is: why did this happen under the Stuarts, when all the prerequisites existed in the previous century? Urban growth resulted from the problem of rising population and lack of employment, which sent migrants flocking to the towns in search of work. The growth of literacy and legal training through grammar schools, the universities and the Inns of Court, largely arose out of changing attitudes created by the English Reformation. Transport improvements, joint stock companies and the patent system all developed out of Tudor initiatives. As in the case of agriculture, the answer appears to be that marketing was transformed by a whole series of changes and minor advances, rather than any one particular breakthrough.

See pages 353–5 for growth of education.

A *London and urban growth*

Although the demographic growth of London was much more rapid than in other towns, the cause was the same: an ability to attract migrants. By no means was it the case that all towns grew in the seventeenth century. Winchester, Beverley, Lavenham, and Salisbury, all of which had been important administrative or industrial towns, stagnated and declined. The prime reason for many people migrating to a town was to find work. This has been called 'subsistence migration', and generally involved young vagrants travelling short distances from the neighbouring countryside to find a job and somewhere to live. It was these unskilled workers who provided the bulk of the extra population flowing into the towns. Crowded in unsalubrious slums and tenement blocks they were vulnerable to the regular urban epidemics because of their lack of resistance to disease. This meant that to grow, a town had to have a constant influx of such itinerant workers.

It was just as important for towns to be able to attract a range of skilled migrants of all types to expand its economic base, and this depended on the number of facilities that they had to offer. These sorts of urban settler or visitor have become known as 'betterment migrants'

DIAGRAM 8
Late Stuart urban growth

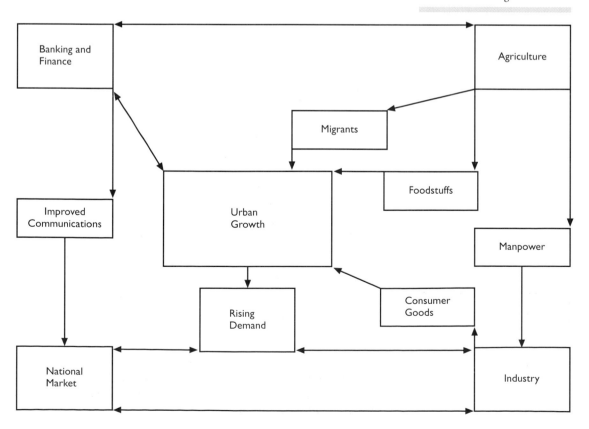

because they were intent on improving their economic and social position, rather than just finding employment. They came mainly, but by no means exclusively, from the elites and the middle orders, and usually travelled longer distances than the subsistence migrants. More parents were sending their sons to attend town schools before they went to university or the Inns of Court. Large numbers of younger sons came to the towns to obtain apprenticeships, or training for a career in business, banking, law, or the Church. Noblemen and the greater gentry maintained town houses for when they visited their bankers, brokers and business managers, or when they and their families stayed in town for the fashionable 'season'. Wealthy businessmen travelled widely for similar purposes, usually staying at one of the increasing number of hotels or coaching houses. Large numbers of skilled craftsman from the Netherlands and France, fleeing from religious persecution, came to settle in towns in the south-east.

LONDON

London, as the capital and the largest city in western Europe, had by far the widest range of facilities to attract the migrant and the visitor. It has been estimated that one person in six of the entire population visited, or settled, in Stuart London. As the political capital, London was the home of the Royal Court and Parliament, and was the centre for patronage and preferment. Apart from the aristocracy, MPs and courtiers, this attracted the ambitious of both sexes in great numbers in the hope of making their fortunes. The Admiralty and the War Department became centres of ever-increasing patronage as careers in the navy and the army became acceptable for the younger sons of the elites. Similarly, the Inns of Court were another attraction because training in law, apart from being very lucrative, had become regarded as an essential part of elite education. The Port of London, the naval dockyards at Chatham and the Royal Arsenal were other centres of great patronage, as well as offering employment to thousands of people from all levels of society. Even before the rapid commercial expansion, London was already the headquarters for the livery companies of all the major craft guilds. Equally, the great trading companies such as the Merchant Adventurers, or the newer Levant and East India companies were centred in London.

By the end of the seventeenth century London was the entrepôt for the whole of western Europe, with the great bulk of world trade being channelled through its port and other commercial facilities. The growth of long distance world trade, while extremely profitable for the merchants, added enormously to the cost and risk of shipping goods. To cater for this, London financiers began to provide increasingly sophisticated credit and insurance arrangements, which culminated in the establishment of the Bank of England by 1715. All these institutions, in themselves, were providers of employment on a very large scale. At the same time, their presence required a vast network of service industries, ranging from bakers, wig makers, tailors, clock makers, gunsmiths, parchment makers and greengrocers with iron founders, brewers, plumbers and masons to support them. It was this seemingly endless

KEY ISSUE

Why was London so successful in attracting migrants?

PICTURE 30
St Paul's Cathedral, designed by Wren after the Great Fire

kaleidoscope of opportunity that attracted the countless stream of migrants to London.

PORTS AND INDUSTRIAL TOWNS

All the other successful towns based their expansion on similar principles to that of London, except on a much smaller scale. Unlike the capital, provincial towns and ports only had one or two major attractions to lure migrants. The growth of oceanic and east coast trade led to the expansion of a number of ports. Bristol continued to expand because of the growing importance of the American and Caribbean trade routes, and the highly lucrative slave trade. Apart from being a thriving port, Bristol also developed as a major centre for processing American tobacco and sugar. The new major west coast ports, Liverpool and Glasgow, grew rapidly for similar reasons.

See pages 301–2 for the origins of the slave trade.

On the east coast, Newcastle benefited both from an increase in Baltic commerce, and from the growing use of coal for domestic fires. By the end of the seventeenth century huge collier fleets were supplying London with coal from Newcastle. Hull also prospered from the thriving Baltic trades, but at the expense of its near neighbour, Beverley. Drainage and development schemes in the Fenlands and Lincolnshire revived the fortunes of Boston, and led to the rapid expansion of Wisbech. A growing demand for fish saw the creation of major fishing ports at Grimsby and Great Yarmouth on the east coast and Whitehaven in the west. The rapid expansion of the Royal Navy encouraged the enlargement of the naval dockyards at Portsmouth and Plymouth. In contrast, the loss of Calais in 1559 and the collapse of the Antwerp trade in the 1580s had caused the decline of other Channel ports, such as Southampton, Romney and Hythe.

The same pattern of growth or decline was to be found among the industrial towns. East Anglia continued to be a major cloth manufacturing centre, and Norwich and Colchester both benefited from large settlements of highly skilled Dutch weavers. On the other hand, cloth making in the south Midlands and the West Country was stagnating and old centres, such as Bath, Newbury and Coventry, were declining. Northampton, another depressed cloth town, was rejuvenated into a major shoe and boot making centre through gaining the contract to supply boots to the New Model Army. Similarly, Banbury revived its fortunes by becoming the largest cattle market in western Europe because it was advantageously cited at the junction of several major drove roads from the north to London. Oxford and Cambridge, although losing their industrial importance, continued to expand because a university education had become an essential feature of an elite lifestyle. However, the most significant industrial urban growth was in the Midlands and the north of England. The rapidly expanding complexes of industrial villages and hamlets around Birmingham, Wolverhampton, Sheffield and Manchester were growing faster than London by 1714. A sign of the pulling power of the new industrial areas was that in 1600 41 per cent of London's apprentices came from the north of England, whereas by the end of the century they were drawn almost entirely from the Home Counties.

LEISURE TOWNS

During the seventeenth century leisure became an important urban industry in its own right. This was because part of the distinguishing feature of the elites was that they did not have to work. The growing numbers of the Stuart elites and the pseudo-gentry made the provision of leisure and recreational facilities a profitable business. This became even more true by the end the century because the prosperous middle orders were emulating the leisured lifestyle of the elites. London, with the Royal Court, was the prime centre of recreation and leisure with its theatres, assembly rooms, libraries and pleasure gardens. All the leading families had their London town houses, which they occupied during the London 'season'. In addition, a host of hotels and inns supplied accommodation for the lesser elites who flocked into the capital to hang around the fringes of the Court and society events. Shopping was becoming a fashionable leisure occupation. Hundreds of shops sprang up to cater for the whims of the elites: milliners, jewellers, tailors, boot makers and swordsmiths, all competed for trade. Similarly, on a smaller scale, all the towns began to cater for the leisure needs of their local elites and resident pseudo-gentry with assembly rooms, ball rooms, libraries, inns and shops, and short provincial seasons.

For some towns leisure and recreation became their major industry. Bath became the fashionable watering place where all those with any social pretensions had to visit and stay at some time during the year. To a lesser extent Scarborough began to perform the same function for the northern elites. In Stuart England all forms of gambling were a passion for both the elites and the masses, but horse racing, popularised by Charles II, became paramount. Towns such as Newmarket, Newbury and Beverley restored their fortunes by building race courses and providing accommodation and entertainment for the growing hordes who flocked to such events.

> **Q**
>
> *Why were inns becoming so numerous and popular in Stuart England?*

B *Banking and the national market*

Part of the explanation of the economic growth taking place in Stuart England was the establishment of a truly national market centred on London. Previously, the exchange of goods had been slowed down by poor communications and a fluctuating money supply. Until the seventeenth century the economy, like society, had remained provincial and localised. There was a sharp divide between the north and the south of the country, with the northerners resenting what they saw as the effete and more prosperous south. Apart from this, England was still divided into county communities, each of which was more interested in its own affairs, and resented interference from London and central government. Such differences were accentuated by local dialects and customs, which were only just beginning to be broken down by the spread of education.

During the seventeenth century, London was becoming recognised as the political and cultural capital. The elites and middle orders increasingly modelled their language, culture and clothes on those in vogue in London. To be provincial was becoming considered as dowdy and unfashionable. In contrast, the lower orders clung to their local customs and popular culture, which increased the gap between the affluent and the masses. The economy was similarly localised at the beginning of the century. Each county and town had its own wage rates, weights and measures, and prices. Day-to-day trading was conducted through a network of local markets and travelling pedlars. Wider exchanges took place at annual fairs, which were attended by merchants and traders from all over the country and from abroad. By the 1650s, the growth of demand from London meant that its markets had to be supplied from all over the country. Not only did this speed up improvement in communications, but it also led to the greater standardisation of prices and measures, which were becoming based on those in London.

BANKING

To a large extent much of this standardisation came as a result of London developing into a major financial centre. Until the seventeenth century goods were bought and sold on a cash basis, or, as frequently occurred in the countryside, by bartering other goods or services in exchange. While the lower social orders largely continued to use barter, business and commerce adapted a much more flexible system based on credit, cheques and paper money. This developed out of the bill of exchange, which had been used in some form since the Middle Ages. The bill of exchange was a type of credit, where a purchaser agreed to pay for goods already supplied by a certain date. As the supplier was risking not being paid, the amount of the bill was higher than the value of the goods. The same principle was used for insuring and underwriting ships and their cargoes. In this case the added value was calculated on the amount of risk being taken by the underwriters, which depended where the ship was going, the type of cargo and whether the country was at war. If the debt was settled before the agreed date, the added value or interest was wholly or partly waived. In the sixteenth century the interest rate had been fixed at 10 per cent, but this had been halved by the end of the Stuart period. This made dealing by credit more attractive, and London financiers offered the cheapest rates in western Europe. By the eighteenth century, London underwriters, such as Lloyd's, had taken over from the Dutch as the main suppliers of commercial and marine insurance.

For the same reason the use of credit became increasingly popular among the elites and middle orders. Bills of exchange became a form of currency that could be used to pay off debts and loans, or be used as a substitute for cash. Out of this developed the banking system. London merchants and goldsmiths came to accept such bills from their clients so as to offer them credit facilities. Businessmen, members of the professions, or landowners visiting London were able to draw cash against their credit to cover expenses while in the capital. From this basis it soon became possible to open accounts for the deposit or withdrawal of cash. Provincial entrepreneurs quickly began to offer similar services, which meant that credit and cash could be moved round the country much more quickly. As this could be an extremely lucrative source of income, some businessmen began to specialise in this form of transaction and established their firms as banks.

There were two main forms of banking: one dealing in commerce and insurance, and the other catering mainly for the private customer. In London commercial banks were located in the East End, while private banks favoured the West End. By the second half of the seventeenth century banks were offering a whole variety of services. The use of current accounts and overdrafts was soon followed by deposit accounts, loans, insurance, stock brokering and the issue of paper bank notes. It was this range of financial facilities that enabled a rapid expansion in the domestic market, and encouraged the growth of consumerism.

See page 294 for growth of consumerism.

The last stage in the establishment of banking was the founding of the Bank of England. This arose from the need for the government to borrow money. Previously, royal and government borrowing had been very haphazard. Long- and short-term loans had been obtained from wealthy individuals and large companies such as the Merchant Adventurers. However, by the late seventeenth century government was becoming more complex and much more expensive. Wars had always been a crippling expense, and in the sixteenth century both Spain and France had been bankrupted by the Wars of the Habsburg Ring. Warfare was becoming more technical and costly. By the 1690s the long wars against Holland and France, and the growing expense of maintaining the Royal Navy, had plunged the government deeply into debts which could not be met by the old methods of raising loans.

See pages 245–6 for the political background to the Bank of England. See pages 239–45 for the wars.

Finally, in 1694, a group of bankers agreed to lend the government £1.2 million, secured against taxes and custom revenues. In return they were given a four-year charter to set up the Bank of England and issue shares. This institution was immediately widely popular, and members of the Royal Court, the City and private individuals all invested in the new concern. The government charter was extended, and by 1715 the Bank of England had become a permanent joint stock limited liability bank with a capital of £10 million. In addition to managing the permanent national debt, which had by then reached £40 million, the new bank had the right to deal in bullion, issue bank notes and cheques, and give overdrafts to other banks. The creation of the Bank of England was the final stage in making London the financial capital of western Europe and consolidating the national market.

KEY ISSUE

Why was banking and finance so important in creating a market economy?

THE NATIONAL MARKET

In order to boost the domestic economy and to break down localism, it was necessary to be able to circulate goods and people more rapidly. For this to happen the quality of communications by road and water had to be improved. The old Roman roads, such as Watling Street and Ermine Street, circulating from London were still in use. They were in a better state of repair than the other roads, which were little more than muddy trackways, and often virtually impassable in the winter. Roads were theoretically kept in repair by the parishes through which they passed, which meant in practice that virtually nothing was done.

Bridges were rare and most rivers had to be crossed by fords. This also made river communications difficult, and even the Thames was only navigable as far as Abingdon in Oxfordshire at the beginning of the seventeenth century. However, the Tudors had begun to improve river navigation by dredging, the clearance of weirs, dams, fish traps and other obstructions, and by building more bridges. This work continued under the Stuarts, and by the end of the century many rivers, such as the Thames, Severn and Ouse, were navigable for most of their lengths. At the same time, there was an increase in building and improving docks and harbours, and the construction of small ships for carrying heavy goods around the coastline. Such vessels could dock in even small harbours and in river estuaries, where their cargoes could be loaded into barges for transportation inland.

Road improvements were slow, even though the building of bridges and the setting up of signposts and milestones did help the traveller. It was the introduction of turnpikes after the 1660s that really improved the road system. These specially constructed stretches of new road usually were built to link neighbouring towns. They were commissioned by groups of local businessmen and landowners anxious to improve the transportation of their goods. Those using such roads had to pay a tariff of tolls, which helped to recoup the original outlay and pay for maintenance. Congestion in many towns was reduced because the large number of major fires during the seventeenth century, such as the Great Fire of London in 1666, enabled the widening, straightening and paving of the old medieval winding, narrow streets. However, it should be remembered that cows, pigs and chickens still foraged in the street, even in central London, and were driven along major roads to be slaughtered.

Although by modern standards transportation was still painfully slow, there had been a marked improvement by the end of the seventeenth century. Large collier fleets, protected from pirates and privateers by the Royal Navy, were sailing regularly down the east coast carrying coal to London and returning with a range of imports and manufactured goods for distribution in the north. Smaller fleets of coasters operated down the west coast carrying mixed cargoes, some of which could be transported inland as far as the Midlands along the River Severn. Watermen from towns along the Thames as far west as Wiltshire were operating regular twice-weekly trips to London carrying passengers and goods. As early as the 1630s there were already over 2,000 such licensed carriers operating by both river and road linking the main provincial towns with London. Although large quantities of goods were still carried by pack horses, mules and donkeys, many more waggons were using the improving road network. The old, two-wheeled carts, capable of carrying 20 hundredweight, were being replaced by larger four-wheeled waggons drawn by 12 horses, which could carry some 70 hundredweight. Fast stage coaches were beginning to run regular services between London and the provincial towns along routes

MAP 7
London in 1603

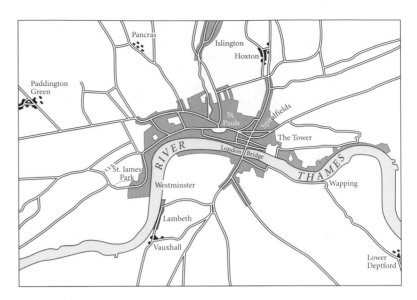

where coaching inns offered overnight accommodation for the passengers and a change of horses.

This developing national market depended mainly on the flow of foodstuffs and raw materials into London, and the distribution of luxury and consumer wares from the capital into the provinces. As the communication network improved so did the flow of goods and people in and out of London. At the same time, there was a considerable increase in the publication of London news sheets, pamphlets and advertising material. By 1712, 20 newspapers were being produced regularly every week with a wide distribution outside London. In turn, this accelerated the spread of ideas and promoted the development of a national culture. Even more importantly from the economic point of view, it promoted consumerism. As more people visited London, looked in the new shop windows or read the advertisements in the newspapers, so they became aware of the rapidly increasing range of goods that was becoming available.

C *Conclusion*

There is no doubt that the establishment of an increasingly integrated national market was vital in promoting economic growth in Stuart England. Without the improvements in road, river and coastal communications and the development of banking, there would not have been the increasing rapid movement of people, goods and money necessary to raise demand. But, like all the other parts of the economy, it cannot be looked at in isolation. The national market developed largely out of the need to maintain London and the other expanding towns. Urban growth was only possible because of the improved performance in the agricultural sector, which produced the food surpluses required to supply the town markets. At the same time, the growth in demand for consumer goods would not have been nearly as great if living standards had not been rising. There is also considerable debate on whether it was

---

Q

How did improvements in communications help to promote a national market?

KEY ISSUE

How did the creation of a national market help to increase demand within the economy?

the rapid growth of overseas trade or the less flamboyant developments in domestic industry that provided the impetus for the late Stuart consumer boom. This question will be discussed in the next two sections.

6 ⌐ COLONISATION, COMMERCIAL EXPANSION AND THE WORLD MARKET

The growth of overseas trade and the development of a colonial empire used to be considered the major Stuart economic achievement. More recently, however, the 'commercial revolution' has come to be regarded as an important, but by no means the paramount, part of the process of economic growth in the seventeenth century. The reason for this change of view is that the Stuart overseas trade was import led, whereas under the Tudors it had been export led. In other words, Tudor merchants were largely dependant on the export of cloth to Europe, while their Stuart counterparts were more concerned with importing and re-exporting cheap raw materials from the Americas and luxury goods from the Far East. Manufacturing and exporting cloth stimulated English industry and created jobs, whereas importing and re-exporting sugar, tobacco and Eastern silks and spices, while creating wealth, did little to promote industry or provide employment. For this reason commercial expansion cannot be said to have had any immediate impact on English economic growth. This issue will be discussed in more detail at the end of the chapter.

Like all other aspects of the economy, Stuart commercial expansion was based on the framework created in the sixteenth century. Tudor exploration had helped to open up oceanic trade routes, while the defeat of the Armada in 1588 had established English sea power. Tudor trade had largely depended on the export of semi-manufactured cloth to the Netherlands. After the collapse of the Antwerp market in the 1580s it was necessary to find new markets. A number of new spheres of influence had been established by 1603. Much of this commercial activity was based on the creation of a new type of trading company. Previously, merchants had tended to trade as individuals, or to form loose confederations, such as the English Merchant Adventurers or German Hanseatic League, to increase their negotiating powers in countries with which they traded. The new joint stock companies were based in London and were made up of several hundred merchants who had a mutual interest in trading in a particular area, such as the Baltic or the Far East. The members shared in the cost of sending a trading fleet, and then shared the profits or the loss if the voyage was unsuccessful. To reduce competition, such companies were granted a royal charter giving them a monopoly over trading in their chosen sphere of interest.

As early as 1555, the Muscovy Company had been founded to open up trade with the Baltic and Russia. This had been followed by the Levant Company in 1579, which traded in the Mediterranean and the Middle East. Both the Levant and Muscovy companies had sent officials overland to try to establish trading contacts with China and the Orient.

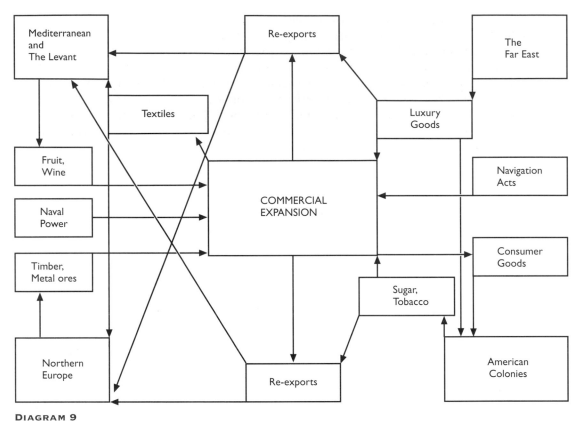

DIAGRAM 9
Late Stuart commercial expansion

Finally, in 1600, the East India Company had been formed to trade in the Far East.

At the same time, some merchants from Bristol and other west coast ports had opened up trading links with Spain and the western Mediterranean, and traded in gold, ivory and slaves along the west coast of Africa. Others, such as Drake and Hawkins, had organised trading and privateering expeditions to the Caribbean and mainland America. Explorers, such as Sir Humphrey Gilbert and John Davis, had investigated and mapped much of the Hudson Bay area in an unsuccessful attempt to find a north-west passage to China. Between 1577 and 1580 Sir Francis Drake had circumnavigated the world. In the 1580s, both Sir Humphrey Gilbert and Sir Walter Raleigh had tried to establish colonies on the east coast of north America in Newfoundland and Virginia. These ventures had established the areas which were to be successfully developed and exploited by the Stuarts (see the map showing Stuart world trade on page 302).

(see the map showing Stuart world trade on page 302).

A *The commercial depression of 1603–40*

By the 1590s, the continental markets had been depressed by over-population, inflation, and the long series of dynastic and religious wars

---

KEY ISSUE

How had the Tudors laid the foundations for Stuart commercial expansion?

fought between France, Spain and the Holy Roman Empire. The revolt of the Netherlands against its Spanish overlord had hastened the eventual collapse of the Antwerp cloth market on which English exporters had largely relied. In any case, the 'old draperies' had fallen out of favour and were being supplanted by the lighter fabrics of the 'new draperies'. This added to the problems of English cloth exporters, who had to adjust to the manufacture and marketing of the new textiles. Although attempts had been made to open alternative markets for exports, these had made little headway by the early seventeenth century.

In 1614, the situation deteriorated still further when Alderman Cockayne, a London merchant with interests in the textile trade, succeeded in persuading the government to ban the export of unfinished cloth to the Netherlands. This, he thought, would boost the English finishing and dyeing trades. The scheme was a total disaster because the Dutch simply bought unfinished cloth from elsewhere, and it was abandoned in 1617, but not before it had caused widespread unemployment amongst textile workers. The beginning of the Thirty Years War on the Continent in 1618 further depressed the European markets. This, allied with indecisive government policies, resulted in increasing unemployment and falling levels of trade in the 1620s and 1630s. However, trade was already beginning to pick up again by the 1640s, which suggests that the Civil War was less economically disruptive than might have been expected. Although Spanish influence was declining in both the Americas and the Far East, Holland and France were beginning to emerge as contestants for the supremacy of the world's seaways.

See pages 312–15 for more information on the 'new draperies'.

See pages 36–7 for the Thirty Years War.

KEY ISSUE

Why was overseas trade still depressed in 1640?

B *Colonisation*

It was from this unpromising base that overseas trade began to expand in the 1650s. There was growing rivalry between England, France and Holland to wrest control of the New World and the Far East from the weakening grasp of Spain. This was the result of the need for the European powers to gain a greater share in the world markets to overcome the economic stagnation in western Europe. Seventeenth-century economists considered that the power of a nation depended on a favourable balance of trade, and that a country had to draw in more wealth (gold and silver) than it spent abroad. To achieve this it was necessary to find new markets in order to gain a greater share in existing markets. England and Holland were particularly anxious to seize control of the highly lucrative Far Eastern trade in silks and spices. Great interest was being shown in establishing colonies on the east coast of north America and in the Caribbean. It was thought that the climate of the Americas was suitable to produce a range of crops that were previously only available from southern Europe. Once established, it was hoped that colonists would be able to produce cheap raw materials, which would save the mother country from spending wealth on expensive Mediterranean imports. Similarly, it was hoped to obtain large supplies of cheap fish from the Newfoundland cod banks, and furs from around Hudson Bay. Historians used to describe this new economic outlook as mercantilism, although like many general theories it has now fallen out of favour.

COLONIES ON MAINLAND AMERICA

Initially, it was the hope of finding gold that reawakened English interest in American colonisation. The Virginia Company was given a royal charter to re-establish the failed Tudor settlement, and in 1607 an expedition of 120 adventurers landed at Chesapeake Bay to search for gold. They built a fort on the James River to protect themselves from hostile Amerindians. Although no gold was found, new colonists continued to arrive and began clearing the forest for farming. Despite constant Amerindian attacks and severe epidemics, by 1610 a steady flow of settlers, including women and children, had successfully established the colony around Jamestown. A governor was appointed in 1611, by which time it had been found that the soil in Virginia was particularly well suited to grow tobacco. The first shipment of 20,000 pounds was sent to England in 1613. The high price of tobacco immediately attracted interest among the elites and wealthy middle orders. They bought tracts of land in the new colony to create large tobacco plantations, which were managed by stewards, or younger sons. To supply labour to work the plantations, regular shipments of indentured servants, orphans, vagrants and convicts were sent over to Virginia.

The growth of the tobacco industry in Bristol and Liverpool encouraged the creation of further coastal colonies immediately to the south of Virginia. Maryland was established in 1632 by Lord Baltimore for the settlement of Catholic refugees. This was followed by the colonisation of the neighbouring areas of North and South Carolina in the 1660s. The population of the southern states continued to expand rapidly, reaching some 300,000 by about 1714. Tobacco remained the principal crop grown on the plantations, and by 1700 22 million pounds was being exported to Britain. At the same time, the southern states proved very suitable for growing cotton and rice, particularly in the Carolinas. By the early eighteenth century increasing quantities of raw cotton and rice were being shipped for processing and re-export in England.

Further north along the American coast a different type of settlement had been taking place. In 1620, the *Mayflower* arrived off Cape Cod carrying Puritan refugees and a group of settlers bound for Virginia. Finally, all 110 passengers signed the 'Mayflower Compact' under which they agreed to set up a free and democratic colony. Although the conditions were much harsher than further south, they established themselves at Plymouth, which became the capital of the colony of New England. Neither the weather, nor the terrain, were suitable for growing tobacco, and the settlers concentrated on small-scale general farming, trading and fishing. In 1628, the Massachusetts Bay Company was formed and was given extensive settlement rights over all the neighbouring land. Puritans and other religious dissidents, escaping persecution under the Laudian Church, came in large numbers, and by 1643 the colony had a population of some 1,600. This attracted a further

What part did tobacco play in Stuart commercial growth?

See pages 70–2 for Laud's reforms.

exodus of people suffering religious persecution, who established colonies at Rhode Island and Maine along similar lines.

Although these northern colonies were unable to supply England with highly lucrative raw materials, they prospered and expanded. By 1700 they had a population that was only slightly smaller than that of the southern states. The Newfoundland cod banks provided a valuable export because fish was in high demand in southern Europe, and large quantities were re-exported from England to the Mediterranean. Ship building became an important industry, and the colonists developed a thriving coastal trade. As settlers moved west into New Hampshire and Pennsylvania they became involved in fur trading along the St Lawrence Seaway and the Great Lakes. This brought them into conflict with the French from their settlements around Quebec, which had become a royal colony of France in 1674. To the south, the Dutch colony of New Amsterdam was finally conquered in 1664 and renamed New York. By 1714 two contrasting groups of English colonies were firmly established in North America: the wealthy, plantation colonies in the south with strong Catholic and Anglican leanings, and the prosperous Protestant colonies in the north organised on a more democratic and equalitarian basis.

> **KEY ISSUE**
>
> *How did the two groups of English mainland colonies differ?*

THE CARIBBEAN

In the West Indies the English were not only in conflict with the French and the Dutch, but also with Spain because the islands fell west of 'the line'. This was an imaginary line running from north to south through the Cape Verde Islands, which the papacy had used in 1494 to grant Spain control of all lands to the west, and Portugal all the lands to the east. Consequently, Spain regarded the Caribbean as their special pre-serve and defended it jealously against all intruders. Spain had already occupied the larger islands such as Hispaniola, Cuba and Jamaica. Until the seventeenth century England had seen the Caribbean as an area for piratical raids and freebooting without having any real intention of set-tlement. Then, in 1612, Bermuda, which was situated well to the north of the main islands, was occupied by a group of 60 English colonists. Some twelve years later the small island of St Kitts was taken over by Sir Thomas Warner and his family, along with a handful of other settlers. Warner soon discovered that tobacco grew well on the island, and a year later he was able to send some 7,000 pounds back to England. In recognition of his services, Charles I granted Warner the right to colonise the neighbouring islands of Bermuda, Nevis and Monserrat.

Taking advantage of the Spanish inertia and lack of sea power, English colonists quickly occupied these and other islands in the Leeward group during the 1630s. Barbados proved to be very popular, and after the first settlers arrived in 1627, the island's population quickly rose to over 1,600. One of the major English acquisitions was Antigua, which had the best natural harbour in the Caribbean, and was to become one of the key naval bases in the region. Although English interest in the West Indies was originally aroused by the possibilities of growing tobacco, it was soon discovered that another crop had even greater potential value. Dutch settlers in the West Indies during the 1630s had adopted the idea of growing sugar cane from Brazil. The Caribbean climate was ideally suited to this crop, and it was rapidly introduced into all the English-held islands. As with the production of tobacco, sugar was best suited to being grown on large plantations, and the English elites and middle orders quickly established a monopoly land holding in the West Indies. The Caribbean was even more unsuited to white labour than the American mainland, and the rapidly expanding demand for sugar and its products gave a further boost to the development of the slave trade.

The establishment of the English Republic under Oliver Cromwell boosted English influence in the Caribbean. Cromwell was determined to expand English influence abroad, and to increase the country's share of world commerce. The military and naval reforms carried through by the new regime gave him the opportunity to intervene in the West Indies. During the early 1650s, 40 heavily armed warships were built, which doubled the size of the navy. Under the command of two former Parliamentary generals, George Monck and Robert Blake, the English navy had decisively defeated the Dutch by 1654. Having gained control of the sea, Cromwell embarked on his 'Western design', which was to drive the Spanish out of the Caribbean. In 1655, a joint military and naval force was sent to capture Hispaniola. The expedition, marred by poor planning, ill-disciplined troops and inept leadership, failed to gain a foothold on Hispaniola. Instead, it did manage to capture the smaller island of Jamaica. Like Antigua, Jamaica had an excellent harbour, and both islands became heavily fortified naval bases to protect British interests in the Caribbean.

See page 152 for defeat of the Dutch.

See page 153 for political background.

Drinking sweetened chocolate, tea and coffee had become highly fashionable among the elites and wealthy middle orders in western Europe, and created an almost insatiable demand for sugar. This turned the West Indian colonies into extremely valuable Crown possessions, and attracted large numbers of settlers to the islands. Many people emigrated from England to escape the Civil War and the Interregnum. These numbers were swelled by large numbers of prisoners of war and convicts transported to the Caribbean to work on the harbour defences or to clear the ground and to plant sugar cane. The population of the islands rose rapidly in the 1640s and 1650s, reaching some 40,000 in Jamaica and Barbados alone. However, just as in the southern colonies on the mainland, all the best agricultural land was quickly acquired by wealthy plantation owners. The small farmers were squeezed out, and the flow of immigrants slowed down. In any case, the Caribbean was a very unhealthy place in which to live, and there was a high death rate from yellow fever and dysentery. Fewer servants, orphans and convicts were shipped to the Caribbean as labourers, because black slaves were cheaper, more efficient and had a higher resistance to disease. For these reasons the white population on the islands steadily declined. In contrast, sugar exports rose rapidly from 150 hundredweight in the 1670s to 400,000 hundredweight worth £630,000 by 1700.

C *The slave and 'triangular' trades*

KEY ISSUE

Why were the West Indian colonies so important to English commerce?

Trading in slaves had been a profitable business in the Mediterranean for centuries. The establishment of plantations in the Portuguese and Spanish colonies in South America and the Caribbean had extended the demand for slave labour. The native Amerindians were found to be reluctant to work on the estates of their new masters. For this reason black slaves began to be shipped across from west Africa. Although both the Dutch and the English did some slave trading in the sixteenth century, it was the Portuguese who had established the trade. In the late fifteenth century, Portuguese explorers had mapped the west African coastline when they pioneered the first sea route to India. They built strongly fortified depots at strategic points along the coast and started to trade with the local tribes. These trading stations became the centre for the collection and shipment of slaves across the Atlantic to the New World. The Portuguese obtained their slaves from the local tribal chieftains, who were very willing to exchange prisoners of war, political rivals and surplus wives and children for European trade goods.

Once the slaves had been sold in the Caribbean or mainland America, the proceeds were used to buy sugar, tobacco, cotton, mahogany and other valuable hard woods, all of which were in high demand in western Europe. This was the basis of what became known as the 'triangular trade'. Cheap trade goods were taken to west Africa and exchanged for slaves. The slaves were transported to the Americas and sold for cash. This was converted into high value goods, which were then shipped back to Europe and sold at a handsome profit. Such a trading pattern was helped by the prevailing winds and currents in the north Atlantic, especially the very constant 'trade wind' blowing from the north-east.

By the early seventeenth century the Dutch had largely succeeded in seizing control of all the major slave stations in west Africa. Not surprisingly, as the triangular trade was so highly profitable, English merchants from the west coast were anxious to gain a share. Taking advantage of early English naval successes in the Dutch wars, a chartered company, the Royal Adventurers of England Trading to Africa, was set up in 1663. Having taken over some of the Dutch trading posts, the company promised its backers to ship 3,000 slaves a year to the Caribbean. However, the Dutch had regained their naval supremacy by 1667, and were able to recapture all but one of their trading posts. This led to the collapse of the company with a loss of £120,000. Despite such reverses, the Royal Africa Company was established in 1672. Taking advantage of the Royal Navy's growing domination of the sea routes, the company gradually gained control of the whole west African coast from Senegal down to Angola.

See page 211–13 for the political background.

With their existing involvement in American commerce, the ports of Bristol, Liverpool and eventually Glasgow became the main centres of the slave trade in Britain. By the 1680s some 50,000 slaves a year were being shipped to the Americas. An indication of the increasing volume of trade is that the number of slaves on Barbados alone rose from about

See page 260 for the
Treaty of Utrecht.

20,000 in the 1650s to some 80,000 by 1700. The Royal Africa
Company's fortunes continued to prosper. Under the terms of the
Treaty of Utrecht in 1713 Britain was given the right to supply slaves to
the Spanish colonies in South America. This enabled the Company to
increase its share of the trade to 50 per cent, and to establish control
over the west African coast from Gambia to the Congo.

D *The Far East*

KEY ISSUE

*How did the slave and
triangular trades
contribute to English
commerce?*

In the Far East, England's main commercial rivals were also the Portuguese and the Dutch. After Vasco da Gama had crossed the Pacific to
reach India in 1498, the Portuguese had established trading posts at
strategic points along the coast. During the sixteenth century they
extended their sea empire to include the East Indian islands, such as
Java, the Molluccas and Sumatra. This gave the Portuguese access to the
fabulously wealthy Oriental trade in silks, cottons, spices, jewels, tea and
coffee. All these commodities were sought after in western Europe to
satisfy the growing demand for luxury goods among the elites. For most

MAP 8
Stuart world trade, 1603–1714

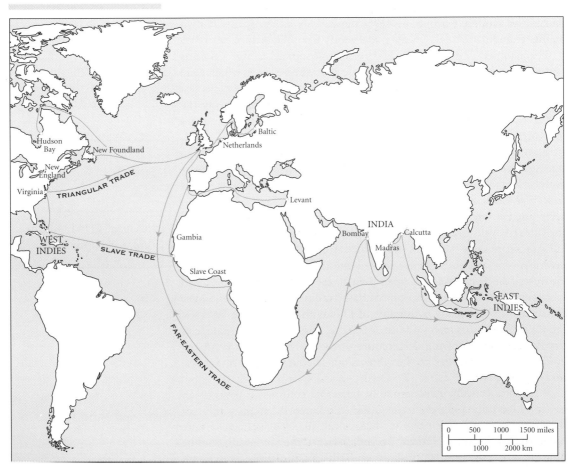

of the sixteenth century there was little attempt to break the Portuguese monopoly of supplying Oriental luxuries to the European markets for fear of incurring the wrath of the all-powerful Habsburgs. However, by the end the century both the English and the Dutch were beginning to try to establish themselves in the Far East. While the Dutch had succeeded in setting up trading posts in the East Indies, similar English attempts in the 1590s had all failed.

In 1600, Elizabeth I granted a charter to 242 London merchants to form the East India Company. A fleet of five ships sailed in 1601 taking £30,000 of silver to buy goods, and a quantity of lead, iron and cloth for exchange and sale. This expedition did succeed in gaining permission to set up a factory (trading post) in Java. The fleet returned to England in 1603 with Eastern goods to the value of some £3 million, although there had been little success in selling any of the trade goods. Encouraged by this success, another fleet was sent out to India to try to negotiate trading rights with the Mughal Emperor Jahangir. This venture failed because Portuguese influence in India was still too strong. Meanwhile, the East India Company continued to extend its influence in the East Indies and several new trading stations were established. At the same time, Portuguese control was growing weaker as the English naval presence increased in the Indian Ocean, and in 1613 company officials succeeded in gaining permission to set up a factory at Surat on the mainland.

These advances quickly brought the English into conflict with the Dutch, who hoped to establish a monopoly in the East Indies. Ten leading company officials were accused of trying to drive the Dutch out of their main base at Amboyna in the Moluccas by assassinating the governor. Their execution in 1623 became known as the 'Amboyna massacre' in England, and it effectively ended the English presence in the East Indies. This reverse forced the East India Company to concentrate its interests in India. By the 1630s it had begun to take control of the highly profitable trade in tea and coffee, and had acquired a major factory at Madras. By this time the Mughal empire was beginning to break up enabling company officials to quickly extend their influence, and another 25 trading stations were established. However, as the political situation in India became more unstable, trading became more difficult. Matters were further complicated by the English Civil War and the Parliamentary victory because of the Company's suspected Royalist sympathies. Relationships with the new English Republic steadily declined until, in 1657, its charter was withdrawn. However, because the Indian trade was so profitable a rival group of merchants was chartered to take over the Company's concessions.

The main problems with Far Eastern commerce was that it was virtually impossible to sell any European goods; Oriental countries were then more technically advanced, and were not particularly anxious to buy what they thought were inferior European goods. Instead, they preferred to exchange their products for silver. This went against current economic thinking, because it took bullion out of the country instead of drawing it in. However, the profits to be made from Oriental trade were so immense that this defect was always conveniently ignored. It was also a difficult area in which to trade, requiring great diplomacy and considerable knowledge of local conditions. For these reasons, and because of its support for the Royalist cause, the Company regained its charter at the Restoration in 1660, and had its privileges extended. Not only was it allowed to issue its own coinage, but also was given jurisdiction over all English subjects in India. Because the political situation in India remained uncertain, the Company was granted the right to recruit and maintain its own private army to protect its interests. As the Company's influence increased so did the size of its fleet of specially built and heavily armed ships.

The Company's position was strengthened still further by the marriage of Charles II to the Portuguese princess, Catherine of Braganza. Part of her dowry was the island of Bombay, which in 1668 the King leased to the Company at a rent of £10 a year. Bombay, Madras and Calcutta became the Company's main military bases in India. The Company became a national institution, and was a popular investment for members of the Royal Court and the wealthy elites. Although William III, suspicious of the Company's links with the former regime, allowed another merchant group to trade with India, Oriental commerce continued to expand. When the rival companies amalgamated in 1708, they had capital assets of over £3 million and an annual turnover of some £650,000. This was very comparable to the equally lucrative trade in West Indian sugar.

KEY ISSUE

How did Far Eastern trade contravene Stuart economic thinking, and why did it remain so popular?

E *Navigation Acts and command of the seas*

An obvious question is: why were Stuart merchants were so successful in opening up trade in the the Americas, the Atlantic and the Far East when their Tudor predecessors had failed? The answer lies more with the changing balance of power within western Europe and greater political governmental will in England than with any difference in initiative and endeavour. Of paramount importance was the growing influence of the Royal Navy, which by 1714 virtually controlled all the major sea routes.

During most of the sixteenth century western European politics had been dominated by the powerful Habsburg dynasty that controlled the Holy Roman Empire, Spain, the Netherlands, northern Italy, and eventually Portugal. When Philip II ascended the throne of Spain in 1555, supported by gold from South America and the industries of the Netherlands, the Habsburg hegemony seemed unassailable. Yet, the long wars against France, and the struggle to stop the spread of Protestantism began to bankrupt even the wealth of the Spanish empire. When Philip II died in 1598, further intervention in France, the loss of the northern Netherlands and the defeat of the Armada had left Spain bankrupt and the economies of Spain and Portugal in ruins. Both countries steadily declined during the seventeenth century, and it was this that enabled England, Holland and France to intervene successfully in their crumbling American and Far Eastern empires.

THE NAVIGATION ACTS

It was not until after the Civil War that England began to benefit fully from the new situation. In 1622, Thomas Munn, a member of the East India Company, published *English Treasure by Foreign Trade*. This book became the basis of economic thinking for the remainder of the century. It stressed the need to acquire markets abroad for the sale of English goods and to protect them against commercial competitors. To achieve this, Munn advocated the close regulation of commerce. Such thinking was not entirely new, but the problem was one of enforcement. It was not until the military and naval reforms carried out by the English Republic began to take effect that England was in a position to safeguard its markets and colonies effectively, or to regulate overseas trade. To achieve this objective, England had to have command of the sea. Not until the Royal Navy had become strong enough to defeat the Spanish, French and Dutch fleets was it possible to effectively control world commerce. The first steps in this direction were taken in the 1650s by the passing of Navigation Acts to restrict the carriage of goods to English ships. This effectively meant that all the raw materials supplied by the colonies could only be transported in English ships, and that the colonists could only buy English goods. At the same time, trade with other foreign countries had to be conducted in either English ships or those of the country of origin. Such regulations, if enforcable, would prevent any other country benefiting from the English colonies, and would cut out competition from middlemen in the carriage of goods. The Navigation Act of 1660 brought together all the previous legislation and became the basis of English control of overseas trade:

> For the increase in shipping and encouragement of the navigation of this nation wherein, under the good providence and protection of God, the wealth, safety and strength of this kingdom is so much concerned; be it enacted ... that from and after the first day of December one thousand six hundred and sixty, and from thenceforward, no goods or commodities whatsoever shall be imported into or exported out of any lands, islands, plantations [colonies] or to territories to his majesty belonging or in his possession ... in Asia, Africa or America, in any ship or ships, vessel or vessels whatsoever, but in ships or vessels as do truly and without fraud belong only to the people of England.

Not surprisingly, England's main commercial competitors resisted any attempt to limit their share of the market, and this was a major cause of the wars with Holland and France during the second half of the century. The English colonists were not particularly happy either, because they thought that lack of competition would mean that they would have to sell their raw materials cheaply and buy English manufactured goods at inflated prices. Such misgivings were expressed clearly in *The Humble Remonstrance* of 1663 on behalf of the inhabitants and planters of Virginia and Maryland:

KEY ISSUE

Why were the Navigation Acts so important in establishing English commercial supremacy?

> First, that traders to Virginia and Maryland from England shall furnish and supply the planters and inhabitants of these colonies with all sorts of commodities and necessaries which they may want or desire, at as cheap rates and prices as the Hollanders used to have when the Hollanders was admitted to trade hither.
>
> Secondly, that the said traders out of England to these colonies shall not buy of the planters [just] such tobacco in the colonies as is fit [needed] for England, but take of all that shall be yearly made by them, at as good rates and prices as the Hollanders used to give.

In fact, such fears proved groundless because of the high demand for tobacco and sugar in England, and the ability of the industrial sector to meet the demand for reasonably priced consumer goods (see pages 316–23).

CONTROL OF THE SEA

See page 73 for opposition to ship money.

The ability of the English government to provide naval protection for its overseas possessions and reduce commercial competition was hampered until the 1660s by lack of money. Most of the Elizabethan naval enterprises had been largely privately financed. After the defeat of the Armada the government was so short of money that it could not afford to pay the crews of the victorious fleet. For fear of riots, the ships were ordered to stay at sea and hundreds of sailors actually died of starvation. Both James I and Charles I faced the same problem of chronic underfunding because of Parliament's unwillingness to provide taxation without a greater share in government. Charles I's attempts to reburbish the navy by imposing the non-parliamentary ship money tax aroused great opposition.

Ironically, it was the English Republic that benefited from the new ship building programme inaugurated by the King. With the restoration of Charles II, government financing was put on a sounder basis. New taxes, such as the Hearth Tax, and the imposition of higher custom and excise duties ensured that there was sufficient money to continue the naval expansion started under the Republic. Commercial interests in Parliament and the City were strong enough to maintain an aggressive government policy in the series of wars that lasted until 1713.

Continental conflicts had previously been dominated by land battles, but sea power was becoming a decisive factor. However, warfare was highly expensive and disrupted trade. It was a sign of the more positive and determined government attitude that the late seventeenth-century wars were fought through to a successful conclusion. Even a series of humiliating naval defeats in the Dutch wars, which had cost £6 million by the time peace was made in 1674, only briefly dented the national resolve. In any case, the conflict had been a serious drain on Dutch resources, and the country was becoming exhausted by the commercial struggle with England.

France was becoming a more dangerous colonial and commercial competitor. The accession of William of Orange to the throne in 1688 created an Anglo-Dutch alliance against France. The wars of the League of Augsburg and the Spanish Succesion proved decisive in establishing English naval superiority. Little attention had been paid to the navy since 1674, and this was made apparent when the combined English and Dutch navies were defeated by the French off Beachy Head in 1690. This reverse immediately led to a very searching overhaul of the navy, and renewed activity in ship building. Although the French navy was decisively beaten at the battle of La Hogue in 1692, French commerce raiders and privateers continued to be a major threat.

The problem was the sheer number of English merchant ships that had to be protected, having trebled to some 300,000 tons in the course of the century. The most dangerous area, with greatest concentration of shipping, was the English Channel and the North Sea. To prevent losses this area had to be patrolled by small squadrons of warships, and enemy ports were blockaded to stop their cruisers going to sea. At the same time, ships had to be found to escort merchant convoys across the Atlantic, to the Far East and to the Mediterranean.

A massive building programme was started to provide enough warships, especially smaller escort vessels such as frigates and sloops, for convoy duties. While this was in progress heavy losses continued, and an estimated 4,000 merchant ships were captured or sunk between 1689 and 1697. In 1693 on one Mediterranean convoy to Turkey the French seized half the 400 merchant ships. However, in 1696 the Board of Trade was set up to co-ordinate and increase the efficiency of the assembling and escorting of convoys. This measure, and the growth in the number of battle ships and escort vessels steadily improved the situation, so that by 1713 losses had been reduced by 50 per cent. Apart from securing control of the sea, England had made some very significant gains from both France and Spain. By the Treaty of Utrecht, Spain ceded the strategic Mediterranean naval bases of Minorca and Gibraltar, while France relinquished its American possessions of Nova Scotia, Hudson Bay and Newfoundland. Although the Dutch retained their monopoly of the East Indies, Britain now virtually controlled all the other areas of world commerce.

> **Q**
> *Why was the capture of Gibraltar so important for English naval and commercial supremacy?*

F *Commercial Expansion 1640–1713*

The striking feature of this period was not just the increasing volume of trade, but also its changing nature and distribution. Until the 1640s the pattern of English overseas trade had changed very little from that of the late sixteenth century. Woollen cloth was still the major export, although sales of the heavy broadcloths and worsteds were being replaced by the lighter fabrics of the 'new draperies'. Northern Europe and the Baltic remained the main destination, taking some 60 per cent of all sales, but exports to the Levant and other parts of the Mediterranean were increasing rapidly. The volume of imports still greatly exceeded exports. Wine, oil, spices, cottons, silks and other luxury goods came from the Mediterranean, with linen, metal wares and a whole range of manufactured items being supplied from northern Europe. American and Oriental imports amounted to only about six per cent of the total. During the 1640s and 1650s there were no radical changes, although demand in Europe had begun to recover, especially after the end of the Thirty Years War.

Holland remained a major competitor in the European markets. The Dutch also dominated the distribution of merchandise through the carrying trade, although English shipyards were building increasing numbers of bulk carriers. The quantity of sugar and tobacco being produced in the English American and Caribbean colonies was beginning to increase very slowly. In any case, the Dutch were buying much of the crop and supplying the colonists with slaves, consumer goods and other necessities. It was not until after the 1660s, when the Navigation Acts and growing English sea power became effective, that the picture started to change. Thereafter, England steadily began to take control of trade outside Europe and the Mediterranean, except for the East Indies. Colonial sugar and tobacco became an English monopoly, and Europe was becoming virtually dependent on re-exports. Similarly, the East India Company's dominance in India gave them control of supplying tea, coffee, calicoes and other cotton goods to European markets. By this time English merchants were also largely in charge of the highly profitable slave and triangular trades, and were replacing the Dutch as the main carriers of goods.

These changes to the commercial pattern meant that imports and not exports had become the major driving force in the expansion of trade. The main target for sales continued to be the traditional markets of northern Europe and the Baltic, and the Mediterranean and southern Europe. In many respects the nature of this commerce remained much the same as earlier in the century. The main export was still woollen cloth from the expanding rural textile industries. However, the fabrics were no longer unfinished because the English dyeing and finishing trades were now working to a high standard. Selling fully finished cloth, which was now being carried largely in English ships, cut out the continental middlemen and gave exporters a much better profit margin. England was still importing timber from the Baltic for ship building, a range of manufactured goods from northern Europe, and wine, exotic fruits and other luxuries from the Mediterranean. But the volume of European imports was falling in relation to exports. English manufacturers were producing an increasingly wide range of consumer goods and so reducing the need for imports from northern Europe. The East India Company imports of silks, spices, cottons, tea and coffee meant that these commodities no longer had to be expensively imported from the Mediterranean. Furs, which previously had to be imported from the Baltic, could now be obtained from northern English American colonies. This contributed significantly to the increasingly favourable balance of trade that was being achieved at the end of the Stuart period.

The other important consideration was the rising volume of raw materials coming from the American and Caribbean colonies. Not only

See pages 312–13 for information on the textile industries.

did this remove the need to import tobacco and sugar from more expensive sources, but also provided a valuable item for re-export. Some mollasses and tobacco leaf were simply shipped across to England and then re-exported to the Continent. The bulk went to the refineries and processing plants at Bristol, Glasgow and Liverpool to be refined into sugar, or processed into cigar or pipe tobacco, and was then re-exported. England had a virtual monopoly and the Dutch sugar and tobacco industries were priced out of the market. As the quantities of raw materials rose so did the incomes and living standards of the colonists. Under the Navigation Acts the colonies were forbidden to produce manufactured goods for themselves, or import anything from any country but England This meant that by the end the century they were dependent on England for consumer and luxury goods. Exports of goods, such as textiles, metal and glass wares, tools, carpets, carriages, silks, cottons, tea and coffee, increased and had risen to some 20 per cent of all English exports and re-exports by 1714. All of these goods, and a large proportion of the re-exports to the Continent, were carried in English ships, which were insured by London brokers. This was a another source of valuable invisible earnings that added to England's favourable balance of trade.

By 1700 the value of exports had reached £6.4 million, while the cost of imports amounted to £5.8 million. This favourable balance of trade was even more impressive than the figures suggest. Only 61 per cent of the total imports were from Europe, while the remainder came from the Americas and the Far East, of which 30 per cent were re-exported. Significantly, this favourable trade balance was the beginning of a long-term upward pattern. By the 1730s exports had risen to £8 million, a rising proportion of which were manufactured goods. Imports had grown to £7.4 million, of which only 48 per cent came from Europe, with 30 per cent of American and Oriental imports being re-exported.

> ### KEY ISSUE
> *How had England achieved a favourable balance of trade by 1700?*

G *Conclusion*

The commercial expansion under the Stuarts was certainly impressive. American and Caribbean colonies were the source of valuable raw materials and provided an expanding market for English goods. The Far Eastern, triangular and slave trades were an almost equally valuable source of income. By 1714 England was the leading trading and naval power in western Europe. The dominance of the Royal Navy had made it possible to enforce the Navigation Acts, which gave England a commercial advantage. Spain was no longer a threat, and major competitors such as Holland and France had been exhausted by the long series of wars that ended in 1713. An expanding English merchant fleet was taking over an increasing share of the carrying trade. By 1714 England had a favourable trade balance, and was able to process and re-export colonial raw materials to a virtually captive European market. Success had boosted national confidence and self-esteem, generating what is known in the media today as the 'feel good' factor.

Although very striking, commercial expansion did not actually add greatly to economic growth. Apart from possibly tobacco, the imports from the Americas and the Far East were destined for the elite market. Even given that demand from the affluent middle orders was growing, this did not represent the breakthrough into a mass market that was needed really to stimulate the economy. Although the import of European goods was reduced, very little headway had been made in exporting English manufactured goods to the Continent. Equally, the expansion of overseas trade did very little directly to create employment. The tobacco and sugar industries only employed a small, skilled workforce. The expansion in the City, financial institutions, or in ship building and its allied trades, did nothing to help the unskilled and semi-skilled masses seeking work. The high performance of overseas trade also has to be considered in the context of the economy as a whole. Without the great urban expansion led by London, and the sound financial structure of the national market, commercial growth would have been more difficult and much slower. Much of the investment in overseas trade came from the profits made in the agricultural sector. In any case, had it not been for the greatly improved agricultural performance, urban expansion would not have been possible and the transfer of people from farming to other occupations would not have taken place. In other words, all the economic sectors were interdependent. What remains to be seen is what part the industrial sector played in the overall creation of economic growth.

7 ⌐ INDUSTRY AND THE DOMESTIC MARKET

The industrial sector was basically very similar to that of the Tudors for most of the Stuart period. Apart from the rural cloth industry, production was on a small scale and geared to meet the needs of the local market. Continental industries, particularly in Germany and the Netherlands, were more advanced and efficient. As a result, they produced a much wider and cheaper range of goods than their English counterparts. For this reason, England had to import a variety of industrial and consumer goods, such as tools, metal and glass wares, linen, silk and cotton fabrics, pins, mirrors, yarn, dyes and pottery. It was this constant inflow of continental manufactured goods that helped to keep the balance of trade in deficit. This situation did not fit into the economic thinking of the period. National prosperity was considered to depend on drawing in wealth, and not spending money abroad. To overcome this problem the industrial sector had to become more productive to supply all the needs of the domestic market, and create a surplus for sale overseas.

A *The problems of early Stuart industry*

Like the other areas of the economy industry was facing severe problems at the beginning of the seventeenth century. Most industrial

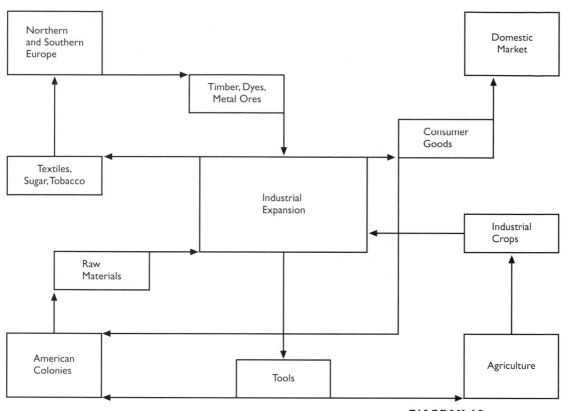

DIAGRAM 10
Late Stuart industrial expansion

activity was localised and on a small scale. Levels of unemployment were still high, which indicates that industry was not absorbing the surplus labour from agriculture. Poor communications and transport meant that goods could not be carried over long distances, and most industries only served a limited local market. This meant that there was little incentive to invest in high cost heavy industries such as mining or metal extraction. Even in the craft industries output was low and hampered by restrictive practices and central government legislation to prevent competition. Another major problem was lack of demand. Only the wealthy elites could afford to buy luxury and manufactured goods, and they preferred to spend their money on better quality products imported from the Continent. The bulk of the population were largely self-sufficient, and in any case could not afford to buy consumer goods.

CRAFT GUILDS

To a large extent industry was still urban based, and controlled by the craft guilds that had been established in the Middle Ages. These were organisations specialising in a particular type of trade, such as butchers, bakers, weavers, spinners, shoe makers, glovers, plumbers, carpenters, swordsmiths or goldsmiths. The members had to be master craftsmen and obey the particular rules governing their craft or mystery. People wishing to enter a guild had to serve a seven-year apprenticeship, and then work as journeymen (day workers) until they could afford to set up on their own. Guilds were to be found in every town, ranging from several hundred in London to five or six in a market town. Employing only a small, highly skilled workforce, this type of craft operation offered very limited scope for employment. Output was low, and the products, although they had to be of good quality, were expensive. However, because no competition was allowed from anyone who was not a member, townspeople and those from the surrounding country-side had to pay the inflated prices.

THE REGULATION OF INDUSTRY

To protect their monopoly, the urban guilds also tried to insist that no one was to be allowed to set up industries in the countryside. Tudor and early Stuart governments misguidedly supported such demands on the grounds that country industries employed unskilled or semi-skilled labour, and therefore produced poor quality goods. Acts, such as the Statute of Artificers of 1563, tried to ensure that only people who had passed their full apprenticeship could set up, or be employed in a craft industry. This legislation remained in place during the seventeenth century, although it was increasingly becoming unenforceable and ignored. Another aspect of this policy was the belief that the nation's welfare would be put at risk if people stopped working on the land to produce grain. The fixation on the importance of 'tillage' was at the root of much of the legislation. Even as late as 1662 the Settlement Act was still trying to prevent people leaving agriculture and moving away from their native parish.

THE RURAL CLOTH INDUSTRY

A notable exception to this general rule was the rural cloth industry, which, although initially disapproved of by the authorities, had become firmly established from the end of the Middle Ages. The main areas of rural clothmaking were East Anglia, the West Country, the south Mid-lands and the East Riding of Yorkshire. In contrast to the guild-based textile trades it was a large scale industry producing cloth for export. It was organised by wealthy entrepreneurs known as clothiers, who bought up large quantities of raw wool. Their agents then distributed the wool among their workforce of semi-skilled spinners and carders. The thread was then collected and put out to the weavers to be made into cloth, which was then collected and shipped abroad. Unlike the master craftsman who made a profit from producing small amounts of highly priced materials, the clothier profited from making large amounts of cheap fabric. The type of textile produced was 'white' or semi-manufactured woollen cloth. The reason for this was that, unlike the urban industry, rural clothmakers did not have skilled nappers, cutters and dyers, who could finish the cloth to the quality required for sale on the Continent. For this reason, it was sent for finishing in the Netherlands, where it was then sold on as fully manufactured cloth.

This type of organisation was known as the 'putting out' system, or cottage industry, because the employees all worked in their own cottages. The spinning, combing or carding was carried out by the women and children, while the men did the better paid weaving. By the end of the seventeenth century spinning was regarded as a sign of poverty, and the word 'spinster' became a term of contempt for a poor or single woman. Even so, cottage industry was an important part of the 'dual economy' through which the rural masses maintained their living standards by having several different seasonal occupations. Cottage industry continued to be the main means of mass textile production until well into the eighteenth century, and became the basis for a whole range of other rural industries by the end of the seventeenth century.

At the beginning of the century rural clothmaking was in as severe difficulties as the remainder of the industrial sector. The problem was that the Antwerp textile trades, the main market for English 'white' cloth, had been declining since the 1580s. The reasons for this were partly the revolt of the Netherlands against Spain, and more importantly that fashions for clothes were beginning to change. The 'new draperies', which were a lighter type of cloth made from mixtures of woollen, linen, cotton and silk threads, were becoming popular. Such fabrics were already being manufactured in various parts of the Netherlands and northern France. This meant that the old, heavy, woollen broadcloths, kerseys and worsteds made in England became increasingly difficult to sell. Attempts to suspend the export of white cloth in 1614 under the Cockayne Scheme proved a total disaster. The continental markets were then depressed still further by the outbreak of the Thirty Years War. The rural cloth industry went into a recession from which it did not emerge until the 1650s.

KEY ISSUE

What were the main problems facing the rural textile industry up to the 1640s?

OTHER CRAFTS AND INDUSTRIES

Other Tudor and Stuart attempts to regulate industry were more beneficial. The patent scheme introduced under Elizabeth I and continued under the Stuarts succeeded in promoting some new industries. The idea behind this programme was to encourage continental craftsmen with a particular industrial skill to settle in England and develop the industry. For this purpose such craftsmen were granted a patent giving them a monopoly over whatever they were manufacturing for 20 years, by which time they were expected to have made a handsome profit. Thereafter the skilled workers trained to use the process were at liberty to set up their own businesses. In this way it was hoped to introduce fresh skills and establish new industries that would make England less dependent upon continental imports. At the same time, it was thought that this would create employment.

By 1603 a number of new industries had been successfully established, such as silk and linen weaving, and making clay tobacco pipes. On a larger scale, processes for the manufacture of paper, glass and bricks, and producing salt from evaporating sea water were introduced. The problem was that by the early seventeenth century they had made very little impact upon the economy. The reason for this was that such enterprises were often expensive to set up and initially production levels were so low that it was still cheaper to buy continental imports. Furthermore, they only required small skilled workforces and so did nothing to ease unemployment.

Although the Tudor patent system was potentially very useful for the expansion of industry, malpractices were already throwing it into disrepute. James I and Charles I did nothing to make the system less open to abuse. The granting of monopolies and projects to courtiers and big City interests became a major issue during the Civil War when there was a rising demand for free trade. Another problem was that as domestic production rose, so the need to import continental goods fell, which damaged the profit margins of some of the influential City companies. Equally, a fall in the level of imports represented a reduction in government revenue from custom and excise duties. For this reason monopolies were often sold off to large business concerns that would agree to pay the government a lump sum to compensate for any loss in revenue. However, the beneficial side of these developments was that a large number of the new industries were run in cottages as family businesses and were too small to be hunted out by rapacious monopolists. It was this type of enterprise that was to promote industrial growth in the Stuart economy.

KEY ISSUE

Why had the new industries introduced by the Tudors failed to create any real economic growth by the 1640s?

HEAVY INDUSTRY

Coal mining, although widespread by 1603, was still comparatively backward. The main areas of coal extraction were the Forest of Dean in Gloucestershire, the Weald in Sussex and Kent, and Northumberland, with some workings in the Midlands, Wales and Lancashire. There had been scarcely any technological advance during the sixteenth century: most coal was still obtained from shallow bell pits, or from open cast mining. Transportation difficulties meant that coal was generally only used locally, and that it was often quicker and cheaper to ship it in from abroad. The general lack of demand provided little incentive for mine owners to invest the large amounts of capital needed to modernise the industry. To increase levels of output it was necessary to sink deeper mine shafts. This in turn created problems of flooding and lack of ventilation, which were expensive to overcome. However, there were some signs of an increase in demand during the early seventeenth century. More coal was being shipped from Newcastle to London for use as domestic fuel, and it was also being used in industrial furnaces to evaporate sea water to obtain salt, as well as in the manufacture of glass and bricks.

Similar problems faced the iron industry. The main centre for iron production remained in the Sussex Weald. The Wealden iron masters were still using blast furnaces introduced from France at the end of the fifteenth century. These were powered by water-driven bellows, and produced cast iron that was used for making cannons. Although situated close to coal workings, charcoal continued to be used as fuel because it had fewer impurities. Most of the ore was of such poor quality that it could only be smelted into crude pig iron, which had to be refined further in finery forges. The resultant bar iron was then distributed on pack animals to metal workers and blacksmiths to be made into a variety of tools and household equipment. In other areas it was cheaper to import Swedish iron ore because it was of a much higher quality and was easier to work than the English sources of supply. Although rural metal crafts were beginning to become established around Sheffield, Birmingham, Wolverhampton and Dudley, they were still very localised

The other metallurgic industries were on an even smaller scale. Tin was mined in Cornwall, and lead, silver and zinc in Shropshire and the Mendips. However, the growing popularity of silver, pewter (an alloy of lead and tin) and brass (an alloy of lead, tin and zinc) for tableware and ornaments, was beginning to promote some expansion.

> ### KEY ISSUE
>
> *What were the main problems facing heavy industry?*

B *The reasons for industrial growth 1660–1714*

There is no one simple explanation for why some Stuart industries showed such a marked improvement after the 1660s. It was a case of a combination of various factors working together at the right time. These changes did not happen overnight but continued to develop and evolve well into the eighteenth century.

After the 1650s, deflation, following the slowdown and stagnation in population increase, led to rising demand. This was not just confined to the wealthy elites and increasingly affluent middle orders. Falling food prices, rising wages and the greater availability of employment also improved the living standards of the lower social orders, and gave them greater spending power. At the same time, the rising prosperity of the American colonists increased demand for manufactured and consumer goods. This was particularly beneficial to English industry because the enforcement of the Navigation Acts had made the colonies a captive market.

Such changes coincided with the rapid growth of London and the expansion of the urban markets. Just as in the case of agriculture, the industrial sector benefited from the resultant creation of a national market. Improved communications and the greater ease of travel and transportation enabled an ever-widening distribution of manufactured goods. Banking, improved insurance facilities and falling interest rates made it easier to raise capital to modernise existing industries and to launch new initiatives. The rapid spread of shops to even the small market towns, provided a valuable outlet for industrial producers. At the same time, shop windows helped to increase the sale of consumer goods because they were on display to the public.

Another boost to the industrial sector were the changing attitudes towards regulation, free trade, competition and employment. During the English Republic many monopolies had been abolished because they were regarded as harmful to the development of free trade. Monopolies, such as the East India Company, remained untouched because they were protected by powerful vested interests in Parliament and the City. However, the corrupt system surrounding the granting of patents was largely removed, and this enabled new industrial processes to spread more quickly. Competition and free trade was increasingly seen as a means of lowering prices and promoting industrial enterprises. The regulations on apprenticeships and conformity to craft guild standards in rural industry were gradually allowed to lapse. As agricultural production rose there were less fears about people leaving agriculture to work in industry, and many of the old 'tillage' laws were relaxed. The expansion of rural industry gradually came to be seen as a means of promoting national prosperity and creating full employment.

This trend was helped because towns were also having to adapt themselves to the changing economic climate. Increasingly, rural industry was no longer being seen as a threat to urban prosperity. Competition gradually became replaced by co-operation. A major objection to rural industry had been that, because the workforce was usually only semi-skilled, their products were of a poorer quality and would not sell abroad. The realisation that the domestic market was just as important as the overseas market changed this attitude. Indeed, the provision of a variety of cheaper goods became seen as an advantage because it offered a range of consumer choice. In any case, it soon became apparent that such goods had an equally popular appeal in both the colonial and European markets. Urban master craftsmen continued to make high quality goods and specialist products, such as clocks, watches, gold and silver ware, and jewellery, for sale to the elites. At the same time, because of the growth of banking and other financial institutions, towns took over the role of financing the surrounding rural industries and of marketing their products.

C *Industrial expansion, 1660–1714*

KEY ISSUE

Why were industrial conditions more favourable after the 1660s?

There was by no means a revolutionary industrial breakthrough. Most industries had been slowly evolving even during the depression in the first half of the century. Expansion was slow and uneven, and some industries had hardly progressed at all by the end of the Stuart period. The lighter, rural industries responded relatively quickly to the more favourable conditions after the 1650s. Many new industries were established, but the technical problems facing some of the heavy industries were more difficult to overcome.

TEXTILES AND ALLIED TRADES

Cloth manufacture remained the main industry after agriculture in late Stuart England. East Anglia became the major centre for the production of the 'new draperies'. The other traditional clothmaking areas in the West Country, the south Midlands and the East Riding of Yorkshire either stagnated or adopted alternative occupations. The reason for this was that large numbers of continental cloth workers, mainly from the Netherlands, had come to East Anglia during the early seventeenth century. By the 1620s some 4,000 immigrants had settled mostly in Norwich and Colchester, where they formed what was called the Dutch Congregations. Apart from introducing the new continental cloth-

MAP 9

The main areas of Stuart farming and industry

making techniques, many were also experts in the dyeing and finishing trades. The industry was centred mainly in Norwich and Colchester, producing lightweight woollen worsteds. Norwich also specialised in manufacturing 'stuffs', which were made from various mixtures of woollen, cotton, silk and linen threads.

A variety of other forms of textile production were established as rural industries in East Anglia and many other parts of the country during the seventeenth century. In many cases the techniques were introduced by skilled craftsmen from the Continent. The Dutch knitting frame became the basis for a widespread cottage industry as well as on a larger scale in small workshops. Woollen stockings were very popular in the seventeenth century, and, as they were slow to make, rising demand provided considerable employment among the lower social orders. There was also an increasing demand among the elites for fine woollen and silk stockings. After Louis XIV had revoked the Edict of Nantes in 1685, there was another influx of French Protestants fleeing persecution. They helped to promote the expansion of the English silk industry already operating at Spitalfields in London and

Sudbury in Suffolk. At the same time, these Huguenot craftsmen were able to improve the techniques and production of fashionable silk stockings, fine linens, lace and other fabrics for the elite market. The small-ware loom was another introduction from Holland, which was used for making ribbons and a range of fabrics known as 'fancy' goods.

Lancashire was increasingly becoming a centre for the manufacture of cheaper cottons, and fustians, which were made from wool and cotton thread. A wide range of ready-made products, such as shirts, petticoats, tablecloths, and aprons, were popular with the lower order market. In Devon, there was an expansion in the manufacture of serge, a hard-wearing, twilled cloth, which was much in demand for working clothes. The West Country also became an important centre for the making of canvas. The technique had originally been brought to Suffolk by Breton immigrants in the sixteenth century. However, flax and hemp, the two materials needed for canvas making, were grown widely in Somerset, and by the 1650s Yeovil was producing large quantities of linen and hemp thread. Consequently, the canvas industry transferred itself to the West Country to be closer to its supply of raw materials. Hemp was also used widely in the manufacture of ropes and sacks.

KEY ISSUE

How had the textile industries expanded by 1714?

OTHER RURAL INDUSTRIES AND OCCUPATIONS

Apart from textiles, a great number and variety of trades, crafts and other occupations were developing quickly in the countryside, and in or around the towns. These could range from quite large putting out enterprises (workshops employing a few journeymen) to small initiatives run by families in their own homes. The reason the number of such industries spread was the relaxing of apprenticeships and other regulations, which made it much easier for people to learn a skill and then to set up in business for themselves. The advantage for individuals just starting up in many trades was that capital outlay for materials was small, they usually had their own tools, and they could generally work in their own homes. If the business expanded they could buy a workshop, or start putting out work among neighbouring cottagers. These industries included a wide range of occupations, not just in the major leather, metal crafts and building trades, but also smaller enterprises, such as making wigs or starch, or hairdressing and dressmaking. However, by 1700, like the textile trades, many of these industries were becoming increasingly capitalistically organised. It was this development that was giving employment to an ever-increasing number of men and women. On the other hand, it also meant that a growing number of families were losing their independence and becoming ever more reliant on wages.

The building trades gave employment to a large number of people all over the country. Even the small towns and villages had resident carpenters, plumbers, glaziers and joiners available for local work, while specialist masons, bricklayers and tilers travelled more widely. The growing affluence of the elites and middle social orders provided great scope for a whole range of craftsmen. The Tudor 'Great Rebuilding' that had been started by the wealthy elites, continued into the seventeenth century, and was taken up by the affluent middle social orders. The elites were employing architects to remodel their country mansions in the latest Palladian style developed by Inigo Jones, and having their pleasure gardens redesigned. The pseudo-gentry were modelling their town houses in similar styles. Fashionable urban squares, terraces and parks were being commissioned, even in new towns such as Birmingham and Liverpool, by the end of the century. Streets were being paved and lighted with oil lamps, and public water supplies constructed. Quite small towns were erecting libraries and assembly rooms. This process was helped by the numerous town fires, which gave architects, such as Sir Christopher Wren, great scope for rebuilding whole city centres. At the same time, house interiors had to be refurbished, decorated and furnished in the fashionable style that the new attitudes towards privacy and comfort demanded. This gave employment to a whole range of decorators, artists, designers and cabinet makers, as well as raising the demand for fabrics, carpets, porcelain, silverware and other furnishings.

Leather goods were very popular in Stuart England. One reason for this was because leather became fashionable among the elites for clothes and furnishings. Another was the widespread use of leather in industry for machinery, harnesses and tools. While all towns had their tanneries and leather workers, it was the Midlands that became the major leather production area during the seventeenth century. This was because the open woodland parishes of the area were particularly suitable for raising cattle and pigs. They were also on the route of the drove roads from the north, which were being increasingly used to supply cattle for the London meat markets. Birmingham and Leicester had a great variety of leather crafts, and produced a wide range of goods such as water pipes, bottles, powder flasks, scabbards, jackets, harnesses, bellows, buckets and hinges. Northampton was the centre of an extensive putting out system specialising in making boots and shoes. Several Oxfordshire towns were centres for cottage industries producing a variety of types of glove. The expansion in agriculture and travel and the greater use of horses raised the demand for many leather goods, ranging from saddles to leather springs and upholstery for the new fast coaches.

The open woodlands of the Midlands were also the setting for a great expansion in the metalworking crafts. This helps to explain why it was such a popular settlement area for young vagrants seeking employment. As in the case of the building and leather trades, all the towns and villages already had their resident metalworkers and blacksmiths. This emphasises the fact that the various developments in the Midlands represented new economic growth to meet rising demand. Shropshire became a major centre for metalsmiths, with specialist crafts also being established in Sheffield, Birmingham, Wolverhampton and Dudley. In the towns, master cutlers, clockmakers, silversmiths, goldsmiths and pewterers catered for rising demand from the elites and the middle social orders. Although this side of the trade was important, the real growth came from the production of cheap consumer goods and industrial items in rural industry. For example, Sheffield metalworkers were famed for their cutlery, but they also organised the production of knives, sickles, scythes, hoes, adzes and a variety of other tools in the surrounding parishes. This type of production benefited from the expansion in agriculture, transport, building and other industries. Even more significant was the rise in demand from the lower social orders for cheap tin and iron consumer goods, such as saucepans, frying pans, cups, plates, jugs, cutlery, ornaments and trinkets. By the early eighteenth century such items were on sale in small back-street shops, but were still mainly distributed by travelling pedlars.

THE PIN INDUSTRY

Possibly the best way of illustrating the significance of the expansion in rural industry is to examine the development of the pin industry. The Scottish political economist, Adam Smith, when writing *The Wealth of Nations* in 1776, selected pin making as a prime example of the industrial progress that had been made in the previous hundred years. What impressed him was not only that the industry created considerable employment, but that its manufacturing process was based on a division of labour.

Previously, in most craft trades, apart from clothmaking, an individual had been responsible for producing a completed item, whether it was a pin, a hat or a saddle. In the new pin industry one person was responsible for making the shank, another the head, and yet another for sharpening the point. These same methods were soon adopted in other industrial processes; one person made a sickle blade, another made the handle, a third person fitted them together, while a fourth person sharpened the blade. Smith considered that by greatly speeding up production methods, the division of labour was the key to Britain's industrial success in the eighteenth century.

Pins were widely used in the textile and allied trades. Pins made from iron or brass wire were produced in several places in England. However, because these individually handmade pins were poorly finished, large quantities of higher quality pins had to be imported from Holland, at a cost of some £40,000 a year by the end of the sixteenth century. In the early seventeenth century Dutch immigrants introduced the much superior process of pin manufacture by division of labour. The new technique was quickly established in various parts of the country. Pin manufacture was cheap and easy to set up and employed a large number of people. The actual manufacturing was a light and repetitive process, which could easily be carried out by children and the disabled. For these reasons, many overseers of the poor adopted it for use in parish workhouses. Production of good quality pins rose rapidly, and by the 1630s England was producing enough to supply all its own needs.

NEW HIGH-COST INDUSTRIES

A number of new industries had been introduced from the end of the sixteenth century largely as a result of techniques introduced from the Continent. Paper mills, salt evaporation plants and potteries, along with the manufacture of glass and gunpowder, were all well established by

> **KEY ISSUE**
>
> *What contribution had the rural industries made to the economy by 1714?*

1714. Although these industries helped to improve the balance of trade by reducing the need to import such goods from Europe, they did not make such a significant contribution to the economy as the rural industries. One reason for this was that the processes required a high capital outlay in buildings and equipment, and production was relatively slow and on a small scale. The other reason was that they employed only small, highly skilled workforces, and did little to lower unemployment levels. Sugar refining and tobacco manufacture were also expensive to set up, and only required skilled workers. However, their position was slightly different because they contributed to the re-export trade. By 1700 England produced all the sugar and tobacco required for home consumption, and re-exports of these commodities accounted for some 30 per cent of total exports. The success of these two industries was largely at the expense of the Dutch, whose own manufacturers were unable to compete with their English rivals.

HEAVY INDUSTRIES

The mining and metal smelting industries did not make any very significant contribution to the Stuart economy compared with rural industry. It has been proposed that there was a seventeenth-century revolution in coal production. J.U. Nef in *The Rise of the British Coal Industry* (1932), claimed that there had been a revolutionary rise of 500 per cent in coal production during the century. He suggested that the increasing use of coal as a fuel in the brewing, brick manufacturing, salt evaporation, distilling and malting industries constituted a major breakthrough for the coal industry. Later research has shown that such claims were over-optimistic, and that coal, along with the other heavy industries, made little impact on the economy until the late eighteenth century.

It is true that coal production did rise during the Stuart period, and that some advances were made to overcome the technical difficulties facing the industry. Even so, there is little evidence of any significant rise in the use of coal in industry. It is estimated that by the end of the century two-thirds of the coal produced was being used for domestic heating. Not until the industrial use of coked coal became widespread in the later eighteenth century did coal output begin to grow rapidly. Until then the high cost of maintaining, ventilating and keeping underground shafts free from flooding, estimated at £1,000 a year, deterred most mine owners from undertaking any expansion. Little interest was shown in the invention of the Savary Pump in the 1690s to replace the traditional horse-driven treadmill to remove water from mine shafts. It was not until the demand for industrial coal rose that mine owners were willing to invest the high capital outlay needed to install the more efficient Newcomen Pump. Although the transport system had improved, the cost of moving coal by road or river was still prohibitive. Consequently, even those industries that were using coal had to be located close to mining areas.

The ever-increasing need to supply London with domestic fuel was the only real major area of growth. By the 1680s shipments from the Durham and Newcastle coalfields had risen to 370,000 tons a year, and were to continue to rise steeply. This was an important contribution to the economy, and the collier fleets shipping the coal to London helped to stimulate east coast trade. However, the fact that the price of coal in London was double that in Northumberland indicates that transport costs, even by sea, were still excessively high. Having a secure market for domestic coal, and further outlets to supply the local salt evaporation plants, north-eastern mine owners were willing to invest money to overcome technical problems. By 1700 some mine shafts had already reached over 400 feet in depth.

The lack of any real economic growth in the Stuart heavy industries has been attributed to the failure to solve the problem of how to use coal instead of expensive charcoal as a fuel for smelting. The difficulty was that, although coal was cheaper, it gave off too many gases and spoilt the smelted metal. Various ways were tried to cook or coke coal in a confined space in the same way as charcoal was produced from wood, but none of them was very successful. By 1709, Abraham Darby, with a foundry at Coalbrookdale in Shropshire, was beginning to produce cast iron cooking pots using coked coal. However, the method was not widely used until later in the century. Production costs remained high and output low in the iron, lead and tin industries. Iron ceased to be worked in the Weald because of its poor quality. As other industries, particularly building, expanded, the demand for metals increased, but the English producers failed to respond. By the 1680s 18,000 tons of high-grade Swedish iron was being imported every year. Similarly, problems of flooding and lack of investment in the tin and lead industries made it cheaper to import these metals from the Continent. By the end of the century there was a considerable recession in these industries, forcing thousands to seek alternative employment.

KEY ISSUE

Why had some areas of the industrial sector failed to expand by 1714?

D *The domestic market*

To a great extent the growth in the industrial sector, apart from the heavy industries, resulted from rising demand in the domestic market. There was a strong contrast between the depressed state of the market in the first half of the century, and the buoyancy that had begun to develop after the 1650s. Much of this must be attributed to the change in the demographic trends after the 1650s when population increase came to an end and population levels fell and then stagnated. It was this deflationary situation that led to a rise in living standards throughout society, and so promoted demand through greater spending power. A related effect of this was the increased levels of agricultural output, which, by reducing the cost of food, left people with more money to spend on manufactured goods. At the same time, industrial expansion, particularly in the rural industries, reduced levels of unemployment and lowered the cost of consumer goods. This was in strong contrast with the Tudor economy, which had experienced rapid population expansion, rising food prices and widespread unemployment. This meant that the Tudor domestic market had been almost exclusively led by elite demand for luxury goods that had to be imported from abroad.

Another marked difference was in social attitudes. The Tudors thought that it would upset the balance of the social order if social inferiors copied the dress, eating habits and lifestyle of their superiors. They also considered that keeping too many servants and making an over-ostentatious display of wealth was socially disruptive. Sumptuary laws were passed throughout the sixteenth century banning ostentation, and listing what types of clothes, hats and food could be worn and eaten by each rank of society ranging from the royal family down to the poor. The Stuarts did not share this view of society and the sumptuary legislation ceased to be enforced. As a result, the upturn in the economy led to a marked increase in what was known as 'to ape one's betters'. This was particularly true after the Restoration, when society in general followed the example of the Royal Court in increasingly lavish expenditure as a reaction to the imposed austerity under the English Republic. The effect of this on the market was to lead to a rising demand for cheaper copies of a whole range of commodities such as clothes, furnishing, jewellery and ornaments. It has been suggested that this situation was beginning to create a consumer society by the end of the Stuart period.

See pages 65–6 for the Royal Court.

THE ELITES

The wealthy landed elites and pseudo gentry continued to lead the market. This was only to be expected because they had to display their genteel status by their leisured and lavish lifestyle. The elites were building or remodelling their country mansions and town houses, and laying out pleasure gardens. They were also employing a growing number of servants ranging from stewards, artists, musicians and tutors, to gardeners, grooms, wet nurses, hairdressers and kitchenmaids. Such expenditure created employment and stimulated the building trades and other rural industries. At the same time, unlike their Tudor predecessors, the landed elites invested money on their estates, on road and river improvements, in the City and the colonies. Their demand for luxury goods, such as tea, coffee, chocolate, spices, sugar, tobacco, silks and satins, helped to expand American and Far Eastern commerce. Not only did this help the re-export trade, but by increasing the volume of luxury items being imported, eventually reduced their price.

THE MIDDLE SOCIAL ORDERS

Both the affluent and lower middle social orders were increasingly modelling their lifestyles on that of the elites in as far as it was within their means. Their clothes, houses, furnishings and behaviour mirrored those of fashionable society. This generally meant that to avoid cost they had to opt for cheaper alternatives, such as fine woollens instead of silk, and pewter dinner services rather than silver. They also began to keep domestic servants. To cut overheads, these were often, like Samuel Pepys's younger, unmarried sister, Paulina, poor relations. For the same reason, young unmarried women were increasingly being employed as servants. This 'feminisation of domestic service' has been applauded by

See page 383 for Pepys's sister.

some women writers as providing a valuable source of employment for young women apart from prostitution. Other feminist writers merely see it, by emphasising that they were only fitted to do housework, as further evidence of the declining status of women. The rising demand from the middle orders for luxuries and consumer goods provided a considerable boost for the domestic industries. At the same time, by encouraging higher production, it helped to lower the price of a whole range of goods.

THE LOWER SOCIAL ORDERS

There is no doubt that the gap between the masses and even the bottom end of the middle social orders was widening rapidly. Poverty was widespread even though it was cushioned by poor relief. The masses were becoming increasingly wage dependent and at the mercy of market forces. Even so, fuller employment and rising wages were giving many of the lower orders more spending power. This was encouraged by falling prices and the production of a cheap range of consumer goods. More of them could afford to buy the tin cups, plates, pans, and cheap ornaments that were becoming available from pedlars or in back street corner shops. They were also buying the cheap cotton, fustians and serges that were being produced by the textile trades, as well as ribbons and other 'fancy' wares. While this was certainly taking place, the authorities still considered that the lower social orders preferred idleness to work. They were seen as exercising this 'leisure preference' by drinking beer and gin and smoking tobacco in the ale-houses, and by gambling at horse races and other sporting events. However, whether it was by buying cheap consumer goods, or drinking beer and gin, lower social order demand was still encouraging domestic industries.

The pattern of demand that was developing in the domestic market is known as the 'trickle down' effect. Demand at the top end of the market created greater production, which lowered prices. A new range of goods became affordable to people lower down the social scale. This increased demand and production still further, and so lowering prices and making goods available to the next level of society. It was this process that is seen as creating the consumer society that was to expand as both production and demand continued to increase during the eighteenth century.

See pages 376–7 for attitudes to the poor.

E *Conclusion*

Apart from the continued depression in the heavy industries there was considerable expansion in the industrial sector. By the end of the seventeenth century the rural industries were successfully beginning to absorb the surplus labour being released from agriculture. This was partially due to the stagnation in population levels, but there was a considerable real increase in the amount of work available outside agriculture. As elsewhere in the economy, there is no evidence of any revolutionary breakthroughs; even during the depression in the first half of the century, most industries were steadily building on the firm foundations

PICTURE 31
A broadsheet likening smokers to heathen Turks

laid down by the Tudors. This is shown by the speed with which rural industry was able to respond to the increased demand from not only the domestic market, but also the captive American colonial market. Not only was domestic industry able to supply the needs of these markets, but by increasing production levels, it progressively reduced prices. This, in turn, created more demand, which the industrial sector was successful in meeting.

Industry, particularly the rural craft trades, was probably the most significant area of growth in the economy. By the end of the Stuart period, industry was supplying most of the manufactured goods and commodities required by the domestic market. This was a major contribution to the favourable balance of trade that had been achieved by 1700. In addition, English textiles were gaining an increasing share of the Mediterranean and Levantine markets. Although English goods had not made much headway in the northern European market, they were meeting all the needs of the American and West Indian colonists. By creating employment, industry was also building up a sustained level of demand within the domestic market that continued to expand throughout the eighteenth century. This was a considerable transformation from the position at the beginning of the century when exports of unfinished cloth were failing to pay for the import of luxury goods to meet the demands of the elite led market.

8 ~ HISTORIOGRAPHICAL DEBATE: STUART WORKING WOMEN

Books about the seventeenth-century economy generally seem to make little reference to the economic role of women. This is possibly not surprising since Stuart society was becoming increasingly male dominated. The development of women's history over the last decade or so has meant that both female and male historians have begun to pay more attention to the place of women in the economy. The overall status of women at all levels of society was declining in the seventeenth century. This certainly seems to have had an impact on the contribution of lower social order women in the home and the workplace. It is suggested that as the better paid employment was increasingly taken by men, so women's economic contribution to the household fell. The husband became the 'bread winner', while the wife merely earned 'pin money'. Remember that there is a good deal of debate on this issue. Some writers think that women, especially single women, were better off because more work was available. Others consider that such changes were only just beginning in the early eighteenth century.

See pages 377–85 for the overall position of women.

Study sources A, B and C, and either discuss or prepare written answers to the following questions. You will find it helpful to read the case study on 'How the other nine-tenths lived' under section 3 of Chapter 10 (pages 392–6).

A *English Society 1580–1680* by K. Wrightson.

Urban wives of craftsmen and tradesmen were busy in the shop as well as above it. What was true of the 'middling sort' was equally true of the labouring poor. The wives of weavers working at piece rates in the cloth townships of the north, the west country and East Anglia were commonly engaged in spinning for their husbands' employers, as indeed were the wives of many agricultural labourers in these districts – in Essex female involvement in spinning for the looms of the cloth towns was widespread throughout the north and centre of the county. If no so such opportunities existed locally, then there was casual labour in weeding, haymaking and harvest time, stone picking, gleaning, washing, perhaps keeping an ale-house and many another way of earning a penny or two towards the family's subsistence. Indeed, for many of the poorest villagers and townspeople the joint endeavour of feeding, clothing and housing themselves and their children may well have dominated the marital relationship, though this is not to suggest that marriage for the poor did not have other satisfactions.

B *Women in Stuart England and America* by R. Thompson.

Not only were conditions, comparatively speaking, worse in England, but as the century progressed, the economic opportunities for women deteriorated. This is the thesis of Alice Clarke's survey, *The Working Life of Women in the Seventeenth Century* [1919]. This decrease in outlets she puts down to various causes, but the all-embracing villain to her is 'the blind force of capitalism' ... The old familial economic partnership of husband and wife was being undermined. The concept of the husband supporting his family was replacing mutuality in earning power. In becoming a dependent, the wife lost her 'psychic and moral influence'; her place might still be in the home, but her husband was no longer an integral part of it. Even in the fields which women had previously dominated, like brewing, baking, or midwifery or the retail trade, specialisation tended to squeeze them out in favour of men.

C *Women, Work, and Sexual Politics in Eighteenth Century England* by B. Hill.

In the first half of the [eighteenth] century, women seem to have worked in a wide range of trades, some of them involving work that was to later become the monopoly of men. The grounds on which they were excluded from such trades were that the work was unsuitable, unfeminine, inclining to immoral habits because it required being in close proximity to men, or that it was physically too demanding. Very rarely is there evidence of open opposition to women working at certain tasks because they were competing with men, although when apprenticeship was already in decline, the efforts of some male craftsmen may well have been partly motivated by competition from unapprenticed female labour. During the course of the century, the range of occupations open to women tended to narrow. Side by side with the 'masculinization' of some tasks and trades went the feminization of others. By the end of the century, female blacksmiths, carpenters, and coopers were becoming rarities. On the other hand, domestic service was in the process of being feminized and the importance of the so-called women's trades – milliners, mantua makers, seamstresses, and dressmakers – was growing.

The same process can be seen in housework. While there had always been certain tasks normally undertaken only by women, there had been others where men, and sometimes all members of the household, co-operated; there was no rigid sexual division of labour.

Q

1. *In source A, marriage is seen as a 'joint endeavour'. Do the wives seem to be making an equal contribution to the family income? (3 marks)*
2. *In source B, 'the blind force of capitalism' is blamed for the loss of equal opportunities for women. What does this mean, and how did it affect women at work and at home? (5 marks)*
3. *What does source C suggest was undermining the place of women in the workplace, and what is meant by the 'sexual division of labour'? (7 marks)*
4. *How do the views expressed in these three extracts agree or differ about the problems facing working women? (10 marks)*

9 ⌐ GENERAL CONCLUSION: ECONOMIC EXPANSION?

The suggestions that there were revolutionary developments in Stuart agriculture and industry have now been largely discounted. Change in the Stuart economy is now thought to have been much slower and more evolutionary. Similarly, the economic impact of the English Civil War is now regarded as less dynamic than once thought. This does not mean that it did not have an effect on attitudes to such things as monopolies and overseas trade. However, it is widely agreed that the economic recovery in the second half of the seventeenth century can be more readily explained in terms of the slowdown in population growth, along with changes in social and governmental attitudes.

Certainly it is safe to say that the economy was in a better state in 1714 than it had been in 1603. This does not mean that the Stuart economy was not still very similar to its sixteenth-century counterpart. Most areas of the economy that were beginning to expand by 1700 had developed out of Tudor initiatives. Even the successful establishment of American and Caribbean colonies owed much to the exploration and pioneering of sea routes carried out under the Tudors. All the techniques and crops used by the Stuart landowners and farmers were in use in the previous century. It had been the Tudor use of patents to attract skilled workers from the Continent that had begun the expansion of rural industry. The programme of road and river improvement and of bridge building had been under way for most of the sixteenth century. As early as 1580 Elizabeth I had been considering establishing a bank in London. While this illustrates the evolutionary nature of the economic change taking place, it does not explain the faster rate of development after the 1650s.

This must be attributed to the period of deflation, and to the new patterns of demand. After the 1650s landowners and other producers could no longer rely on inflation providing a constant source of demand. This meant that they had to invest some of the easy profits made during the inflationary period into modernising their businesses to improve output and so lower prices. They also had to invest in road and river improvements in order to meet the growing demand from London and the other urban markets. Private and governmental investment was also needed to protect and supply the growing colonial population. This, in turn, required improvements in the banking and other financial institutions to ensure that money supply flowed more easily. The great problem with the Tudor economy had been lack of investment, so this marks a significant difference between the Tudor and late Stuart economies.

Another marked difference was the slackening in population pressure, which eased the problems of food shortages, poverty and unemployment, and reduced social tensions. This led to changes in social and governmental attitudes. The masses were no longer seen as a threat, whose duty it was to be usefully employed in producing food. The relaxing of regulations on apprenticeships made it easier for people to seek and to find work in industry and other occupations. The removal of restrictive monopolies helped this process still further. It was such changes, and a fall in the number of young adolescents seeking work, that helped to absorb much of the surplus workforce by 1714. It was the changed outlook towards both investment and the redeployment of manpower that was important in maintaining the larger armies and navies to fight the wars against Holland and France. Without this considerable expenditure England would not have gained the naval supremacy that enabled the enforcement of the Navigation Acts. Even if the Stuart economy was not as dynamic as it was once claimed to be, it had certainly expanded. The agricultural and industrial sectors were able to meet the needs of the domestic market without relying on continental imports. Moreover, domestic industries fully supplied the rapidly growing colonial market. By 1714 commercial supremacy had been secured over the world trade routes, and the balance of trade was steadily becoming more favourable. These were considerable achievements for a pre-industrial economy.

10 ∽ CONTRASTING ECONOMIES: SCOTLAND AND IRELAND

The Scottish and Irish economies did not begin to expand until the end of the Stuart period. The reason for this striking contrast with the English economy was political as well as economic.

Scotland had not merged with England when James VI became the King of England in 1603, and it was not until the Act of Union in 1707 that the two countries were united. Since the late sixteenth century, Ireland had become regarded as a colonial settlement. It was only after William III had established firm military control and the Protestant Ascendancy in the 1690s that links with England became stronger. Until these changes had taken place, both Scotland and Ireland had remained politically and religiously divided and strongly resentful of intervention from England (see Chapter 12). Another cause of friction was that neither country was allowed free access to the English market. Not only did this mean that they were restricted in exporting goods to England, but that they were also largely excluded from the expanding colonial market. Consequently, neither the Scottish, nor the Irish economies benefited from the expansion of the English economy until the eighteenth century.

Another reason for the lack of economic progress in Scotland and Ireland was that, unlike England, both countries still had peasant subsistence economies similar to those on the Continent. The age of marriage was in the late teens or early twenties, so that unlike England there were rapid fluctuations in population levels. Demographic growth frequently outstripped food production and both countries were subject to famines and 'malthusian crises'. By 1714 each country had a population of some one million people. Most of the people were small-scale, general farmers, so there was very little market demand and production levels remained low. Industry continued to be organised on a guild and cottage basis producing goods mainly for sale locally. Apart from Edinburgh and Dublin, Scottish and Irish towns were small and showed no sign of expansion, so there was no strong urban market to encourage higher agricultural production. In any case, a lack of good road and river communications made the transport of goods difficult. In these circumstances the dominant landowners had little incentive to spend money, either to improve their estates, or to invest in any other part of the economy.

SCOTLAND

Agriculturally, Scotland was divided into two regions: the Highlands in the north and west and the Lowlands in the south and east. In the Highland zone, self-sufficient crofters eked a precarious living from their small farms, livestock and fishing. The richer lands of the Lowlands were dominated by the semi-feudal landowners, who lived off the rents of their smallholders. It was not until the Scots gained access to the English food markets that the Lowland landowners began to introduce enclosure, and the new farming techniques developed in England. At the same time the Highlanders started to specialise in raising cattle, which were driven south to sell in England. Progress was slow because it was not until the middle of the eighteenth century that any real attempts were made to build roads and bridges. Even in the late eighteenth century, travellers wishing to cross the river Yarrow near Selkirk had to sit on the shoulders of a ferryman on stilts, who carried their luggage in his teeth.

See pages 5–6 and 423 for Scotland in 1603.

Industry and commerce were equally backward. No attempt was made to exploit the Scottish coal and iron reserves until the late eighteenth century. The widespread woollen textile industry remained very localised, although the Edinburgh textile trades had a wider distribution in the Lowlands. The Scottish linen and cotton industries only began to develop after greater investment was introduced from England. After 1707, Glasgow became an important centre for importing and processing tobacco and sugar, and slave trading. Edinburgh, although losing its political power, became the major cultural and academic centre for Scotland during the eighteenth century.

Possibly the best example of Scotland's economic isolation before 1707 is the Darien Scheme. In 1695, a plan to set up a Scottish company to trade with the West Indies, Africa and the East Indies was approved by the Scottish Parliament and endorsed by William III. The proposal immediately aroused opposition in London from the East India Company and other City interests who regarded it as an infringement of their trading monopoly. The Dutch were equally antagonistic since they saw it as a threat to their East Indian trade. Worse was to follow when it leaked out that the Scots also intended to establish a colony at Darien on the Isthmus of Panama. This infuriated Spain, who owned the Isthmus of Panama, and its ally, France. Increasing pressure was put on William III to disown the scheme. To avoid the threat of war, William III withdrew his approval and forbade any financial investment from England. The Scots were determined to continue with their project. Two fleets were fitted out to transport colonists to Darien, but the whole undertaking was undermined by lack of funds, and poor planning and leadership. The first group of colonists landed in 1698 and established a fort and a base at Darien. However, they had used up virtually all their supplies, and the English government had issued orders that the American colonies were not to sell them provisions. In 1699, starving and faced by a strong Spanish army, the colonists were forced to abandon Darien before the second group of colonists arrived. The second expedition, finding the site deserted, had similar difficulties and were finally allowed to withdraw by the Spanish military commander. Of the 1,500 colonists who set out, only 180 survived.

See page 433 for the political implications of the Darien Scheme.

IRELAND

During the seventeenth century, large areas of the best farming land in Ulster and Munster were confiscated from Catholic Irish landowners and given to English and Scottish Protestant settlers. These new landowners gradually dispossessed their Irish tenants and rented out farms to English and Scottish emigrants. They improved the land and introduced new techniques from England. It was from these areas that an increasing amount of timber, meat and dairy produce was exported to England. Elsewhere, particularly in the poorer agricultural regions such as Connacht in the west, traditional small-scale, general farming continued to be practised. Native Irish landlords were poor by English standards and relied on rents as their sole source of income. As the population rose during the seventeenth century, native tenant farms became progressively smaller as they were divided up between all the sons of a family. Consequently, the bulk of the population became steadily poorer, and were frequently reduced to starvation in poor harvest years. This situation only started to improve slowly during the eighteenth century as more landlords began to improve their land in order to profit from exporting foodstuffs to England. At the same time, Dublin's increasing status as a political and cultural centre led to

See pages 413–14 for Ireland in 1603 and pages 418–19 for Ireland during the Interregnum.

improvements in the surrounding road and river systems. This, in turn, meant that goods could be transported more easily.

The major industry in Ireland was the manufacture of woollen and linen textiles. This was largely a cottage-based industry since the rural population needed to supplement their meagre living standards by spinning and weaving. For a brief spell in the 1690s there was considerable demand for Irish woollens and linens in England. However, the rise in cheap Irish imports worried the English textile producers, who eventually persuaded the government to impose steadily increasing restrictions on Irish exports. The main consequence of this was that by the early eighteenth century Ireland was producing large quantities of woollen and linen thread for the English textile manufacturers. By the end of the Stuart period Ireland was continuing to export meat and other agricultural produce to England through the ports of Dublin, Cork and Wexford. At the same time, foodstuffs and some textiles were being sent to the colonial markets.

11 ⌁ BIBLIOGRAPHY

The following books provide contrasting views and interpretations of the Stuart economy and its place in the world economy, and illustrate how these have changed over the last two decades.

Economic Expansion and Social Change by C.G.A. Clay (CUP, 1984); *The Economy of England 1450–1750* by C. Coleman (OUP, 1977); *London and the English Economy 1500–1700* by F. Fisher (Hambledon, 1988); *Stuart Economy and Society* by N. Heard (Hodder and Stoughton, Access to History series, 1995); *A Century of Revolution*, second edition by C. Hill (Nelson, 1980); *The Population History of Britain and Ireland 1500–1750* by R.A. Houston (Macmillan, 1992); *Women in English Society 1500–1800* by M. Prior (ed) (Methuen, 1985); *Economic Policy and Projects* by J. Thirsk (Clarendon Press, 1987); *Creating a World Economy: Merchant Capital, Colonialism and World Trade, 1400–1825* by A.K. Smith (Westview Press, 1991); and *The Modern World System*, Vols 1 and 2 by I. Wallerstein (Academic Press, 1974).

C. Hill makes a popular and lively, old-style Marxist defence of the revolutionary nature of the century, while D.C. Coleman presents what is still a very orthodox account of the economy.

12 ⌁ DISCUSSION POINTS AND ESSAY QUESTIONS

A *This section consists of questions that might be used for discussion (or written answers) to test your knowledge of the chapter and to help with your note-taking.*

1. Why and how might deflation after 1650 have helped to raise living standards among the masses?
2. 'Enclosure was the main means of improving agricultural output.' Discuss.
3. Did the economy benefit from the release of labour from agriculture?
4. How did the growth of London help to create a national market?
5. Assess the significance of the creation of the Bank of England.
6. Why was the improvement of road and river communications so important?
7. What part did the Navigation Acts play in enabling England to achieve commercial supremacy by 1714?
8. 'The American colonies made the most significant contribution to England's favourable balance of trade by 1700.' Comment.
9. To what extent can it be said that rural industry made the major contribution to industrial growth?
10. Why had demand in the domestic market grown by 1714?

B *Essay questions.*
1. How significant was the period of deflation between 1650 and 1714 in creating demand in the economy?
2. 'The expansion of overseas trade was the most significant factor in creating growth in the Stuart economy.' Discuss.
3. Assess the significance of a national market in promoting economic expansion.
4. 'There had been a significant improvement in the living standards of the masses by 1714.' Comment.
5. Is it true to say that improved agricultural output was the most important economic advance in Stuart England?

13 ∽ ANSWERING SIGNIFICANCE ESSAY QUESTIONS

Examiners often set significance questions in order to test your ability to organise your material and to put forward balanced arguments for and against a particular factor or event being significant. This means that you must not try to answer such questions by writing a narrative type of essay just describing what happened. Nor is it advisable to agree too readily with the statement. This is particularly true when something is described as being the most important or significant cause of a series of events. In this case the examiner is often expecting you to argue against the suggestion that it was the most important factor. The five essay questions in the previous section are all examples of the significance question, and in all of them there is a good case to be made for and against the statement made in the question. The secret of answering these questions is to organise your essay so that you give an equal balance to both sides of the argument.

The best way to do this is to divide your essay into four parts: an introduction; the case for the statement; the case against the statement; and a conclusion.

When answering question 5 in the previous section, your opening paragraph should explain how agricultural output had improved by 1714. Remember that you are not explaining why output had improved, so there is no need to discuss such things as enclosure, specialisation or new crops. You need to make the point that unlike the beginning of the century farmers were producing food surpluses from less land with a smaller workforce. This led to such things as no local famines, lower food prices, London and other town markets being fully supplied, fewer people working in farming, more industrial crops being grown, and grain being exported to the Continent.

Your next section should show how this significantly helped the economy. This means that you need to write paragraphs on such points as lower food prices raising living standards, not having to import grain helping the balance of payments, increased food supply enabling town populations to grow, industrial crops providing raw material for industry, enclosure creating more employment, or landowners investing in overseas trade and road improvements.

The third section should discuss all those things that you consider were making an equal or greater contribution to the economy such as overseas trade, rural industry, improved communications, banking, the colonies, the end of population growth, the growth of London, or new towns. Remember that your arguments both for or against are generally interconnected, and that they all tend to have an effect on each other.

In the conclusion weigh up the arguments that you have made for or against the statement, and then decide whether increased agricultural output was more significant, just as significant, or less significant than other causes of economic growth.

14 ∽ DOCUMENTARY EXERCISE ON THE LABOURING POOR

1. There is in England more labour than hands to perform it, and consequently a want of people, not of employment.
2. No man in England, of sound limbs and senses, can be poor merely for want of work.

The poverty and exigence of the poor in England is plainly derived from one of these two particular causes,

Casualty or Crime

By Casualty, I mean sickness of families, loss of limbs or sight, and any natural or accidental, impotence as to labour. The crimes of our people, and from whence their poverty derives, as the visible and direct fountains are:

1. Luxury
2. Sloth
3. Pride

This is so apparent in every place, that I think it needs no explication; that English labouring people eat and drink, but especially the latter, three times as much in value as any sort of foreigner of the same dimensions of the world.

There is a general taint of slothfulness upon our poor, there is nothing more frequent, than for an Englishman to work till he has got his pocket full of money, and then go to and be idle, or perhaps drunk, till it is all gone, and perhaps he himself in debt; and ask him in his cups what he intends, he will tell you honestly, he will drink as long as it lasts, and then go to work for more.

From *Giving Alms No Charity* by Daniel Defoe (1704).

Q

1. *Which section of the labouring poor does Defoe think deserve charity? (3 marks)*
2. *Why does Defoe think that the able-bodied remained poor? (5 marks)*
3. *How does the extract suggest that there was more employment to be found in 1704 than earlier in the Stuart period? (5 marks)*
4. *How far do you think that the opinions expressed in these three extracts give a genuine picture of the life of the labouring poor? (10)*
5. *How does this extract fit in with historians' views of the working lives of women? (10 marks)*

9 Church, State and Individual

INTRODUCTION

Historians differ in their judgements on whether the seventeenth century produced a political revolution, and of what kind. Political revolution is often defined in terms of the relationship between king and Parliament, or between the different components of the United Kingdom. There is, however, a third area that requires examination, which is the nature of the relationship between the government and the governed. This can best be defined as the relationship between the State and the individual. By the word 'State', we mean more than a particular government – it includes the permanent apparatus and institutions that enable a government to exercise power. By the word 'individual' we do not mean a particular person, but *all* particular persons, whatever their precise views and circumstances. The issue therefore addresses primarily the aims and purposes of government, what it is assumed to exist for, and how much of an individual's life it should try to control.

These questions are still hotly debated today, but the debate tends to be in economic and social terms: how far is the State responsible for the welfare of citizens in terms of their health, diet, housing and employment prospects, and how far should it control them? In the seventeenth century such issues were regarded as much less important (or controllable) than the matter of spiritual welfare. For a conscientious king such as Charles I, a primary duty was to care and provide for the well-being of his subjects' souls. Not only did he and his predecessors claim to rule by Divine Right, they also believed that the State had a divine purpose. By taking control of the Church in the 1530s, Henry VIII had strengthened and extended a much longer tradition of Christian monarchy. A monarch was expected to provide for the defence of the kingdom, the enforcement of law and order within it, and the safety of his subjects in this world and the next. Political loyalty and religious conformity were inseparable. The Church taught that rebellion was a sin and upheld the existing hierarchy, while the monarch carried the responsibility of ensuring that the organisation and doctrines of the Church supported the queen's or king's subjects in their search for God and salvation. Having laid down the necessary rules, it was the monarch's duty to ensure that they were obeyed. This responsibility created divisions and differences that contributed greatly to the political crisis of the seventeenth century, but neither a monarch's conscience nor his critics would have allowed him to ignore or evade it.

KEY ISSUE

The seventeenth-century State controlled the individual's spiritual life.

By 1714, George I had neither the desire nor the capacity to make such claims. Early eighteenth-century government dealt with law and order, peace and war, and had even taken a new interest in promoting the well-being of the economy, but increasingly, a man's soul was regarded as his own responsibility. The Church still enjoyed a privileged position, but attendance was no longer compulsory and the existence of separate and independent religious groups and denominations was accepted. Religious pluralism of this kind was a matter of political debate and political convenience, but it reflected a different perception of religion in society, and a very different perception of what the role of government should be. It could be argued, therefore, that the most revolutionary changes produced by the seventeenth century lay with the development of a secular (non-religious) State, and the extension of personal freedom accorded to the individuals within it.

How had such changes come about? They did not result from any single event or dominant influence, but from a combination of events and ideas that evolved through the sixteenth and seventeenth centuries to produce results that were unintended and unforeseen. Diagram 11 on page 338 outlines the process of development. The chapter that follows provides a more detailed analysis of the factors that produced this change, and how they interacted.

KEY ISSUE

By 1714, the State was no longer responsible for the individual's spiritual welfare.

1 ⌐ THE CONFESSIONAL STATE AND ITS SUPPORTERS, 1603–46

A *The role of the Church*

A 'confessional state' is one in which the government establishes a national religious faith, and regards the enforcement of it as one of the primary duties of government. In this situation, religion is a means of providing unity and a bond between governors and governed. It influences and defines both political and social relationships, and determines both rights and responsibilities. The head of State bears both the authority and duties of God's deputy on earth. In seventeenth-century England, these assumptions were expressed in practice through the functions of the Church of England.

The Church served to reinforce the authority of government, but its influence went much further than preaching the duty of obedience. In the words of Derek Hirst, it was 'a social and political cement' used to 'bind together the community'. Stress laid on the fifth commandment in preaching and prayer enjoined the duty to 'honour thy father and thy mother', establishing a duty of obedience to authority and a climate of respect for elders. Therefore, obedience to a king, as the father of the nation, was mirrored in the authority of fathers within the family and masters or employers within the community. Unity was created by a

KEY ISSUE

The Church buttressed authority in a hierarchical society.

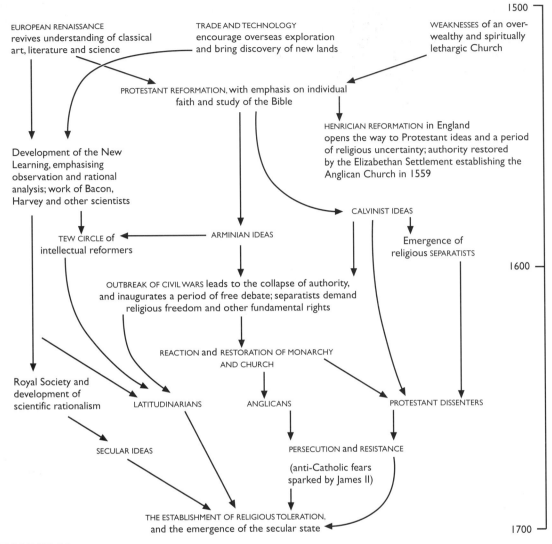

1500

EUROPEAN RENAISSANCE
revives understanding of classical
art, literature and science

TRADE AND TECHNOLOGY
encourage overseas exploration
and bring discovery of new lands

WEAKNESSES of an over-
wealthy and spiritually
lethargic Church

PROTESTANT REFORMATION, with emphasis on individual
faith and study of the Bible

Development of the New
Learning, emphasising
observation and rational
analysis; work of Bacon,
Harvey and other scientists

HENRICIAN REFORMATION in England
opens the way to Protestant ideas and a period
of religious uncertainty; authority restored
by the Elizabethan Settlement establishing the
Anglican Church in 1559

CALVINIST IDEAS

TEW CIRCLE of
intellectual reformers

ARMINIAN IDEAS

Emergence of
religious SEPARATISTS

1600

OUTBREAK OF CIVIL WARS leads to the collapse of authority,
and inaugurates a period of free debate; separatists demand
religious freedom and other fundamental rights

Royal Society and
development of
scientific rationalism

REACTION and RESTORATION OF MONARCHY
AND CHURCH

LATITUDINARIANS

ANGLICANS

PROTESTANT DISSENTERS

SECULAR IDEAS

PERSECUTION and RESISTANCE

(anti-Catholic fears
sparked by James II)

THE ESTABLISHMENT OF RELIGIOUS TOLERATION,
and the emergence of the secular state

1700

DIAGRAM 11

*The development of religious
toleration*

See pages 20–5 for the
general context of the
Church's role.

series of overlapping hierarchies linking family, community and government, based on a single, divinely ordained principle.

This sense of communal identity was also expressed by the Church in a number of practical ways. The parish church was both the social and administrative centre of many towns and villages. It was often the largest building, and could be used for communal activities. Many contained a 'village chest' in which parishioners could store their valuables; prudently, these chests had two locks and required two keys to open them, usually kept by two different people. In most parishes the great religious festivals were marked by a communion service, which virtually all parishioners attended, reinforcing communal identity through corporate worship. Parish officials – constables, churchwardens and overseers of the poor – carried out many aspects of local government.

A king's responsibility for the souls of his subjects was also expressed through the work of the Church courts, whose authority extended to the laity in many matters. The prerogative Court of High Commission dealt with serious matters, but issues such as adultery, drunkenness and disputes between neighbours were brought before the local Church courts. Known as the 'bawdy courts', they were sometimes accused of unnecessary interference, but they often played a useful part in maintaining social harmony. Their sanctions were usually intended to reform rather than punish, and their contribution to social discipline and order was significant; they provided one practical way in which government could influence manners and morality. Source A provides some examples of the kind of cases that they dealt with.

See pages 392–6 for the bawdy courts in action.

A Church court records

Case 1 (1592)
William Hills of Sandon was reported to be a very lewd and uncharitable man with his wife, [having] used her most ungodly, not only by refusing her company, but also by beating her most cruelly ... Hills came and confessed that, upon occasion that his wife had beated and misused his sister and some fatherless children, whom he keepeth in his house, he gave her eight strokes with a wand; for which he is sorry for now, and promiseth never to use himself in the like sort hereafter.

Case 2 (1598)
Upon Sunday before Michaelmas in time of afternoon service, William Haynes of Southbemfleet was dancing with minstrels on a green by Thomas Harris his house.

Case 3 (1599)
Thomas Ward, of Purleigh, 'was presented as by report, to seek help at a sorcerer's hands. Confessed that, having lost certain cattle ... he went to one Taylor in Thaxted, a wizard, to know whether they were bewitched, and to have his help.

Case 4 (1600)
William Wallis and wife of Stanford Rivers reported for that they have made their habitation in the south porch of the parish church; and therewithal he doth not otherwise provide, but suffereth his wife to travail in childbirth therein, and to continue there her whole month.

Case 5 (1600)
Thomas Perrin of Rayleigh reported for a common drunkard and railer and chider, to the grief of the Godly and great danger of his soul.

The Church was therefore essential to the good order of both government and society. It expressed and reinforced royal authority, buttressed both communal identity and political loyalty, and enabled the individual soul to find God. It enhanced social order and personal morality for the benefit of both the State and the individual. Its functions demonstrated both the powers and responsibilities of a Christian monarchy, and these functions could only be fulfilled by a single, national and compulsory institution. What divided most men between 1603 and 1640, was not whether such an institution should exist, but how the existing Church could best meet these requirements.

B *The problems of the Church*

KEY ISSUE

The poverty, ignorance and inadequacy of the Anglican clergy.

See pages 69–72 for the Church's problems in the political context.

In 1603, the Church of England faced significant problems. The Reformation of the 1530s had entailed a massive transfer of wealth and property from the Church to the laity, and the situation had been made worse by Queen Elizabeth's habit of leaving some dioceses vacant for considerable periods in order to enjoy their revenues before appointing the next bishop. Difficulties stemmed from three overlapping problems: the need for an effective and educated clergy; the poverty and inequality of clerical livings; and the control of appointments to many of them.

The qualities required to make an effective minister had changed with the advent of Protestant beliefs. In the pre-Reformation Church the role of parish priests had been mainly to hear confessions and administer sacraments and ceremonies laid down by the Church. Provided that they could recite the set forms effectively, they were able to perform adequately even without extensive theological knowledge. The Protestant religion, with its emphasis on preaching, teaching and explanation of the Bible, created much greater demands, and required an educated ministry. In 1600, however, fewer than half of the clergy had university degrees.

This problem was compounded by the economic difficulties of a Church whose wealth had been plundered by successive monarchs. The medieval Church had possessed great wealth, but much of it was in the hands of the monasteries, and had passed to the Crown with their dissolution. In 1584, Archbishop Whitgift had calculated that only 600 livings out of the 9,000 parishes in England carried sufficient salary to support a minister and his family in any degree of comfort. While this may have been an exaggeration, it is clear that clerical incomes varied widely. Where a living included the possession of 'glebe' land attached to the parish church, and the right to the 'great' tithes levied on arable land and produce, its holder could live in some comfort. Where this was not the case, livings were often inadequate, and ministers were forced to find some method of earning an income, or to hold more than one living (pluralism) with an inevitable effect on their availability to parishioners.

The problem of inadequate provision was made worse by the varying size of parishes. Some town parishes had been established at a time when population distribution was very different to that of the seventeenth century. Sheffield, for example, was a town of several thousand people, with one parish church. Colchester had eight parishes, capable of supporting only two ministers. The sizeable port of Hull lay technically within the parish of Hessle, less than half its size; the vicar of Hessle employed a curate to serve in the church of Holy Trinity, Hull, which was considerably larger than the parish church in Hessle itself. Outside the towns, much depended on the nature of the area. Many 'fielden' parishes (in arable farming areas) were well catered for, but in the more remote 'forest' areas parishes were often impossibly large and the people's spiritual welfare was neglected. The inhabitants of the Forest of Dean were renowned for irreligious behaviour, while other areas such as the Weald of Kent became centres of radical dissent. The parish of Whalley in Lancashire covered 180 square miles, forty townships and over 10,000 people; in the same county there were 51 curates earning less than £15 a year.

KEY ISSUE

The vast size of some parishes.

Successive Archbishops were well aware of these problems, and sought to deal with them, but there were complications that went beyond limited resources. In 1604, Archbishop Bancroft put forward an ambitious scheme for reform, which had the support of the King. It failed because it involved taking control of large numbers of parishes that were effectively in the hands of laymen, and this was regarded as an attack on their property rights. The monasteries had controlled around 45 per cent of English parishes before 1536, and these had passed into the hands of those who acquired the monastery lands. In some cases the patron had the right of 'advowson' (the right to choose the minister), while others had been 'impropriated' so that the patron had the right to collect tithes and pay the minister a salary. These rights were not necessarily abused (many lay patrons nominated and supported good preaching ministers), but it did make the task of reform more complex and infinitely more difficult to carry out.

C Reformation in Church and society

In spite of these difficulties, a great deal of progress was made. In 1604, King James was concerned to control Puritan ambitions, and encouraged Bancroft to enforce uniformity, but by 1611, when he appointed George Abbot to succeed him, he had realised the value of accommodation and partnership. The difficulty of defining 'Puritans' has been discussed in Chapter 2 (see page 21), but their role in strengthening the Church is easier to describe. Two Puritan characteristics – a concern to support good preaching and to promote a 'reformation of manners' – worked particularly strongly to benefit the Church and its functions within a confessional state. Puritan gentry were often generous patrons, willing to supplement the salaries of local clergy and employ young ministers within their households. In east Yorkshire, for example, the Stricklands of Boynton, near Bridlington, maintained the living of Boynton, supported a curate at Sewerby and supplemented the salaries of the vicar and curates in Bridlington itself. In the 1630s, Lady Dorothy Norcliffe gave £20 a year to each of eight different ministers in the East Riding. These examples could be replicated in almost all parts of England.

KEY ISSUE

Reforms achieved by idealistic individuals, especially Puritans.

Similar activities were undertaken by borough authorities, who paid ministers and endowed weekday lectures to supplement Sunday preaching. In Hull, the curate of Holy Trinity was paid a salary by the Mayor and Aldermen for preaching on Wednesdays as well as alternate Sundays, and given charge of the town almshouse, the Charterhouse, in order to provide accommodation and an extra income. Wealthy merchants were another source of patronage, especially if they were established in the great London companies. Many, such as Leonard Chamberlain of Hull, made generous provision for their home district. Chamberlain endowed a lecture in Howden, where he was born, provided an annual grant for the poor, and paid an extra pension for the curate of St Mary's in Beverley to visit the area and preach.

Not all such gifts and endowments came from known 'Puritans', but the Puritan emphasis on preaching and the need to encourage godly behaviour provided a powerful stimulus towards making this provision. Leading Puritans, such as William Perkins, published guides to a plain, accessible style of preaching in order to ensure that the word of God reached all levels of society, and sought especially to encourage young ministers to take the crusade into the 'darkest' and most remote areas. The work of the Feoffees, who bought up impropriations and endowed preaching ministers, has been described in Chapter 2. While the King was prepared to allow such efforts to continue, the Church could harness this individual enthusiasm to the needs of the confessional state.

A great deal was achieved by these efforts. By 1640 the proportion of the parish clergy who held university degrees had risen to around 75 per cent and preaching of reasonable quality was available in most areas. Unfortunately, from the point of view of those in authority, the process of reforming society through preaching the word of God involved significant disadvantages. Sources B and C explain the results from different viewpoints.

See page 24 for Feoffees.

KEY ISSUE

Those in authority were worried about maintaining control.

B From *History of the Great Rebellion* by Clarendon, explaining the distribution of support in 1642.

Training as volunteers for parliament began ... only in those corporations and by those inferior people who were notorious for faction and schism in religion ... The people generally (except in great towns and corporations where, besides the natural malignity, the factious lecturers ... had poisoned the affections) and especially those of quality were loyally inclined ...

Q *To what extent does Hirst agree with Clarendon's arguments and explanations?*

C From *Authority and Conflict* by Derek Hirst (1987).

The gradual dispersal throughout England of ministers capable of preaching the Word had at last, by the eve of the civil war, seemed to make a practical possibility of the early Reformers' dream of rendering England a fully protestant nation. Indeed, one of the most important features of the early-modern period was the attempt to persuade the whole population to internalise and apply to itself the teachings of the Reformation. The pre-civil war church was thus a missionary church, as well as a political arm. It aimed not merely to preach Christianity to an unschooled peasantry, but also to extract an intense protestant response from the individual.

The problem lay in this intense individual response. Preaching and Bible reading encouraged souls to find God and improved the behaviour of individuals in society, but might also involve a level of individual opinion and independent thought that was unacceptable to those in authority. The confessional state required obedience and uniformity as well as high moral standards. The path to God had to be the one chosen by the monarch.

See pages 23–5 for James I's Church

While James I lived, a level of compromise contained these tensions. James accepted the role of lay patrons and was prepared to allow ministers a measure of freedom in their preaching, within a broad framework of authority. In the name of Christian unity, valued and respected by all, the majority of ministers were prepared to demonstrate their obedience and respect for the national establishment. The great defender of the Anglican Church, Richard Hooker, had argued that few issues of Church government and ceremonial involved matters that were essential for salvation, and most could therefore be left to the monarch to decide. As long as they were permitted to pursue the essential work of spreading the word of God, many ministers were able to accept this for much of the time. In 1625, however, England came under the control of a monarch with a different and more dynamic view of the confessional state, and of his own duties within it.

KEY ISSUE

Compromise achieved by James I.

D *The influence of Charles I*

Between 1625 and 1640 Charles I embarked on a programme of reform in Church and State, which alienated a significant section of the political community. Although the measures were mainly enacted by William Laud as Archbishop of Canterbury, there is no doubt that the programme was initiated and supervised by Charles himself. Indeed, some historians have suggested that by 1637 the pace of reform was moving more quickly than Laud himself considered wise, and reflected the growing influence of Charles's private chaplain, Matthew Wren. It is clear that Charles planned to create uniformity in religion across three kingdoms, based on a Church that emphasised ritual and sacraments rather than preaching; order and beauty rather than religious passion; and communal rather than individual worship.

KEY ISSUE

Compromise upset by Charles I and by Laud.

This process and the policies involved have been outlined in Chapter 3, but if the outcome is to be fully understood, the measures adopted and the opposition that was generated need to be carefully analysed. Historians have often labelled as 'Puritan' those who objected to the Laudian reforms of the 1630s, but the reality is more complex than this. When the issues were fully aired in the Long Parliament in 1640–1, it became clear that the focus of complaint varied considerably among

See pages 69–72 for the political consequences of Charles's Church policies.

different groups of MPs. Having obstructed Charles and defeated Laud,
the opposition proved unable to agree on an acceptable alternative.
Nevertheless, the reforms sponsored by Charles and the methods used
to enforce them created an alliance of opposition groups that was
strong enough to ensure his failure. By alienating different groups at
different levels, he became a common enemy whose downfall took priority over any differences between their own schemes and plans.

'Puritan' reformers favoured a Church organised on Presbyterian
lines, as in Scotland. Few wished to see an exact replica of the Scottish
model; it was the central role accorded to a preaching minister in each
parish and his ability to maintain discipline among his parishioners that
was most important. By the work of these ministers, the Puritan
reformers hoped to bring souls to God and create a 'reformation of
manners', as the twin pillars of the godly society. Such men were alienated by most of the Laudian programme. The emphasis on ceremonies
preserved elements of popish idolatry, which distracted people from the
word of God, the restrictions on preaching prevented them from
acquiring knowledge and understanding, and the rejection of predestination threatened the distinctively Protestant identity shared with
European churches. The key objective for these men was not to reduce
the authority of the Church, nor to change its role in the confessional
state. What they sought was a reformed version, more suited to the
godly state and society that they wanted to create in England.

The views of Puritan reformers were intensified by the millenarian
mood of the time and the events taking place in Europe. Millenarianism, the belief that Christ would return to earth in person and reign for
a thousand years was shared by most Protestants, including men of
'science' such as Sir Isaac Newton who tried to use mathematical principles to estimate when this would take place. The evidence for this
kingdom of God on earth was to be found in the Bible, which depicted
history as a continuing struggle between good and evil ending in a great
battle, which would bring about the collapse of earthly kingdoms. It was
not difficult for enthusiastic souls to identify the late medieval age, with
its wars and visitations of the plague, as the beginning of such a collapse, and to see the Protestant Reformation, the religious wars that followed, and the contemporary Thirty Years War in Europe, as its final
stage. These arguments added urgency to the task of the Puritan
reformers in England. As the largest of the Protestant powers, it was
England's duty and destiny to lead the forces of God and ensure their
triumph over evil. Instead, Charles was undermining the Protestant
faith within England, and, willingly or otherwise, helping the forces of
evil. Although many English Protestants did not share the more
extreme millenarian perceptions or the desire for Presbyterian reform,
the fear of Catholicism was widespread. The experience of persecution
under Mary Tudor, the Protestant propaganda of Foxe's *Book of
Martyrs*, and the threat of Catholic and Spanish invasion in the reign of
Elizabeth had created an unshakeable belief in Catholic tyranny and a
conspiracy led by the Catholic Church to destroy Protestant England.
Therefore, many who cared little for the finer points of theology or the

precise role allotted to bishops were very sure that a clearly and defin-
ably Protestant Church of England was essential to their religious and
political security.

This combination of beliefs allowed the Puritan reformers to appeal
to a significant section of the political community, and to be convinced
that they could organise the rejection of Charles's vision of the Church
in favour of their own.

Others, however, were alienated less by the changes that had been
made in the Church than by the manner of their making and the wider
political role of the bishops. It is difficult to gauge the extent of support
for the Anglican model of the Church, but there is no doubt that it
existed. The work of Richard Hooker had established the theoretical
justification for the Elizabethan settlement and the claim that the
Anglican Church represented the best of ancient Christianity, stripped
of the corruption and unnecessary ceremonies introduced by Rome.
The Anglican Church represented tradition and purity, both valued in
equal measure by the seventeenth-century mind. It is also clear that
usage and familiarity had created a place in popular affections for the
services and sacraments laid out in the Prayer Book. The continued use
of the book in many places during the Civil War, when it had been forbidden by Parliament, is evidence of its popularity. According to
Clarendon, in Cornwall, the existing Church and especially 'that part of
the Church as concerned the liturgy, or Book of Common Prayer ...
was a most general object of veneration with the people. And the jealousy and apprehension that the other party intended to alter it was a
principal advancement of the King's service' during the years of civil
war.

For those who accepted or preferred the Anglican model to any
Puritan alternative, the offensive elements in Charles's vision of the
Church related to the role and pretensions of the Laudian bishops.
There were three main sources of complaint, apart from the general
dislike of the Arminian reforms and the extent to which they were
enforced. The first was the claim that bishops received their spiritual
authority from Christ Himself, and were therefore above human law in
that capacity. This doctrine, known as Apostolic Approbation, held that
Jesus had entrusted the care of his Church to Peter the Apostle (disci-
ple) who had, in turn, handed on his power to the early popes, and to
the bishops that they ordained. Although the temporal power of
bishops (the power to enforce rules) came from the King, their spiritual
authority was held independently through the pre-Reformation
Church. Not only did this claim indicate a measure of spiritual
pride and stress the existence of a separate clerical order in society, it
also emphasised the common heritage of the English and Roman
Churches.

The second and third categories of complaint related to the political
role of the bishops. By virtue of their office they were members of the
House of Lords, and formed a block of 26 votes that could be commanded by the King. Although membership of the Lords had increased
from 55 (excluding bishops) in 1603, to 126 in 1628 (after Bucking-

KEY ISSUE

*Enthusiasm for
moderate Anglicanism.*

See pages 97–8 for
Royalist sympathy with
Anglicanism.

KEY ISSUE

*Dislike of Laudian
bishops.*

See pages 72–3 and 89 for the political results of hatred of bishops.

What were Lord Brooke's objections to bishops? **Q**

ham's sale of peerages), the influence of the bishops would obviously be significant. Given that average attendance of the Lords was around half of this number, and that the buying of titles also increased the influence of the King and favourites who sold them, it is not surprising that the older nobility felt their position and influence to be under threat. Their point of view is expressed by Lord Brooke in source D. It is perhaps worth noting that he fought for Parliament in 1642, raising a volunteer regiment that was noted for its religious tolerance.

D From *A Discourse Opening the Nature of that Episcopacy which is exercised in England,* second edition by Robert Greville, Lord Brooke (1642).

I humbly propound as worthy [of] mature consideration, how fit these spiritual lords may be to sit as law-makers in that highest court [the House of Lords], by whose fundamental orders, as also by the law of nature, none ought to have vote but free men. And how can they possibly be deemed free, that wholly depend on another's thought (for I need not say, beck, smile or frown) not only for their first creation, but continual preservation in this state and power of giving vote in that court?

Though all branches of nobility first sprouted out from the root of royalty ... yet estates and revenues did not, which are parts and supports of noble honours. And these also in Bishops depend on the prince's will ... , whose baronies are only annexed to their office and not invested in them by blood ... When they look upon themselves as peers and grandees of the kingdom, and again, reflect on their wives and children, as those which, after their decease, must soon be reduced from such a height ... , must not this be a great temptation by any means, right or wrong, to seek the private enrichment of themselves and families, even before the public good of the commonwealth ...

To make matters worse, Charles had extended the political influence of the bishops by appointing them to important offices of state. In 1635, Bishop Juxon became Lord Treasurer, while Laud himself dominated the Privy Council. This ran counter to the whole trend of administrative development since the Reformation, which had opened the opportunity for service to the State to an increasingly educated laity. While the Tudors had accrued huge power through the changes of the 1530s, they had exercised it in partnership with the ruling class in both central and local government. Whether deliberately or not, the powers and functions given by Charles to his bishops were a threat to that partnership. The reactions of the political community are described by Clarendon in source E, and it is significant that, although eventually a Royalist and the King's close adviser, he shared some of these feelings himself.

E From *History of the Great Rebellion* by Edward Hyde, Earl of Clarendon (1702).

The Treasurer's is the greatest office of benefit in the kingdom, and the chief in precedence next the archbishop and the Great Seal [the Lord Chancellor] ... and the greatest of the nobility who were in the chiefest employments looked upon it as the prize of one of them ...; when on a sudden the staff was put into the hands of the bishop of London, [William Juxon] a man so unknown that his name was scarce heard of in the kingdom, who had been within two years before but a private chaplain to the King and the president of a poor college in Oxford. This inflamed more men than were angry before, and no doubt did not only sharpen the edge of envy and malice against the archbishop [Laud], who was the known architect of this new fabric, but most unjustly indisposed many towards the Church, which they looked upon as the gulf ready to swallow all the great offices, there being others in view, of that robe [i.e. bishops], who were ambitious enough to expect the rest.

Q

Why did Clarendon object to the appointment of Juxon as Lord Treasurer?

These grievances were outlined in the Root and Branch Petition, presented to Parliament in December 1640, which called for the complete abolition of bishops. The petition listed their transgressions, and included complaints based on political, personal and spiritual grievances. There was no doubt about the widespread unpopularity of the bishops at this time, but the debates that followed revealed the variety of views regarding what should be done about them. While some wanted the abolition of bishops and the introduction of a Presbyterian structure in their place, others were concerned about the safety of the Church, while yet others were determined to defend the freedom of the laity from an intrusive clergy. As Lord George Digby put it: 'We all agree upon this, that a Reformation of Church Government is most necessary ... but [not] to strike at the root and attempt a total alteration ... I am confident that instead of every bishop we put down in a diocese, we should set up a pope in every parish'.

The problem facing the English State in 1641 and the years that followed, was that while the majority of the political community continued to believe that a compulsory national Church was essential to good order, there was no consensus as to what its powers and organisation should be. It was clear that the model favoured by Charles and Laud, and the extensive role that they gave to the Church as the pillar of Divine Right monarchy was unacceptable. What became clear in the months that followed the calling of the Long Parliament was that the alternative favoured by the opposition leaders was equally unacceptable. The reservations expressed by Digby were echoed in the debates over the Bishops' Exclusion Bill of May 1641 and the Root and Branch Bill of June. The first was aimed at the removal of the bishops from the House of Lords, and passed the Commons only to be rejected by the Lords after intervention from the King reinforced the opposition of the

KEY ISSUE

Disagreements about the future role of bishops from 1640 onwards

See pages 89–90 for the political context of Root and Branch.

bishops themselves. This reinforced the need for 'Root and Branch' abolition, which would replace bishops in the Church by committees of ministers, but such radical changes raised fears that authority itself would be undermined.

While the gentry had an aversion to being instructed by the clergy in their own lives, they regarded the Church as essential in teaching obedience and maintaining control of the lower social orders. As cement for the fabric of a hierarchical society, authority in the Church must be maintained. The view was put by Sir Henry Slingsby, a good example of the moderate gentry who opposed the actions of Charles I while remaining attached to Divine Right monarchy as the guarantee of social stability.

> **KEY ISSUE**
>
> *Would the abolition of bishops undermine authority in general in society?*

F From the *Diary of Sir Henry Slingsby* (1660).

'I went with the Bill' he wrote in his diary, 'for their taking of [the bishops'] votes in the house of Peers and for meddling with temporal affairs, but I was against the Bill for taking away the function and calling of Bishops ... I could never be of that opinion that the government of the Church as it is now established by bishops and archbishops to be of absolute necessity ...; but I am of opinion that the taking them out of the church ... may be of dangerous consequence to the peace of the church ..., considering that this government hath continued from the Apostles; ... it were not safe to make alteration from so ancient a beginning.'

These fears were crucial in dividing Parliament and enabling the King to rally support to fight the Civil War. Research has shown that those who, like Slingsby and Clarendon, opposed Charles on political and constitutional issues were likely to support him when faced with the radical strategies adopted by the opposition leaders, and that affection for the Anglican Church or fear that its removal would threaten social stability played a significant part in the process. In this sense, many of the MPs who ultimately chose to support Charles I can be described as 'conservatives' – seeking to preserve and conserve the existing social fabric by supporting Church and King. Such attitudes reflect the power and appeal of the Confessional State to men who were not necessarily motivated by personal religious faith. At the same time, however, their removal from Westminster allowed those who favoured more sweeping changes in the Church to carry out their plans. In 1642, they excluded the bishops from the Lords, and later abolished them. In December 1643, under pressure from their Scottish allies, they called a conference of ministers to meet in Westminster, in order to plan a new, Presbyterian organisation for the Church. This Assembly of Divines, also known as the Westminster Assembly, began to debate the possibilities, and produced a Directory of Worship as the basis of a reformed national Church in 1646. They were never able to put their plans into practice, because, by then, the opponents of the confessional state had emerged in sufficient numbers to prevent them.

*Study sources A–F on pages 339–48 in the context of the
information above, and attempt the questions that follow:*

Q

1. *In what ways did the Church support the monarch in maintaining
order?*
2. *How far were the Puritan reformers and Charles I pursuing the
same objectives?*
3. *Why were their methods incompatible?*
4. *Why was there so much hostility to the Laudian bishops?*
5. *Why was it so difficult to establish agreement about the role of the
Church in government and society?*

2 ⌐ THE CHALLENGE TO THE CONFESSIONAL STATE, 1603–60

A *The influence of the Renaissance*

The European Renaissance (the word means rebirth) was traditionally
portrayed as a challenge to medieval orthodoxy in the late fifteenth
century, which coincided with the discovery of previously unknown
lands overseas and contributed to the Protestant Reformation of the
early sixteenth century. This neat package of intellectual, scientific and
religious change has been shown by more recent research to be an over-
simplification, although some of its key elements remain important.
The idea that medieval man was devoid of curiosity and unable to challenge authority has been exploded, and instead, the roots of the intellectual exploration that flourished after 1500 have been shown to lie deep
in medieval society.

Medieval scholars were capable of original thought, but they were
respectful of tradition. The institutions that they respected had their
origins in the classical world of ancient Greece and Rome, and they
believed that classical scholars had discovered the essential truths about
the world. Much knowledge had been lost with the collapse of the
Roman Empire, and the most that they could achieve was to rediscover
this knowledge through studying the texts of the writers whose work
had been preserved by the Christian Church in Rome and Byzantium.
As a result, the works and authors approved by the Church, such as
Galen in medicine and Ptolemy in astronomy and geography, had
enormous authority. In time, however, studying the work of such men
led to better translations, often from the original Greek, which revealed
not only their discoveries but also their approaches to the process of
study, emphasising personal observations, empirical research and 'scientific' methods. The Renaissance involved a rebirth of classical thinking as well as greater knowledge of classical achievements.

The influence of classical scholarship and its spread across Europe

> **KEY ISSUE**
>
> *The Renaissance
> encouraged challenges
> to authority and
> tradition.*

arose from many different factors. The invention and development of printing, the growing wealth of the Italian cities and their trading links with the eastern world where Greco-Roman traditions lived on, their patronage of artists and architects who studied Greek and Roman originals, and the search for new routes to the east (which led to exploration of Africa and the discovery of America) – all these developments and more encouraged a stronger spirit of enquiry and a willingness to challenge traditional assumptions. In the mid-sixteenth century, the discoveries of Copernicus, that the earth and planets revolved around the sun, and of Vesalius, who showed that Galen's ideas about the human anatomy were wrong in many ways, proved conclusively that new ideas were possible, that modern men could extend knowledge further than the ancient authorities, and that the concepts of progress and improvement had a place in society.

It was this idea above all, that human societies could improve their ways and conditions by the application of scientific thought and rational thinking, which inspired further development and opened up new possibilities. Before 1640 the main contribution of English scholars to the growing body of new knowledge lay in the fields of mathematics and medicine, but the significance of the new thinking was much wider than any specific scientific advances. The scientific methods of experiment and observation, the demand for traditional beliefs to be justified on a rational basis, and the willingness to challenge authority created a climate of intellectual exploration that affected political and religious assumptions as well as more obviously practical applications. The new approach was summed up by Sir Francis Bacon, whose essay entitled *The Advancement of Learning* was published in 1605. Although his ideas were not widely influential until after 1640, Bacon encouraged scholars to subject all aspects of society to rational examination, and sparked off a response among an influential minority. While it is important not to exaggerate the influence of the new learning in the years before the Civil War, it did inspire a number of influential men to challenge the religious and intellectual restrictions imposed by the confessional state.

While Bacon (and others who became associated with 'science') applied rational analysis to the natural world, others were more interested in the implications for society and religion. Among them was Lucius Carey, Lord Falkland, who made his house at Great Tew in the Cotswolds a centre for learning, and welcomed friends and acquaintances from the University of Oxford nearby. Encouraged by the study of classical humanists, which formed a significant part of the university curriculum at the time, they engaged in intellectual debates that were, in some ways, far removed from the practical problems of the Church. They were therefore able to explore uncharted waters. The result was an approach to religious debate that emphasised rational logic and the need for intellectual freedom.

Among those who benefited from the patronage of Falkland was William Chillingworth, who published a tract entitled *The Religion of Protestants a Safe Way to Salvation* in 1638. Chillingworth began with the conventional Protestant belief that the truth about God was to be

---

KEY ISSUE

English intellectual liveliness was typified by Bacon.

found in the Bible. Applying a rational approach, he pointed out that there were many books in, and versions of, the Bible, and that much of it was contradictory and required interpretation. Therefore, he concluded, errors were unavoidable and beliefs would inevitably vary. Since God wished souls to be saved, it was inconceivable that He would allow errors to be propagated in essential beliefs. Chillingworth's conclusion, therefore, was that only a few of the many elements of Christianity were essential to salvation, and those were the fundamental beliefs found in all texts. The existence of God, the birth and death of Jesus, His sacrifice to save humanity through the inner Holy Spirit: these were made plain and simple in the Scriptures, and these alone were essential to salvation.

If such arguments were accepted, then it was possible to establish religious harmony within a broadly tolerant Church. It therefore seems ironic that Chillingworth was the godson of the arch-persecutor, William Laud, who also patronised and encouraged Chillingworth's friend and supporter, John Hales. The apparent contradiction can be explained by the fact that Chillingworth, Hales, Falkland, Morley and others of the Great Tew circle were engaged in scholarly debate, while Laud carried responsibility for the practical outcomes. While their concern was with the logic of ideas, Laud sought to maintain the ability of the Church to protect order in society and buttress the social hierarchy on which it depended. When religious and political divisions came to an open breach in 1642, the members of the Tew circle were solidly Royalist, and Falkland was second only to Edward Hyde in rallying moderate support of the King. What is equally significant is that both men seem to have been motivated by dislike of militant Puritanism and fear of social disorder.

This does not mean that the views put forward by Anglicans such as Chillingworth were entirely without significance. In the long-term they laid the foundations of a campaign for tolerance within the Church that would become stronger after 1660, and even at the time they argued strongly against the attempts to stifle debate. It was Falkland who accused the Laudian bishops of keeping the people in darkness 'so that they might sow more tares [weeds] in the night'. In so doing, they were helping to develop ideas that would emerge more clearly after 1642, in a concerted campaign for religious toleration. This was not their intention – like Laud, they believed in an inclusive national Church, but sought to make it sufficiently tolerant and flexible to encompass a variety of views. Nevertheless, their insistence that variety was inevitable, and that error must be accepted as part of the search for truth, opened the way to a more radical challenge to the compulsory Church and the confessional state.

This challenge was to come from several sources, but some of the most persuasive efforts and arguments came from the same classical humanist influences that inspired Falkland and his associates. Among them was a man who could be seen as the Parliamentarian counterpart to Falkland, a similarly idealistic aristocrat, Robert Greville, Lord Brooke. Like Falkland, Brooke was influenced by Sir Francis Bacon to see humans as engaged in a rational search for truth, and like Falkland

> **KEY ISSUE**
>
> *Long-term contribution of the Tew circle to religious toleration.*

> **KEY ISSUE**
>
> *The influence of Lord Brooke.*

he accepted that error and variety were an inevitable part of this. Unlike the Tew circle, however, he was prepared to extend this freedom to all sections of society, and to argue that it was no threat to the State. Where the Anglicans argued that the Church and the nation were one and the same, and that therefore a threat to the Church was an act against the State, Brooke suggested that a state could contain many Churches, and religious differences that did not directly threaten political authority should be treated as having no public significance. In arguing this case, Brooke and his supporters had taken the huge step of arguing that religious belief was, in itself, a matter for private conscience, and denying the need for a confessional state.

What is more, they were determined that these private beliefs could and should be freely expressed. If the justification for allowing error was a human search for truth, then that search had to be conducted openly, so that new arguments could be proposed, tested and debated. There was no room for censorship, except in cases of obvious danger. The influence of rational humanism therefore extended beyond religious freedom to allow freedom of expression. At the time when Brooke was publishing his ideas, in 1640–1, the normal machinery of censorship, based on the Church courts and the authority of bishops, was already breaking down under the pressure of hostility between the King and Parliament. Political and religious debate extended beyond the confines of Parliament, and the views and concerns of ordinary people were expressed with growing freedom. To many of the governing class, this was cause for concern, and there is no doubt that fear of popular upheaval played a major part in rallying many of the gentry to the King. For a few, such as Brooke, it was entirely natural and acceptable:

> The ways of God's spirit are free and not tied to a university man or to any man, to any bishop, or magistrate or church. The light shines where it will among men, no matter how humble or ignorant, moves them to utterance, to inquiry and discussion, to ceaseless search for more light, until truth in its entirety shall become known to all, and men have once more become one with God.

Such views, if widely adopted, would spell the death of the confessional state and much more besides.

B *Popular culture – education, literacy and Protestant influence*

Brooke's claim that men and women of all classes were capable of contributing to the search for truth was encouraged by a growing availability of education and a resulting spread of literacy. It is difficult to estimate what proportion of the population could read, but it is likely that the wealthy and 'middling sort' (at least in towns) were almost universally literate, and that some of the poor were also able to read to some degree. It has been estimated that, by the end of Elizabeth's reign, about 38 per cent of the male population were able to read, rising to around 78 per cent in London, which tended to attract literate migrants in search of opportunity, and was also well-endowed with schools. Writing was less widely distributed. The dangers inherent in this situation were described by the Earl of Newcastle in a letter to Charles II in 1660:

> The Bible in English under every weaver's and chambermaid's arms hath done us much hurt. That which made it one way is the universities [which] abound with too many scholars... But that which hath done us most hurt is the abundance of grammar schools and Inns of court... And there are so many schools now as most read. So indeed there should be, but such a proportion as to serve the church and moderately the law and the merchants, and the rest for the labour; for else they run out to idle and unnecessary people that becomes a factious burden to the Commonwealth. For when most was unlettered, it was much a better world both for peace and war.

In Newcastle's view, the spread of education and literacy, combined with unsupervised Bible reading, had sown the seeds of rebellion.

See pages 121–3 for the political context of religious radicalism.

Educational provision had been increasing for a considerable time. In the fifteenth century King Henry VI had founded Eton and King's College, Cambridge, for example, and the establishment of chantry and grammar schools mirrored these developments at local and parish level. The Christian humanists of the Renaissance, such as John Colet who refounded St Paul's Grammar School in London in 1509, believed in the power of education to reform and improve society. While the Henrician reformation had adversely affected some of these arrangements through the dissolution of the monasteries, the spread of Protestant ideas in the reign of Edward VI repaired the damage and encouraged further expansion. 'King Edward VI' grammar schools remain in many places today. Thereafter, there was a steady increase in the licensing of 'petty' schools, which taught basic literacy, and of grammar schools that extended this to the study of the classics. In towns this was supported by charitable endowments from wealthy citizens and merchant guilds, reflecting both sober citizenship and religious fervour. In addition, many children were taught to read a little at private 'dame' schools or in their own homes.

The motives for this emphasis on literacy varied. Religious and humanist influences played their part, but there were many economic advantages in being able to read, for example property records, apprentices' indentures and contracts. Career opportunities were enhanced in a variety of trades and professions. Social mobility was encouraged, and helped to spread awareness of the benefits of education. At the higher levels of society, the acquisition of a suitable education was an essential step in moving from the merchant or yeoman class into the ranks of the gentry. Wealthy men from these middling ranks sent their sons to grammar schools and universities to acquire knowledge of the classics, which marked out a gentleman, and even allowed their daughters to acquire some of the same knowledge at home. As the gentry played an increasing role in local government and administration, they equipped themselves with the necessary skills by attending the universities and Inns of Court for a sufficient period, although usually short of the time required for a degree. At every level of society, education was increasingly seen as a useful, if not a necessary, part of preparing the young for life.

What did these institutions provide? The answer was quite variable, but there was a broad progression through to the universities, whose preoccupation with the classics influenced the curriculum as a whole. Local schools were often small, run by a single teacher, and focused on basic literacy and religious instruction. Able students who learnt to read quickly would also be instructed in arithmetic, but writing was not usually taught at this level. Some of them acted as 'feeder' schools for the grammar schools, which were situated in many market towns. For example, at Shrewsbury there were schools at St Alkmund's and St Chad's that fed scholars through to Shrewsbury Grammar School, and smaller market towns such as Rugby and Burton drew from the surrounding countryside in the same way. As their name suggests, these schools offered a classical education – the grammar in question being Latin – and an emphasis on religion. The Latin texts used were often christianised, and by the late sixteenth century tended to be chosen to reinforce Protestant ideas. The parodies in which the reformer Erasmus mocked the pre-Reformation Church, for example, were widely studied. Some more practical subjects were offered, such as accounting, and there is evidence in some schools of a form of streaming, with less able students concentrating on English and accounting, while the more able applied themselves to the classical curriculum in preparation for further study at the universities.

The university curriculum was also dominated by the classics, although the transfer of control from the Church to the Crown, which followed from the Reformation, allowed a more secular atmosphere to develop. The full curriculum consisted of a four-year BA course focused on logic, rhetoric and some philosophy, followed by a further three-year course leading to an MA, which included Greek, natural and moral philosophy, metaphysics, geometry and astronomy. While those who were seeking entry to the professions (law and the Church) might pursue the full course at least to BA level, many undergraduates attended for a shorter period before moving on to the Inns of Court in London to study a shortened course in law. The growing practice among the gentry of seeking this kind of training was accommodated at Oxford and Cambridge by the development of the college system. Originally associations of scholars, the colleges began to welcome students whose fees supplemented scholarly incomes, and were able to offer more flexible arrangements than the university authorities. It was increasingly possible to arrange individual courses of study for those who could afford to pay, and by 1640 the sons of gentry were able to receive tuition in more modern subjects such as history, geography, literature, mathematics and divinity.

Between the Reformation and the Civil War, therefore, there was a period of considerable expansion in educational provision, in terms of both quantity and quality. Literacy increased, the new learning of the Renaissance gained ground, and education was increasingly seen as a civilising influence. Among enthusiasts such as Bacon, there were plans and schemes for a new academy, and this project was developed further in the Civil War period by reformers such as Samuel Hartlib who sought to encourage scientific learning. In many ways, however, it was religious belief, and Protestant influence in particular, which was most responsible for the spread of literacy, especially among the middling and lower social orders; and it was this aspect of educational development that would prove most immediately dangerous to the authority of the confessional state.

The core of Protestant theology was that salvation for the soul was obtained as a gift of free grace from God. To receive this gift, the individual need only believe in the gospel of Christ and His sacrifice of atonement for the sins of humanity. Belief, however, came from knowledge of the word of God as presented in the Bible, which contained all that was needed for the individual soul to understand Christ's message and for Churches to plan and organise the practice of Christianity. The role of the minister was therefore to teach and preach, to guide the individual in their personal search and to shed light on the more obscure aspects. While the early reformers undoubtedly saw this as a major role, and expected that the laity would need and accept the guidance of an educated ministry, the logic of Protestant beliefs also placed great emphasis on private prayer, private reading and study of the Bible, including an individual understanding of its message.

Such beliefs encouraged education on several levels. The need for an educated ministry has already been discussed above, but the implications for the laity were more far-reaching. Individuals needed to be able to read in order to study the Bible. Given the difficulty of some texts, it was useful for ministers to hold Bible meetings, at which the meaning of more obscure passages could be discussed and debated. Such meetings were attended by the more intensely religious parishioners, and tended to distinguish them from the average sinner, encouraging the Calvinist distinction between the predestined 'saints' and the unregenerate multitude who would be damned. Debate and discussion tended to blur the line between the minister and the more educated or gifted laymen, allowing greater confidence and willingness to challenge the views and interpretations put forward by existing authority. The logic of the Protestant faith was to involve the individual in his own salvation, to extend his responsibility for his own soul, and to provide him with the tools to make his own judgements.

For the vast majority of individuals, this was as far as it went, even among the 'hotter sort' of Protestants who came to be called Puritans. Bible reading within the home and the discussion of sermons that had been heard and noted down was widely practised, without ever causing

KEY ISSUE

The threat of literacy to the confessional state.

the Church or the ministry to be seriously challenged. For a few, however, the enthusiasm generated by a fiery preacher and the mystical obscurities of the Bible itself produced different results. Told that they were among those predestined to salvation, that true equality was spiritual equality, and that it was the duty of God's chosen saints to exercise their talents, it was hardly surprising that some should feel able and willing to follow their own ideas and their own path. Encouraged to believe that the Bible was the infallible Word of God, it was not surprising that some placed greater faith in what they perceived the Bible to be saying than in the words of men, however well-educated. If the Church, for whatever reason, was unable or unwilling to go with them on the road to salvation, it is hardly surprising that they should choose to go without it. For this minority, the logic of Protestant ideas led to separation and the development of independent Churches to challenge the confessional state.

C *The separatist challenge*

It is difficult to trace the early development of separatist groups, since they were illegal, persecuted and therefore secretive. Evidence of their existence tends to come from records of persecution, which by definition only record the point when they were revealed, and from the writings of ministers who led them. Since many preachers held meetings and classes as part of their pastoral work, attended by those who also attended church, it is difficult at times to distinguish a separatist congregation from a group of enthusiastic parishioners. In many cases, one merged into the other or took the momentous decision to separate because of external factors, often because the minister that they followed was suspended or removed from his living for failing to conform to the rules of the Church. Most of the early separatist groups were originally led by ordained ministers, although they did not always remain so thereafter.

The motives for separation varied. In some cases it stemmed from the Calvinist belief in predestination, which created a sense of separate identity among those who believed themselves to be saved. This might take the form of a desire to be exclusive, to withdraw from the contact of the unrepentant sinners around them, and to enable the minister and elders to establish order and discipline within the congregation along the lines of Calvin's arrangements at Geneva. It might be occasioned by a desire to be free of the unwanted ceremonies of the Church, or by a belief that a purer, more supportive Church could be established by separation. There is no doubt that before 1640 much separation was enforced rather than voluntary, formed due to the insistence of the authorities that the rules of the Church be obeyed. One indication of this is the increase in separatism at times when the government sought to assert its authority, for example between 1604 and 1610 when Bancroft was Archbishop of Canterbury, and again in the 1630s under the leadership of Laud.

In many cases the moment of separation was marked by some form

KEY ISSUE

Varied motives for separation.

of agreement or covenant, by which the members bound themselves together and established rules. These can indicate the motives of those who participated. For example, the Covenant of the Canterbury Congregational Church, established in 1645, describes a perfectly orthodox theology of salvation by God's grace, but refers to the desire of members to 'cleave to, and walk with one another . . . in a way of Christian and brotherly love, admonishing, exhorting, reproving, counselling, comforting, and helping one another forward in the way to heaven'. Clearly they believed that the combination of discipline and support offered by these arrangements would increase their ability to hold to God and secure salvation.

It would therefore appear that separation did not necessarily imply unorthodox beliefs, but it is also the case that both beliefs and behaviour tended to become more distinctive after separation. There were a number of reasons for this. Separate groups tended to be more inward-looking, and gradually became divorced from the mainstream of debate. Internal debate encouraged members to put forward ideas and interpretations that were not then tested and refined outside their own ranks. Regular debate and discussion encouraged the lay members to develop their own ideas, especially as the need for the minister to find some means of earning a living tended to blur the lines between laity and clergy. Increasingly, as ministers who had gathered a group died or moved on, separate Churches had to rely on preaching by members and Elders, therefore challenging the clerical monopoly. Above all, the intense commitment that was required for separation combined with isolation and reliance on internal discipline to make separatist groups vulnerable to internal divisions and splits. Sometimes this destroyed them; sometimes it led them to divide and multiply.

The evolution of separatism can be most effectively demonstrated by considering some of the more important examples, such as the careers of John Smyth and John Robinson. Both were originally Lincolnshire men, educated at Cambridge and ordained to the ministry. In 1602, Smyth was preaching in Lincoln and Robinson at Norwich. In that year, Smyth lost his post, presumably because of his Puritan views, and little is known of him until he is recorded as leading a separatist group in Gainsborough in 1606. Shortly after, Robinson appears to have left Norwich in order to preach to a similar group at Scrooby, near Gainsborough; whether this was linked to Smyth's group or not is hard to say, but there seems to have been a measure of co-operation between the two. By 1608, both had been forced into exile in Holland to avoid persecution, where they settled in Leyden. There they were joined by a number of separatists from Sandwich, led by a woolcomber named Richard Masterson. In Holland, the paths of the two groups diverged. Robinson's congregation seems to have prospered until they tired of living in Holland and set out to find a new home in America in 1621. As the Pilgrim Fathers they settled in Massachusetts, New England, and established the first of many Puritan colonies in the area. In the 1630s, their numbers were swelled by a steady stream of immigrants, driven out of England by the policies and persecutions of Laud. The example

KEY ISSUE

The links between separatism and independent thought.

KEY ISSUE

The influence and significance of Smyth and Robinson.

of independent, self-governing Churches that became the accepted pattern in New England did much to encourage the movement towards Independency in England itself.

Smyth's group remained in Holland, where contact with continental reformers inspired him to rebaptise them as a sign of their conscious, adult choice in becoming members of the Church. This implied a rejection of the Anglican practice of infant baptism as a relic of popery. The practice of baptising children at birth was based on the idea that all humans inherited 'original' sin, handed down from Adam, and that the Church had the power to wash this away by accepting the child into membership. For many Puritans this claim gave too much power to the Church as an institution, and denied the need for the individual to understand and personally commit themselves to membership. The congregation seem to have accepted Smyth's advice on this matter, but when he went further and began to challenge the doctrine of predestination many of them left him. Smyth argued that God would not sacrifice His Son to save humanity, and then deny that salvation to all but a few, an argument that was very close to that put forward at much the same time by Arminius and adopted by that enemy of all separatists, William Laud. In this period of religious debate and exploration, the challenge to rigid Calvinism, like the challenge to the confessional state, was not limited to one part of the religious spectrum.

While Smyth's claim that God offered salvation to all men who were willing to accept the message of Christ divided his congregation, it also led to important developments in religious separatism. His congregation became the first English Baptists, and some returned to England. By 1626 there were Baptist Churches in London, Canterbury, Salisbury and Tiverton in Devon. Most of these held on to their Calvinist beliefs, and adopted the name of Particular Baptists – exclusive gatherings of 'saints' believing in predestination. Although it is difficult to trace their development in the years of persecution they clearly prospered. In 1641, there were seven Particular Baptist Churches in London alone, and in 1643 they issued a joint Confession of Faith in order to distinguish themselves from the emerging Independent congregations. More importantly in the long run, some of Smyth's followers accepted his views and established a General Baptist movement, which encouraged ideas of spiritual equality and freedom of choice. In 1616, Thomas Helwys established the first General Baptist congregation in Spitalfields in London. Little is known of them, but their emphasis on human choice and reason laid the basis for arguments in favour of religious toleration, and for the emergence of Leveller ideas.

Until 1641, separatist development was inevitably fragmentary and uncertain, but the rapid emergence of separatist groups in that year is evidence of their prior existence. With the calling of the Long Parliament and the attack on the authority of the Church, they were now able to expand and flourish. The collapse of press censorship permitted a flood of pamphlets and publications, lay preachers and 'tub-thumpers' such as Thomas Lambe and Samuel Oates who were active in London, and all kinds of ideas were advocated and debated. According to

KEY ISSUE

The establishment of the English Baptist movement.

KEY ISSUE

In the liberal atmosphere of 1641 the separatists spread their ideas.

Clarendon: 'the licence of preaching and printing increased to that degree that all pulpits were freely delivered to the schismatical [separatist] and silenced preachers who till then had lurked in corners or lived in New England: and the presses were at liberty for the publishing the most invective, seditious and scurrilous pamphlets that their wit and malice could invent'.

The majority of MPs shared Clarendon's concerns, and as early as 1643 Parliament attempted to reimpose some form of censorship, but this was impossible in wartime. The attempt drew condemnation from the former Presbyterian supporter, John Milton, whose *Areopagitica*, published in 1644, made a convincing case for freedom of expression. By this time the activities of the separatists had developed into a concerted campaign for the establishment of religious toleration. It began at the end of 1643, when five of the ministers called to the Westminster Assembly and charged with devising a reformed system for the Church revealed their Independent connections and put forward the case for tolerating separate congregations alongside the new Church. Their demands were extremely limited: the right for orthodox Protestants to establish self-governing congregations, provided that they did not infringe on doctrinal or legal conventions. Their views were dismissed by the Presbyterian majority, whereupon they embarked on a campaign of debate and delay that was designed to prevent a new system being established and to prolong the unofficial freedom that existed. By the middle of 1644 a pamphlet campaign was under way, in which men such as William Walwyn, a wealthy London merchant, and Roger Williams, the founder of the religiously tolerant colony of Rhode Island, carried the debate much further and demanded religious toleration as a matter of human right.

This campaign drew together men who had been treading different paths towards the same destination and brought into the open a number of developments that now began to interact. The political and religious radicalism that threatened to turn a quarrel within the ruling elite into a political and social revolution had been slowly evolving for a century or more, drawing on the variety of cultural traditions outlined above. Now different strands of thought were able to stimulate and influence one another, to create and defend new ideas, and therefore to develop wider and increasingly radical plans and schemes. Moreover, they were not debating in isolation. The emergence of separatism alerted conservative Puritans to the enemy within and their fears were increased by the activities of radicals within the New Model Army, whose movement around the country encouraged more separatist congregations. In 1644, the first Independent congregation in England had been established in Hull, where the Army chaplain, John Canne, preached with the support of a well-known Independent minister, Philip Nye. By 1646, there were six such congregations in Yorkshire alone. The efforts of conservatives to control the development of increasingly radical ideas were not only ineffectual, but counter-productive. By imprisoning John Lilburne on the authority of Parliament alone, they sparked off the campaign for his release that shaped the

> **KEY ISSUE**
>
> *Censorship versus freedom.*

> **KEY ISSUE**
>
> *The merging of religious and political radicalism*

See pages 117–23 for
political radicalism in
the New Model Army.

KEY ISSUE

*Religious enthusiasm
became a political
campaign.*

Levellers into a political movement. By attempting to disband the Army
and remove its more radical officers, they drove it into political action
in 1647, and afforded the Levellers a new ally. By seeking to come to an
agreement with the King to restore normal authority, they provoked the
Army leaders into the establishment of a republic. The fact was that the
collapse of censorship and other controls and the momentous events
surrounding King and Parliament had opened the way to intellectual
ferment and visions of a new earth, as well as a new heaven that could
not be controlled. One after another, the different forms of authority
were challenged and rejected.

By 1647, religious and political radicals in London and within the
New Model Army had rejected the authority of both King and Parliament. The separatists had rejected the authority of government and
Church in the name of the Bible. In the intense excitement that followed, others began to go further and reject all external authority,
arguing that God spoke first in the human heart and to the individual
spirit. The logic of separatist ideas about spiritual equality, the Baptist
and Leveller insistence that all were capable of salvation and that God
had made human beings as creatures of reason and free will, carried
implications that were now being explored to the full. As early as 1647
Joseph Salmon was arguing that God, the Devil, heaven and hell all had
their existence in the human mind, while others, influenced by scientific
study and natural philosophy, suggested that since God had created the
natural world He existed within it. This was not necessarily an extreme
or eccentric idea since many of the early scientists such as Robert Boyle
and Isaac Newton believed that in studying the workings of the natural
world they were coming to a better understanding of the God who had
created it. The idea could, however, have more radical applications. The
Diggers argued that God had created the earth as a resource to be
shared by all, and the Ranters argued that nothing was sinful if it was
natural. Groups and individuals who have been labelled 'seekers' came
to the conclusion that God did not exist in any of the Churches or in
the Bible, and that they must seek until He chose to reveal Himself. In
1652, George Fox united many of these seekers in the Quaker movement, whose central message was that God exists within the human
spirit and speaks directly in the human heart.

The common feature among these later radicals was the repudiation
of all external authority in religion, in favour of the inner spirit. Unlike
the Puritan separatists, many of whom were shocked by these later
developments, they did not issue formal declarations of faith or lists of
members; nor did they accept the Bible as the word of God. They
regarded the Bible as a useful guide, containing the story of Christ and
much more, but only if interpreted and enlightened by the individual
spirit. The expression of these concepts was often eccentric and short-
lived, but in the ideas of George Fox this view found a coherent and
lasting expression. If the key features of religious radicalism are defined
as an individual search for truth, an emphasis on the free expression of
ideas derived from this search, and the right of all to find God in their
own way, then Quaker ideas might be said to embody religious radical-

ism in its most complete form. It is perhaps no coincidence that so many radicals (Salmon, Winstanley, and Lilburne himself) ended their lives as Quakers.

D *Source investigation: The evolution of radicalism*

The most significant characteristic of religious and political radicalism was the way in which it evolved, first from within the ranks of Puritan reformers, and then in a complex variety of forms during the heady excitement of civil war and regicide. The sources collected here are supported by brief biographical accounts of Lilburne and Milton, which illustrate the emergence of Puritan radicalism.

> **A** From *The Ancient Bounds*, an anonymous pamphlet published in 1645.
>
> There are two things contended for in this liberty of conscience: first to instate every Christian in his right of free, yet modest, judging and accepting what he holds; secondly, to [seek] the truth, and this is the main end and respect of this liberty. I contend not for variety of opinions; I know there is but one truth. But this truth cannot easily be brought forth without this liberty; and a general restraint, though intended but for errors ... may fall upon the truth. And better errors of some kind suffered than one useful truth be obstructed or destroyed.

> **B** From *The Bloody Tenent of Persecution* by Roger Williams (1644).
>
> It is the will and command of God that ... a permission of ... consciences and worships be granted to all men in all nations and countries; ... God requireth not an uniformity of religion to be enacted and enforced in any civil state; which enforced uniformity, sooner or later, is the greatest occasion of civil war, ravishing of conscience, persecution of Christ Jesus his servants, and of hypocrisy and destruction of millions of souls.

> **C** From *Radical Religion in the English Revolution* by J.F. McGregor and B. Reay (eds) (1986).
>
> The General Baptists regarded their doctrine [of general redemption] as the foundation of their faith. [Smyth had declared that Christ lived in every man, saints and sinners alike; the difference was that the one acknowledged him the other did not; 'God lives in all, but all know it not'.] ... To all Baptists, the foundation of Puritan reformation was the guarantee of liberty of worship for the saints, and in defence of

this liberty they made a substantial contribution to the cause of toleration. They argued that the true Church was the creation of divine grace, not of man. Since it was not of this world, it must necessarily be completely separate from the state.

This provided the elements of a radical reform programme ... but the leaders were content with the Independents' strategy of discreetly lobbying their sympathisers in government as they feared that any attempt at popular agitation would awake memories of bloody Anabaptist rebellions in Germany. Their timidity allowed the Levellers to mobilise rank and file discontent, turning the principle of religious liberty into a secular theory of natural rights ... If [as Smyth claimed] all mankind had God in them and were potentially to be saved, there could be no distinction between the civil rights of saints and of citizens. To guarantee the liberties of the saints, it was necessary to seek rights and freedoms for all.

PICTURE 32

An engraving of John Lilburne by Glover. Glover was a reliable engraver, so this is probably what Lilburne looked like in 1641. The engraving shows the face of a man who has already experienced pain but will not be browbeaten

JOHN LILBURNE C.1614–57

Though Lilburne originated from County Durham and was educated at the Royal Grammar School, Newcastle, he was apprenticed to a London cloth merchant. As a young man he would certainly have listened to the radical preachers who made London a centre of religious and intellectual ferment, and he was associated with the London Baptist congregations. He was powerfully affected by the mutilation and imprisonment of Burton, Prynne and Bastwick, and arranged the printing in Holland and illegal importation of Bastwick's *Letany* (an attack on bishops). As a result Lilburne found himself before the Star Chamber. His defiance earned him a £500 fine, a public whipping, the pillory and imprisonment in the Fleet. Standing in the pillory he harangued the crowd on their rights to freedom of conscience and expression, and on the illegality of his own treatment – until he was brutally gagged.

Lilburne was released by the Long Parliament, ironically after an impassioned plea by Cromwell – whom he was later to attack bitterly. He was involved in the disturbances that drove the bishops from the Lords. When war came, Lilburne was commissioned in the tolerant Lord Brooke's regiment and supported Cromwell in his quarrel with Manchester. In 1645 when he was accused by Presbyterians of slandering Speaker Lenthall, he lectured a Parliamentary committee on Magna Carta and was imprisoned again. Released in 1646, he was sent to the Tower by the Lords for attacking Manchester and defending himself as 'a freeborn commoner'. The campaign for his release, orchestrated by Walwyn, Overton and Lilburne's wife, gave birth to the Leveller movement. Lilburne continued to criticise every regime up to and including the Protectorate. Much of his remaining life was spent in prison. From his cell he inspired Leveller protests, and wrote *England's New Chains Discovered* after the establishment of the

Republic. Twice exiled, he twice returned to contest the legality of his treatment. Finally, imprisoned in Jersey, he became a Quaker. He died at the early age of 43, exhausted by his efforts and privations.

Lilburne was clearly an impossible man, but his popularity, illustrated by the widespread delight at his acquittals after his various trials, is a tribute to his attractive personality. He was not a practical politician, but rather an individualist, a maverick loose cannon. But he performed an invaluable service in standing up to authority and campaigning for individual liberty and defining what we know today as human rights. How to react to awkward customers such as Lilburne is a test of any supposedly fair regime, for he was an irrepressible enemy of injustice and oppression. When he died, someone wrote this epitaph for his tomb:

> Is John departed and is Lilburne gone?
> Fairwell to both, to Lilburne and to John.
> Yet being dead, take this advice from me.
> Let them not both in one grave buried be.
> But lay John here, lay Lilburne hereabout.
> For if they ever meet, they will fall out.

See pages 132–3 for Lilburne during the Rump and page 138 for his trial during the Barebones Parliament.

D From *The True Levellers Standard Advanced* by Gerrard Winstanley (1649).

In the beginning of time the great Creator, Reason, made the earth to be a common treasury, to preserve beasts, birds, fishes, and man, the lord that was to govern this creation. For man had domination given to him over the beasts, birds and fishes. But not one word was spoken in the beginning, that one branch of mankind should rule over another.

And the reason is this. Every single man, male and female, is a perfect creature of himself. And the same Spirit that made the globe dwells in man to govern the globe; so that the flesh of man, being subject to Reason, his maker, hath him to be his teacher and ruler within himself, therefore need not run abroad after any teacher and ruler without him[self].

E From *The Great Mystery of the Great Whore Unfolded* by George Fox (1659).

We found this light to be a sufficient teacher, to lead us to Christ, from whence this light came ... to dwell in us ... And so we ceased from the teachings of men and their words and their worships and their temples ... that we might become truly wise, and by this light of Christ in us we were led out of false ways and false preachings and false ministers; and we met together often and waited upon the Lord.

JOHN MILTON 1608–74

The son of a London notary, Milton was educated at Christ's College, Cambridge, where he got his degree with a one-line answer on the miracle at Cana in Galilee ('The water recognised its creator, and blushed'). Alienated by Laud's Arminian offensive, he left Cambridge as a freelance scholar and poet. He published *Lycidas* in 1638, which was a thinly-veiled attack on bishops. Although he defended Presbyterian reform in 1641, he was too much of an individualist to accept Presbyterian discipline. His claim as a layman to guide and inform the English people threatened the clergy's monopoly of truth. When he defended divorce in 1642 after his wife had left him, he was labelled immoral by his previous friends. Infuriated by their censure, Milton published *Aeropagitica* – a powerful plea for intellectual freedom. Religion, he argued, was a personal search for truth and no man could predict where truth and the knowledge of God might be found. Therefore, all should be allowed to express themselves freely and to hear the views of others.

In 1649, as Cromwell's secretary, Milton defended regicide because the people were the source of power. In 1659, he argued fiercely for the preservation of the Republic. After the Restoration, blind, lonely and disgraced, he wrote his noblest works, *Paradise Lost* and *Samson Agonistes*, in which he struggled to come to terms with God's apparent abandonment of his elect. Throughout his career Milton fought for the individual's intellectual freedom to search for truth in his own way. Now he satisfied himself that the great truths of the goodness of God and the eventual triumph of right over wrong still prevailed despite appearances to the contrary.

See page 159 for Milton's reaction to defeat and disgrace.

1. *How does the demand for religious toleration widen and develop according to sources A–C and the chapter so far?*

2. *How did ideas about spiritual equality turn into a demand for civil and political rights according to sources A–C and the chapter so far?*

3. *What similarities and differences are there in sources D and E of the two explanations offered by Winstanley and Fox of how God exists?*

4. *What factors influenced the development of Lilburne and Milton as radical campaigners?*

5. *Why do you think they supported Presbyterian ideas before 1640, when they disagreed with them so radically in the years that followed?*

6. *How important were such individuals in developing radical ideas in this period?*

7. *What other factors encouraged such ideas at this time?*

8. *Did they have any lasting importance?*

9. *What does the portrait of Lilburne tell us about his personality?*

3 ⌐ REACTION AND REVENGE – THE RESTORATION OF THE CONFESSIONAL STATE

A *Reaction and fear, 1650–60*

By the 1650s the heady excitement of radical ideas found expression in a variety of ways. The historian David Underdown described some effects in his study entitled *Pride's Purge*:

> Out of the multiplicity of sects, out of the excited chorus of political debate, voices were heard calling for absolute freedom. The Diggers repudiated the tyranny of private property, the Ranters the restraints of conventional morality, Zionism, vegetarianism, a dozen other modern 'isms' were in the air. The mad hatter of Chesham, Roger Crab, reached the irreducible dietary minimum of dock leaves and grass at about the time he gave all his wordly goods to the poor. During a sermon by Peter Sterry in the austere surroundings of Whitehall Chapel in 1652, a woman in the congregation stripped naked, with joyful cries of 'Welcome the Resurrection'! All things were possible, the world was to be made new, the reign of king Jesus was just around the corner.

Just as worrying to those in positions of authority were cases such as the two Wiltshire weavers who argued in the tavern at Laycock that 'there was no God or power ruling above the planets, and that there was no Christ, but the scripture . . . ; and that if the scripture was to be made again, then Tom Lampire of Melksham should do it . . .'. They were accused of being Ranters, and of having said further 'that heaven and hell were only in a man's conscience. God was in everything, so if he was drunk, God was drunk with him . . . and that he would sell all religions for a jug of beer'. If ordinary men were to place such robust interpretations on the arguments of the radicals, and to lose their fear of sin, how were they to be kept under control?

It is hardly surprising, therefore, that radical ideas created a reaction among the ruling classes and a determination to restore normal controls. As early as 1646 those who had sought to create a godly state and a reformed national Church were becoming primarily concerned to destroy the monster that they had created. The first attacks on radicals came from the Presbyterian clergy and MPs such as William Prynne, who orchestrated the campaign against toleration and arranged the imprisonment of Lilburne for slandering the speaker of the House of Commons. The bitter invective hurled at separatists, lay preachers and radicals by supporters of the Parliamentary cause reflects a sense of disappointment and betrayal at the failure of their own reforming plans. By 1649 the destruction of political radicalism had begun. The Levellers had been first outmanoeuvred and then isolated by the New Model Army leaders, and their attempts to strike back by inciting mutiny in

> **KEY ISSUE**
>
> *The conservative backlash against the freedom of ideas.*

the Army led to the execution of the mutineers at Burford and the imprisonment of the leaders. In 1650, the Diggers were driven out of their commune in Surrey, while the Ranter scare led to a harsh Blasphemy Act, which could be used to control the more eccentric. By 1653 it was clear that the Commonwealth was not the prelude to political or social revolution, and that the dreams of freedom and equality would not become reality. In one aspect, however, the claim to a measure of religious freedom, the radicals fared better.

For much of the period of the Commonwealth and Protectorate, religious radicals had some friends in high places, and were protected from the worst effects of persecution. Cromwell might destroy the Levellers as a political movement, but he was not unsympathetic to many radical hopes, and was prepared to regard many of their excesses as over-enthusiasm rather than evil. Separatist groups were able to meet and practise their faith in peace, and the broad, tolerant Church that Cromwell sought to create allowed for varied beliefs and practice both within and alongside the parish structure. It was by no means unusual for ministers such as Christopher Ness and Philip Nye, who had Independent beliefs, to hold a parish living where they offered services to all while also holding meetings of their own gathered congregation at other times. In theory, Catholic worship and the use of the Anglican Prayer Book were illegal, but in practice those who used them discreetly were often left undisturbed.

Such tolerance was not, however, widespread within the ruling class, and the freedom given to radicals served only to increase fear of them. After 1654, when the Quakers, who had operated largely in remote northern districts, brought their message to the south, examples of persecution increased. These early Quakers were not the restrained pacifists of later years, but aggressive missionaries who entered churches and abused the ministers as 'hirelings of the devil', argued for non-payment of tithes and lectured the Justices of the Peace who were given the responsibility of curbing them. Not only were they eccentric and emotional in their faith (hence the nickname, Quakers, derived from the ecstatic tremblings that often accompanied their sermons), but they were clearly subversive. Refusing to remove their hats before their betters, insisting on the familiar address of 'thee' and 'thou' rather than the respectful 'you', they threatened the social hierarchy in all that they did. Above all, they were successful. The Quaker message, with its promise of an escape from sin, its depiction of a loving God, and its clear instructions on how to find Him, had a huge attraction for those who had been struggling to find comfort and certainty. In these circumstances, it was not unusual for Quaker preachers to convert tens and hundreds of followers at one meeting. To the conventionally minded and to the ruling classes, the threat that they posed seemed huge. By 1659 there were perhaps 60,000 Quakers in England, and fear of them played a significant part in bringing Charles II to the throne in 1660.

The fear and hatred that radicals could engender had already been demonstrated in the case of James Nayler, the Quaker leader who had entered Bristol in a procession emulating Christ's entry into Jerusalem.

KEY ISSUE

The provocative behaviour of the early Quakers.

For this act of blasphemy he had been flogged, bored through the tongue and imprisoned for life on the instructions of Parliament. The intervention of Cromwell had helped to avert a death sentence, but that was what the punishment actually proved to be. Nayler was released in 1659, broken in health, and died on the journey back to his native Yorkshire. Nevertheless, before 1660 his case had been unusual. Quakers were more likely to be prosecuted under the vagrancy laws or for non-payment of tithes than for blasphemy or sedition. Within a year or two, however, this situation was to change. The Restoration brought a wave of persecution that would almost destroy the Quaker movement and engulf many others besides.

See pages 146–7 for Cromwell's attempts to spare Nayler.

B   *Royalists and Anglicans – the making of Dissent*

The restoration of the monarchy took place in two parts: the first supervised by the Convention Parliament of 1660–1; and the second under the influence of the Cavalier Parliament elected in 1661. In the first period the emphasis appeared to be on reconciliation, in the second, on revenge. The same can be said of the restoration of the Anglican Church. In September 1660, an Act of Parliament restored to their parishes some 695 ministers who had been ejected between 1642 and 1660, but left others who had been appointed in that period in their places. This was followed in October by the King's Worcester House Declaration, which suggested several measures of reconciliation, and led to the calling of a conference to meet at Savoy House in London and decide on a settlement. It was intended that this would embody a compromise between Presbyterian and Anglican views, and Charles had signalled his interest in reconciliation by appointing Presbyterians as royal chaplains and offering a bishopric to the Presbyterian leader, Richard Baxter. While it was always clear that religious radicals such as the Baptists and Quakers would be restricted, there were high hopes of a broad Church that could encompass a range of mainstream views.

KEY ISSUE

The failure of comprehension in 1660–1.

KEY ISSUE

Anglican persecution made official.

By the time the conference met, however, the situation had changed. In January 1661, an abortive rising of millenarian radicals in London, led by Thomas Venner, had raised old fears of Puritan radicalism, while an Anglican party led by Gilbert Sheldon, Bishop of London, had determined that the restored Church must be built on the foundations laid by Laud. When the conference met in April they obstructed debates and insisted on the retention of ceremonies that the Presbyterians regarded as popish. To a considerable extent the Presbyterians played into their hands by allowing such specific differences to overshadow the broad areas of agreement that existed (regarding limits on the power of bishops, and a State Church based on parishes and supported by tithes), and there were areas of unimaginative rigidity on both sides. Nevertheless, the high-handed attitude of the Anglican party was clearly adopted deliberately, and it was certainly the Presbyterians who suffered from the failure of the conference.

By late 1661 the Anglican and Cavalier desire for revenge had been

PICTURE 33
*A portrait of George Morley,
Bishop of Winchester, by Lely.
One of the Calvinist clergy given
preferment (promotion) by
Charles II on his restoration.
Morley had been a member of
the Great Tew Circle (see page
351). When Morley was once
asked, 'What do the Arminians
hold [believe]?' he replied, 'All
the best livings in England?'*

See pages 170–1 for the
political context of the
Clarendon Code.

demonstrated in the first of a series of persecuting laws that became known as the Clarendon Code. The Confessional State had returned.

C *The survival of Dissent, 1662–89*

KEY ISSUE

*Uneven persecution of
Dissenters.*

This was the case in theory, but never in practice: the Clarendon Code caused great suffering to Dissenters, but it never succeeded in enforcing uniformity. The incidence of persecution varied. At its worst it could be inhuman. The Quakers bore the brunt in many areas, because they were unpopular, vulnerable and refused to hide. Not only did they insist on meeting openly, it was easy to bring them into court on some trumped-up charge and then imprison them under the Quaker Act for refusing to swear an oath in court. Four Quakers from Hollym in east Yorkshire were accused by their local vicar of having taken part in a plot against the King in 1663. The four were arrested and imprisoned in York castle until the Assizes, when the vicar failed to appear; nevertheless, they were ordered to take the Oath of Allegiance, and returned to prison when they refused. Despite offering to make a declaration of their loyalty, they were kept in York castle by this ploy for some years, until their families finally persuaded the JPs at Beverley to enquire about their condition. By the time that they were released in 1669, two had died of fever and one had lost his farm. His family had been kept alive by the charity of other Quakers.

This example could have been matched by others in most parts of the country, and by 1666, when George Fox was released from imprisonment in Scarborough castle, most of the early Quaker leaders were dead, and the movement was near collapse. However, by tireless travelling from 1666–9, Fox was able to visit most areas and establish a new organisational structure that ensured the survival of a Quaker Church. If it was more disciplined and less idealistic than in earlier years, most felt this to be a price worth paying. By the early 1670s the Quakers had a national organisation capable of supporting members and even of bringing prosecutions against those who abused the law in pursuing them. In addition, missionary work overseas had succeeded in establishing Quaker meetings in America and elsewhere – far from destroying the movement, the fires of persecution had hardened it into an international Church.

The Quakers were the most extreme example of resistance and success, but other Dissenters also survived. The Presbyterians had probably fared worst, since their separation was enforced and reluctant. They were therefore never able to establish an effective organisation, since the organisation that they believed in was the State Church. Nevertheless, Presbyterian meetings survived in many areas for some years before joining with local Independents or eventually succumbing to Unitarian ideas. Persecution was at its worst in the 1660s, when political bitterness was at its height, but even then some places were relatively safe. In Hull, there were complaints that Dissenters operated unhindered, and that Puritan ministers were even invited to preach in Holy Trinity Church. In 1666, there were angry scenes when the Mayor, John Tripp, allowed Joseph Wilson, who had been ejected from Beverley in 1662, to preach in Holy Trinity at the end of morning service. When local Royalists objected and tried to interrupt, the remaining congregation drove them out. Hull housed two regular conventicles, one Presbyterian and one Independent, throughout the period of persecution, and when the governor, the Earl of Plymouth, ordered the corporation to enforce the law against them in 1682, he was plainly told by one alderman that he would rather resign than apply such unjust laws against peaceable neighbours.

These incidents offer some clues as to why Protestant Dissent was able to survive the onslaught of persecution. Popular support for persecution in the 1660s was to some extent a reaction to fears that, in the preceding decade, the radicals had brought society to the point of collapse. As well as a simple desire for revenge among those who had suffered (as one ex-Royalist put it to the Independent ex-soldier, Captain John Hodgson of Coley in Yorkshire: 'now that the sun shines on our side of the hedge') there was an overwhelming desire for peace, order and security. Puritans of all shades provided a convenient target for blame and a symbol of all that threatened those characteristics. The party of revenge in Church and State therefore had a particular opportunity to impose their views on more neutral or indifferent elements.

The intention of persecuting Anglicans had been to isolate and eradicate Puritan views, but by defining the Anglican Church so narrowly as to exclude Presbyterians such as Baxter, they had swelled the numbers of potential Dissenters and excluded many whose views were known to be moderate. Such men had friends and allies who had been able to remain within the Church and used their position to protect and

> ### KEY ISSUE
>
> *The survival of Protestant Dissent.*

support those who were excluded. Had they established a broadly comprehensive Church in 1662, only those who held determinedly separatist views would have chosen to remain outside, and lacking both numbers and social connections, they might well have dwindled further. As it was, the Dissenters had friends and allies in many quarters who were able to protect them until the desire for revenge had begun to die away. This help came in many forms, but the three main sources were Puritan gentry, occasional conformists and Latitudinarians. These were not necessarily distinct categories; some men could come within all three, but each offered a different way in which individuals who were sympathetic to Dissenters might be able to avoid persecution themselves, and offer support to others who were vulnerable to it.

There is abundant evidence that gentry of Puritan views offered places to ejected ministers as chaplains and tutors, allowing them to earn a living and often to preach to groups of supporters. Outside the boroughs and urban areas where supporters were numerous enough to maintain a minister, this was the main reason for the survival of Presbyterian and Independent groups among the rural population. In the West and North Ridings of Yorkshire, these denominations relied on support from the clothing districts with their concentrations of craft workers and a network of contacts among the gentry. In 1672, an ejected minister, Richard Frankland, set up an academy at Rathmell in North Yorkshire, where potential ministers were educated alongside the sons of gentry before the latter moved on to the universities. The second generation of Nonconformist ministers in Yorkshire was largely a product of this academy. In many ways the Nonconformist academies would be at the forefront of educational development in the century that followed, since they were often more receptive to new ideas and technology than the classically hidebound universities and grammar schools.

A second source of allies was provided by the practice of occasional conformity, in which many moderate Puritans found themselves able to attend their parish church sufficiently often to fulfil the requirements of the law, while also maintaining links among the Dissenters and even attending conventicles at times. This was particularly prevalent in corporate boroughs such as Hull, and explains why the corporation there was notoriously sympathetic to Dissent (although not to the Quakers). Similar contacts existed in most boroughs and the larger towns. Occasional conformity was made easier by the existence of a party within the Church who have been labelled Latitudinarian, who interpreted the rules of the Church to emphasise its breadth and capacity to embrace a variety of views. Some were men who held views similar to the Nonconformists; for example, John Tillotson, who became Archbishop of Canterbury in 1691, did not himself conform until 1664. Others were simply men who regarded persecution as irrational, unchristian and counter-productive.

As the heirs of Chillingworth and Hales, the Latitudinarians were concerned above all to establish religious peace. They represented a brand of Christianity that emphasised forgiveness and brotherhood and sought to minimise dispute. Some drew on scientific principles, arguing that reli-

See pages 252–5 for the political context of occasional conformity.

KEY ISSUE

Latitudinarian toleration.

gion needed to be supported by reason; that which was not demonstrable was not sufficient cause for harshness and persecution. At its best, the Latitudinarian spirit portrayed Christ as a loving saviour, at its worst it could undermine faith itself. Either way it emphasised the virtues of toler-ance and dismissed persecution as illogical and unworkable. Like the political Whigs with whom they often allied, these men were as likely to have Parliamentarian history as Royalist connections, although many were of a generation that barely remembered the war. John Wilkins, who became Bishop of Chester in 1668, had married Cromwell's daughter, and was an early supporter of the Royal Society. Edward Stillingfleet, who became Bishop of Worcester in 1689, sheltered ejected ministers in his Bedfordshire vicarage and opened a school to employ one of them. These men were not occasional conformists – they held office in the Church, although few were promoted under the regime of Sheldon, Sancroft and their high Anglican allies, and were committed supporters of the national Church of England. The Church to which they were committed, however, was a broad, welcoming and ecumenical institution, unsympa-thetic to any attempt to destroy fellow Christians. In the years of persecu-tion, they could not create such an institution, but they were able to soften the worst effects of the Anglican and Cavalier alternative.

It could therefore be said that the failure to re-establish the confes-sional state after 1660 owed much to the activities of enemies within, and chief among these was the King himself. It is difficult to assess the motives and convictions of Charles II, but on several occasions he showed himself to be unsympathetic to persecution. To some extent his attitude was that of a rational Latitudinarian – personally unsympathetic to persecution, regarding it as irrational and unnecessary. In 1660 and 1662 he tried to soften its effects by suspending the application of the law, and in 1672 his proclamation of an Indulgence proved a turning point for Dissent. In that year's grace the ministers and meetings were able to organise themselves, obtain premises and establish funds. Their open exercise of their faith also had a significant psychological effect. Stillingfleet, who befriended many ejected ministers, always believed that their psychological separation from the Church stemmed from 1672.

Although Parliament forced the King to withdraw the Indulgence in 1673, the climate of persecution had changed. Attempts were made to provide parliamentary toleration, which were blocked by the bishops and the King himself. It is this, and the vindictiveness with which the King supported a new wave of persecution in the aftermath of the Exclusion Crisis, that raises doubts about his motives and offers support to the view that his sympathy for Dissent was always a cover for a desire to ease the situation for Catholics. There is, in fact, no reason to see these motives as contradictory. What is clear is that Charles was a politi-cian, and his concern was to use the weapons available to control the State. In that sense, as in much else, he embodied the interests and values of the more secular society that was now emerging in the aftermath of civil war and regicide. One legacy of the upheaval was a revulsion against the intense spirituality and the concern with other men's souls that had marked those years.

KEY ISSUE

The role of Charles II in mitigating persecution.

KEY ISSUE

Persecution becomes self-evidently immoral and absurd.

This outlook was reinforced by the emphasis on rational argument and practical observation that accompanied the scientific revolution. While theoretical science remained of interest mainly to an intellectual minority, the emphasis on sensible practice was more widely influential, and this also helped the Dissenters. It was perfectly clear to many that the Dissenters of the 1670s and 1680s were not the dangerous radicals of the past. They were respectable, hard-working neighbours, often craftsmen and businessmen, who played a useful part in the community. In this area, the Quakers were particularly influential. Fox's insistence on a strict code of morality and the Quaker habit of supporting their own poor and settling their debts had made them a byword for honesty and integrity, which helps to explain their later success as ironmasters, bankers and chemists. The Dissenters' Academies, which had been founded to provide a new generation of ministers, also offered a practical curriculum that compared favourably with the grammar schools and universities, where political reaction had renewed the tyranny of the classics and brought Baconian schemes of reform to an abrupt halt. What was clear on the basis of practical observation and rational thought, was what the Hull alderman had told the Earl of Plymouth – apart from their religious eccentricity, which should be largely their own business, the Dissenters were perfectly normal citizens who should be left in peace.

These arguments did not convince everyone, and it is ironic that what finally drove the Anglican authorities into alliance with Dissent was the re-emergence of an older enemy – Catholicism. It is in keeping with the changes that had taken place in 'Puritan' thinking that the Dissenters played a largely negative part in driving out the 'Catholic tyrant', James II. By refusing the alliance that he offered, they enabled the Whig and Anglican leaders to carry out a coup and replace one monarch with a more acceptable candidate. Their price was religious toleration, although some had hoped for more. In an echo of earlier disputes, the conscientious refusal of some High Churchmen to betray their King, and the intransigence of Scottish Calvinists in abolishing bishops soured the religious climate and destroyed the Comprehension Bill that would have allowed moderate Presbyterians such as Baxter to rejoin the Church. In a sense, the failure was prophetic. The Toleration Act of 1689 did not mean the end of religion as a political issue. It had the power to raise passions and prejudices (for example, the Sacheverell Riots of 1710 and the Schism Bill of 1711, and even the Gordon Riots of the 1780s), and the issue of the validity of a State Church remains today. What the Toleration Act did signify, however, was the end of the confessional state.

See page 229 for the political background.

4 ⌐ CONCLUSION: WAS THERE A POLITICAL REVOLUTION IN THE SEVENTEENTH CENTURY?

This chapter began by raising a question that has divided and continues to divide historians. The debate, however, usually focuses on the more tangible and measurable aspects of political activity – the role of Parliament, the nature of Britain and the functions of the monarchy. Disagreement usually centres on how far the abortive changes introduced between 1640 and 1660 were reversed, and on the relative importance of long-term, evolutionary changes as opposed to the political explosion of those years. The same issues arise in assessing the impact of political theory and changes in attitudes and ideas. Between 1689 and 1714, England ceased to operate as a confessional state. Religion had become a private matter, and intensity was in bad taste. As Derek Hirst expressed it: 'in religion piety and morality were all, zeal had become a dirty word'. Was this the result of long-term intellectual changes, emanating from the classical humanism of the Renaissance and development of science? Or was it the result of Protestant individualism and the sectarian vision of freedom? If so, it was a vision that had clearly been watered down in the process.

See pages 160–1 for a general discussion of the 'English Revolution'.

The answer is that it was both; and it is in the precise mix of ingredients and the process by which they interacted that debate continues to lie. What is clear is that both the intellectual and religious developments of the late Middle Ages in Europe posed a challenge to the existing authorities, and that this had results across Europe. The process by which they came together in England was influenced by local conditions and by historical accident. The personality of Henry VIII and of his daughter Elizabeth created the confessional state of England. The ability of Puritan preachers to inspire religious enthusiasm without having control of its effects created a revolutionary force outside the Church. The personality of Charles I created a cauldron in which enthusiasms of all kinds could be developed. The influence of classical models, Christian humanism and Protestant convictions came together in unique circumstances, which allowed them to create new visions to change the human condition. The idea of progress, of the ability to improve the lot of mankind, and to establish certain fundamental rights for all human beings, drew on all of these traditions.

In the prevailing circumstances, the visionaries went too far. They created a backlash that destroyed their revolution and drove them from power. It also led to a rejection of enthusiasm itself. Yet certain changes could not be reversed. The political revolution that required new institutions or organised movements was easily crushed, but the religious convictions that motivated many of them were harder to eradicate. They underwent change in the process of survival, and it was a limited concept of freedom that became reality after 1689. In many ways, the results of the radical revolution were negative – it destroyed both the Anglican vision and its Puritan counterpart. It failed to provide an alternative, and toleration came from debate partly through weariness. Nevertheless, by removing restrictions on belief, by establishing the right of individuals to follow their own conscience within the limits required by social peace, and by destroying the ideal of the confessional state, the events of the seventeenth century laid the foundations of liberal democracy and the concept of fundamental human rights.

Society

10

INTRODUCTION

The purpose of this chapter is to convey the atmosphere of life in Stuart Britain, to open windows into a world in many ways similar to our own, and in many ways dramatically different. Particular aspects – such as the role of women, popular protest, the prevalence of squalour, disease and death – have been selected to convey both the contrasts and the similarities. On the face of it the contrasts are more striking. If we could be transported by some miraculous time-machine to Stuart Britain, we would at once be assaulted by the stench of bad drains and open sewers, the sight of diseased and impoverished people, and the sounds of an unfamiliar language. After a while, however, we would find our bearings and discover that in some respects little has changed. These similarities and contrasts are vital to our understanding of 'the years of turmoil'.

In one chapter it is impossible to cover every aspect of Stuart Britain. For 'Britain' comprised many different societies and ways of life. The crofter in the north of Scotland spoke a different language, ate a different diet and acknowledged different loyalties to a Londoner. Furthermore much changed between 1603 and 1714, especially in the first half of the century. Conrad Russell has written that 'a social history of Britain in the early seventeenth century would be a stark impossibility'. The approach in this chapter is therefore impressionistic. It is hoped that the topics selected will convey those key contrasts and similarities that will enable the reader to understand the developments described in the other chapters of this book.

1 ∼ RICH, MIDDLING AND POOR

Straightaway, three crucial points of a general nature must be emphasised and discussed. First, while there has always been a gulf between rich and poor, the differences during the seventeenth century would strike us as extraordinary. Secondly, during the 'years of turmoil' this gap actually widened, both in terms of wealth and lifestyle. The significance of protest movements such as the Levellers (see pages 121–3) cannot be grasped without an awareness of this ever-widening gulf between 'haves' and have-nots'. Thirdly, whereas in 1603 society was predominantly rural with squires and peasants both owning land, economically linked and making a living in more or less the same world, by 1714 the pattern of both society and land ownership had changed. The era of large-scale farming for profit had dawned, so that there was not enough land for everyone to own. Peasants were driven off their farms, forced to sell up and labour for wages. Many of the rich too were now divorced from the land, living in luxurious town houses, making fortunes in trade or in professions such as law and government service. There were many reasons for this, but above all was the emergence of Britain as the commercial centre of the world. While throughout the period land remained a status symbol and a source of wealth, rich people invested their gains in trade, urban property or investments in the stock market. These developments are crucial to the understanding of politics during the reigns of William III and Anne.

On the whole rank and wealth coincided. This was achieved when aristocrats married money. But the rich were frequently ennobled in their own right. 'Riches do make gentlemen in every country of England', as a contemporary observed. Indeed, when the Crown was financially embarrassed, rank was offered in return for cash. On behalf of the spendthrift James I, the Duke of Buckingham flogged peerages for £10,000 and baronetcies for £1,000. A significant seventeenth-century development lower down the social scale was the marketing by churchwardens of places in church, since a pew reflected social status. In 1688, an acute observer, Gregory King, calculated the average income of a peer at £2,800 a year, a knight at £650 and a gentleman at £280. Others were less well-paid. A naval officer received £60 a year, a country parson £45. A labourer's earnings would vary according to the time of year, but might total £10 if he was lucky. A woman in domestic service was paid £2 a year plus her keep. So when Shakespeare's Prince Hal jokingly offered Francis the publican's lad £1,000, this was an immense fortune and a gateway to respectability.

The rich also included what historians call the pseudo gentry, that is to say men without titles. These might well be successful merchants, lawyers, doctors, higher clergy and senior government employees. Often such men were the younger sons of titled parents who continued to maintain links with their families, since there was far less prejudice against 'trade' and the professions than in contemporary France. Successful careerists who were *not* aristocrats copied the lifestyle of their social superiors, dressing ostentatiously, living in magnificent town or country houses and employing armies of servants. The titled and the pseudo gentry, or in other words the rich, between them may have amounted to five per cent of the population by 1714.

Then there were 'the middling sort', as contemporaries called them. At the beginning of the seventeenth century the backbone of the middling sort was the yeomanry, the independent, self-employed, landowning peasants – the traditional crop-growers of old England. By the end of the century, however, the yeomanry was much decayed, weakened by inflation, pressures from enclosing landlords and by competition from rival food producers. Many yeomen sold their land and became tenant-farmers. Others moved to the towns. The middling sort now included lesser merchants, parish clergy, craftsmen, country doctors and schoolmasters. Clearly the boundaries between the middling sort and the rich could become blurred. There was much social mobility. Hard work,

> **KEY ISSUE**
>
> *Social divisions in Stuart Britain.*

> See pages 322–4 for details of economic progress.

ability and luck could make a man wealthy and lift him out of the middling sort. Conversely, bad luck or bad habits could bring a man down: gambling, drink and an inability to manage his affairs. Perhaps the middling sort accounted for about 30 per cent of the population in 1714.

Finally there were the poor. It was no use fining a pauper, nor could he object to corporal punishment. 'No goods – to be whipped', was therefore a magistrate's typical decision. The middling sort dreaded the descent into the indignity and anonymity that was the pauper's lot. 'A poor woman who died in a barn at the parsonage whose name we could not learn', recorded the parish officials at the beginning of our century. At the end of Anne's reign, a typical task performed by comparable parish officials would be to dump a poor woman in labour across the ditch that separated the parishes, in order to avoid the expense of a pauper's child. The poor were distinguished from the middling by their ragged appearance. They were landless and illiterate. Often they would be vagrants, migrating from neighbourhood to neighbourhood in search of work, begging off the charitable, endeavouring to escape the penalties for the petty crimes that they had committed in their desperation, and drifting to the towns in search of work. Society was prejudiced against 'the masterless men' who, by their refusal to settle down challenged the basis of social order. Vagrants were treated brutally in the economically advanced south-east, but more kindly in the backward north. In general, they were persecuted – and feared. 'Hark, hark, the dogs do bark . . .' reminds us of the general unease when beggars came to town. Did the poor actually starve? In times of dearth some must have done, while others perished from diseases related to malnutrition. However, Englishmen were supposed to be better off than the French who wore wooden shoes and ate black bread. Irish, Scottish and Welsh were less fortunate than the English.

On the whole, historians today agree that seventeenth-century English folk were saved from total destitution by the Poor Law, created by a number of statutes in Elizabeth's reign. This severely practical code has been much criticised by historians, yet in its way was a remarkable achievement, unique in Europe. It reflected the morality of the age by distinguishing between 'sturdy beggars', that is to say able-bodied paupers who were put to work in 'houses of correction' or whipped and branded if they refused to work, and the 'impotent poor', that is the old, the very young, the mad and the sick. It was assumed that there were jobs available for the 'sturdy', though clearly this was not always the case. Those who could not work were maintained by the parish out of the poor rate, fed, housed and clothed. The rich and middling paid their share of the poor rate because if they refused they were imprisoned and their goods were confiscated. It also made sense to save the locality from the threat of riot and disorder to which the poor might resort if they were not relieved. On the whole, the poor rioted less during the seventeenth than the sixteenth century. There was another reason for paying the poor rate: you never could tell, anyone could be reduced to penury. Administered by the Overseers of the Poor and supplemented

See pages 276–7 for the living conditions of the poor.

KEY ISSUE

How harsh was the Old Poor Law?

by private charity, the Poor Law served as a safety-net, offering a minimum guarantee against starvation and homelessness. It may have been harsh, but it worked. In fact, the Old Poor Law was arguably less barbaric than the New Poor Law which replaced it in 1834.

Recent research has revised some previously accepted beliefs. For instance, elderly people in middling and poor families did *not* live with their younger relations. A typical family consisted of husband, wife, children and servants (often young relations) – but no grandfather or grandmother. Again, English society was surprisingly mobile. Here is another contrast with France where the majority of peasants were born, married and died within sight and sound of their village church. Not so in seventeenth-century England, where parish registers often indicate that over half the inhabitants' families had recently moved into the locality.

A further surprising point: standards of living may have been rising at the end of the period, as glass and pewter replaced earthenware and wood on the dinner table, people drank coffee, tea and chocolate and an Essex contemporary remarked on 'the multitude of chimneys lately erected'. Yet post-Restoration Britain, the age of reason, the Royal Society, and the age of Newton and Locke saw a deterioration in overall educational standards since the literate proportion of the population actually declined. The gap widened between the educated rich and the illiterate poor, and between well-educated men and half-educated women. Particularly with regard to the education of women, the seventeenth century compared badly with the sixteenth century. By the beginning of the eighteenth century, education was as ever the gateway to success, but it was a gateway that a decreasing number of people could enter. Not only was it 'all right for some', but such contrasts were deliberately encouraged. This polarisation of society between the rich and the fairly rich, or middling, on the one hand and the poor on the other, between the ruling classes and the governed, between the educated and the illiterate, and between men and women was perceived to be the essential background for economic success. Both in towns and in the countryside the ever-widening gap between the 'haves' and the 'have-nots', between the respectable and the disreputable was not only accepted but was welcomed in the name of progress. Reason dictated that everyone had different jobs to do, and different roles to fill.

> **KEY ISSUE**
>
> *Three previously accepted beliefs now discredited.*

> See page 324 for the economic aspects of the widening gap.

> **KEY ISSUE**
>
> *Why did the gap widen between rich and poor?*

2 ⌐ WOMEN IN THE SEVENTEENTH CENTURY: A CASE STUDY

A *A Woman's Place?*

Nothing better illustrates the contrast between seventeenth-century society and our own than the role of women. It is no coincidence that books on the seventeenth century are almost entirely about men, the female half of the human race being ignored. This imbalance is easily explained. To describe seventeenth-century Britain as sexist would be an understatement. Not only were women excluded from jobs, money, privileges and education, but grotesque justifications were advanced for such injustice. Women were called 'the weaker vessel' – the phrase used in the First Epistle of St Peter where husbands were told 'to give honour to the wife as to the weaker vessel'. But women were dishonoured by contemporary understanding of 'weakness'. Rochester, the Restoration poet, typified this male chauvinism:

> Love a Woman! You're an Ass
> Tis a most insipid passion
> To choose out for your Happiness
> The silliest part of God's Creation.

Q

How could an intelligent man like Rochester write such nonsense?

PICTURE 34

A portrait of Lucy Hutchinson by Walker. She failed to rescue her husband from prison after the Restoration though she had pleaded successfully for his life

Women were perceived to be not only physically weak but also mentally and morally weak. They were allegedly irrational, emotional chatterboxes and intellectually second rate. They were also regarded as feckless, devious, malicious and dedicated to man's corruption. Their only strength was supposed to be their sexual appetite, which proverbially exceeded the male's. What was the justification for these sexist views? The first chapters of Genesis tells of how the Devil, in the form of a serpent, corrupted Eve who then corrupted Adam, her husband. This story was used against women by the Bible-worshipping males, though they no doubt believed what they wanted to believe. Some men doubted whether women had souls at all, 'no more than a goose'.

Did anyone question this widely received orthodoxy? Antonia Fraser, in her book entitled *The Weaker Vessel* (1984), records the successful defiance and protests of several women. She shows how in practice scores of men gave their wives and daughters the affection and admiration they so clearly deserved. Furthermore, several redoubtable women (Brilliana, Lady Harley; Lucy Hutchinson; Aphra Behn; Sarah, Duchess of Marlborough, to name but a few) refuted the notion that women were in any way inferior. They are the practical, real-life heroines of this chapter. But what about the theory, supposedly based on Scripture? George Fox, who founded the Quakers (see pages 368–9), scorned the argument that women had no souls. How could the Virgin Mary sing 'My soul doth magnify the Lord', if she did not have one? Emilier Lanier wittily defended her sex's supposed 'Grandmother Eve':

Q

What was Lanier's argument in defence of women?

> But surely Adam cannot be excused,
> Her fault though great, yet he was more to blame;
> What weakness offered, strength might have refused,
> Being lord of all, the greater was his shame.

Despite such comments, it will come as no surprise that the woman's place was perceived to be the home. But there were homes and homes. While all Eve's grandchildren inherited from her the pains of childbirth, a woman's duties and lifestyle varied according to her wealth and station in society. The grand lady on a country estate or the rich wife of a London merchant would manage the labours of others rather than get her own hands dirty. She would even employ a wet-nurse to breastfeed her children, an unhygienic practice that caused the deaths of many infants from monied homes. On the other hand, the wife of a peasant would breast-feed her own children. She would spend her day not only cooking and cleaning and minding the children, but supplementing her husband's income with agricultural labour or weaving. The wives of the middling sort often had to do the work themselves, especially if they wanted it done properly. A London minister's wife, Elizabeth Walker, used to react indignantly when she heard her husband praised for the cider served to their guests: 'His cider! 'Tis my cider! I have all the pains and care, and he has all the praise who never meddles with it'.

See pages 326–8 for women employed in agriculture.

Elizabeth Walker's husband hastened to point out that when she protested in this way she was not wholly serious, but 'half way between jest and earnest'. This was just as well since seventeenth-century society was merciless towards 'uppity' women. A man's rightful place was believed to be on top – in the professions, at home, and even during sexual intercourse. The woman on top was unnatural, to be disciplined and brought down. In village society the hen-pecked husband and his bossy wife were humiliated by the riotous shaming ritual called the **skimmington ride**. Two men, often the neighbours of the couple being ridiculed, rode through the village on a horse. Both riders faced backwards, with one dressed as a woman. The suggestion was that everything was wrong, back to front as it were, when the woman bossed the man. The ride was accompanied by 'rough music' and, no doubt, uproarious laughter (see page 401). Again, this was semi-humorous but even more cruel punishment was meted out to a woman who was allegedly a scold, bullying her husband or her neighbours with offensive, domineering language. A scold could be fined, padlocked in a bridle or a ducking stool and thrown into a pond. The worst and most horrifying fate of the woman who could not hold her tongue in a meek and feminine way was to be branded as a witch with the consequence of being hanged in England or burnt alive in Scotland (see pages 404–7).

skimmington ride was derived from the skimming ladel used by housewives in the process of making cheese. It was a riotous ritual to humiliate scolds and their husbands.

B *Bucking the system*

KEY ISSUE

Aristocratic women in the Civil War.

See page 167 for the Act of Indemnity and page 178 for a portrait of Bennet.

Act of Indemnity was a statute by which Charles II pardoned all who had fought against the Crown – with a very few named exceptions.

The greatest opportunities for women occurred during the 20-year period between 1640 and 1660 when the world was turned upside down. The 'weaker vessel' often *had* to be strong. Aristocratic women managed estates when their husbands departed for the wars. They appealed to hostile committees against the confiscation of their husbands' properties. Elizabeth, Lady Cholmley, battled for the ancestral home in Whitby after her husband Sir Hugh sailed to the Continent, having unsuccessfully defended Scarborough Castle for the King. The Parliamentarians occupied their house in Whitby until plague drove them out. The redoubtable Lady Cholmley then travelled across the North Yorkshire moors on foot in midwinter from Malton to Whitby, to repossess her property, plague or no plague. Lucy Hutchinson fought for her husband's life when he was indicted as a regicide in 1660. Sure enough, his name is on the death warrant, but Lucy pleaded with Charles II's Secretary of State, Sir Henry Bennet, that her husband was covered by the **Act of Indemnity**. She was only partially successful in that John Hutchinson escaped the rope but died in prison. When the Royalist Colonel Charles Townley was killed at Marston Moor, his widow was to be seen next morning seeking her husband's corpse among the slain. Cromwell gave her an escort, since a battlefield in his opinion was no place for a woman, however courageous.

Even braver deeds were sometimes required. Brilliana, Lady Harley, took charge of Brampton Bryan Castle, Herefordshire, while her husband was away in London on the business of Parliament. Initially, her chief concerns were to send him veal pies and new shoes, while persuading her son, Ned, to remain at Oxford University out of harm's way. But when the Royalist army summoned the castle, Brilliana defiantly refused to surrender. The King's cannon demolished the walls, but still this paragon of female courage held out until a relieving Parliamentary army arrived. Unfortunately, Brilliana was so exhausted by her ordeal that she died of apoplexy. Equally celebrated, but on the Royalist side, was Charlotte, Countess of Derby, who held Lathom House in Lancashire for the King while her husband operated from the Isle of Man. According to a Parliamentarian journal, 'three women have ruined this kingdom, Eve, the Queen and the Countess of Derby'. The Countess was certainly too warlike for the Parliamentary commander besieging Lathom House, Colonel Alexander Rigby, the MP for Wigan. When he summoned the castle, the Countess replied, 'Tell that insolent rebel, he shall neither have persons, goods nor house; when our strength and provision is spent, we shall find a fire more merciful than Rigby'. This was in fact calculated bravado. The true state of the Countess' mind was indicated by her desperate appeal to Prince Rupert: 'from a distressed woman whose only hope next to Almighty God is in Your Highness' help'. Rupert responded to the 'distresssed woman' when he relieved Latham House during his whirlwind campaign in Lancashire on the road to Marston Moor.

Less aristocratic women were actively involved as nurses, messengers and companions. Some followed their husbands to the wars. Others accompanied the armies as 'leaguer bitches', that is to say prostitutes serving the needs of the soldiers. One such group was massacred by the infantry of the New Model Army after the Royalists' defeat at Naseby, on the grounds that they were Irish papists (they were more probably Welsh, equally incomprehensible to their bigoted killers). On both sides some women dressed in men's clothes and fought in battle. A ballad of 1655 recalled the exploits of one celebrated 'she-soldier' who went by the name of 'Mr Clarke' until she became pregnant. 'Tom, why do you grow so fat?', asked her commanding officer'. 'Tis strong beer and tobacco which is the cause of that', she replied. But she could only conceal her condition for so long, her preoccupation now being her reputation as an 'honest woman'. 'Mr Clarke's' husband was the father of her child, she insisted. Mother and baby were nevertheless much visited by her fellow troopers, who still asked for 'Mr Clarke'.

In general, the climate of the times removed the shackles that had imprisoned the female sex. Contemporaries were astonished by the crowd of women who petitioned Parliament for peace in August 1643. Estimates ranged from 200 to 6,000. Hostile witnesses described a mob of 'whores, bawds, oyster-women, kitchen-stuff women, beggar women and the very scum of the suburbs besides abundance of Irish women' (the ultimate insult). Other reports simply referred to citizens' wives with their babies at their breasts. There seems no doubt, however, that the protest was noisy and disrespectful. The women had to be ejected by soldiers.

Even more shocking was the involvement of women in the campaign

KEY ISSUE

War work for women of all classes.

KEY ISSUE

The emerging emancipation of women.

to release Lilburne the Leveller in April 1649. Elizabeth Lilburne was rebuked for unfeminine presumption when she organised a petition on her husband's behalf. This rebuke was countered by 'The Humble Petition of divers well-affected Women inhabiting the City of London' in April 1649, which Antonia Fraser calls 'the high point of political female activity at this period'. Signed by 10,000 women and presented to Parliament, this was a Leveller-inspired demand for equal rights. The Petition began with a punchy, well-argued preamble: 'Since we are assured of our creation in the image of God, and of an interest in Christ equal unto men, as also of a proportionate share in the freedom of this Commonwealth ...'. The repartee that followed its presentation repays study. 'You are desired to go home and look after your own business, and meddle with your house-keeping ... It is not for women to petition ... Wash your dishes.' 'Sir, we have scarce any dishes left to wash, and those we have are not sure to keep.' 'It is strange for women to petition.' 'It was strange that you cut off the King's head.' When 20 women were admitted into the lobby, they grabbed Cromwell's cloak. 'What will you have?' 'Those rights and freedom of the Nation that you promised us.'

Fighting talk! But the women failed to achieve Lilburne's release and failed again when they petitioned the Barebones Parliament in April 1653. Women continued to play a prominent role in the Leveller movement, but primarily in support of their militant and often persecuted husbands. The most radical of all the Leveller pamphleteers, the Digger, Gerald Winstanley advocated total freedom for women to marry whom they pleased and to control their own property – revolutionary ideas at the time. But not even 'the mad weaver of Wigan' argued that women should be given the vote, though it should also be remembered that the Levellers, for all their revolutionary characteristics, did not advocate complete male suffrage.

What really shocked contemporaries was that women preached. In the permissive climate of the 1640s ordinary soldiers in the Parliamentary armies frequently occupied pulpits. So why not women? There was a tradition of women preaching in the late sixteenth-century congregationalist movements on the Continent. This tradition manifested itself occasionally in England in the 1630s, and it was a woman, Jenny Geddes, who threw a stool at the Dean of St Giles's in 1637. So not surprisingly 'she-preachers' blossomed in the 1640s among the sects, especially in London and especially among the Baptists. Mrs Attoway for instance impressed her congregation by regularly preaching for more than an hour – but then she damaged the cause by running off with another woman's husband. The greatest chance for women to play a prominent role was provided by the Quaker movement. Its founder, George Fox, believed that the Holy Spirit spoke to everyone, both female and male, and that everyone, male and female, had the right to impart the Spirit's teaching. Quaker women were famous, indeed notorious, for using the Spirit's guidance to interrupt services of other denominations. Quakers were fearless and lacking in deference, and that applied especially to their women.

KEY ISSUE

Leveller women.

KEY ISSUE

Women preached in public.

See page 75 for Jenny Geddes's protest.

This heady atmosphere encouraged not only saints and heroines, but also cranks and exhibitionists. Perhaps 'Little Elizabeth' Fletcher personified all four attributes. At the age of 14 she believed that she had a mission to the university of Oxford. After being roughed up by the undergraduates and suffering 'shameful abuses' she sought to bring home to them their hypocrisy by running naked through the city. When she refused to stop preaching, the vice-chancellor had her whipped for blasphemy. 'Serve her right' was the popular comment. Yet during those 20 years in which so many social way-posts were uprooted there was a real chance that women might be emancipated as never before. Or so it might have seemed.

C *Companions, she-authors and brimstone*

But appearances were deceptive. 'The contribution of women has surprised and delighted the nation', was Neville Chamberlain's well-meant but patronising comment on the role of British women in the First World War, and it is a textbook commonplace that as a result women were rewarded with the vote. No such compliment was paid to British women after the end of the seventeenth-century civil wars. After the Restoration of 1660 the supremacy of the male sex was reinstated just as much as the supremacy of King, Parliament, squire and parson. The tone was set by Charles II, one of the most selfish male-chauvinists in history. 'I meddle not with ladies' souls', he remarked complacently, the implication being that he certainly meddled with their bodies. Perhaps appropriately the only identifiable area in which women achieved a breakthough was the stage. In the permissive, self-indulgent society led by the King, women for the first time in the history of the British stage regularly played female roles. Many of these emancipated actresses found their way into the King's bed.

Apart from marrying and becoming a housewife, or someone's mistress, there was little on offer. Virtually the only alternative for most upper class women who were not married was to become the companion of a woman who was more fortunate. Samuel Pepys recorded in his diary the problem of finding the right companion for his difficult and demanding wife. His own sister, Pall, was lazy, grumpy and prone to self-pitying tears, the girl Barker was devious and dishonest, Mary Mercer could speak French but could do little else. As for Deb Willett, Mrs Pepys caught her husband groping this nubile wench while she was supposedly combing his hair. So she had to go as well. The doyenne of companions was Abigail Hill (later Mrs Abigail Masham), who became Queen Anne's friend, companion and lover. Kind, loyal, self-effacing Abigail became indispensable to her royal mistress, offering her undemanding affection and resourceful attention to her many ailments. There was a real problem when the grateful Queen wished to reward her companion by ennobling her, for how could 'Baroness Masham' sleep on the floor by the Queen's bed and empty her slops every morning? Abigail was therefore given the resounding title of 'Woman of the Bedchamber to the Queen'.

KEY ISSUE

Women failed to defend and develop their emancipation.

KEY ISSUE

The role of the companion

See pages 258–9 for the dismissal of Marlborough.

Abigail Masham's greatest feat was to displace her predecessor and patron, Sarah, Duchess of Marlborough. Sarah represents the brilliant and formidable career woman who would have succeeded in any age and place. Clever, beautiful and self-confident, she was devoted to the interests of her husband, John Churchill, who was in due course made a duke in recognition of his victories over the French in the War of the Spanish Succession. Sarah's friendship with the Queen guaranteed her husband's retention of his post despite the jealousy of his many enemies. But with all her brilliance Sarah committed the supreme blunder of quarrelling with the Queen. John's dismissal as commander-in-chief followed inexorably. Actually, Sarah quarrelled with everybody. 'Why do they call me Bellisarius?' (Bellisarius was a Roman general), Churchill asked the tactless and forthright Bishop of Salisbury, Gilbert Burnet. 'Because he had a brimstone of a wife', was the reply. Sarah was on speaking terms with neither her daughters nor her grandchildren. Sir John Vanbrugh who designed Blenheim Palace for the Marlboroughs, referred to her as 'that b b b of a b'. She had just refused him admittance to his own masterpiece. He had to spend the day in a pub at Woodstock.

A handful of women rose above the deplorable education provided for their sex and succeeded as educators or as authors, following the example of Louis XIV's mistress and second wife, Madame de Maintenon, who had led the way with her school at St Cyr for aristocratic but impoverished girls. So inevitably Basua Makin and Mary Astell were accused of being papists when they founded girls' schools. Aphra Behn wrote witty plays that delighted Charles II, but which his brother James was too solemn and stupid to understand. Anne Conway wrote philosophy. Anne Killigrew, the poetess, spoke for all women who dared to defy the supposed male monopoly of talent and wisdom:

What was Anne Killigrew's response to male prejudice? Why were some women nevertheless able to achieve fame as writers?

Did I my lines intend for public view
How many censures would their faults pursue . . .
Alas! a woman that attempts the pen
Such an intruder on the rights of men
Such a presumptuous creature is esteemed
The fault, can by no virtue be redeemed.

KEY ISSUE

Women in business.

Then there were the businesswomen such as Mrs Constance Pley who supplied Pepys's navy with sailcloth. There was always a close link between the Quakers and business, exemplified by Joan Dant who made a fortune through supplying haberdashery. 'I got it by the rich and mean to leave it to the poor', she exclaimed, bequeathing over £9,000 to widows and the fatherless. Even more unusual was Mrs Bridget Bendish, the child of Henry Ireton and Oliver Cromwell's daughter, Bridget. Mrs Bendish managed a saltpan and refinery, which supplied the East Anglian herring industry. She resembled her famous grandfather in looks, personality and eccentricity. Once a fellow traveller in a stagecoach made derogatory remarks about the late Protector unaware

PICTURE 35
A portrait of Sarah, Duchess of Marlborough, by Kneller. Sarah was seen to be a difficult and fascinating woman

of the identity of the homely woman opposite him. To his astonishment the lady instantly challenged him to a duel – with swords. It cannot be said that Mrs Bendish was a successful businesswoman. For one thing she gave away the profits with impulsive generosity. But her workforce respected her for sharing their privations in all weathers, with an old blanket across her shoulders. She would drop in on friends unannounced, drink heavily and depart for home in the darkness, riding on her old mare and singing Isaac Watts's hymns at the top of her voice. No-one called her a weaker vessel.

Nevertheless, the overall picture of the role of women in the 'years of turmoil' is depressing. According to Antonia Fraser, 'where the status of the so-called weaker vessel was concerned, the seventeenth century saw very little improvement in real terms'. If the world was turned upside down between 1640 and 1660, men saw to it that it was turned the right side up again after the Restoration. Women were still confined to the home, obliged to wash dishes. Husbands still controlled their wives' property and could beat them if they were insubordinate. Women's education lagged behind men's even more than in James I's day. In particular Lucy Hutchinson's competence in Latin was still beyond virtually every other woman's reach. So the conclusion to this case study, while interesting and important, is basically negative.

> **KEY ISSUE**
>
> *Women's failure to buck the system.*

See pages 326–7 for women's place in the Stuart economy.

PICTURE 36
A portrait of Barbara Villiers,
Duchess of Cleveland, by Lely

3 ~ COURTSHIP, MARRIAGE, LOVE AND SEX

A *Marriage à la mode*

Nothing better illustrates the divisions between rich and poor with which this chapter began than the contrasting attitudes to marriage. For the rich, marriage was a business transaction as a result of which fortunes could be made and lost. For the poor, money inevitably played a part, but it was not nearly such a consideration. A Somerset peasant tried to palm off his pregnant girlfriend with the assertion that 'she is a most capable servant for anything within doors and without, for she can get a man's living and her own too'. But he still did not marry her himself. Another revealing contrast is provided by rich and poor widows. The nearest approach to an emancipated female in the seventeenth century was a rich widow. Unlike an unmarried girl who obeyed her father or a wife who obeyed her husband, the wealthy widow could do as she pleased. A poor widow on the other hand was to be pitied, dependent on the kindness of others and vulnerable to exploitation. Another consistent contrast is the age of marriage. The rich could afford to get married in their late teens or early twenties, while the poor on average waited until men were 29 and women were 27. The rich had more children: they were more fertile since they were better fed; they married younger; poor women breastfed their children (a natural form of contraception); and the poor had to limit the size of their families to what they could afford, by whatever methods of birth control they could devise (coitus interruptus is the most plausible guess).

For the upper classes a rich heiress attracted suitors from far and wide. When in April 1628 Richard Bennett, a rich London merchant, died, he left his widow, Elizabeth, extremely well off. Among several suitors for her fortune were, to the entertainment of the general public, Sir Heneage Finch, Sir Sackville Crowe and Dr Raven. Remembering the proverbial reward for the early bird, Dr Raven climbed into Mrs Bennett's bedroom, assuming that being a widow she would be sex-starved and find him irresistible. Quite the reverse. Mrs Bennett shrieked for help, had Dr Raven ejected by her servants and prosecuted him for 'ill demeanour'. Who should the magistrate be but Sir Heneage Finch whom the widow eventually married.

Equally dramatic but not so amusing was the experience of Sara Cox. In August 1637, this monied 14-year-old orphan, who was in the care of the City of London, was abducted from her boarding school in Hackney and forcibly married to Roger Fulwood, her best friend's brother. She was then stripped and made to get into bed with Roger so that the marriage could be consummated – for a consummated marriage could not be annulled. Fortunately, Sara's friends alerted the law, she was rescued and Roger was arrested and brought before the Lord Mayor. He denied that sex had in fact occurred, and after a spell in prison was fined £2,000. A notorious forced marriage was Frances Coke's to Sir John Villiers. The motive was political as well as financial, the bride's father, the disgraced Lord Chief Justice Coke, being anxious to recover royal favour by his daughter's marriage into the Buckingham family. Coke kidnapped his daughter from his estranged wife after battering down the front door and tied Frances to her bed so that she could be whipped into compliance. The marriage duly took place, but with predictably disastrous results. Villiers went mad, Frances committed adultery, lost her property and was exiled by the King.

Historians now maintain that forced marriages, even among the upper classes where so much money was often at stake, were the exceptions rather than the rule. Scholars with Marxist sympathies such as Laurence Stone emphasised the English monied classes' interest in money. But it is now clear that parents appreciated out of common sense if not human kindness that a marriage was more likely to work if the two young people involved were reasonably content. Arranged

> **KEY ISSUE**
>
> *Upper class marriage.*

See page 32 for Coke's role.

KEY ISSUE

Were seventeenth-century people able to marry for love?

marriages certainly did occur. The bride's dowry had to be discussed, to say nothing of her jointure (what she would keep if her husband predeceased her). Lady Sunderland commented on her niece's marriage: 'He is not a pleasant man – very few are . . . One thing pleased: when he said "With all my worldly goods I thee endow" he put a purse upon the book with two hundred guineas'. This was indeed an encouraging start to married life. But it made sense to have consulted the preferences of the prospective bride and groom beforehand.

Young men and women of the poorer and middling sorts had much more freedom of choice. For one thing, as we have seen, they were older than their social superiors when they got married, and so were presumably less easily dominated by their parents – if they were still alive. Quite often the couple had been living together on a trial basis. Recent research suggests that something like one-third of English brides in the seventeenth century were pregnant on their wedding day. It was common custom for a man who wanted to have sex with a woman to go through a form of betrothal with her in which he would give her a symbolic coin in front of witnesses. Only after this semi-official commitment would she agree to sleep with him. If she became pregnant he would honour his promise and formally marry her in church.

Rich, middling and poor shared one experience in particular that separates them from us. A high proportion of marriages were prematurely terminated by death. In fact, one social historian has estimated that a similar number of marriages were ended by death within say ten years of the marriage taking place as are terminated by divorce in late twentieth-century Britain and America.

KEY ISSUE

The termination of marriage.

Even for the rich it was extremely difficult to get a divorce. It involved much expense, appeals to the House of Lords and notoriously unprovable circumstances such as non-consummation, justifying a decree of nullity. A famous test case was the termination of the Earl of Essex's marriage to Frances Howard on the grounds of his alleged impotence. Maybe he did 'lack ink in his pen' as contemporaries put it, or maybe he was so discouraged by his wife's frostiness that he could not manage to have sex with her. The important point is that Frances only got her divorce due to her desire to marry James I's favourite, Robert Carr, Duke of Somerset. Divorce was out of the question for ordinary people. Unhappily married couples jogged along as best they could, or simply went their separate ways, seeking sexual fulfilment where they could get it. As was invariably the case the man was in a better position than the woman. A woman who was caught committing adultery lost her dowry if her husband opted for separation, while a man who was unfaithful paid no penalty whatsoever.

See page 34 for the political context of the Essex divorce.

'The oldest profession' was always available to men, both rich and poor, who were bored with their wives. Aubrey described Sir Walter Raleigh dining out with his wild, unreliable son, young Walter:

Mr Walter humbled himself to his father and promised he would behave himself mighty mannerly. He sat next to his father and was very demure half of dinner time. Then said he, 'I, this morning, not having the fear of God before my eyes, went to a whore. I was very eager of her, kissed and embraced her, and went to enjoy her, but she thrust me from her, and vowed I should not, "For your father lay with me but an hour ago" '. Whereupon Sir Walter gives his son a damned blow over the face. His son, rude as he was, would not strike his father, but strikes over the face the gentleman that sat next to him and said, 'Box about, t'will come to my father anon'.

London society resorted to prostitutes, witness the bawdy house riots of March 1668 when mobs of apprentices demolished high-class brothels in Shoreditch and Holborn as protests against a dissolute and Romish court. During the Exclusion Crisis of 1678–81 (see pages 187–94) the Lord Chamberlain's officials were frequently sent round the 'ale-houses and stews' surrounding Westminster in order to winkle out the government's supporters when they were needed. Charles II may not have resorted to brothels but he certainly patronised prostitutes. There was a celebrated exchange between the King and his Lord Chancellor, the Earl of Shaftesbury (whom he nicknamed 'Little Sincerity'): 'Here comes the greatest whoremaster in all England', quipped the King to which Shaftesbury with a bow replied '. . . of a subject, Sire'.

> **KEY ISSUE**
>
> *The availability of prostitutes.*

See page 180 for the portrait and profile of Shaftesbury.

B *Source investigation: A profile of the mistresses of Charles II and James II*

A *History of his Own Time* by Bishop Gilbert Burnet (1707) describes Barbara Villiers, later Countess of Castlemain, later Duchess of Cleveland.

One of the race of the Villiers, then married to Palmer, a papist, soon after made Earl of Castlemain, who, afterwards being separated from him, was advanced to be Duchess of Cleveland, was his first and longest mistress, by whom he had five children. She was a woman of great beauty, but most enormously vicious and ravenous; foolish but imperious, very uneasy to the king, and always carrying on intrigues with other men . . .

B John Evelyn, *Diary, 1697,* describes Charles II shortly before his death.

The king sitting and toying with his concubines, Portsmouth, Cleveland and Mazarin, etc.; a French boy singing love songs in that gorgeous gallery, whilst about twenty of the great courtiers and other dissolute persons were at basset round a large table, a bank of at least £2000 in gold before them . . . but six days after all was in dust.

A portrait of the Duchess of Portsmouth by Mignard

c *Charles II* by Ronald Hutton (OUP, 1991) explains how Charles seduced Louise-Renee de Penancoet de Keroualle, subsequently Duchess of Portsmouth.

Charles coaxed and cajoled and made her presents. Louis XIV believed that a French lover would further predispose his English cousin to his interests and added his pleas through de Croissy. Arlington professed himself anxious to see his master set up with a polite, sweet-natured woman like Louise instead of 'a lewd and bouncing orange-girl' or a 'termagent' . . . He and de Croissy even told Louise that the Queen wished her to submit. They arranged a house-party at Arlington's mansion at Euston, Suffolk, where she at last gave in. Thus two monarchs, an ambassador, and a great minister had combined to push an unwilling virgin into a royal bed.

People take after their grandfathers as much as their parents. Certainly Charles II and James II resembled the promiscuous Henry of Navarre rather than their chaste father. Lucy Walter, Elizabeth Killigrew, Catherine Pegg, Barbara Villiers, Nell Gwyn, Moll Davies, Winifred Wells, Jane Roberts, Louise de Keroualle, Hortense de Mancini and various unknown prostitutes kept Charles happy. James had several extremely ugly mistresses, provoking Charles's witticism that they were imposed as a penance. Catherine Sedley and Arabella Stuart were clever as well as hideous.

Some of these women are better known than others. Burnet's malicious portrait of Barbara Villiers (source A) is matched by Evelyn's description of Lucy Walter, 'a brown, beautiful, bold but insipid creature'. 'Pretty, witty Nell Gwyn' (Pepys), orange-seller, actress and prostitute, was immortalised by Charles's death-bed request, 'Let not poor Nelly starve'. She showed her wit when she defused a raging, anti-Catholic mob: 'Peace, good people, I am the *Protestant* whore'. She was getting at her rival, Louise de Keroualle, Duchess of Portsmouth, whose ravishment is described in source C. However much a victim to male heartlessness, Louise was fully capable of cruelty to others. For instance, she reduced Queen Catherine of Braganza to tears by insinuating herself among the maids who waited on her at dinner. The cleverest of Charles's mistresses was Hortense de Mancini, Cardinal Mazarin's niece. Charles's evident enjoyment of her conversation prompted Nell Gwyn to call the jealous Duchess of Portsmouth 'the weeping willow'. Catherine Sedley was baffled by James's behaviour: 'Why does he choose us? We are none of us handsome, and if we had wit, he has not enough to discover it.' She needed her wits to survive the hostility of James's queen, Mary of Modena, and of his daughter, Mary, who, despite her betrayal of her father, disliked his mistress. 'If I have broken one commandment, you have broken another', Catherine told Mary, 'and my offence is more natural'.

Did Charles's and James's sexual exploits matter? Do their mistresses concern the serious historian? Most certainly. Apart from the light shed on their personalities, their sex-life definitely influenced the history of their time. While Louis XIV and others were wrong to attribute political influence to Charles's mistresses, for he listened to them no more than to his ministers, he led – or misled – aristocratic society by his example. So far as the political community as a whole was concerned, he undoubtedly damaged the Crown's prestige by his shamelessly open profligacy. Evelyn (source B) was not the only contemporary to disapprove. When the Royal Court visited Winchester in 1682, the hymn-writer Thomas Ken refused to accommodate Nell Gwyn because 'a woman of ill-repute ought not to be endured in the house of a clergyman'. While Charles acknowledged Ken's integrity by making him Bishop of Bath and Wells, even though 'he would not give poor Nelly a lodging', he could not disarm criticism.

Both brothers provoked widespred disapproval when they ennobled their many acknowledged bastards, therefore debasing the peerage.

Similarly, the extravagance of Charles II's 'family' was notorious. The guilt that James eventually felt for his promiscuity diminished his self-confidence and what little political ability he had. This guilt caused his total collapse in 1688 when he made last-minute concessions. In J.P. Kenyon's words: 'he repented of his sins, but the wrong ones'. Whether historians are justified in expressing disapproval (as Hutton does implicitly in source C) is a good question. Certainly the ruthless lust that Charles displayed on that occasion dispels his 'naughty but nice' image.

> **Q**
>
> **1.** *Hutton writes about Barbara Villiers: 'In a sense her achievement had been impressive, for at a time when women had few opportunities for advancement she had succeeded in winning for herself a fortune, a title, and independence by the age of thirty'. Did Charles II's and James II's mistresses advance the cause of women?*
> **2.** *Did Charles II and James II behave irresponsibly in their sexual relationships? Were they more culpable than James I, Louis XIV, David Lloyd George, the Kennedy brothers – or even Bill Clinton?*
> **3.** *'The historians will forgive – it is their trade'. Does Ronald Hutton go too far in his implied criticism of Charles II?*

C How the other nine-tenths lived – a case study

KEY ISSUE

How sexually promiscuous were the lower classes?

If the rich followed their sovereign, what about the middling sort and the poor? What was the prevalent sexual morality of the typical inhabitants of the British countryside? This is an important and controversial question, justifying this case study. Laurence Stone and Edward Shorter have argued that, both from economic prudence and under the influence of the moral teaching of the Puritan revolution, English peasants refrained from premarital or extramarital sex. Here was a contrast from the late Middle Ages when an amoral approach to sex prevailed and with contemporary France where feckless peasants under the permissive approval of the Roman Church allegedly slept around. They have argued that there was a particularly restrained period during the middle years of the century under the influence of Puritan ethics, with a return to 'medieval' licence and permissiveness after the Restoration. This overall picture has been questioned by Peter Laslett who has shown that bastardy statistics by no means suggest more stringent sexual theory and practice in mid-seventeenth century England. G.R. Quaife, in his *Wanton Wenches and Wayward Wives* (Croom Helm, 1979), has demonstrated that in Somerset there is little evidence to suggest that a stricter Puritan code was in operation. Where does the truth lie? If the Puritans were indeed successful in imposing their standards on ordinary folk, if they actually made British people sexually moral, it demonstrates the widespread power and influence of the movement.

See page 339 for the courts.

The available evidence is inconclusive. There is little autobiographical material from the hands of a largely illiterate peasantry. Bastardy statistics are derived from parish registers and courts of law dealing with maintenance disputes. The problem here is the unreliability of the keepers of parish registers, usually parish priests who may or may not have been conscientious, while it is impossible to assert what proportion of bastardy cases came before the courts. Quaife's findings, derived from the proceedings of lay and ecclesiastical courts, are fine as far as they go. But as Quaife himself admits it is impossible to say what pro portion of people led an irregular, illicit sex-life that never came before the courts, which were primarily concerned with threats to law and order, or public decency. Nor for that matter can we tell how many led a restrained sex-life, never indulging in practices that the law of God or man could call illicit, and for that reason never entering the documentary records.

Any alleged contrast, however, between a sexually immoral British aristocracy and a chaste, self-restrained peasantry seems unsound. There is not a contrast with contemporary France either. Even allowing for the argument that premarital conceptions occurred because of a promise to marry, the statistics do not justify a contrast with largely Catholic France where the proportion of pregnant brides was in fact rather less. Quaife's findings impress by their volume and variety. Clearly young men and women had various options with regard to sexual gratification before they were married, while plenty of married men and women slept around. While the precise extent of illicit sex in seventeenth-century Somerset may be 'a stupid question' (Quaife), one can perhaps form a general impression based on two facts. There were always men like the peasant from West Hatch 'who for those 20 years past hath been the seeker of the chastity of divers [several] women and maids' and equally, in addition to vulnerable women who fell victim to the wiles of such men, there were plenty of 'wanton wenches and wayward wives'.

Certainly there were victims, such as mentally defective village girls who were preyed upon by unscrupulous lechers. A magistrate investigating one such case noted: 'This Ann Evil seems to be an idiot'. Sometimes naive girls would be betrayed by spurious offers of marriage, sometimes terrified by threats. Or take the case of Agnes Peek of Sutton Mallet:

> She is a single woman and was never married and is now great with child. This examinate being at Glaston market and going into an inn, there happened into the company of a strange man, tall of stature and apparrelled in blue apparel and yellow haired, but what his name is or where he dwelleth she knoweth not ... The strange man seeing her come in took her by the hand and desired her to walk into a room and drink with him, she became light-headed, and was in such a trance that she knew not what she did ... About a week or two after Christmas last she found to be with child and then assured herself that the strange man had the carnal knowledge of her body.

KEY ISSUE

What opportunities were there for extramarital sex?

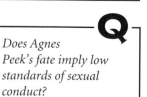

Does Agnes Peek's fate imply low standards of sexual conduct?

Agnes Peek's sad story may well have been true. However, unscrupulous men often bullied or bribed single women into naming somebody else as the father of their child or conjuring up a mythical explanation. In any case if the true father refused to be named, not only did the woman have to live with the physical consequences of pregnancy and childbirth, but would in all probability be blamed for her condition, ostracised and disgraced.

On the other hand, there are plenty of examples of married women committing adultery. Often they did so willingly, due to boredom, sexual dissatisfaction with their husbands or the wish to continue a pre-marital relationship, such as a wealthy or domineering employer. Matthew Tully told how his wife, Marjery, cheated on him at a friend's house:

> While there my wife went upstairs into one of the chambers. Two other men there tried to stop me going up. I went up and found her on a bed with Thomas Goddard who pretended to be asleep and whom Mills and Gadd had tried to conceal under some petticoat. They said, 'take no offence, it was a woman that lay besides your wife'.

A little later Tully found his wife carrying on with Mills and after a feeble protest went home alone. A few days later his wife broke in, took some dishes and left him for good. Frequently women had sex with wealthy employers. A rich yeoman asked a neighbouring wife to winnow his corn. 'But the said John was too strong for her, and with long striving did with force use her body against her will, throwing her against a board in such violent manner, that he brake the skin of her hand'. There was no suggestion of violence, however, when Margaret Holloway went fern-raking for Edward Cross and a witness 'about twelve of the clock saw Cross lie upon Margaret Holloway, wagging his body'. A Walton woman exploited her husband's absence by sleeping with her lover, but her bed was too near the window so that neighbours overheard the following exchange: 'Thou liest so close thou will throw me out of the bed', to which her paramour replied, 'I lie so close unto thee because I love thee'. Wives' infidelities were often overlooked by husbands who were bribed by the adulterer.

Indeed, the readiness of husbands to condone their wives' infidelities for cash amounted to prostitution of which there were many forms. The most organised and professional prostitutes operated in the larger towns, especially London. An Act of Charles I's austere reign complained that citizens were 'pestered with many immodest, lascivious and shameless women generally reputed for notorious common and professed whores'. *The Wandering Whore*, published in the more permissive atmosphere of the Restoration, listed London's most celebrated brothels, paying tribute to such notable prostitutes as the Queen of Morocco, Welsh Nan Peg the Seaman's Wife, Madame Creswell and Mrs Osbridge's Scolding Daughter. Cambridge boasted 13 brothels in 1676. Mall Perman brought sophistication to Bath:

Q *Why was Matthew Tully humiliated by his wife?*

> Of all the whores that I have known
> From Court that came unto our town,
> There's none compares with Muddy Mall,
> That plays the whore from spring to fall.

Wells too catered for the sex-starved. Ann Morgan was overheard negotiating with a client who offered her a shilling. 'No', she replied, 'I will have eighteen pence for thou hast torn my coat and has hindered me the knitting of half a hose.' Ann was indeed an entrepreneur. When she had 'lewd company' she would send round for three or four of her female neighbours who were glad to help her out. Ale-houses such as the Bear in Wells and the Swan in Wellington were notorious as brothels. Lucy Francis was a travelling whore who concentrated on weavers' workshops, 'putting her back towards the side of the looms and saying, "here is a good place to go at trading" – because there was a firm footing where she would not slide'.

Some women were driven to prostitution by hard times or by misfortune. Joan Eaton of Doulting was thrown to George Goring's troops in late 1645 by her fellow villagers. 'Goring's crew' had an evil reputation in the West Country. On entering the village 'they were very rude and beat up most of the people'. When they demanded a 'woman to dress meat for them' everyone knew what they meant. 'Whereupon Joan Eaton was brought thither and remained with the soldiers all the day and night.' This was apparently Joan's first sexual experience. But she was for ever afterwards shunned by her neighbours.

Q *Why was Joan Eaton treated so harshly by her neighbours?*

Moral crusaders must have been embarrassed by the number of clergy who came before the courts. 'If impressionistic evidence could be converted into an irrefutable statistical statement there would be the temptation to argue that the clergy were the most lecherous, bastard-making class in seventeenth-century Somerset' (Quaife). The vicar of Cutcombe seduced the wife of a dying parishioner by promising to marry her, and continued to string her along after he had made her pregnant. The Reverend John Musgrave had four or five bastards by his servant girls. The Reverend David Jenkins committed bigamy. The Reverend John Gast molested little girls. The most enterprising was the Reverend John Wolfall who had sex with a parishioner, with his son's mistress, with the mistress of a neighbouring parson, imported whores from London and organised a circuit of whores for neighbouring clergy. Even allowing for the tendency to blame the vicar when girls became pregnant or for the unpopularity of Laudian clergy whom everyone wanted to blame, this record hardly suggests that the clergy were moral crusaders. Anglicans were not the only reprobates. Titus Oates's father, 'Dipper Oates', was a Baptist who was notorious for what he got up to at his midnight baptisms, while the Wiltshire minister, Thomas Webbe, claimed that 'heaven is women, marriage is hell'.

KEY ISSUE

The immorality of the clergy.

What could any moral crusader do with Mary Combe the publican's wife who appeared before the justices on several occasions on account of her outrageous lewdness? Drinkers at her pub were groped by her, and she often 'layd her down in the highway between Axbridge and Crosse, and called to all persons passing, by spreading her legs abroad' to make her husband a cuckold. She organised drunken orgies for cuckolds and cuckold-makers. She wandered around the parish naked and urinated in public. Quaife suggests that Mary Combe represented a deliberate challenge to the values of the conservative establishment, witness her reputation for plucking up her clothes and sitting astride any man she found lying on his back. Did she represent 'the woman on top', produced by 'the world turned upsidedown'? Or was she typical of people who have defied the accepted standards of any society? There is certainly something timeless about the Taunton man whom Quaife describes at Broomfield Fair:

How impressive is the evidence for sexual permissiveness?

As evening settled he discovered a willing wench and began to have his way with her against what must have appeared a reasonably firm tree. It was in fact the ceremonial pole erected for the festival and their unrestrained sexual movements were such that 'it made a bell hanging on top of the pole to ring out whereby he was discovered'.

To sum up, the evidence put forward in this case study does not support the argument that Puritan reformers succeeded in tidying up the morals of ordinary seventeenth-century people. It is true that the political and religious leaders of the Parliamentarian and Republican governments between 1646 and 1660 aimed at moral reformation. They passed laws laying down the death penalty for adultery, they closed alehouses as centres of depravity, they charged the Major-Generals with the prevention of loose living. But the question remains, did this campaign work? Two conclusions seem valid. First, a number of people defied the reformers. Secondly, people resented this campaign. 'Didst thou never see a cow bulled?', asked a young peasant when caught in the act by a Puritan vicar and genuinely puzzled and angered when rebuked. So were thousands of his contemporaries who longed for emancipation from do-gooders and busybodies. This was politically important in that, rightly or wrongly, it was believed that a Stuart restoration would bring back permissive freedom.

KEY ISSUE

Why did seventeenth-century British people give their governments so little trouble?

4 ⌐ VIOLENCE, CRIME, LAW AND ORDER

However unsuccessful Puritan politicians may have been as moral crusaders, it is extraordinary how docile Britain was, given the lack of coercive force available to governments. The contrast is striking with continental regimes, able to call upon standing armies, bureaucracies and secret agents. Certainly the Stuart kings had few of the weapons of absolutism that kings of France enjoyed. Yet compared with the French, with the striking exception of the rebellions between 1638 and 1651, the British seem to have given their governments relatively little trouble.

Perhaps the problems facing British people and their governments were less severe. Certainly taxation was less oppressive in Britain than in the France of the Cardinals and Louis XIV, where the peasants in particular were the victims of the rule that those least able to pay paid most. While times were frequently hard, the British poor were not taxed directly, though there was popular agitation against such indirect taxes as the excise during the Interregnum and the Hearth Tax after 1660. As we shall see, there were protests against other unpopular measures. Yet for all the Englishman's reputation for violence (and Scots, Irish and Welsh had even worse reputations), the people made few protests.

This was just as well, since the early Stuarts in particular had no standing army, apart from the trained bands which, with the significant exception of London's, were about as formidable as the Home Guard of World War Two days. Charles II had a few regiments, James II rather more, while William III and Anne presided over vast continental coalitions that never featured in Britain, apart from William's brief initial campaigns in Scotland and Ireland. The exception that illustrates the rule is the standing army of the Interregnum. The firm view of the British people after the Restoration was 'no more sword government, no more Major-Generals'. The government employed a few civil servants at the centre, a few customs and excise men in the provinces and the occasional hangman, though even he was sometimes replaced by an amateur. There were virtually no police force or secret service.

The whole of royal government was otherwise executed by amateurs. The county was administered by the lord lieutenant, his deputies and a sheriff, and the localities by the Justices of the Peace and the officials of the village and the manor, such as the constables and churchwardens. All these officials were unpaid, untrained and voluntary. They did their jobs partly because of the prestige involved, partly because they believed in what they were doing. Shakespeare's lovable parish constable, Dogberry, is a parody of the truth. County and parish officials were obeyed for the most part because the people accepted their authority. In other words, the whole operation was based on consent. Conditions varied in Scotland, Ireland and Wales, though here again the consent of the upper classes was crucial. When this consent broke down the government was in trouble. The classic illustration is the Great Rebellion.

At a local level there was always the danger of a calculated, wilful withdrawal of consent that highlighted the government's weakness. For example, in 1631, the Sheriff of Wiltshire failed to expel Thomas Carr from Clayhill Farm in Selwood Forest. The Sheriff represented the law of the land, acting on behalf of the rightful owner and supported by 50 pikemen and 50 musketeers from the trained bands. But Carr defended the farm with 'a multitude of base and desperate persons'. In the end the Sheriff withdrew due to 'the foulness of the weather and the nearness of the night'. A compromise was conceded.

Such activities also raise the issue of organised crime in the seventeenth century. Clearly there were examples, notably among the smugglers, poachers and coiners whom we have mentioned. The

PICTURE 38
St Stephen's Walbrook, a London church designed by Wren. How relevant was the Church of England to London's poor?

KEY ISSUE

The means of coercion available to governments

See pages 14–16 for details of local government.

KEY ISSUE

The defiance of the authorities.

KEY ISSUE

How much organised crime was there?

Smorthwaites brothers operated in Westmoreland in the 1680s, specialising in burglaries, highway-robbery, coin-clipping and cattle-lifting. Horse-thieving was the seventeenth-century equivalent to the used car racket of modern times. Some measure of organisation was required to steal a horse, move it to a different part of the county and recolour it just as nowadays stolen cars are resprayed and given new number plates. Again, coin-clipping was a profitable criminal activity. In 1682, Yorkshire JPs, following a tip-off, arrested 13 coin-clippers at 'a retired house in the country', 'at work in their drawers and shirts', along with £30 to £40 of clipped silver. In the larger towns and especially in London there were gangs of professional criminals, and indeed apprentice schemes run by 'godfathers' reminiscent of Dickens's Fagan. Recent research suggests, however, that even in London such activity was haphazard, with an ever-changing membership of amateur criminals, down on their luck and in need of employment. Most crime was the work of impoverished individuals.

KEY ISSUE

Crime in London.

London certainly was the Mecca for criminals. The huge capital had a population of 575,000 by the end of the period, most of them immigrant, young and poor. It was known as 'Gineva' due to the increasing availability of cheap gin – a dangerous and sinister development. There were tempting opportunities for petty thieves: plenty of vulnerable, rich people with valuable, movable property, great houses to be burgled, merchants set up for trade and carrying large sums of cash, and narrow streets and alleyways filled with crowds of passers-by into whom it was easy to merge. The police authorities were virtually non-existent, and the rate of detection was very low. Here were ideal conditions for petty burglars, pickpockets, cardsharpers and whores. But there is little evidence of mass crime or of the existence of a criminal sub-culture. Still less is this the case for the rest of the British Isles. Few contemporaries expressed fear of organised crime.

KEY ISSUE

The pattern of criminal activity in general.

The pattern emerges of criminal activity by the poor against the poor. The sixteenth-century phenomenon of aristocratic or 'fur-collar crime' (often reminiscent of the bastard feudalism of the later Middle Ages) becomes increasingly rare. Similarly, the popular tradition of the have-nots robbing the haves is a myth. In the real world, peasants stole from each other, damaged each other's property, and assaulted each other. A typical example was the two East Riding labourers who raped a girl after she had rejected half a crown for sex. Furthermore, to an increasing extent during the seventeenth century people in trouble before the local courts were accused of crimes against the community. John Ayly, keeper of the Unicorn at Kelvedon, Essex, kept a disorderly house and sold liquor on the sabbath, while Osias Johnson assaulted the constables, fought with his neighbours, refused to pay church rates and obstructed the highway with a dunghill. Henry Abbott of Earls Colne used scandalous words against his neighbours, cut trees down without permission and played cards and dice on the Lord's Day.

The number of women prosecuted for crime was low, around ten per cent in the countryside, rather higher in towns where women had greater liberty. As we have seen, there were crimes of which women

PICTURE 39
A portrait of Sir Christopher Wren by Kneller. Wren drew up designs for the rebuilding of the whole city embracing wide streets and green spaces. The plans were never fully implemented and the narrow alleyways of London remained a hot bed for crime

were uniquely guilty, such as scolding (see page 380) and witchcraft. A poignant example of largely feminine crime was infanticide. In 1632, Somerset JPs referred to the many unfortunate young women indicted for murdering 'bastard children begotten at wakes and revels'. A more typical scenario was the servant girl who was sexually exploited by her employer and became pregnant. Having failed to obtain an abortion, she faced disgrace and dismissal when her bastard child was born. So she murdered her infant. Infanticide was made a specific capital offence by a statute of 1624, which was not repealed until 1803.

Given the nature and extent of crime in seventeenth-century Britain, how did the authorities punish and deter the criminal? Several crimes received the death penalty: murder, treason, coin-clipping, piracy, 'grand larceny' (theft of goods worth more than a shilling), and adultery (by an act of 1650). The usual method of execution was hanging, though traitors were cut down before they were dead, disembowelled and quartered. Gentlemen were decapitated, including Charles I and the Earl of Derby (September 1651), though Clarendon was shocked that Derby was executed in Bolton marketplace, 'a town of his own'. Adulteresses and witches were hanged in England and burnt in Scot-

> ## KEY ISSUE
>
> *The deterrence of crime.*

land. Convicted pirates were chained at low water and drowned by the incoming tide. Executions took place in public. The condemned man was accompanied by a minister of religion and was expected to make a penitent and edifying death. When Sir Walter Raleigh and his execution party had difficulty pushing their way through the crowd surrounding the scaffold, Raleigh shouted to a friend, 'I'm sure they'll find me a place', shocking contemporaries by his flippancy. The largest crowd recorded – allegedly 100,000 – watched Strafford's execution on Tower Hill in May 1641.

What is very striking is the dramatic fall both in convictions for capital offences and in executions during the period. The figures for Devonshire reflect the national situation: 250 felons executed in the first decade of the seventeenth century, 30 in the first decade of the eighteenth. In James I's reign, 150 felons were hanged annually in London, whereas the annual average a century later was 20. Why this fall occurred is a matter for speculation. Perhaps the authorities were influenced by the age of reason and became more humane, though the alternative punishments handed down should prevent facile sentimentalisation of the past. As ever the prime objective remained the deterrence of the criminal, though the possibility of repentance and reform explains the growing preference for alternatives such as transportation or imprisonment. At the beginning of the period prisons were simply parking places for criminals awaiting trial, or for bankrupts unable to pay their debts. In addition there were houses of correction where people of both sexes unwilling to work were forced to undertake humiliating and unpleasant tasks. A good example was Bridewell, founded by the dying Edward VI, to rescue poor children, which soon became a cross between Bedlam and Borstal.

Whipping was the normal punishment unless the culprit happened to be a gentleman, which accounts for the outrage when Strafford recommended that Hampden should be whipped. Everything was done to ensure that whipping was not only painful but degrading. The convicted felon was whipped either 'at the cart's tail' – that is to say, his or her hands would be tied to a cart that would be drawn along while the whipping was administered – or at the local whipping-post, prominently sited and the centre of popular attention on marketday. Neither the nature of the whip nor the number of lashes was stipulated. But it was normal procedure for the criminal, male or female, to be stripped to the waist and for blood to be drawn. Watching the female inmates of Bridewell being whipped was a popular Sunday afternoon entertainment for Londoners. When it proved impossible for Titus Oates's enemies to obtain a capital sentence, they persuaded the officials concerned to whip him to death. It was not their fault that he survived punishment so atrocious that onlookers cried 'enough!' ('Not enough for the truth!' was that irrepressible scoundrel's reply.)

It became increasingly common for criminals facing the death penalty to be acquitted, or to have their punishment commuted to whipping. One escape route was to claim 'benefit of clergy'. This was a medieval wheeze by which criminous clergy could evade the death

KEY ISSUE

Deterrence apart from the death penalty.

See page 73 for Hampden's 'crime'.

See pages 185–6 for Titus Oates's offences.

penalty by claiming the right to be tried by their own courts. All a man (or indeed a woman) had to do was to prove elementary literacy, and therefore by definition clerical status, by reading a verse from the Psalms. The criminal would then be branded and released. A similar way of avoiding the death penalty was for a woman to claim 'benefit of the belly'. If she was pregnant, it was wrong that her unborn child should be punished. This practice was widely and mercifully abused, no further action being taken if the pregnancy failed to materialise.

Criminals were sometimes condemned to shaming punishments. In 1663, a Southwark man was put in the pillory for 'a foul and great trespass in attempting an act of uncleanness with a girl about eight years old'. Pilloried homosexuals or child-abusers were occasionally stoned to death. Church courts might require people convicted of sexual crimes to appear in church on Sunday, clad in a white sheet with a placard round their necks detailing their offences. Sometimes the community spontaneously inflicted a shaming punishment. Whores were 'carted', that is to say, drawn through the town or village in a cart while they were pelted with stones and filth. When a peasant who was notorious for stealing his neighbours' timber built himself a new oven, gunpowder was secreted in the timber so that the oven blew up in his face. In cases such as these no resort to the law was necessary, for the community had acted. The role of the community in implementing its own rules is discussed in the following section.

KEY ISSUE

How humane was the criminal code?

5 ⌁ PLEASURE, PROTEST AND REPRESSION

Traditionally, until the middle years of the seventeenth century the community had to a great extent governed itself. The leaders of society (squire, parson, local officials and the better sort) had taken the lead in imposing the law of the land and local custom on the lower social orders. It was a patriarchal regime based on status and deference, but the inhabitants of a typical village saw themselves as a community in which everyone had his or her place but in which there were obligations and charitable deeds as well. This community spirit manifested itself in the festivals of the Christian year and on such traditional rural occasions as May Day when everyone had a good time. Peasants danced round the maypole and got drunk on liquor provided by the squire. In general, the community looked after its old and sick, and took appropriate steps to control what was perceived to be antisocial behaviour. The classic example of the skimmington ride, when the domineering wife and her hen-pecked husband were publicly ridiculed by two male neighbours riding a horse facing the wrong way, has already been noted.

During the latter part of the sixteenth century the ideal of the community was beginning to be challenged by Puritan emphasis on the individual, as opposed to the generality. The essential group was no longer seen to be the town or village, but God's chosen people. It was

KEY ISSUE

Did villages constitute a caring society?

the privilege and the duty of this elite to discipline and control the rest. The social implication of this belief was clear. God favoured the clean-living, hard-working upper and middling sort who increasingly dominated urban and rural Britain. They repaid God by imposing godly rule. So the new ideal was a docile, orderly society in which the poor, ignorant and feckless were disciplined for their own good by the prosperous, literate and righteous people of God.

How puritanical were the Puritans? Part of their code involved the abolition of corrupting practices such as drinking in ale-houses, gambling, cock-fighting and cutting church services in favour of ungodly pursuits on the Lord's Day. Many Puritans were paranoid about dancing. Morris dancing for instance was condemned by the minister at Marlborough because those who danced 'served the devil and not God'. John Hammond, the minister at Bewdley, stopped his parishioners' 'lewd and lascivious' dancing by battering down the maypole. Samuel Bird attacked mixed dancing as 'a chief sin and arch-enemy to religion' and 'a nursery of bastardy'. Laud's *bête noir*, Prynne, claimed that dancing broke all ten commandments, plus a special Puritan addition, 'thou shalt not waste time by enjoying thyself'. Perhaps the quintessential Puritan was William Perkins. Like so many moral absolutists Perkins had a past. Known at university as 'drunken Perkins' he had fathered an illegitimate child. Now he made up for former backslidings by fighting the Devil. Even laughter was dangerous – the use of it must be both 'moderate and seldom'. As for the dancers round the maypole, they made a ring 'whose centre was the Devil'. Perkins justifies the generalisation that popular culture and Puritanism were incompatible. The ungodly must be forced into line by the godly.

What if the ungodly did not wish to be forced into line? Worse still, what if backsliders were supported by churchmen, unsympathetic to Puritanism? Such men might even defend traditional community life on the grounds that the poor were looked after, the antisocial were checked, links were forged binding the community together, possible causes of tension and discontent were defused and everyone was happy, enjoying themselves in harmless pastimes. In 1632, the Bishop of Bath and Wells justified boisterous and riotous misrule, church-ales, dancing on May Day and so forth 'for the civilising of people, for their lawful recreations, for composing of differences by making of friends, for increase of love and amity, as being feasts of charity, for relief of the poor, the richer sort keeping open house . . .'. An idealised picture, no doubt, for the abuse of drink and sex often played a larger part than dancing round the maypole, producing hedgerow bastards. But if the Puritans had a case, so had the bishop.

Furthermore, what if the King and his government supported such a point of view? To the disgust of Puritan MPs and all godly folk, this was indeed James I's policy. In May 1618, he issued his Declaration of Sports, prompted supposedly by the growth of popery in Lancashire, which the King attributed to overzealous implementation of laws against sabbath-breaking. So when people had been to church on Sunday morning they were not to be 'disturbed, letted or discouraged

KEY ISSUE

Puritan discipline.

KEY ISSUE

Controversy about 'discipline'.

Q

What was the Bishop of Bath and Wells's argument for popular sports?

from any lawful recreation such as dancing, archery, leaping, vaulting or any other such harmless recreation, nor from having May games, Whitsun ales and morris dancing and the setting up of maypoles ...'. Needless to say this was anathema to the Puritan-dominated House of Commons, which petitioned for the stricter keeping of the Lord's Day and for the withdrawal of the Declaration of Sports for the next 30 years. It was anathema too for Puritan clergy who admonished their parishioners for such crimes as 'dancing the morris in evening prayer time'. Charles I and Laud beefed up James I's policy even more by issuing the Book of Orders in January 1631 which required JPs and their subordinates to do their jobs properly in caring for the poor and maintaining a healthy, charitable community spirit.

KEY ISSUE

The Stuarts' policies concerning village activities.

The Puritans found their chance when Charles's government was brought down in the 1640s. The Long Parliament duly cancelled the Declaration of Sports. The republican regimes issued ordinances disciplining the ungodly and the disaffected. Maypoles were chopped down, allegedly popish Christmas festivities were abolished, morris dancing was banned, people guilty of sexual peccadilloes were persecuted as were users of the Anglican Book of Common Prayer. Magistrates who were reluctant to impose such discipline were kept up to the mark by Cromwell's major-generals or were dismissed. The result was patchy. Some parts of the country became havens of righteous living, others were hardly affected. Obstinate loyalty to the Book of Common Prayer was as widespread as obtinate sexual immorality, drunkenness and playing at cards. While 'gadding to sermons' attracted some enthusiasts, Puritan preaching had never been widely popular. Witness the views of James Nicholson of Aysgarth, Yorkshire: 'The preaching of the gospel is but bibble babble and I care not a fart of my tail for any black coat in Wensleydale and I would rather hear a cuckoo sing'. There was much mirth when Cromwell's chaplain, Hugh Peter, a most unpopular 'black coat', got into trouble for eating a mince pie on Christmas Day – or 'Christ-tide' as it was now called. Puritan discipline was resented and divisive. It helps to explain the revival of royalism:

> Let us drink, let us sing,
> Here's a health to our King,
> And 'twill never be well
> Till we have one again

KEY ISSUE

To what extent did dislike of Puritanism cause a revival of royalism?

Only monarchy could apparently bring back the good old days of merry England when everyone was happy and free. 'It was a myth, but it was a powerful one' (David Underdown).

The reality was different. Ironically the demise of the dictator and of his regime did not usher in an age of tolerance and happiness, for indeed Cromwell himself was by contemporary standards exceptionally tolerant. The Restoration gave the green light to a different set of persecutors throughout Britain who had until now been checked and frustrated. In Scotland, for example, the ecclesiastical authorities now burnt and flayed a backlog of witches, sexual deviants and sabbath-breakers whom previously they had been obliged to tolerate. Thomas Akenhead was burnt as a heretic in Glasgow as late as 1694. Likewise, in England, a persecuting Church and squirearchy were restored, though that easy-going hedonist Charles II regretted the way things turned out. It was a grim time for Nonconformists and for anyone sympathetic to 'the good old cause'.

A far more significant milestone in the growth of tolerance and civilisation was the Revolution of 1688. William III despised the intolerant Anglicans whom he had rescued from Roman Catholic persecution. He promoted broadchurchmen such as the notoriously tolerant John Tillotson, and the ultra-Whig Gilbert Burnet. Though Thomas Tenison who succeeded Tillotson at Canterbury in 1695 was also a broadchurchman, he was a keen moral reformer. As vicar of St Martin in the Fields he had persuaded the dying Nell Gwyn to bequeath her wealth to the poor. 'Hot and heavy as a tailor's goose', Tenison attempted to reform the King ('Sire, we must repent of our sins.' 'Yes, my lord, I must repent of my sins, and you must repent of yours.') and led a vigorous campaign to make England a better place. Societies were founded 'for the reformation of manners', for the propagation of the gospel and for the creation of charity schools. Meanwhile, the asthmatic little Dutchman forged ahead on his own. Oblivious of his subjects' disapproval, he employed Jewish financiers and Catholic soldiers. He drove the Toleration Act through an unenthusiastic Parliament. When he used Dutch troops to suppress riots against Catholics in London, he relished his unpopularity. Britain was slowly becoming a less oppressive place. The courage of Nonconformists who had defied persecution was rewarded, combined with increasing scepticism about religious truth.

So far as the ordinary people of Britain were concerned, however, the outcome was uninspiring. An unattractive feature of the 'Puritan revolution' survived into the latter half of the seventeenth century and into the eighteenth century: the divine right of the respectable. British society was now even more divided between rich and poor, educated and illiterate, socially acceptable and socially disreputable. The rich and their allies, the middling sort, dominated the poor, patronising, exploiting and domineering them. Political and social stagnation was represented by the corpulent Sir Robert Walpole. British society was now characterised by complacency, conservatism, deference and graft, unchallenged until the interventions of Wesley and Wilkes.

KEY ISSUE

Did Britiain become a happier place by the end of the century?

6 ～ SUPERSTITION AND WITCHCRAFT

If complacency, deference and graft are still with us, can it be argued that superstition is a thing of the past? Perhaps it would be more true to say that superstition has changed as credulity has changed. In the reign of Charles II distinguished members of the Royal Society such as Sir Isaac Newton dabbled in alchemy and astrology. The Duke of Monmouth proved that he was a genuine Stuart by 'touching for the king's evil'. Above all, the climate was still religious rather than secular. We have noted the reliance on Scripture to justify the inferiority of women. A more trivial example, though equally ludicrous, was the belief that the potato was the creation of the Devil because it is not mentioned in the Bible.

There was a horrible logic in beliefs about witches, given the state of knowledge, or rather ignorance, in the seventeenth-century world. Disease, sudden death, crop failures, and cattle plagues were not only unpleasant but inexplicable disasters. The Bible taught the goodness of God. What more logical than the attribution of evil to the Devil and his agents? Although Catholics as well as Protestants persecuted witches, it has been argued that the upsurge in Britain and Scandinavia was due to the withdrawal of the Catholic rituals; worship of the saints and belief in miracles it was believed used to combat the powers of evil. Now the only solution was to tackle the problem head on and kill the Devil's agents. Add the typical fears and prejudices of the English village which, according to Laurence Stone, 'was a place filled with malice and hatred, its only unifying bond being the occasional bout of mass hysteria which temporarily bound together the majority in order to harry and persecute the local witch'.

While about 25 per cent of continental victims of witchcraft trials were male, the typical British 'witch' was female. In addition, she was usually elderly and poor. Again, there is a logical explanation. We have noted that old people were not taken into the homes of their children, they were left to fend for themselves. Given that many old women were widows, this cannot have been easy. An old, lonely, destitute woman, begging for charity, was a reproach to her neighbours. They might well credit her with feelings of resentment caused by their own hardness of heart. How much more so if the poor old soul permitted herself a few well-chosen curses. Even the *fear* of being cursed could cause psychosomatic illnesses among a witch's supposed victims. What if a child falls sick, a cow's milk dries up, a barn burns down? The old woman's curse, imagined or actual, is then called to mind. Add the current prejudice against the female sex (morally weak and therefore susceptible to the Devil's powers), add the preoccupation with 'scolding' and 'cursing' as women's weapons – and we have a witch. After all, what else could a destitute old woman do when cold-shouldered by her neighbours except curse? She may well have believed in the powers attributed to her. They were all she had.

The more pathetic and vulnerable, the more convincing. John Gaule, a Hertfordshire minister, remarked in 1646: 'Every old woman with a wrinkled face, a furred brow, a hairy lip, a gobber tooth, a squint eye, a squeaking voice or a scolding tongue, a dog or a cat by her side, is not only suspected but pronounced for a witch'. This generalisation is backed by the description of Anne Whittle, one of the Pendle Forest witches tried at Lancaster in 1612: 'A very old, withered, spent and decrepid creature, her sight almost gone, her lips ever chattering and working, but no man knew what'. There was a pseudo-science involved in identifying a witch. She was supposed to commune with 'familiars' – the snakes and toads of Shakespeare's witches – but more commonly a

KEY ISSUE

Why did people believe in witches?

KEY ISSUE

The prosecution of witches.

dog or a cat (what more likely than that a lonely widow should have a domestic pet?). A witch was supposed to have extra teats secreted on her person with which she gave suck to the Devil or to her familiars. Midwives would be deputed to identify such features. If the witch had been seen flying on a dark night, that settled the matter. Visions, trances and prophesyings likewise distinguished the witch, though occasionally fraud was detected, as when James I ended a woman's 'trance' by suddenly removing her bedclothes.

KEY ISSUE

The Belvoir witches.

The combination of rational and irrational is illustrated by the story of the Belvoir witches. In 1612, the Earl and Countess of Rutland held benevolent sway at Belvoir Castle, Leicestershire. Among the many local people they employed was their char woman (it is a seventeenth-century term), Joan Flower, and her daughter, Margaret. The Countess put up with the Flowers longer than most. Old Mother Flower was a malicious trouble-maker and the daughter stole food. In the end the Countess sacked them both, though she gave Margaret £2, the equivalent of a year's pay. Then disaster struck. The Rutlands' heir, Henry Lord Roos, died suddenly. Their second son, Francis, fell sick and their daughter, Catherine, had a breakdown. Mother Flower and her daughter unfortunately had indiscreetly vowed vengeance on the Earl and Countess, so they were duty prosecuted. In court, Margaret Flower testified that her mother had stolen a glove belonging to Lord Roos, which she wore when she stroked her cat Rutterkin. She did the same with another glove, belonging to Lord Francis. A handkerchief belonging to Lady Catherine was applied to Rutterkin's belly, prompting the cat to mew. Mother and daughters were clearly guilty and were condemned to hang. Mother Flower cheated the gallows. She challenged a morsel of bread and butter to choke her if she was a witch – with fatal results. Margaret and her sister Philippa (who, it transpired, had bewitched her lover) were hanged at Lincoln in March 1619, 'to the terror of all beholders'.

KEY ISSUE

The Bideford witches.

If the Flowers come across as unpleasant people, though hardly deserving their gruesome end, the majority of witches can only excite pity – and horror. The Bideford witches, executed in 1682, were elderly, poor and not very bright. Lord Chief Justice North who conducted the trial described them as 'the most old, decrepid, despicable, miserable creatures that ever he saw'. The usual posse of respectable women found two teats concealed on Temperance Lloyd's person which she confessed the Devil had sucked, sometimes disguised as a magpie. Susanna Edwards had conferred with the Devil, 'a fine gentleman apparrelled in black'. Mary Trembles had bewitched a housewife for refusing her meat and tobacco. Temperance had little understanding of the danger facing her, cheerfully incriminating herself and her companions. They went to the gallows asking 'the Lord Jesus to receive my soul'. The judge regretted that 'we cannot reprieve them without appearing to deny the very being of witches'.

Since witches were prosecuted as a result of malice and fear, usually by their neighbours rather than by the magistrates, prosecutions increased in times of dearth or national disaster. A spectacular example was the campaign conducted in East Anglia in 1645 by Matthew Hopkins, the 'Witch-finder General'. This sinister, self-appointed persecutor exploited people's fears and discontent caused by poor harvests and the disruption by civil war to bring 147 poor wretches to the gallows. How was Hopkins able to get so many convictions? Indeed, why was anybody convicted? In England, in contrast to continental practice, torture was not normally applied. But ignorant and helpless old women were browbeaten and bullied. An unfair test, given the virtual non-existence of female literacy and education, required the accused to recite the creed and the Lord's Prayer as a proof of innocence. A strange and seemingly inexplicable aspect is geography. Between 1560 and 1700, 299 witches were prosecuted in Essex, but only 91 in Kent, 52 in Hertfordshire, 54 in Surrey and 17 in Sussex.

However poisonous the atmosphere in Essex, Scotland's record was worse. While prosecutions for witchcraft tailed away in England after the Restoration, in Scotland there was a veritable Indian summer of credulity and cruelty. 'Thou shalt not suffer a witch to live', said the Old Testament, and the text was faithfully implemented with the approval and support of the Scottish Church. An 'expert' such as Alexander Chisholm was allowed to imprison and torture suspects in his own house, one of whom went mad and another died of her injuries. Any tale, however preposterous, however suspect the source, was believed. Midnight orgies, black masses, witches' covens of old women with hooves and no shadows – the stories impressed by their repetitiveness. Children denounced their own parents. A servant girl discovered a clay image of Sir George Maxwell who had mysteriously sickened, so the occupants of the house where the image was found were prosecuted as witches. The girl was now unstoppable and a whole batch of her victims were burnt at Paisley. Confessions were extracted by tortures such as sticking pins into the victim to prove that she had had contact with the Devil. The allegations of the very young, the very old, the malicious and the mad brought scores of innocent women to the pyre before sanity at last brought the nightmare to an end. For only sanity and scepticism could have saved unlucky Alice Molland, the last woman to be executed as a witch in England. She died at Exeter in 1685. In 1712, Jane Wenham was condemned as a witch because she had been seen flying on a broomstick. But she was reprieved by Lord Chief Justice Powell because there was no law against flying.

> **KEY ISSUE**
>
> *The persecution of witches in Scotland.*

> **KEY ISSUE**
>
> *Why did the persecution of witches end?*

7 ⌐ DISEASE, FAMINE AND DEATH

If ignorance and prejudice caused the persecution of witches, they also inspired the medical profession. Indeed, the rich who could afford doctors were at greater risk than the poor. Queen Elizabeth the Great ascribed her health and longevity to her refusal ever to see a doctor. In contrast to her good sense, the French statesman Cardinal Richelieu's life was made wretched by medically inflicted pain, his last moments spent drinking 'medicine' consisting of white wine and horse dung. As for the mighty Louis XIV, he was regularly tortured by Fagel, his arrogant and incompetent court physician, who also murdered virtually the whole French royal family. Meanwhile, Charles II was killed by his doctor who compounded the effects of a minor stroke by bleeding his royal patient and inflicting on him five painful days of purging and vomiting while his head was covered with pigeon dung. Queen Anne suffered appallingly from toothache and her doctors' attempts to cure her gout. Sir John Clerk, one of the Scottish commissioners who drew up the Act of Union, has left this description:

> One day I had occasion to observe the calamities which attend human nature even in the greatest dignities of life. Her majesty was labouring under a fit of the gout, and in extreme pain and agony, and on this occasion everything about her was much in the same disorder as about the meanest of her subjects. Her face, which was red and spotted, was rendered frightful by her negligent dress, and the foot affected was tied up with a poultice and some nasty bandages.

Q

Was Queen Anne fortunate or unfortunate to afford medical expertise?

Not that the poor lived healthy lives. Indeed their appearance was enough to indicate the contrary: bodies wasted by rickets and gout, faces disfigured by smallpox and teeth infections, expressions indicating congenital halfwittedness. Malnutrition dictated that the poor were physically shorter than the rich, a contrast accentuated by lameness and humped backs. Bad food and contaminated water caused stomach disorders, skin complaints and failing eyesight. These problems were accentuated by the famines that inevitably followed poor harvests. Unfortunately, crop failures tended to occur in consecutive years such as 1627–9 and 1647–9. Magistrates did what they could to release food for the desperate, but especially in backward areas, such as Westmoreland, people actually starved to death. Acute malnutrition also caused outbreaks of typhus, as well as turning measles, whooping-cough and the common cold into killers.

While the rich certainly enjoyed better health than the poor (unless they consulted their doctors), everyone was at risk due to the unhygienic conditions of seventeenth-century life. Everywhere there was the stench of decay, rotting sewage and rubbish. The poor tipped their excrement onto dunghills, while for the rich it was a constant battle to keep their houses smelling sweet, especially in summer, since there was no public water supply and no water-closets. Ironically, our word 'loo' comes from the cry 'guardez l'eau' when Edinburgh chambermaids emptied the slops out of the window onto passers-by. Animals were everywhere, fouling the place uninhibitedly and spreading fleas. Butchers tipped their offal into the street and left carcases to rot. While countryside conditions were deplorable, the towns were worse. According to a foreigner London streets had a 'foundation which sometimes remains for twenty years nursing a collection of spittle, vomits, excrements of dogs and human beings, spilt beer and fish bones'. Rats and mice abounded. Even the rich seldom changed their clothes or bathed:

KEY ISSUE

The conditions for the spread of disease.

witness the great lady in Anne's reign who boasted that she had a bath once a month whether she needed it or not. Samuel Pepys regularly had his hair combed for lice. In these conditions disease flourished, for the connection between squalour and infection was dimly perceived.

Society's vulnerability and the helplessness of the medical profession is illustrated by the plague. Throughout the Middle Ages bubonic plague had ravaged Europe, coming and going with mysterious unpredictability. In the seventeenth century it continued its ravages before dying out in the 1690s. The outbreak that hit London in 1665 has been immortalised by Pepys and Defoe. It may or may not have been the most serious of the century. When plague devastated Cheshire in 1629, a Malpas man buried his wife and six children before dying himself. It is now well known that infection was spread by fleas living off black rats. No-one was able to work that one out or guess the truth. Pym was able to create a convincing sensation in the House of Commons by producing a 'plague sore', that is to say a cloth defiled by a plague sufferer, which papists had allegedly sent in an attempt to murder him. Doctors produced herbal remedies, recommended 'pocketfuls of posies', and wore hoods to protect themselves from infection. All to no avail. The only effective cure was to run away, a measure more available to the rich than to the poor. The great fire of 1666 killed off some of the rats.

Several complaints were the subject of animated discussion. What if one was unfortunate enough to suffer from gallstones? Everyone knew that the answer was to have the stone removed. But the knife was a killer as well as a saviour, due to the lack of skill and cleanliness of the surgeons. Furthermore, the ordeal had to be endured without anaesthetics. Some literally bit the bullet and risked the operation, Pepys for example who proudly kept his stone on the mantelpiece. But he was fortunate to survive. Others could not face the knife – and suffered. Some drank to ease the pain, such as Lord Chief Justice Jeffreys. The medical profession had no answer to smallpox, which killed both high and low. Gout similarly tortured everyone from Queen Anne downwards. It was wrongly attributed to drink, abstinence bringing little relief. Syphilis was a killer with no respect and various quack remedies were applied. The Earl of Shaftesbury's doctor, the philosopher John Locke, inserted a tap into his noble patient's stomach to draw off the fluid caused by 'the French complaint'. He was lucky not to kill Shaftesbury.

Childbirth brought anxiety to everyone, bereavement to some, suffering and death to many. It was above all a dreadful hazard for the mother. Seventeenth-century women were expected to have babies. That was their chief *raison d'être*. Many upper class women were more or less permanently pregnant. For some women once was too many. A tombstone summed it up:

> Twenty years a maiden,
> Nine months a wife,
> Half an hour a mother,
> Then ended life.

KEY ISSUE

Society's helplessness against the plague.

KEY ISSUE

The perils of childbirth.

forceps surgical pincers used to extract the baby from the womb.

puerperal fever infection caused by dirty hands and instruments used in childbirth.

KEY ISSUE

Infant mortality.

KEY ISSUE

How successful were seventeenth-century people in coming to terms with death?

Whether a woman in labour was at greater risk from a midwife or a doctor was a good question. Midwives were handicapped by ignorance of basic anatomy as all medical textbooks were written in Latin. Doctors were handicapped by their arrogant complacency, but also by inadequate equipment. Dr Peter Chamberlen invented the **forceps** in James I's reign, but with selfish jealousy kept his life-saving discovery a family secret so that it had to be re-invented in the eighteenth century. While doctors knew enough to try to turn a baby in the womb, anything irregular such as a breech delivery condemned mother and child to cutting and hacking, only too likely to be fatal to both. Worst of all neither doctors nor midwives washed their hands, so that their patients became infected and died from **puerperal fever**.

While the poor often gave birth unattended, royalty experienced the opposite – a practice both embarrassing and unhygienic. A good example was the birth of the 'Old Pretender' when a baby was allegedly smuggled into Mary of Modena's bed in a warming-pan. An amazing number of people failed to notice. For the room contained, as well as Mary Beatrice herself, who was in labour for five hours, her husband James II, Lady Sunderland, Lady Roscommon, Lady Bellasis, Jane Wilks the midwife and her French assistant, Lady Fingall, six bedchamber-women, the Queen Dowager, the Countess of Arran, Lord Chancellor Jeffreys, Lords Sunderland, Arundel, Middleton and Mulgrave, the Earls of Feversham, Huntingdon, Melfort and Peterborough, Sidney Godolphin, Gold Stick in Waiting, two doctors and a laundress. All agreed that the baby was male though there was disagreement as to whether he was heard to cry before being removed from the room by the midwife. In other words, was the baby healthy? He did well to survive infection from such a crowd.

Infant mortality was very high. Statistics vary, but a conservative estimate is that one in five babies died more or less at once, and four out of every ten born did not reach the age of fifteen. The figures for London were worse, 30 per cent dying in the parish of St Botolph before the age of one. Of 27 children born to a Warwickshire couple, not one lived beyond a month – a statistic that also confirms the impression that seventeenth-century women were more or less permanently pregnant. Why did infants die? One cause that affected upper-class families was the practice of wet-nursing. Apart from infection passed by the wet-nurse's milk, babies were crushed to death when the wet-nurse rolled on them in bed. Babies of all classes were menaced by filthy conditions, wrapped in swaddling clothes that were seldom changed. Unwashed and undernourished, they were vulnerable to the most trivial complaints.

At the end of the Stuart era life expectancy was still only in the mid-thirties, even for the highest in society. Mary, the wife of William III, died of smallpox aged 32 and her sister, Anne, at 49 after producing six children, all of whom died in infancy. Whether the prevalence of suffering and death inured our ancestors to grief is anyone's guess. Laurence Stone has suggested that parents deliberately refrained from getting too fond of their infants. But we know of parents grief-stricken when their child died. Mary Verney, for example, was delirious with sorrow for two days. Or take Adam Martindale's grief at the death of his son:

> I was gone to Chester when he died, my business being urgent and he in a hopeful way of recovery when I set out, and being there I had an irresistible impression upon my spirit that I must needs go home that night so that I left some considerable business undone, and went home that evening, where I found a sad distracted family that needed much consolation and assistance from me . . .

Q
What does Adam Martindale's account reveal about his attitude to bereavement?

As for their own deaths some were able to joke about it, such as the courageously flippant Charles II who apologised for being 'such an unconscionable time a-dying'. Set against this was the haunting deathbed cry of his sister-in-law, Anne Hyde, the first wife of James, Duke of York: 'Ah Duke, Duke, death is terrible!'. Contemplating their imminent deaths, Charles I looked forward to an incorruptible crown, Cromwell to a deserved rest 'which shall be hereafter' Or there was the whimsical tombstone at Ripon: 'Here lies poor but honest Bryan Tunstall, he was a most expert angler until Death envious of his merit threw out his line, hooked and landed him here, the 21st day of April 1709'. Ben Johnson sought to comfort his contemporaries by arguing that the quality of a life mattered more than its length:

> It is not growing like a tree
> In bulk doth make Man better be:
> Or standing long an oak, three hundred year
> To fall a log at last, dry, bald and sere:
> A lily of a day
> Is fairer far in May,
> Although it fall and die that night,
> It was the plant and flower of light.
> In small proportions we just beauties see;
> And in short measures life may perfect be.

Q
Is Johnson making a valid point or not?

8 ✑ BIBLIOGRAPHY

The following books can all be cordially recommended, though some are very demanding and should only be attempted by those with an interest in the book's specialism (e.g. witchcraft or crime). Those by Antonia Fraser and G.R. Quaife are particularly enjoyable for their quite exceptional insights into the seventeenth-century world. Nigel Heard's book, in the Access to History series, specially designed for sixth-form students, is helpful.

Crime and Punishment in England by John Briggs, Christopher Harrison, Angus McInnes and David Vincent (UCL, 1996); *Witches and*

Neighbours by Robin Briggs (HarperCollins, 1996); *The Weaker Vessel* by Antonia Fraser (Mandarin, 1984); *Stuart Economy and Society* by Nigel Heard (Hodder & Stoughton, 1995); *The World We Have Lost* by Peter Laslett (Methuen, 1976); *Wanton Wenches and Wayward Wives* by G.R. Quaife (Croom Helm, 1979); *Crime in Early Modern England* by J.A. Sharpe (Longman, 1984); *Early Modern England* by J.A. Sharpe (Arnold, 1987); *Religion and the Decline of Magic* by Keith Thomas (New York, 1971); *The European Witch-craze of the Sixteenth and Seventeenth Centuries* by H.R. Trevor-Roper (Penguin, 1988); *Revel, Riot and Rebellion* by David Underdown (Oxford University Press, 1985); *English Society 1580–1680* by Keith Wrightson (Hutchinson, 1982).

9 ⌐ DISCUSSION POINTS AND ESSAY QUESTIONS

Examiners tend to ignore social questions, so the following are really for class or seminar discussion.

1. 'It was all right for some.' To what extent was there equality of opportunity in Stuart Britain?
2. Was Stuart Britain 'a caring society'?
3. How easy was it for women in Stuart Britain to 'get out of the home'?
4. Did people in Stuart times marry for love or money?
5. Was British society in Stuart times sexually immoral?
6. How much organised crime was there in Stuart Britain?
7. How did Stuart governments keep order?
8. How can the persecution of witches be explained?
9. Had the rich a better chance of being healthy than the poor?
10. What was the attitude of seventeenth-century people to death and bereavement?

Towards a United Kingdom

In 1603 only reluctant allegiance to James I united his disparate kingdoms. By 1714 the situation had changed dramatically. England, Ireland, Scotland and Wales were now politically and economically integrated. 'Great Britain' – James I's bombastic slogan – had become fact. Traditionally this development has been attributed to *English* aggression, spearheaded by Cromwell and William III. There is clearly much truth in this explanation. This chapter, however, investigates the story from the Scottish, Irish and Welsh angles. Their histories are explored in their own rights. Furthermore the impact of the smaller kingdoms on the developing history of England is emphasised. For it was by no means a one-way process.

1 ⌐ IRELAND

A *The Tudor legacy*

At the beginning of the seventeenth century Ireland had a population of approximately one million at a rough density of 20 people to the square mile, compared to 50 per square mile in England. Most of the population were engaged in subsistence agriculture, mainly of a pastoral kind, and indeed the Irish diet consisted almost entirely of dairy products and meat. There were few towns; Dublin was still largely timber-built, and with the exception of Kilkenny, most of the other urban centres such as Waterford, Youghal, Limerick and Galway were on the coast. The northern province of Ulster was even less urbanised than the other three (Munster, Connacht and Leinster), and only Armagh and Carrickfergus could realistically be described as towns. Trade was unsurprisingly of agricultural products (cattle, corn, fish, hides and timber) to other parts of the British Isles.

Politically Ireland was, in theory, under English sovereignty, but in reality the monarch's writ extended hardly beyond the Pale (an area of land centred on Dublin and reaching only as far west as Athlone). The English regarded the Pale as a movable colonial frontier, and during the sixteenth century had used the technique of plantation to entrench settlers further west (e.g. in Ulster, Leix, Offaly and Munster). The sovereign, whom the London Parliament had recognised as 'King of Ireland'

Poyning's Law the decisions of the Irish Parliament were effectively under English control.

in 1541, was represented in Dublin by a lord deputy, presiding over a Privy Council and summoning from time to time an Irish Parliament, which still operated under **Poyning's Law**, first promulgated in 1495. According to this the Irish Parliament could only meet by royal licence, and all its business must be approved by the King's deputy, his Council in Ireland and by the King and his Council in England.

In religion a further contradiction was apparent. In 1537, Henry VIII's assertion that he was Supreme Head on Earth of the whole Church of Ireland contrasted with the reality that papal leadership was accepted by most of the inhabitants of the island of Ireland. The Gaelic Irish and the so-called 'Old English' (those descended from the twelfth-century Anglo-Norman conquest of Ireland) shared a common allegiance to Roman Catholicism. Only the 'New English' – the settlers of the sixteenth-century plantations – could be said to adhere to the new Protestant faith, to which most English people had been converted by the end of Elizabeth I's reign.

It was against this background that the most serious Irish rebellion since the Anglo-Norman conquest erupted towards the end of Elizabeth's reign. Hugh O'Neill, created Earl of Tyrone in 1582, joined forces with the Fitzgerald Earl of Desmond to challenge English rule. In 1600, O'Neill progressed from Westmeath via Kilkenny and Cork to Ulster, at that time wild, Gaelic, and the least inhabited and developed of the four provinces. Elizabeth's response was to send out a new lord deputy, Charles Blount, Lord Mountjoy, who arrived in Ireland in February 1600. Philip III of Spain, with whose country England had been at war since 1585, sent an invading force of 3,500 troops to Kinsale in County Cork to assist O'Neill, but in December 1601 Mountjoy defeated the Spanish at Kinsale. In 1603, O'Neill made his peace with the English Crown as Elizabeth lay dying. She could reasonably claim to be the first English monarch properly to claim control of most of the Crown's second kingdom.

See page 6 for information on Ireland in 1603.

B *James I: the plantations*

KEY ISSUE

The plantations of land in Ulster and elsewhere aroused great resentment.

The defeat of O'Neill was followed in September 1607 by the 'Flight of the Earls', when he and his ally, O'Donnell, the Earl of Tyrconnell left in a French ship from Rathmullin on Lough Swilly in County Donegal with over 90 followers. Both earls died in Rome, and bills of attainder were passed so that their considerable landholdings in Donegal, Tyrone, Coleraine (later County Londonderry), Armagh, Cavan and Fermanagh were escheated to the Crown. The Committee on Plantations therefore had over 500,000 acres at its disposal when it issued the Articles of Plantation in 1609 to attract English and Scots settlers to take blocks of between 1,000 and 2,000 acres. A consortium of 12 City of London livery companies was granted the northern part of County Derry (thereafter known, at least to Protestants, as County Londonderry), and by 1622 around 13,000 adult settlers were established in Ulster. Further plantations followed until 1625 in Wexford, Carlow, Wicklow, Longford, Leitrim and Offaly, continuing the trend that had started in the previous century.

The Ulster plantations are a highly significant event in Irish history, since they introduced a Protestant minority into what had been traditionally a Gaelic and Catholic province. By 1641 three million Ulster acres were owned by Protestants and a mere 500,000 acres by Catholics, but it is an exaggeration to state that the native Irish were driven *en masse* to the hills and bogs of the west. Many labourers were needed for work on large landholdings, or as tenants, and some kind of Gaelic aristocracy remained in Ulster, many of whom (O'Neills, Maguires, Magennis and MacMahons) emerged as leaders of the 1641 rebellion. The original plan to segregate Irish and 'adventurers' therefore was not put into effect, contributing to the feelings of insecurity still felt by Northern Ireland Protestants surrounded by a Catholic sea, and reinforced by their Calvinist sense of being an elect minority.

In 1613, Lord Deputy Sir Arthur Chichester summoned the first Irish Parliament for 27 years to confirm the plantations. Skilful management produced a Protestant majority in the Commons (132 to 100 Old English Catholics), although many of the latter believed in the compatibility of Roman Catholicism and loyalism. Its work done, Parliament was dissolved in 1615, to meet again only in 1633. The government was left to try to enforce the Acts of Recusancy and Supremacy, and while the latter successfully kept a good many Old English out of office, the former was widely evaded with some Justices of the Peace remaining as Catholics, and priests being harboured in gentry households. Catholics were, however, debarred from practising law, running schools and proceeding to university degrees.

The Archbishop of Armagh, James Ussher, a product of Trinity College, Dublin, issued in 1627 with 12 other bishops a declaration that 'the religion of the Papists is superstitious and heretical and toleration is a grievous sin'. In 1615, while still a professor at Trinity, he had presided over the meeting of Convocation that had framed 104 Articles of Religion, both more numerous (Anglicans accepted 39) and more Calvinistic than those agreed in England. Ussher's policy no doubt contributed to the conversions among Irish peers that marked the early seventeenth century: James Butler, Earl and later, Duke of Ormond became the first convinced Protestant member of his family, and by 1640 the Earls of Kildare, Barrymore, Thomond and Inchiquin were all converted. Clanrikarde and Antrim were the chief remaining Catholic peers, but Richard Boyle, Earl of Cork from 1620 is the outstanding example of the new magnate type that had supplanted the old lords and chiefs of Ireland. Boyle had arrived penniless in Ireland in 1588, but he was soon able to buy up Raleigh's estates for £1,000, to acquire former abbey lands and the Earl of Desmond's old college at Youghal, and to construct the new town of Bandon. He brought in fresh English settlers, commanded eight votes in the Irish House of Commons and founded iron and linen industries. His four sons all became peers too, including Roger who became Lord Broghill and then the Earl of Orrery. Under the likes of Cork, Munster was rapidly becoming a Protestant province, yet the Earl was soon to fall foul of Charles I's best known lord deputy, Thomas Wentworth.

C *Wentworth's rule as Lord Deputy*

KEY ISSUE

The arrival of Wentworth made English government more unpopular in Ireland.

See pages 76–7 and 86–7 for Wentworth's relationship with Charles I.

To Charles I Ireland's religious divisions and its political intractability were affronts to the dignity of a powerful monarch – the more so since Ireland had not in the King's view paid its fair share of taxation during the wars of the 1620s. Accordingly, in 1632, Charles appointed Thomas Wentworth as Lord Deputy of Ireland.

Wentworth, who had cut his political teeth as President of the Council of the North at York, shared many of Laud's personal attributes. He was single-minded, domineering, decisive and not averse to feathering his own financial nest in Ireland (his personal income rose from £2,000 per annum in 1628 to £23,000 in 1639). He arrived in Ireland determined to follow a policy of 'Thorough', in other words to restore the position of Crown and Church, and, in the Irish context, to make every Irishman a loyal and prosperous English citizen. In short, Ireland was to be used as an administrative experiment that was intended eventually for the mainland itself. Moreover, if Wentworth was successful in Ireland he could look for promotion in England.

The new Lord Deputy summoned Parliament in 1634 to obtain statutory support for his financial reorganisation. The subsidies granted by Parliament were intended to wipe out Ireland's £20,000 deficit, and to enable it to contribute to the expense of a royal army, which would cost at least £70,000 to maintain. To further this end Wentworth was prepared to take on every powerful group on the island. He alienated the Old English landowners of Connacht (especially the most eminent, the Earl of Clanrikarde) by his confiscations of land in County Galway, and he struck also at New English figures such as the Earl of Cork. Cork was fined £15,000 for failing to fulfil the terms of the original grant, and was compelled to surrender his former Church lands into the bargain. To add insult to injury Wentworth even removed his wife's tomb from St Patrick's Cathedral in Dublin. The City of London was not immune from the depredations of 'Thorough', since their charter in the north was forfeit, a swingeing fine of £70,000 was imposed and Coleraine and Derry customs reverted to the Crown.

See pages 69–71 for Laud's religious policies.

In religious policy Wentworth showed his Laudian colours, and indeed his mentor, William Laud, had been a member of the Irish Committee of the English Privy Council that had chosen him as the Lord Deputy in 1631. Laudians such as Bramhall, who became Bishop of Derry, were appointed to Irish bishoprics (a move that angered many of the Old English), the 39 Articles were imposed on the Church of Ireland and new Laudian statutes were applied to Trinity College, Dublin. The revived ceremonialism that lay at the heart of Laudianism seemed to many Protestants to threaten the reformed ascendancy; neither Ulster Scots nor their mainland kinsfolk were impressed.

However, Wentworth's work was under threat by 1638 from the looming war in Scotland, and in the following year he mustered an Irish army of 9,000 men at Carrickfergus sustained by the Dublin Parliament's grant of £200,000 over three years. His parting shot to the Ulster Scots was to impose an Oath of Abjuration (the hated 'Black Oath') on them to abjure their covenant and to bind them to the King. At the end of 1639 a sick and strained Wentworth was called back to England, cheered by his elevation to the earldom of Strafford, but dismayed by the Long Parliament's decision to impeach him. In fact, 20 out of 28 Articles of Impeachment referred to his Irish administration, and in May 1641 Strafford was executed under Act of Attainder. Charles I had chosen to abandon his minister to the Parliamentary wolves, and his fresh attempts to win Irish support were thwarted by the events of 1641. The true legacy of 'Thorough', a policy that had enjoyed some successes, but which had also alienated every interest group on the island, can be seen in the Irish Rebellion of 1641.

Wentworth had this to say when he addressed the Council of the North for the first time in December 1628: 'the authority of a king is the keystone which closeth up the arch of order and government, which contains part in due relation to the whole, and which once shaken, infirmed, all the frame falls together into a confused heap of foundation and battlement, of strength and beauty . . .'.

D *The Irish Rebellion: fact and fiction*

The Irish Rebellion of 1641 was inspired by Ulster gentry of Irish origin smarting from the dispossessions of the previous 35 years. Sir Phelim O'Neill, Rory O'More and others complained about the unjust treatment of the native Irish, the favour shown to colonists and the lack of civil rights for Catholics; they further demanded a viceroy acceptable to native Irish feeling, and a parliament free of the constraints of Poyning's Law. The rebels never formally repudiated the English monarchy, and indeed O'Neill stressed that they were not in arms against Charles I, therefore lending credibility to English Parliamentary claims that the King was in sympathy, if not actually in league, with the rebels.

English Protestant fears were further inflamed as news arrived of massacres of Ulster Protestant settlers. It seems unlikely that more than 2,000 to 4,000 were killed, but tales reaching England suggested a death toll of many times that figure. Compared with the horrors occurring at exactly the same time on the Continent, which was in the throes of the Thirty Years War, the Ulster atrocities seemed unimportant, but the Long Parliament was sufficiently alarmed to declare the rebels' estates forfeit. As a result, £1 million was raised under the Adventurers' Act of February 1642, owing to 2.5 million acres in all four Irish provinces becoming available for plantation. Events became even more confused as Charles I sent a royal army under General Munro to Carrickfergus to reinforce the Duke of Ormond's royalist army. However, by the end of 1642 it was clear that the King no longer controlled Ireland, if he ever

Q

Why was Wentworth's rule so unpopular in Ireland?

KEY ISSUE

The 1641 Irish Rebellion had huge repercussions, in Ireland and elsewhere.

See pages 90–1 for the English background to the Irish revolt.

had, and was not in control of his other two kingdoms either, since civil war had erupted on the mainland from August 1642.

Meanwhile, in Ireland, the Catholic party met in May 1642 to form the Catholic Confederacy of Kilkenny, a combination of clergy and laity, who reiterated many of the demands of the 1641 rebels at the same time as upholding royal authority. Anglo-Irish Catholics such as Clanrikarde, Muskerry, Antrim and Mountgarret rubbed shoulders rather uneasily with Old Irish Gaels, but their cause received a powerful shot in the arm from the arrival of Irish officers from Spanish service like Preston and Owen Roe O'Neill, a committed zealot of the continental Counter-Reformation. The sense of involvement in the wider perspective of Catholic resurgence and the Thirty Years War was strengthened by the arrival of a papal nuncio, the Florentine Giovanni Battista Rinuccini, Bishop of Fermo, in October 1645.

Continental Catholic interest in Ireland made English Parliamentary Protestants more determined to reconquer the island, particularly as, after the Battle of Naseby in July 1645, the King could no longer effectively deploy an army and his surrogate Ormond surrendered Dublin and went into exile in 1647. The landing of a Parliamentary army under General Jones in June 1647 led to the defeat of the Catholic forces at Dangan Hill, and a further victory against the returning Ormond at Baggotrath in 1648. Rinuccini left Ireland in 1649. The coast was now clear for the arrival of Cromwell, to mop up Catholic resistance following his victory in the English Civil War, and the execution of Charles I on 30 January 1649.

KEY ISSUE

The motives for Cromwell's visit to Ireland.

See pages 133–4 for Cromwell's Irish campaign in the English context.

KEY ISSUE

Cromwell was responsible for two notorious massacres in Ireland.

E *The Cromwellian reconquest*

'Few men's footprints have been so deeply imprinted upon Irish history and historiography', writes Roy Foster. Oliver Cromwell set foot on Irish soil on 15 August 1649 as 'Lord Lieutenant and General for the Parliament of England', with an army of 20,000 men, 'as much a conscripted infantry bent on plunder as a corps of radicals bearing God's word' in Roy Foster's words. Cromwell's aims were clear: to recover Ireland for the Republic (there were still strong Royalist armies in Ireland effectively in alliance with Catholic rebels), to ensure the progress of the new Protestant land settlement by enforcing the Adventurers' Act of 1642 and to punish the Irish for the Ulster massacres (Cromwell held all papists responsible for what had happened).

Cromwell's notoriety in Ireland stems from two atrocities: at Drogheda in September 1649 and at Wexford in October. At the former, 3,500 were put to the sword, although the garrison was led largely by English officers, including Sir Arthur Aston, who had been the Royalist governor of Reading in the English Civil War and was beaten to death with his own wooden leg. Moreover, Drogheda lay within the Pale, and its inhabitants had taken no part in the 1641 rising. At Wexford, 2,000 died, mainly civilians, as the town was stormed while surrender negotiations were still going on. It is strictly true that seventeenth century rules of war allowed the slaughter of garrisons unsuccessfully defending a town after refusing to surrender, and indeed this 'rule' was ruthlessly followed with far greater bloodletting during the Thirty Years War. Cromwell added to this a further argument: that his tactics were saving lives in the long run. It is, however, incontestable that Cromwell's tactics quickly passed into Irish nationalist demonology. After Drogheda and Wexford resistance rapidly crumbled: Owen Roe and Ormond left Ireland; Kilkenny – the heartland of Confederacy – surrendered in March 1650; and Cromwell left the island on 26 May 1650, having broken the back of the Irish resistance. He left his son-in-law, Ireton, as Lord Lieutenant, and by July 1650 Commonwealth armies controlled all of Ireland except for Connacht. In that year Preston and Inchiquin followed other Royalists into exile, abandoned by Charles II in his declaration from Dunfermline. As Galway and Limerick fell by 1652, the remainder of 35,000 Irish troops sought refuge in France and Spain. Ireland, writes Edmund Curtis, 'was almost a blank sheet on which the English Commonwealth could write as it wished'.

The Cromwellian Settlement of 1652 installed the 'Adventurers' as permanent colonisers. Nine counties were confiscated to pay for the arrears of army pay and to satisfy the Adventurers' claims. In other words, Ireland was to pay for its own conquest, as Irish landowners were given more inhospitable land in the west (Sligo, Leitrim, Mayo and Clare), and the 1,000 Adventurers and 35,000 demobilised Parliamentary soldiers received 11 million acres of fertile land in the east. By the end of 1655 all the land west of the River Shannon had been transplanted, and in theory the death penalty applied to any Irish landowner found east of that river after 1 May 1654. A few stayed or drifted back to work, but the 26 counties were now in English hands.

All towns were taken over with New English, the Church of Ireland was disestablished, and full toleration was extended to all Protestant sects. Cromwell himself was made Lord Protector of England and Ireland, although his authority in Ireland was exercised directly by another of his sons-in-law, Fleetwood, and then by his younger son, Henry. In 1653, the Rump Parliament declared a union of the three kingdoms, and Ireland, as part of the Protectorate, was allotted 30 members of Parliament out of 460, while the Dublin Parliament itself was abolished. With a new political framework in place, a new landlord class entrenched on Irish soil and bitter memories of the Cromwellian 'settlement', the Lord Protector himself died in September 1658.

Q *What was Cromwell's legacy in Ireland?*

F *Restoration in Ireland*

Charles II was proclaimed in Dublin a mere two weeks after his proclamation in London, and he was seen by Catholics as the only hope for religious toleration or the recovery of confiscated property. An Irish parliament was restored in Dublin, supreme in internal affairs, but still subject to Poyning's Law and effectively a Protestant assembly, in spite of Ireland's renewed political separation from England. The presidencies of the four Irish provinces were revived, and Parliament began to grapple with the vexed question of a land settlement. The 1662 Act of

See pages 185–6 for
information on the
Popish plot.

Ultramontanes those
Catholics who believed
that the Pope had the
right to assert control
over the Catholic
Church in Roman
Catholic states.

Settlement confirmed the status of the Adventurers' lands, but restored
lands to a few Irish papists – especially to those who had received
'Decrees of Innocence'. Those adjudged to be 'not innocent', i.e. those
who had joined the nuncio Rinuccini, or who had belonged to the Confederacy, gained less. Therefore, many Catholics returned from beyond
the Shannon, if their cases prospered at the Court of Claims set up by
Charles II, so that Catholic-held land increased, temporarily, from a
nine per cent portion in 1660 to 20 per cent a few years later. Nonetheless the Act of Settlement did remain a standing grievance with
those Catholic landowners who lacked a voice in Parliament and
Council, and were handicapped in asserting their claims. The Gaelic
Irish in Ulster suffered worst in the emergence of a Protestant Anglican
ascendancy.

The Church of Ireland was restored as the only officially recognised
religion, and in January 1661 two archbishops and ten bishops were
consecrated in St Patrick's Cathedral, Dublin. Catholics, meanwhile,
were weakened by the division between moderates and **Ultramontanes**.
Further grievances included the Irish Cattle Bill of 1666, the result of
English resentment at the import of cheap Irish cattle, the Navigation
Acts of 1663 and 1670, which excluded Ireland from the burgeoning
imperial trade, and the Popish Plot of 1678, which revived Protestant
fears of Catholic conspiracies. Oliver Plunkett, the Catholic bishop of
Armagh, was arrested on a charge of complicity in the Plot, and in 1681
he was tried and executed in London. When Charles II died in 1685,
Ireland's Catholics could be forgiven for placing rather higher hopes in
his brother, James, Duke of York, a declared Catholic himself.

G *The Protestant ascendancy under William III*

If Catholics contemplated the accession of James II in 1685 with optimism, Protestants greeted it with trepidation. There were early signs
that James intended to favour Irish Catholics, who formed the great
majority of the population and held only 22 per cent of the land. He
appointed Richard Talbot ('lying Dick'), Earl of Tyrconnell as
Lieutenant-General of the army with orders to increase markedly the
proportion of Catholic officers and men. Tyrconnell replaced 3,500
troops in less than a year, but in political matters he had to defer to the
Lord Lieutenant, Clarendon, James II's brother-in-law, who arrived in
Dublin in January 1686. Clarendon's orders were to admit Catholics to
the Council, the law and other professions, to remodel the charters of
Irish towns to re-accommodate Catholics, and to advance Catholics
further as judges and sheriffs. In January 1687, Clarendon was dismissed and replaced in all but name by Tyrconnell, who enjoyed the
title of Lord Deputy.

Tyrconnell set to work with a will: he extended the terms of James's
two Declarations of Indulgence to Ireland in 1687 and 1688; he continued the policy of Catholicising the army; imposed a new charter on
Dublin; rescinded the charters of other towns; and dismissed all the
sheriffs. As he was poised to begin to reverse the disparity in land distri-

bution, the looming crisis in England caused by James's kingship erupted. In June 1688, James's wife, Mary of Modena, gave birth to a son and heir, and Protestants contemplated with dread a Catholic dynasty. In September 1688, 13 apprentice boys in Derry (one of only two Irish garrisons not held by Tyrconnell) closed the gates of the town to the army led by the Catholic Lord Antrim, while the Bishop of Londonderry and the garrison's commander, Colonel Lundy, escaped in disguise. When William of Orange landed in Devon in November 1688, and James II fled the following month, it was only a question of time before Ireland would be dragged into the new situation.

Irish Protestants were quick to acclaim William, although Ireland was quite likely to become embroiled in the War of the League of Augsburg, since William had come to England largely for reasons of foreign policy (he planned nothing less than a revolution in English diplomacy: an anti-French alignment). James's arrival at Kinsale with a French fleet was partly to use Ireland as a stepping-stone for recovering his throne, but it also underlined the wider context of European warfare into which Ireland was being dragged.

As the siege of Derry began, James summoned the Irish Estates to Dublin in May 1689 to form the so-called 'Patriot Parliament'; the last Irish Parliament in fact to contain Catholic MPs until 1921. There were actually only six Protestant members, and the sessions were dominated by famous names from the Gaelic and Norman past: Clanrikarde, Antrim, Clancarthy, Megennis, Roche, O'Dempsey, Fleming, Plunkett, Purcell, Burke and Butler. In his opening speech James stressed freedom of conscience, and promised that Protestant clergy could keep their land. The Parliament went on to repeal the Act of Settlement, and to assert its independence from London; in future, they stated, the English Parliament was to have no right to pass laws that bound Ireland. This was followed up by an Act of Attainder against the 2,400 landowners who had left Ireland in the wake of James's return, but soon the focus of attention switched to the town of Derry.

Derry was under siege with 30,000 Protestant refugees sheltering within its walls, when food ships managed to break the boom blocking the River Foyle and relieve the beleaguered town. Derry therefore has a second hallowed place in the Protestant collective memory, since both the actions of the apprentice boys and the raising of the siege are still commemorated by marches to this day – as is the Battle of the Boyne, which swiftly followed.

William's senior commander, Marshal Schomberg, landed at Bangor with 20,000 troops on 13 August 1689, and William himself arrived early in the following year to confront James and his French allies under Marshal Lauzun. The Battle of the Boyne, fought on 1 July 1690, was both to change the destiny of Ireland and to represent a significant international defeat for Louis XIV of France. Indeed, in one sense it was literally an international conflict with Irish, French, Germans and Walloons confronting other Irish, English, Dutch, other Germans and Danes. William, unable to follow up his victory at the Boyne, returned to England, leaving John Churchill to take Cork and Kinsale in

> **KEY ISSUE**
>
> *Protestants in Ireland welcomed the arrival of William III.*

> See pages 230–4 for William III and Ireland.

> **Q**
>
> *Why are the events of 1689–90 still commemorated in Northern Ireland?*

Munster, and sending Ginkel to take over his command. Ginkel captured Athlone, the gateway to the west in June 1691, before winning the decisive battle of Aughrim in County Wicklow in July. Indeed for Roy Foster it is 'the last great pitched battle in Irish history'. In October 1691 Ginkel took Limerick, and then returned to England in December, his work done.

The Treaty of Limerick of October 1691 set out William's terms for Ireland. The Jacobite army was dispersed: some to their homes and some to enlist with their conqueror, Ginkel; others, 12,000 in all (known as the 'Wild Geese' and including their commander, Sarsfield) were allowed to enter French service. Some of the latter even reached the rank of marshal in Austria, Russia, Spain and France. The civil terms confirmed for Catholics the same liberties of religion as they had enjoyed under Charles II, and allowed those who took the Oath of Allegiance to be pardoned and to practise in the professions. There was, however, no general safeguard for Catholic property, and bitterness against the settlement was widespread as the Gaelic/Old English majority considered their fate: a Protestant ascendancy created by the traumatic events of James II's short reign and its aftermath.

The terms of Limerick, as ratified by the Dublin Parliament, formed the first of a series of penal laws, many of which were to last until 1829. Members of Parliament themselves had to take an oath of allegiance, to make a declaration against the Mass, and an oath abjuring the Pope's spiritual supremacy. In 1692, 1695 and 1697, the 300 commons, 12 bishops and 16 peers enacted further legislation to tighten the screw on the Catholic majority. 'Papists' were forbidden to bear arms, or to study abroad (they were already debarred from degrees, fellowships and scholarships at Trinity College), and Catholic bishops and regular clergy, i.e. the members of religious orders, were formally banished. Further persecution followed in the 1704 Act that followed James II's death in 1701, and the recognition by Louis XIV of James Edward (the 'Old Pretender') as King of England. **Partible inheritance** had already been prescribed for Catholics in 1697, but now two acres became the maximum holding that could be bequeathed; purchase and leasing rights were restricted, and the guarantee of access to the professions enshrined at Limerick was now circumscribed. Finally, sacramental tests according to Church of Ireland usage, and oaths of allegiance and abjuration were demanded from all office-holders.

Meanwhile, the proportion of land owned by Catholics decreased further, as the Court of Claims at Chichester House in Dublin did its work. By 1703 a mere 14 per cent of the useful land was owned by Catholics, and this had gone down even further to five per cent by 1753. One beneficiary of this was the Church of Ireland, which required tithes from everyone, even though it represented only one-sixth of the population, and was closely linked to the Church of England and Irish landowners. The Church made little effort to proselytise, as the large population of Dissenters in the north certifies. Their legal position was little better than that of Catholics, but their ministers did benefit from

Partible inheritance
the division of an estate equally among the children on the landowner's death.

KEY ISSUE

The proportion of land owned by Catholics decreased steadily.

overseas education (usually at Glasgow University), and they were immune from the effects of the Clarendon Code and Test Acts.

As the great age of the Protestant Ascendancy dawned in Ireland after 1714, it was clear that the island had undergone cataclysmic changes over the previous century. Roy Foster writes:

> Irish society and politics had undergone a series of seismic shocks. Indigenous elites had been wiped out, along with the culture they represented. The descendants of settler gentry asserted their ascendancy in a polity that had the status of a dependent kingdom, but psychologically and pragmatically partook of attitudes best called colonial. The uniqueness of Irish development from that time to this owes everything to the fundamental and protracted revolution of the seventeenth century.

2 ∾ SCOTLAND

A *James I of 'Great Britain': an opportunity missed*

James VI of Scotland acceded to the English throne on Elizabeth's death in 1603 through his descent via his great-grandmother, Margaret Tudor, sister of Henry VIII. He had been nominal King of Scotland since 1566, and in the full sense since his mother's execution in 1587, and by 1603 he had considerable achievements to his credit. Scotland was still a poor and peripheral state compared to England, with a linguistic divide roughly along the Highland line between Gaelic and English-speakers, and few large towns (Edinburgh had only one-tenth of London's population). Moreover, strong bonds of kin united many Scots around powerful clan leaders such as the Gordons in Aberdeenshire, the Kers in the Borders and the MacDonalds and Campbells in the Highlands. Yet James had increased central power, usually by playing off one magnate against another, and by creating a growing service nobility as part of his bureaucracy. In religious terms there were still strong divisions between the Catholic north and the Calvinist Lowlands, but law and order had improved and greater mobility was beginning to erode feudal loyalties.

See pages 5–6 for information on Scotland in 1603.

Once installed in London, James made clear that he favoured a 'perfect union' between England and Scotland, but the scheme advanced by a special Union Commission, which eventually came before Parliament in 1607, was rejected. James had underestimated English suspicions of Scottish motives, and he was baffled by the legalistic arguments put forward by his advisers. In short, English MPs could not see any advantages for England in a full merger between the two states, which was likened by one member to two fields separated by a hedge, 'one pasture bare, the other fertile and good'. It was feared that

KEY ISSUE

James I was keen on a full union with Scotland.

trade would be to Scotland's advantage, and that Scots would come flooding into England in search of work (James himself lost little time in appointing Scottish advisers such as Carlisle and Somerset). The King's relationship with Parliament had got off to a bad start, an omen for the future.

Thereafter, James's direct interest in Scottish affairs was fitful: he used the Duke of Lennox as his representative north of the border, and he made only one visit of 11 weeks in 1617 despite his original promise to return every three years. This visit was connected with James's desire to achieve greater convergence between the Scottish Kirk and the Church of England, and shortly after his return south in 1618 the Kirk's General Assembly passed the Five Articles of Perth. These would impose the traditional dates of the Christian year, permit communion to be taken kneeling, allow confirmation of the laity only by a bishop, provide for private communion and baptism for the infirm, and sanction Holy Communion at Easter. These proposals were adopted by the Scottish Parliament, but only by the relatively narrow margin of 86 votes to 59. James was discouraged by what Michael Lynch has called 'a virtual vote of no confidence in a central plank of the King's policy'. Plans for further reform of the liturgy were abandoned, and Dissenters formed conventicles, breaking away from the Kirk. At James's death in March 1625 he was succeeded by his surviving son, Charles, who had seen nothing of the land of his birth since 1603.

See page 25 for information on James I's failure to persuade Parliament to agree to his plans for union.

B *The Act of Revocation, the new Prayer Book and the Covenant*

Charles I had been born in Scotland in 1600, but he had not returned since his father's accession to the English throne. His main wish for Scotland was that it should provide a greater income – both for the parish clergy and for the King, who contemplated foreign wars. Accordingly, Charles secured the passage of the Act of Revocation, whereby land grants made by any of Charles's predecessors during their minority could be annulled. Most nobles would be affected, and the whole plan seemed to them nothing less than a vast confiscation: 'the groundstone of all the mischief that followed', as one gentleman put it. There is no doubt that the Church benefited, for bishoprics could now be re-endowed and ministers' stipends increased, but the danger of a split between the nobility and the bishops was looming. Similar royal policies had been extremely dangerous for nobles' property rights in sixteenth-century France and the Netherlands, and were to be a factor in the Catalonian revolt of 1640.

Charles was accompanied by Archbishop Laud on his visit to Scotland in 1633 to be crowned. Already unpopular, Charles increased the distrust of many of his Scottish subjects by his use of bishops on the Scottish Council, his snub to a delegation of nobles led by the Earl of Montrose, and his behaviour at the 1633 session of the Scottish Parliament, when he ostentatiously took notes of the proceedings. At the coronation service itself Charles, accompanied by the Arminian Laud, who had replaced the Calvinist Abbot, insisted on using the English form of service, and then promptly scurried back to London. Resentment still smouldered, however, and was strengthened in 1635 during the trial of Lord Balmerino, one of those who had organised Montrose's petition two years before. Balmerino was convicted on only one of the three counts, and that conviction was only secured through the casting vote of Lord Traquair, one of Charles's Scottish placemen. He was sentenced to death, although he escaped execution. Scotland therefore experienced its equivalent of the ship money case and the trial of Prynne.

JAMES GRAHAM, FIRST MARQUIS OF MONTROSE 1612–50

As an Elder of the Kirk he opposed Laud's attempt to impose the new Prayer Book on Scotland, signed the National Covenant and fought for the Covenanters in 1640. However, he opposed Argyll's extremism, and fought for Charles I in the Civil War, raising his standard at Blair Atholl in August 1644. During 1644–5, he won a series of victories: Tippermuir, Aberdeen, Inverlochy, Aldearn and Alford. Having entered Glasgow, he planned to march on England, but he was heavily defeated at Philiphaugh in September 1645 by David Leslie's Covenanters. After a period in exile abroad he returned to Scotland in 1650 to fight for Charles II, only to be defeated again by Leslie at Carbisdale. He was captured and hanged without trial the same year.

In 1636, encouraged by Laud who had been unimpressed by the state of the Scottish Church, Charles introduced his Book of Canons for the Kirk, without reference to the General Assembly or the Scottish Parliament. Authority would in future lie with the bishops in the dioceses, whose licence would be required for a minister to preach in another's parish. Charles was therefore confronting head on the presbytery system in his quest for a 'British' Church. Other canons ordered the preaching of the need for good works, baptism on demand, 'bending the knee' at Holy Communion, short sermons, no extempore prayers and a new liturgy, which eventually appeared in the form of the 1637 Prayer Book.

The notorious 1637 Prayer Book was in fact not the work of Laud, who would have preferred to have imposed the English Prayer Book, but of the Scottish bishops. Reactions to it in Scotland were immediately hostile: any change to established forms of worship was resented; it bore an ominous resemblance in places to the Catholic Mass; long extempore prayers were omitted; and once again the General Assembly had not been consulted. The mood in Scotland was already volatile on the eve of the Prayer Book's first reading, for three important sections of the nation were already annoyed by royal policy: the Scottish Privy Council; the Scottish Parliament; and the General Assembly of the Church. In this atmosphere the Prayer Book was read for the first time on 23 July 1637 in St Giles's Cathedral, Edinburgh in the presence of the Scottish Privy Council, two archbishops, eight bishops and many nobles. The service ended in a riot, precipitated by Jenny Geddes who hurled a three-legged stool at the Dean to mark her disapproval. Within a week the new Prayer Book was abandoned and a form of counter-government was rapidly assembled.

Laud told the Star Chamber in June 1637:

> Our main crime is (would they all speak out, as some of them do) that we are bishops; were we not so, some of us might be as passable as other men. And a great trouble 'tis to them that we maintain that our calling of bishops is *jure divino*, by divine right: of this I have said enough, and in this place, in Leighton's case, nor will I repeat it. Only this will I say, and abide by it, that the calling of bishops is *jure divino*, by divine right, though not all adjuncts to their calling. And this I say in as direct opposition to the Church of Rome, as to the Puritan humour. And I say further, that from the Apostles' times, in all ages, in all places, the Church of Christ was governed by bishops, and lay elders never heard of till Calvin's newfangled device at Geneva.

Q *Why was Charles's Church policy so unpopular in Scotland?*

The 'Tables' emerged in December 1637 to demand the withdrawal of the new liturgy and the removal of bishops from the Privy Council. Representatives of burghs (towns), parishes (i.e. ministers of the Kirk), nobles and lairds (i.e. lesser landowners) met to draw up a supplication that eventually became the famous National Covenant, formally drawn up by a lawyer, Archibald Johnston of Wariston, and a minister, Alexander Henderson. In one sense this was a conservative document, for the signatories bound themselves 'to maintain the Kirk, Sovereign, laws and liberties of the kingdom, and to be bound together in this enterprise'. In another sense it was revolutionary, since it stemmed from the mass of the nation and not from the Crown. One-third of the Scottish nobility were the first to sign, according to the conventions of a hierarchical society, followed by lairds and ministers, and then by burgesses, who included an impressive number of lawyers. The general public had their chance to sign (or at least to affirm their support in public) in early March 1638. Rosalind Mitchinson writes: 'subscription to the Covenant was a threat to the Crown's authority. The Covenant bound the Scots together on a revolutionary enterprise, and in so doing destroyed the frail apparatus of royal control'.

C *The Bishops' Wars and the Scottish intervention in England*

In this revolutionary situation Charles sent the Marquis of Hamilton to try to browbeat the General Assembly meeting at Glasgow Cathedral in

November 1638. Hamilton failed, and the Assembly went on to abolish the office of bishop, the Five Articles of Perth, the Canons of Charles I, the 1637 Prayer Book and the Court of High Commission. Episcopacy was replaced by a new office of 'Ruling Elders', and a show trial ensued of 11 bishops, who were formally tried in their absence, deposed and excommunicated. As more Scottish councillors defected to the revolution (the Earl of Argyll, Alexander Leslie returned from Swedish service, and Alexander Hamilton and Robert Munro among others), Charles resorted to armed force to try to bring the Covenanters to heel in the two Bishops' Wars.

The First Bishops' War in the summer of 1639 ended in the Pacification of Berwick, which both sides regarded as merely the prelude to further hostilities. In the Second Bishops' War of 1640, a Scots invasion of northern England led to the Scots' victory at Newburn in Northumberland and the Treaty of Ripon of October 1640, in which Charles bought the promise of no further Scottish advance with a payment of £850 per day for the Scottish army's subsistence. Scotland was now effectively free of royal control, and Charles's power in England was also dwindling, as he found when the 'Short Parliament' of April–May 1640 refused him supply to resume military operations in Scotland, and the 'Long Parliament' proved equally obdurate. In 1641, there was still some hope that a civil war could be averted in England, but the Irish Rebellion, which erupted in the autumn of 1641, increased fears that Charles could not be relied on to deal with 'popery'. When the English Civil War did break out in 1642 the Scots insisted on hearing both the appeals addressed to them, i.e. from Charles I and from Parliament, and Pym opened serious negotiations with the Covenanters in August 1643 during the inconclusive military campaign of that year.

The Solemn League and Covenant was the fruit of these talks, whereby Parliament would pay for a Scottish army of 20,000 men to be deployed in England, and in return the Churches in England and Ireland would be reformed 'according to the Word of God and the example of the best reformed churches'. The army of the Covenant crossed the border in January 1644 under Alexander Leslie, now Earl of Leven, and besieged Newcastle before proceeding to York, from where it was deployed at the Battle of Marston Moor on 2 July 1644, helping to defeat the Royalist commander Prince Rupert. Meanwhile, Montrose embarked on a Royalist campaign in central Scotland, winning no less than six battles in 13 months before he was defeated by David Leslie, Leven's nephew, at the decisive engagement of Philiphaugh outside Selkirk on 13 September 1645. Charles himself was determined to parley with the peace party in Scotland, and in May 1646 he slipped out of his Oxford headquarters disguised as a servant, and gave himself up to the Scottish army encamped at Newark.

Charles's flight to Newark presented the Scots with a problem: if no agreement was forthcoming, he might form a focus for Montrose and other anti-Covenanter elements as he was escorted up to Newcastle. Yet Charles could not be persuaded to set up a Presbyterian Church in all three of his kingdoms by signing up to the Solemn League and

> **KEY ISSUE**
>
> *Charles's policy in Scotland provoked two wars.*

> See pages 105–8 for information on Scotland's contribution to the first civil war.

Covenant. A deal was reached, however, in January 1647, whereby the Scots received a payment of £100,000 for arrears of pay, and walked back across the border, while talks continued with the King over the other outstanding issues.

In June 1647, Charles was abducted by Cornet Joyce of Fairfax's New Model Army, and eventually imprisoned in Carisbrooke Castle on the Isle of Wight, from where he continued to negotiate with the Covenanters. Here he signed the 'Engagement', an undertaking to deal with English Independency (i.e. to suppress religious sectaries), to guarantee Scottish Presbyterianism, to set up a Presbyterian system in England for three years, and to offer Scottish nobles a role in his government (in return for military support). Most members of the Scottish Parliament accepted the agreement, but Cromwell himself defeated the 'Engagers', led by Hamilton at Preston, in August 1648. Hamilton was executed in London, and the 'Whiggamore Raid' established the opponents of the Engagement in Edinburgh and central Scotland. A Whig Parliament passed the Act of Classes in January 1649, banning from office for life all those who had promoted the Engagement or had backed Montrose. When Charles I was executed on 30 January 1649, the Scottish Parliament proclaimed Charles II on condition that he would adhere to the Covenant. War now seemed inevitable between the Scots and the Republic's new leader, Oliver Cromwell.

See pages 119–20 for information on the Second Civil War.

D *The Cromwellian settlement*

KEY ISSUE

Cromwell turned his attention to Scotland after Ireland.

Charles II arrived in Scottish waters in June 1650, and ostentatiously signed the Covenant, appearing to be the King whom the Covenanters had been seeking since 1638, and on 1 January 1651 he was crowned King of Scotland, yet again affirming his allegiance to the Covenant for good measure. War with England was now certain, and in July 1650 Cromwell crossed the border with 16,000 men. He defeated David Leslie's larger army at Dunbar on 3 September, but he was entering a country where there were still four armies in the field: the remnants of Leslie's United Kirk party; the 'holie' army of the Western Remonstrance, who refused to compromise with anyone; the surviving 'malignant' Royalist army in the north; and his own. By the end of the year Cromwell or his lieutenants, Lambert and Monck, had either defeated or reached an accommodation with the other three, and Cromwell himself headed south to defeat Charles II at Worcester on 3 September 1651 ('God's crowning mercy') in the fourth Scottish invasion of England since 1639. Now for the first time since the early fourteenth century an English army had conquered and occupied Scotland, and the Wars of the Covenant were over, as the crisis of the three kingdoms seemed to subside.

Cromwell continued to occupy Scotland with an army of over 18,000 men garrisoned at Inverness, Perth, Leith and Stirling. The Scottish Parliament was abolished after several failed attempts in the Ordinance of Union in 1654, which eventually became an act in the Protector's second parliament of 1656–7. Scotland sent 30 MPs to Westminster to

See pages 134–5 for Cromwell's attitudes to Scotland.

join the remaining 430 in a unicameral parliament: 20 from the shires and 10 from the burghs, of whom half were to be English army officers. The estates of active Royalists were confiscated to meet English military expenses, and many of the political community were disfranchised for their role in the wars, but liberty of worship was respected. There was nevertheless one serious Royalist rising in the Highlands in 1653–4, which was led by Glencairn and Middleton, and provoked by the arbitrary extension of English law and the encouragement of sectarian Independents against the Kirk. The Lord Protector's death in 1658 raised starkly the question of whether the *status quo* in Scotland could continue, given the substantial residual support for the Stuarts and the huge cost (around £100,000 per year) of occupation. Cromwell's aspiration for Scotland was that it should become a testing ground for the New Jerusalem that he hoped to build in England. At his death there was still some way to go before his ideal 'union and right understanding between the godly people', the English, and ' our brethren of Scotland' could be achieved.

E *Restoration in Scotland*

The death of Lord Protector Cromwell in 1658 curtailed the Rump Parliament's plan for a bill to give a fuller union, and in the winter of 1659–60 Monck left Scotland, vaguely stating that he was going to press for a restoration of the three nations' liberties. Events, however, moved rapidly towards a restoration: some Scottish notables had been in touch with Charles in exile, and his proclamation as King in London was swiftly followed by his affirmation as King of all three of his kingdoms in Edinburgh on 14 May 1660. In a sense he had been the King of Scotland at least for the last ten years, as he had taken the Covenant, and had been crowned before the Battle of Worcester, underlining the irony that while Scotland had been the most loyal kingdom to the Stuarts, it was also the kingdom where the civil wars had begun.

See pages 156–7 for Monck's intervention.

A Convention Parliament met on 1 January 1661, and on 28 March passed the Act Recissory, annulling all legislation passed since 1633, and offering the King £40,000 a year in taxation, triple the amount of the 1620s. This set the tone for the re-establishment over the next two years of Scotland as a separate kingdom, with a restored monarch, its own Privy Council, a separate parliament and judiciary and the revival of bishops in the Church. Charles was quick to appoint his own men to key positions: Middleton as Commissioner of Parliament; Glencairn as Chancellor; Cassillis as Justice-General; Rothes as Lord President of the Council; and Lauderdale as Secretary of the Council. Lauderdale was by far the most important; as a member of the Cabal he spent almost all his time on Scottish affairs, and his record inspired Charles's confidence, since he had been an original Covenanter, an Engager who had proclaimed Charles in 1650, and had fought by his side at Worcester. Indeed, Lauderdale had spent the years from 1651 to 1660 languishing in the Tower. Finally, while there were no regicides in Scotland against whom to proceed, there were a few vindictive executions of those who had complied with Cromwell's regime: the Marquis of Argyll, Guthrie, and Wariston being the main ones. At the same time the Restoration found its martyr; Montrose's remains were exhumed and he received a state funeral.

The return of episcopacy to the Scottish Church was heralded by the consecration of an advance guard of four at Westminster in December

PICTURE 40

A portrait of the Duke of Lauderdale by Jacob Huysmans. Lauderdale was a cynical and ruthless careerist who ruled Scotland as Charles II's 'gauleiter' (JP Kenyon's word)

See pages 177–81 for information on the Cabal.

JOHN MAITLAND, DUKE OF LAUDERDALE 1616–82

'Red John' Maitland was an uncouth, foul-mouthed Scottish aristocrat who supported Charles I in the Second Civil War, accompanied Charles II to Scotland for his coronation at Scone, fought for him at Worcester in 1651 and spent the rest of the Interregnum in prison. At the Restoration, Maitland was rewarded with a peerage and was appointed Secretary of State for Scotland. From 1667 to 1673 he was the 'L' in the CABAL (**C**lifford **A**rlington **B**uckingham **A**shley **L**auderdale). He spent much of his time in Scotland, maintaining royal authority by such desperate expedients as calling in the 'Highland Host' to plunder and harry the Presbyterian Lowlanders. Envied and hated in England and faced with mounting hostility in Scotland, Lauderdale resigned in 1680 due to 'ill health'. In fact, Charles II had decided to replace him with the even more unpopular James, Duke of York.

Bishop Burnet left this unforgettable pen-portrait of Lauderdale (from *History of His Own Time* (1727)):

> He made a very ill appearance: he was very big: his hair red, hanging oddly about him: his tongue was too big for his mouth, which made him bedew all that he talked to: and his whole manner was rough and boisterous, and very unfit for a court. He was very learned, not only in Latin, in which he was a master, but in Greek and Hebrew. He was haughty beyond expression, abject to those he saw he must stoop to, but imperious to all others. He was the coldest friend and the most violent enemy I ever knew: I felt it too much not to know it.

Burnet's description is supported by the National Portrait Gallery's painting. Here, caught on canvas, is the brutal, greedy, cynical careerist whom J.P. Kenyon felicitously described as 'Charles II's Scottish *gauleiter*'. Lauderdale retained Charles's confidence for 20 years by keeping Scotland in order. As a courtier, he knew what he had to do, entertaining the King with coarse jokes and obscene horseplay. Lauderdale was a strange man: a decadent thug who was at the same time an erudite scholar and a Presbyterian who persecuted his own co-religionists. He illustrates the anomalies of the Restoration Court.

1661, among them Sharp of St Andrews and Leighton of Dunblane. The following year the Privy Council banned presbyteries and synods without bishops' authority, and the great expulsions of Dissenting ministers began: around 30 per cent left the ministry, i.e. around 262 ministers, who became an obvious focus for opposition and disobedience. Most of the dissent centred on the three south-west synods of Galloway, Glasgow and Ayr, where Dissident prayer meetings formed into armed bands in the rather half-hearted rising of 1666. In this so-called 'Pentland Rising' 1,000 ill-armed men never posed a real threat, and were easily dispersed on 28 November 1666 by Tam Dalyell of the Binns at Rullion Green. The Act of Supremacie of 1669 declared that the King had supreme authority in all causes ecclesiastical, but synods and presbyteries continued to meet despite Lauderdale's use of the 'Highland Host' – a permanent militia to harry Dissenters. The Scottish Church remained a State Church in an insecure state.

In 1679, more serious disorders broke out in Scotland, partly in response to the more punitive statutes of 1677 against Scottish Presbyterians, denying them office, restricting their civil rights and requiring them to subscribe to bonds guaranteeing their tenants' behaviour. The primate of the Scottish Church, Archbishop Sharp of St Andrews, was murdered in May 1679, an armed uprising erupted in the west in favour of the exclusion of the Duke of York, government forces under John Graham of Claverhouse were defeated at Drumclog, and Richard Cameron and his Covenanters came out in favour of open war against Charles II. Charles sent his illegitimate son, the Duke of Monmouth, to put the rebellion down and he won a signal victory at Bothwell Bridge on 22 July 1679. Lauderdale lost office, and James, Duke of York arrived in Edinburgh – partly to secure his own succession, and partly to support the 1678 Test Act, which required all office-holders to accept the confession of 1660, recognising Charles II as supreme in spiritual as well as in temporal matters. Even the ninth Earl of Argyll subscribed to the Test Act (with certain qualifications) before escaping to Holland. Charles II, who had never visited Scotland during his reign of 25 years, died in 1685. The accession of the openly Catholic James seemed likely to put at risk the *status quo* in Scotland as much as south of the border.

> **KEY ISSUE**
>
> *Charles II's position in Scotland seemed more insecure than ever during the final part of his reign.*

F *Jacobite reaction defeated*

James II was proclaimed as King of the Scots on 10 February 1685, and his subordinates easily dealt with the invasion of the Earl of Argyll from Holland via Orkney, Kintyre and Glasgow in May of that year. The Scottish Parliament was as accommodating to James as the Westminster assembly, granting him the right to collect the excise in perpetuity, and accepting his proposal that Catholics should enjoy the right to worship freely. This suggestion was formulated by James in his announcement of February 1686, allowing private worship to Catholics and Quakers, and suppressing Conventiclers. Meanwhile, James advanced Catholics or Catholic converts to positions of power: Perth and Melfort became Chancellor and Secretary of State respectively, and Sir John Dalrymple

> **KEY ISSUE**
>
> *James II was welcomed at his accession in Scotland.*

See pages 203–6 for James II's policies of toleration.

See pages 234–6 for William III's attitudes towards Scotland.

KEY ISSUE

The notorious Massacre of Glencoe soured William's relations with many of his Scottish subjects.

of Stair replaced Lord MacKenzie as Lord Advocate. Yet there was no mass capture of public office, unlike in England (by 1688, for example, only one-fifth of Scottish JPs were Catholics). Emboldened, James announced in June 1687 a general toleration of worship in his Letters of Indulgence, permitting those Presbyterian ministers who had been forced out of their livings in 1662 to return to their parishes.

The events of December 1688 took Scotland by surprise, and there was some unease at the disinheriting of a Stuart king and of his heir, mingled with fears of a fresh interregnum. While there was no significant rallying to James, only a few Protestants supported William of Orange; many felt too confused by the turn of events to take sides. From 14 March 1689 a Convention Parliament met and issued the Claim of Right on 11 April, declaring the Crown forfeit and offering it to William and Mary. They condemned the proceedings against Argyll, asserted their independence and announced the abolition of bishops in the Kirk ('an insupportable grievance and trouble to this nation'). They followed this up two days later in the Articles of Grievances outlining James II's tyrannous acts. The Church did indeed change from June 1690 from an Episcopalian to a Presbyterian one, and at least 60 pro-Episcopalian ministers were forced out of their livings.

First, however, William and Mary had to deal with a full-scale Jacobite rising in the Highlands led by Sir John Graham of Claverhouse, otherwise known as Viscount Dundee, who had been irked by the promotion of the Duke of Hamilton, the tenth Earl of Argyll, Sir James Montgomerie and Sir John Dalyrmple, and who hoped to assist the simultaneous Jacobite rising in Ireland. On 27 July 1689 Dundee's forces narrowly defeated Hugh MacKay of Scourie's government troops at Killiekrankie, but Dundee himself was killed by a stray bullet, depriving the movement of effective leadership. The Jacobites received their come-uppance at Dunkeld on 21 August 1689 and at Cromerdale on 1 May 1690. William's government was now faced with the problem of what to do with the Jacobite clans who were still holding out, in spite of the conclusion of the war in Ireland by the end of 1690.

In mid-August 1691, the Earl of Breadalbane gave all chiefs and vassals until the end of the year to swear allegiance to William III. James II (or James VII as he was to Scots) wrote from his exile in France releasing his supporters from their undertakings to him. By 1 January 1692 only the MacIains of Glencoe had failed to conform, and Dalyrmple countersigned additional instructions to Sir Robert Livingstone on 16 January, ordering that those who had not taken the oath were to be obliged to surrender, and to this were added the following significant words: 'If Mac Ian of Glen Co and that tribe can be well separated from the rest, it will be a proper vindication of public justice to extirpate that set of thieves'.

At the notorious Massacre of Glencoe on 13 February 1692, troops under the command of Captain Robert Campbell of Glenlyon killed 38 MacIains or MacDonalds, including women and children. This was by no means the worst government atrocity in the seventeenth century, but it especially rankled since the perpetrators had recently received hospitality from their victims. After two inconclusive enquiries Dalrymple left office, but Jacobite sympathies remained a problem. The Highlands remained ungovernable, and more Jacobite rebellions were likely with Glencoe as a rallying cry. It is fair to say that William faced an intractable situation in Scotland.

Q

Why did the incident at Glencoe arouse so much anger?

G *The Act of the Union of 1707*

If the aftermath of the Massacre of Glencoe was unpropitious for better Anglo-Scottish relations, the events that followed make it still harder for the historian to explain why England and Scotland eventually agreed on a union in 1707. The first such development was the Darien Scheme, a Scottish enterprise set up under the 1695 Company of Scotland Act to plant a colony on Spanish territory in the isthmus of Panama, and intended to be a diversion from the Glencoe scandal. William III tried every possible impediment (blocking Hamburg loans and obstructing the supply of ships from Holland) because Darien was claimed by Spain, and the enterprise threatened William's delicate diplomacy on the eve of the War of Spanish Succession. Scots saw the scheme rather differently: for nationalist sentiment it was a panacea for the Scottish economy, and eventually no less than a quarter of all Scotland's liquid assets found their way into the venture. Two disastrous expeditions ensued, and relations between England and Scotland worsened when English capital was withdrawn, leading to the collapse of the Company of Scotland.

KEY ISSUE

The Darien Scheme caused Anglo-Scottish relations to deteriorate.

Meanwhile, the issue of Jacobitism revived when Anne's only surviving child from 17 pregnancies, William, Duke of Gloucester, died in 1700 at the age of 11. As a result, in 1701 the English Parliament passed the Act of Succession, which established the succession to the English throne in the House of Hanover (initially to the Electress Sophia and then to her son George), in the likely event that Princess Anne, William's successor, would die childless. Scottish opinion was furious since Scotland had not been consulted, and Anne went on to accede on William's death in 1702. As negotiations for a union fizzled out in 1702–3, Jacobite gains in the 1703 election suggested that more and more Scots were opting for the choice of the 'Pretender' (James VIII and III) over Anne, who is described by Michael Lynch as 'the first genuine unionist since James VI'.

See pages 251–59 for the political background in Anne's reign.

The Edinburgh Parliament passed two pieces of legislation in 1703, which illustrated the mood of the Scottish political community: the Act Anent Peace and War insisted on the right of a Scottish parliament to decide Scottish issues, i.e. if necessary to stop Scotland being dragged into a foreign war by Anne's successor, and the Act of Security, which claimed the right for Scotland to make a different choice of monarch after Anne's death, if it had not by then been granted freedom of trade with England and English colonies. By 1704 the prospect of union seemed further away than ever, but two factors encouraged greater integration: growing trading difficulties encouraged farmers and merchants to look more closely at the English market, and Godolphin's Alien Act of 1705 may well have ultimately forced the unity of the two kingdoms, which occurred two years later. Under this measure the new Whig ministry proposed that all Scots (except for those domiciled in England) would be treated as aliens, and that the main sectors of trade with England would be banned unless Scotland accepted the Hanoverian succession by 25 December 1705.

There is no doubt that trading advantages were the main Scottish motive for union, and the Scottish Parliament contained many (both landowners and merchants) whose economic interests would be promoted by it: half of all Scottish exports were after all taken up by the English market. On the other hand, the Church was opposed, fearing that the Presbyterian order would be put at risk, not least by a return to episcopacy, which would enable Scottish bishops to join their colleagues in the House of Lords. The real political pressure for union, however, came from within the Scottish Parliament itself, where elements within both the new 'Squadrone Volante' party, such as the Marquess of Tweeddale, and the 'Country' party saw union as a way of lining their pockets. It was agreed that a commission of 62 (31 from each country), nominated by the Queen, should negotiate union, on condition that the Alien Act was repealed. Honours were given to those such as the Duke of Hamilton, suggesting the largesse that might come the way of those who co-operated.

By the spring of 1706 the details of the plan had been worked out: the Scots would accept the Hanoverian succession; would receive compensation for the demise of the Darien Scheme; and would benefit from an 'Equivalent' tax to raise £400,000 a year as compensation to the Scots for their future share in funding the English debt. Scottish MPs would sit in the Westminster Parliament: 16 peers chosen by open election by their fellows to join the 190 English peers, and 45 members of the House of Commons (30 from the shires and 15 from the burghs) to join the 513 MPs from England and Wales. The two countries would merge as Great Britain, and would share a common flag, great seal, coinage, weights and measures, militia, navy and monarch. Scotland would, however, keep her own law and judicature and her Privy Council. Despite these provisions to allay Scottish fears, it is reasonable to ask how the Scottish Parliament was brought to accept the treaty.

The Kirk was to remain separate under the Act for Securing the Protestant Religion and Presbyterian Church Government of 1706, which assured the Scottish Church establishment. The treaty was ratified by both parliaments, and Seton of Pitmedden's remarks in the Edinburgh assembly give the flavour of the clinching argument (other than the sweeteners offered to some prominent politicians): 'this nation, being poor, and without force to protect its commerce, cannot reap great advantage by it, till it partake of the trade and protection of some powerful neighbour nation'. Scotland therefore gained a guarantee of her revolutionary settlement in Church and State, and a chance

Q

Why did the Act of Union succeed in 1707?

for economic development; England gained security against French hostility, and the acceptance of the Hanoverian succession.

There were several successful amendments to the treaty after 1707. In May 1708, the separate Scottish Privy Council was abolished, in 1709 the English law and penalties for treason were extended to Scotland, and in 1712 the Toleration Act allowed Episcopalians the freedom of worship, arousing fears that bishops might return. There were also more serious attempts to undermine the settlement: in 1708 a French fleet set sail from Dunkirk with the Pretender aboard, but failed to land, and in 1713 the Earl of Seafield, Chancellor of Scotland and originally a supporter of union, tried to get the union dissolved. Certainly the union settlement would take a while to be established, and in reality a genuine British State did not emerge until after the Battle of Culloden in 1746. After Anne died in 1714, the 1715 Jacobite Rebellion served as a reminder that the union was as yet a tender growth.

> **KEY ISSUE**
>
> *The Union was in no way firmly established by 1715.*

3 ~ WALES

A *Establishment of squirearchy*

Political developments during the sixteenth century favoured the aspirations of the Welsh landowning gentry. The 1536 statute ended the distinction between Wales and the Marches, and Thomas Cromwell's Act of 1543 extended English law and institutions further into Wales. In particular, Welsh shires were now organised on similar lines to English ones, with opportunities for Justices of the Peace, which the Welsh squirearchy were not slow to take advantage of.

> **KEY ISSUE**
>
> *During the sixteenth century, Welsh government and law were brought into line with English practice.*

Welsh gentlefolk were already adept at accumulating and consolidating landholdings: by the acquisition of former monastic lands; by benefiting from rewards for service; through enclosures of pasture and arable land in a region where there was always plenty of land; and through useful marriage alliances. They were not slow to seize opportunities for sheriffs and magistrates. JPs were responsible for law and order, tax collection, road maintenance, poor relief, the issuing of licences, militia organisation and the recruitment and the hunting out of recusants. As landowners the gentry were in a good position to exploit the mining of coal, iron or lead on their land and to profit from fishing. As their wealth and confidence increased they could become more proficient in English and extend their intellectual and artistic horizons – perhaps to the extent of sending their progeny to the Inns of Court in London or to one of the universities (Jesus College, Oxford was founded in 1571, to cater for Welshmen).

The majority of the Welsh elite welcomed the accession of James I in 1603, since he was the great-great-grandson of Henry VII, a Welshman. Elizabeth I herself had recognised him as her heir, and a strong king could protect parts of south-west Wales vulnerable to a Spanish Catholic invasion. James seemed in no way to threaten the order established by the Tudors; indeed his accession promised more of the same – hopes of reward, lucrative employment in the State, law, Church and great households. Indeed, several Welshmen were prominent in the professions and public office in the early seventeenth century, especially in the Anglican Church where Richard Vaughan secured the key appointment of Bishop of London in 1604. The Welsh squirearchy looked forward to a mutually beneficial partnership as a new dynasty acceded.

B *Catholic and Nonconformist influence*

KEY ISSUE

It was easier to spread the Protestant reformation into Wales, as many key religious texts were translated into Welsh.

The established Anglican Church had benefited during the sixteenth century from the rapid translation into Welsh of key religious texts, and Elizabeth I's preference of native Welshmen in Welsh sees (13 out of 16 of her Welsh bishops were native-born, including William Morgan of St Asaph who encouraged a translation of the entire Bible). The trend continued after 1603: in 1606 a Welsh 'book of homilies' appeared, in 1620 a new authorised version of the Bible and a new Prayer Book, and in 1621 an edition of the Psalms in Welsh was published. There was therefore no difficulty in conducting church services in the vernacular: the problem was more likely to be the church's poverty and the resulting lack of preachers, leading to pluralism and non-residence.

As discussed earlier, the Welsh landowning elite welcomed James I's accession. It is true that a small number of Welsh Catholics was involved in the Watson Plot of 1603 to seize the King and to free him from his Protestant advisers, but most Welsh Catholics accepted James as king, hoping for a relaxation of the laws against recusants, and noting that the Queen, Anne of Denmark, was herself a Catholic convert. The Anglican Church offered a useful area of patronage, from which a number of Welshmen benefited, including Richard Vaughan, Bishop of London from 1604, and John Williams, Archbishop of York from 1641. Catholics were quick to complain of continuing recusancy fines, but they were less harshly treated than in the previous reign. Clearly, James I's reign stirred up little religious excitement in Wales.

Resentment by some Welshmen against Charles I's religious policy was slightly more evident, for there was criticism of the Court of High Commission's activities and in particular of William Laud, who had been Bishop of St David's from 1621 to 1627. Laud, who obtained rapid promotion from Bath and Wells to London and then to Canterbury in 1633, was identified with a form of High Anglicanism that was attacked by its Nonconformist critics as 'popish'. Laudian bishops began to appear in Wales: Murray and Morgan Owen at Llandaff, John Owen at St Asaph and Manwaring at St David's. These prelates began to follow the Laudian path of improving the appearance of churches, and stressing seemliness, dignity and the 'beauty of holiness'. The Monmouthshire Petition of 1642 emanated no doubt from a Puritan minority in a border area, but it expresses articulately the strength of anti-Catholic feeling on the eve of the Civil War: '. . . we in Wales of all

See pages 69–72 for Charles I's religious policies.

others, and in Monmouthshire above the rest, cannot but be most sensible and suspicious of our own imminent destruction, as being compassed about with papists, more in number, and stronger in power, arms, horse and ammunition than any other country (as we conceive) in the Kingdom besides'.

The Irish Revolt of 1641 and the widespread impression that Charles was concerned to promote Catholicism fuelled fear of the 'papists', but, as civil war loomed, most Welshmen rallied to the King's side.

C *Wales and the civil wars*

Two facts stand out about Welsh opinion in the Civil War: few in Wales wanted a civil war, and most supported the King once war had broken out. There were several peculiarly Welsh factors that restricted commitment: relative economic backwardness; the lack of influential families; the paucity of towns and only a small commercial lobby; the small number of Puritans (most Welsh Puritans fled to England on the outbreak of hostilities); Wales's remoteness and its poor communications; and the language barrier, which reduced access to propaganda from either side. In a few more sophisticated parts there was some support for Parliament, for example among Pembrokeshire merchants under the influence of Robert Devereux, Earl of Essex, who owned land in south-west Wales, and in the Wrexham area of Denbighshire. Other parts of Wales held a few supporters: perhaps Puritan enthusiasts who feared a Roman Catholic despotism, landowners anxious to further local feuds, aspirant soldiers of fortune or businessmen critical of royal financial policy. The pressures to support the King were, however, greater.

Many Welshmen held Charles I in affection and respect, and many regarded the Parliamentary challenge to him as illegal, and indeed sinful. Moreover, staunch Anglicans supported the Church as a unifying force, and as an avenue for promotion and patronage: religious freedom as advocated by Parliament would, they believed, threaten national cohesion and the King's authority. They blamed Parliament for the outbreak of civil war and for the horrors that ensued; the ravages of the Thirty Years War on the Continent would, they feared, be repeated in Britain (famine, pestilence, fire, economic dislocation, etc.). They were essentially conservative with a respect for the old order, and had a sense that they had done well out of the 1536 and 1543 statutes. Finally, Catholics backed Charles out of necessity, taking their cue from the Catholic Marquis of Worcester, who unreservedly backed Charles for fear of a Puritan-controlled Parliament.

In conclusion, it is only fair to stress that the reaction of many in Wales, as elsewhere, was one of indifference or of fickle commitment. Fear of death, war, disorder and economic depression encouraged neutralism, and the instinct to opt out, or at least to limit the war's disastrous consequences. These fears could also encourage hedging and trimming among the committed as circumstances changed. 'The only

Q *To what extent was the Monmouthshire gentry's fear of 'papists' alarmist?*

KEY ISSUE

Few Welshmen felt strongly about the Civil War.

Q *Why was there more support for the King than for Parliament in Wales?*

constant thing about the Welsh', writes G.H. Jenkins, 'was their inconstancy'.

When war did break out, how was Wales affected? Charles was confident of support from Wales, and he left Nottingham in September 1642 to establish bases along the Welsh border at Shrewsbury and Chester, before returning to London. Meanwhile, the Prince of Wales made for Raglan, the seat of Charles's ally, the Marquis of Worcester. Welsh troops fought for Charles at Edgehill and Brentford in 1642. Wales was also valued by Parliament as a good recruiting area and source of victuals and as a strategic base with easy access to Ireland. The next area of contention was the Marches, with the King holding Chester and Shrewsbury, and capturing Bristol in July 1643; Parliament held Hereford and Gloucester. There was bad news for Welsh Royalists in 1644 when Charles suffered a stunning defeat at Marston Moor, and the Royalists were also defeated at the biggest battle of the First Civil War in Wales at Montgomery in September. This baleful trend continued in 1645 with a further major defeat for Charles at Naseby in June. Shrewsbury fell to Parliament in February, and Raglan (now Charles's headquarters) in August. The New Model Army took Chester in February 1646, and Parliamentary forces could now surge into Wales and capture Royalist castles one by one: Chirk and Ruthin in April, followed by Caernarfon, Beaumaris, Rhuddlan, Flint and Denbigh by October. Conway, Holt and Harlech followed suit by March 1647. In the Second Civil War Welsh Royalists were defeated in May 1648 by Colonel Horton's Ironsides at St Fagan's, and Cromwell retook Pembroke in July.

By 1649 Welshmen could begin to count the cost of seven years of war, which most of them had not wanted. There were numerous complaints of forcible conscription and commandeering, and rumours of atrocities, plundering and destruction (ironically by the Royalists considering the staunch Welsh support for the Stuart cause). Trade and local administration had been disrupted, property had been sequestered and fines had been levied. Many Welshmen had been put to considerable expense to equip themselves for war – Worcester who spent £900,000 is perhaps an extreme example. In short, the Welsh elite were ready to come to terms in 1649, and were opposed to too radical a change once it was clear that a republic was on the cards. There was strong Welsh opposition to the trial of Charles I, and Wales produced only two regicides: John Jones and Thomas Wogan.

D *Impact of the Interregnum*

Welsh reaction to the execution of Charles I was one of horror; only a handful of Welshmen saw it as the dawn of a new era, including the two regicides mentioned above. But there were more horrors to come: in March 1649 the monarchy and the House of Lords were abolished, and in May the English Republic was proclaimed. From 1648 to 1653 Wales was effectively governed by the Rump Parliament, which imposed sequestration and fines on those who had supported the losing side in

---

KEY ISSUE

Both sides regarded Wales as an important strategic objective.

See page 105 for Charles I's recruitment campaign.

the wars, and introduced a new constitution, whereby each Welsh county would have two seats in the Commons, and Cardiff and Haverfordwest were advanced to borough status. The Rump also made partially successful attempts to Puritanise Wales and to set up a state-supported education system. It also set up a commission to evict Anglican priests (278 were deprived between 1650 and 1653), and to appoint preaching ministers to take their places. Few keen and able candidates presented themselves as preachers, and those who did found the language barrier almost insuperable. After 1653 the Act to Propagate and Preach the Gospel in Wales was quietly allowed to lapse, while many of the sectaries, such as Vavasor Powell of the Fifth Monarchy Men who invaded Wales, made little impact. The Quakers alone had some limited success.

> See page 136 for the Rump Parliament's religious policies.

Between April and December 1653 a nominated Parliament named after Praise-God Barebones ruled, but still failed in its experiment to set up 'godly rule'. Ejected clergy still had some influence in their former parishes, and there was considerable lay hostility to 'innovations' such as civil marriage, the non-observance of Christmas and other holy days, and penalties against swearing and drunkenness. Resentment at taxation demands and quarrels among Puritan propagandists are other factors, yet Hugh Thomas believes that some religious progress was made in the Interregnum: 'but if their propaganda had not achieved wholesale conversion, it had succeeded in directing the attention of Welshmen to basic religious issues; it had also established pockets of Puritanism in Wales. By so doing it contributed substantially to the religious awakening that occurred in Wales during the century that followed'. Nonetheless, when Oliver Cromwell died in September 1658, few mourned him, and by 1659, after Richard Cromwell's short-lived regime and the dissolution of the Rump, the general mood in Wales was for restoration. On 7 August Sir Thomas Myddleton, the leader of an earlier failed Royalist rising in Cheshire that coincided with Sir George Booth's revolt, proclaimed Charles II in Wrexham.

> **Q**
> *What effect did the Civil War have on Wales?*

E *Re-establishment of the squirearchy*

Wales seemed to revert to its customary stability and moderation after the Restoration. One-third of the Welsh members of the Convention Parliament of 1660 were Cavaliers, and few of the elections were contested, while half of the members eventually elected had previous parliamentary experience. The elections to the 1661 Cavalier Parliament, when only six constituencies were contested, produced a Welsh representation of whom half were Cavaliers, and in the 24 by-elections between 1661 and 1679 two-thirds of the successful members were loyalists. Only the Venner Rising of 1661 seemed to disturb the calm until the fall of Clarendon in 1667, when Welsh MPs were divided in their loyalty to him; the same happened at the fall of Danby in 1679.

The Popish Plot of 1678 aroused a certain amount of anti-Catholic feeling in Wales, as it did elsewhere. Opposition was focused against the Marquis of Worcester, who had been made President of the Council of

Wales and the Marches in 1672 and Lord Powis, who was said to be planning to seize Chepstow Castle on his way to Milford Haven to meet an invading force of 20,000 Spanish troops. One of Titus Oates's associates, William Bedloe, was a Monmouthshire man and known criminal. In the Exclusion Parliaments themselves Welsh voices were raised on both sides: in the first, Welsh Exclusionists were well represented, and indeed the first Exclusion Bill was drawn up by a Welsh lawyer, after the second Powis was consigned to the Tower, and the third saw a larger contingent of Welsh Tories. By Charles II's death in 1685 it would have been difficult to detect much difference in the behaviour and views of Welsh and English Parliamentarians.

The accession of James II was greeted much the same as elsewhere in the realm, and Monmouth's Rebellion received very little support in Wales. Indeed, Judge Jeffreys himself was Welsh, the proprietor of Acton Park near Wrexham and the youngest Lord Chancellor in English history. James came to Wales in 1686 on a pilgrimage to the well of St Winifred in Flintshire, whose supernatural powers were revealed (according to some) when a son was born to the Queen, Mary of Modena, two years later. Contemporaries noted that Lady Powis was appointed as James Francis Edward's governess, and that Welsh students at Jesus College, Oxford refrained from lighting candles or ringing bells to mark the event. Moreover, the seven bishops who refused to instruct their clergy to read the Second Declaration of Indulgence from the pulpit in 1688 included William Lloyd of St Asaph. Finally, Huguenot refugees began to arrive in Wales from France with dire tales of Catholic persecution. Welsh opinion emulated opinion elsewhere: James II had outstayed his welcome.

The Glorious Revolution in Wales passed off as peacefully as anywhere else, although the Convention Parliament abolished the Council in the Marches in 1688–9, making Wales no longer a separate unit of government. The Toleration Act was hailed by Welsh Dissenters, but there was some resentment at the handing over of the Powis estate to Bentinck, one of William's Dutch cronies. A mere 19 non-juring clergy refused to take the oath to William and Mary.

Anne's reign was just as quiet, disturbed only by the agitation surrounding the Henry Sacheverell case in 1709. After his sermon 'In Perils among False Brethren', preached at St Paul's on the twenty-first anniversary of William's landing at Torbay, 17 Welsh Tory MPs voted for him, and seven Welsh Whigs voted for impeachment. On his release the good doctor made a triumphal tour of the Welsh borders in 1710, before settling down in the living of Sellatyn in Shropshire. By the accession of George I in 1714 Welsh MPs were being drawn from an increasingly narrow circle of Bulkeleys, Myddletons, Mostyns, Vaughans, Harleys, Mansells and Morgans, especially after the 1711 Property Qualifications Act, which laid down that parliamentary candidates must have real estate worth £600 per year in the counties, or £300 per year in boroughs. This was at a time when the franchise was restricted to those whose freehold property was valued at 40 shillings a year, which pro-

KEY ISSUE

James II was greeted in Wales at his accession, but soon disillusionment set in.

See pages 254–5 for the Sacheverell case.

duced an electorate of 21,000, or four per cent of the Welsh population. The voters themselves were usually apolitical and apathetic, and Whig versus Tory ideological rivalry rarely came between one Welsh member and another. Local jealousies and territorial interests tended to be more important. Apart from one or two reverses during the Civil War and Interregnum, the leading Welsh squirearchical families had prospered and thrived in a generally stable environment from the sixteenth century to the eighteenth century.

4 ⌐ THE CIVIL WAR AS A BRITISH SETTLEMENT

The traditional account of the English Civil War stresses the issues that set the King against Parliament by 1642, ensured a return to violence in the Second Civil War from 1648 and led to the purge of Parliament, the execution of the King, the abolition of monarchy and the House of Lords, and the setting up of an English Republic in 1649. Such a view in no way precludes mention of Scottish and Irish dimensions. After all from 1603 all three kingdoms shared the same monarch, Scotland precipitated the crisis of 1642 by rising against Charles I in the 1630s and effectively defeating him, and the 1641 Irish Revolt widened the conflict, and sharpened the burgeoning disagreement between Charles I and Parliament. Moreover, once the civil war had started both sides looked to Scotland and Ireland for help, successfully in the case of Parliament, whose victory by 1646 in the First Civil War owed much to Scottish intervention. Parliament went on to secure victory in both Scotland and Ireland, leading to more effective English control.

Such an anglocentric view has been challenged by a group of historians including Pocock, Morrill and Russell, who have urged a greater awareness of the depth and importance of Scottish and Irish factors. They emphasise the common factors in the resistance to Charles I from 1639 to 1642, and the intimate and repeated intertwining of the three kingdoms throughout the period. They even use a different nomenclature to describe the wars ('the War of the Three Kingdoms' or 'the British Wars') and maintain that the conflicts are only intelligible within a British context. Other writers are more sceptical: Cannadine, Canny and Brown stress the danger of ignoring or underestimating the internal factors unique to each of the three kingdoms, and Peter Gaunt encapsulates their argument: 'a three kingdom approach may give us a fuller and more accurate picture of this period, but it is unlikely to answer every question, to convince every historian or to command the field for evermore'.

Examining military events it is not difficult to identify certain common features. In all three parts there were changes in central and local government to put them on a war footing, and to enable them to tap resources effectively. In all three, military leaders gained more power and prominence than they would have enjoyed in peacetime, and

KEY ISSUE

To what extent were the three kingdoms intertwined during the Civil War?

See pages 92–9 for a discussion of the causes of the Civil War.

there was widespread killing and destruction throughout the British Isles. However, it is also striking that the nature of warfare and the timescale are different in each case: in Scotland and Ireland, for example, the periods of fighting were relatively short, while England and Wales saw an intensive four years of war. The same argument could be made for the settlement between 1648 and 1651. By 1651 the English Republic had imposed a form of union on Ireland and Scotland, forging a more unified British State. Yet this settlement took a different form in each part: in England a military coup occurred without great social or economic upheaval; in Scotland military conquest led to an enforced union but avoided large-scale colonisation; and in Ireland a brutal military conquest led to enforced union and dispossession, involving virtual ethnic cleansing and persecution of the majority Catholic religion. Peter Gaunt comments: 'in Ireland, at least, the legacy of the British wars still lurks near the surface'.

The sceptics summarise their criticisms as follows: the British approach is too politically focused to the neglect of social, economic and other factors; it still fails to avoid the charge of anglocentrism; it exaggerates the unity and integrity of the component kingdoms; it ignores links with continental Europe, and it stretches too far the abilities of any one historian to handle successfully such a mass of material. In particular they point to the significant differences between the three kingdoms. The struggle in England, they argue, was between two groups from within the same polity and sharing the same religion; in Ireland the conflict took on the dimensions of a clear racial and religious struggle. The consequences of the war differed too: in England the war unleashed new radical political and religious ideas encouraged by a free press. Such radical activity was much less a feature in the other two kingdoms with their powerful churches, landed elites, weaker press and small urban sector. The emphasis on the 'British' dimension offers a useful insight, but it cannot offer a total interpretation of a complicated problem.

5 ⌐ TOWARDS A UNITED KINGDOM?

Now the more general question must be faced regarding how far progress had been made towards a co-ordinated, truly unified and mutually beneficial united kingdom by 1715 after the turmoil of the previous century. In the case of Wales it may be reasonable to conclude that the real progress towards the absorption of the Principality into 'England and Wales' had been achieved in the previous century. By 1603, the Tudors, themselves originally a Welsh family, had established strong government and legal institutions in Wales that continued to cement England and Wales closer together throughout 1603–1714. The hiatus of the English Civil War was unwelcome in Wales, and by 1715 Welshmen were once again profiting from their link with England. The lucrative employment opportunities afforded to the Welsh landowning elite and the absence, after more than a century of reformation, of significant religious differences between the two parts may have led England to take Welsh acquiescence in the union for granted, but the relationship between England and Wales was much more straightforward, and much less oppressive, than that between England and Scotland and England and Ireland.

The 1707 Act of Union between England and Scotland was never popular, and its very passing astonished contemporaries. Greed, fear and bribery may be a cynical explanation, but this was not a meeting of minds and cultures as equals. Indeed, the Union only survived its infancy with difficulty, and it faced a severe test in the 1715 Jacobite rebellion. Any union, once established, would be hard to dissolve, and Scottish merchants appreciated their share in the huge free trade area that the deal had opened up. English commercial gains were complemented by a greater sense of security, as the notorious 'postern gate' seemed to be permanently barred. It would be a rash historian indeed, however, who would conclude that the Union at this stage was in any sense secure.

See pages 433–5 for a critical assessment of the union of England and Scotland.

In Ireland it could be said that the penetration of English government had been very successful compared with the weakness of most Tudor monarchs beyond the Pale. The successive legacies of Jacobean plantations, Wentworth's 'Thorough', Cromwell's massacres and William III's victory at the Boyne undoubtedly gave England much greater control over the whole island of Ireland. A mass of Protestant settlers had swarmed into Ulster and elsewhere, pushing the Catholic Gaelic population further west and south. Catholic Ireland was no doubt intimidated after the onslaught of the previous century, but it would be difficult to claim that Ireland was any more genuinely integrated into a British State on a basis of consent than it had been before. It is too early to celebrate a real British kingdom by 1715, and indeed from the standpoint of George I's accession such an achievement still must have seemed very far off.

6 ⌐ BIBLIOGRAPHY

The best general survey of the Stuart era, which also contains substantial material on all the kingdoms, is *A Monarchy Transformed: Britain, 1603–1714* by Mark Kishlansky (Penguin, 1996).

The best recent general history of Ireland with a decidedly revisionist tone is *Modern Ireland, 1600–1972* by Roy Foster (Penguin, 1988), while *A History of Ireland* by Edmund Curtis, first published in 1936, is still useful (Routledge, sixth edition 1995). Also on Ireland see *A Short History of Ireland* by J. O'B. Ranelagh (CUP, second edition 1994) and *Ireland, a History* by Robert Kee (Abacus, revised edition 1995), which is a journalistic account anxious to explain the troubles in Northern Ireland from 1968 in terms of aspects of past Irish history. Finally, for Cromwell's role see *Oliver Cromwell* by Barry Coward (Longman, 1991).

The most concise treatment of Scotland during the period is *A*

History of Scotland by J.D. Mackie (Penguin, second edition 1978). An original treatment is in *Scotland, a New History* by Michael Lynch (Pimlico, 1992), while *Lordship to Patronage, Scotland 1603–1745* by Rosalind Mitchison (Edinburgh University Press, 1983) is also useful.

On Wales the standard accounts of this period are still *Recovery and Reorientation in Wales, 1415–1642* by Glanmor Williams (Oxford University Press and the University of Wales Press, 1987), and *Foundations of Modern Wales* by Geraint Jenkins (Oxford University Press and the University of Wales Press, 1993). See also the essay 'The English Crown, the Principality of Wales and the Council in the Marches, 1534–1641' by P. Roberts in *The British Problem, c.1534–1707, State Formation in the Atlantic Archipelago* edited by Brendan Bradshaw and John Morrill (Macmillan, 1996).

On the 'British' dimension in seventeenth-century history see 'The British Problem, c.1534–1707' by John Morrill and 'The Atlantic Archipelago and the War of the Three Kingdoms' by J.G.A. Pocock in *The British Problem, c.1534–1707, State Formation in the Atlantic Archipelago* edited by Brendan Bradshaw and John Morrill (Macmillan, 1996). For a critique of the above see 'The Triple-crowned Islands' by Ronald Hutton in *The Reigns of Charles II and James VII and II* edited by Lionel K.J. Glassey (Macmillan, 1997), and *The British Wars, 1637–1651* by Peter Gaunt (Routledge, 1997).

7 ⌐ HOW TO WRITE A SYNOPTIC ESSAY (LOOKING AT THEMES ACROSS THE PERIOD)

A synoptic essay is one that requires you to write about a particular theme over a long period of time. The following essay title also presents the added difficulty of expecting you to deal with several parts of the British Isles at the same time, on top of the problem of handling detail from no less than six reigns, not to mention the Interregnum from 1603 to 1714.

'To what extent was religion a factor among the three British kingdoms during the Stuart period?'

As usual the introduction is crucial. Outline the problem and put it into the widest possible context. The problem is partly the reality of religious diversity, for example a Protestant settlement established in England by 1603 against a background of a largely Catholic Ireland, a strong Presbyterian influence in Scotland and a generally compliant Wales, which was in any case very much more closely linked to England in the first place. You will also need to show an awareness of the importance of religion at this time: almost everyone regularly went to church and governments were expected to establish a religious settlement. Moreover, religious toleration was most unusual, as a glance at continental Europe will show: after the French 'Wars of Religion' from 1560 to 1598, the Thirty Years War ensued quite quickly in 1618, and Louis XIV (reigned 1661–1715) had a strong religious plank in both his foreign and domestic policy. In short, Protestants and Catholics distrusted each other, and the British archipelago provided examples of both types of religious experience and considerable variations within each.

In the body of the essay you will have to cover developments in the three Celtic areas, but you would be well advised to start with England as the dominant polity. All English rulers strove for religious uniformity, and none more so than Charles I. It is quite easy to point to Laudianism as a major factor in inducing mistrust of Charles I within his English kingdom. It also, of course, bedevilled his relationship with Scotland and, for that matter, with Ireland. The Interregnum encouraged the rise of radical sects within an overall Protestant establishment, but the Anglican Church revived under Charles II. There was then a short-lived Catholic interlude under Charles's brother, James II, before William and Mary presided over a redefinition of the English Reformation. This was to be continued under Anne.

Ireland shows the resilience of Catholicism, and the readiness to resort to arms in the face of a perceived threat to religious orthodoxy. The Ulster plantations in James I's reign also aroused fears of dispossession from landed rights, but the Irish Revolt of 1641 was seen in England as a religious crusade in favour of the old faith. Moreover, Cromwell's brutal policy of repression in Ireland stemmed mainly from a religious motive. Finally, William III continued the policy of Protestant hegemony under both republican and monarchical regimes. You will need to show an awareness of these religious factors, and be able to relate them to political and ethnic realities.

In Scotland Laud was seen as a Catholicising threat, as the imposition of an unpopular Prayer Book prompted the two Bishops' Wars against Charles I. Examine the religious policy in Scotland of Cromwell, Charles II, James II, William and Mary and Anne. Finally, you should deal with the 1707 Union. Was this purely an economic and political issue, or did religion play a part as well?

In Wales it is much less clear that religious issues raised the intensity of passion that led, or helped to lead to armed conflict elsewhere. You will have to look, however, at Laudianism in Wales and at the impact of the religious enthusiasms released there, and in England, by the emergence of the English Republic. Finally, for the Principality, there is some evidence of the reaction of the Welsh elite to the Sacheverell incident of 1709–10.

The conclusion is an opportunity to reach a view, to tie up any loose ends and to summarise your argument as it has emerged. No less than in the body of the essay, you will have to omit much detail in the interests of economy. You will need to point out that there were other issues that affected relations among the various component parts – political ideology, questions of land settlement, trade and the economy, international diplomacy and war. You should, however, ensure a place for the religious factor, based on your assertion in the introduction of its importance at the time, and include your examination of the accuracy of that assertion in the light of circumstances over time in four areas.

8 ~ DISCUSSION POINTS AND ESSAY QUESTIONS

A *This section consists of questions that might be used for discussion (or written answers) as a way of expanding on the chapter and testing understanding of it.*

1. Why were the Ulster plantations undertaken?
2. What successes did Wentworth enjoy as Lord Deputy of Ireland?
3. Why did the Irish Rebellion break out in 1641?
4. What were Cromwell's motives in his reconquest of Ireland?
5. What role did Ireland play in the Glorious Revolution?
6. What was Archbishop Laud trying to achieve in his Scottish Church settlement?
7. Why was the new Prayer Book of 1637 so resented in Scotland?
8. Why did Charles I lose the Bishops' Wars?
9. Account for the persistence of Jacobitism after James II's abdication.
10. Why did the Union of 1707 come about?
11. Account for the Royalist sympathies of many Welsh gentlemen at the outbreak of the English Civil War.

B *Essay questions.*

1. Why was Ireland so embroiled in the Civil War?
2. Why was William III so concerned to subjugate Ireland?
3. What role did Scotland play in the Parliamentary victory of the Civil War?
4. Account for the continuing instability in Scotland after the Restoration.
5. How popular was the Act of Union of 1707 in England and Scotland?
6. To what extent did Welshmen take sides in the English Civil War?
7. How important was Wales to either side during the course of the English Civil War?

9 ∾ DOCUMENTARY EXERCISE ON THE UNION BETWEEN ENGLAND AND SCOTLAND

Study sources A to E and attempt the questions that follow.

A   The New Scottish Prayer Book of 1637, from J. Rushworth *Historical Collections* (1659).

That in the new Service-book which most startled the Scots, was the omission at delivery of the Bread in the sacrament of these words, *"And take and eat this, in remembrance that Christ died for thee, and feed on him in thy heart by faith with thanksgiving"*; and the omission at the delivery of the wine of these words, *"And drink this, in remembrance that Christ's blood was shed for thee, and be thankful"* although these passages are both in the English Liturgy, and do expressly take away all opinion of any Transubstantiation, or corporeal eating of Christ's body, or drinking his Blood in the Sacrament; so that there was nothing left at the delivery of the Bread and Wine, but the preceding words in the English Liturgy, *"The Body of our Lord Jesus Christ etc."* and, *"The Blood of our Lord Jesus Christ etc."* which the aforesaid words expunged out of the Scottish Liturgy did qualify and explain. But thus standing alone in this new Liturgy, these are the very same words that are in the Roman Missal, without any other addition than *"Amen"*, to be pronounced by the receiver. What the meaning hereof was, appears not; but the Scots apprehended it the prologue to the bringing in among them a principal point of Popery, to wit, the Doctrine of Transubstantiation.

B   *'A solemn league and covenant for reformation and defence of religion, the honour and happiness of the King, and the peace and safety of the three kingdoms of England, Scotland and Ireland',* from J. Rushworth, *Historical Collections* (1659).

II. That we shall in like manner, without respect of persons, endeavour the extirpation of popery, prelacy (that is, Church government by archbishops, bishops, their chancellors and commissaries, deans, deans and chapters, archdeacons, and all other ecclesiastical officers depending on that hierarchy), superstition, heresy, schism, profaneness, and whatsoever shall be found to be contrary to sound doctrine and the power of godliness, lest we partake in other men's sins, and thereby be in danger to receive of their plagues; and that the Lord may be one and his name one in the three kingdoms.

C Scottish Claim of Right, April 1689.

(i) declared that James had 'forfeited the right to the crown' because of his violation of the 'fundamental constitution of the kingdom';

(ii) laid down that no papist could rule or hold office in Scotland;

(iii) forbade use of judicial torture 'without evidence' or in ordinary case;

(iv) forbade dragonnades;

(v) laid down that Parliament should meet frequently and freely and must give its consent to raising of revenue;

(vi) reversed two Court of Session rulings extending law of treason to include unspoken personal opinions;

(vii) condemned prelacy as 'a great and insupportable grievance and trouble to this nation', and advocated its abolition.

D Act of Security (Scotland), 1704. (Note: This was passed by the Scottish Parliament in 1703, but was refused royal assent until 1704.)

(1) Scotland's Parliament was to meet on the Queen's death and offer the crown to the next heir on condition of his acceptance of Claim of Right.

(2) Heir to be a Protestant, descended from House of Stuart, chosen by Parliament.

(3) *But* (unless suitable terms securing Scotland's sovereignty, trade and religion could be negotiated with England during Anne's lifetime) heir not to be same person as inherited throne of England.

E Act of Union.

(1) From 1 May 1707 England and Scotland to be united into one Kingdom, 'Great Britain', with a common 'Union' flag, the succession of their joint monarchies settled in the House of Hanover, and a common 'Parliament of Great Britain'.

(2) All subjects of new state of Great Britain to enjoy freedom of trade both internally and with their [in effect, English] overseas 'dominions and plantations'.

(3) Scotland not to be liable to taxation to service the existing English National Debt.

(4) All monies unavoidably so taken to be returned annually in a lump-sum, the 'Equivalent', to be used in first instance to compensate stockholders of the bankrupt 'Company of Scotland' (Darien).

(5) Scotland not to be liable to a malt tax until end of War of Spanish Succession, but *was* to be liable to the English Excise, with exception of that on beer. Scotland to pay £48,000 in Land Tax for every £1,997,763 paid by the English.

(6) Coin to be 'of the same standard and value throughout the United Kingdom', along with common weights and measures.

(7) Scotland to retain her own fully autonomous legal system.

(8) The worship, discipline and government of the (Presbyterian) Church of Scotland to be 'effectually and unalterably secured', and the Kirk to be free of English episcopal supervision.

(9) Heritable jurisdictions, and privileges of royal burghs in Scotland, to be continued and preserved.

(10) Scotland to have 45 representatives in House of Commons of the Union Parliament, elected under existing Scottish electoral system.

(11) Only 16 Scottish peers to sit in House of Lords, elected at each General Election by Scottish peerage.

(12) Otherwise, Scots nobility to have all legal privileges enjoyed by English counterparts.

Q

1. *Summarise the argument against the new Prayer Book in source A. (6 marks)*
2. *How reliable are soures B and C as evidence of opinion in Scotland between 1643 and 1689? (6 marks)*
3. *Account for the truculence of the tone of source D. (6 marks)*
4. *Using your own knowledge and all the sources, discuss the view that the Union of 1707 was 'an astonishing development'. (12 marks)*

12 Conclusion

'What was the end of all the show?' From *The Widow's Party* by Rudyard Kipling.

1 ⌐ GAINS AND LOSSES

To conclude *Years of Turmoil* with a quotation from Kipling makes sense. The most spectacular and indisputable development that occurred between 1603 and 1714 was the emergence of Britain as a great power. The unimpressive off-shore islands that James I had inherited now dominated Europe. The Treaty of Utrecht, extracted from a beaten and humiliated Louis XIV, at once reflected Britain's new-found might and formed the basis for continued imperial expansion.

This remarkable success of *Great* Britain depended on several factors. First, the financial revolution of the 1690s enabled British statesmen to wage a European war without bankrupting the treasury – a trick that France and its Habsburg rivals never learnt. Meanwhile, London was now replacing Amsterdam as the commercial capital of the world. Secondly, Britain's army and navy had come of age – from La Rochelle to Ramillies. The amateur, aristocratic leadership of the first two Stuarts had been transformed as a result of the civil wars into the professional corps of Marlborough and Rooke. The British army and navy had been 'blooded' by William III. Now well trained, well equipped and well led they could take on the French and Spanish super-powers that had dominated Europe. Thirdly, British agriculture was the most efficient in the world. While famine could still strike, British fighting men were nurtured mainly on British beef, beer and bread. British farmers could not only feed themselves, but also supply the growing centres of commerce and industry on which the war effort depended.

Equally indisputable as a positive achievement was the Union of England and Scotland. Chapter 11 indicated that this was the result of greed, fear and bribery. Furthermore, the Union was never popular in either country and survived some rocky moments between 1707 and the Jacobite rising of 1715. But survive it did, partly because the Scots 'discovered that it is harder to dissolve any union than it is to enter it' (Barry Coward). Both parties benefited from the Union. Together, England and Scotland constituted the largest free-trade area in Europe. During the rest of the eighteenth century Scotland experienced a cultural, intellectual and social renaissance, while England was protected against invasion through the back door.

Political 'gains' are more debatable. We have come a long way from the complacency of Whig historians such as Trevelyan. Jonathan Clarke argues that the monarchy, far from being subordinated to Parliament, emerged from the civil wars and the Glorious Revolution with its powers intact and increasing. J.P. Kenyon questions the virility of Parliament: 'Weak and disorganised as the monarchy often was, Parliament was more so'. He quotes Parliament's failure to impose the political community's will on the Crown during the Exclusion Crisis, while between 1639 and 1644 only the intervention of the Scots enabled Parliament to defeat Charles I. As for the Glorious Revolution when Parliament is supposed to have dictated terms, it needed the intervention of another foreigner, William III, with a 'Danish, Swedish, German, Anglo-Scotch army' at his back to defeat a monarch whose stupidity amounted to senile dementia.

See page 161 for Clarke's views.

It is true that if the monarchy was still very powerful in 1714 it was due to its partnership with the political community. But then that was true of all despotic rulers (even Louis XIV) until dictators such as Stalin could exploit modern technology and rule through terror. The question is: what were the terms of the partnership? Two aspects of this interdependence between the Crown and political community tarnish the British 'freedom' admired by Whig historians. The real victors of the seventeenth-century conflict were not the Pyms and Hampdens, the sturdy country squires who sat as MPs in the Commons, but the great magnates in the Lords. According to John Adamson, the aristocratic leaders on the Parliamentary side called the shots from the 1640s onwards, with their arrogant demands that Charles I, like some latter-day Moonie, should be de-programmed. Great magnates certainly dominated the reigns of William III and Anne, and monopolised power under the approving Hanoverians. While no royal palaces were built during the years of turmoil, the aristocracy littered the countryside with self-advertising mansions, culminating in Blenheim *Palace* – financed by the Crown for a nobleman! The second aspect of this political achievement is the reliance neither on force, nor on eloquence but on corruption. 'Sir, do you not hold a commission in His Majesty's Guards?', asked an indignant whip when a young aristocrat had voted against the government. 'Indeed I do, Sir, but my father died last week, leaving me £5,000 a year.' Few enjoyed such independence. Success in politics was achieved by turning sleaze into an art form.

Have the alleged achievements of the years of turmoil virtually disappeared under the historians' scrutiny? Not entirely. Britain was certainly a parliamentary monarchy. There were now steps that no monarch could take. Parliament had insisted that for good or ill Britain had to be ruled by Protestants, and the monarch could not conduct foreign policy without Parliament's approval. The most important political result of the financial revolution was that the monarch needed parliamentary support in order to borrow money. That meant frequent parliaments, genuine consultation of both Houses by the government and parliamentary scrutiny of expenditure. As for the composition of govern-

PICTURE 41

Blenheim Palace. Designed by Sir John Vanbrugh and built between 1705–25, this residence was a gift from Queen Anne to the Duke of Marlborough as a monument to his victories over the French

ments, both William III and Anne had to accept ministers who were personally objectionable to them – since only they could guarantee the necessary parliamentary support. All this may sound uninspiring, but it did make Britain a uniquely parliamentary state.

The triumph of religious liberty was equally uninspiring. 'Toleration' was not the wish of the British people. In fact, what emerged hardly deserved to be called toleration (even with a small 't'). Dissenters continued to be treated as second-class citizens until the nineteenth century, Roman Catholics were brutally persecuted in Ireland and the Scots only agreed to the Act of Union if their beloved Kirk retained its persecuting hegemony. Meanwhile, the persecuting Church of England reaped its reward, having seen off the challenges of militant Nonconformity in the 1650s and militant Catholicism between 1685 and 1688. It is true that the confessional state was no more. Not even in Ireland were Catholics actually massacred – though they were allowed to die from starvation. But the abandonment of the Anglican Church's claim to monopolise the religious allegiance of all the Crown's subjects was not due to idealistic tolerance and love. It was a recognition of such inconvenient facts as the virulence of Nonconformity and Irish Catholicism, combined with growing scepticism and indifference.

Considerable reservation should greet references to 'personal liberty'. Alas, the old cliché 'it's all right for some' applies here. Marxists such as Hill are right to stress the meaningless nature of 'liberty' when there is material disparity. The grotesque gulf between rich and poor meant that the triumphs of the British political community were worthless so far as three-quarters of the people were concerned; and 'the people' did not just include the English. Not only the poor wretch evading the press-gang in the streets of London, but the starving crofter in the Highlands, the dispossessed Catholic in Ulster and the manacled slave in Jamaica can have felt little enthusiasm for British 'freedom'. The only politicians whose victory could possibly have helped such people were the Levellers. And unfortunately they lost.

Two other 'gains and losses' should be stressed. The first was the result of war. A vast bureaucratic machine had been created in order to administer the armed forces and run the war effort. This machine increased both the expense and the power of government, and also the opportunities for corruption. No wonder few eighteenth-century governments lost elections. The second development was the result of peace. After the Restoration when the country returned to its former ways, the county community was restored and within it the parish. Great aristocrats, wholly independent of government interference, dominated their county communities, just as squire and parson once again controlled the parish, with their armies of beadles, constables, churchwardens and overseers of the poor.

2 ↠ UNFINISHED BUSINESS

While it is right to acknowledge the political, economic and intellectual achievements of seventeenth-century Britain, there was still much to be done. For example, considerable unfinished business remained in the field of medicine. The discoveries of vaccination and anaesthetics still lay in the future, and contemporaries still did not have an inkling about the dangers of contaminated water. Childbirth was hazardous for mother and baby so that life expectation remained in the low thirties. 'Dental care' amounted to extraction and the 'care of lunatics' meant the straightjacket.

Similarly, it is important not to exaggerate British economic advances. Britain was still an agrarian society, with the majority of working people employed on the land. British people rightly believed that their agriculture was more efficient than that of the French. While bad harvests still caused distress and unemployment, few actually starved. But to talk of a proto-industrial revolution at this stage is wrong. Only in coal mining and shipbuilding were people employed in their tens, never mind hundreds. Manufacture was still domestic, and still labour-intensive. There were no factories, no labour-saving machines. The crucial marriage of coal and iron was barely envisaged, and the invention of steam power was impossible until that marriage was consummated. While roads were improving, it still took a fortnight to travel from London to Edinburgh while, away from the sea and the few navigable rivers, transport of bulk goods was by packhorse and horse-drawn waggon.

The socially and politically disadvantaged still awaited their emancipation. Twenty-four years after Anne's death, the poor would be told by John Wesley that they had souls. By the end of the eighteenth century trade unions emerged to care for their bodily needs. Only in the nineteenth century would free education cultivate their minds. Black slaves and Irish Catholics had to wait a long while before they were treated justly. The emancipation of women made little progress during the years of turmoil. Sarah, Duchess of Marlborough was entitled to complain: 'I am confident I should have been the greatest hero that ever was known in the Parliament house, if I had been so happy as to have been a man.' The only power that most women enjoyed was over men who loved them (in 1707, Jeremiah Clarke, the gifted organist of St Paul's Cathedral, fell in love, was rejected and shot himself). Sarah and her John stayed together despite her appalling tantrums. Long after his death, she remarked sadly, 'An old woman is a very insignificant thing'.

3 ⌐ TURMOIL AND STABILITY

Uppity women demonstrating for the release of Lilburne the Leveller, Irish Catholics in arms against their Protestant tormentors, Scottish Covenanters rescuing the English Parliamentarians, Quakers, Shakers, Diggers and Fifth Monarchy men, Republicans, Saints and Major-Generals, the last forlorn radicals who fought and died for King Monmouth – all these and many more gave the leaders of the establishment the fright of their lives during the years of turmoil. *And it had been their own fault!* So never again would the rich and the well-born fall out among themselves, giving the outsiders a chance to break in. Once it was clear who best guaranteed their privileges, the elite rallied to the sinister, sleazy Charles II, the impossible James II (until he threatened their monopoly of power) William the Dutchman who radiated anti-charm and George of Hanover who was William III cubed, so to speak.

It only remained for the leaders of the political community to win the confidence of the monarch and create a political and social paradise for the upper classes. Walpole was the man for this particular job. The Scots co-operated, having calculated the dire consequences of the alternative, namely Jacobitism, while the Irish were driven from the sight of respectable society. The English were personified by the corpulent, complacent and deferential John Bull. Woe betide anyone who threatened to upset this comfortable stability. This was why the troublemaker John Wilkes was victimised by the House of Commons and explains the hysterical paranoia with which the upper classes treated John Wesley who preached 'what is a lord but a sinner born to die?'. No-one must rock the boat in case the British once again shed each others' blood. They must be free to shed other people's blood in what Kipling euphemistically called 'The Widow's Party'.

Chronological Summary

1603	Accession of James I
1604	Hampton Court Conference
1604–10	First Parliament of James I
1605	Gunpowder Plot
1608	Bate's case
1610	Debate over the Great Contract
1612	Deaths of Salisbury and Prince Henry
1613	Murder of Overbury
1614	The Addled Parliament (James I's second Parliament)
1615	Cranfield Surveyor-General of the Customs
1616	Promotion of George Villiers (Buckingham)
1616–18	Raleigh's expedition to Guiana
1617	James I's visit to Scotland
1618	Dismissal of Lord Treasurer Suffolk for corruption
1621	Third Parliament of James I The Commons' Protestation
1623	The visit of Charles and Buckingham to Madrid
1624	Fourth Parliament of James I
1625	Death of James I: Accession of Charles I Charles's marriage to Henrietta Maria First Parliament of Charles I Failure of Buckingham's expedition to Cadiz
1625–6	Second Parliament of Charles I
1627	Failure of Buckingham's expedition to La Rochelle The Five Knights case
1628–9	Third Parliament of Charles I The Petition of Right Assassination of Buckingham Wentworth President of the Council of the North
1629	The Three Resolutions
1629–30	The 'personal rule' of Charles I
1632	Wentworth Lord Deputy in Ireland Death of Eliot in the Tower

1633	Laud becomes Archbishop of Canterbury
1635	Ship money imposed on the whole country
1637	Prynne, Bastwick and Burton branded and de-eared Riots in St Giles's Cathedral, Edinburgh Trial of John Hampden
1638	The Scottish National Covenant
1638–9	The First Bishops' War
1639	Peace of Berwick
1640	The Short Parliament Second Bishops' War – the Treaty of Ripon
1640–60	The Long Parliament The Root and Branch Petition
1641	Trial and execution of Strafford Abolition of ship money and prerogative courts etc. Charles I's visit to Scotland: the Incident Outbreak of rebellion in Ireland The Grand Remonstrance
1642	The attempted arrest of the Five Members The Militia Ordinance The Nineteen Propositions Outbreak of First Civil War The battle of Edgehill Confrontation at Turnham Green
1643	The abortive Treaty of Oxford Royalists' triple advance on London Battle of Roundway Down Solemn League and Covenant The cessation Death of Pym
1644	Sack of Bolton Battle of Marston Moor Parliamentary forces surrendered at Lostwithiel

	Battle of Tippermuir		Committee of Public Safety
1645	Self-Denying Ordinance	**1660**	Monck invades from Scotland
	Creation of the new Model Army		The Rump recalled – and dissolved
	Battles of Naseby and Langport		The Convention Parliament
	Surrender of Bristol		Declaration of Breda
1646	Surrender of Oxford ends the First		Restoration of Charles II
	Civil War	**1661**	Savoy House Conference
	Propositions of Newcastle	**1661–4**	The Clarendon Code
1647	Charles I kidnapped by the New	**1661–79**	The Cavalier Parliament
	Model Army	**1665**	Great Plague of London
	The Heads of the Proposals	**1665–7**	Second Dutch war
	Debate in Putney church	**1666**	Great Fire of London
	The mutiny crushed at Ware	**1667**	The Dutch in the Medway
	The Engagement		Fall of Clarendon
1648	Royalist revolts all over the country	**1667–73**	The Cabal
	The Second Civil War	**1668**	The Triple Alliance between England,
	Scottish invasion: the battle of Preston		Holland and Sweden
	The treaty of Newport	**1670**	Secret Treaty of Dover
	Pride's Purge	**1672**	Second Declaration of Indulgence
1649	Trial and execution of Charles I		Third Dutch war
	Creation of the Commonwealth (the	**1673**	Declaration of Indulgence withdrawn:
	Rump)		the Test Act
	Suppression of the Levellers and the		Break-up of the Cabal
	Diggers	**1673–9**	Ministry of Danby
	Invasion of Ireland	**1677**	Betrothal of Mary to William of
	Massacres of Drogheda and Wexford		Orange
1650	Invasion of Scotland: battle of Dunbar	**1678**	Popish Plot: execution of Coleman
1651	Battle of Worcester	**1679**	First Exclusion Parliament
	Navigation Act		Defeat of Scottish Covenanters at
1652–4	First Dutch war		Bothwell Bridge
1653	Dissolution of the Rump	**1680**	Second Exclusion Parliament
	Barebones Parliament	**1681**	Third Exclusion Parliament
	The Instrument of Government: the		Acquittal of Shaftesbury
	Protectorate	**1683**	Rye House Plot
1654–5	First Parliament of the Protectorate	**1685**	Death of Charles II
	Cony's case	**1685–8**	Reign of James II
	The Western design begins		First Parliament of James II
1655	Penruddock's rising suppressed		Defeat of Monmouth's rebellion: the
	The Major-Generals		Bloody Assize
	Jews admitted to England	**1686**	*Godden v. Hales*
1656–8	Second Parliament of the Protectorate		The Court of Ecclesiastical Commis-
	James Nayler arrested		sion
1657	The Humble Petition and Advice	**1688**	Birth of the 'Old Pretender'
1658	Battle of the Dunes		Trial of the seven bishops
	Death of Oliver Cromwell: Richard		Invitation sent to William by the
	Cromwell Protector		Immortal Seven
1659	Third Protectorate Parliament		William of Orange's invasion
	Abdication of Richard Cromwell		James II fled to France
	Defeat of Booth's rising	**1688–1702**	The reign of William III and Mary II

1689	The Convention Parliament
	The Declaration and Bill of Rights
	Battle of Killiekrankie
1689–97	The Nine Years War
1690	Battle of the Boyne
1692	The Massacre of Glencoe
	Battle of Steenkirk
1693	Battle of Neerwinden
1694	Foundation of the Bank of England
	Death of Queen Mary
1695	William III recaptured Namur
1697	The peace of Ryswick
1698	The first Partition Treaty
1700	Second Partition Treaty
	Deaths of the Duke of Gloucester and of Carlos II
1701	Death of James II: Louis XIV recognised James III
	Act of Settlement
1702	Death of William III

1702–14	Reign of Anne
1704	Capture of Gibraltar by Rooke
	Battle of Blenheim
1706	Battle of Ramillies
1707	Act of Union between England and Scotland
1708	Battle of Oudenarde
	The Whig Junto in power
1709	Battle of Malplaquet
1710	Trial of Sacheverell
	Whigs replaced by Tories led by Harley (Oxford)
1711	Swift's *Conduct of the Allies*
	Marlborough dismissed
1713	Treaty of Utrecht
1714	Death of Electress Sophia
	Oxford replaced by Shrewsbury as Lord Treasurer
	Death of Anne
1714–27	Reign of George I

Glossary

Index